Physics
A First Course

Light and Color
Forces and Motion
Kinetic Energy
Resistance
Electricity
Positive +
Van de Graaff

Tom Hsu, Ph.D.

cpo science

A member of
School Specialty
Science

About the Author

Dr. Thomas C. Hsu is a nationally recognized innovator in science and math education and the founder of CPO Science (formerly Cambridge Physics Outlet). He holds a Ph.D. in Applied Plasma Physics from the Massachusetts Institute of Technology (MIT), and has taught students from elementary, secondary and college levels across the nation. He was nominated for MIT's Goodwin medal for excellence in teaching and has received numerous awards from various state agencies for his work to improve science education. Tom has personally worked with more than 12,000 K-12 teachers and administrators and is well known as a consultant, workshop leader and developer of curriculum and equipment for inquiry-based learning in science and math. With CPO Science, Tom has published textbooks in physical science, integrated science, and also written fifteen curriculum Investigation guides that accompany CPO Science equipment.

Physics A First Course

Copyright © 2005, 2008 CPO Science, a member of School Specialty Science

ISBN-10: 1-58892-141-7

ISBN-13: 978-1-58892-141-3

2 3 4 5 6 7 8 9 - QWE- 12 11 10 09

CPO Science

80 Northwest Boulevard

Nashua, NH 03063

http://www. cposcience.com

Printed and Bound in the United States of America

Dear Student,

I am also a student. I like to learn how things work then use what I know to show others. As one student to another, I hope you enjoy this course! I hope you learn how electricity works and how light and color are created. I hope you learn some secrets of nature that lie deep within the tiny atoms that make up our universe and yourself. I hope you learn what it means to accelerate and how to apply force to cause things to stop and go. Most of all, I hope you learn how to take a new situation and figure out how things work for yourself.

The secret to success is not in knowing the answers, but in knowing how to *find* the answers. Someday, each of you will come across many problems that are not in this book or any other book. I hope this course will teach you how to begin solving any problem involving the man-made or natural world. My knowledge of physics has allowed me to solve problems as simple as why my car will not start, and as complex as making a nuclear fusion reactor work.

I love learning new things. From one student to another, I hope you have fun in this course and that you will also come to love learning new things about the wonderful universe we live in.

Tom Hsu

CPO Science Staff

Editorial

Lynda Pennell – Educational Products, Executive Vice President

B.A., English, M.Ed., Administration, Reading Disabilities, Northeastern University; CAGS Media, University of Massachusetts, Boston

Nationally known in high school restructuring and for integrating academic and career education. Served as the director of an urban school with 17 years teaching/administrative experience.

Contributing Writers

Scott Eddleman – Project Manager and Principal Writer

B.S., Biology, Southern Illinois University; M.Ed., Harvard University

Taught for 13 years in urban and rural settings; nationally known as trainer of inquiry-based science and mathematics project-based instruction; curriculum development consultant.

Mary Beth Abel Hughes – Curriculum Specialist and Principal Writer

B.S., Marine Biology, College of Charleston; M.S., Biological Sciences, University of Rhode Island

Taught science and math at an innovative high school; expertise in scientific research and inquiry-based teaching methods and curriculum development.

Erik Benton – Professional Development Specialist and Principal Investigation Editor

B.F.A., University of Massachusetts

Taught for 8 years in public and private schools, focusing on inquiry and experiential learning environments.

Art, Design Illustration

Polly Crisman – Graphic Manager; Designer and Illustrator

B.F.A., University of New Hampshire

Graphic artist with expertise in advertising and marketing design, freelance illustrating, and caricature art.

Bruce Holloway – Senior Creative Designer

Pratt Institute, N.Y.; Boston Museum School of Fine Arts

Expertise in product design, advertising, and three-dimensional exhibit design. Commissioned for the New Hampshire Duck Stamp for 1999 and 2003.

Equipment Design

Thomas Narro – Product Design, Senior Vice President

B.S., Mechanical engineering, Rensselaer Polytechnic Institute

Accomplished design and manufacturing engineer; experienced consultant in corporate reengineering and industrial-environmental acoustics.

Dave Zucker – Industrial Designer

B.A., Physics, Brandeis University

Talented designer with a strong background in physics and problem solving. Also contributed to several connections articles.

Curriculum Consultants

Stacy Kissel – Principal Writer

B.S., Civil and Environmental Engineering, Carnegie Mellon University; M.Ed., Physics Education, Boston College

Nine years teaching experience physics, math and integrated science.

Laine Ives – Principal Writer

B.A., English, Gordon College; graduate work, biology, Cornell University, Wheelock College

Experience teaching middle and high school, here and abroad; expertise in developing middle school curriculum and hands-on activities.

Sonja Taylor – Contributing Writer

B.S., Chemistry, Stephen F. Austin State University

Taught chemistry and biology for four years. Expertise in teaching with inquiry and technology.

Patsy DeCoster – Contributing Writer

B.S., Biology/Secondary education, Grove City College; M.Ed., Tufts University

Curriculum and professional development specialist. Taught science for 12 years. National inquiry-based science presenter.

Mary Ann Erickson – Assessment Specialist

B.S., Naval Architecuture; B.S. Marine Engineering, Massachusetts Institute of Technology

Twenty-five years experience in engineering and technical writing; also, contributed to many assessment pieces, glossary, and index.

Consultants

Contributing Writers

Patricia Tremblay – Math Coach, Boston Public Schools, Boston, Massachusetts

B.A., Mathematics; Boston State College; M.Ed., Boston State College; Doctoral work, Curriculum, Boston College

Twenty-five years experience in the Boston Public Schools as a teacher, department head of mathematics, assistant headmaster, and presently as a mathematics curriculum coach.

David Bliss – Physics Teacher, Mohawk Central High School, New York, New York

Art, Design Illustration

James Travers – Graphic designer and animator

Associate Degree of Applied Business and Commercial Art, Akron University

Has held positions as graphic designer, art department manager, and currently is a commissioned painter.

David Rosolko – Graphic designer and illustrator

B.F.A, Massachusetts College of Art

Has worked as a graphic artist, illustrator, painter, and sculptor.

Technical Support

Tracy Morrow – Framemaker Expert, Technical Editor, Technical Trainer

B.A., English, Texas A&M University; M.A., English, Sam Houston State University

Taught middle school in Houston, Texas, and English at Tomball College; has also worked as a technical writer and trainer in many industries.

Julie Dalton – Senior Copy Editor, Journalist, and former Sportswriter and English teacher.

B.A., English Literature, University of Iowa; M.A., English Education, State University of New York at Albany.

Taught middle and high school English, and has worked for newspapers as a writer, editor, and copy editor for more than 25 years. She is a copy editor at the Boston Globe.

"Connections" Writers

William G. Fleischmann – Science Teacher, Wood Hill Middle School, MA

Edmund Hazzard – Research Associate, The Concord Consortium, MA

Besides his research and development responsibilities, experiments with hybrid cars by taking data about performance; he is also a carpenter and architect, specializing in designing energy-efficient buildings.

Nick Nicastro – Physics Teacher, Wachusett Regional High School, MA

Thirty-two years experience teaching physics. He developed high energy particle physics curriculum at European Center of Nuclear Research (CERN). He is a member of the executive board for the New England Section of the American Association of Physics Teachers.

Dr. Nicholas Benfaremo – Lecturer, Adjct Faculty, and a Professional Baker, University of Southern Maine, ME

Kenneth Rideout – Physical Science Teacher, Swampscott High School, MA

Ed Wiser – Physics Teacher, Brookline High School, MA

Ten years experience teaching physics.

Content Reviewers

George Whittemore
Physics Instructor
Leominster High School, MA

Dr. David Guerra
Associate Professor
Department Chair Physics,
St. Anselm College, NH

Ken Rideout
Physical Science Teacher
Swampscott High School, MA

Brett Malas
National Board Certified Science Teacher
Naperville North High School, IL

William G. Fleischmann
Science Teacher
Wood Hill Middle School, MA

Ruby Ashley
Project Coordinator, Georgia Southern Museum
Outreach Programs, GA

Mary Jo Carabatsos PhD
Science Teacher,
Andover High School, MA

Angela Benjamin
AP Physics Instructor
Woodrow Wilson Senior High School, DC

Richard Famiglietti
Science Teacher
Lynn Classical High School, MA

Elizabeth A. Jensen
Science Teacher
James Blair Middle School, VA

Colleen M O'Shell
Chemistry Teacher
Cambridge Rindge and Latin School, MA

Ian Smith
Physics Teacher
Bellows Free Academy, VT

Jean Lifford
Reading Coach
Boston Public Schools, MA

Ed Wiser
Physics Teacher
Brookline High School, MA

David Harris
Head of Science Department
Hackley School, NY

Sarah Segreti
Science Teacher
Naperville North High School, IL

Nick Nicastro
Physics Teacher
Wachusett Regional High School, MA

Cecilia A. Cherill
Physical Science Teacher
Churchill Junior High School, NJ

Kristy Beauvais
Physics Teacher
Concord-Carlisle Regional High School, MA

On each page of the student text you will find aids to help find information, understand concepts and answer questions. The following introduction includes sample pages with indicators that point out the page contents and reading aids.

Unit Pages and Chapter Pages

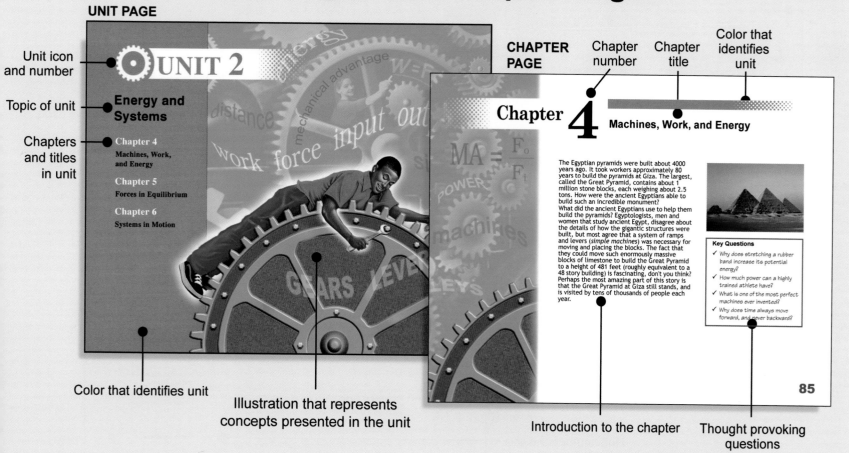

UNIT PAGE

Unit icon and number

UNIT 2

Topic of unit — **Energy and Systems**

Chapters and titles in unit

Chapter 4
Machines, Work, and Energy

Chapter 5
Forces in Equilibrium

Chapter 6
Systems in Motion

Color that identifies unit

Illustration that represents concepts presented in the unit

CHAPTER PAGE

Chapter number — Chapter title — Color that identifies unit

Chapter 4
Machines, Work, and Energy

The Egyptian pyramids were built about 4000 years ago. It took workers approximately 80 years to build the pyramids at Giza. The largest, called the Great Pyramid, contains about 1 million stone blocks, each weighing about 2.5 tons. How were the ancient Egyptians able to build such an incredible monument?
What did the ancient Egyptians use to help them build the pyramids? Egyptologists, men and women that study ancient Egypt, disagree about the details of how the gigantic structures were built, but most agree that a system of ramps and levers (*simple machines*) was necessary for moving and placing the blocks. The fact that they could move such enormously massive blocks of limestone to build the Great Pyramid to a height of 481 feet (roughly equivalent to a 48 story building) is fascinating, don't you think? Perhaps the most amazing part of this story is that the Great Pyramid at Giza still stands, and is visited by tens of thousands of people each year.

Key Questions
✓ Why does stretching a rubber band increase its potential energy?
✓ How much power can a highly trained athlete have?
✓ What is one of the most perfect machines ever invented?
✓ Why does time always move forward, and never backward?

Introduction to the chapter — Thought provoking questions

Student Text Pages

FIRST PAGE OF THE SECTION

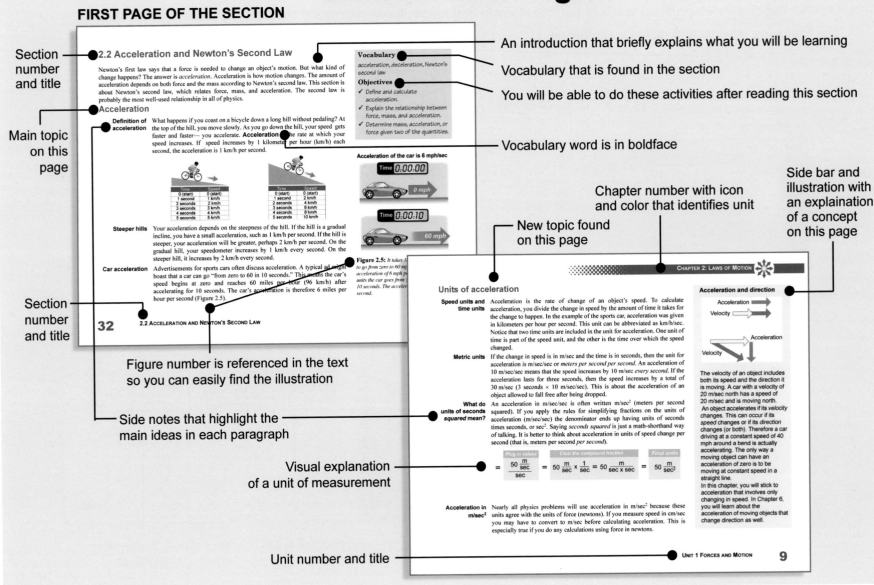

Section number and title → 2.2 Acceleration and Newton's Second Law

An introduction that briefly explains what you will be learning

Vocabulary that is found in the section

You will be able to do these activities after reading this section

Main topic on this page → Acceleration

Vocabulary word is in boldface

Side bar and illustration with an explanation of a concept on this page

Chapter number with icon and color that identifies unit

New topic found on this page

Section number and title

Figure number is referenced in the text so you can easily find the illustration

Side notes that highlight the main ideas in each paragraph

Visual explanation of a unit of measurement

Unit number and title

Student Text Pages

Main topic found on this page

Side notes that highlight the main ideas in each paragraph

Formula that is important for understanding in this section

Words that explain each letter symbol

Figure number referenced in the problem

A problem that is solved using a step-by-step method

Two problems for you to solve with the answers

Section number and title

Figure number referenced in the text

Chapter number with icon and color that identifies unit

Side notes that highlight the main ideas in each paragraph

Example graphs

Questions for you to answer after reading this section

Unit number and title

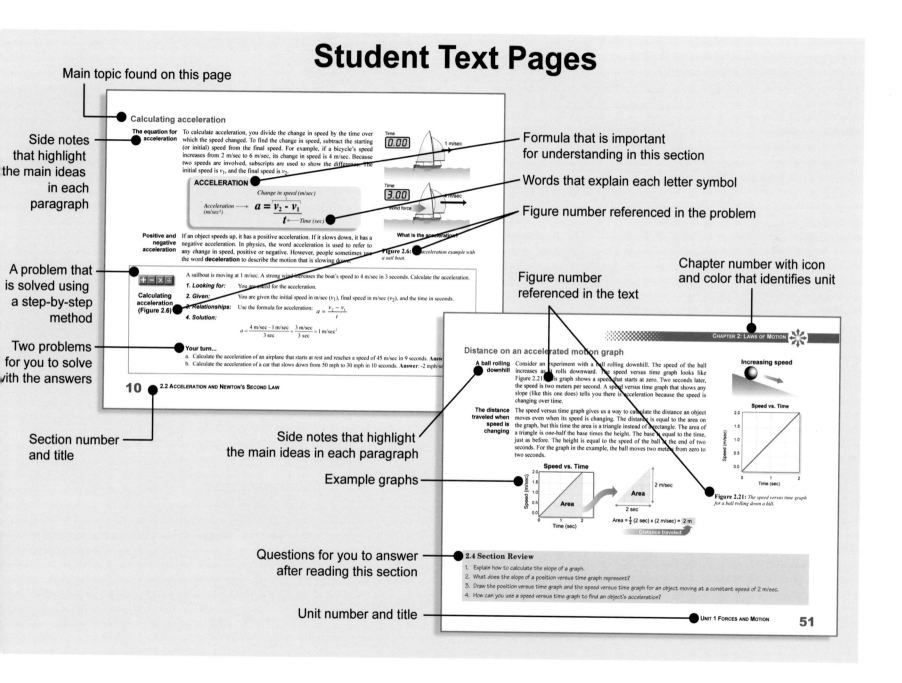

Chapter Review Pages

This part of the review asks you to fill in sentences with vocabulary words

Vocabulary words to fill in the sentences below

These questions help you check your understanding of concepts you have learned in the chapter

Section numbers identify where you can find the information to answer the questions

Chapter number with icon and color that identifies unit

You will use this graphic to answer question #12.

These questions help you practice solving problems found in the chapter

These questions ask you to think about what you have learned in the chapter and apply this knowledge to another situation

Graphics to help you solve the problem

Colorful illustrations to support the questions

Unit number and title

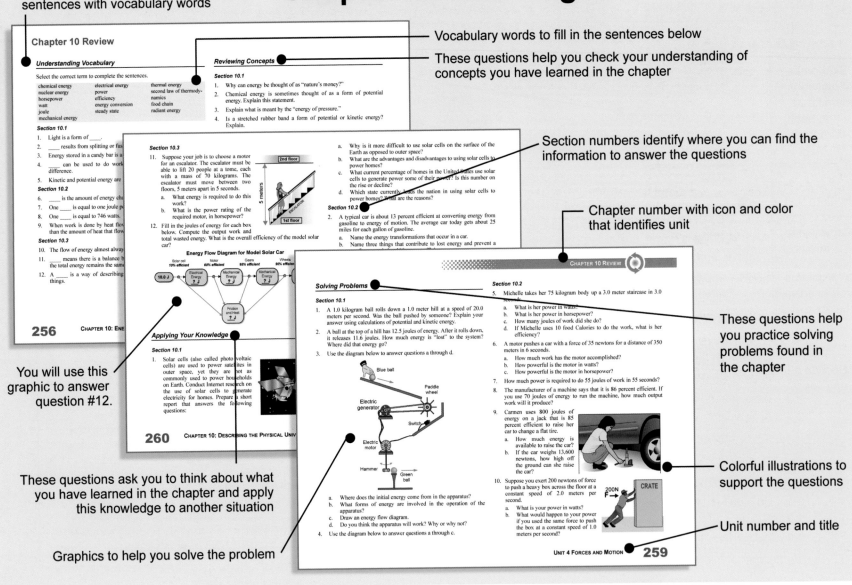

Physics
A First Course

Table of Contents

Forces and Motion

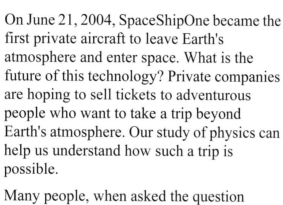

Chapter 1

Describing the Physical Universe

On June 21, 2004, SpaceShipOne became the first private aircraft to leave Earth's atmosphere and enter space. What is the future of this technology? Private companies are hoping to sell tickets to adventurous people who want to take a trip beyond Earth's atmosphere. Our study of physics can help us understand how such a trip is possible.

Many people, when asked the question "What is physics?" respond with "Oh, physics is all about complicated math equations and confusing laws to memorize." This response may describe the physics studied in some classrooms, but this is not the physics of the world around us, and this is definitely not the physics that you will study in this course! In this chapter you will be introduced to what studying physics is REALLY all about, and you will begin your physics journey by studying motion and speed.

Key Questions

✓ Does air have mass and take up space? What about light?
✓ How can an accident or mistake lead to a scientific discovery?
✓ What is the fastest speed in the universe?

1.1 What Is Physics?

What is physics and why study it? Many students believe physics is a complicated set of rules, equations to memorize, and confusing laws. Although this is sometimes the way physics is taught, it is not a fair description of the science. In fact, physics is about finding the simplest and least complicated explanation for things. It is about observing how things work and finding the connections between *cause* and *effect* that explain why things happen.

Three aspects of physics

1. Describing the organization of the universe

The *universe* is defined as everything that exists. Everything in the universe is believed to be either matter or energy (Figure 1.1). *Matter* is all of the "stuff" in the universe that has mass. You are made of matter, and so is a rock and so is the air around you. *Energy* is a measure of the ability to make things change. Energy flows any time something gets hotter, colder, faster, slower, or changes in any other observable way.

2. Understanding natural laws

A **natural law** is a rule that tells you how (or why) something happens the particular way it does. We believe that all events in nature obey natural laws that do not change. For example, one natural law tells you a ball rolling down a ramp of a certain height will have a certain speed at the bottom. If the same ball rolls down the same ramp again, it will have the same speed again. Physics is concerned with understanding the natural laws that relate matter and energy.

3. Deducing and applying natural laws

A third important part of physics is the process of figuring out the natural laws. The natural laws are human explanations based on human experience. A ball will still roll down a ramp regardless of whether you know why or how. It is up to us to figure out how and why. This part of physics often uses experiments and analysis. An **experiment** is a situation you carefully set up to see what happens under controlled conditions. **Analysis** is the detailed thinking you do to interpret and understand what you observe. Both of these activities lead to the development and refinement of natural laws. You will learn many natural laws in this course. We don't yet know all the natural laws. There is a lot left for us to learn.

Matter
Material that has mass and takes up space

Solid Liquid Gas

Energy
The ability to cause changes in factors like temperature, height, or speed

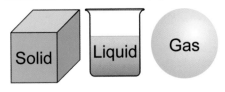

Figure 1.1: *The universe contains matter and energy.*

Matter and energy

Matter and mass   *Matter* is defined as anything that has mass and takes up space. **Mass** is the measure of the amount of matter that makes up an object. A car has more mass than a bicycle. But why does the car have more mass? The answer is that the car contains more matter. Steel, plastic, and rubber are different forms of matter and the car has a lot more than the bicycle.

Is air matter?   How can you tell if something takes up space? Does the air around you take up space? Think about how you could test whether or not air takes up space. An "empty" glass contains air. Imagine a cylinder you could push into the empty glass. If the cylinder formed a seal so that the air inside couldn't escape, you wouldn't be able to push the cylinder all the way to the bottom. Why? Because air is matter and takes up space (Figure 1.2). You don't always notice the mass of air because it is spread thinly, but the mass of air in an average classroom is about equal to the mass of one student.

Is light matter?   Just as an empty glass is actually filled with air, it also fills with light in front of a window. Is light a kind of matter? Because light does not take up space and has no mass, it does not fit the definition of matter. Imagine pumping all of the air out of that empty glass while the cylinder is pulled back. Even if the glass were near a light source and filled with light, you could push the cylinder all the way down because light does not take up space (Figure 1.3). The glass also has the same mass in a dark room and a room full of sunlight. Later in the course we will see that light is a pure form of *energy*.

Energy   Imagine dropping a stone. In your hand, the stone is described by its mass and height off the ground. Once it is falling, the stone speeds up and its height changes. If you investigate, you learn that you cannot get *any* speed by dropping the stone. You cannot make the stone go 100 miles per hour by dropping it only one meter from your hand to the floor. But why not? What limits how much speed the stone can have? The answer is energy. Energy is how we measure the amount of change that is possible. Changing the speed of the stone from zero to 100 mph takes a certain amount of energy. Lifting the stone up (changing its height) also takes energy. Change takes energy and the amount of change you can have is limited by the amount of energy available.

AIR
Air takes up space.

Figure 1.2: *Air is matter because it has mass and takes up space.*

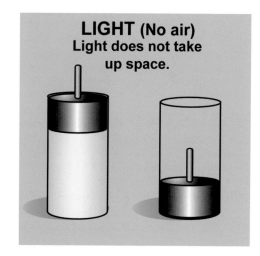

LIGHT (No air)
Light does not take up space.

Figure 1.3: *Light is not matter because it has no mass and does not take up space.*

Systems and variables

Defining a system
The universe is huge and complex. The only way to make sense of it is to think about only a small part at a time. If you want to understand a car rolling down a ramp, you don't need to confuse yourself with the sun, or the Milky Way galaxy or even the room next door. When you want to understand something, you focus your attention on a small group called a **system**. A system is a group of objects, effects, and variables that are related. You choose the system to include the things you wish to investigate and exclude the things you think are not relevant.

Variables
A **variable** is a factor that affects the behavior of the system. When you are trying to find out how a system works, you look for relationships between the important variables of the system. For example, imagine you are doing an experiment with a car rolling down a ramp. The car and ramp are the system. The car's speed is one important variable. Time, position, and mass are other variables.

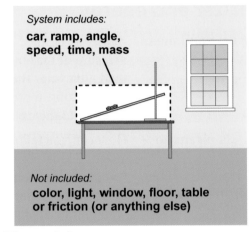

Figure 1.4: *Choose variables that are important to your investigation.*

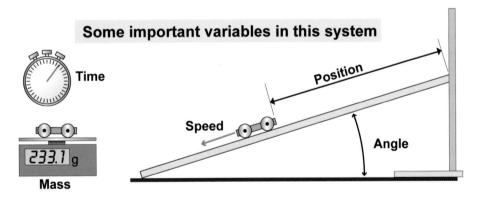

Some important variables in this system

Time

Mass

233.1 g

Speed

Position

Angle

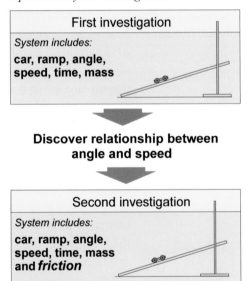

Figure 1.5: *You may change the system later to include new objects, effects, or variables. You may also remove things if they are not necessary to explain what you observe.*

What to include
The ideal choice of a system includes all the objects, effects, and variables that affect what you are trying to understand (Figure 1.4). To understand the motion of a car on a ramp you might include the car, the ramp, and the mass, angle, and speed. The fewer the variables, the easier it is to find important relationships. You can include more variables, like friction from the wheels, after you understand how the more important variables fit together (Figure 1.5).

The scale of a system

An example of different scales A system almost always shows different and important behavior at different *scales*. Figure 1.6 shows a road at three different scales. To calculate driving time between cities, you use the largest scale. To design the road to be wide enough to fit a car, you use the middle scale. To understand how water drains through cracks in the road, you need to look on the smallest scale. In a similar way, the universe can be understood differently on different scales. It depends on what you are trying to understand.

The macroscopic scale Observations are on the **macroscopic** scale when they are large enough for us to see or directly measure. The mass of a car and the temperature of a pot of water are macroscopic variables. Virtually all the things you measure in experiments in this course are macroscopic. Many of the natural laws you learn will relate macroscopic variables, such as speed, temperature, and mass.

Variables that can be observed and measured directly are on the macroscopic scale.

The scale of atoms Temperature is related to energy but it is not possible to understand *how* on the macroscopic scale. To understand temperature we must investigate the composition of matter. To understand the connection between temperature and energy we must look on the scale of atoms and molecules.

Atoms Almost all of the matter you experience is made of atoms. Atoms are tiny particles, far too small to see directly. However, many of the macroscopic properties of matter you can observe depend on the behavior of atoms. Physics shows us that to understand certain aspects of the macroscopic world (such as temperature) we need to understand the behavior of atoms. We will use the term "*atomic*" to mean "*on the scale of atoms.*"

Variables that are on the scale of atoms and are far too small to be observed are on the atomic scale.

10 cm

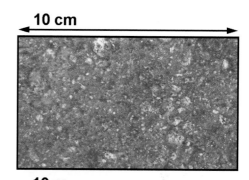

10 m

10 km

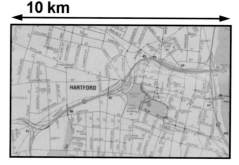

Figure 1.6: *Three different scales for looking at a road.*

Investigating systems

Experiments An experiment is a situation set up to investigate the relationship between variables in a system. Experiments usually have a question associated with them. An example would be: "How does the steepness of a ramp affect the speed of a ball at the bottom?" (Figure 1.7) The process used to conduct an experiment is called the **scientific method** (Figure 1.8).

Types of variables To answer the question you do an experiment to measure the cause-and-effect relationship between the ramp's angle and the speed of the ball. The variable that is the cause of change in the system is called the **independent variable**. This is the variable that you change in an experiment. The ramp's angle is the independent variable in this example. The variable that shows (or may show) the effect of those changes is called the **dependent variable**. The speed of the ball is the dependent variable.

Making a hypothesis A **hypothesis** is an educated guess that predicts the relationship between the independent and dependent variables in an experiment. Coming up with a good hypothesis means you must have some experience with the system you are investigating. However, don't worry if you are unsure about what will happen in an experiment. Scientists often make hypotheses that they end up proving to be incorrect. The first hypothesis is just a *starting point* for developing a correct understanding.

Designing experiments In an ideal experiment you change only one variable at a time. You keep ALL of the other variables the same. This way you can be certain any change you see in the system must be associated with the one variable you changed. A variable that is kept the same is called a **control variable**, and the variable that is changed is called the **experimental variable**. In a ball and ramp experiment, the ramp angle, the ball's mass, and the starting point are all important variables that affect the speed. In a well-designed experiment you choose only one variable at a time.

How does the angle of a ramp affect the speed of the ball?

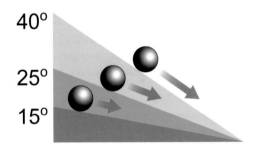

Figure 1.7: *How does the angle of the ramp affect the ball's speed?*

The scientific method

1. Ask a question.
2. Formulate a hypothesis.
3. Design a procedure to test the hypothesis.
4. Conduct the experiment and collect the data.
5. Analyze the data.
6. Use the data to make a conclusion.
7. If necessary, refine the question and go through each step again.

Figure 1.8: *Follow these steps when conducting an experiment.*

Energy and systems

Energy *Energy* is an important concept that is difficult to define. **Energy** is a measure of a system's ability to change or create change in other systems. A car at the top of a ramp is able to move because it has energy due to its height on the ramp. The car's increase in speed as it moves is a change in the system that could not occur without energy.

Energy can appear in many forms, such as heat, motion, height, pressure, electricity, and chemical bonds between atoms. The key to understanding how systems change is to trace the movement of energy between objects and also between the various forms of energy.

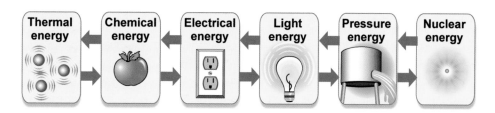

The stability of systems Systems in nature tend to go from higher energy to lower energy. A system at higher energy is often unstable, while a system at lower energy is stable. The car is unstable at the top of the ramp where its energy is greatest. It will naturally move to a more stable position at the bottom of the ramp.

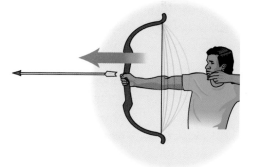

Figure 1.9: *A stretched bowstring on a bent bow has energy, so it is able to create change in itself and in the arrow.*

Creating change The stretched bowstring on a bow is another example of a system that has energy (Figure 1.9). Released, the string springs back to its unstretched, stable position. The bow uses its energy to change its own shape. It also can create change in the arrow. While the bow and bowstring move from high to low energy, the arrow moves from low to high energy. The energy originally in the bowstring is used to change the speed of the arrow.

Macroscopic and atomic changes Energy can create macroscopic and atomic scale changes to systems. The changes in the bow and arrow are macroscopic because they can be directly observed. If you shoot many arrows one after another, the bowstring gets warm from the heat of friction. The warmth comes from energy flowing between atoms on the atomic scale.

Models

An example system Consider the following system. A stretched rubber band is used to launch a car along a track that is straight for a distance and then turns uphill. If the rubber band is stretched more, the car has more speed. If the car has more speed it gets higher on the hill. How do we explain the relationship between the height the car reaches and the speed it has at the bottom of the hill?

What is a model? Explanations in physics typically come in the form of models. In physics, a **model** is an explanation that links the variables in a system through cause and effect relationships.

An example model Figure 1.10 shows a model of the car and ramp system. Launching the car gives it energy due to its speed. Climbing the hill takes energy. The car climbs only so high because it only has so much energy. Making the car go faster gives it more energy and that is why it goes higher. This explanation is a model that links the height and speed through the idea of energy. This model is known as the *law of conservation of energy* and is one of the natural laws of physics. The model in Figure 1.10 is *conceptual* because it is not precise enough to predict exactly how much height the car gets for a given speed. In chapter 3 you will encounter a more detailed version of the law of conservation of energy.

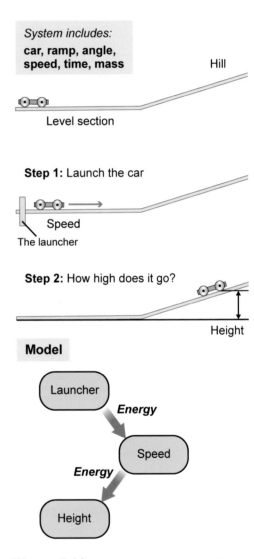

Figure 1.10: *A conceptual model of the car and ramp system.*

1.1 Section Review

1. What are the main activities involved in studying physics?

2. Which has more mass: a dollar bill or a quarter? Why?

3. Imagine that you are doing an experiment to find out if more expensive batteries will run your radio for a longer amount of time than cheaper batteries will. List a question, a hypothesis, the independent variable, the dependent variable, and the control variables for this experiment. Then write a procedure that would allow you to test your hypothesis.

4. What is needed to create change in a system?

1.2 Distance and Time

To do science you need a precise way to describe the natural world. In physics, many things are described with measurements. For example, two meters is a measurement of length that is a little more than the height of an average person. Measurements such as length, mass, speed, and temperature are important in science because they are a language that allows us to communicate information so everyone understands exactly what we mean. In this section you will learn about measuring distance and time.

Measuring distance

Measurements   A *measurement* is a precise value that tells how much. How much *what*, you ask? That depends on what you are measuring. The important concept in measurement is that it communicates the amount in a way that can be understood by others. For example, two meters is a measurement because it has a *quantity,* 2, and gives a *unit,* meters.

Units   All measurements must have units. Without a unit, a measurement cannot be understood. For example, if you asked someone to walk 10, she would not know how far to go: 10 feet, 10 meters, 10 miles, and 10 kilometers are all 10, but the units are different and therefore the distances are also different. Units allow people to communicate amounts. For communication to be successful, physics uses a set of units that have been agreed upon around the world.

What is distance?   **Distance** is the amount of space between two points (Figure 1.11). You can also think of distance as how far apart two objects are. You probably have a good understanding of distance from everyday experiences, like the distance from one house to another, or the distance between California and Massachusetts. The concept of distance in physics is the same, but the actual distances may be much larger and much smaller than anything you normally refer to as a distance.

Distance is measured in units of length   Distance is measured in units of **length**. Some of the commonly used units of length include inches, miles, centimeters, kilometers, and meters. It is important to always specify which length unit you are using for a measurement.

Distance

Distance is the amount of space between two points.

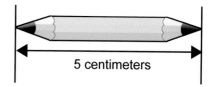

5 centimeters

Figure 1.11: *The definition of distance.*

The two common systems for measuring distance

Systems of units   There are two common systems of standardized (or agreed upon) units that are used for measuring distances, the **English system** and the International System of Units, commonly called the **metric system** in the United States. The English system uses inches (in), feet (ft), yards (yd), and miles (mi). The metric system uses millimeters (mm), centimeters (cm), meters (m), and kilometers (km). The names of units in the metric system use prefixes that are based on powers of ten (Figure 1.12).

Scientists use metric units   Almost all fields of science use metric units because they are easier to work with. In the English system, there are 12 inches in a foot, 3 feet in a yard, and 5,280 feet in a mile. In the metric system, there are 10 millimeters in a centimeter, 100 centimeters in a meter, and 1,000 meters in a kilometer. Factors of 10 are easier to remember than 12, 3, and 5,280. The diagram below will help you get a sense for the metric units of distance.

Prefix	Meaning	
giga (G)	1 billion	1,000,000,000
mega (M)	1 million	1,000,000
kilo (k)	1 thousand	1,000
centi (c)	1 one-hundredth	0.01
milli (m)	1 one-thousandth	0.001
micro (μ)	1 one-millionth	0.000001

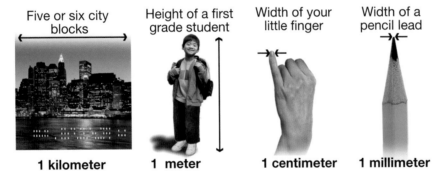

Five or six city blocks — **1 kilometer**
Height of a first grade student — **1 meter**
Width of your little finger — **1 centimeter**
Width of a pencil lead — **1 millimeter**

Figure 1.12: *Metric prefixes*

You will use both systems of measurement   To solve problems by applying science in the real world, you will need to know both sets of units, English and metric. For example, a doctor will measure your height and weight in English units. The same doctor will prescribe medicine in milliliters (mL) and grams (g), which are metric units. Plywood is sold in 4-by-8-foot sheets — but the thickness of many types of plywood is given in millimeters. Some of the bolts on an automobile have English dimensions, such as $^1/_2$ inch. Others have metric dimensions, such as 13 millimeters. Because both units are used, it is a good idea to know both metric and English units.

Measuring time

Two ways to think about time In physics, just as in your everyday life, there are two ways to think about time (Figure 1.13). One way is to identify a particular moment in time. The other way is to describe a quantity of time. The single word, "time," means two different things.

What time is it? If you ask, "What time is it?" you usually want to identify a moment in time relative to the rest of the universe and everyone in it. To answer this question, you would look at a clock or your watch at one particular moment. For example, 3 P.M. Eastern Time on May 21, 2007, tells the time at a certain place on Earth.

How much time? If you ask, "How much time?" (did something take to occur, for instance), you are looking for a quantity of time. To answer, you need to measure an interval of time that has both a beginning and an end. For example, you might measure how much time has passed between the start of a race and when the first runner crosses the finish line. A quantity of time is often called a **time interval**. Whenever you see the word *time* in physics, it usually (but not always) means a time interval. Time intervals in physics are almost always in seconds, and are represented by the lower case letter *t*.

Units for measuring time You are probably familiar with the common units for measuring time: seconds, hours, minutes, days, and years. But you may not know how they relate to each other. Table 1.1 gives some useful relationships between units of time. In everyday life, time is often expressed in mixed units rather than with a single unit (Figure 1.14)

What time is it?

3:00 PM (Eastern time) May 21, 2007

Figure 1.13: *There are two different ways to understand time.*

Table 1.1: *Time relationships*

Time unit	. . . in seconds . . .	. . . and in days
1 second	1	0.0001157
1 minute	60	0.00694
1 hour	3,600	0.0417
1 day	86,400	1
1 year	31,557,600	365.25
1 century	3,155,760,000	36,525

Figure 1.14: *A microwave oven can understand time in either mixed units (minutes and seconds) or in a single unit (seconds). Both 1:30 and 0:90 will result in the same cooking time.*

Time scales in physics

One second The **second** (sec) is the basic unit of time in both the English and metric systems. One second is about the time it takes to say "thousand." There are 60 seconds in a minute and 3,600 seconds in an hour. The second was originally defined in terms of one day: There are 86,400 seconds in an average day of 24 hours (24 hr × 3,600 $^{sec}/_{hr}$).

Time in physics Things in the universe happen over a huge range of time intervals. Figure 1.15 gives a few examples of time scales that are considered in physics and in other sciences. The average life span of a human being is 2.2 billion seconds. The time it takes a mosquito to beat its wings once is 0.0005 second. The time it takes light to get from this page to your eyes is 0.000000002 seconds.

Time in experiments In many experiments, you will observe how things change with time. For example, when you drop a ball, it falls to the ground. You can make a graph of the height of the ball versus the time since it was released. The *time* is the time interval measured from when the ball was released. This graph shows how the height of the ball changes with time. The graph shows that it takes the ball about 0.45 seconds to fall a distance of 1 meter. Many of the experiments you will do involve measuring times between 0.0001 seconds and a few seconds. When making graphs of results from experiments, the time almost always goes on the horizontal (or *x*) axis.

An experiment involving time

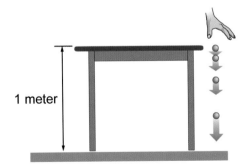

Height vs. Time

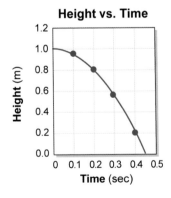

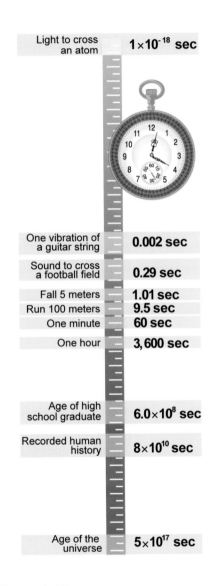

Light to cross an atom	1×10^{-18} sec
One vibration of a guitar string	0.002 sec
Sound to cross a football field	0.29 sec
Fall 5 meters	1.01 sec
Run 100 meters	9.5 sec
One minute	60 sec
One hour	3,600 sec
Age of high school graduate	6.0×10^{8} sec
Recorded human history	8×10^{10} sec
Age of the universe	5×10^{17} sec

Figure 1.15: *Some time intervals in physics.*

Unit conversions

Measuring time
When doing an experiment or solving a physics problem, you often need to convert from one unit to another. This happens a lot with time. If you used a stopwatch to measure the time it took a runner to finish a marathon, the stopwatch would display the time in hours, minutes, and seconds (Figure 1.16). The measurements of hours, minutes, and seconds are usually separated with colons. Accurate timers, such as those used for races, usually also have a decimal that shows fractions of a second.

Converting units
Hours, minute, and seconds are *mixed units*, but people are used to hearing time this way. However, if you want to do any calculations with the race time, such as figuring out the runner's average speed, you must convert the time into a single unit. When converting to seconds the first thing you do is convert each quantity of hours and minutes to seconds. Then you add up all the seconds to get the total. Seconds are often used as the unit of time for experiments.

Figure 1.16: *Digital timers have displays that show time in mixed units.*

Converting time units

Convert the time 2:30:45 into seconds.

1. Looking for: You are asked for the time in seconds.

2. Given: You are given the time in mixed units.

3. Relationships: There are 60 seconds in one minute and 3,600 seconds in one hour.

4. Solution:

$$2 \text{ hr} \times 3600 \text{ sec/ hr} = 7200 \text{ sec} \qquad 30 \text{ min} \times 60 \text{ sec/ min} = 1800 \text{ sec}$$

Add all of the seconds: 7200 sec + 1800 sec + 45 sec = 9045 seconds

Your turn...

a. Convert 3:45:10 into seconds.   **Answer:** 13,510 seconds
b. One year equals 365.25 days. How many seconds are in 5 years?   **Answer:** 157,790,000 seconds

---

Distance and time graphs

Graphs A graph is a picture that shows how two variables are related. Graphs are easier to read than tables of numbers, so they are often used to display data collected during an experiment. The graph to the right shows distance and time measurements taken during a long trip in a car.

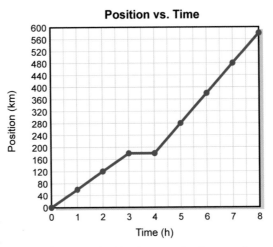

Position vs. Time

The independent variable By convention, or common agreement, graphs are drawn with the *independent variable* on the horizontal or *x*-axis. In the graph above, time is the independent variable. We say it is independent because we are free to decide the times when we take measurements. The graph shows that measurements were taken every hour.

The dependent variable The *dependent variable* goes on the vertical or *y*-axis. Distance is the dependent variable because the distance depends on the time. If a time interval other than one hour had been chosen, the distance measurements would be different.

1.2 Section Review

1. List two common systems of units and give examples of distance measurements for each.
2. Explain the two meanings in physics of the word "time."
3. If you wait in a long line for 1 hour and 10 minutes, how many seconds have you waited?
4. List the steps you should follow when making a graph.

How to make a graph

Each box = 1	Each box = 20	Each box = 40
15	300	600
10	200	400
5	100	200
0	0	0

Letting each box = 40
fits the biggest data point (580 km)

1. Decide which variable to put on the *x*-axis and which to put on the *y*-axis.
2. Make a scale for each axis by counting boxes to fit your largest value for each axis. Count by multiples of 1, 2, 5, 10, or a larger number if needed. Write the numbers on each axis at evenly spaced intervals and label each axis with its corresponding variable and unit.
3. Plot each point by finding the *x*-value and tracing the graph upward until you get to the right *y*-value. Draw a dot for each point.
4. Draw a smooth curve that shows the pattern of the points.
5. Create a title for your graph.

1.3 Speed

Nothing in the universe stays still. A book on a table appears to be sitting still, but Earth is moving in its orbit around the sun at a speed of 66,000 miles per hour. You and the book move with Earth. Speed is an important concept in physics and saying that something is "fast" is not descriptive enough to accurately convey its speed. A race car may be fast compared with other cars, but it is slow compared with a jet airplane. In this section, you will learn a precise definition of speed.

Speed

An example of speed
Consider a bicycle moving along the road. The diagrams below show the positions of two bicycles at different times. To understand the concept of speed, think about the following two questions.

- How many meters does the bicycle move in each second?
- Does the bicycle move the same number of meters every second?

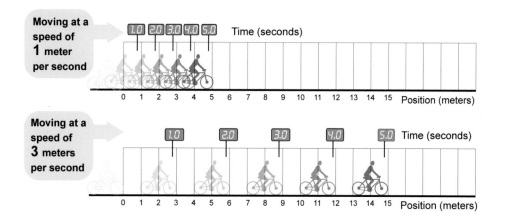

The precise meaning of speed
The **speed** of a bicycle is the distance it travels divided by the time it takes. At 1 m/sec, a bicycle travels one meter each second. At 3 m/sec, it travels three meters each second. Both bicycles in the diagram are moving at **constant speed**. Constant speed means the same distance is traveled every second.

Vocabulary

speed, constant speed

Objectives

✓ Define speed.
✓ Express an object's speed using various units.
✓ Calculate speed, distance, or time given two of the three quantities.
✓ List the steps for solving physics problems.

The speed limit of the universe

300,000,000 m/sec

The fastest speed in the universe is the speed of light. Light moves at 300 million meters per second (3×10^8 m/sec). If you could make light travel in a circle, it would go around the Earth 7 $\frac{1}{2}$ times in one second! We believe the speed of light is the ultimate speed limit in the universe.

Calculating speed

Speed is distance divided by time
Speed is a measure of the *distance* traveled in a given amount of *time*. Therefore, to calculate the speed of an object, you need to know two things:

- The distance traveled by the object.
- The time it took to travel the distance.

Average speed
Speed is calculated by dividing the distance traveled by the time taken. For example, if you drive 150 kilometers in 1.5 hours (Figure 1.17), then the average speed of the car is 150 kilometers divided by 1.5 hours, which is equal to 100 kilometers per hour.

What does "per" mean?
The word "per" means "for every" or "for each." The speed of 100 kilometers per hour is short for saying 100 kilometers *for each* hour. You can also think of "per" as meaning "divided by." The quantity before the word per is divided by the quantity after it. For example, 150 kilometers divided by 1.5 hours (or per every 1.5 hours) equals 100 miles per hour.

Units for speed
Since speed is a ratio of distance over time, the units for speed are a ratio of distance units over time units. In the metric system, distance is measured in centimeters, meters, or kilometers. If distance is in kilometers and time in hours, then speed is expressed in kilometers per hour (km/h). Other metric units for speed are centimeters per second (cm/sec) and meters per second (m/sec). Speed is also commonly expressed in miles per hour (mph). Table 1.2 shows different units commonly used for speed.

$$\frac{150 \text{ kilometers}}{1.5 \text{ hours}} = 100 \text{ kilometers (km/h)}$$

Figure 1.17: *A driving trip with an average speed of 100 km/h.*

Table 1.2: *Common units for speed*

Distance	Time	Speed	Abbreviation
meters	seconds	meters per second	m/sec
kilometers	hours	kilometers per hour	km/h
centimeters	seconds	centimeters per second	cm/sec
miles	hours	miles per hour	mph
inches	seconds	inches per second	in/sec, ips
feet	minutes	feet per minute	ft/min, fpm

Relationships between distance, speed, and time

Mixing up distance, speed, and time

A common type of question in physics is: "How far do you go if you drive for two hours at a speed of 100 km/h?" You know how to get speed from time and distance. How do you get distance from speed and time? The answer is the reason mathematics is the language of physics. A mathematical description of speed in terms of distance and time can easily be rearranged while preserving the original connections between variables.

Calculating speed

Let the letter v stand for "speed," the letter d stand for "distance traveled," and the letter t stand for "time taken." If we remember that the letters stand for those words, we can now write a mathematically precise definition of speed.

SPEED

$$\text{Speed (m/sec)} \longrightarrow v = \frac{d}{t}$$

d — Distance traveled (meters)

t — Time taken (seconds)

There are three ways to arrange the variables that relate distance, time, and speed. You should be able to work out how to get any one of the three variables if you know the other two (Figure 1.18).

Using formulas

Remember that the words or letters stand for the values that the variables have. For example, the letter t will be replaced by the actual time when we plug in numbers for the letters. You can think about each letter as a box that will eventually hold a number. Maybe you do not know yet what the number will be. Once we get everything arranged according to the rules, we can fill the boxes with the numbers that belong in each one. The last box left will be our answer. The letters (or variables) are the labels that tell us which numbers belong in which boxes.

Why v is used to represent speed

When we represent speed in a formula, we use the letter v. If this seems confusing, remember that v stands for *velocity*.

It is not important for this chapter, but there is a technical difference between speed and velocity. Speed is a single measurement that tells how fast you are going, such as 80 kilometers per hour. Velocity means you know both your speed and the *direction* you are going. If you tell someone you are going 80 km/h directly south, you are telling them your velocity. If you say only that you are going 60 mph, you are telling them your speed.

Forms of the speed equation

Equation	gives you	if you know
$v = d \div t$	speed	distance and time
$d = vt$	distance	speed and time
$t = d \div v$	time	distance and speed

Figure 1.18: *Different forms of the speed equation.*

How to solve physics problems

Physics problems You will be asked to analyze and solve many problems in this course. In fact, learning physics will make you a better problem-solver. This skill is important in all careers. For example, financial analysts are expected to look at information about businesses and determine which companies are succeeding. Doctors collect information about patients and must figure out what is causing pain or an illness. Mechanics gather information about a car and have to figure out what is causing a malfunction and how to fix it. All these examples use problem-solving skills.

A four-step technique The technique for solving problems has four steps. Follow these steps and you will be able to see a way to the answer most of the time and will at least make progress toward the answer almost every time. Figure 1.19 illustrates these steps, and the table below explains them.

Table 1.3: *Steps to solving physics problems*

Step	What to do
1	Identify clearly what the problem is asking for. If you can, figure out exactly what variables or quantities need to be in the answer.
2	Identify the information you are given. Sometimes this includes numbers or values. Other times it includes descriptive information you must interpret. Look for words like *constant* or *at rest*. In a physics problem, saying something is constant means it does not change. The words "at rest" in physics mean the speed is zero. You may need conversion factors to change units.
3	Identify any relationships that involve the information you are asked to find and the information you are given. For example, suppose you are given a speed and time and asked to find a distance. The relationship $v = d \div t$ relates what you are asked for to what you are given.
4	Combine the relationships with what you know to find what you are asked for. Once you complete steps 1-3, you will be able to see how to solve most problems. If not, start working with the relationships you have and see where they lead.

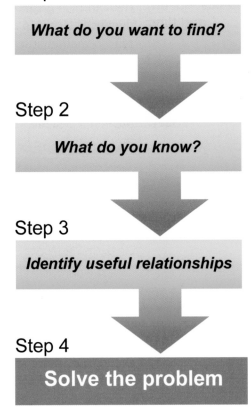

Step 1

What do you want to find?

Step 2

What do you know?

Step 3

Identify useful relationships

Step 4

Solve the problem

Figure 1.19: *Follow these steps and you will be able to see a way to the answer most of the time.*

Example problems

Solved example problems are provided   Throughout this book you will find example problems that have been solved for you. Following each solved example, there are two practice problems. The answers to the practice problems are provided so that you can check your work while practicing your problem-solving skills. Always remember to write out the steps when you are solving problems on your own. If you make a mistake, you will be able to look at your work and determine where you went wrong. Here is the format for example problems:

Calculating speed

An airplane flies 450 meters in 3 seconds. What is its speed in meters per second?

1. Looking for: You are asked for the speed in meters/second.

2. Given: You are given the distance in meters and the time in seconds.

3. Relationships: Use this version of the speed equation:
$$v = d \div t$$

4. Solution: $v = 450 \text{ m} \div 3 \text{ sec} = 150 \text{ m/sec}$

Your turn...

a. A snake moves 20 meters in 5 seconds. What is the speed of the snake in meters per second? **Answer:** 4 m/sec

b. A train is moving at a speed of 50 kilometers per hour. How many hours will it take the train to travel 600 kilometers? **Answer:** 12 hours

1.3 Section Review

1. List three commonly used units for speed.

2. State the steps used to solve physics problems.

3. Calculate the average speed (in km/h) of a car that drives 140 kilometers in two hours.

4. How long (in seconds) will it take you to swim 100 meters if you swim at 1.25 m/sec?

5. How far (in meters) will a dog travel if he runs for 1 minute at a constant speed of 5 m/sec?

Scientific Method and Serendipity

Have you ever made a mistake that resulted in something very positive happening? Usually, we try to avoid mistakes. However, sometimes making a mistake — like taking a wrong turn — leads to a place you would not have seen if you had taken a right turn!

Serendipity is a term used to describe an event that happens by accident that results in an unexpected discovery. An example of an accident might be losing your keys. An example of a serendipitous event would be that looking for your keys causes you to find the watch that you lost a week ago.

Scientists tend to follow the scientific method or some version of it to "do science." However, while searching for answers to nature's mysteries or looking for a cure to a disease, many important discoveries have come about unexpectedly. Sometimes small chance events or observations are just enough for a curious person to begin to unravel an important mystery.

A scientist made famous by serendipity

In 1928, Alexander Fleming, a British bacteriologist, was investigating the influenza virus as well as his own interests in the antibacterial properties of mucus. He was working at St. Mary's Hospital in London.

In one experiment, Fleming smeared mucus in a petri dish that had a culture of a harmful strain of bacteria called staphylococcus. Infections of staphylococcus would spread uncontrollably, and often caused the death of the infected person.

Alexander Fleming in his laboratory

Important observation brings fame and saves lives

At one point in his research, Fleming took a two-week vacation. He happened by chance to leave a petri dish containing staphylococcus on his laboratory bench. What happened next is a good example of serendipity.

When Fleming returned from his vacation he noticed that mold had grown in the plate. The growth was a simple mold that grows as green and white, fuzzy masses on food that is left out too long and exposed to the air. In Fleming's case, a mold spore had entered his lab from another lab in his building. This mold spore had traveled through the air and had landed by chance on the petri dish.

When Fleming examined the plate he saw that the staphylococcus was growing on the plate, but it was not growing near the mold. At this point, Fleming came up with a hypothesis that brought him great fame and helped save the lives of many people. His hypothesis was that a substance produced by the mold could kill harmful bacteria.

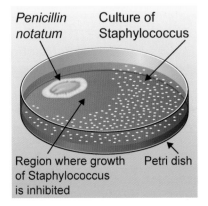
Penicillin notatum
Culture of Staphylococcus
Region where growth of Staphylococcus is inhibited
Petri dish

A miracle drug

After Fleming made his important hypothesis, that mold has antibiotic properties, he investigated the mold on the petri dish. He grew a pure sample of the mold and learned that it produced a substance that stopped some of the bacteria from growing. Fleming named the substance *penicillin* after the fungus (or mold) growing in the plate, *Penicillin notatum*. You may be familiar with the drug, penicillin. It is a very common and effective antibiotic.

Although Fleming was not able to purify penicillin enough for use as an antibiotic, he published his findings so others could. In 1945, Fleming received the Nobel Prize along with two other scientists (Ernst B. Chain and Sir Howard Florey) who helped develop penicillin. Ernst B. Chain and Sir Howard Florey were very important in developing the techniques needed to make large quantities of penicillin. During World War II penicillin saved the lives of thousands of injured soldiers and civilians. Not surprisingly, penicillin became known as a "miracle drug."

More discoveries

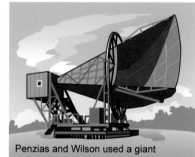

Alexander Fleming made an important discovery by recognizing the importance of mold in a petri dish. He took advantage of a serendipitous event and opened the door for a life-saving medical breakthrough!

Penzias and Wilson used a giant antenna to record cosmic background radiation which is accepted as evidence of the Big Bang.

It is through education, and a strong sense of curiosity, tempered with a bit of creativity, (and yes, sometimes a little luck) that people can make great scientific discoveries. So, the next time you make a mistake or something does not seem to be working as you think it should, be patient and think about it. You may discover something yourself!

Here are some other serendipitous events that resulted in scientific breakthroughs. Take the time to research these important events and get inspired. Maybe one day you will make an important discovery!

- An apple falling from a tree inspires Isaac Newton to develop the idea of gravity.
- An unusual, accidental photograph revealing the bone structure of a hand leads to the discovery of X rays by Wilhelm Röntgen.
- Two photographs of the same star field, taken a few days apart by astronomy student Clyde Tombaugh, reveal that one of the "stars" moved during that time. The "star" turned out to be a previously undiscovered object in our solar system—Pluto.
- After developing safely-stored photographic film, Henri Becquerel discovers a "ghostly" image on new photographic paper. That something turned out to be coming from uranium salts stored in the same drawer. The accidental exposure of the film led to the pioneering work of Marie and Pierre Curie on "radioactivity"—a term coined by Marie Curie.
- Background radio noise coming from space led technicians Arno Penzias and Robert Wilson to the realization that they were actually listening to the *Big Bang*, an event that formed the universe billions of years ago.

Questions:

1. What serendipitous event led to the discovery of penicillin?
2. Lewis Thomas, a medical research scientist and former president of Memorial Sloan-Kettering Cancer Center, once stated "You create the lucky accidents." What do you think he meant by this statement?
3. Why is the scientific method important to follow when confirming an accidental discovery?
4. Do some research to find three additional serendipitous events (besides the ones mentioned in this reading) that led to important scientific discoveries.

Chapter 1 Review

Understanding Vocabulary

Select the correct term to complete the sentences.

experiment	metric system	seconds
dependent	length	hypothesis
speed	natural laws	constant speed
time interval	English system	atomic
	mass	

Section 1.1

1. It is believed all events in nature obey a set of ____ that do not change.

2. ____ is the measure of the amount of matter in an object.

3. A(n) ____ can help you understand the natural laws that relate matter and energy.

4. When you formulate a(n) ____, you make an educated guess or prediction that can be tested by an experiment.

5. ____ properties are too small to be directly observed.

6. The ____ variable goes with the *y*-axis of a graph.

Section 1.2

7. Distance is measured in units of ____.

8. A quantity of time is known as a(n) ____.

9. The ____ uses length measurements of millimeters, centimeters, meters, and kilometers.

10. In physics, time is usually measured in units of ____.

11. The ____ uses length measurements of inches, feet, yards and miles.

Section 1.3

12. ____ is the distance traveled divided by the time taken.

13. A car traveling the same distance every second is moving at ____.

Reviewing Concepts

Section 1.1

1. List and define the two categories we use to classify everything in the universe.

2. How have physicists come to understand the natural laws?

3. What property does matter have that energy does not?

4. Is light matter? Why or why not?

5. Define the term *system* as it relates to experiments.

6. When designing an experiment, how do you choose the system to investigate?

7. Explain the main difference between the macroscopic scale and the atomic scale.

8. List the steps of the scientific method.

9. A hypothesis is a random guess. True or false? Explain your answer.

10. What do you call variables that are kept the same in an experiment?

11. Why is it important to only change one experimental variable at a time in an experiment?

12. You wish to do an experiment to determine how a ball's radius affects how fast it rolls down a ramp. List the independent and dependent variables in this experiment.

13. Explain the role of energy in a system that is changing.

Section 1.2

14. Why are units important when measuring quantities?

15. State whether you would measure each quantity in kilometers, meters, centimeters, or millimeters.
    a. The length of a car
    b. A single grain of rice
    c. The thickness of your textbook
    d. The distance from your house to school

16. Why is it important to understand both English and metric units?

17. Give an example of a quantity that is often measured in metric units and a quantity that is often measured in English units.

18. What are the two different meanings of the word time?

19. Summarize how to make a graph by listing the steps you would follow.

20. You wish to make a graph of the height of the moon above the horizon every 15 minutes between 9:00 p.m. and 3:00 am during one night.
    a. What is the independent variable?
    b. What is the dependent variable?
    c. On which axis should you graph each variable?

Section 1.3

21. Write the form of the speed equation that you would use in each of the following scenarios. Let v = speed, t = time, and d = distance:
    a. You know distance and speed and want to find the time.
    b. You know time and distance and want to find the speed.
    c. You know speed and time and want to find the distance.

22. What is the speed of an object that is standing still?

23. Your friend rides her bicycle across town at a constant speed. Describe how you could determine her speed.

24. Fill in the missing information in the table showing common units for speed below:

Distance	Time	Speed	Abbreviation
meters	seconds		
			km/h
		centimeters per second	

25. Summarize the four steps for solving physics problems mentioned in the text.

Solving Problems

Section 1.1

1. You want to find out whether the birds near your school prefer thistle seed or sunflower seed. You have a bag of thistle seed, a bag of sunflower seed, and two bird feeders. Describe the experiment you would do to see which type of seed birds prefer. Write down your question, your hypothesis, and the procedure you would follow when doing your experiment.

2. You are doing an experiment to determine whether a dropped ball's mass affects the rate at which it falls. Describe the system you are studying. Write down your question, your hypothesis, and the procedure you would follow when doing your experiment.

Section 1.2

3. Order the following lengths from shortest to longest.
    a. 400 millimeters
    b. 22 kilometers
    c. 170 meters
    d. 3.3 centimeters

4. Convert:
    a. 3 kilometers = ____ meters
    b. 1.5 meters = ____ centimeters
    c. 110 centimeters = ____ meters
    d. 2.5 centimeters = ____ millimeters

5. Convert:
    a. 3 minutes = ____ seconds
    b. 200 seconds = ____ minutes, ____ seconds
    c. 2 days = ____ minutes
    d. 1,000 minutes = ____ hours

6. Determine your age in each of the following units.
    a. months
    b. days
    c. hours
    d. seconds

7. Luis rides his new bike while his brother records his position and time. They create the data table shown below.

Position (m)	0	105	270	400	540	600
Time (sec)	0	30	60	90	120	150

    a. Which is the dependent variable?
    b. Which is the independent variable?
    c. On which axis should you graph each variable?
    d. Construct a graph of Luis' bike ride.

Section 1.3

8. A bicyclist, traveling at 22 miles per hour, rides a total of 44 miles. How much time (in hours) did it take?

9. A mouse is moving in a straight line at a steady speed of 2 m/sec for 10 seconds. How far (in meters) did the mouse travel?

10. The gray wolf is a threatened animal that is native to the United States. A wildlife biologist tracks a gray wolf that moves 250 meters in 100 seconds. Calculate the wolf's speed in meters per second.

11. It takes Brooke 10 minutes to run 1 mile. What is her speed in miles per minute?

12. If it takes 500 seconds for the light from the sun to reach Earth, what is the distance to the sun in meters? (The speed of light is 300,000,000 meters/second).

13. Use the data from Luis' bike ride in question 7 to answer the following questions:
    a. What was Luis' speed (in meters per second) for the entire ride, from 0 to 150 seconds?
    b. What was Luis' speed (in meters per second) between 60 and 90 seconds?
    c. During which 30 second interval did Luis have the greatest speed? Calculate this speed in meters per second.

Applying Your Knowledge

Section 1.1

1. Read an article in a science magazine and identify how scientists have used the scientific method in their work.

2. Given a ruler, a stopwatch, a tennis ball, a 1-meter long piece of string, a rubber band, tape, and 10 pieces of paper, design an experiment. List a question, a hypothesis, the independent variable, the dependent variable, the control variables, and the procedure for your experiment.

Section 1.2

3. Research the number system and length units of an ancient civilization. What types of things did this ancient group of people need to measure? What were the smallest and largest units of length used? Write a short report on what you learn.

4. Research what the time standard is for the United States. What determines the correct time? Where is this national clock kept and how can you set your clocks at home to it? Write a short report on what you learn.

5. Find an example of a graph used to model a system in your everyday life. You might check magazines, newspapers, or the internet. Copy the graph, describe what it is modeling, and list the dependent variable, independent variable, and measurement scales used.

Section 1.3

6. Research the speeds of many kinds of animals and make a table showing slowest to fastest.

7. Determine your average walking speed. How long would it take you to walk 2,462 miles (3,962 km) from New York to Los Angeles?

8. Prepare a short report on important speeds in your favorite sport.

9. Use the Internet to find the world record times for running races of different lengths (100-meter, 200-meter, mile, marathon, etc.). Calculate and compare speeds for the different races.

Chapter 2

Laws of Motion

In January 1993, the 53rd space shuttle mission crew, in addition to their usual science experiments, brought some toys on board! During the flight, crew members took the toys out and played with them to see how they would work in what NASA calls "microgravity." Many people think astronauts float because there is no gravity in space. Not true! If there were no gravity, the space shuttle would not stay in orbit around Earth. So why do astronauts float?

This chapter will help you explain many aspects of motion as it occurs here on Earth, and even how things like simple toys would act in microgravity. You will be able to use Newton's laws of motion to explain why it's possible to throw a basketball through a hoop. What if that hoop and basketball were on the space shuttle? Would the crew members be able to shoot baskets in a microgravity environment?

Sir Isaac Newton, who lived from 1642-1727, attempted to answer similar questions and soon you will know the answers too!

Key Questions

✓ Why do thrown objects fall to Earth instead of flying through the air forever?

✓ Is it possible for a feather and a hammer to hit the ground at the same time when dropped?

✓ What does a graph of motion look like?

2.1 Newton's First Law

Sir Isaac Newton (1642-1727), an English physicist and mathematician, was one of the most brilliant scientists in history. Before age 30, he had made several important discoveries in physics and had invented a new kind of mathematics called calculus. Newton's three laws of motion are probably the most widely used natural laws in all of science. The laws explain the relationships between the forces acting on an object, the object's mass, and its motion. This section discusses Newton's first law of motion.

Changing an object's motion Suppose you are playing miniature golf and it is your turn. What action must you take to make the golf ball move toward the hole? Would you yell at the ball to make it move? Of course not! You would have to hit the ball with the golf club to get it rolling. The club applies a force to the ball. This force is what changes the ball from being at rest to being in motion (Figure 2.1).

What is force? A **force** is a *push* or *pull*, or *any action that has the ability to change motion*. The golf ball will stay at rest until you apply force to set it in motion. Once the ball is moving, it will continue to move in a straight line at a constant speed, unless another force changes its motion. You need force to start things moving and also to make any change to their motion once they are moving. Forces can be used to increase or decrease the speed of an object, or to change the direction in which an object is moving.

How are forces created? Forces are created in many different ways. For example, your muscles create force when you swing the golf club. Earth's gravity creates forces that pull on everything around you. On a windy day, the movement of air can create forces. Each of these actions can create force because they all can change an object's motion.

Force is required to change motion Forces create changes in motion, and *there can be no change in motion without the presence of a force.* Anytime there is a change in motion a force must exist, even if you cannot immediately recognize the force. For example, when a rolling ball hits a wall and bounces, its motion changes rapidly. That change in motion is caused by the wall exerting a force that changes the direction of the ball's motion.

Vocabulary

force, Newton's first law, inertia, newton, net force

Objectives

✓ Recognize that force is needed to change an object's motion.
✓ Explain Newton's first law.
✓ Describe how inertia and mass are related.

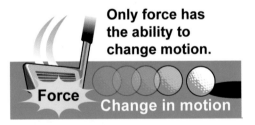

Figure 2.1: *Force is the action that has the ability to change motion. Without force, the motion of an object cannot be started or changed.*

Forces, mass, and inertia

Stopping a moving object Let's keep playing golf. Once the golf ball is moving, how can you stop it? The only way to stop the ball is to apply a force in a direction opposite its motion. In general, objects continue doing what they are already doing. This idea is known as Newton's first law of motion.

Newton's first law **Newton's first law** states that objects tend to continue the motion they already have unless they are acted on by forces. In the absence of forces an object at rest will stay at rest. An object that is moving will keep moving at the same speed and in the same direction. In other words, objects resist changes in their motion.

An object at rest will stay at rest and an object in motion will continue in motion with the same speed and direction UNLESS acted on by a force.

Inertia Some objects resist changes in motion better than others. **Inertia** is the property of an object that resists changes in its motion. To understand inertia, imagine trying to move a bowling ball and a golf ball. Which requires more force? Of course, the bowling ball needs more force to get it moving at the same speed as the golf ball (assuming the forces act for the same length of time). The bowling ball also requires more force to stop. A bowling ball has more inertia than a golf ball. The greater an object's inertia, the greater the force needed to change its motion. Because inertia is an important idea, Newton's first law is sometimes called the law of inertia.

Mass Inertia comes from mass. Objects with more mass have more inertia and are more resistant to changes in their motion. Mass is measured in kilograms (kg). A golf ball has a mass of 0.05 kilograms, and the average bowling ball has a mass of 5 kilograms (Figure 2.2). A bowling ball is 100 times as massive, so it has 100 times the inertia. For small amounts of mass, the kilogram is too large a unit to be convenient. One gram (g) is one-thousandth of a kilogram. A dollar bill has a mass of about a gram, so 1,000 dollar bills have a mass of approximately 1 kilogram.

One dollar bill =
1 gram
0.001 kilogram

A golf ball
50 grams
0.050 kilogram

One liter of soda
1000 grams
1 kilogram

A bowling ball
5000 grams
5 kilograms

Figure 2.2: *Mass can be measured in grams or kilograms. One kilogram equals 1000 grams.*

Units of force

Pounds If you are mailing a package at the post office, how does the clerk know how much to charge you? The package is placed on a scale and you are charged based on the package's weight. For example, the scale shows that the package weighs 5 pounds. The pound is a unit of *force* commonly used in the United States. When you measure weight in pounds on a scale, you are measuring the *force of gravity* acting on the object (Figure 2.3).

The origin of the pound The pound measurement of force is based on the Roman unit *libra*, which means "balance" and is the source for pound's abbreviation, "lb." The word "pound" comes from the Latin word *pondus*, which means "weight." The definition of a pound has varied over time and from country to country.

The newton Although the pound is commonly used to express force, scientists prefer to use the newton. The **newton (N)** is the metric unit of force. A force of one newton is the exact amount of force needed to cause a mass of one kilogram to speed up by one meter per second each second (Figure 2.3). We call the unit of force the newton because force in the metric system is defined by Newton's laws. The newton is a useful way to measure force because it connects force directly to its effect on mass and speed.

Converting newtons and pounds The newton is a smaller unit of force than the pound. One pound of force equals 4.448 newtons. How much would a 100-pound person weigh in newtons? Remember that 1 pound = 4.448 newtons. Therefore, a 100-pound person weighs 444.8 newtons.

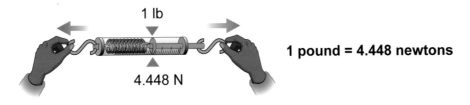

1 pound = 4.448 newtons

The force unit of newtons When physics problems are presented in this book, forces will almost always be expressed in newtons. In the next section, on Newton's second law, you will see that the newton is closely related to the metric units for mass and distance.

Pound

One pound (lb) is the force exerted by gravity on a mass of 0.454 kg.

Newton

One newton (N) is the force it takes to change the speed of a 1 kg mass by 1 m/sec in 1 second.

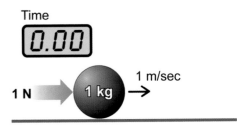

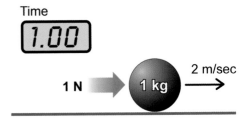

Figure 2.3: *The definition of the pound and the newton.*

The net force

Multiple forces   When you hit a golf ball, the force from the club is not the only force that acts. Gravity also exerts a force on the ball. Which force causes the change in the ball's motion: gravity or the force from the golf club? Does gravity stop while the golf club exerts its force?

Forces act together   You are right if you are thinking "all forces together." The motion of objects changes in response to the *total force* acting on the object, including gravity and any other force that is present. In fact, it is rare that only one force acts at a time since gravity is always present.

Net force   Adding up forces can be different from simply adding numbers because the *directions* of the forces matter. For this reason the term **net force** is used to describe the total of all forces acting on an object. When used this way, the word "net" means *total* but also implies that the direction of the forces has been taken into account when calculating the total.

Forces in the same direction   When two forces are in the same direction, the net force is the sum of the two. For example, think about two people pushing a box. If each person pushes with a force of 300 newtons in the same direction, the net force on the box is 600 N (Figure 2.4 top). The box speeds up in the direction of the net force.

Forces in opposite directions   What about gravity acting on the box? Gravity exerts a force downward on the box. However, the floor holds the box up. In physics, the term "holds up" means "applies a force." In order to "hold up" the box, the floor exerts a force upward on the box. The net force on the box in the "up-down" direction is *zero* because the force from the floor is opposed to the force of gravity. When equal forces are in the opposite direction they cancel (Figure 2.4 bottom). The motion of the box in the up-down (vertical) direction does not change because the net force in this direction is zero.

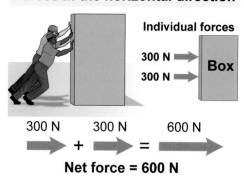

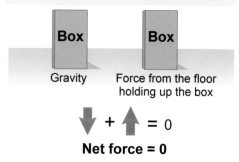

Figure 2.4: *The net force acting on a box being pushed.*

2.1 Section Review

1. State Newton's first law in your own words.

2. How is mass related to inertia?

3. What is the net force and how is it determined?

2.2 Acceleration and Newton's Second Law

Newton's first law says that a force is needed to change an object's motion. But what kind of change happens? The answer is *acceleration*. Acceleration is how motion changes. The amount of acceleration depends on both the force and the mass according to Newton's second law. This section is about Newton's second law, which relates force, mass, and acceleration. The second law is probably the most well-used relationship in all of physics.

Acceleration

Definition of acceleration   What happens if you coast on a bicycle down a long hill without pedaling? At the top of the hill, you move slowly. As you go down the hill, your speed gets faster and faster—you accelerate. **Acceleration** is the rate at which your speed increases. If speed increases by 1 kilometer per hour (km/h) each second, the acceleration is 1 km/h per second.

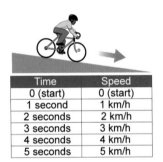

Time	Speed
0 (start)	0 (start)
1 second	1 km/h
2 seconds	2 km/h
3 seconds	3 km/h
4 seconds	4 km/h
5 seconds	5 km/h

Time	Speed
0 (start)	0 (start)
1 second	2 km/h
2 seconds	4 km/h
3 seconds	6 km/h
4 seconds	8 km/h
5 seconds	10 km/h

Steeper hills   Your acceleration depends on the steepness of the hill. If the hill is a gradual incline, you have a small acceleration, such as 1 km/h per second. If the hill is steeper, your acceleration will be greater, perhaps 2 km/h per second. On the gradual hill, your speedometer increases by 1 km/h every second. On the steeper hill, it increases by 2 km/h every second.

Car acceleration   Advertisements for sports cars often discuss acceleration. A typical ad might boast that a car can go "from zero to 60 in 10 seconds." This means the car's speed begins at zero and reaches 60 miles per hour (96 km/h) after accelerating for 10 seconds. The car's acceleration is therefore 6 miles per hour per second (Figure 2.5).

Acceleration of the car is 6 mph/sec

Figure 2.5: *It takes 10 seconds for a car to go from zero to 60 mph if it has an acceleration of 6 mph per second. In metric units the car goes from zero to 96 km/h in 10 seconds. The acceleration is 9.6 km/h per second.*

Units of acceleration

Speed units and time units
Acceleration is the rate of change of an object's speed. To calculate acceleration, you divide the change in speed by the amount of time it takes for the change to happen. In the example of the sports car, acceleration was given in kilometers per hour per second. This unit can be abbreviated as km/h/sec. Notice that two time units are included in the unit for acceleration. One unit of time is part of the speed unit, and the other is the time over which the speed changed.

Metric units
If the change in speed is in meters per second and the time is in seconds, then the unit for acceleration is m/sec/sec or *meters per second per second*. An acceleration of 10 m/sec/sec means that the speed increases by 10 m/sec *every second*. If the acceleration lasts for three seconds, then the speed increases by a total of 30 m/sec (3 seconds × 10 m/sec/sec). This is approximately the acceleration of an object allowed to fall free after being dropped.

What do units of seconds *squared* mean?
An acceleration in m/sec/sec is often written m/sec^2 (meters per second squared). If you apply the rules for simplifying fractions on the units of acceleration (m/sec/sec), the denominator ends up having units of seconds times seconds, or sec^2. Saying *seconds squared* is just a math-shorthand way of talking. It is better to think about acceleration in units of speed change per second (that is, meters per second *per second*).

$$\text{Acceleration} = \frac{\text{Change in speed}}{\text{Change in time}}$$

How we get units of m/sec²

Plug in values	Clear the compound fraction	Final units
$\dfrac{50\,\frac{m}{sec}}{sec}$	$= 50\,\frac{m}{sec} \times \frac{1}{sec} = 50\,\frac{m}{sec \times sec}$	$= 50\,\frac{m}{sec^2}$

Acceleration in m/sec^2
Nearly all physics problems will use acceleration in m/sec^2 because these units agree with the units of force (newtons). If you measure speed in centimeters per second, you may have to convert to meters/second before calculating acceleration. This is especially true if you do any calculations using force in newtons.

Acceleration and direction

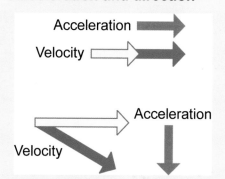

The velocity of an object includes both its speed and the direction it is moving. A car with a velocity of 20 m/sec north has a speed of 20 m/sec and is moving north. An object accelerates if its *velocity* changes. This can occur if its *speed* changes or if its *direction* changes (or both). Therefore, a car driving at a constant speed of 40 mph around a bend is actually accelerating. The only way a moving object can have an acceleration of zero is to be moving at constant speed in a straight line.
This chapter covers acceleration that involves only changes in speed. In chapter 6, you will learn about the acceleration of moving objects that change direction as well.

Calculating acceleration

The equation for acceleration To calculate acceleration, you divide the change in speed by the time over which the speed changed. To find the change in speed, subtract the starting (or initial) speed from the final speed. For example, if a bicycle's speed increases from 2 m/sec to 6 m/sec, its change in speed is 4 m/sec. Because two speeds are involved, subscripts are used to show the difference. The initial speed is v_1, and the final speed is v_2.

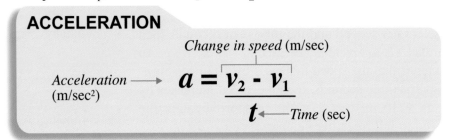

ACCELERATION

Change in speed (m/sec)

Acceleration (m/sec²) → $a = \dfrac{v_2 - v_1}{t}$ ←—Time (sec)

Time

0.00 1 m/sec

Time

3.00 4 m/sec

Wind force

What is the acceleration?

Positive and negative acceleration If an object *speeds up*, it has a *positive acceleration*. If it *slows down*, it has a *negative acceleration*. In physics, the word acceleration is used to refer to any change in speed, positive or negative. However, people sometimes use the word **deceleration** to describe the motion that is slowing down.

Figure 2.6: *An acceleration example with a sailboat.*

Calculating acceleration

A sailboat moves at 1 m/sec. A strong wind increases its speed to 4 m/sec in 3 seconds (Figure 2.6). Calculate the acceleration.

1. Looking for: You are asked for the acceleration in meters per second.

2. Given: You are given the initial speed in m/sec (v_1), final speed in m/sec (v_2), and the time in seconds.

3. Relationships: Use the formula for acceleration: $a = \dfrac{v_2 - v_1}{t}$

4. Solution:

$$a = \frac{4\ \text{m/sec} - 1\ \text{m/sec}}{3\ \text{sec}} = \frac{3\ \text{m/sec}}{3\ \text{sec}} = 1\ \text{m/sec}^2$$

Your turn...

a. Calculate the acceleration of an airplane that starts at rest and reaches a speed of 45 m/sec in 9 seconds. **Answer:** 5 m/sec²

b. Calculate the acceleration of a car that slows from 50 m/sec to 30 m/sec in 10 seconds. **Answer:** -2 m/sec²

Force, mass, and acceleration

Newton's second law

Newton's second law relates the net force on an object, the mass of the object, and acceleration. It states that the stronger the net force on an object, the greater its acceleration. If twice the net force is applied, the acceleration will be twice as great. The law also says that the greater the mass, the smaller the acceleration for a given net force (Figure 2.7). An object with twice the mass will have half the acceleration if the same force is applied.

Direct and inverse proportions

In mathematical terms, the acceleration of an object is directly proportional to the net applied force and inversely proportional to the mass. These two relationships are combined in Newton's second law (below).

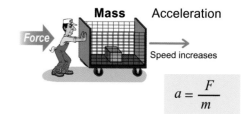

NEWTON'S SECOND LAW

$$\text{Acceleration (m/sec}^2) \rightarrow a = \frac{F}{m} \begin{matrix} \leftarrow \text{Force (N)} \\ \leftarrow \text{Mass (kg)} \end{matrix}$$

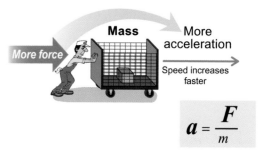

Changes in motion involve acceleration

Force is not necessary to keep an object in motion at constant speed. A moving object will keep going at a constant speed in a straight line until a force acts on it. Once a skater is moving, she will coast for a long time without any force to push her along. However, she does need force to speed up, slow down, turn, or stop. Changes in speed or direction always involve acceleration. *Force* causes *acceleration*, and *mass* resists *acceleration*.

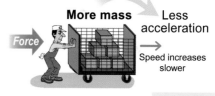

Figure 2.7: *Increasing the force increases the acceleration, and increasing the mass decreases the acceleration.*

Applying the second law

Some guidelines To use Newton's second law properly, keep the following important ideas in mind. They are a good guideline for how to apply the second law to physics problems.

1. The *net* force is what causes acceleration.
2. If there is *no* acceleration, the net force *must* be zero.
3. If there *is* acceleration, there *must* also be a net force.
4. The force unit of newtons is based on kilograms, meters, and seconds.

Net force When two forces are in the same direction, the net force is the sum of the two forces. When two forces are in opposite directions the net force is the difference between them. To get the direction right we usually assign positive values to one direction and negative values to the other direction. Figure 2.8 shows how to calculate the net force for different forces.

Examples with and without acceleration Objects at rest or moving with constant speed have zero acceleration. This means the net force must also be zero. You can calculate unknown forces by using the knowledge that the net force must be zero. The motion of a kicked ball or a car turning a corner are examples where the acceleration is not zero. Both situations have net forces that are not zero.

Using newtons in calculations The newton is *defined* by the relationship between force, mass, and acceleration. A force of one newton is the exact amount of force needed to cause a mass of one kilogram to accelerate at one m/sec^2 (Figure 2.9). The newton is a useful way to measure force because it connects force directly to its effect on matter and motion. A net force of one newton will always accelerate a 1-kilogram mass at 1 m/sec^2 no matter where you are in the universe. In terms of solving problems, you should always use the following units when using force in newtons:

- mass in kilograms
- distance or position in meters
- time in seconds
- speed in m/sec
- acceleration in m/sec^2

Calculating the net force

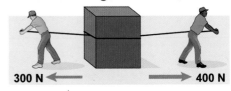

1. Assign positive and negative directions.

2. Add up all the forces using the positive and negative values.

$$+ 400\text{ N}$$
$$-300\text{ N}$$
$$\overline{+ 100\text{ N}}$$

The net force is 100 N to the right (positive).

Figure 2.8: *Calculating the net force.*

Newton

One newton (N) is the force it takes to change the speed of a 1 kg mass by 1 m/sec in 1 second.

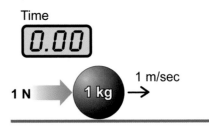

Figure 2.9: *The definition of a newton.*

Doing calculations with the second law

Writing the second law The formula for the second law of motion uses *F*, *m*, and *a* to represent force, mass, and acceleration. The way you write the formula depends on what you want to know. Three ways to write the law are summarized below.

Table 2.1: *Three forms of the second law*

Use . . .	. . . if you want to find . . .	. . . and you know . . .
$a = F/m$	acceleration (*a*)	force (*F*) and mass (*m*)
$F = ma$	force (*F*)	acceleration (*a*) and mass (*m*)
$m = F/a$	mass (*m*)	acceleration (*a*) and force (*F*)

Net force Remember, when using the second law, the force that appears is the net force. Consider all the forces that are acting and add them up to find the net force before calculating any accelerations. If you work in the other direction, calculating force from mass and acceleration, it is the net force that you get from the second law. You may have to do additional work if the problem asks for a specific force and there is more than one force acting.

Units and the second law

When using $F = ma$, the units of force (newtons) must equal the units of mass (kilograms) multiplied by the units of acceleration (m/sec²). How is this possible? The answer is that 1 newton is 1 kg·m/sec². The unit "newton" was created to be a shortcut way to write the unit of force. It is much simpler to say 5 N rather than 5 kg·m/sec².

Newton's second law

A car has a mass of 1,000 kg. If a net force of 2,000 N is exerted on the car, what is its acceleration?

1. Looking for: You are asked for the car's acceleration.

2. Given: You are given its mass in kilograms and the net force in newtons.

3. Relationships: $a = \dfrac{F}{m}$

4. Solution: $a = \dfrac{2000 \text{ N}}{1000 \text{ kg}} = \dfrac{2 \text{kg} \cdot \text{m/sec}^2}{\text{kg}} = 2 \text{ m/sec}^2$

Your turn...

a. What is the acceleration of a 1,500-kilogram car if a net force of 1,000 N is exerted on it? **Answer:** 1.5 m/sec²

b. As you coast down the hill on your bicycle, you accelerate at 0.5 m/sec². If the total mass of your body and the bicycle is 80 kg, with what force is gravity pulling you down the hill? **Answer:** 40 kg·m/sec² or 40 N

c. You push a grocery car with a force of 30 N and it accelerates at 2 m/sec². What is its mass? **Answer:** 15 kg

Force and energy

Energy moves through force
Force is the action through which energy moves. This important idea will help you understand why forces occur. Consider a rubber band that is stretched to launch a car. The rubber band has energy because it is stretched. When you let the car go, the energy of the rubber band is transferred to the car. The transfer of energy from the stretched rubber band to the car occurs through the force that the rubber band exerts on the car (Figure 2.10).

Energy differences create force
Forces are created any time there is a difference in energy. A stretched rubber band has more energy than a rubber band lying relaxed. The difference in energy results in a force that the rubber band exerts on whatever is holding it in the stretched shape.

An example of energy difference
Energy differences can be created in many ways. A car at the top of a hill has more energy than when the car is at the bottom. This tells you there must be a force that pulls the car toward the bottom of the hill. You can predict that a downhill force must exist even though you may not know the cause of that force.

An important idea
Suppose there is an energy difference between one arrangement of a system (car at the top) and another arrangement (car at the bottom). Some force will *always* act to bring the system from the higher energy arrangement to the lower energy one. We will find many examples of this important principle throughout the course. The principle is true in all of science, not just physics. It is true in chemistry, earth science, and biology, too.

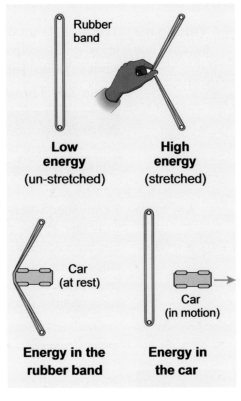

Figure 2.10: *Energy differences cause forces to be created. The forces can transfer energy from one object to another.*

2.2 Section Review

1. List three units in which acceleration can be measured.

2. According to Newton's second law, what causes acceleration? What resists acceleration?

3. An 8,000 kg helicopter's speed increases from 0 m/sec to 25 m/sec in 5 seconds. Calculate its acceleration and the net force acting on it.

4. Define the term "net force."

5. Describe the conceptual relationship between energy and force.

2.3 Gravity and Free Fall

Imagine dropping a baseball out of a second-floor window. What happens? Of course, the ball falls toward the ground. Is the speed constant or does the ball accelerate? If it accelerates, at what rate? Do all objects fall at the same rate? You will learn the answers to these questions in this section.

The acceleration due to gravity

The definition of free fall
An object is in **free fall** if it is accelerating due to the force of gravity and no other forces are acting on it. A dropped baseball is in free fall from the instant it leaves your hand until it reaches the ground. A ball thrown upward is also in free fall after it leaves your hand. Although you might not describe the ball as "falling," it is still in free fall. Birds, helicopters, and airplanes are *not* normally in free fall because forces other than gravity act on them.

The acceleration of gravity
Objects in free fall on Earth accelerate downward at 9.8 m/sec^2, the **acceleration due to gravity**. Because this acceleration is used so frequently in physics, the letter g is used to represent its value. When you see the letter g in a physics question, you can substitute the value 9.8 m/sec^2.

Speed in free fall
If you know the acceleration of an object in free fall, you can predict its speed at any time after it is dropped. The speed of a dropped object will increase by 9.8 m/sec every second (Figure 2.11). If it starts at rest, it will be moving at 9.8 m/sec after one second, 19.6 m/sec after two seconds, 29.4 m/sec after three seconds, and so on. To calculate the object's speed, you multiply the time it falls by the value of g. Because the units of g are m/sec^2, the speed must be in m/sec and the time must be in seconds.

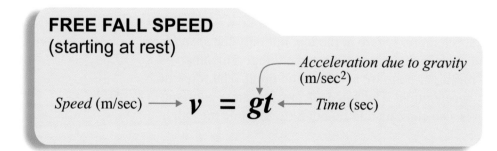

FREE FALL SPEED
(starting at rest)

$$v = gt$$

Speed (m/sec) — v

Acceleration due to gravity (m/sec^2) — g

Time (sec) — t

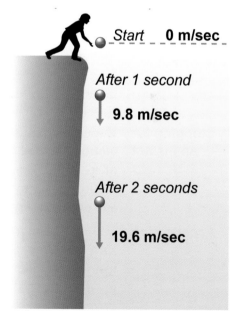

Start 0 m/sec

After 1 second

9.8 m/sec

After 2 seconds

19.6 m/sec

Figure 2.11: *The speed of a ball in free fall increases by 9.8 m/sec every second.*

Upward launches

Throwing a ball upward When an object is in free fall, it accelerates *downward* at 9.8 m/sec². Gravity causes the acceleration by exerting a downward force. So what happens if you throw a ball *upward*? The ball will slow down as it moves upward, come to a stop for an instant, and then fall back down. As it moves upward, the speed *decreases* by 9.8 m/sec every second until it reaches zero. The ball then reverses direction and starts falling down. As it falls downward, the speed *increases* by 9.8 m/sec every second.

Velocity When an object's direction is important, we use the *velocity* instead of the speed. **Velocity** is speed with direction. In Figure 2.12, the ball's initial velocity is +19.6 m/sec and its velocity four seconds later is -19.6 m/sec. The positive sign means upward and the negative sign means downward.

Speed The acceleration of the ball is -9.8 m/sec² (-*g*). That means you subtract 9.8 m/sec from the speed every second. Figure 2.12 shows what happens to a ball launched upward at 19.6 m/sec. The speed decreases for two seconds, reaches zero, and then increases for two seconds. *The acceleration is the same all the time* (-9.8 m/sec²) even though the ball is slowing down as it goes up and speeding up as it comes back down. The acceleration is the same because the change in speed is the same from one second to the next. The speed always changes by -9.8 m/sec every second.

Stopping for an instant Notice the ball's speed is 0 m/sec at the top of its path. If you watch this motion, the ball looks like it stops, because it is moving so slowly at the top of its path. To your eye it may look like it stops for a second, but a slow-motion camera would show the ball's speed immediately reverses at the top and does not stay zero for any measurable amount of time.

Acceleration You may want to say the acceleration is zero at the top, but only the *speed* is zero at the top. Speed and acceleration are not the same thing, remember — just like 60 miles and 60 miles per hour are not the same thing. The force of gravity causes the ball's acceleration. The force of gravity stays constant; therefore, the acceleration is also constant and cannot be zero while the ball is in the air.

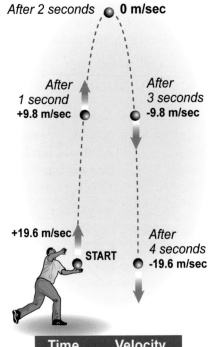

Time (sec)	Velocity (m/sec)
0.0	19.60
1.0	9.80
2.0	0.00
3.0	-9.80
4.0	-19.60

Figure 2.12: *The motion of a ball launched upward at 19.6 m/sec.*

Free fall and distance

Changing speeds   In chapter 1, you used $d = vt$ to calculate distance. You cannot calculate distance in the same simple way when speed is not constant, as happens in free fall. An object in free fall increases its speed by 9.8 m/sec each second (or 9.8 m/sec^2), so it moves a greater distance each second.

Average speed   One way to calculate distance is to use the *average speed*. In free fall and other situations of *constant* acceleration, the average speed is the average of the starting or initial speed (v_i) and the final speed (v_f). Taking the average accounts for the fact that the speed is not constant. Be careful when doing this calculation. The average speed may *not* be ($v_f + v_i$) ÷ 2, if the acceleration is not constant.

$t = 0$

$t = 5$ seconds

Figure 2.13: *What is the average speed of a rock that falls for 5 seconds?*

AVERAGE SPEED

Average speed (m/sec) → $V_{avg} = \dfrac{v_f + v_i}{2}$

Final speed (m/sec)
Initial speed (m/sec)

Average speed

A rock falls off a cliff and splashes into a river 5 seconds later (Figure 2.13). What was the rock's average speed during its fall?

1. Looking for: You are asked for the average speed in meters per second. You need to find the final speed in meters per second.

2. Given: You may assume zero initial speed and are given the air time in seconds.

3. Relationships: $v_f = gt$ and $v_{avg} = \dfrac{v_i + v_f}{2}$ where $g = 9.8$ m/sec^2

4. Solution:

$$v_f = (9.8 \text{ m/sec}^2)(5 \text{ sec}) = 49 \text{ m/sec} \qquad v_{avg} = \frac{0 + 49 \text{ m/sec}}{2} = 24.5 \text{ m/sec}$$

Your turn...

a. What is the average speed of a baseball dropped from rest that falls for 2 seconds? **Answer:** 9.8 m/sec

b. What is the average speed of a ball with an initial downward speed of 10 m/sec that falls for 2 seconds? **Answer:** 14.8 m/sec

Calculating distance Now that you know how to calculate the average speed for an object in free fall, you can use the average speed to find out the distance it falls.

FREE FALL DISTANCE

$$Distance\ (m) \longrightarrow d = v_{avg}\, t \xleftarrow{} \begin{array}{c} Average\ speed\ (m/sec) \\ Time\ (sec) \end{array}$$

Calculating free fall speed and distance

A skydiver falls for 6 seconds before opening her parachute. Calculate her actual speed at the 6-second mark and the distance she has fallen in this time.

1. Looking for: You are asked to find the final speed and the distance.

2. Given: You may assume zero initial speed and are given the time in seconds.

3. Relationships: $v_f = gt \qquad v_{avg} = \dfrac{v_i + v_f}{2} \qquad d = v_{avg}t$

4. Solution: $v_f = (9.8\ \text{m/sec}^2)(6\ \text{sec}) = 58.8\ \text{m/sec}$

The speed after 6 seconds is 58.8 m/sec.

$v_{avg} = \dfrac{0 + 58.8\ \text{m/sec}}{2} = 29.4\ \text{m/sec}$

$d = (29.4\ \text{m/sec})(6\ \text{sec}) = 176.4\ \text{m}$

The skydiver falls 176.4 meters.

Your turn...

a. Calculate the final speed and distance for a skydiver who waits only 4 seconds to open his parachute. **Answer:** 39.2 m/sec and 78.4 m
b. An apple falls from the top branch of a tree and lands 1 second later. How tall is the tree? **Answer:** 4.9 m

Another way to calculate free-fall distance

Using the average speed to calculate the distance traveled by an object in free fall requires multiple steps. If you are only given the air time, you must first find the final speed, then you must calculate the average speed, and finally you can find the distance. These three steps can all be combined into one formula. The general version of the formula is more complicated than the scope of this book, but can be simplified if the object starts at rest ($v_i = 0$).
1) If the initial speed is zero and the object falls for t seconds, then the final speed is gt.
2) The average speed is half the final speed or $^1/_2 gt$.
3) The distance is the average speed multiplied by the time or $^1/_2 gt^2$.
The general formula is therefore:

$$d = \frac{1}{2}g\,t^2$$

Remember, this formula only works when the object starts at rest and is in free fall.

Gravity and weight

Gravity's force depends on mass

The force of gravity on an object is called **weight**. The symbol F_g stands for "force of gravity" and is used to represent weight. At Earth's surface, gravity exerts a force of 9.8 N on every kilogram of mass. That means a 1-kilogram mass has a weight of 9.8 N, a two-kilogram mass has a weight of 19.6 N, and so on. On Earth's surface, the weight of any object is its mass multiplied by 9.8 N/kg. Because weight is a force, it is measured in units of force such as newtons and pounds.

Weight and mass

We all tend to use the terms *weight* and *mass* interchangeably. Heavy objects have lots of mass and light objects have little mass. People and things such as food are "weighed" in both kilograms and pounds. If you look on the label of a bag of flour, it lists the "weight" in two units: 5 pounds in the English system and 2.3 kilograms in the metric system. As long as we are on Earth, where g = 9.8 N/kg a 2.3-kilogram object will weigh 5 pounds. But on the moon, g = 1.6 N/kg, so a 2.3 kilogram object will weigh only 0.8 pounds (Figure 2.14).

Weight and the second law

You should recognize that the value of 9.8 N/kg is the same as g (9.8 m/sec^2) but with different units. This is no coincidence. According to the second law, a force of 9.8 newtons acting on one kilogram produces an acceleration of 9.8 m/sec^2. For this reason the value of g can also be used as 9.8 N/kg. Which units you choose depends on whether you want to calculate acceleration or the weight force. Both units are actually identical: 9.8 N/kg = 9.8 m/sec^2.

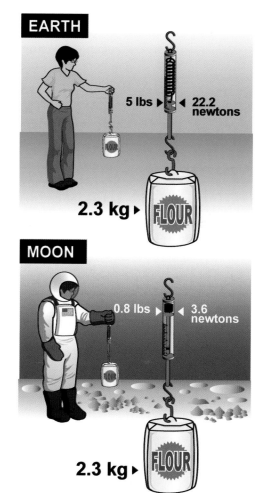

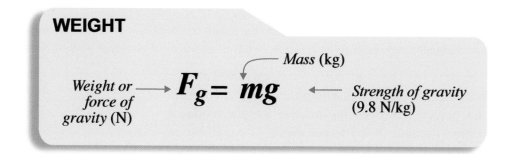

WEIGHT

$$F_g = mg$$

Weight or force of gravity (N) ⟶ $F_g = mg$ ⟵ Mass (kg), Strength of gravity (9.8 N/kg)

Figure 2.14: *An object that weighs 5 pounds on Earth weighs only 0.8 pounds on the moon. It has the same mass but different weights because gravity is stronger on Earth.*

Mass is fundamental Although mass and weight are related quantities, always remember the difference when doing physics. Mass is a fundamental property of an object measured in kilograms (kg). Weight is a *force* measured in *newtons (N)* that depends on mass and gravity. A 10-kilogram object has a mass of 10 kilograms no matter where it is in the universe. A 10-kilogram object's weight, however, can vary greatly depending on whether the object is on Earth, on the moon, or in outer space.

Weight and mass

Legend has it that around 1587 Galileo dropped two balls from the Leaning Tower of Pisa to see which would fall faster. Suppose the balls had masses of 1 kilogram and 10 kilograms.
a. Use the equation for weight to calculate the force of gravity on each ball.
b. Use your answers from (a) and Newton's second law to calculate each ball's acceleration.

1. Looking for:	You are asked to find the force of gravity (weight) and the acceleration.
2. Given:	You are given each ball's mass in kilograms.
3. Relationships:	$F_g = mg$ $a = F/m$
4. Solution:	For the 1-kg ball: a) $F_g = (1 \text{ kg})(9.8 \text{ m/sec}^2)$ $F_g = 9.8 \text{ N}$ b) $a = (9.8 \text{ N})/(1 \text{ kg})$ $a = 9.8 \text{ m/sec}^2$

For the 10-kg ball:
a) $F_g = (10 \text{ kg})(9.8 \text{ m/sec}^2)$ $F_g = 98 \text{ N}$
b) $a = (98 \text{ N})/(10 \text{ kg})$ $a = 9.8 \text{ m/sec}^2$ Both balls have the same acceleration.

Your turn...
a. Calculate the weight of a 60-kilogram person (in newtons) on Earth and on Mars ($g = 3.7 \text{ m/sec}^2$). **Answer: 588 N, 222 N**
b. A 70-kg person travels to a planet where he weighs 1,750 N. What is the value of g on that planet? **Answer: 25 m/sec^2**

Why accelerations are the same The example problem shows the weight of a 10-kilogram object is 10 times the weight of a 1-kilogram object. However, the heavier weight produces only one-tenth the acceleration because of the larger mass. The increase in force (weight) is exactly compensated by the increase in inertia (mass). As a result, the acceleration of all objects in free fall is the same.

Air resistance

Air resistance
We just said the acceleration of all objects in free fall is the same. So why does a feather fall slower than a baseball? The answer is that objects on Earth are not truly in free fall because gravity is *not* the only force acting on falling objects. When something falls through air, the air exerts an additional force. This force, called **air resistance**, acts against the direction of the object's motion.

Factors affecting air resistance
The size and shape of an object affect the force of air resistance. A feather has its weight spread out over a comparatively large area, so it must push a lot of air out of the way as it falls. The force of air resistance is large compared with the weight. According to the second law of motion of motion, acceleration is caused by the net force. The net force is the weight minus the force of air resistance. The feather accelerates at much less than 9.8 m/sec^2 because the net force is very small.

Why the baseball falls faster
A baseball's shape allows it to move through the air more easily than a feather. The force of air resistance is much smaller relative to the baseball's weight. Since the net force is almost the same as its weight, the baseball accelerates at nearly 9.8 m/sec^2 and falls much more rapidly than the feather.

Terminal speed
If you observe a falling feather it stops accelerating after a short distance and then falls at constant speed. That is because air resistance increases with speed. A feather only accelerates until the force of air resistance equals the force of gravity. The net force then becomes zero and the feather falls with a constant speed called the **terminal speed**. The terminal speed depends on the ratio of an object's weight to its air resistance. A tightly crumpled ball of paper has a faster terminal speed than a flat piece of paper because the flat sheet has more air resistance even though the papers' weights are the same.

Skydiving and terminal speed

Parachutes use air resistance to reduce the terminal speed of a skydiver. Without a parachute, the skydiver has a small area and can reach a speed of over 100 mph. The parachute increases the area dramatically and creates greater air resistance. The skydiver's terminal speed is then slow enough to allow for a safe landing.

2.3 Section Review

1. Describe the motion of a freely falling object. Use the words speed, acceleration, and distance in your answer.

2. What is the difference between mass and weight?

3. If you drop a feather and a baseball in a place where there is no air (a vacuum), how will their motions compare? Why?

2.4 Graphs of Motion

Motion graphs are an important tool used to show the relationships between distance, speed, acceleration, and time. For example, meteorologists use graphs to show the motion of hurricanes and other storms. Graphs can show the location and speed of a storm at different points in time to help in predicting its path and the time when it will reach a certain location. In this section, you will use graphs of position versus time and speed versus time to represent motion.

The position vs. time graph

Position versus time

The position versus time graph in Figure 2.15 shows the constant-speed motion of two cars, A and B. Using the numbers on the graph, you see that both cars move for 5 seconds. Car A moves 10 meters while car B moves only 5 meters. Using the equation $v = d/t$ the speed of car A is 2 m/sec. The speed of car B is 1 m/sec. Notice that line A is steeper than line B. A steeper slope on a position versus time graph means a faster speed.

The definition of slope

The **slope** of a line is the ratio of the "rise" (vertical change) to the "run" (horizontal change). The diagram below shows you how to calculate the slope of a line. The rise is equal to the height of the triangle. The run is equal to the length along the base of the triangle. Here, the *x*-values represent time and the *y*-values represent distance. The slope of a position versus time graph is therefore a distance divided by a time, which equals speed.

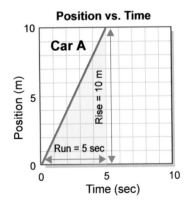

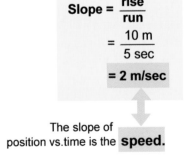

The slope of position vs.time is the **speed.**

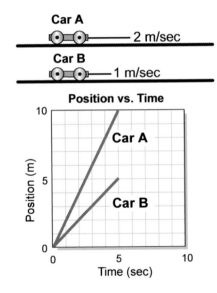

Figure 2.15: *Both cars have constant speed, but Car A is moving faster than Car B.*

Position graphs of accelerated motion

Graphing free fall A position versus time graph can tell you whether an object's speed is constant or changes. If the speed is constant, the graph is a straight line with a constant slope. If the speed is changing, the slope changes, so the graph curves. Consider the speed of an accelerating ball in free fall. As time passes, the ball's speed increases. Because the slope equals the speed, the slope must also become greater with time. The graph is a curve that gets steeper as you move along the *x*-axis (time). A position versus time graph for a ball in free fall is shown below.

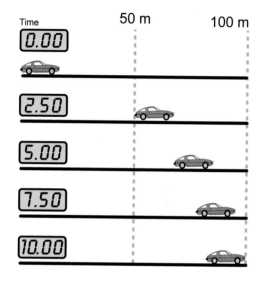

Free Fall Position vs. Time

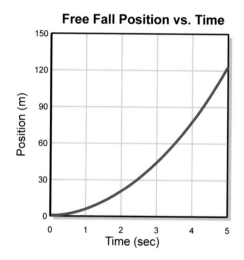

Time (sec)	Position (m)
0	0
1	4.9
2	19.6
3	44.1
4	78.4
5	122.5

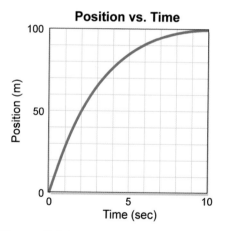

Figure 2.16: *The position versus time graph for a car coming to a gradual stop at a red light.*

Slowing down The graph of an object slowing down is also curved. One example might be a car gradually coming to a stop at a red light. As time passes, the car's speed decreases. The slope of the graph must therefore decrease as you trace the line to the right. Figure 2.16 shows the graph of a car coming to a stop.

The speed vs. time graph for constant speed

The speed versus time graph The speed versus time graph has speed on the *y*-axis and time on the *x*-axis. The graph in Figure 2.17 shows the speed versus time for a ball rolling at constant speed on a level floor. On this graph, constant speed is shown with a straight horizontal line. If you look at the speed on the *y*-axis, you see that the ball is moving at 1 m/sec for the entire 10 seconds. Figure 2.18 is the position versus time graph for the ball. Both of the graphs in the sidebar show the exact same motion. If you calculate the slope of the lower graph, you will find that it is 1 m/sec, the same as the speed in Figure 2.17.

Calculating distance A speed versus time graph also can be used to find the *distance* the object has traveled. Remember, distance is equal to the speed multiplied by the time. Suppose we draw a rectangle on the speed versus time graph between the *x* - axis and the line showing the speed. The area of the rectangle (shown below) is equal to its length times its height. On the graph, the length is equal to the time and the height is equal to the speed. Therefore, the area of the graph is the speed multiplied by the time. This is the distance the ball traveled.

Constant speed

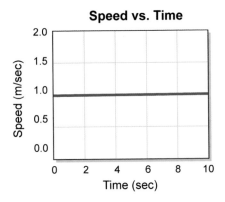

Figure 2.17: *The speed versus time graph for a ball rolling on a level floor at a constant speed of 1 m/sec.*

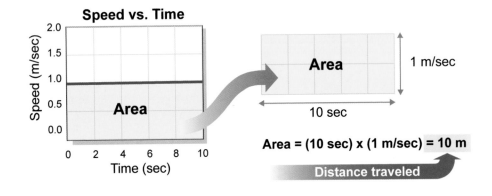

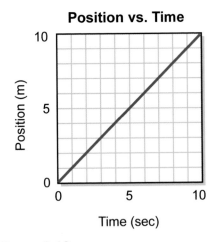

Figure 2.18: *The position versus time graph that shows the exact same motion as the speed versus time graph above.*

The speed vs. time graph for accelerated motion

The speed versus time graph If an object is accelerating it is easier to work with the speed versus time graph instead of the position versus time graph. The speed versus time graph is the best tool for understanding acceleration because it clearly shows how an object's speed changes with time.

Constant acceleration The speed versus time graph below is for a ball in free fall. Because the graph is a straight line, the speed increases by the same amount each second. This means the ball has a *constant acceleration*. Make sure you do not confuse constant speed with constant acceleration. As long as it is moving in one direction, an object at constant speed has zero acceleration (Figure 2.19, bottom). Constant speed means an object's position changes by the same amount each second. Constant acceleration means an object's *speed* changes by the same amount each second.

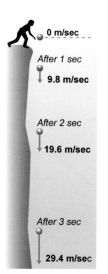

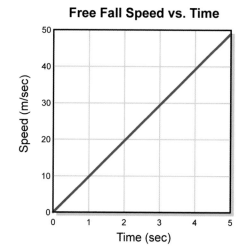

Free Fall Speed vs. Time

Time (sec)	Speed (m/sec)
0	0
1	9.8
2	19.6
3	29.4
4	39.2
5	49.0

Positive acceleration
(speeding up)

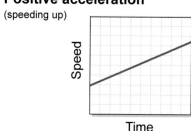

Negative acceleration
(slowing down)

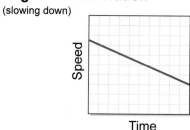

No acceleration
(constant speed)

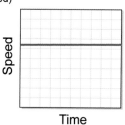

Figure 2.19: *Examples of graphs showing different accelerations.*

Calculating acceleration The slope of a speed versus time graph represents the object's acceleration. Figure 2.19 shows some examples of graphs with and without acceleration. Note that there is acceleration any time the speed versus time graph is *not perfectly horizontal* (or zero slope). If the graph slopes down, it means the speed is decreasing. If the graph slopes up, the speed is increasing.

Calculating acceleration from the speed vs. time graph

Slope You know that the slope of a graph is equal to the ratio of *rise* to *run*. On the speed versus time graph, the rise and run have special meanings, as they did for the distance versus time graph. The *rise* is the amount the speed changes. The *run* is the amount the time changes.

Acceleration and slope Remember, acceleration is the change in speed over the change in time. This is *exactly the same* as the rise over run for the speed versus time graph. The slope of an object's speed versus time graph is equal to its acceleration. Figure 2.20 shows how to find the acceleration of a ball in free fall from a speed versus time graph.

Make a triangle to get the slope To determine the slope of the speed versus time graph, take the rise (change in speed) and divide by the run (change in time). It is helpful to draw a triangle on the graph to help figure out the rise and run. The rise is the height of the triangle. The run is the length of the base of the triangle. The graph is for a ball in free fall, so you should not be surprised to see that the slope is 9.8 m/sec^2, the acceleration due to gravity.

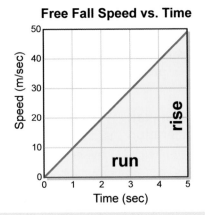

Free Fall Speed vs. Time

$$\text{Slope} = \frac{\text{rise}}{\text{run}} = \frac{49 \text{ m/sec}}{5 \text{ sec}} = 9.8 \text{ m/sec}^2$$

Figure 2.20: *The slope of a speed versus time graph equals the acceleration.*

Calculating acceleration

Calculate the acceleration shown by the speed versus time graph at right.

1. Looking for: You are asked for the acceleration in meters per second per second.

2. Given: You are given a graph of speed versus time.

3. Relationships: The acceleration is equal to the slope of the line.

4. Solution: The rise is 40 m/sec, and the run is 10 sec. Dividing the two gives an acceleration of 4 m/sec^2.

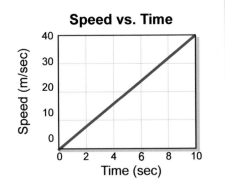

Speed vs. Time

Your turn...

a. Calculate the acceleration shown by the graph in Figure 2.21. **Answer:** 1.0 m/sec^2

b. Calculate the acceleration shown by the graph in Figure 2.17. **Answer:** 0 m/sec^2 because the rise is 0 m/sec.

Distance on an accelerated motion graph

A ball rolling downhill Consider an experiment with a ball rolling downhill. The speed of the ball increases as it rolls downward. The speed versus time graph looks like Figure 2.21. This graph shows a speed that starts at zero. Two seconds later, the speed is two meters per second. A speed versus time graph that shows any slope (like this one does) tells you there is acceleration because the speed is changing over time.

The distance traveled when speed is changing The speed versus time graph gives us a way to calculate the distance an object moves even when its speed is changing. The distance is equal to the area on the graph, but this time the area is a triangle instead of a rectangle. The area of a triangle is one-half the base times the height. The base is equal to the time, just as before. The height is equal to the speed of the ball at the end of two seconds. For the graph in the example, the ball moves two meters from zero to two seconds.

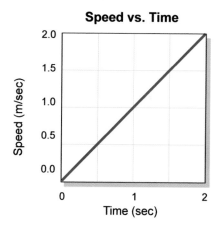

Figure 2.21: *The speed versus time graph for a ball rolling down a hill.*

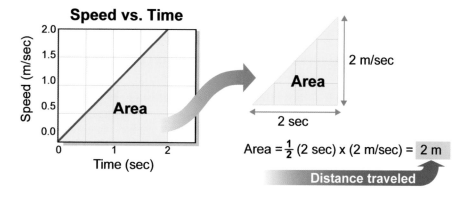

$$\text{Area} = \tfrac{1}{2}\,(2\text{ sec}) \times (2\text{ m/sec}) = \boxed{2\text{ m}}$$

Distance traveled

2.4 Section Review

1. Explain how to calculate the slope of a graph.

2. What does the slope of a position versus time graph represent?

3. Draw the position versus time graph and the speed versus time graph for an object moving at a constant speed of 2 m/sec.

4. How can you use a speed versus time graph to find an object's acceleration?

CONNECTIONS

Revealing the Secrets of Motion

How can a tiny hummingbird fly backward? How does it manage to hover in mid-air as it sips nectar from a flower? For years, answers to these questions eluded naturalists, because a hummingbird's wings beat an average of sixty times per second, so fast that their movement appears blurred to our eyes.

In 1936, a young MIT professor unlocked the secrets of hummingbird flight using a tool he invented to study rotating engines. Harold Edgerton, Ph.D., created a system for taking high-speed photographs of moving objects using a *strobe light* in a darkened room.

Edgerton left his camera shutter open while his strobe light flashed quick, bright pulses of light that lasted only 1/100,000 of a second, with a period of darkness 1/500 of a second between each flash. He invented a device to pull film at a constant speed through his camera, enabling him to take about 540 separate pictures in a single second. The resulting photos revealed that hovering hummingbirds don't beat their wings up and down like other birds. Instead, they move them forward and backward, tracing a figure-eight. This pattern allows them to generate lift during both parts of their wings' beat making hovering possible.

Newton's laws caught on film

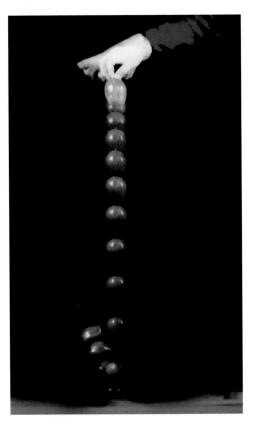

"Doc" Edgerton spent a lifetime using his strobe light to illuminate aspects of motion that we aren't normally able to see. His famous photo, *Newton's apple*, is a striking demonstration of acceleration due to gravity. To create this photo, he set his strobe light to flash sixty times per second, and had an assistant drop the apple in a darkened room. By capturing all of the resulting images on a single piece of film, he shows very clearly how the apple accelerates as it falls.

Capturing the moment of impact

Prior to World War II, Edgerton studied another of Newton's laws, an action-reaction pair—the firing of a bullet and the "kickback" of the pistol. Edgerton proved that the pistol's upward "kick" did not affect the bullet's path as was previously thought. Edgerton's photos showed that the gun did not begin its upward motion until after the bullet had left the barrel.

Photos © Harold & Esther Edgerton Foundation, 2004, courtesy Palm Press, Inc.

When U.S. Army officials learned of Edgerton's work, they asked him to assist in testing the effects of various types of shells on armor. They wanted to photograph the exact moment of impact. Edgerton invented a new way to trigger the flash—he placed a microphone in front of the target and connected it to his flash unit. The sound wave from the bullet set off the flash and Edgerton obtained clear photos of the moment the bullet pierced the armor. Edgerton's work helped the Army develop better materials for fighting World War II.

Edgerton also developed a strobe flash that allowed Allied troops to take aerial reconnaissance photos of nighttime movements of enemy troops. His strobes were used in the nights immediately preceding the D-Day invasion of Normandy. In 1946, Edgerton was awarded the Medal of Freedom for this work.

Finding the perfect swing

Edgerton's photographic techniques are also used to analyze motion in sports. In this photograph of a golfer's swing, you can see

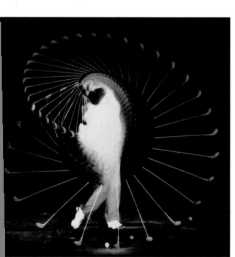

that the head of the golf club gets faster toward the bottom of the swing because it moves a greater distance between flashes of the strobe. Photographs like these can help an athlete evaluate and improve his or her technique and performance. For example, a high-speed photograph records a player's stance and timing through a swing so that improvements can be made.

An irrepressible curiosity

Although Edgerton is perhaps best remembered as a photographer, he saw himself primarily as a scientist. He wanted to know what could be revealed about motion in all sorts of contexts. Strobe photography was his tool for doing that. His curiosity extended beyond studies of birds, falling apples, ammunition, and sports. In his lifetime, he showed us how red blood cells move through capillaries, how tiny marine animals dart about, and how an atomic bomb explodes. Yet he never lost his appreciation for the beauty of the simplest motions like the splash of a milk drop on a table.

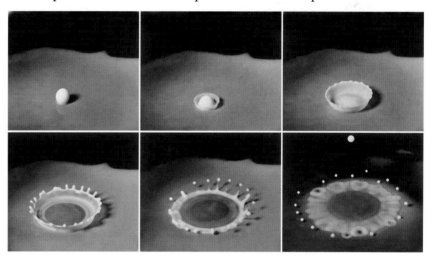

Photos © Harold & Esther Edgerton Foundation, 2004, courtesy Palm Press, Inc.

Questions:

1. What did Edgerton's photos reveal about hummingbird flight?
2. Describe how Edgerton's photo of an apple's falling motion shows that the apple is accelerating.
3. Make a list of other examples where high-speed photography could be used to better understand what is happening in a situation involving motion.

Chapter 2 Review

Understanding Vocabulary

Select the correct term to complete the sentences.

velocity	force	acceleration
Newton's first law	inertia	net force
newton	free fall	terminal speed
Newton's second law	weight	acceleration due to gravity
slope		

Section 2.1

1. A ____ is required to change motion.

2. "Objects continue moving in the same way" is a way of stating ____.

3. An object with more mass also has more ____.

4. The total of all the forces acting on an object is called the ____.

5. The ____ is the metric unit of force.

Section 2.2

6. The rate at which speed changes is called ____.

7. ____ relates force, mass, and acceleration in the equation $F = ma$.

Section 2.3

8. A falling object under the influence of only gravity is in ____.

9. The ____ on Earth is equal to 9.8 m/sec^2.

10. Speed with direction is called ____.

11. The force of gravity on an object is its ____.

12. When the force due to gravity equals the force due to air resistance, the speed of a falling object is called its ____.

Section 2.4

13. The ____ of a line is found by dividing the rise by the run.

Reviewing Concepts

Section 2.1

1. Define the term *force* and give three examples of forces.

2. Give an example of Newton's first law in everyday life.

3. Explain why Newton's first law is also known as the law of inertia.

4. List two units for measuring mass and two units for measuring force.

5. One newton is the ____ it takes to change the ____ of a ____ mass by ____ in one second.

Section 2.2

6. If an object has an acceleration of 20 cm/sec^2, what do you know about how its speed changes over time?

7. Give two ways the unit "meter per second per second" can be abbreviated.

8. An object accelerates if its speed changes. What is the other way an object can accelerate (without changing speed)?

9. Write the equation for Newton' second law that you would use in each of the following scenarios. Let F = force, m = mass, and a = acceleration:
    a. You know mass and acceleration and want to find the force.
    b. You know mass and force and want to find the acceleration.
    c. You know force and acceleration and want to find the mass.

10. What is the acceleration of a car moving at a steady speed of 50 mph?

11. Give an example of Newton's second law in everyday life.

12. Explain how the unit of 1 newton is defined.

Section 2.3

13. By how much does the speed of an object in free fall change each second?

14. A ball is thrown straight up into the air. As it moves upward, its speed ____ by ____ each second. As it falls back down, its speed ____ by ____ each second.

15. What is the difference between speed and velocity?

16. Can an object have a negative speed? Can it have a negative velocity?

17. Can an object have a speed of zero while it has an acceleration that is not zero? Explain.

18. An astronaut carries a rock from the moon to Earth. Is the rock's mass the same on Earth as on the moon? Is its weight the same? Explain.

19. What is the direction of air resistance on a falling object?

20. Which two forces are equal when an object is at its terminal speed?

Section 2.4

21. Explain how to calculate the slope of a line.

22. The slope of a position vs. time graph is equal to the object's _____.

23. Sam rolls down his driveway on a skateboard while Beth keeps track of his position every second for 15 seconds. When they make a graph of the data, the position vs. time graph is a curve that gets steeper as time increases. What does this tell you about Sam's speed?

24. A graph is made of the speed vs. time of a plane as it flies from San Francisco to the Kahului Airport on Maui. How could the distance traveled by the plane be calculated from the graph?

25. The slope of a speed vs. time graph is equal to the object's _____.

26. Sketch the speed vs. time graph for an object moving at a constant speed of 3 m/sec.

Solving Problems

Section 2.1

1. Order the following mass measurements from smallest to largest: 0.5 kilograms, 1,000 grams, 5 kilograms, 50 grams.

2. Dani and Gina are pushing on a box. Dani pushes with 250 N of force and Gina pushes with 100 N of force.
   a. What is the net force if they both push in the same direction?
   b. What is the net force if they push in opposite directions?

Section 2.2

3. A car accelerates from 0 to 20 m/sec in 10 seconds. Calculate its acceleration.

4. During a race, you speed up from 3 m/sec to 5 m/sec in 4 seconds.
   a. What is your change in speed?
   b. What is your acceleration?

5. Marcus is driving his car at 15 km/h when he brakes suddenly. He comes to a complete stop in 2 seconds. What was his acceleration in km/h/sec? Was his acceleration positive, negative, or zero?

6. You start from rest and ski down a hill with an acceleration of 2 m/sec^2. Find your speed at the following times:
   a. 1 second
   b. 2 seconds
   c. 3 seconds
   d. 10 seconds

7. Use your knowledge of Newton's second law to answer the following questions:
   a. What is the net force required to accelerate a 1,000-kg car at 3 m/sec^2?
   b. You pull your little cousin in a wagon. You must pull with a net force of 50 N to accelerate her at 2 m/sec^2. What's her mass?
   c. When a 10-kg object is in free fall, it feels a force of 98 N. What is its acceleration?

Section 2.3

8. You drop a ball from the edge of a cliff. It lands 4 seconds later.
   a. Make a table showing the ball's speed each second for 4 seconds.
   b. What is the ball's average speed during the first second it is in free fall?
   c. What is the ball's average speed for the whole 4 second?
   d. What distance does the ball fall during the 4 seconds?

9. During a science experiment, your teacher drops a tennis ball out of a window. The ball hits the ground 3 seconds later.
   a. What was the ball's speed when it hit the ground? Ignore air resistance.
   b. What was the ball's average speed during the 3 seconds?
   c. How high is the window?

10. Answer the following questions about mass and weight:
    a. How many newtons does a 5-kg backpack weigh on Earth?
    b. How many newtons does a 5-kg backpack weigh on the moon?
    c. Aya's mass is 45 kg. What is her weight in newtons on Earth?
    d. What is Aya's mass on the moon?
    e. What is Aya's weight in newtons on the moon?

Section 2.4

11. Rank the four points on the position vs. time graph in order from slowest to fastest.

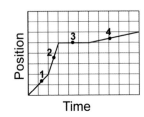

12. Draw the position vs. time graph for a person walking at a constant speed of 1 m/sec for 10 seconds. On the same axes, draw the graph for a person running at a constant speed of 4 m/sec.

13. Calculate speed from the position vs. time graph to the right. Show your work.

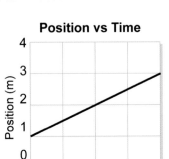

14. Draw the position vs. time graph for an object that is not moving.

15. Why is the position vs. time graph for an object in free fall a curve?

16. Draw the speed vs. time graph showing the same motion as the position vs. time graph to the right.

17. Draw a speed vs. time graph for a car that starts at rest and steadily accelerates until it is moving at 40 m/sec after 20 seconds. Then calculate the car's acceleration and the distance it traveled during the 20 seconds.

18. Draw a speed vs. time graph for an object accelerating from rest at 2 m/sec^2.

Applying Your Knowledge

Section 2.1

1. Aristotle, Galileo Galilei, and Sir Isaac Newton all developed their own theories about motion. Research to find out how each scientist changed what people believed about motion. Were all of their theories correct?

2. Write about Newton's three laws of motion, giving examples from your own life. If you have ever ridden in an automobile, taken a bike ride, played a sport, or walked down the street you have experienced Newton's laws. Be sure to describe the effects of all three of Newton's laws on the activities you choose.

Section 2.2

3. Research the accelerations from 0-60 mph for ten different car models and make a table showing: the model of car, the mass of the car, the amount of time to go from 0-60 mph (in seconds), and the acceleration (in mph/sec). Is there any relationship between the masses of the cars and their accelerations? Explain possible reasons.

4. Research the following: What is the fastest acceleration of a human in a sprint race? Which animal using only its muscles is capable of the fastest acceleration?

Section 2.3

5. A falling object reaches terminal speed when the force of gravity is balanced by the air resistance of the object. Explain this in terms of Newton's first and second laws.

6. Imagine what it would be like if there suddenly were no air resistance. Explain three differences you might notice in the world around you.

Section 2.4

7. As Joseph starts to ride his bike, he accelerates at a constant 1 m/sec^2 from rest to final speed of 10 m/sec.
    a. Make a table of his speed each second from zero to ten seconds. Make a speed vs. time graph from your table.
    b. Make a table of his position each second from zero to ten seconds. Make a position vs. time graph from your table.

Chapter 3

Conservation Laws

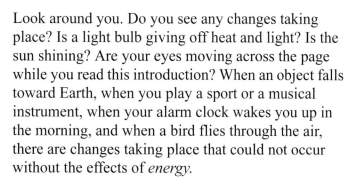

Look around you. Do you see any changes taking place? Is a light bulb giving off heat and light? Is the sun shining? Are your eyes moving across the page while you read this introduction? When an object falls toward Earth, when you play a sport or a musical instrument, when your alarm clock wakes you up in the morning, and when a bird flies through the air, there are changes taking place that could not occur without the effects of *energy*.

Energy is everywhere! Energy is responsible for explaining "how the world works". As you read this chapter think about the examples and see if you can identify the forms of energy that are responsible for the changes that take place in each. Skateboarding, astronauts, car crashes, ball throwing, billiards, and tennis are just some of the physical systems you will encounter. Studying physics also requires energy, so always eat a good breakfast!

Key Questions

- ✓ Do objects at rest ever have any forces acting on them?
- ✓ Why does a faster skateboarder take more force to stop than a slower one with the same mass?
- ✓ How can energy be so important when it cannot be smelled, touched, tasted, seen, or heard?

3.1 Newton's Third Law and Momentum

For every action there is an equal and opposite reaction. This section is about the true meaning of this statement, known as Newton's third law of motion. In the last section, you learned that forces cause changes in motion. However, this does not mean that objects at rest experience no forces! What is that keeps your book perfectly still on the table as you read it even though you *know* gravity exerts a force on the book (Figure 3.1)? "Force" is a good answer to this question and the third law is the key to understanding why.

Newton on a skateboard

An imaginary skateboard contest   Imagine a skateboard contest between Newton and an elephant. They can only push against each other, not against the ground. The fastest one wins. The elephant knows it is much stronger and pushes off Newton with a huge force thinking it will surely win. But who does win?

The winner   Newton wins — and will always win. No matter how hard the elephant pushes, Newton always moves away at a greater speed. In fact, Newton doesn't have to push at all and he still wins. Why?

Forces always come in pairs   You already know it takes force to make both Newton and the elephant move. Newton wins because *forces always come in pairs*. The elephant pushes against Newton and that *action* force pushes Newton away. The elephant's force against Newton creates a *reaction* force against the elephant. Since the action and reaction forces are equal in strength and because of Newton's second law of motion ($a = F/m$), Newton accelerates more because his mass is smaller.

Objectives

✓ Use Newton's third law to explain various situations.
✓ Explain the relationship between Newton's third law and momentum conservation.
✓ Solve recoil problems.

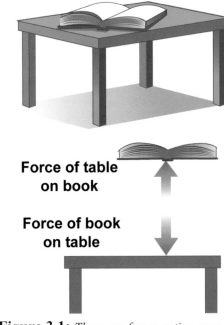

Force of table on book

Force of book on table

Figure 3.1: *There are forces acting even when things are not moving.*

The third law of motion

The first and second laws
The first and second laws of motion apply to single objects. The first law says an object will remain at rest or in motion at constant velocity unless acted upon by a net force. The second law says the acceleration of an object is directly proportional to force and inversely proportional to the mass ($a = F/m$).

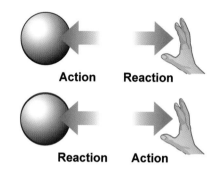

Figure 3.2: *It doesn't matter which force you call the action and which the reaction. The action and reaction forces are interchangeable.*

The third law operates with pairs of objects
In contrast to the first two laws, the third law of motion deals with pairs of objects. This is because *all forces come in pairs*. **Newton's third law** states that every action force creates a reaction force that is equal in strength and opposite in direction.

> *For every action force, there is a reaction force equal in strength and opposite in direction.*

Forces *only* come in action-reaction pairs. There can never be a single force, alone, without its action-reaction partner. The force exerted by the elephant (action) moves Newton since it acts on Newton. The reaction force acting back on the elephant is what moves the elephant.

The labels "action" and "reaction"
The words action and reaction are just labels. It does not matter which force is called action and which is reaction. You choose one to call the action and then call the other one the reaction (Figure 3.2).

A skateboard example
Think carefully about moving the usual way on a skateboard. Your foot exerts a force backward against the ground. The force acts *on* the ground. However, *you* move, so a force must act on you. Why do you move? What force acts on you? You move because the action force of your foot against the ground creates a reaction force of the ground against your foot. You "feel" the ground because you sense the reaction force pressing on your foot. The reaction force is what makes you move because it acts on *you* (Figure 3.3).

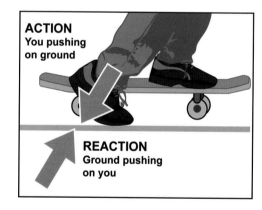

Figure 3.3: *All forces come in pairs. When you push on the ground (action), the reaction of the ground pushing back on your foot is what makes you move.*

Action and reaction forces

Action and reaction forces do not cancel
It is easy to get confused thinking about action and reaction forces. Why don't they cancel each other out? The reason is that action and reaction forces act on different objects. For example, think about throwing a ball. When you throw a ball, you apply the action force to the ball, creating the ball's acceleration. The reaction is the ball pushing back against your hand. The action acts on the ball and the reaction acts on your hand. The forces do not cancel because they act on different objects. You can only cancel forces if they act on the same object (Figure 3.4).

Draw diagrams
When sorting out action and rea7ction forces it is helpful to draw diagrams. Draw each object apart from the other. Represent each force as an arrow in the appropriate direction.

Identifying action and reaction
Here are some guidelines to help you sort out action and reaction forces:

- Both are always there whenever any force appears.
- They always have the exact same strength.
- They always act in opposite directions.
- They always act on different objects.
- Both are real forces and either (or both) can cause acceleration.

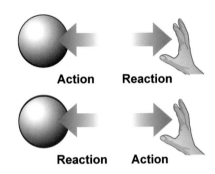

Figure 3.4: *An example diagram showing the action and reaction forces in throwing a ball.*

Action and reaction

A woman with a weight of 500 N is sitting on a chair. Describe an action-reaction pair of forces.

Sitting on a chair

1. Looking for: You are asked for a pair of action and reaction forces.

2. Given: You are given one force in newtons.

3. Relationships: Action-reaction forces are equal and opposite, and act on different objects.

4. Solution: The force of 500 N exerted by the woman on the chair seat is an action. The chair seat acting on the woman with an upward force of 500 N is a reaction.

Your turn...

a. A baseball player hits a ball with a bat. Describe an action-reaction pair of forces. **Answer:** The force of the bat on the ball accelerates the ball. The force of the ball on the bat (reaction) slows down the swinging bat (action).

b. Earth and its moon are linked by an action-reaction pair. **Answer:** Earth attracts the moon (action) and the moon attracts Earth (reaction) in an action-reaction pair. Both action and reaction are due to gravity.

Momentum

Faster objects are harder to stop
Imagine two kids on skateboards are moving toward you (Figure 3.5). Each has a mass of 40 kilograms. One is moving at one meter per second and the other at 10 meters per second. Which one is harder to stop?

You already learned that inertia comes from mass. That explains why an 80-kilogram skateboarder is harder to stop than a 40-kilogram skateboarder. But how do you account for the fact that a faster skateboarder takes more force to stop than a slower one with the *same* mass?

Momentum
The answer is a new quantity called **momentum.** The momentum of a moving object is its mass multiplied by its velocity. Like inertia, momentum measures a moving object's resistance to changes in its motion. However, momentum includes the effects of speed and direction as well as mass. The symbol *p* is used to represent momentum.

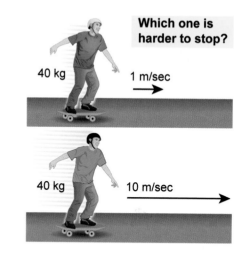

Figure 3.5: *Stopping a fast-moving object is harder than stopping a slow-moving on.*

MOMENTUM

$$\underset{\textit{Momentum (kg·m/sec)}}{} \quad p = m v \quad \underset{\textit{Velocity (m/sec)}}{\overset{\textit{Mass (kg)}}{}}$$

Units of momentum
The units of momentum are the units of mass multiplied by the units of velocity. When mass is in kilograms and velocity is in meters per second, momentum is in kilogram·meters per second (kg·m/sec).

Calculating momentum
Momentum is calculated with velocity instead of speed because the direction of momentum is always important. A common choice is to make positive momentum to the right and negative momentum to the left (Figure 3.6).

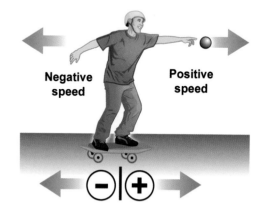

Figure 3.6: *The direction is important when calculating momentum. We use positive and negative numbers to represent opposite directions.*

Impulse

Force changes momentum
Momentum changes when velocity changes. Since force is what changes velocity, that means that force is also linked to changes in momentum. The relationship with momentum gives us an important new way to look at force.

Impulse
A change in an object's momentum depends on the net force and also on the amount of time the force is applied. The change in momentum is equal to the net force multiplied by the time the force acts. A change in momentum created by a force exerted over time is called **impulse**.

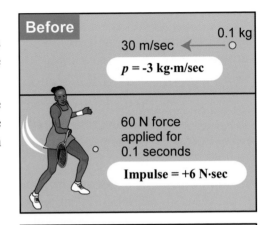

Before
30 m/sec ← 0.1 kg

$p = -3$ kg·m/sec

60 N force applied for 0.1 seconds

Impulse = +6 N·sec

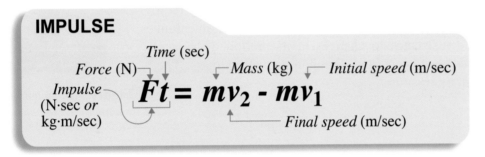

IMPULSE

$$Ft = mv_2 - mv_1$$

Force (N) — Time (sec) — Mass (kg) — Initial speed (m/sec)
Impulse (N·sec or kg·m/sec) — Final speed (m/sec)

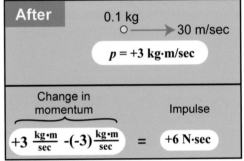

After
0.1 kg → 30 m/sec

$p = +3$ kg·m/sec

Change in momentum   Impulse

$+3 \frac{\text{kg·m}}{\text{sec}} - (-3) \frac{\text{kg·m}}{\text{sec}} = +6$ N·sec

Units of impulse
Notice that the force side of the equation has units of N·sec, while the momentum side has units of momentum, kg·m/sec. These are the same units, since 1 N is 1 kg·m/s^2. Impulse can be correctly expressed either way.

Force and momentum

A net force of 100 N is applied for 5 seconds to a 10-kg car that is initially at rest. What is the speed of the car at the end of the 5 seconds.

1. Looking for: You are asked for the speed.

2. Given: You are given the net force in newtons, the time the force acts in seconds, and the mass of the car in kilograms.

3. Relationships: impulse = force × time = change in momentum; momentum = mass × velocity.

4. Solution: The car's final momentum = 100 N × 5 seconds = 500 kg·m/sec.
Speed is momentum divided by mass, or v = (500 kg·m/sec) ÷ 10 kg = 50 m/sec

Your turn...

a. A 15-N force acts for 10 seconds on a 1-kg ball initially at rest. What is the ball's final momentum? **Answer:** 150 kg·m/sec

b. How much time should a 100-N force take to increase the speed of a 10-kg car from 10 m/sec to 100 m/sec? **Answer:** 9 sec

The law of momentum conservation

An important new law
We are now going to combine Newton's third law with the relationship between force and momentum. The result is a powerful new tool for understanding motion: the law of conservation of momentum. This law allows us to make accurate predictions about what happens before and after an interaction even if we don't know the details about the interaction itself.

Momentum in an action-reaction pair
When two objects exert forces on each other in an action-reaction pair, their motions are affected as a pair. If you stand on a skateboard and throw a bowling ball, you apply force to the ball. That force changes the momentum of the ball.

The third law says the ball exerts an equal and opposite force back on you. Therefore, *your* momentum also changes. Since the forces are exactly equal and opposite, the changes in momentum are also equal and opposite. If the ball gains +20 kg·m/sec of forward momentum, you must gain -20 kg·m/sec of backward momentum (Figure 3.7).

The law of conservation of momentum
Because of the third law, the total momentum of two interacting objects stays constant. If one gains momentum, the other loses the same amount, leaving the total unchanged. This is the **law of conservation of momentum**. The law says the total momentum in a system of interacting objects cannot change as long all forces act only between the objects in the system.

If interacting objects in a system are not acted on by outside forces, the total amount of momentum in the system cannot change.

Forces inside and outside the system
Forces outside the system, such as friction and gravity, can change the total momentum of the system. However, if ALL objects that exert forces are included in the system, the total momentum stays perfectly constant. When you jump up, the reaction force from the ground gives you upward momentum. The action force from your feet gives the *entire Earth* an equal amount of downward momentum and the universe keeps perfect balance. No one notices the planet move because it has so much more mass than you so its increase in momentum creates negligible velocity (Figure 3.8).

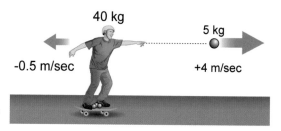

Figure 3.7: *The result of the skateboarder throwing a 5-kg ball at a speed of +4 m/sec is that he and the board, with a total mass of 40 kg, move backward at a speed of -0.5 m/sec, if you ignore friction.*

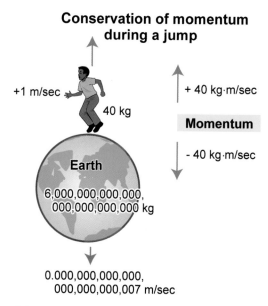

Figure 3.8: *When you jump, your body and Earth gain equal and opposite amounts of momentum.*

Using the momentum relationship

An astronaut floating in space throws a 2-kilogram hammer to the left at 15 m/sec. If the astronaut's mass is 60 kilograms, how fast does the astronaut move to the right after throwing the hammer?

1. Looking for: You are asked for the speed of the astronaut after throwing the hammer.

2. Given: You are given the mass of the hammer in kilograms and the speed of the hammer in m/sec and the mass of the astronaut in kilograms.

3. Relationships: The total momentum before the hammer is thrown must be the same as the total after. Momentum = mass × velocity. A negative sign indicates the direction of motion is to the left.

4. Solution: Both the astronaut and hammer were initially at rest, so the initial momentum was zero. Use subscripts (a and h) to distinguish between the astronaut and the hammer.

$$m_a v_a + m_h v_h = 0$$

Plug in the known numbers:
$$(60 \text{ kg})(v_a) + (2 \text{ kg})(-15 \text{ m/sec}) = 0$$

Solve:
$$(60 \text{ kg})(v_a) = +30 \text{ kg·m/sec}$$
$$v_a = +0.5 \text{ m/sec} \quad \text{The astronaut moves to the right at a speed of 0.5 m/sec.}$$

Your turn...

a. Two children on ice skates start at rest and push off from each other. One has a mass of 30 kg and moves back at 2 m/sec. The other has a mass of 15 kg. What is the second child's speed? **Answer:** 4 m/sec

b. Standing on an icy pond, you throw a 0.5 kg ball at 40 m/sec. You move back at 0.4 m/sec. What is your mass? **Answer:** 50 kg

3.1 Section Review

1. List three action and reaction pairs shown in the picture at right.

2. Why don't action and reaction forces cancel?

3. Use impulse to explain how force is related to changes in momentum.

4. Explain the law of conservation of momentum and how it relates to Newton's third law.

3.2 Energy and the Conservation of Energy

Energy is one of the fundamental quantities in our universe. Without energy, nothing could ever change. Yet pure energy itself cannot be smelled, tasted, touched, seen, or heard. However, energy does appear in many forms, such as motion and heat. Energy can travel in different ways, such as in light and sound waves and in electricity. The workings of the universe (including all of our technology) can be viewed from the perspective of energy flowing from one place to another and changing back and forth from one form to another.

What is energy?

A definition of energy **Energy** is a quantity that measures the ability to cause change. Anything with energy can change itself or cause change in other objects or systems. Energy can cause changes in temperature, speed, position, momentum, pressure, or other physical variables. Energy can also cause change in materials, such as burning wood changing into ashes and smoke.

> *Energy is a quantity that measures the ability to cause change in a physical system.*

Examples
- A gust of wind has energy because it can move objects in its path.
- A piece of wood in a fireplace has energy because it can produce heat and light.
- You have energy because you can change the motion of your own body.
- Batteries have energy because they can be used in a radio to make sound.
- Gasoline has energy because it can be burned in an engine to move a car.
- A ball at the top of a hill has energy because it can roll down the hill and move objects in its path.

Units of energy The unit of measurement for energy is the **joule (J)**. One joule is the energy needed to push with a force of one newton over a distance of one meter (Figure 3.9). The joule is an abbreviation for one newton multiplied by one meter. If you push on your calculator with a force of one newton while it moves a distance of one meter across a table, one joule of your energy is converted into the energy of the calculator's motion.

1 joule is the energy needed to push with 1 newton for 1 meter.

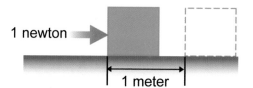

Figure 3.9: *Pushing with a force of one newton over a distance of one meter requires one joule of energy.*

Calories

The *Calorie* is a unit of energy often used for food. One Calorie equals 4,187 joules.

What is work?

"Work" means different things

The word "*work*" is used in many different ways.

- You should always check over your *work* before handing in a test.
- You go to *work*.
- Your toaster doesn't *work*.
- You *work* with other students on a group project.

What "work" means in physics

In physics, **work** has a very specific meaning. Work is the transfer of energy that results from applying a force over a distance. To calculate work you multiply the force by the distance the object moves in the direction of the force. If you lift a block with a weight of one newton for a distance of one meter, you do one joule of work. One joule of energy is transferred from your body to the block, changing the block's energy. Both work and energy are measured in the same units because work is a form of energy.

Work is done on objects

When thinking about work you should always be clear about which force is doing the work on which object. Work is done *on* objects. If you lift a block one meter with a force of one newton, you have done one joule of work *on the block* (Figure 3.10).

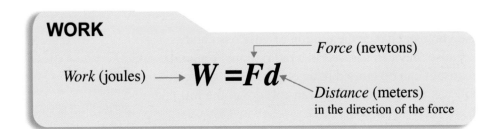

WORK

$$W = Fd$$

Work (joules) → $W = Fd$ ← *Force* (newtons)

Distance (meters) in the direction of the force

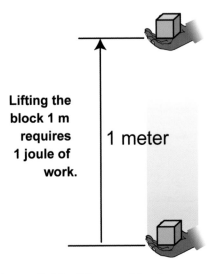

Lifting the block 1 m requires 1 joule of work.

1 meter

Energy is needed to do work

An object that has energy is able to do work; without energy, it is impossible to do work. In fact, one way to think about energy is as *stored work*. A falling block has kinetic energy that can be used to do work. If the block hits a ball, it will do work on the ball and change its motion. Some of the block's energy is transferred to the ball during the collision.

Figure 3.10: *When you lift a 1-newton block a height of 1 meter, you do 1 joule of work on the block.*

Potential energy

What is potential energy? **Potential energy** is energy due to *position*. The word "potential" means that something is capable of becoming active. Systems or objects with potential energy are able to exert forces (exchange energy) as they change to other arrangements. For example, a stretched spring has potential energy. If released, the spring will use this energy to move itself (and anything attached to it) back to its original length.

Gravitational potential energy A block above a table has potential energy. If released, the force of gravity moves the block down to a position of lower energy. The term *gravitational potential energy* describes the energy of an elevated object. The term is often shortened to just "potential energy" because the most common type of potential energy in physics problems is gravitational. Unless otherwise stated, you can assume "potential energy" means gravitational potential energy.

How to calculate potential energy How much potential energy does a raised block have? The block's potential energy is exactly the amount of work it can do as it goes down. Work is force multiplied by distance. The force is the weight (*mg*) of the block in newtons. The distance the block can move down is its height (*h*) in meters. Multiplying the weight by the distance gives you the block's potential energy at any given height (Figure 3.11).

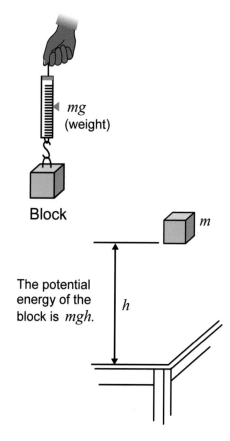

POTENTIAL ENERGY

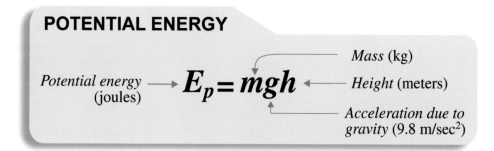

Potential energy (joules) $\longrightarrow E_p = mgh \longleftarrow$ — Mass (kg), Height (meters), Acceleration due to gravity (9.8 m/sec²)

Figure 3.11: *the potential energy of the block is equal to the product of its mass, the strength of gravity, and the height the block can fall from.*

Kinetic energy

Kinetic energy is energy of motion

Objects that are moving also have the ability to cause change. Energy of *motion* is called **kinetic energy**. A moving billiard ball has kinetic energy because it can hit another object and change its motion. Kinetic energy can easily be converted into potential energy. The kinetic energy of a basketball tossed upward converts into potential energy as the height increases.

Kinetic energy can do work

The amount of kinetic energy an object has equals the amount of work the object can do by exerting force as it stops. Consider a moving skateboard and rider (Figure 3.12). Suppose it takes a force of 500 N applied over a distance of 10 meters to slow the skateboard down to a stop (500 N × 10 m = 5,000 joules). The kinetic energy of the skateboard and rider is 5,000 joules since that is the amount of work it takes to stop the skateboard.

Kinetic energy depends on mass and speed

If you had started with twice the mass — say, two skateboarders — you would have to do twice as much work to stop them both. Kinetic energy increases with mass. If the skateboard board and rider are moving faster, it also takes more work to bring them to a stop. This means kinetic energy also increases with speed. Kinetic energy is related to *both* an object's speed and its mass.

The formula for kinetic energy

The kinetic energy of a moving object is equal to one half its mass multiplied by the square of its speed. This formula comes from a combination of relationships, including Newton's second law, the distance equation for acceleration ($d = \frac{1}{2}at^2$), and the calculation of energy as the product of force and distance.

Moving skateboard and rider

A force of 500 N applied for 10 m ...

500 N

... brings the skateboard and rider to a stop.

10 m

Work done = 500 N x 10 m = 5,000 joules

Therefore ...

The kinetic energy is 5,000 joules because that is the amount of work the skateboard can do as it stops.

KINETIC ENERGY

$$\underset{\substack{\text{Kinetic energy} \\ \text{(joules)}}}{\longrightarrow} E_k = \frac{1}{2}mv^2 \quad \overset{\text{Mass (kg)}}{\underset{\text{Speed (m/sec)}}{}}$$

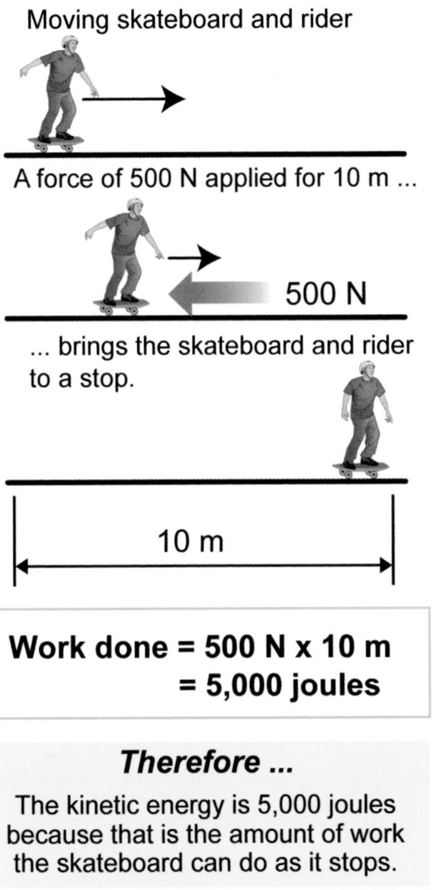

Figure 3.12: *The amount of kinetic energy the skateboard has is equal to the amount of work the moving board and rider can do as they come to a stop.*

Kinetic energy increases as the square of the speed

Kinetic energy increases as the square of the speed. This means that if you go twice as fast, your energy increases by four times ($2^2 = 4$). If your speed is three times as fast, your energy is nine times bigger ($3^2 = 9$). A car moving at a speed of 100 km/h (62 mph) has *four times* the kinetic energy it had when going 50 km/h (31 mph). At a speed of 150 km/h (93 mph), it has *nine times* as much energy as it did at 50 km/h. The stopping distance of a car is proportional to its kinetic energy. A car going twice as fast has four times the kinetic energy and needs four times the stopping distance. This is why driving at high speeds is so dangerous.

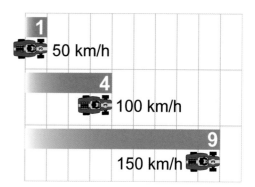

Figure 3.13: *Stopping distances.*

Potential and kinetic energy

A 2 kg rock is at the edge of a cliff 20 meters above a lake. It becomes loose and falls toward the water below. Calculate its potential and kinetic energy when it is at the top and when it is halfway down. Its speed is 14 m/sec at the halfway point.

1. Looking for: You are asked for the potential and kinetic energy at two locations.

2. Given: You are given the mass in kilograms, the height at each location in meters, and the speed halfway down in m/sec. You can assume the initial speed is 0 m/sec because the rock starts from rest.

3. Relationships: $E_p = mgh$ and $E_k = \frac{1}{2}mv^2$

4. Solution:

Potential energy at the top: $m = 2$ kg, $g = 9.8$ N/kg, and $h = 20$ m
$E_p = (2 \text{ kg})(9.8 \text{ N/kg})(20 \text{ m}) = 392$ J

Potential energy halfway down: $m = 2$ kg, $g = 9.8$ N/kg, and $h = 10$ m
$E_p = (2 \text{ kg})(9.8 \text{ N/kg})(10 \text{ m}) = 196$ J

Kinetic energy at the top: $m = 2$ kg and $v = 0$ m/sec
$E_k = (1/2)(2 \text{ kg})(0^2) = 0$ J

Kinetic energy halfway down: $m = 2$ kg and $v = 14$ m/sec
$E_k = (1/2)(2 \text{ kg})(14 \text{ m/sec})^2 = 196$ J

Your turn...

a. Calculate the potential energy of a 4 kilogram cat crouched 3 meters off the ground. **Answer:** 117.6 J

b. Calculate the kinetic energy of a 4 kilogram cat running at 5 m/sec. **Answer:** 50 J

Conservation of energy

Energy converts from potential to kinetic
What happens when you throw a ball straight up in the air (Figure 3.14)? The ball leaves your hand with kinetic energy it gained while your hand accelerated it from rest. As the ball goes higher, it gains potential energy. However the ball slows down as it rises so its kinetic energy *decreases*. The increase in potential energy is exactly equal to the decrease in kinetic energy. The kinetic energy converts into potential energy, and the ball's total energy stays the same.

Law of conservation of energy
The idea that energy converts from one form into another without a change in the total amount is called the **law of conservation of energy**. The law states that energy can never be created or destroyed, just converted from one form into another. The law of conservation of energy is one of the most important laws in physics. It applies to not only kinetic and potential energy, but to all forms of energy.

Energy can never be created or destroyed, just converted from one form into another

Using energy conservation
The law of conservation of energy explains how a ball's launch speed affects its motion. As the ball in Figure 3.14 moves upward, it slows down and loses kinetic energy. Eventually it reaches a point where all the kinetic energy has been converted to potential energy. The ball has moved as high as it will go and its upward speed has been reduced to zero. If the ball had been launched with a greater speed, it would have started with more kinetic energy. It would have had to climb higher for all of the kinetic energy to be converted into potential energy. If the exact launch speed is given, the law of conservation of energy can be used to predict the height the ball reaches.

Energy converts from kinetic to potential
The ball's conversion of energy on the way down is opposite what it was on the way up. As the ball falls, its speed increases and its height decreases. The potential energy decreases as it converts into kinetic energy. If gravity is the only force acting on the ball, it returns to your hand with exactly the same speed and kinetic energy it started with — except that now it moves in the opposite direction.

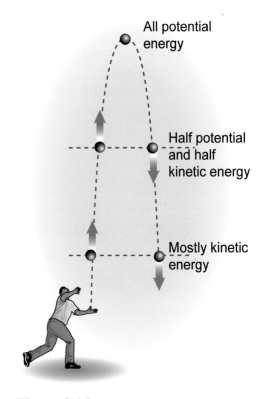

Figure 3.14: *When you throw a ball in the air, the energy transforms from kinetic to potential and then back to kinetic.*

Using energy conservation to solve problems

How to use energy conservation
Energy conservation is a direct way to find out what happens before and after a change (Figure 3.15) from one form of energy into another. The law of energy conservation says the total energy before the change equals the total energy after it. In many cases (with falling objects, for instance), you need not worry about force or acceleration. Applying energy conservation allows you to find speeds and heights very quickly.

Before change → Change → After change

Total energy = Total energy

Figure 3.15: *Applying energy conservation.*

Energy conservation

A 2 kg car moving with a speed of 2 m/sec starts up a hill. How high does the car roll before it stops?

2 kg   2 m/sec   How high?

1. Looking for: You are asked for the height.

2. Given: You are given the mass in kilograms, and starting speed in m/sec.

3. Relationships: From the law of conservation of energy, the sum of kinetic and potential energy is constant. The ball keeps going uphill until all its kinetic energy has been turned into potential energy.

$$E_K = \tfrac{1}{2}mv^2 \quad , E_P = mgh$$

4. Solution: Find the kinetic energy at the start:
$E_K = (1/2)(2 \text{ kg})(2 \text{ m/sec})^2 = 4 \text{ J}$
Use the potential energy to find the height
$mgh = 4 \text{ J}$ therefore:
$h = (4 \text{ J}) \div ((2 \text{ kg})(9.8 \text{ N/kg}))$
$= 0.2 \text{ m}$
The car rolls upward to a height of 0.2 m above where it started

Your turn...

a. A 500 kg roller coaster car starts from rest at the top of a 60-meter hill. Find its potential energy when it is halfway to the bottom. **Answer:** 147,000 J

b. A 1 kg ball is tossed straight up with a kinetic energy of 196 J. How high does it go? **Answer:** 20 m

---

"Using" and "conserving" energy in the everyday sense

"Conserving" energy   Almost everyone has heard that is good to "conserve energy" and not waste it. This is good advice because energy from gasoline or electricity costs money and uses resources. But what does it mean to "use energy" in the everyday sense? If energy can never be created or destroyed, how can it be "used up"? Why do smart people worry about "running out" of energy?

"Using" energy   When you "use" energy by turning on a light, you are really converting energy from one form (electricity) to other forms (light and heat). What gets "used up" is the amount of energy *in the form of electricity*. Electricity is a valuable form of energy because it is easy to move over long distances (through wires). In the "physics" sense, the energy is not "used up" but converted into other forms. The total amount of energy stays constant.

Power plants   Electric power plants don't *make* electrical energy. Energy cannot be created. What power plants do is convert other forms of energy (chemical, solar, nuclear) into electrical energy. When someone advises you to turn out the lights to conserve energy, they are asking you to use less electrical energy. If people used less electrical energy, power plants would burn less oil, gas, or other fuels in "producing" the electrical energy they sell.

"Running out" of energy   Many people are concerned about "running out" of energy. What they worry about is running out of certain *forms* of energy that are easy to use, such as oil and gas. When you use gas in a car, the chemical energy in the gasoline mostly becomes heat energy. It is impractical to put the energy back into the form of gasoline, so we say the energy has been "used up" even though the energy itself is still there, only in a different form.

3.2 Section Review

1. What are the units of energy and what do they mean?
2. What is work in physics and what is the relationship between work and energy?
3. How can you increase an object's potential or kinetic energy?
4. What happens to the kinetic and potential energy of a ball as it falls toward the ground?
5. Explain what it means to say energy is conserved.

Please turn out the lights when you leave!

There are about 285,000,000 people living in the United States. If an average house has four light bulbs per person, it adds up to 1,140,000,000 light bulbs. The average bulb uses 100 joules of electrical energy each second. Multiplying it out gives an estimate of 114,000,000,000 joules every second, just for light bulbs!

A big electric power-plant puts out 2,000,000,000 joules each second. That means 67 big power plants are burning up resources just to run your light bulbs. If everyone were to switch their incandescent bulbs to fluorescent lights we would save 75 percent of this electricity. That means we could save 50 big power plants' worth of pollution and wasted resources!

3.3 Collisions

A **collision** occurs when two or more objects hit each other. When we hear the word collision, we often picture cars crashing. But a collision also takes place when a tennis ball hits a racket, your foot hits the ground, or your fingers press on a keyboard. During a collision, momentum and energy are transferred from one object to another. Different factors like mass, initial velocity, and the type of collision determine the velocity of objects after they collide. In this section, you will learn about the two types of collisions, elastic and inelastic, and the momentum and energy changes that result.

Elastic and inelastic collisions

Elastic collisions There are two main types of collisions, elastic and inelastic. When an **elastic collision** occurs, objects bounce off each other with no loss in the total kinetic energy of the system. The total kinetic energy before the collision is the same as the total kinetic energy after the collision. The collision between billiard balls is very close to a perfectly elastic collision (Figure 3.16).

Inelastic collisions In an **inelastic collision**, objects change shape or stick together, and the total kinetic energy of the system decreases. The energy is not destroyed, but it is transformed into forms other than kinetic energy, such as permanently changing shape. An egg hitting the floor is one example of an inelastic collision; two vehicles colliding is another. In both cases, some of the kinetic energy is used to permanently change an object's shape.

Perfectly elastic collisions Collisions you see in everyday life are mixed. When two billiard balls collide, it looks like they bounce without a loss of kinetic energy. But the sound of the collision tells you a small amount of kinetic energy is being changed into sound energy. However, we approximate the collision as elastic because it is more like an elastic collision than an inelastic one. The balls bounce off each other and do not change shape. Perfectly elastic collisions *do* occur on an atomic scale. The collision between two individual atoms in the air is an example of a perfectly elastic collision. The kinetic energy may be *transferred* between atoms, but no kinetic energy is *transformed* into heat or sound. The movement of atoms and collisions between them are responsible for air pressure in balloons and tires.

Vocabulary

collision, elastic collision, inelastic collision

Objectives

✓ Distinguish between elastic and inelastic collisions.

✓ Use momentum conservation to solve collision problems.

✓ Explain how momentum, impulse, force, and time are related.

Figure 3.16: *The collision of two billiard balls is elastic. The collision of an egg with the floor is inelastic.*

Momentum conservation in collisions

Elastic and inelastic collisions
As long as there are no outside forces (such as friction), momentum is conserved in both elastic and inelastic collisions. This is true even when kinetic energy is not conserved. Conservation of momentum makes it possible to determine the motion of objects before or after colliding.

Problem-solving steps
Using momentum to analyze collisions takes practice. Use the steps below to help you find solutions to problems.

1. Draw a diagram.
2. Decide whether the collision is elastic or inelastic.
3. Assign variables to represent the masses and velocities of the objects before and after the collision.
4. Use momentum conservation to write an equation stating that the total momentum before the collision equals the total after. Then solve it.

Before collision

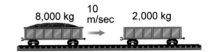

After collision

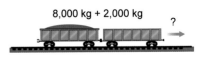

Figure 3.17: *An inelastic collision of two train cars.*

Momentum and collisions

An 8,000-kg train car moves to the right at 10 m/sec. It collides with a 2,000-kg parked train car (Figure 3.17). The cars get stuck together and roll along the track. How fast do they move after the collision?

1. Looking for: You are asked for the velocity of the train cars after the collision.

2. Given: You are given both masses in kilograms and the initial velocity of the moving car in m/sec. You know the collision is inelastic because the cars get stuck together.

3. Relationships: Apply the law of conservation of momentum. Because the two cars get stuck together, consider them to be a single giant train car after the collision. The final mass is the sum of the two individual masses.
initial momentum of car 1 + initial momentum of car 2 = final momentum of combined cars
$m_1v_1 + m_2v_2 = (m_1+m_2)v_3$

4. Solution: $(8{,}000 \ \text{kg})(10 \ \text{m/sec}) + (2{,}000 \ \text{kg})(0 \ \text{m/sec}) = (8{,}000 \ \text{kg} + 2{,}000 \ \text{kg})v_3$
$v_3 = 8$ m/sec. The train cars move to the right together at 8 m/sec.

Your turn...
a. Repeat the above problem but with each car having a mass of 2000 kg. **Answer:** 5 m/sec
b. A 5-kg bowling ball with a velocity of +10 m/sec hits a stationary 2-kg bowling pin. If the ball's final velocity is +8 m/sec, what is the pin's final velocity? **Answer:** +5 m/sec

Forces in collisions

Collisions involve forces
Collisions create forces because the colliding objects change their motion. Since collisions take place quickly, the forces change rapidly and are hard to measure directly. However, momentum conservation can be used to estimate the forces in a collision. Engineers need to know the forces so they can design things not to break when they are dropped.

Force and collisions
A rubber ball and a clay ball are dropped on a gymnasium floor (Figure 3.18). The rubber ball has an elastic collision and bounces back up with the same speed it had when it hit the floor. The clay ball has an inelastic collision, hitting the floor with a thud and staying there. Both balls have the same mass and are dropped from the same height. They have the same speed as they hit the floor. Which ball exerts a greater force on the floor?

Force changes momentum
The total change in momentum is equal to the force multiplied by the time during which the force acts. Because force and time appear as a pair, we define the impulse to be the product of force and time.

Bounces have greater momentum change
Suppose each ball shown in Figure 3.18 has a mass of 1 kilogram and hits the floor at a velocity of -5 m/sec (negative is downward). The momentum of the clay ball changes from -5 kg·m/sec to zero. This is a change of 5 kg·m/sec. The rubber ball also starts with a momentum of -5 kg·m/sec. If the collision is perfectly elastic, it bounces up with the same momentum but in the opposite direction. Its momentum then goes from -5 kg·m/sec to +5 kg·m/sec, a change of +10 kg·m/sec. The rubber ball (elastic collision) has twice the change in momentum (Figure 3.19). The momentum change is always greater when objects bounce compared with when they do not bounce.

Bouncing vs. stopping
Because we don't know the collision times, it is impossible to calculate the forces exactly. We can only say for certain that the impulse (force × time) is 10 N·sec for the rubber ball. This could be a force of 10 N for 1 second, or 100 N for 0.1 seconds, or any combination that results in 10 N·sec. However, we can be pretty sure the force from the rubber ball is greater because the momentum of the rubber ball changed twice as much as the momentum of the clay ball. Bouncing nearly always results in a greater force than just stopping because bouncing creates a larger change in momentum.

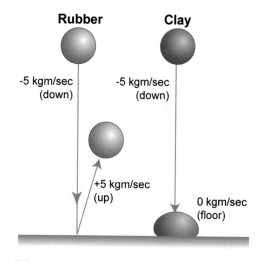

Figure 3.18: *Bouncing results in a greater change in momentum and therefore almost always creates a greater force.*

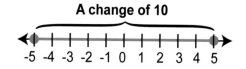

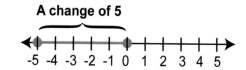

Figure 3.19: *A number line can help you see clearly that a change from -5 to +5 is twice as great as a change from -5 to 0.*

Solving impulse problems

Motion problems Impulse can be used to solve many practical problems. For example, how much force does it take to stop a 1,000-kilogram car in 10 seconds if the car is moving at 30 m/sec (67 mph)? To solve this kind of problem, calculate the change in momentum, then use the impulse to calculate the force. For the car, the change in momentum is 30,000 kg·m/sec (1,000 kg × 30 m/sec). That means the impulse must be 30,000 N·sec. Since you know the time is 10 seconds, the force is 3,000 N because 3,000 N × 10 sec = 30,000 N·sec.

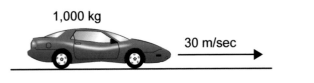

1,000 kg

30 m/sec

3,000 N for 10 seconds will stop the car

Collision force problems If you know the time during which the colliding objects touch each other you can calculate the average force of the collision. The maximum force is larger than the average because forces in collisions tend to rise as the colliding objects come together, reach a maximum, and then drop off as the objects move apart. However, knowing the average force is useful.

Why does impulse equal the force multiplied by the time?

To find the relationship between momentum, force, and time, start with Newton's second law:

$$F = ma$$

Substituting for acceleration:

$$F = m \frac{(v_2 - v_1)}{t}$$

Rearranging:

$$Ft = m(v_2 - v_1)$$

$$Ft = mv_2 - mv_1$$

Therefore the change in momentum (impulse) equals the product of the force and time.

Impulse

A 1 kg clay ball hits the floor with a velocity of -5 m/sec and comes to a stop in 0.1 second. What force did the floor exert on it?

2. Given: You are given the ball's mass, initial speed, final speed, and stopping time.

3. Relationships: $Ft = mv_2 - mv_1$

4. Solution: $F(0.1 \text{ sec}) = (1 \text{ kg})(0 \text{ m/sec}) - (1 \text{ kg})(-5 \text{ m/sec})$

$F(0.1 \text{ sec}) = 5 \text{ kg} \cdot \text{m/sec}$

$F = 50 \text{ N}$

Your turn...

a. What braking force is needed to stop a 1000 kg car moving at 30 m/sec in a time of 2 seconds? **Answer:** 15,000 N

b. You pedal your bicycle with a force of 40 N. If you start from rest and have a mass of 50 kg, what is your final speed after 10 seconds? **Answer:** 8 m/sec

Car crash safety

Stopping in an accident
The relationship between impulse, force, and time has been used by auto manufacturers to make vehicles safer in accidents. When a car crashes to a stop, its momentum drops to zero. The shorter the amount of stopping time, the greater the force on the car. Car bodies are designed to crumple in an accident to extend the stopping time. The ideal car crumples enough to stop gradually, but not so much that the passenger compartment is affected.

Seat belts
The stopping time of a car in a collision is very short even when crumpling occurs. A passenger without a seat belt will have a momentum that drops from a large value to zero when hitting the windshield, steering wheel, or dashboard. Seat belts are made of a very strong fabric that stretches slightly when a force is applied. Stretching extends the time over which the passenger comes to a stop and results in less force being exerted on the person's body.

Air bags
Air bags work together with seat belts to make cars safer (Figure 3.20). An air bag inflates when the force applied to the front of a car reaches a dangerous level. The air bag deflates slowly as the person's body applies a force to the bag upon impact. The force of impact pushes the air out of small holes in the air bag, bringing the person to a gradual stop. Many cars now contain both front and side air bags.

Crash test dummies
Automakers use crash test dummies to study the effects of collisions on passengers (Figure 3.21). Crash test dummies contain electronic sensors to measure the forces felt in various places on the body. Results of these tests have been used to make changes in automobile design, resulting in cars that are much safer than they were in the past.

Figure 3.20: *Seat belts and air bags work together to safely stop passengers in automobile collisions.*

Figure 3.21: *Crash test dummies are used in car safety tests.*

3.3 Section Review

1. List three examples of elastic collisions and three examples of inelastic collisions not mentioned in this chapter.
2. Are momentum and kinetic energy conserved in all collisions?
3. What is the definition of impulse?
4. Why will an egg break if it is dropped on the ground but not if it is dropped on a pillow?

Rockets: Out of This World Travel

What if you wanted to travel to space? What type of vehicle would get you there? Your vehicle would need to reach incredible speeds to travel huge distances. Speed is also important in overcoming the gravitational pull of planets, moons, and the sun. Your vehicle would need to be able to travel in a *vacuum* because space has no air. It would also need a very powerful engine to get into space.

So what would be your vehicle of choice? A rocket, of course!

Rockets and Newton's third law

A rocket is a vehicle with a special type of engine. The basic principle behind how a rocket works is Newton's third law, *for every action, there is an equal and opposite reaction*.

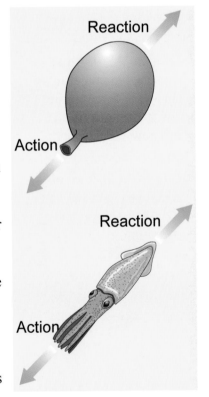

What happens when you blow up a party balloon, then let it go, allowing the air to blow out the open end? The balloon darts around the room, travelling through the air. With the balloon, the *action* is the air being expelled. The *reaction* is the movement of the balloon in the opposite direction. Another example is the movement of squid. A squid takes water into its body chamber and rapidly expels it out of backward-directed tube. What are the action and reaction forces in this example?

Rocket science

The action/reaction forces demonstrated by the balloon and squid are the main idea behind how a rocket engine works. A rocket engine forces material out the nozzle in one direction causing the rocket to move in the opposite direction.

The mass that is ejected in a rocket's exhaust is the same as the mass of fuel that is burned. The speed of the exhaust is very high, often more than 1,000 meters per second. Since the backward-moving exhaust carries negative momentum, the rocket must increase its positive momentum to keep the total momentum constant.

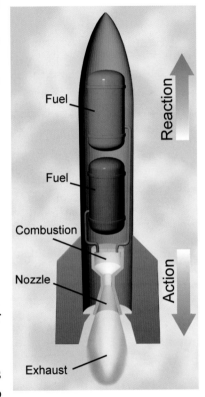

To break free from Earth's gravity and get into space, a rocket must reach a speed of over 40,250 kilometers per hour (called *escape velocity*). Attaining this speed requires a rocket engine to achieve the greatest possible action force, or *thrust*, in the shortest time. To do this, the engine must burn a large mass of fuel and push the gas out as fast as possible. The fuel required to achieve this thrust weighs over 30 times more than the rocket and its payload (what it carries). Rockets that travel into space are so huge because you need to carry lots of fuel!

Rocket scientists

Robert Goddard (1882 to 1945), an American scientist, concluded that it was possible to travel to space by applying the kind of thrust demonstrated by the balloon example. Goddard was able to take his ideas beyond theory and actually designed and built rockets. In fact he launched the first liquid-fueled rocket in 1926. Perhaps more importantly, Goddard proved rockets can propel objects in a vacuum. This touched off a revolution in thinking about space travel that continues to this day. His patents and technology innovations would solve the large problems of rockets in space. There are over 200 patents from Goddard's work.

A little help from gravity

In August 2004, NASA launched MESSENGER, a spacecraft headed for the planet Mercury. The entire trip will cover almost 7.9 billion kilometers (4.9 billion miles) rounding the sun 15 times. At 1,100 kilograms, MESSENGER is considered lightweight for a rocket. While more than half of the weight is fuel, it would not be enough to cover this great distance without some external help. Thankfully, not all of the trip is to be powered by the energy of the rocket. MESSENGER will get a slight boost from the sun and different planets it passes.

While rocket technology will continue to power the space exploration industry for years to come, we need to develop newer energy sources or whole new technologies to take us deeper into

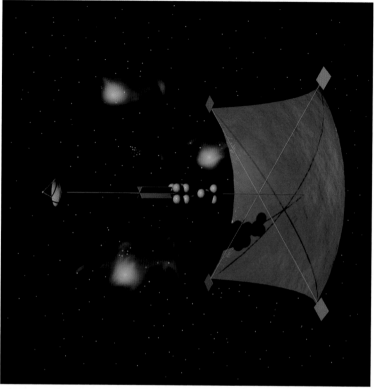

space. Scientists estimate that if we were to travel to distant regions of our own solar system using today's fuel technologies, 99% of the spacecraft launch weight would have to be fuel and only 1% would be payload. Can you think of ways to do this without having to carry so much fuel on board?

The future of rockets

Some new technologies being developed and tested for deep space travel minimize the fuel storage burden by having their energy sources located behind them. One of these technologies uses the photons (light particles) from the sun as a "wind" to accelerate the spacecraft like a sail boat. Another idea uses extremely light gases for fuels to reduce the mass required and increase the distances that can be covered. Still another idea is to find ways to accelerate atomic particles to extremely high speeds, creating thrust more efficiently. Even with these advanced technologies, all rockets rely on the ideas in Newton's laws.

Questions:

1. Is a rocket's thrust the action or reaction force?
2. Why are rockets for deep space travel so huge?
3. How is a rocket engine different than an automobile engine?
4. What are the major obstacles to bringing humans deeper into space?

Chapter 3 Review

Understanding Vocabulary

Select the correct term to complete the sentences.

energy	momentum	elastic collision
work	inelastic collision	kinetic energy
Newton's third law	joule	potential energy
law of conservation of energy	collision	impulse
law of conservation of momentum		

Section 3.1

1. The _____ states that the total amount of momentum in a closed system cannot change.

2. _____ is calculated by multiplying a force and the time needed for the force to act.

3. According to _____, for every action force, there is a reaction force equal in strength and opposite in direction.

4. The mass of an object multiplied by its velocity equals its _____.

Section 3.2

5. The _____ states that energy can never be created or destroyed, just changed from one form to another.

6. The unit of energy needed to push with a force of one newton over a distance of one meter is one _____.

7. Energy due to position is known as _____.

8. Energy of motion is called _____.

9. _____ is needed to cause change to an object, such as changing its speed or height.

10. _____ is force times distance moved in the direction of the force.

Section 3.3

11. When two or more objects hit each other, a _____ occurs.

12. When two objects collide and stick together or change shape, it is called a(n) _____.

13. Two billiard balls bouncing off each other is an example of a(n) _____.

Reviewing Concepts

Section 3.1

1. State Newton's third law in your own words.

2. Action and reaction forces always have the _____ strength and act in _____ directions.

3. You and a friend are sitting across from each other on chairs with wheels. You push off each other and move in opposite directions. Explain the following:
   a. How does the force you feel compare to the force your friend feels?
   b. If your mass is greater than your friend's mass, how do your accelerations compare?

4. A book rests on a table. The force of gravity pulls down on the book. What prevents the book from accelerating downward?

5. Give three examples of Newton's third law in everyday life. List the action and reaction forces in each example.

6. What two things does an object require to have momentum?

7. Consider an airplane at rest and a person walking through the airport.
   a. Which has greater mass?
   b. Which has greater velocity?
   c. Which has greater momentum? Explain.

8. Explain the two different ways to calculate impulse.

9. Is the unit used to represent impulse the same as the unit for momentum? Explain.

10. State the law of conservation of momentum in your own words.

11. You and your little cousin are standing on inline skates. You push off of each other and both move backwards.
    a. Which of you moves back at a greater speed? Use the law of conservation of momentum to explain your answer.
    b. How does your impulse compare to your cousin's impulse?

12. When you jump, you move upward with a certain amount of momentum. Earth moves downward with an equal amount of momentum. Why doesn't anyone notice Earth's motion?

Section 3.2

13. What is anything with energy able to do?

14. The joule is an abbreviation for what combination of units?

15. When work is done, _____ is transferred.

16. How can you increase the gravitational potential energy of an object?

17. Explain why a bicycle at rest at the top of a hill has energy.

18. Which two quantities are needed to determine an object's kinetic energy?

19. What happens to a car's kinetic energy if its speed doubles? What if its speed triples?

20. A ball is thrown up into the air. Explain what happens to its potential and kinetic energies as it moves up and then back down.

21. Explain what it means to say energy is conserved as a ball falls toward the ground.

22. Will we ever run out of energy on Earth? Might we run out of certain forms of energy? Explain.

Section 3.3

23. Distinguish between elastic and inelastic collisions.

24. Classify each collision as elastic or inelastic.

    a. A dog catches a tennis ball in his mouth.

    b. A ping-pong ball bounces off a table.

    c. You jump on a trampoline.

    d. A light bulb is knocked onto the floor and breaks.

25. Is momentum conserved during elastic collisions? Is it conserved during inelastic collisions?

26. Why does bouncing nearly always cause a greater force than simply stopping during a collision?

27. Cars that crumple in a collision are safer than cars that bounce when they collide. Explain why this is so.

28. What is the secret to catching a water balloon without breaking it? Explain using physics.

Solving Problems

Section 3.1

1. You throw a basketball by exerting a force of 20 newtons. According to Newton's third law, there is another 20-newton force created in the opposite direction. If there are two equal forces in opposite directions, how does the ball accelerate?

2. What is the momentum of a 2-kg ball traveling at 4 m/sec?

3. How fast does a 1000 kg car have to move to have a momentum of 50,000 kg-m/sec?

4. Idil's momentum is 110 kg-m/sec when she walks at 2 m/sec. What's her mass?

5. Which has more momentum: a 5000-kg truck moving at 10 m/sec or a sports car with a mass of 1200 kg moving at 50 m/sec?

6. Two hockey players on ice skates push off of each other. One has a mass of 60 kilograms. The other has a mass of 80 kilograms.

m = 60 kg   m = 80 kg

    a. If the 80-kilogram player moves back with a velocity of 3 m/sec, what is his momentum?

    b. What is the 60-kilogram player's momentum?

    c. What is the 60-kilogram player's velocity?

7. A 75 kg astronaut floating in space throws a 5 kg rock at 5 m/sec. How fast does the astronaut move backwards?

8. A 2-kilogram ball is accelerated from rest to a speed of 8 m/sec.
    a. What is the ball's change in momentum?
    b. What is the impulse?
    c. A constant force of 32 newtons is used to change the momentum. For how much time does the force act?

9. A 1000-kg car uses a braking force of 10,000 N to stop in 2 seconds.
    a. What impulse acts on the car?
    b. What is the change in momentum of the car?
    c. What was the initial speed of the car?

Section 3.2

10. A 5-kg can of paint is sitting on top of a 2-meter high step ladder. How much work did you do to move the can of paint to the top of the ladder? What is the potential energy of the can of paint?

11. How much work is done to move a 10,000-N car 20 meters?

12. Which has more potential energy, a 5 kg rock lifted 2 meters off the ground on Earth, or the same rock lifted 2 meters on the moon? Why?

13. At the end of a bike ride up a mountain, Chris was at an elevation of 500 meters above where he started. If Chris's mass is 60 kg, by how much did his potential energy increase?

500 m

14. Alexis is riding her skateboard. If Alexis has a mass of 50 kg:
    a. What is her kinetic energy if she travels at 5 m/sec?
    b. What is her kinetic energy if she travels at 10 m/sec?
    c. Alexis's 50 kg dog Bruno gets on the skateboard with her. What is their total kinetic energy if they move at 5 m/sec?
    d. Based on your calculations, does doubling the mass or doubling the speed have more of an effect on kinetic energy?

15. A 1-kilogram coconut falls out of a tree from a height of 12 meters. Determine the coconut's potential and kinetic energy at each point shown in the picture. Its speed is zero at point A.

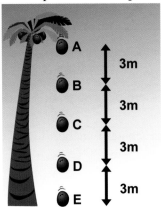

Section 3.3

16. A demolition derby is a car-crashing contest. Suppose an 800-kg car moving at 20 m/sec crashes into the back of and sticks to a 1200-kg car moving at 10 m/sec in the same direction.

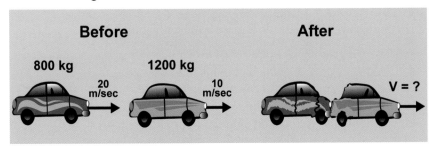

    a. Is this collision elastic or inelastic? Why?
    b. Calculate the momentum of each car before the collision.
    c. What is the total momentum of the stuck together cars after the collision? Why?
    d. What is the speed of the stuck together cars after the collision?

17. A 5-kg ball moving at 6 m/sec collides with a 1-kg ball at rest. The balls bounce off each other and the second ball moves in the same direction as the first ball at 10 m/sec. What is the velocity of the first ball after the collision?

Before

5 kg

6 m/sec

1 kg

at rest

After

V = ?

10 m/sec

18. Yanick and Nancy drive two identical 1500-kilogram cars at 20 m/sec. Yanick slams on the brakes and his car comes to a stop in 1 second. Nancy lightly applies the brakes and stops her car in 5 seconds.

a. How does the momentum change of Yanick's car compare to the momentum change of Nancy's car?

b. How does the impulse on Yanick's car compare to the impulse on Nancy's car?

c. How does the force of Yanick's brakes compare to the force of Nancy's brakes?

d. Calculate the stopping force for each car.

19. Your neighbor's car breaks down. You and a friend agree to push it two blocks to a repair shop while your neighbor steers. The two of you apply a net force of 800 newtons to the 1000-kilogram car for 10 seconds.

a. What impulse is applied to the car?

b. At what speed is the car moving after 10 seconds? The car starts from rest.

Applying Your Knowledge

Section 3.1

1. Think up some strange scenarios that might happen if the universe changed so that Newton's third law were no longer true.

2. Identify at least *three* action-reaction force pairs in the picture of the firefighter below.

3. The greatest speed with which an athlete can jump vertically is around 5 m/sec. Determine the speed at which Earth would move down if you jumped up at 5 m/sec.

Section 3.2

4. A car going twice as fast requires four times as much stopping distance. What is it about the kinetic energy formula that accounts for this fact?

5. The energy in food is measured in Calories rather than joules. One Calorie is equal to 4187 joules. Look on the nutrition labels of three of your favorite foods. Determine the amount of energy in joules in one serving of each type of food.

Nutrition Facts
Serving Size 1 oz (40grams/about 1/2 cup)
Servings Per Container 20

Amount per serving

Calories 240	Calories from Fat 120
	% Daily Value*
Total Fat 10g	11%
Saturated Fat 5g	22%
Trans Fat 0g	
Cholesterol 2mg	0%
Sodium 240mg	10%
Total Carbohydrate 24g	8%
Dietary Fiber Less tahn 1g	4%
Sugars 5g	
Protein 2g	

Ingredients: Unbleached wheat flower, potatoes, water, sugar, Partially hydroginated palm oil, corn starch, artifical flavors, preservatives.

Section 3.3

6. Major League Baseball requires players to use wooden bats, and does not allow the use of aluminum bats. Research to find out why this is. Relate what you find to what you learned in this chapter.

7. Use the Internet to learn more about how cars are designed to be safer in collisions and how they are tested. Make a poster that summarizes what you learn.

UNIT 2

Energy and Systems

Chapter 4

Machines, Work, and Energy

The Egyptian pyramids were built about 4,000 years ago. It took workers approximately 80 years to build the pyramids at Giza. The largest, called the Great Pyramid, contains about 1 million stone blocks, each weighing about 2.5 tons. How were the ancient Egyptians able to build such an incredible monument?

What did the ancient Egyptians use to help them build the pyramids? Egyptologists, men and women that study ancient Egypt, disagree about the details of how the gigantic structures were built, but most agree that a system of ramps and levers (*simple machines*) was necessary for moving and placing the blocks. The fact that they could move such enormously massive blocks of limestone to build the Great Pyramid to a height of 481 feet (roughly equivalent to a 48-story building) is fascinating, don't you think? Perhaps the most amazing part of this story is that the Great Pyramid at Giza still stands, and is visited by tens of thousands of people each year.

Key Questions

- ✓ Why does stretching a rubber band increase its potential energy?
- ✓ How much power can a highly trained athlete have?
- ✓ What is one of the most perfect machines ever invented?
- ✓ Why does time always move forward, and never backward?

4.1 Work and Power

Energy is a measure of an object's ability to do work. Suppose you lift your book over your head. The book gets potential energy which comes from your action. Now suppose you lift your book fast, then lift it again slowly. The energy is the same because the height is the same. But it feels different to transfer the energy fast or slow. The difference between moving energy fast or slow is described by *power*. Power is the rate at which energy flows or at which work is done. This section is about power and its relation to work and energy.

Reviewing the definition of work

What "work" means in physics In the last chapter you learned that work has a very specific meaning in physics. Work is the transfer of energy that results from applying a force over a distance. If you push a block with a force of one newton for a distance of one meter, you do one joule of work. Both work and energy are measured in the same units (joules) because work is a form of energy.

Work is done on objects When thinking about work you should always be clear about which force is doing the work. Work is done by forces *on* objects. If you push a block one meter with a force of one newton, you have done one joule of work (Figure 4.1).

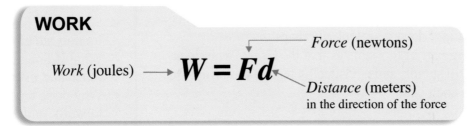

WORK

$$Work\ (joules) \longrightarrow W = Fd$$

Force (newtons)

Distance (meters)
in the direction of the force

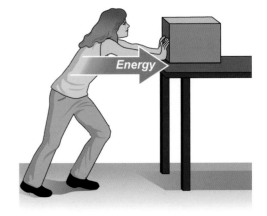

Figure 4.1: *A force of 1 newton applied for 1 meter does one joule of work on the block.*

Energy is needed to do work An object that has energy is able to do work; without energy, it is impossible to do work. A block that slides across a table has kinetic energy that can be used to do work. If the block hits a ball, it will do work on the ball and change its motion. Some of the block's kinetic energy is transferred to the ball. An elastic collision is a common method of doing work.

Work and energy

Work and potential energy

Doing work always means transferring energy. The energy may be transferred to the object you apply the force to, or it may go somewhere else. You can increase the potential energy of a rubber band by exerting a force that stretches it. The work you do stretching the rubber band is stored as energy by the rubber band. The rubber band can then use the energy to do work on a paper airplane, giving it kinetic energy (Figure 4.2).

Work may not increase the energy of an object

You can do work on a block by sliding it across a level table. In this example, though, the work you do does not increase the energy of the block. Because the block will not slide back all by itself, it does not gain the ability to do work *itself*, therefore gains no energy. Your work is done to overcome friction. The block does gain a tiny bit of energy because its temperature rises slightly from friction. However, that energy comes from the force of friction, not from your applied force.

Not all force does work

Sometimes force is applied to an object, but no work is done. If you push down on a block sitting on a table and it doesn't move, you have not done any work on the block (force A below). If you use $W=Fd$ to calculate the work, you will get zero no matter how strong the force because the distance is zero.

Force at an angle to distance

There are times when only *some* of a force does work. Force B is applied at an angle to the direction of motion of a block. Only a portion of the force is in the direction the block moves, so only that portion of the force does work.

Doing the most work

The more exact calculation of work is the product of the portions of force and distance that are *in the same direction*. To do the greatest amount of work, you must apply force in the direction the object will move (force C). If forces A, B, and C have equal strengths, force C will do the most work because it is entirely in the direction of the motion.

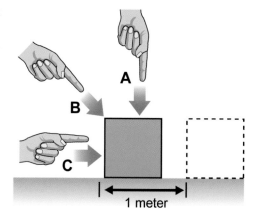

Work done stretching a rubber band increases its potential energy.

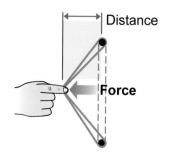

The rubber band can then do work on the plane, giving it kinetic energy.

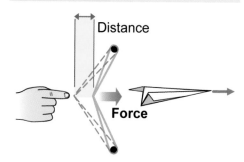

Figure 4.2: *You can do work to increase an object's potential energy. Then the potential energy can be converted to kinetic energy.*

Work done against gravity

Lifting force equals the weight
Many situations involve work done by or against the force of gravity. To lift something off the floor, you must apply an upward force with a strength equal to the object's weight. The work done while lifting an object is equal to its change in potential energy. It does not matter whether you lift the object straight up or you carry it up the stairs in a zigzag pattern. The work is the same in either case. Work done against gravity is calculated by multiplying the object's weight by its change in height.

Why the path does not matter
The reason the path does not matter is found in the definition of work as the force times the distance moved *in the direction of the force*. If you move an object on a diagonal, only the vertical distance matters because the force of gravity is vertical (Figure 4.3). It is much easier to climb stairs or go up a ramp but the work done *against gravity* is the same as if you jumped straight up. Stairs and ramps are easier because you need less force. But you have to apply the force over a longer distance. In the end, the total work done against gravity is the same no matter what path you take.

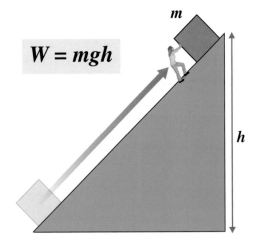

$$W = mgh$$

Figure 4.3: *The work done when lifting an object equals its mass multiplied by the strength of gravity multiplied by the change in height.*

Calculating work

Alexander has a mass of 70 kilograms. His apartment is on the second floor, 5 meters up from ground level. How much work does he do against gravity each time he climbs the stairs to his apartment?

1. Looking for: You are asked for the work.

2. Given: You are given the mass in kilograms and the height in meters.

3. Relationships: $F_g = mg$ $W = Fd$

4. Solution: The force is equal to Alexander's weight.
$F_g = (70 \text{ kg})(9.8 \text{ m/sec}^2)$ $F_g = 686 \text{ N}$

Use the force to calculate the work.
$W = (686 \text{ N})(5 \text{ m})$ $W = 3430 \text{ J}$ He does 3430 joules of work.

Your turn...
a. How much additional work does Alexander have to do if he is carrying 5 kilograms of groceries? **Answer:** 245 J
b. A car engine does 50,000 J of work to accelerate at 10 m/sec^2 for 5 meters. What is the mass of the car? **Answer:** 1,000 kg

---

Power

What is power? Suppose Michael and Jim each lift a barbell weighing 100 newtons from the ground to a height of two meters (Figure 4.4). Michael lifts quickly and Jim lifts slowly. Because the barbell is raised the same distance, it gains the same amount of potential energy in each case. Michael and Jim do the same amount of work. However, Michael's *power* is greater because he gets the work done in less time. **Power** is the rate at which work is done.

Units of power The unit for power is equal to the unit of work (joules) divided by the unit of time (seconds). One **watt** is equal to one joule per second. The watt was named after James Watt (1736-1819), the Scottish engineer who invented the steam engine. Another unit of power that is often used for engine power is the **horsepower**. Watt expressed the power of his engines as the number of horses an engine could replace. One horsepower is equal to 746 watts.

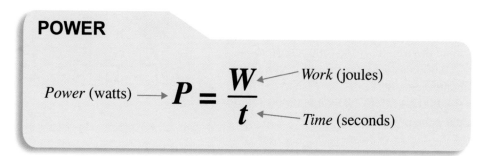

POWER

$$Power\ (watts) \longrightarrow P = \frac{W}{t}$$

Work (joules) — W

Time (seconds) — t

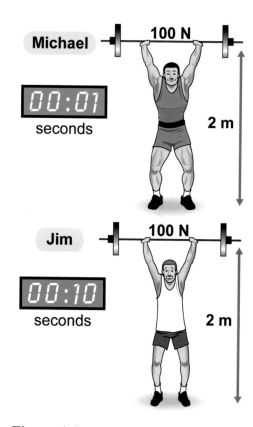

Michael 100 N

00:01 seconds

2 m

Jim 100 N

00:10 seconds

2 m

Figure 4.4: *Michael and Jim do the same amount of work but do not have the same power.*

Calculating work So how much power do Michael and Jim use? You must first calculate the work they do, using $W = Fd$. The force needed to lift the barbell is equal to its weight (100 N). The work is therefore 100 newtons times two meters, or 200 joules. Each of them does 200 joules of work.

Calculating power To find Michael's power, divide his work (200 joules) by his time (1 second). Michael has a power of 200 watts. To find Jim's power, divide his work (200 joules) by his time (10 seconds). Jim's power is 20 watts. Jim takes 10 times as long to lift the barbell, so his power is one-tenth as great.

Calculating power

Human power The maximum power output of a person is typically around a few hundred watts. However, it is only possible to keep up this power for a short time. Highly trained athletes can keep up a power of 350 watts for about an hour. An average person running or biking for a full hour produces an average power of around 200 watts.

Calculating power

A roller coaster is pulled up a hill by a chain attached to a motor. The roller coaster has a total mass of 10,000 kg. If it takes 20 seconds to pull the roller coaster up a 50-meter hill, how powerful is the motor?

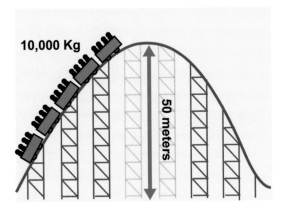

10,000 Kg

50 meters

1. Looking for: You are asked for power.

2. Given: You are given the mass in kilograms, the time in seconds, and the height in meters.

3. Relationships: $F_g = mg$ $W = Fd$ $P = W/t$

4. Solution: Calculate the weight of the roller coaster:
$F_g = (10,000 \text{ kg})(9.8 \text{ m/sec}^2)$ $F_g = 98,000 \text{ N}$
Calculate the work:
$W = (98,000 \text{ N})(50 \text{ m})$ $W = 4,900,000 \text{ J or } 4.9 \times 10^6 \text{ J}$
Calculate the power:
$P = (4.9 \times 10^6 \text{ J}) \div (20 \text{ sec})$ $P = 245,000 \text{ watts}$

Your turn...
a. What would the motor's power be if it took 40 seconds to pull the same roller coaster up the hill? **Answer:** 122,500 watts
b. What is the power of a 70-kilogram person who climbs a 10-meter-high hill in 45 seconds? **Answer:** 152 watts

4.1 Section Review

1. Explain how work is related to energy.
2. Who does more work, a person who lifts a 2-kilogram object 5 meters or a person who lifts a 3-kilogram object 4 meters?
3. While sitting in class, your body exerts a force of 600 N on your chair. How much work do you do?
4. Is your power greater when you run or walk up a flight of stairs? Why?

4.2 Simple machines

How do you move something that is too heavy to carry? How did the ancient Egyptians build the pyramids long before the invention of powered machines? The answer to these questions has to do with the use of simple machines. In this section, you will learn how simple machines multiply forces to accomplish many tasks.

Using machines

What technology allows us to do
Today's technology allows us to do incredible things. Moving huge steel beams, digging tunnels that connect two islands, and building 1,000-foot skyscrapers are examples. What makes these accomplishments possible? Have we developed super powers since the days of our ancestors?

What is a machine?
In a way we *have* developed super powers. Our powers come from the clever human invention of machines. A **machine** is a device with moving parts that work together to accomplish a task. A bicycle is made of a combination of machines that work together. All the parts of a bicycle work as a system to transform forces from your muscles into motion. A bicycle allows you to travel at faster speeds and for greater distances than possible on foot.

Work output is forward motion

Work input forces applied to pedals

The concepts of input and output
Machines are designed to do something. To understand how machines work it is useful to define an **input** and an **output**. The *input* includes everything you do to make the machine work, like pushing on the bicycle pedals, for instance. The *output* is what the machine does for you, like going fast or climbing a steep hill. For the machines that are the subject of this chapter, the input and output may be force, power, or energy.

Vocabulary

machine, input, output, fulcrum, simple machines, mechanical advantage, fulcrum, input arm, output arm, tension

Objectives

✓ Describe how a machine works in terms of input and output.
✓ Define simple machines and name some examples.
✓ Calculate the mechanical advantage of a simple machine given the input and output force.

Parts of a bicycle

Wheels   Pedals   Gears

Figure 4.5: *A bicycle contains machines working together.*

Simple machines

The beginning of technology
The development of the technology that created cars, airplanes, and other modern conveniences began with the invention of **simple machines**. A simple machine is a mechanical device that accomplishes a task with only one movement (such as a lever). A lever allows you to move a rock that weighs 10 times (or more) what you weigh. Some important types of simple machines are shown below.

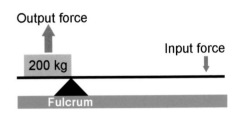

Figure 4.6: *A small input force can create a large output force if the lever is arranged correctly.*

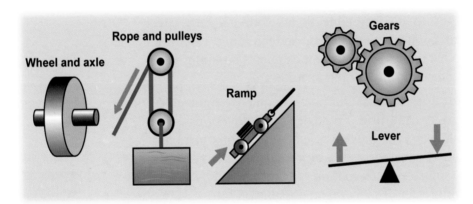

Input force and output force
Simple machines work with forces. The *input force* is the force you apply to the machine. The *output force* is the force the machine applies to what you are trying to move. Figure 4.6 shows how a lever can be arranged to create a large output force from a small input force.

Ropes and pulleys
A rope and pulley system is a simple machine made by connecting a rope to one or more pulleys. You apply the input force to the rope and the output force is exerted on the load you are lifting. One person could easily lift an elephant with a properly designed system of pulleys (Figure 4.7).

Machines within machines
Most of the machines we use today are made up of combinations of different types of simple machines. For example, the bicycle uses wheels and axles, levers (the pedals and kickstand), and gears. If you take apart a complex machine such as a video cassette recorder, a clock, or a car engine, you will find many simple machines inside. In fact, a VCR contains simple machines of every type including screws, ramps, pulleys, wheels, gears, and levers.

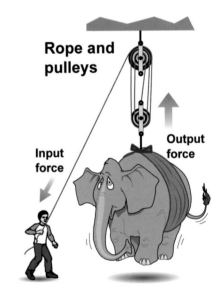

Figure 4.7: *A simple machine made with a rope and pulley allows one person to lift tremendous loads.*

Mechanical advantage

Ratio of output to input force Simple machines are best understood through the concepts of input and output forces. The **mechanical advantage** of a machine is the ratio of the output force to the input force. If the mechanical advantage of a machine is larger than one, the output force is larger than the input force. A mechanical advantage smaller than one means the output force is smaller than the input force. Mechanical advantage is a ratio of forces, so it is a pure number without any units.

MECHANICAL ADVANTAGE

$$\text{Mechanical advantage} \rightarrow \text{MA} = \frac{F_o \leftarrow \textit{Output force (N)}}{F_i \leftarrow \textit{Input force (N)}}$$

Calculating mechanical advantage

What is the mechanical advantage of a lever that allows Jorge to lift a 24-newton box with a force of 4 newtons?

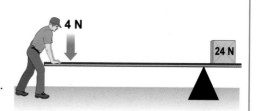

1. Looking for: You are asked for the mechanical advantage.

2. Given: You are given the input force and the output force in newtons.

3. Relationships: $MA = F_o/F_i$

4. Solution: $MA = (24\text{ N})/(4\text{ N})$
$MA = 6$

a. Calculate the mechanical advantage of a rope and pulley system that requires 10 newtons of force to lift a 200-newton load.
   Answer: 20

b. You use a block and tackle with a mechanical advantage of 30. How heavy a load can you lift with an input force of 100 N?
   Answer: 3000 N

Work and machines

Input and output work A simple machine does work because it exerts forces over a distance. If you are using the machine you also do work, because you apply forces to the machine that move its parts. By definition, a simple machine has no source of energy except the immediate forces you apply. That means the only way to get output work *from* a simple machine is to do input work *on* the machine. In fact, the output work done by a simple machine can never exceed the input work done on the machine. This is an important result.

Perfect machines In a *perfect* machine the output work equals the input work. Of course, there are no perfect machines. Friction always converts some of the input work to heat and wear, so the output work is always *less* than the input work. However, for a well-designed machine, friction can be small and we can often assume input and output work are approximately equal.

An example Figure 4.8 shows a simple machine that has a mechanical advantage of two. The machine lifts a 10-newton weight a distance of one-half meter. The output work is five joules (10 N × 0.5 m).

You must do at least five joules of work on the machine to lift the weight. If you assume the machine is perfect, then you must do exactly 5 J of input work to get 5 J of output work. The input force is only five newtons since the machine has a mechanical advantage of two. That means the input distance must be 1 meter because 5 N × 1 m = 5 J. You have to pull one meter of rope to raise the weight one-half meter.

The cost of multiplying force The output work of a machine can never be greater than the input work. This is a rule that is *true for all machines*. Nature does not give something for nothing. When you design a machine that multiplies force, you pay by having to apply the force over a greater distance.

The force and distance are related by the amount of work done. In a perfect (theoretical) machine, the output work is exactly equal to the input work. If the machine has a mechanical advantage greater than one, the input force is less than the output force. However, the input force must be applied over a longer distance to satisfy the rule about input and output work.

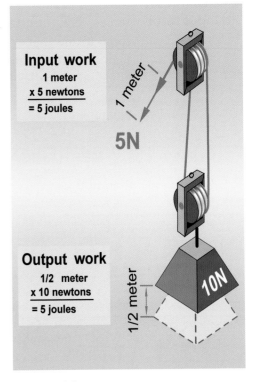

Figure 4.8: *The work output equals the work input even though the forces differ.*

Using work to solve problems

Mechanical advantage
To solve mechanical advantage problems, start by assuming a perfect machine, with nothing lost to friction. Set the input and output work equal and use this relationship to find the mechanical advantage.

Force or distance
Many problems give three of the four quantities: input force, input distance, output force, and output distance. If the input and output work are equal then force × distance at the input of the machine equals force × distance at the output. Using this equation, you can solve for the unknown force or distance.

Work and machines

A jack is used to lift one side of a car in order to replace a tire. To lift the car, the jack handle moves 30 centimeters for every one centimeter that the car is lifted. If a force of 150 newtons is applied to the jack handle, what force is applied to the car by the jack? You can assume all of the input work equals output work.

1. Looking for: You are asked for the output force in newtons.

2. Given: You are given the input force in newtons, and the input distance and output distance in centimeters. Convert these distances to meters.

3. Relationships: *Work = Force × distance*   and   Input work = output work

4. Solution: Input work: $W = (150 \text{ N})(0.30 \text{ m}) = 45$ joules
Output work: 45 J of input work = *Force* × 0.01 m
$F = 45 \text{ J} / 0.01 \text{ m} = 4{,}500$ newtons
The jack exerts an upward force of 4,500 newtons on the car.

Your turn...

a. A mover uses a pulley to lift a 2,400-newton piano up to the second floor. Each time he pulls the rope down 2 meters (input distance), the piano moves up 0.25 meter (output distance). With what force does the mover pull on the rope? **Answer:** 300 newtons

b. A nutcracker is a very useful lever. The center of the nutcracker (where the nut is) moves one centimeter for each two centimeters your hand squeezes down. If a force of 40 newtons is needed to crack the shell of a walnut, what force must you apply? **Answer:** 20 newtons

How a lever works

Example of a lever
A lever can be made by balancing a board on a log (Figure 4.9). Pushing down on one end of the board lifts a load on the other end of the board. The downward force you apply is the input force. The upward force the board exerts on the load is the output force.

Parts of the lever
All levers include a stiff structure that rotates around a fixed point called the **fulcrum**. The side of the lever where the input force is applied is called the **input arm**. The **output arm** is the end of the lever that applies the output force. Levers are useful because you can arrange the fulcrum and the input and output arms to make almost any mechanical advantage you need.

Changing direction
When the fulcrum is in the middle of the lever, the input and output forces are the same. An input force of 100 newtons makes an output force of 100 newtons. The input and output forces are different if the fulcrum is not in the center of the lever (Figure 4.10). The side of the lever with the longer arm has the smaller force. If the input arm is 10 times longer than the output arm, the output force is 10 times greater than the input force.

Mechanical advantage of a lever
You can find the mechanical advantage of a lever by looking at two triangles. The output work is the output force multiplied by the output distance. The input work is the input distance multiplied by the input force. By setting the input and output work equal, you see that the ratio of forces is the inverse of the ratio of distances. The larger (input) distance has the smaller force. The ratio of distances is equal to the ratio of the lengths of the two arms of the lever. Using the lengths of the arms is the easiest way to calculate the mechanical advantage of a lever (below).

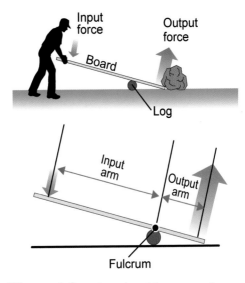

Figure 4.9: *A board and log can make a lever used to lift a rock.*

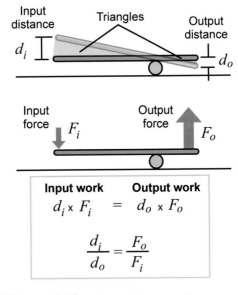

Input work		Output work
$d_i \times F_i$	$=$	$d_o \times F_o$

$$\frac{d_i}{d_o} = \frac{F_o}{F_i}$$

Figure 4.10: *How to determine the mechanical advantage of a lever.*

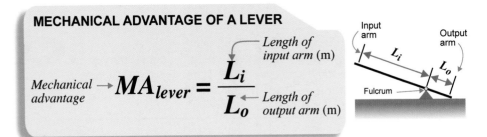

MECHANICAL ADVANTAGE OF A LEVER

$$\underset{\text{advantage}}{\overset{\text{Mechanical}}{\longrightarrow}} MA_{lever} = \frac{L_i}{L_o} \quad \begin{array}{l} \text{Length of} \\ \text{input arm (m)} \\ \\ \text{Length of} \\ \text{output arm (m)} \end{array}$$

Types of levers

The output force can be *less* than the input force
You can also make a lever in which the output force is less than the input force. The input arm is shorter than the output arm on this kind of lever. You might design a lever this way if you need the motion on the output side to be larger than the motion on the input side. A very small downward motion on the input side can cause the load to lift a large distance on the output side.

The three types of levers
Levers are used in many common machines, including, for example, pliers, a wheelbarrow, and the human biceps and forearm (Figure 4.11). You may have heard the human body described as a machine. In fact, it is a machine. Bones and muscles work as levers when you do something as simple as biting an apple. Levers are classified as one of three types or classes defined by the location of the input and output forces relative to the fulcrum. The mechanical advantage is always the ratio of lengths of the input arm to the output arm.

The Three Classes of Levers

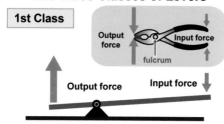

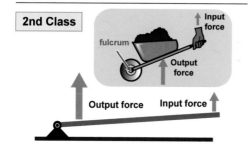

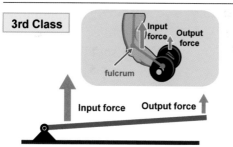

Figure 4.11: *There are three classes of levers.*

Mechanical advantage of levers

A lever has a mechanical advantage of 4. Its input arm is 60 centimeters long. How long is its output arm?

1. Looking for: You are asked for the output arm in centimeters.

2. Given: You are given the mechanical advantage and the length of the input arm in centimeters.

3. Relationships: $MA_{lever} = \dfrac{L_i}{L_o}$

4. Solution:

$$4 = \frac{60 \text{ cm}}{L_o} \qquad 4L_o = 60 \text{ cm}$$

$$L_o = \frac{60 \text{ cm}}{4} = 15 \text{ cm}$$

a. What is the mechanical advantage of a lever with an input arm of 25 centimeters and an output arm of 100 centimeters? **Answer:** 0.25

b. A lever has an input arm of 100 centimeters and an output arm of 10 centimeters. What is the mechanical advantage of this lever? Given this mechanical advantage, how much input force is needed to lift a 100-newton load?
Answer: $MA_{lever} = 10$; 10 newtons of force would be needed.

How a rope and pulley system works

Tension in ropes and strings

Ropes and strings carry forces along their length. The force in a rope is called **tension** and is a pulling force that acts along the direction of the rope. The tension is the same at every point in a rope. If the rope is not moving, its tension is equal to the force pulling on each end (below). Ropes or strings do *not* carry pushing forces. This is obvious if you ever tried pushing a rope.

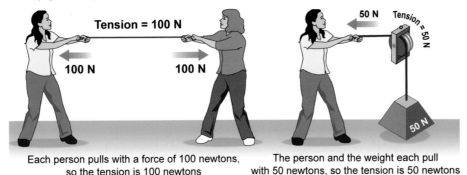

Each person pulls with a force of 100 newtons, so the tension is 100 newtons

The person and the weight each pull with 50 newtons, so the tension is 50 newtons

The forces in a pulley system

Figure 4.12 shows three different configurations of ropes and pulleys. Imagine pulling with an input force of 5 newtons. In case A, the load feels a force equal to your input force. In case B, there are two strands of rope supporting the load, so the load feels twice your input force. In case C, there are three strands so the output force is three times the input force.

Mechanical advantage

The mechanical advantage of a pulley system depends on the number of strands of rope directly supporting the load. In case C, three strands directly support the load, so the output force is three times the input force. The mechanical advantage is 3. To make a rope and pulley system with a greater mechanical advantage, you can increase the number of strands directly supporting the load by taking more turns around the pulleys.

Work

To raise the load 1 meter in case C, the input end of the rope must be pulled for 3 meters. This is because *each* of the three supporting strands must shorten by 1 meter. The mechanical advantage is 3 but the input force must be applied for three times the distance as the output force. This is another example of the rule stating that output and input work are equal for a perfect machine.

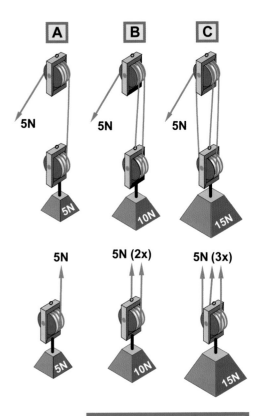

	A	B	C
Input force	5N	5N	5N
Output force	5N	10N	15N
Mechanical advantage	1	2	3

Figure 4.12: *A rope and pulley system can be arranged to have different mechanical advantages.*

Gears and ramps

Rotating motion Many machines require that rotating motion be transmitted from one place to another. The transmission of rotating motion is often done with gears (Figure 4.13). Some machines that use gears, such as small drills, require small forces at high speeds. Other machines, such as the paddle wheel on the back of a steamboat, require large forces at low speed.

How gears work The rule for how two gears turn depends on the number of teeth on each gear. The teeth don't slip, so moving 36 teeth on one gear means that 36 teeth have to move on any connected gear. Suppose a large gear with 36 teeth is connected to a small gear with 12 teeth. As the large gear turns once around, it moves 36 teeth on the smaller gear. The smaller gear must turn three times $(3 \times 12 = 36)$ for every single turn of the large gear (Figure 4.13).

Ramps A ramp is another type of simple machine. Using a ramp allows you to push a heavy car to a higher location with less force than is needed to lift the car straight up. Ramps reduce the input force needed by increasing the distance over which the input force acts. For example, suppose a 10-meter ramp is used to lift a car one meter. The output work is work done against gravity. If the weight of the car is 500 newtons, then the output work is 500 joules $(w = mgh = 500 \text{ N} \times 1 \text{ m})$.

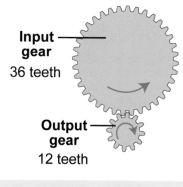

Input gear
36 teeth

Output gear
12 teeth

$$\text{Gear ratio} = \frac{\text{output}}{\text{input}}$$

Figure 4.13: *The smaller gear makes three turns for each one turn of the larger gear.*

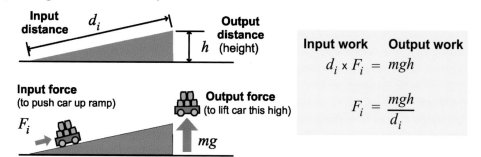

Input distance d_i

Output distance h (height)

Input force (to push car up ramp) F_i

Output force (to lift car this high)

mg

Input work	Output work
$d_i \times F_i$	$= mgh$

$$F_i = \frac{mgh}{d_i}$$

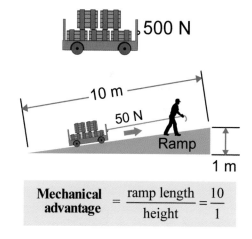

500 N

10 m

50 N

Ramp

1 m

$$\text{Mechanical advantage} = \frac{\text{ramp length}}{\text{height}} = \frac{10}{1}$$

Figure 4.14: *The car must be pulled 10 meters to lift it up one meter, but only one-tenth the force is needed*

Mechanical advantage of a ramp The input work is the input force multiplied by the length of the ramp (10 meters). If you set the input work equal to the output work, you quickly find that the input force is 50 newtons $(Fd = F \times 10 \text{ m} = 500 \text{ J})$. The input force is one-tenth of the output force. For a frictionless ramp, the mechanical advantage is the length of the ramp divided by the height (Figure 4.14).

Screws

Screws   A screw is a simple machine that turns rotating motion into linear motion (Figure 4.15). A screw works just like a ramp that curves as it gets higher. The "ramp" on a screw is called a thread. Imagine unwrapping one turn of a thread to make a straight ramp. Each turn of the screw advances the nut the same distance it would have gone sliding up the ramp. The *lead* of a screw is the distance it advances in one turn. A screw with a lead of one millimeter advances one millimeter for each turn.

A screw and screwdriver   The combination of a screw and screwdriver has a very large mechanical advantage. The mechanical advantage of a screw is found by thinking about it as a ramp. The vertical distance is the lead of the screw. The length of the ramp is measured as the average circumference of the thread. A quarter-inch screw in a hardware store has a lead of 1.2 millimeters and a circumference of 17 millimeters along the thread. The mechanical advantage is 14. If you use a typical screwdriver with a mechanical advantage of 4, the total mechanical advantage is 14 × 4 or 56 (theoretically). Friction between the screw and the mating surface causes the actual mechanical advantage to be somewhat less than the theoretical value, but still very large (Figure 4.16).

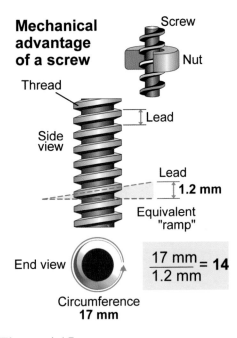

Figure 4.15: *A screw is a rotating ramp.*

4.2 Section Review

1. Name two simple machines that are found on a bicycle.
2. Calculate the mechanical advantage of the crowbar shown at right.
3. Classify each of these as a first-, second-, or third-class levers: see-saw, baseball bat, door on hinges, scissors (Figure 4.16).
4. A large gear with 48 teeth is connected to a small gear with 12 teeth. If the large gear turns twice, how many times must the small gear turn?
5. What is the mechanical advantage of a 15 meter ramp that rises 3 meters?

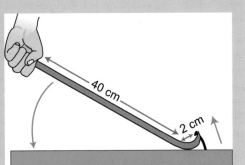

Figure 4.16: *Which type of lever is shown in each picture?*

4.3 Efficiency

So far we have talked about perfect machines. In a perfect machine there is no friction and the output work equals the input work. Of course, there are no perfect machines in human technology. This section is about *efficiency,* which is how we measure how close to perfect a machine is. The bicycle comes as close to perfect as any machine ever invented. Up to 95 percent of the work done by the rider on the pedals becomes kinetic energy of the bicycle (Figure 4.17). Most machines are much less perfect. An automobile engine converts less than 15 percent of the chemical energy in gasoline into output work to move a car.

Friction

Friction   Friction is a catch-all term for many processes that oppose motion. Friction can be caused by rubbing or sliding surfaces. Friction can also be caused by moving through liquid, such as oil or water. Friction can even be caused by moving though air, as you can easily feel by sticking your hand out the window of a moving car.

Friction and energy   Friction converts energy of motion to heat and wear. The brakes on a car use friction to slow the car down and they get hot. Over time, the material of the brakes wears away. This also takes energy because the bonds between atoms are being broken as material is being worn down. When we loosely say that energy is "lost" to friction, the statement is not accurate. The energy is not lost, but converted to other forms of energy that are difficult to recover and reuse.

Machines   In an actual machine, the output work is less than the input work because of friction. When analyzing a machine it helps to think like the diagram below. The input work is divided between output work and "losses" due to friction.

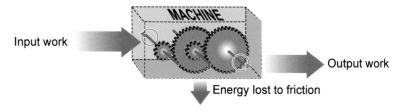

Vocabulary

efficiency, reversible, irreversible

Objectives

✓ Describe the relationship between work and energy in a simple machine.
✓ Use energy conservation to calculate input or output force or distance.
✓ Explain why a machine's input and output work can differ.

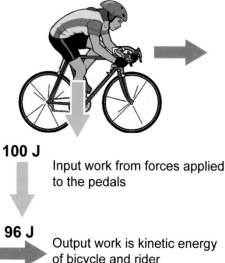

100 J   Input work from forces applied to the pedals

96 J   Output work is kinetic energy of bicycle and rider

4 J   Work done against friction

Figure 4.17: *A bicycle is highly efficient.*

Efficiency

100 percent efficient
A machine has an **efficiency** of 100 percent if the work output of the machine is equal to the work input. If a machine is 100 percent efficient, no energy is diverted by friction or other factors. Although it is impossible to create a machine with 100 percent efficiency, people who design machines try to achieve as high an efficiency as possible.

The definition of efficiency
The efficiency of a machine is the ratio of work output to work input. Efficiency is usually expressed in percent. A machine that is 75 percent efficient can produce three joules of output work for every four joules of input work (Figure 4.18). One joule out of every four (25 percent) is lost to friction. You calculate efficiency by dividing the work output by the work input. You can convert the ratio into a percent by multiplying by 100.

Improving efficiency
An important way to increase the efficiency of a machine is to reduce friction. Ball bearings and oil reduce rolling friction. Slippery materials such as Teflon^{TM} reduce sliding friction. Designing a car with a streamlined shape reduces air friction. All these techniques increase efficiency.

A machine with 75% efficiency

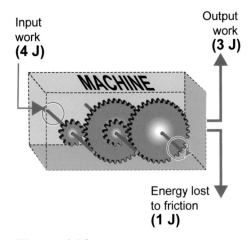

Input work (4 J)

Output work (3 J)

Energy lost to friction (1 J)

Figure 4.18: *If the input work is four joules, and the output work is three joules, then the efficiency is 75 percent.*

Calculating efficiency

A person uses a 75-newton force to push a 51-kilogram car up a ramp. The ramp is 10 meters long and rises one meter. Calculate the efficiency.

1. Looking for: You are asked for the efficiency.

2. Given: You are given the input force and distance, and the mass and height for the output.

3. Relationships: Efficiency = Output work / Input work. Input: $W = FD$. Output: work done against gravity ($W = mgh$)

4. Solution:
Output work = (51 kg)(9.8 N/kg)(1 m) = 500 joules
Input work = (75 N)(10 m) = 750 joules
Efficiency = 500 J ÷ 750 J = 67%

Your turn...

a. If a machine is 80 percent efficient, how much input work is required to do 100 joules of output work?. **Answer:** 125 J

b. A solar cell needs 750 J of input energy to produce 100 J of output. What is its efficiency? **Answer:** 13.3%

Efficiency and time

A connection The efficiency is less than 100 percent for virtually all processes that convert energy to any other form except heat. Scientists believe this is connected to why time flows forward and not backward. Think of time as an arrow pointing from the past into the future. All processes move in the direction of the arrow, never backward (Figure 4.19).

Reversible processes Suppose a process were 100 percent efficient. As an example, think about connecting two marbles of equal mass by a string passing over an ideal pulley with no mass and no friction (Figure 4.20). One marble can go down, transferring its potential energy to the other marble, which goes up. The motion of the marble is **reversible** because it can go forward and backward as many times as you want. In fact, if you watched a movie of the marbles moving, you could not tell if the movie were playing forward or backward.

Friction and the arrow of time Now suppose there is a tiny amount of friction so the efficiency is 99 percent. Because some potential energy is lost to friction, every time the marbles exchange energy, some is lost and the marbles don't rise quite as high as they did the last time. If you made a movie of the motion, you could tell whether the movie was running forward or backward. Any process with an efficiency less than 100 percent runs only one way, *forward with the arrow of time.*

Irreversible processes Friction turns energy of motion into heat. Once energy is transformed into heat, the energy cannot ever completely get back into its original form. Because heat energy cannot get back to potential or kinetic energy, any process with less than 100% efficiency is **irreversible**. Irreversible processes can only go forward in time. Since processes in the universe almost always lose a little energy to friction, time cannot run backward.

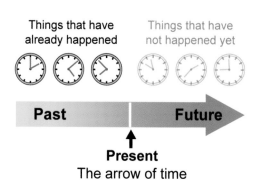

Figure 4.19: *Time can be thought of as an arrow pointing from the past into the future.*

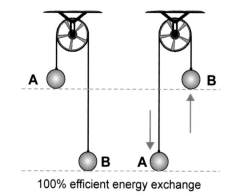

Figure 4.20: *Exchanging energy with a perfect, frictionless, massless pulley.*

4.3 Section Review

1. What is the relationship between work and energy in a machine?

2. Why can the output work of a simple machine never be greater than the input work?

3. Use the concept of work to explain the relationship between input and output forces and distances.

4. How does the efficiency of a car compare to the efficiency of a bicycle? Why do you think there is such a large difference?

Prosthetic Legs and Technology

The human leg is a complex and versatile machine. Designing a *prosthetic* (artificial) device to match the leg's capabilities is a serious challenge. Teams of scientists, engineers, and designers around the world use different approaches and technologies to develop prosthetic legs that help the user regain a normal, active lifestyle.

Studying the human gait cycle

Each person has a unique way of walking. But studying the way humans walk has revealed that some basic mechanics hold true for just about everyone. Scientists analyze how we walk by looking at our "gait cycle." The gait cycle consists of two consecutive strides while walking, one foot and then the other. By breaking the cycle down into phases and figuring out where in the sequence prosthetics devices could be improved, designers have added features and materials that let users walk safely and comfortably with their own natural gait.

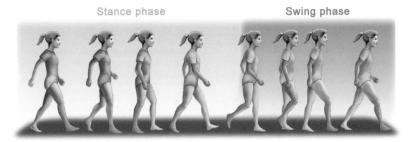

Stance phase   Swing phase

Designing a better prosthetic leg

In many prosthetic leg designs, the knee is the component that controls how the device operates. In the past, most designs were basic and relied on the *user* learning how to walk properly. This effort required up to 80% more energy than a normal gait and often made walking with an older prosthetic leg a work out!

The knee joint in those older designs was often a hinge that let the lower leg swing back and forth. The hinge could also lock in place to keep the leg straight and support the user's weight to make standing easier. This type of system worked relatively well on level surfaces, but could be difficult to use on inclines, stairs, slightly irregular terrain (like a hiking trail), or slippery surfaces.

Current prosthetic legs have improved upon old designs by employing hydraulics, carbon fiber, mechanical linkages, motors, computer microprocessors, and innovative combinations of these technologies to give more control to the user. For example, in some designs a device called a damper helps to control how fast the lower leg can swing back and forth while walking. The damper accomplishes this by changing the knee's resistance to movement as needed.

New knee designs allow users to walk, jog, and with some models even run with a more natural gait. In fact, in 2003 Marlon Shirley became the first above-the-knee amputee in the world to break the 11-second barrier in the 100-meter dash with a time of 10.97 seconds! He accomplished this feat with the aid of a special prosthetic leg designed specifically for sprinting.

Designs that learn

By continuously monitoring the velocities of the upper and lower leg, the angle of knee bend, changes in the terrain, and other data, computer microprocessors in the knee calculate and make adjustments to changing conditions in milliseconds. This makes the prosthetic leg more stable and efficient, allowing the knee, ankle, and foot to work together as a unit. Some designs have built-in memory systems that store information from sensors about how the user walks. These designs "learn" how to make fine-tuned adjustments based on the user's particular gait pattern.

New foot designs

New foot designs also reduce the energy required to walk with prosthetic leg systems. They also smooth out the user's stride. Using composite materials, these designs allow the foot to flex in different ways during the gait cycle. Both the heel and the front part of the foot act like springs to store and then release energy. When the foot first strikes the ground, the heel flexes and absorbs some of the energy, reducing the impact. Weight gets shifted toward the front of the foot as the walker moves through the stride.

As this happens, the heel springs back into shape and the energy released helps to flex the front part of the foot, once again storing energy. When the foot leaves the ground in the next part of the gait cycle, the flexed front part of the foot releases its' stored energy and helps to push the foot forward into the next stride.

Designers have realized the advantage of making highly specialized feet that match and sometimes exceed the capabilities of human feet. Distance running and sprinting feet are built to different specifications to efficiently deal with the forces and demands related to these activities.

A rock-climbing inventor

Hugh Herr, Ph.D., a physicists and engineer at the Harvard-MIT Division of Health Sciences and Technology (Boston, Massachusetts), studies biomechanics and prosthetic technology. In addition to holding several patents in this field, he has developed highly specialized feet for rock climbing that are small and thin— ideal for providing support on small ledges. Being an accomplished climber and an amputee allows Herr to field test his own inventions. While rock climbing, he gains important insights into the effectiveness and durability of each design.

Questions:

1. What are some technologies used by designers of prosthetic legs to improve their designs?
2. How are computers used to improve the function of prosthetic devices?
3. Explain how new foot designs reduce the amount of energy required to walk with a prosthetic leg.
4. Research the field of biomechanics. In a paragraph:
   (1) describe what the term "biomechanics" means, and
   (2) write about a biomechanics topic that interests you.

Chapter 4 Review

Understanding Vocabulary

Select the correct term to complete the sentences.

mechanical advantage	input arm	output
machine	horsepower	power
irreversible	input	simple machines
watt	work	efficiency
tension	fulcrum	

Section 4.1

1. A unit of power equal to 746 watts is called one ____.

2. ____ is the rate of doing work.

3. Force multiplied by distance is equal to ____.

4. The measurement unit of power equal to one joule of work performed in 1 second is called the ____.

Section 4.2

5. The ramp, the lever, and the wheel and axle are examples of ____.

6. Pushing on the pedals of a bicycle is an example of the ____ to a machine.

7. Moving a heavy load is an example of the ____ from a lever.

8. To calculate a machine's ____, you divide the output force by the input force.

9. A ____ is a device with moving parts that work together to accomplish a task.

10. The pivot point of a lever is known as its ____.

11. The side of a lever where the input force is applied is the ____.

12. The pulling force in a rope is known as ____.

Section 4.3

13. ____ is the ratio of work output to work input and is usually expressed as a percent.

14. A process with less than 100% efficiency is ____.

Reviewing Concepts

Section 4.1

1. Why are work and energy both measured in joules?

2. If you lift a box of books one meter off the ground, you are doing work. How much more work do you do by lifting the box 2 meters off the ground?

3. Decide whether work is being done (using your physics definition of work) in the following situations:
   a. Picking up a bowling ball off the floor.
   b. Two people pulling with the same amount of force on each end of a rope.
   c. Hitting a tennis ball with a tennis racket.
   d. Pushing hard against a wall for an hour.
   e. Pushing against a book so it slides across the floor.
   f. Standing very still with a book balanced on your head.

4. In which direction should you apply a force if you want to do the greatest amount of work?

5. What is the difference between work and power?

6. What is the meaning of the unit of power called a watt?

Section 4.2

7. List five types of simple machines.

8. Which two types of simple machines are in a wheelbarrow?

9. A certain lever has a mechanical advantage of 2. How does the lever's output force compare to the input force?.

10. Can simple machines multiply input forces to get increased output forces? Can they multiply work input to increase the work output?

11. Draw a diagram of each of the three types of levers. Label the input force, output force, and fulcrum on each.

12. You and a friend pull on opposite ends of a rope. You each pull with a force of 10 newtons. What is the tension in the rope?

13. A pulley system has four strands of rope supporting the load. What is its mechanical advantage?

14. A screw is very similar to which other type of simple machine?

Section 4.3

15. Why can't the output work for a machine be greater than the input work? Explain.

16. Can a simple machine's efficiency ever be greater than 100%? Explain your answer.

17. List two examples of ways to increase efficiency in a machine.

Solving Problems

Section 4.1

1. Calculate the amount of work you do in each situation.
   a. You push a refrigerator with a force of 50 N and it moves 3 meters across the floor.
   b. You lift a box weighing 25 N to a height of 2 meters.
   c. You apply a 500 N force downward on a chair as you sit on it while eating dinner.
   d. You lift a baby with a mass of 4 kg up 1 meter out of her crib.
   e. You climb a mountain that is 1000 meters tall. Your mass is 60 kg.

2. Sal has a weight of 500 N. How many joules of work has Sal done against gravity when he reaches 4 meters high on a rock climbing wall?

3. You do 200 joules of work against gravity when lifting your backpack up a flight of stairs that is 4 meters tall. What is the weight of your backpack in newtons?

4. You lift a 200 N package to a height of 2 meters in 10 seconds.
   a. How much work did you do?
   b. What was your power?

5. One machine can perform 500 joules of work in 20 seconds. Another machine can produce 200 joules of work in 5 seconds. Which machine is more powerful?

6. Two cranes use rope and pulley systems to lift a load from a truck to the top of a building. Crane A has twice as much power as crane B.
   a. If it takes crane A 10 seconds to lift a certain load, how much time does crane B take to lift the same load?
   b. If crane B can do 10,000 joules of work in a minute, how many joules of work can crane A do in a minute?

7. An elevator lifts a 500 kg load up a distance of 10 meters in 8 seconds.
   a. Calculate the work done by the elevator.
   b. Calculate the elevator's power.

Section 4.2

8. A lever has an input force of 5 newtons and an output force of 15 newtons. What is the mechanical advantage of the lever?

9. A simple machine has a mechanical advantage of 5. If the output force is 10 N, what is the input force?

10. You use a rope and pulley system with a mechanical advantage of 5. How big an output load can you lift with an input force of 200 N?

11. A lever has an input arm 50 cm long and an output arm 20 cm long.
    a. What is the mechanical advantage of the lever?
    b. If the input force is 100 N, what is the output force?

12. You want to use a lever to lift a 2000 N rock. The maximum force you can exert is 500 N. Draw a lever that will allow you to lift the rock. Label the input force, output force, fulcrum, input arm, and output arm. Specify measurements for the input and output arms. State the mechanical advantage of your lever.

13. A rope and pulley system is used so that a 20 N force can lift a 60 N weight. What is the minimum number of ropes in the system that must support the weight?

14. A rope and pulley system has two ropes supporting the load.
    a. Draw a diagram of the pulley system.
    b. What is its mechanical advantage?
    c. What is the relationship between the input force and the output force?
    d. How much can you lift with an input force of 20 N?

15. You push a heavy car weighing 500 newtons up a ramp. At the top of the ramp, it is 2 meters higher than it was initially.

    a. How much work did you do on the car?

    b. If your input force on the car was 200 newtons, how long is the ramp?

Section 4.3

16. A lever is used to lift a heavy rock that weighs 1000 newtons. When a 50-newton force pushes one end of the lever down 1 meter, how far does the load rise?

17. A system of pulleys is used to lift an elevator that weighs 3,000 newtons. The pulley system uses three ropes to support the load. How far would 12,000 joules of input work lift the elevator? Assume the pulley system is frictionless.

Section 4.4

18. A 60 watt light bulb uses 60 joules of electrical energy every second. However, only 6 joules of electrical energy is converted into light energy each second.

    a. What is the efficiency of the light bulb? Give your answer as a percentage.

    b. What do you think happens to the "lost" energy?

19. The work output is 300 joules for a machine that is 50% efficient. What is the work input?

20. A machine is 75% efficient. If 200 joules of work are put into the machine, how much work output does it produce?

Applying Your Knowledge

Section 4.1

1. Imagine we had to go back to using horses for power. The power of one horse is 746 watts (1 horsepower). How many horses would it take to light up all the light bulbs in your school?

    a. First, estimate how many light bulbs are in your school.

    b. Estimate the power of each light bulb, or get it from the bulb itself where it is written on the top.

    c. Calculate the total power used by all the bulbs.

    d. Calculate how many horses it would take to make this much power.

Section 4.2

2. Look for simple machines in your home. List as many as you can find.

3. A car is made of a large number of simple machines all working together. Identify at least five simple machines found in a car.

4. Exactly how the ancient pyramids of Egypt were built is still a mystery. Research to find out how simple machines may have been used to lift the huge rocks of which the pyramids are constructed.

Section 4.3

5. A perpetual motion machine is a machine that, once given energy, transforms the energy from one form to another and back again without ever stopping. You have probably seen a Newton's cradle like the one shown below.

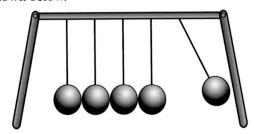

    a. Is a Newton's cradle a perpetual motion machine?

    b. According to the laws of physics, is it possible to build a perpetual motion machine?

    c. Many people have claimed to have built perpetual motion machines in the past. Use the internet to find one such machine. Explain how it is supposed to work and why it is not truly a perpetual motion machine.

6. A food Calorie is equal to 4184 joules. Determine the number of joules of energy you take in on a typical day.

Chapter 5

Forces in Equilibrium

Many people would not consider it extraordinary to get into an elevator and zoom to the top of a 50 story building. They might not be so nonchalant if they knew the balance of enormous forces that keeps a tall building standing up. Or, they might feel even more secure, knowing how well the building has been engineered to withstand the forces.

Tall buildings are an impressive example of equilibrium, or the balancing of forces. The average acceleration of a building should be zero! That means all forces acting on the building must add up to zero, including gravity, wind, and the movement of people and vehicles. A modern office tower is constructed of steel and concrete beams that are carefully designed to provide reactions forces to balance against wind, gravity, people, and vehicles.

In ancient times people learned about equilibrium through trial-and-error. Then, as today, different builders and architects each wanted to make a building taller than the others. Without today's knowledge of equilibrium and forces, many builders experimented with designs that quickly fell down. It is estimated that ten cathedrals fell down for every one that is still standing today! Over time, humans learned the laws of forces and equilibrium that allow us to be much more confident about the structural strength of modern tall buildings.

Key Questions

- ✓ How do you precisely describe a force?
- ✓ How is the concept of equilibrium important to the design of buildings and bridges?
- ✓ What is friction?
- ✓ How is torque different from force?

109

5.1 The Force Vector

Think about how to accurately describe a force. One important piece of information is the strength of the force. For example, 50 newtons would be a clear description of the strength of a force. But what about the direction? The direction of a force is important, too. How do you describe the direction of a force in a way that is precise enough to use for physics? In this section you will learn that force is a *vector*. A vector is a quantity that includes information about both size (strength) and direction.

Scalars and vectors

Scalars have magnitude
A **scalar** is a quantity that can be completely described by a single value called **magnitude**. Magnitude means the size or amount and always includes units of measurement. Temperature is a good example of a scalar quantity. If you are sick and use a thermometer to measure your temperature, it might show 101°F. The magnitude of your temperature is 101, and degrees Fahrenheit is the unit of measurement. The value of 101°F is a complete description of the temperature because you do not need any more information.

Examples of scalars
Many other measurements are expressed as scalar quantities. Distance, time, and speed are all scalars because all three can be completely described with a single number and a unit.

Vectors have direction
Sometimes a single number does not include enough information to describe a measurement. In giving someone directions to your house, you could not tell him simply to start at his house and drive four kilometers. A single distance measurement is not enough to describe the path the person must follow. Giving complete directions would mean including instructions to go two kilometers to the north, turn right, then go two kilometers to the east (Figure 5.1). The information "two kilometers to the north" is an example of a **vector**. A vector is a quantity that includes both magnitude and direction. Other examples of vectors are force, velocity, and acceleration. Direction is important to fully describe each of these quantities.

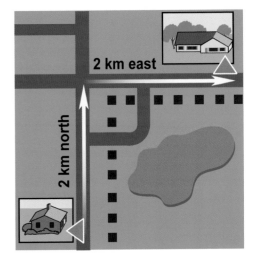

Figure 5.1: *Vectors are useful in giving directions.*

The force vector

What is a force vector?

A force vector has units of newtons, just like all forces. In addition, the force vector also includes enough information to tell the direction of the force. There are three ways commonly used to represent both the strength and direction information: a graph, an *x-y* pair, and a magnitude-angle pair. You will learn all three in this chapter because each is useful in a different way.

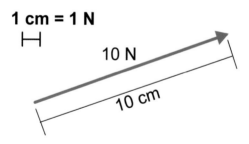

Figure 5.2: *A 10-newton force vector, with a scale of one centimeter to one newton.*

Three ways to describe the same force

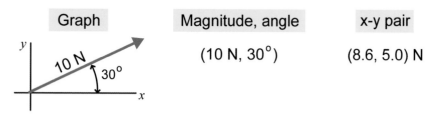

Graph	Magnitude, angle	x-y pair
10 N at 30°	(10 N, 30°)	(8.6, 5.0) N

Drawing a force vector

The graph form of the force vector is a picture showing the strength and direction of a force. It is just like an ordinary graph except the *x*- and *y*-axes show the strength of the force in the *x* and *y* directions. The force vector is drawn as an arrow. The length of the arrow shows the magnitude of the vector, and the arrow points in the direction of the vector.

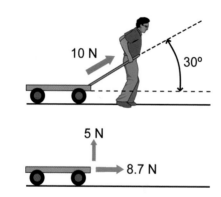

Scale

When drawing a vector, you must choose a scale. A scale for a vector diagram is similar to a scale on any graph. For example, if you are drawing a vector showing a force of five newtons pointing straight up (*y*-direction) you might use a scale of one centimeter to one newton. You would draw the arrow five centimeters long pointing along the *y*-direction on your paper (Figure 5.2). You should always state the scale you use when drawing vectors.

x and y forces

When you draw a force vector on a graph, distance along the *x*- or *y*-axes represents the strength of the force in the *x*- and *y*-directions. A force at an angle has the same effect as two smaller forces aligned with the *x*- and *y*-directions. As shown in Figure 5.3, the 8.6-newton and 5-newton forces applied together have the exact same effect as a single 10-newton force applied at 30 degrees. This idea of breaking one force down into an equivalent pair of *x*- and *y*-forces is very important, as you will see.

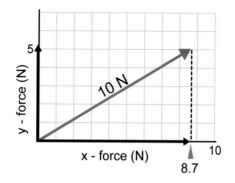

Figure 5.3: *A force at an angle has the same effect as two smaller forces applied at the same time along the x- and y- directions.*

Vector components

Components Every force vector can be replaced by perpendicular vectors called **components**. You can think of components as adding up to make the original force. When adding and subtracting forces, it is usually much easier to work with the components than it is with the original force.

Finding components Figure 5.4 shows how to find the components of a force vector using a graph. There are three steps. The first step is to draw the force vector to scale and at the correct angle. Second, extend lines parallel to the *x*- and *y*-axes. Third, read off the *x*- and *y*-components from the scales on the *x*- and *y*-axes. In the example, the *x*-component is 8.6 newtons, the *y*-component 5 newtons.

Using a triangle Another way to find the components of a force vector is to make a triangle (Figure 5.5). The *x*- and *y*-components are the lengths of the sides of the triangle parallel to the *x*- and *y*-axes. You can check your work with the Pythagorean theorem. The components are the legs of the triangle, or sides *a* and *b*. The original vector is the hypotenuse, or side *c*. According to the Pythagorean theorem $a^2 + b^2 = c^2$. In terms of the forces in the example, this means $(5 \text{ N})^2 + (8.6 \text{ N})^2 = (10 \text{ N})^2$.

Writing an (x, y) vector If you know the *x*- and *y*-components you can write a force vector with parentheses. The force in Figure 5.4 is written (8.6, 5) N. The first number is the *x*-component of the force, the second number the *y*-component. It is much easier to add or subtract forces when they are in *x*- and *y*-components. Mathematically, when we write a vector as *(x, y)* we are using *cartesian coordinates*. Cartesian coordinates use perpendicular *x*- and *y*- axes like graph paper.

Polar coordinates The third way to write a force vector is with its magnitude and angle. The force in Figure 5.4 is (10 N, 30°). The first number (10 N) is the magnitude, or strength of the force. The second number is the angle measured from the *x*-axis going counterclockwise. Mathematically, this way of writing a vector is in *polar coordinates*.

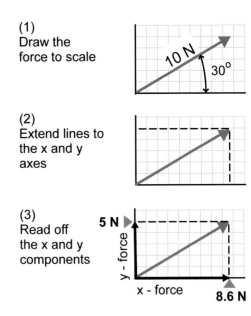

Figure 5.4: *Finding the components of a 10-newton force vector at a 30-degree angle.*

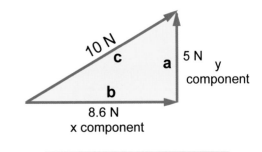

Pythagorean theorem
$$a^2 + b^2 = c^2$$

Figure 5.5: *Finding the components using a triangle.*

Free-body diagrams

Drawing free-body diagrams

A **free-body diagram** is a valuable tool used to study forces. It is a diagram that uses vectors to show all of the forces acting on an object. The free-body diagram for a book sitting on a table is shown in to the right. A free-body diagram shows only the forces acting *on* an object, and does not include the forces an object exerts on other things. When making a free-body diagram, draw only the object you are studying, not any other objects around it. Be sure to clearly label the strength of the force shown by each vector.

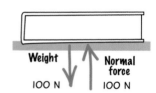

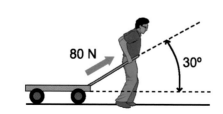

Figure 5.6: *Find the x and y components of the force.*

Components of a force

A man pulls a wagon with a force of 80 N at an angle of 30 degrees. Find the *x* (horizontal) and *y* (vertical) components of the force (Figure 5.6).

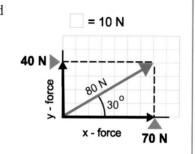

1. **Looking for:** You are asked for the *x*- and *y*-components of the force.

2. **Given:** You are given the magnitude and direction of the force.

3. **Relationships:** The *x*- and *y*-components can found by graphing the force.

4. **Solution:** *x*-component is 70 N, *y*-component is 40 N (see diagram at right).

Your turn...

a. What is the vertical (*y*) component of a 100-newton force at an angle of 60 degrees to the *x*-axis? **Answer:** 86.6 N

b. Two people push on a heavy box. One pushes with a force of 100 newtons toward 90°, and the other pushes with a force of 70 newtons toward 180°. Use a scaled drawing (1 cm = 10 N) to find the net force. **Answer:** 122 N

5.1 Section Review

1. What is the difference between a scalar and a vector?

2. Is each of these a scalar or a vector: speed, time, mass, weight, velocity, temperature.

3. Draw a force vector to scale that represents a force of 200 N at 120°.

4. Draw the force vector (6, 8) N. Is this the same as the force vector (100 N, 53°)?

5. A ball is hanging straight down on a string. Draw a free body diagram of the ball.

5.2 Forces and equilibrium

Sometimes you want things to accelerate and sometimes you don't. Cars should accelerate, bridges should not. In order for a bridge to stay in place, *all* the forces acting on the bridge must add up to produce zero net force. This section is about *equilibrium*, which is what physicists call any situation where the net force is zero. The concept of equilibrium is important to the design of buildings, bridges, and virtually every technology ever invented by humans.

Equilibrium

Definition of equilibrium   The net force on an object is the vector sum of all the forces acting on it. When the net force on an object is zero, we say the object is in **equilibrium**. Newton's first law says an object's motion does not change unless a net force acts on it. If the net force is zero (equilibrium), an object at rest will stay at rest and an object in motion will stay in motion with constant speed and direction.

The second law   The second law says the acceleration of an object in equilibrium is zero because the net force acting on the object is zero. Zero acceleration means neither the speed nor the direction of motion can change.

Normal force   Any object at rest is in equilibrium and has a net force of zero acting on it. Imagine a book sitting on a table. Gravity pulls the book downward with a force equal to the book's weight. But what force balances the weight? The table exerts an upward force on the book called the **normal force**. The word normal here has a different meaning from what you might expect. In mathematics, normal means *perpendicular*. The force the table exerts is perpendicular to the table's surface.

Newton's third law   Newton's third law explains why normal forces exist (Figure 5.7). The book pushes down on the table, so the table pushes up on the book. The book's force on the table is the action force, and the table's force on the book is the reaction force. The third law says that these forces are equal in strength. If the book is at rest, these forces *must* be equal but opposite in direction. If the book were heavier, it would exert a stronger downward force on the table. The table would then exert a stronger upward force on the book.

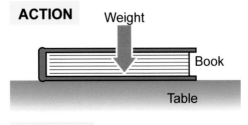

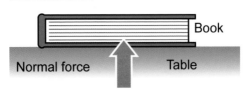

Figure 5.7: *The book pushes down on the table, and the table pushes up on the book. The force exerted by the table is called the normal force.*

Adding force vectors

An example Suppose three people are trying to keep an injured polar bear in one place. Each person has a long rope attached to the bear. Two people pull on the bear with forces of 100 N each (Figure 5.8). What force must the third person apply to balance the other two? The bear will not move if the net force is zero. To find the answer, we need to find the net force when the forces are not in the same direction. Mathematically speaking, we need a way to *add vectors*.

Graphically adding vectors On a graph you add vectors by drawing them end-to-end on a single sheet. The beginning of one vector starts at the end of the previous one. The total of all the vectors is called the **resultant.** The resultant starts at the origin and ends at the end of the last vector in the chain (Figure 5.9). The resultant in the example is a single 141 newton force at 225 degrees. To cancel this force, the third person must pull with an equal 141 N force in the opposite direction (45°). Adding force vectors this way is tedious because you must carefully draw each one to scale and at the proper angle.

Adding x-y components Adding vectors in x-y components is much easier. The *x*-component of the resultant is the sum of the *x*-components of each individual vector. The *y*-component of the resultant is the sum of the *y*-components of each individual vector. For the example, (-100, 0) N + (0, -100) N = (-100, -100) N. The components are negative because the forces point in the negative-x and negative-y directions. The resultant vector is (-100, -100) N.

Equilibrium To have zero net force, the forces in both the *x* and *y* directions must be zero. The third force must have *x* and *y* components that add up to zero when combined with the other forces. The solution to the problem is written below.

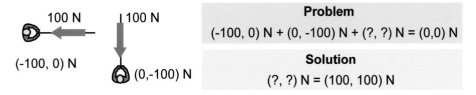

Problem
(-100, 0) N + (0, -100) N + (?, ?) N = (0,0) N
Solution
(?, ?) N = (100, 100) N

Following the rules we just gave, the third force must be (100, 100) N. This is the same as a force of 141 N at 45°.

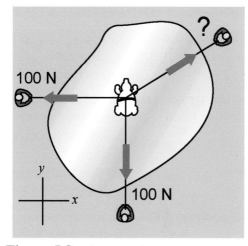

Figure 5.8: *Three people trying to keep a polar bear in the center of an ice floe.*

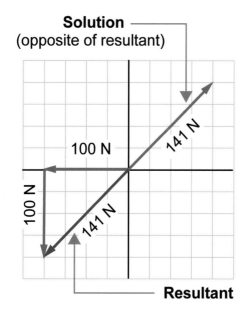

Figure 5.9: *Finding the resultant and solving the problem graphically.*

Solving equilibrium problems

Finding the net force For an object to be in equilibrium, all the forces acting *on the object* must total to zero. In many problems you will need the third law to find reaction forces (such as normal forces) that act on an object.

Using vectors In equilibrium, the net force *in each direction* must be zero. That means the total force in the *x*-direction must be zero and total force in the *y*-direction also must be zero. You cannot mix *x*- and *y*-components when adding forces. Getting the forces in each direction to cancel separately is easiest to do when all forces are expressed in *x*-*y* components. Note: In three dimensions, there also will be a *z*-component force.

Balancing forces If you are trying to find an unknown force on an object in equilibrium, the first step is always to draw a free-body diagram. Then use the fact that the net force is zero to find the unknown force. To be in equilibrium, forces must balance both horizontally and vertically. Forces to the right must balance forces to the left, and upward forces must balance downward forces.

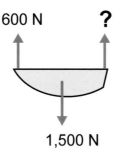

Figure 5.10: *The free-body diagram for the boat in the example problem.*

Equilibrium

Two chains are used to lift a small boat weighing 1500 newtons. As the boat moves upward at a constant speed, one chain pulls up on the boat with a force of 600 newtons. What is the force exerted by the other chain?

1. Looking for: You are asked for an unknown force exerted by a chain.

2. Given: You are given the boat's weight in newtons and the force of one chain in newtons.

3. Relationships: The net force on the boat is zero.

4. Solution: Draw a free-body diagram (Figure 5.10).
The force of the two chains must balance the boat's weight.
$600 \text{ N} + F_{chain2} = 1500 \text{ N}$ $F_{chain2} = 900 \text{ N}$

Your turn...

a. A heavy box weighing 1000 newtons sits on the floor. You lift upward on the box with a force of 450 newtons, but the box does not move. What is the normal force on the box while you are lifting? **Answer:** 550 newtons

b. A 40-newton cat stands on a chair. If the normal force on each of the cat's back feet is 12 newtons, what is the normal force on each front foot? (You can assume it is the same on each.) **Answer:** 8 newtons

The force from a spring

Uses for springs Springs are used in many devices to keep objects in equilibrium or cause acceleration. Toasters use springs to pop up the toast, cars use springs in their suspension, and retractable pens use springs to move the pen's tip. Springs can also be used as a way to store energy. When you push the handle down on a toaster, potential energy is stored in the spring. Releasing the spring causes the potential energy to convert into kinetic energy as the toast pops up.

Stretching and compressing a spring The most common type of spring is a coil of metal or plastic that creates a force when you stretch it or compress it. The force created by stretching or compressing a spring always acts to return the spring to its natural length. When you stretch a spring, it *pulls* back on your hand as the spring tries to return to its original length. When you compress a spring and make it shorter, it *pushes* on your hand as it tries to return to its original length.

Newton's third law Newton's third law explains why a spring's force acts opposite the direction it is stretched or compressed. The top spring in Figure 5.11 stretches when you apply a force to the right. The force of your hand on the spring is the action force. The spring applies a reaction force to the left on your hand.

The bottom picture shows what happens when the spring is compressed. You must exert an action force to the left to compress the spring. The spring exerts a reaction force to the right against your hand. In both cases, the spring's force tries to return it to its original length.

Normal force and springs How does a table "know" how much normal force to supply to keep a book at rest? A table cannot solve physics problems! The answer is that the normal force exerted by a surface is very similar to the force exerted by a spring in compression (Figure 5.12). When a book sits on a table, it exerts a downward force that compresses the table's top a tiny amount. The tabletop exerts an upward force on the book and tries to return to its natural thickness. The matter in the table acts like a collection of very stiff compressed springs. The amount of compression is so small you cannot see it, but it can be measured with sensitive instruments.

Stretching a spring

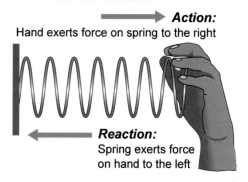

Action:
Hand exerts force on spring to the right

Reaction:
Spring exerts force on hand to the left

Compressing a spring

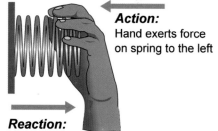

Action:
Hand exerts force on spring to the left

Reaction:
Spring exerts force on hand to the right

Figure 5.11: *The direction of the force exerted by the spring is opposite the direction of the force exerted by the person.*

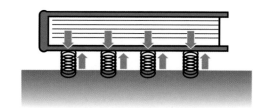

Figure 5.12: *The normal force exerted by a surface is similar to the force exerted by a compressed spring.*

Hooke's law

Hooke's law The relationship between a spring's change in length and the force it exerts is called **Hooke's law**. The law states that the force exerted by a spring is proportional to its change in length. For example, suppose a spring exerts a force of five newtons when it is stretched two centimeters. That spring will exert a force of 10 newtons when it is stretched four centimeters. Doubling the stretching distance doubles the force.

Spring constant Some springs exert small forces and are easy to stretch. Other springs exert strong forces and are hard to stretch. The relationship between the force exerted by a spring and its change in length is called its **spring constant**. A large spring constant means the spring is hard to stretch or compress and exerts strong forces when its length changes. A spring with a small spring constant is easy to stretch or compress and exerts weak forces. The springs in automobile shock absorbers are stiff because they have a large spring constant. A retractable pen's spring has a small spring constant.

How scales work The relationship between force and change in length is used in scales (Figure 5.13). When a hanging scale weighs an object, the distance the spring stretches is proportional to the object's weight. An object that is twice as heavy changes the spring's length twice as much. The scale is calibrated using an object of a known weight. The force amounts are then marked on the scale at different distances. A bathroom scale works similarly but uses a spring in compression. The greater the person's weight, the more the spring compresses.

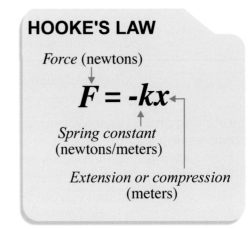

HOOKE'S LAW

$$F = -kx$$

Force (newtons)

Spring constant (newtons/meters)

Extension or compression (meters)

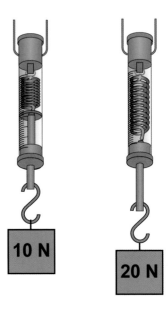

5.2 Section Review

1. Can a moving object be in equilibrium? Explain.
2. Draw a free-body diagram of a 700-newton person sitting on a chair in equilibrium.
3. The spring in a scale stretches 1 centimeter when a 5-newton object hangs from it. How much does an object weigh if it stretches the spring 2 centimeters?
4. How is normal force similar to the force of a spring?

Figure 5.13: *A hanging scale uses a spring to measure weight.*

5.3 Friction

Friction forces are constantly acting on you and the objects around you. When you are riding a bicycle and just coasting along, friction is what finally slows you down. But did you know that friction also helps you to speed up? Tires need friction to push against the road and create the reaction forces that move you forward. In this section you will learn about different types of friction, the cause of friction, and how it affects the motion of objects. You will also find out how friction is useful to us and learn how to reduce it when it's not.

What is friction?

Vocabulary

friction, sliding friction, static friction, lubricant

Objectives

✓ Distinguish between sliding and static friction.
✓ Explain the cause of friction.
✓ Discuss reasons to increase or decrease friction.

What is friction?   **Friction** is a force that resists the motion of objects or surfaces. You feel the effects of friction when you swim, ride in a car, walk, and even when you sit in a chair. Because friction exists in many different situations, it is classified into several types (Figure 5.14). This section will focus on sliding friction and static friction. **Sliding friction** is present when two objects or surfaces slide across each other. **Static friction** exists when forces are acting to cause an object to move but friction is keeping the object from moving.

The cause of friction   If you looked at a piece of wood, plastic, or paper through a powerful microscope, you would see microscopic hills and valleys on the surface. As surfaces slide (or try to slide) across each other, the hills and valleys grind against each other and cause friction. Contact between the surfaces can cause the tiny bumps to change shape or wear away. If you rub sandpaper on a piece of wood, friction affects the wood's surface and makes it either smoother (bumps wear away) or rougher (they change shape).

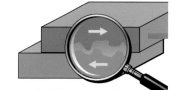

Microscopic hills and valleys cause friction between smooth surfaces.

Two surfaces are involved   Friction depends on *both* of the surfaces in contact. The force of friction on a rubber hockey puck is very small when it is sliding on ice. But the same hockey puck sliding on a piece of sandpaper feels a large friction force. When the hockey puck slides on ice, a thin layer of water between the rubber and the ice allows the puck to slide easily. Water and other liquids such as oil can greatly reduce the friction between surfaces.

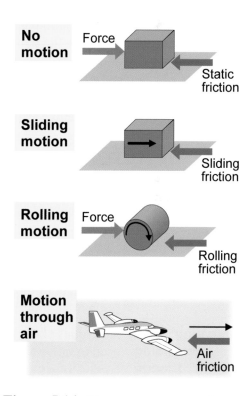

Figure 5.14: *There are many types of friction.*

Identifying friction forces

Direction of the friction force

Friction is a force, measured in newtons just like any other force. You draw the force of friction as another arrow on a free-body diagram. To figure out the direction of friction, always remember that friction is a *resistive* force. The force of friction acting *on* a surface always points opposite the direction of motion *of that surface*. Imagine pushing a heavy box across the floor (Figure 5.15). If you push to the right, the sliding friction acts to the left on the surface of the box touching the floor. If you push the box to the left, the force of sliding friction acts to the right. This is what we mean by saying friction resists motion.

Static friction

Static friction acts to keep an object at rest from starting to move. Think about trying to push a heavy box with too small a force. The box stays at rest, therefore the net force is zero. That means the force of static friction is equal and opposite to the force you apply. As you increase the strength of your push, the static friction also increases, so the box stays at rest. Eventually your force becomes stronger than the maximum possible static friction force and the box starts to move (Figure 5.16). The force of static friction is equal and opposite your applied force up to a limit. The limit depends on details such as the types of surface and the forces between them.

Sliding friction

Sliding friction is a force that resists the motion of an object already moving. If you were to stop pushing a moving box, sliding friction would slow the box to a stop. To keep a box moving at constant speed you must push with a force equal to the force of sliding friction. This is because motion at constant speed means zero acceleration and therefore zero net force. Pushing a box across the floor at constant speed is actually another example of *equilibrium*. In this case the equilibrium is created because the force you apply cancels with the force of sliding friction.

Comparing static and sliding friction

How does sliding friction compare with the static friction? If you have ever tried to move a heavy sofa or refrigerator, you probably know the answer. It is harder to get something moving than it is to keep it moving. The reason is that static friction is greater than sliding friction for almost all combinations of surfaces.

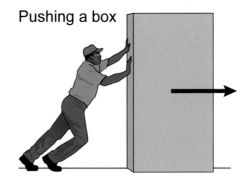

Pushing a box

Free body diagram

Figure 5.15: *The direction of friction is opposite the direction the box is pushed.*

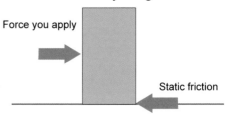

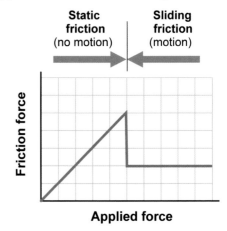

Figure 5.16: *How the friction forces on the box change with the applied force.*

A model for friction

Different amounts of friction   The amount of friction that exists when a box is pushed across a smooth floor is greatly different from when it is pushed across a carpeted floor. Every combination of surfaces produces a unique amount of friction depending upon types of materials, degrees of roughness, presence of dirt or oil, and other factors. Even the friction between two identical surfaces changes as the surfaces are polished by sliding across each other. No one model or formula can accurately describe the many processes that create friction. Even so, some simple approximations are useful.

An example   Suppose you pull a piece of paper across a table. To pull the paper at a constant speed, the force you apply must be equal in strength to the sliding friction. It is easy to pull the paper across the top of the table because the friction force is so small; the paper slides smoothly. Do you believe the friction force between the paper and the table is a value that cannot be changed? How might you test this question?

Friction and the force between surfaces   Suppose you place a brick on the piece of paper (Figure 5.17). The paper becomes much harder to slide. You must exert a greater force to keep the paper moving. The two surfaces in contact are still the paper and the tabletop, so why does the brick have an effect? The brick causes the paper to press harder into the table's surface. The tiny hills and valleys in the paper and in the tabletop are pressed together with a much greater force, so the friction increases.

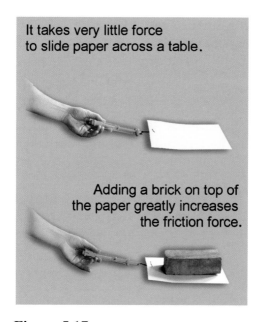

It takes very little force to slide paper across a table.

Adding a brick on top of the paper greatly increases the friction force.

Figure 5.17: *Friction increases greatly when a brick is placed on the paper.*

The greater the force squeezing two surfaces together, the greater the friction force.

The friction force between two surfaces is approximately proportional to the force the surfaces exert on each other. The greater the force squeezing the two surfaces together, the greater the friction force. This is why it is hard to slide a heavy box across a floor. The force between the bottom of the box and the floor is the weight of the box. Therefore, the force of friction is also proportional to the weight of the box. If the weight doubles, the force of friction also doubles. Friction is present between all sliding surfaces.

Reducing the force of friction

All surfaces experience some friction

Any motion where surfaces move across each other or through air or water always creates some friction. Unless a force is applied continually, friction will slow all motion to a stop eventually. For example, bicycles have low friction, but even the best bicycle slows down if you coast on a level road. Friction cannot be eliminated, though it can be reduced.

Lubricants reduce friction in machines

Keeping a fluid such as oil between two sliding surfaces keeps them from touching each other. The tiny hills and valleys don't become locked together, nor do they wear each other away during motion. The force of friction is greatly reduced, and surfaces do not wear out as fast. A fluid used to reduce friction is called a **lubricant**. You add oil to a car engine so that the pistons will slide back and forth with less friction. Even water can be used as a lubricant under conditions where there is not too much heat. A common use of powdered graphite, another lubricant, is in locks; spraying it into a lock helps a key work more easily.

Ball bearings

In systems where there are rotating objects, ball bearings are used to reduce friction. Ball bearings change sliding motion into rolling motion, which has much less friction. For example, a metal shaft rotating in a hole rubs and generates a great amount of friction. Ball bearings that go between the shaft and the inside surface of the hole allow it to spin more easily. The shaft rolls on the bearings instead of rubbing against the walls of the hole. Well-oiled bearings rotate easily and greatly reduce friction (Figure 5.18).

Magnetic levitation

Another method of reducing friction is to separate the two surfaces with a cushion of air. A hovercraft floats on a cushion of air created by a large fan. Magnetic forces can also be used to separate surfaces. A magnetically levitated (or maglev) train uses magnets that run on electricity to float on the track once the train is moving (Figure 5.19). Because there is no contact between train and track, there is far less friction than with a standard train on tracks. The ride is smoother, allowing for much faster speeds. Maglev trains are not yet in wide use because they are much more expensive to build than regular trains. They may yet become popular in the future.

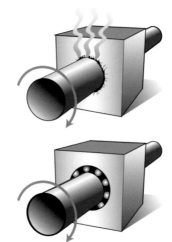

Figure 5.18: *The friction between a shaft (the long pole in the picture) and an outer part of a machine produces a lot of heat. Friction can be reduced by placing ball bearings between the shaft and the outer part.*

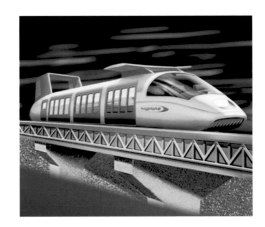

Figure 5.19: *With a maglev train, there is no contact between the moving train and the rail — and thus little friction.*

Using friction

Friction is useful for brakes and tires

There are many applications where friction is both useful and necessary. For example, the brakes on a bicycle create friction between two rubber *brake pads* and the rim of the wheel. Friction between the brake pads and the rim slows the bicycle. Friction is also necessary to make a bicycle go. Without friction, the bicycle's tires would not grip the road.

Weather condition tires

Rain and snow act like lubricants to separate tires from the road. As a tire rolls over a wet road, the rubber squeezes the water out of the way so that there can be good contact between rubber and road surface. Tire treads have grooves that allow space for water to be channeled away where the tire touches the road (Figure 5.20). Special irregular groove patterns, along with tiny slits, have been used on snow tires to increase traction in snow. These tires keep snow from getting packed into the treads and the design allows the tire to slightly change shape to grip the uneven surface of a snow-covered road.

Nails

Friction is the force that keeps nails in place (Figure 5.21). The material the nail is hammered into, such as wood, pushes against the nail from all sides. Each hit of the hammer drives the nail deeper into the wood, increasing the length of the nail being compressed. The strong compression force creates a large static friction force and holds the nail in place.

Cleated shoes

Shoes are designed to increase the friction between their soles and the ground. Many types of athletes, including football and soccer players, wear shoes with cleats that increase friction. Cleats are projections like teeth on the bottom of the shoe that dig into the ground. Players wearing cleats can exert much greater forces against the ground to accelerate and to keep from slipping.

Figure 5.20: *Grooved tire treads allow space for water to be channeled away from the road-tire contact point, allowing for more friction in wet conditions.*

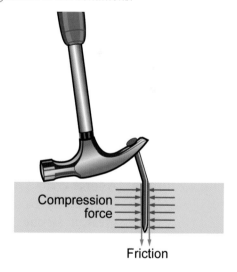

Figure 5.21: *Friction is what makes nails hard to pull out and gives them the strength to hold things together.*

5.3 Section Review

1. Explain the causes of sliding friction and static friction.
2. What do you know about the friction force on an object pulled at a constant speed?
3. What factors affect the friction force between two surfaces?
4. Give an example of friction that is useful and one that is not useful. Use examples not mentioned in the book.

5.4 Torque and Rotational Equilibrium

A canoe is gliding between two docks. On each dock is a person with a rope attached to either end of the canoe. Both people pull with equal and opposite force of 100 newtons so that the net force on the canoe is zero. What happens to the canoe? It is *not* in equilibrium even though the net force is zero. The canoe rotates around its center! The canoe rotates because it is not in *rotational* equilibrium even though it *is* in force equilibrium. In this section you will learn about torque and rotational equilibrium.

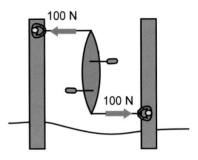

What is torque?

Torque and force **Torque** is a new action created by forces that are applied off-center to an object. Torque is what causes objects to **rotate** or spin. Torque is the rotational equivalent of force. If force is a *push* or *pull*, you should think of torque as a *twist*.

The axis of rotation The line about which an object turns is its **axis of rotation.** Some objects have a fixed axis: a door's axis is fixed at the hinges. A wheel on a bicycle is fixed at the axle in the center. Other objects do not have a fixed axis. The axis of rotation of a tumbling gymnast depends on her body position.

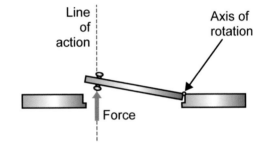

The line of action Torque is created whenever the **line of action** of a force does not pass through the axis of rotation. The line of action is an imaginary line in the direction of the force and passing through the point where the force is applied. If the line of action passes through the axis the torque is *zero*, no matter how strong a force is used!

Creating torque A force creates more torque when its line of action is far from an object's axis of rotation. Doorknobs are positioned far from the hinges to provide the greatest amount of torque (Figure 5.22). A force applied to the knob will easily open a door because the line of action of the force is the width of the door away from the hinges. The same force applied to the hinge side of the door does nothing because the line of action passes through the axis of rotation. The first force creates torque while the second does not.

Figure 5.22: *A door rotates around its hinges and a force creates the greatest torque when the force is applied far from the hinges.*

The torque created by a force

Calculating torque   The torque created by a force depends on the strength of the force and also on the **lever arm**. The lever arm is the perpendicular distance between the line of action of the force and the axis of rotation (Figure 5.23). Torque is calculated by multiplying the force and the lever arm. The Greek letter "tao" (τ) is used to represent torque; the lever arm is represented with a lower-case *r* from the word radius; and force, remember, is an upper-case F.

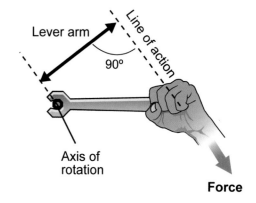

Figure 5.23: *The lever arm is the perpendicular distance between the line of action of the force and the axis of rotation.*

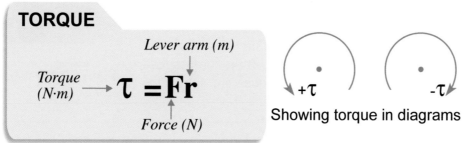

TORQUE

Torque (N·m) → $\tau = Fr$ ← *Lever arm (m)*

Force (N)

Showing torque in diagrams

Direction of torque   The direction of torque is often drawn with a circular arrow showing how the object would rotate. The words *clockwise* and *counterclockwise* are also used to specify the direction of a torque.

Units of torque   When force is in newtons and distance is in meters, the torque is measured in newton·meters (N·m). To create one newton·meter of torque, you can apply a force of one newton to a point one meter away from the axis. A force of only one-half newton applied two meters from the axis creates the *same* torque.

How torque and force differ   Torque is created by force but is not the same thing as force. Torque depends on both force and distance. Torque (N·m) has different units from force (N). Finally, the same force can produce *any* amount of torque (including zero) depending on where it is applied (Figure 5.24).

Torque is not work   The newton·meter used for torque is *not* the same as the newton·meter for work, and is *not* equal to a joule. Work is done when a force *moves* an object a distance in the direction of the force. The distance that appears in torque is the distance away from the axis of rotation. The object does not move in *this* direction. The force that creates torque causes no motion in *this* direction, so no work is done.

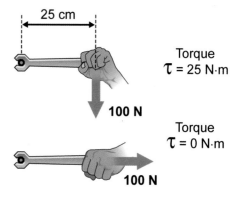

Figure 5.24: *The same force can create different amounts of torque depending on where it is applied and in what direction.*

Solving problems with torque

Reaction torque If you push *up* on a doorknob, you create a torque that tries to rotate the door upward instead of around its hinges. Your force *does* create a torque, but the hinges stop the door from rotating this way. The hinges exert reaction forces on the door that create torques in the direction opposite the torque you apply. This reaction torque is similar to the normal force created when an object presses down on a surface.

Combining torques If more than one torque acts on an object, the torques are combined to determine the net torque. Calculating net torque is very similar to calculating net force. If the torques tend to make an object spin in the same direction (clockwise or counterclockwise), they are added together. If the torques tend to make the object spin in opposite directions, the torques are subtracted (Figure 5.25).

Force A makes **negative** (clockwise) torque

Force B makes **positive** (counterclockwise) torque

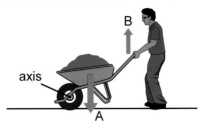

Figure 5.25: *Torques can be added and subtracted.*

Calculating torque

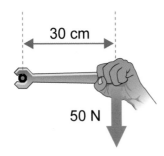

A force of 50 newtons is applied to a wrench that is 0.30 meters long. Calculate the torque if the force is applied perpendicular to the wrench at left.

1. Looking for: You are asked for the torque.

2. Given: You are given the force in newtons and the length of the lever arm in centimeters.

3. Relationships: Use the formula for torque, $\tau = rF$.

4. Solution: $\tau = (0.30 \text{ m})(50 \text{ N}) = 15$ N·m

Your turn...

a. You apply a force of 10 newtons to a doorknob that is 0.80 meters away from the edge of the door on the hinges. If the direction of your force is straight into the door, what torque do you create? **Answer:** 8 N·m

b. Calculate the net torque in diagram A (at right). **Answer:** 10 N·m

c. Calculate the net force and the net torque in diagram B (at right). **Answer:** 5 N and 0 N·m

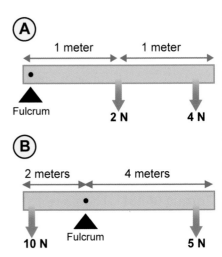

Rotational equilibrium

Rotational equilibrium An object is in **rotational equilibrium** when the net torque applied to it is zero. For example, if an object such as a seesaw is not rotating, you know the torque on each side is balanced (Figure 5.26). An object in rotational equilibrium can also be spinning at constant speed, like the blades on a fan.

Using rotational equilibrium Rotational equilibrium is often used to determine unknown forces. Any object that is not moving must have a net torque of zero *and* a net force of zero. Balances used in schools and scales used in doctors' offices use balanced torques to measure weight. When using a scale, you must slide small masses away from the axis of rotation until the scale balances. Moving the mass increases its lever arm and its torque. Engineers study balanced torques and forces when designing bridges and buildings.

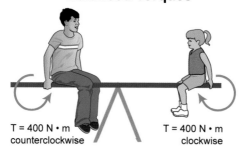

Balanced Torques

T = 400 N • m counterclockwise   T = 400 N • m clockwise

Figure 5.26: *A seesaw is in rotational equilibrium when the two torques are balanced.*

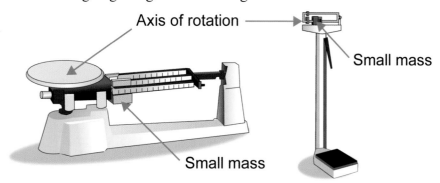

Axis of rotation

Small mass

Small mass

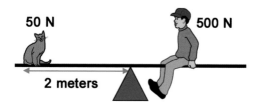

50 N   500 N

2 meters

Figure 5.27: *How far must the boy sit from the center of the seesaw in order to balance?*

5.4 Section Review

1. List two ways in which torque is different from force.

2. In what units is torque measured?

3. Explain how the same force can create different amounts of torque on an object.

4. What is the net torque on an object in rotational equilibrium?

5. A boy and a cat sit on a seesaw as shown in Figure 5.27. Use the information in the picture to calculate the torque created by the cat. Then calculate the boy's distance from the center of the seesaw.

Architecture: Forces in Equilibrium

Even though the builders of the Pyramids of Egypt lived more than 4,000 years ago, they understood how a building needed to be designed to remain standing. They used back-breaking efforts and many attempts to refine their design, keeping ideas that worked and discarding those that didn't. Some pyramids collapsed while they were being built, others lasted decades or centuries before failing, and some are still standing—over 80 pyramids remain in Egypt.

Over time the trial and error process of designing buildings has evolved into a hybrid of science, engineering, and art called architecture. Modern buildings can be very complex and intricate. Yet just as with the most primitive buildings, the structural forces involved must be in equilibrium for the building to stand the test of time. The Pyramids of Giza have lasted about 5,200 years. How do modern buildings compare to the pyramids?

Most buildings today are not pyramids, but are rectangular with four walls and a roof. Also, few buildings are now constructed entirely of limestone and granite like the pyramids. Even though the shape and construction materials are quite different, the ultimate goal is the same—creation of a free-standing structure. A basic box shaped building must have walls that support a roof. But what does "support" mean in terms of forces and equilibrium?

The physics of walls

By staying upright, walls provide a platform for a roof. Walls that carry the weight of the roof are called load-bearing walls. Here is where Newton's second law applies—force equals mass times acceleration ($F = ma$). Gravity pulls down on the mass of the roof, creating a force (*weight*). Why doesn't the roof accelerate down toward the ground because of this force? This is where Newton's third law applies—for every action there is an equal and opposite reaction. If the roof isn't moving down, the load bearing walls must be pushing back on the roof in the upwards direction with a force equal to the weight of the roof. This action-reaction pair is in equilibrium, both forces balancing out one another, bringing up Newton's first law. An object at rest remains at rest until acted on by an unbalanced force.

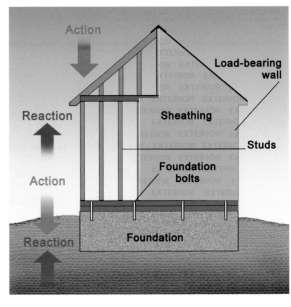

The foundation

The weight force of the walls and roof combined pushes down on the foundation. Just like the action-reaction force pair of the roof and wall, the wall and foundation create an action-reaction pair. Hopefully, this will be in equilibrium too. If the foundation can't provide an equal and opposite reaction, the building will not be in equilibrium. This is the case with the Leaning Tower of Pisa.

The tower began leaning even before construction was finished. The soft soil under the tower began to compress, indicating that the foundation was not large enough to provide the force to equal the weight of the tower. The tower has actually sunk into the ground quite a few feet. One side has compressed more than the other, causing the tower to lean. Towers need to be built with very stable and solid foundations. New York City is an island with a thick layer of extremely stable bedrock just below the topsoil, making it an ideal place for skyscrapers.

The roof

The roof is one of the most important design features of a building. While its major function is to protect the inside of the building from outside elements, it also contributes to the beauty of the structure. The design of the roof therefore must be a balance of form and function. And, it must be able to be supported by the walls and foundation. One of the most famous roofs in the world is the dome that tops the church of Santa Maria del Fiore in Florence, Italy. Called the Duomo, this roof seems to defy the laws of physics.

Filippo Brunelleschi (1377-1446), an accomplished goldsmith and sculptor, travelled to Rome for a two-year study of ancient roman architecture with fellow artist and friend Donatello. The Pantheon, an amazing dome finished in A.D. 126 was of particular interest to Brunelleschi.

Upon his return to Florence, he finished a design for his dome in 1402, but kept it secret. He claimed to be able to build a self-supporting dome without the use of scaffolding, an outlandish claim many deemed impossible. Yet even without explaining how he would accomplish the feat, construction began.

Brunelleschi knew that large domes tended to sag in the middle, lowering the roof and creating huge forces that pushed outward on the supporting base. He used an ingenious double-walled design, one to be seen from inside the church and another on the outside. He also used intricate herringbone patterns of brickwork and huge timbers linked together with metal fasteners around the dome to balance the forces like hoops on a barrel. This design was so innovative and beautiful it is said to have inspired many of the Renaissance's greatest artists including Leonardo da Vinci and fellow Florentine Michelangelo.

Questions:

1. What are the action-reaction pairs in a typical building?
2. Why is New York City an ideal place for skyscrapers?
3. Explain the elements of Brunelleschi's dome design that keeps it standing.

Chapter 5 Review

Understanding Vocabulary

Select the correct term to complete the sentences.

scalar	components	friction
magnitude	normal force	lubricant
equilibrium	torque	lever arm
static friction	resultant	vector
Hooke's law	rotational equilibrium	free-body diagram

Section 5.1

1. A _____ has both magnitude and direction.

2. A _____ has magnitude and no direction.

3. _____ is the size or amount of something and includes a unit of measurement.

4. Every vector can be represented as the sum of its _____.

5. A _____ shows all of the forces acting on an object.

Section 5.2

6. If a book sits on a table, the table exerts an upward _____ on the book.

7. The sum of two vectors is called the _____.

8. _____ is the relationship between a spring's change in length and the force it exerts.

9. When the net force acting on an object is zero, the object is in _____.

Section 5.3

10. _____ is a force that resists the motion of objects.

11. The type of friction between objects that are not moving is called _____.

12. A fluid used to reduce friction is called a _____.

Section 5.4

13. _____ is the action that causes objects to rotate.

14. An object is in _____ if the net torque on it is zero.

15. The longer the _____ of a force, the greater the torque.

Reviewing Concepts

Section 5.1

1. Give two examples of vector quantities and two examples of scalar quantities.

2. List the three different ways in which a force vector can be described.

3. Explain how to find the components of a vector.

4. Explain the Pythagorean theorem using an equation and a picture.

5. A 200-newton television sits on a table. Draw a free-body diagram showing the two forces acting on the television.

Section 5.2

6. What is the net force on an object in equilibrium?

7. What is the mathematical meaning of the word *normal*?

8. As you sit on a chair, gravity exerts a downward force on you.
   a. What other force acts on you?
   b. What is the direction of this other force?
   c. What do you know about the magnitude or strength of this other force?

9. If an object is in equilibrium, then the forces in the x-direction must add to _____, and the forces in the y-direction must add to _____.

10. You pull one end of a spring to the right.
   a. What is the action force?
   b. What is the reaction force?
   c. How do the directions of the two forces compare?
   d. How do the strengths of the two forces compare?

11. What happens to a spring's force as you stretch it a greater amount?

12. What do you know about a spring if it has a large spring constant?

Section 5.3

13. List four types of friction.

14. In which direction does friction act?

15. What is the difference between static friction and sliding friction?

16. What causes friction?

17. Why is it much easier to slide a cardboard box when it is empty compared to when it is full of heavy books?

18. Explain two ways friction can be reduced.

19. Is friction something we always want to reduce? Explain.

Section 5.4

20. How are torque and force similar? How are they different?

21. Which two quantities determine the torque on an object?

22. In what units is torque measured? Do these units have the same meaning as they do when measuring work? Explain.

23. Why is it easier to loosen a bolt with a long-handled wrench than with a short-handled one?

24. In which of the case would a force cause the greatest torque on the shovel? Why?
    a. You press straight down on the shovel so it stays straight up and down.
    b. You twist the shovel like a screwdriver.
    c. You push to the right on the shovel's handle so it tilts toward the ground.

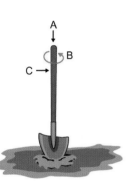

25. What does it mean to say an object is in rotational equilibrium?

Solving Problems

Section 5.1

1. Use a ruler to draw each of the following vectors with a scale of 1 centimeter = 1 newton.
    a. (5 N, 0°)
    b. (7 N, 45°)
    c. (3 N, 90°)
    d. (6 N, 30°)

2. Use a ruler to draw each of the following vectors. State the scale you use for each.

    a. (40 N, 0°)
    b. (20 N, 60°)
    c. (100 N, 75°)
    d. (500 N, 90°)

3. Use a scaled drawing to find the components of each of the following vectors. State the scale you use for each.
    a. (5 N, 45°)
    b. (8 N, 30°)
    c. (8 N, 60°)
    d. (100 N, 20°)

Section 5.2

4. Find the net force on each box.

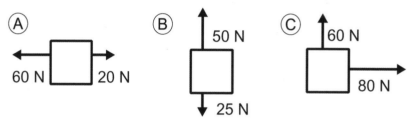

5. A 20-kilogram monkey hangs from a tree limb by both arms. Draw a free-body diagram showing the forces on the monkey. Hint: 20 kg is not a force!

6. You weigh a bear by making him stand on four scales as shown. Draw a free-body diagram showing all the forces acting on the bear. If his weight is 1500 newtons, what is the reading on the fourth scale?

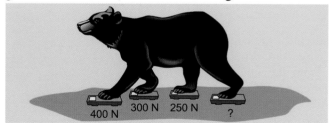

7. A spring has a spring constant of 100 N/m. What force does the spring exert on you if you stretch it a distance of 0.5 meter?

8. If you stretch a spring a distance of 3 cm, it exerts a force of 50 N on your hand. What force will it exert if you stretch it a distance of 6 cm?

Section 5.3

9. Your backpack weighs 50 N. You pull it across a table at a constant speed by exerting a force of 20 N to the right. Draw a free-body diagram showing all *four* forces on the backpack. State the strength of each.

10. You exert a 50 N force to the right on a 300 N box but it does not move. Draw a free-body diagram for the box. Label all the forces and state their strengths.

Section 5.4

11. You push down on a lever with a force of 30 N at a distance of 2 meters from its fulcrum. What is the torque on the lever?

12. You use a wrench to loosen a bolt. It finally turns when you apply 300 N of force at a distance of 0.2 m from the center of the bolt. What torque did you apply?

13. A rusty bolt requires 200 N-m of torque to loosen it. If you can exert a maximum force of 400 N, how long a wrench do you need?

14. Calculate the net torque on the see-saw shown below.

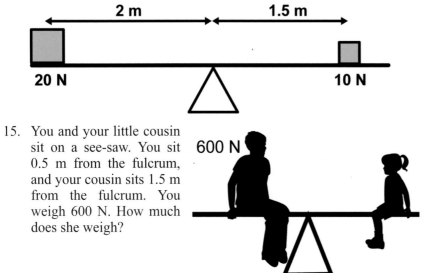

15. You and your little cousin sit on a see-saw. You sit 0.5 m from the fulcrum, and your cousin sits 1.5 m from the fulcrum. You weigh 600 N. How much does she weigh?

Applying Your Knowledge

Section 5.1

1. Is it possible to arrange three forces of 100 N, 200 N, and 300 N so they are in equilibrium? If so, draw a diagram. This is similar to balancing the forces acting on a post.

2. Draw the forces acting on a ladder leaning against a building. Assume you are standing half-way up the ladder. Assume the wall of the building and the ground exert only normal forces on the ladder.

Section 5.2

3. Civil engineers analyze forces in equilibrium when designing bridges. Choose a well-known bridge to research. Some of the questions you might want to answer are listed below.

   a. Who designed the bridge?
   b. How long did it take to build?
   c. Which type of bridge is it?
   d. How much weight was it designed to hold?
   e. What makes this bridge special?

Section 5.3

4. Many cars today have "antilock breaks" that help prevent them from skidding. Research to find out how antilock breaks work.

Section 5.4

5. Can an object be in rotational equilibrium but not have a net force of zero exerted on it? Can an object have a net force of zero but not be in rotational equilibrium? Explain your answers using diagrams.

Chapter 6

Systems in Motion

There is a recurring theme in cartoon film clips. One character is racing toward another, perhaps to cause some harm. The other character turns a road sign the wrong way, sending the chaser over a cliff. What happens next in the cartoon sequence? The chaser runs off the cliff, keeps running straight out over the canyon until it sees that there is no ground directly below, and at that moment, the chaser begins falling. Perhaps the character holds up a "help" sign before hitting the canyon floor and sending up a dust cloud.

The cartoon gag provides lots of laughs, but the physics is all wrong! Do you know what the correct path of the cartoon character would be when it runs off a cliff? Projectiles, bicycle wheels, planets in orbit, and satellites are just some of the interesting systems of motion you will study in this chapter. By the way, the true path of the unfortunate cartoon character is a curve, and the name given to this curved path is trajectory. The only thing more miraculous than defying physics during the fall is that the cartoon character survives every incredible disaster, only to return to the screen more determined than ever!

Key Questions

- ✓ How should you hit a golf ball so it goes as far as possible?
- ✓ Why does a skater spin faster when she pulls her arms in toward her body?
- ✓ Why are you thrown to the outside edge of the car seat when the car makes a sharp turn?
- ✓ How do satellites continuously move around Earth without crashing into it?

133

6.1 Motion in Two Dimensions

The systems we have learned about so far included only forces and motions that acted in straight lines. Of course, real-life objects do not only go in straight lines; their motion includes turns and curves. To describe a curve you need at least two dimensions (*x* and *y*). In this chapter you will learn how to apply the laws of motion to curves. Curves *always* imply acceleration and you will see that the same laws we already know still apply, but with *vectors*.

Displacement

The displacement vector — A vector that shows a change in position is called a **displacement** vector. Displacement is the distance and direction between the starting and ending points of an object's motion. If you walk five meters east, your displacement can be represented by a five-centimeter arrow pointing east.

Writing the displacement vector — Displacement is always a vector. Like the force vector, you can write a displacement vector three ways.

- With a vector diagram
- As a magnitude-angle pair
- As an *x-y* pair

Telling direction — For example, the diagram above, right shows a displacement of five meters at 37 degrees. This vector can be abbreviated (5 m, 37°). Angles are measured from the positive *x*-axis in a counterclockwise direction, as shown in Figure 6.1.

A displacement vector's direction is often given using words. Directional words include left, right, up, down, north, south, east, and west. Which coordinates you use depends on the problem you are trying to solve. Sometimes you will make *x* horizontal and *y* vertical. Other times, you should choose *x* to be east and *y* to be north.

A displacement vector of (5 m, 37°)

5 m 37°

Scale: 1 cm = 1 meter

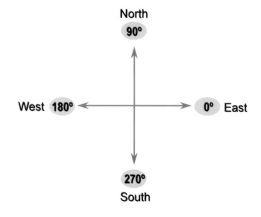

Figure 6.1: *Angles can be used to represent compass directions.*

Solving displacement problems

Displacement vectors for moving objects

When working in a straight line, you can tell the position of an object with just one distance. If the motion is curved, it takes at least two distances to tell where an object is. The motion of a basketball is described by both the *x*- and *y*-coordinates of each point along the basketball's path. The basketball's position at any time is represented by its displacement vector (Figure 6.2). To describe the motion of the basketball we need to describe how the displacement vector changes over time.

Adding displacement vectors

Displacement vectors can be added just like force (or any) vectors. To add displacements graphically, draw them to scale with each subsequent vector drawn at the end of the previous vector. The resultant vector represents the displacement for the entire trip.

For most problems, however, it is much easier to find the *x*- and *y*-components of a displacement vector. The *x*-component is the distance in the *x* direction. The *y*-component is the distance in the *y* direction.

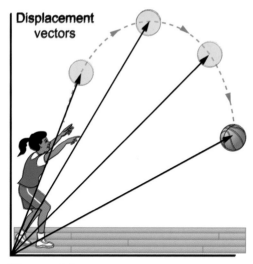

Figure 6.2: *When you throw a ball, it follows a curved path. The position of the ball is described by its displacement vector.*

Vector addition

A mouse walks 5 meters north and 12 meters west. Use a scaled drawing to find the mouse's displacement, and then use the Pythagorean theorem to check your work.

1. Looking for: You are asked for the displacement.

2. Given: You are given the distances and directions the mouse walks.

3. Relationships: Pythagorean theorem $a^2 + b^2 = c^2$

4. Solution: Make a drawing with a scale of 1 cm = 1 meter.
Pythagorean theorem:
$5^2 + 12^2 = c^2$ $169 = c^2$ $13 = c$
The mouse walks 13 meters at 157°.

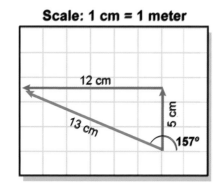

Scale: 1 cm = 1 meter

12 cm
13 cm
5 cm
157°

Your turn...

a. Your school is 5 kilometers south and 5 kilometers east of your house. Use a scaled drawing to find your displacement as you ride from home to school. Then check your answer with the Pythagorean theorem. **Answer:** 7.1 km southeast (or 315°)

b. A helicopter flies straight up for 100 meters and then horizontally for 100 meters. What is the displacement vector of the helicopter relative to where it started? Give your answer in x-y form assuming upward is "y." **Answer:** (100, 100) m

---

The velocity vector

Velocity and force vectors
Velocity is speed with direction, so velocity is a vector. As objects move in curved paths, their velocity vectors change because the direction of motion changes. The symbol $\vec{v}$ is used to represent velocity. The arrow tells you it is the velocity vector, not the speed.

What the velocity vector means
Suppose a ball is launched at five meters per second at an angle of 37 degrees (Figure 6.3). At the moment after launch the velocity vector for the ball in polar coordinates is written as $\vec{v} = (5 \text{ m/sec}, 37°)$. In x-y components, the same velocity vector is written as $\vec{v} = (4, 3)$ m/sec. Both representations tell you exactly how fast and in what direction the ball is moving at that moment. The x-component tells you how fast the ball is moving in the x-direction. The y-component tells you how fast it is moving in the y-direction.

Speed is the magnitude of the velocity vector
The *magnitude* of the velocity vector is the *speed* of the object. The ball in the example is moving with a speed of 5 m/sec. Speed is represented by a lower case v *without* the arrow. When a velocity vector is represented graphically, the length is proportional to speed, not distance. For example, the graph in Figure 6.3 shows the velocity vector $\vec{v} = (4, 3)$ m/sec as an arrow on a graph.

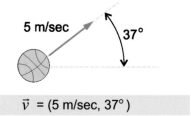

$\vec{v} = (5 \text{ m/sec}, 37°)$

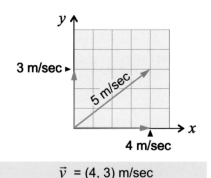

$\vec{v} = (4, 3)$ m/sec

Figure 6.3: *Different ways to write a velocity vector. The length of a velocity vector is proportional to speed.*

Velocity vector

A train moves at a speed of 100 km/hr heading east. What is its velocity vector in x-y form?

1. Looking for: You are asked for the velocity vector.

2. Given: You are given speed in km/hr and direction. The train is moving east.

3. Relationships: x-velocity is east and y-velocity is north

4. Solution: $\vec{v} = (100,0)$ km/hr   Note: The y-component is 0 because the train has 0 velocity heading north.

a. A race car is moving with a velocity vector of (50, 50) m/sec. Sketch the velocity vector and calculate the car's velocity. You can use the Pythagorean theorem to check your sketch. **Answer:** (70.7 m/sec, 45°)

b. A hiker walks 1,000 meters north and 5,000 meters east in 2 hours. Calculate the hiker's average velocity vector in x-y form. **Answer**: (2500, 500) m/hr or (2.5, 0.5) km/hr; [the polar coordinates are (2.6 km/hr, 11°)]

Projectile motion

Definition of projectile Any object moving through air and affected only by gravity is called a **projectile**. Examples include a kicked soccer ball in the air, a stunt car driven off a cliff, and a skier going off a ski jump. Flying objects such as airplanes and birds are *not* projectiles, because they are affected by forces generated from their own power and not just the force of gravity.

Trajectories The path a projectile follows is called its **trajectory**. The trajectory of a projectile is a special type of arch- or bowl-shaped curve called a **parabola**. The **range** of a projectile is the horizontal distance it travels in the air before touching the ground (Figure 6.4). A projectile's range depends on the speed and angle at which it is launched.

Two-dimensional motion Projectile motion is two-dimensional because both horizontal and vertical motion happen at the same time. Both speed and direction change as a projectile moves through the air. The motion is easiest to understand by thinking about the vertical and horizontal components of motion separately.

Independence of horizontal and vertical motion A projectile's velocity vector at any one instant has both a horizontal (v_x) and vertical (v_y) component. Separating the velocity into the two components allows us to look at them individually. The horizontal and vertical components of a projectile's velocity are *independent* of each other. The horizontal component does not affect the vertical component and vice versa. The complicated curved motion problem becomes two separate, straight-line problems like the ones you have already solved.

The horizontal and vertical components of a projectile's velocity are independent of each other.

Subscripts Notice the subscripts (x, y) on the velocity components. Subscripts tell you the direction of the motion. Distance and velocity in the x-direction are identified by using x as a subscript. Distance and velocity in the y-direction are identified by using y as a subscript. It is important to carefully write the subscripts as you do projectile problems. Otherwise, you will quickly lose track of which velocity is which (Figure 6.5)!

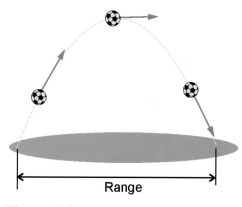

Figure 6.4: *A soccer ball in the air is a projectile. The ball's trajectory is a parabola.*

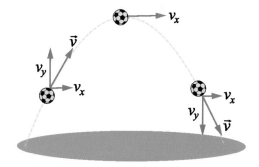

Figure 6.5: *The velocity vector of the ball has both x and y components that change during the ball's flight.*

A ball rolling off a table

Constant horizontal velocity   A ball rolling off a table is a projectile once it leaves the tabletop. Once the ball becomes a projectile it feels no horizontal force, so its horizontal velocity is *constant*. A projectile moves the same distance horizontally each second. A ball rolling off a table at 5 meters per second moves five meters horizontally each second it is in the air (Figure 6.6). The horizontal motion looks exactly like the motion the ball would have were it rolling along the ground at 5 m/sec.

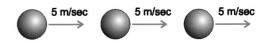

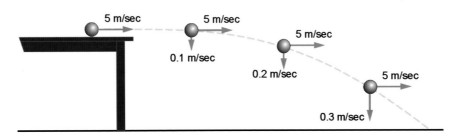

Figure 6.6: *A projectile's horizontal velocity does not change because no horizontal force acts on it.*

Horizontal and vertical velocities

Vertical velocity changes   The vertical motion of the ball is more complicated because of gravity. The ball is in *free fall* in the vertical direction. Just like other examples of free fall, the ball's vertical speed increases by 9.8 m/sec each second (Figure 6.7).

VERTICAL VELOCITY
Projectile motion

$$v_y = gt$$

Vertical velocity (m/sec, downward) → v_y

Acceleration due to gravity (m/sec²)

Time (sec)

The velocity vector   The diagram shows the velocity vector as the ball falls. The horizontal (x) velocity stays constant. The vertical (y) velocity increases because of the acceleration of gravity. As a result, both the magnitude (speed) and direction of the velocity vector change.

The ball's vertical velocity (v_y) is accelerated by 9.8 m/sec²

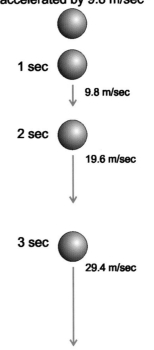

1 sec — 9.8 m/sec

2 sec — 19.6 m/sec

3 sec — 29.4 m/sec

Figure 6.7: *A projectile's vertical velocity increases by 9.8 m/sec each second.*

Horizontal and vertical distance

Horizontal distance The horizontal distance a projectile goes is the horizontal speed (v_x) multiplied by the time (t). Because the horizontal speed is constant, the relationship between distance, speed, and time is the same as you learned in Chapter 1. If you know any two of the variables, you can use the equation below to find the (unknown) third variable.

HORIZONTAL DISTANCE
Projectile motion

Horizontal velocity (m/sec)

Distance (m) ⟶ $d_x = v_x\,t$ ⟵ *Time* (sec)

Vertical distance The vertical distance the ball falls can be calculated using the equation $d=v_{avg}t$, as we did for free fall in Chapter 2. The *average* velocity must be used because the vertical motion is accelerated. A more direct way to find the vertical distance is with the equation $d=1/2at^2$. The vertical acceleration in free fall is 9.8 m/sec^2, so the equation then becomes $d = 4.9\,t^2$. Keep in mind that this equation is only correct on Earth, when the object starts with a vertical velocity of zero (Figure 6.8).

VERTICAL DISTANCE
Projectile motion

Vertical distance (m) ⟶ $d_y = 4.9t^2$

⟵ *Time* (seconds)

Caution! The equations above are suitable ONLY for situations where the projectile starts with zero vertical velocity, such as a ball rolling off a table. If the projectile is launched up or down at an angle, the equations are more complicated.

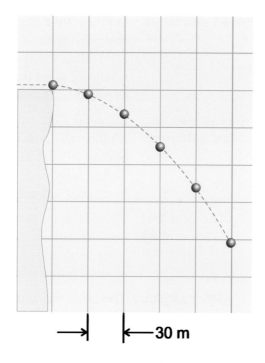

← 30 m

Time (sec)	Horizontal position (m)	Vertical drop (m)
0	0	0
1	30	4.9
2	60	19.6
3	90	44.1
4	120	78.4
5	150	122.5

Figure 6.8: *The horizontal and vertical positions of a ball rolling off a cliff at 30 meters per second.*

The range of a projectile

Speed and angle   Suppose you are hitting golf balls and you want the ball to go as far as possible on the course. How should you hit the ball? The two factors you control are the speed with which you hit it and the angle at which you hit it. You want to hit the ball as fast as you can so that it will have as much velocity as possible. But what is the best angle at which to hit the ball?

90 degrees and zero degrees   Launching the ball straight upward (90 degrees) gives it the greatest air time (Figure 6.9) and height. However, a ball flying straight up does not move horizontally at all and has a range of zero. Launching the ball completely horizontally (0 degrees) makes it roll on the ground. The ball has the greatest horizontal velocity but it hits the ground immediately, so the range is zero.

The greatest range at 45 degrees   To get the greatest range, you must find a balance between horizontal and vertical motion. The vertical velocity gives the ball its air time, and the horizontal velocity causes it to move over the course. The angle that gives the greatest range is 45 degrees, halfway between horizontal and vertical.

Other angles   The more the launch angle differs from 45 degrees, the smaller the range. A ball launched at 30 degrees has the same range as one launched at 60 degrees because both angles are 15 degrees away from 45. The same is true for any pair of angles adding up to 90 degrees.

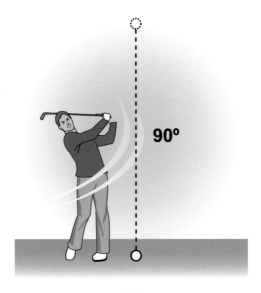

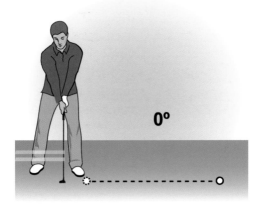

Figure 6.9: *The air time and height are greatest when a ball is hit at an angle of 90 degrees. The air time and range are zero when a ball is hit at an angle of zero degrees.*

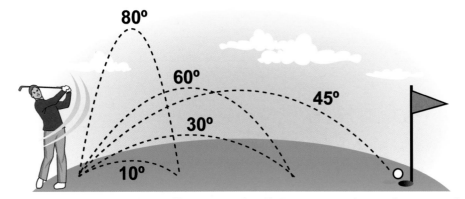

Air resistance   Air resistance can also affect a projectile's range. The trajectory of a projectile is usually not a perfect parabola, and the range is less than would be expected, both because of air resistance.

Projectile motion problems

Distinguishing between horizontal and vertical Projectile motion problems can be tricky because you have to keep track of so many variables. When solving a problem, you should first figure out what the problem is asking you to find and whether it is a horizontal or a vertical quantity. Then you can use the right relationship to answer the question. Remember the horizontal velocity is constant and uses the distance equation for constant velocity motion. The vertical velocity changes by 9.8 m/sec each second and the vertical motion is the same as free fall.

Projectile motion

A stunt driver steers a car off a cliff at a speed of 20 m/sec. He lands in the lake below two seconds later. Find the horizontal distance the car travels and the height of the cliff.

1. Looking for: You are asked for the vertical and horizontal distances.

2. Given: You are given the time in seconds and initial horizontal speed in m/sec.

3. Relationships: Horizontal: $d_x = v_x t$ Vertical: $d_y = 4.9t^2$

4. Solution: Horizontal: $d_x = (20 \text{ m/sec})(2 \text{ sec}) = 40$ meters
Vertical: $d_y = (4.9 \text{ m/sec}^2)(2 \text{ sec})^2 = (4.9 \text{ m/sec}^2)(4 \text{ sec}^2) = 19.6$ meters

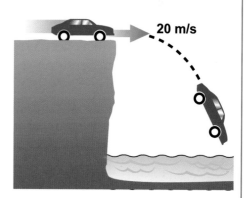

20 m/s

Your turn...

a. Repeat the above problem with a time of three seconds instead of two.   **Answer:** 60 meters, 44.1 meters

b. You kick a soccer ball and it travels a horizontal distance of 12 meters during the 1.5 seconds it is in the air. What was the ball's initial horizontal speed? **Answer:** 8 m/sec

6.1 Section Review

1. What is the word for the horizontal distance a projectile travels?
2. What does it mean to say a projectile's horizontal and vertical velocity are independent of each other?
3. A football is kicked down a field. Describe what happens to its horizontal and vertical velocities as it moves through the air.
4. What launch angle gives a projectile its greatest range?

6.2 Circular Motion

Circular motion occurs when a force causes an object to curve in a full circle. The planets orbiting the sun, a child on a merry-go-round, and a basketball spinning on a fingertip are examples of circular motion.

Describing circular motion

Rotating and revolving A basketball spinning on your fingertip and a child on a merry-go-round both have circular motion. Each moves around its axis of rotation. The basketball's axis runs from your finger up through the center of the ball (Figure 6.10). The child's axis is a vertical line in the center of the merry-go-round. While their motions are similar, there is a difference. The ball's axis is *internal* or inside the object. We say an object **rotates** about its axis when the axis is internal. A child on a merry-go-round moves around an axis that is *external* or outside him. An object **revolves** when it moves around an external axis.

Angular speed When an object moves in a line, we can measure its linear speed. Linear speed is the distance traveled per unit of time. **Angular speed** is the amount an object in circular motion spins per unit of time. Angular speed can describe either the rate of revolving or the rate of rotating.

Vocabulary

circular motion, revolve, angular speed, linear speed, circumference

Objectives

✓ Distinguish between rotation and revolution

✓ Calculate angular speed

✓ Explain how angular speed, linear speed, and distance are related

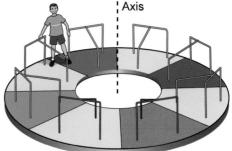

Figure 6.10: *The basketball rotates and the child revolves.*

Linear Speed

Distance traveled per time

Angular Speed

Amount of spin per time

Angular speed

Units of angular speed

Circular motion is described by angular speed. The angular speed is the rate at which something turns. The rpm, or rotation per minute, is commonly used for angular speed. Another common unit is angle per unit of time. There are 360 degrees in a full rotation, so one rotation per minute is the same angular speed as 360 degrees per minute (Figure 6.11).

Calculating angular speed

To calculate angular speed you divide the number of rotations or the number of degrees an object has rotated by the time taken. For example, if a basketball turns 15 times in three seconds, its angular speed is five rotations per second (15 rotations ÷ 3 sec).

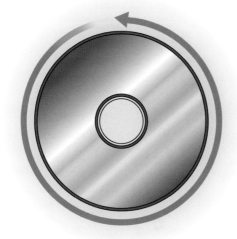

Figure 6.11: *One rotation is the same as 360 degrees.*

ANGULAR SPEED

$$Angular\ speed = \frac{rotations\ or\ degrees}{time}$$

Calculating angular speed

A merry-go-round makes 10 rotations in 2 minutes. What is its angular speed in rpm?

1. Looking for: You are asked for the angular speed in rotations per minute and degrees per minute.

2. Given: You are given the number of rotations and the time in minutes.

3. Relationships: $\text{angular speed} = \dfrac{\text{rotations or degrees}}{\text{time}}$

4. Solution: $\text{angular speed} = \dfrac{10\ \text{rotations}}{2\ \text{minutes}} = 5\ \text{RPM}$

Your turn...

a. Calculate the angular speed of a bicycle wheel that spins 1,000 times in 5 minutes. **Answer:** 200 rpm

b. A bowling ball rolls at two rotations per second. What is its angular speed in degrees per second? **Answer:** 720 degrees/sec

Relating angular speed, linear speed, and distance

Angular speed is the same
Each point on a rotating object has the same angular speed. Suppose three children sit on a merry-go-round (Figure 6.12). When the merry-go-round rotates once, each child makes one revolution. The time for one revolution is the same for all three children, so their angular speeds are the same.

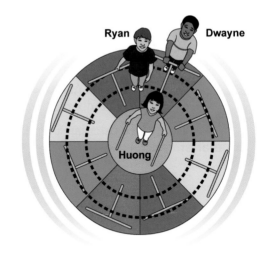

Ryan   Dwayne

Huong

Distance during a revolution
The linear speed of each child is *not* the same because they travel different distances. The distance depends on how far each child is sitting from the center. Dwayne sits near the edge. He moves in the biggest circle and travels the greatest distance during a revolution. Ryan moves in a medium circle and travels a smaller distance. Huong sits exactly in the center of the merry-go-round, so she does not revolve at all. She rotates about the axis in the center.

Figure 6.12: *Each child has the same angular speed, but Dwayne has the fastest linear speed.*

Linear speed depends on radius
The linear speed of a person on a merry-go-round is the distance traveled around the circle divided by the time. The distance depends on the radius of the circle in which the person moves. Therefore the linear speed also depends on the radius. Dwayne moves in a circle with the largest radius, so his linear speed is the fastest. Two people sitting at different places on the same merry-go-round always have the same *angular* speed. But the person sitting farther from the center has the faster **linear speed**.

Circumference
The distance traveled during one revolution equals the **circumference** of the circle. The radius of the circle equals the person's distance from the axis of rotation at the center. A person sitting two meters from the center of a merry-go-round travels in a circle with twice the circumference of that of a person sitting one meter from the center. The person sitting two meters away therefore has twice the linear speed.

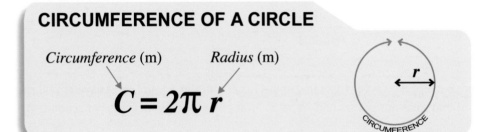

CIRCUMFERENCE OF A CIRCLE

Circumference (m)   *Radius* (m)

$$C = 2\pi\, r$$

CIRCUMFERENCE

Solving linear speed problems

Calculating linear speed The linear speed of any point on a rotating object is directly proportional to the distance between the point and the axis of rotation. You can calculate the linear speed of any point if you know the time it takes to make one revolution and the distance it is from the axis of rotation. If you are given the angular speed, you can determine how much time it takes to make one revolution.

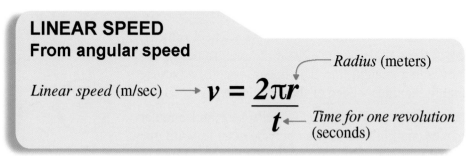

LINEAR SPEED
From angular speed

Radius (meters)

Linear speed (m/sec) ⟶ $v = \dfrac{2\pi r}{t}$ ⟵ *Time for one revolution* (seconds)

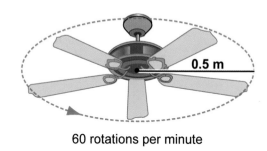

0.5 m

60 rotations per minute

Figure 6.13: *What is the linear speed of the tip of the fan blade?*

Calculating linear speed

The blades on a ceiling fan spin at 60 rotations per minute (Figure 6.13). The fan has a radius of 0.5 meter. Calculate the linear speed of a point at the outer edge of a blade in meters per second.

1. Looking for: You are asked for the linear speed in meters per second.

2. Given: You are given the angular speed in rpm and the radius in meters.

3. Relationships: $v = \dfrac{2\pi r}{t}$

4. Solution: The blades spin at 60 rotations per minute, so they make 60 rotations in 60 seconds. Therefore it takes one second to make one rotation.

$$v = \frac{(2\pi)(0.5\text{ m})}{1\text{ sec}} = 3.14\text{ m/sec}$$

Your turn...

a. Calculate the linear speed of a point 0.25 meter from the center of the fan. **Answer:** 1.57 m/sec
b. The fan slows to 30 rpm. Calculate the linear speed of a point at the outer edge of a blade and 0.25 meter from the center.
   Answer: 1.57 m/sec, 0.79 m

Rolling

Linear and rotational motion
Rolling is a combination of linear motion and rotational motion (Figure 6.14). Linear motion occurs when an entire object moves from one place to another. Holding a bicycle wheel up in the air and moving it to the right is an example of linear motion. Rotational motion occurs when an object spins around an axis that stays in place. If you lift a bicycle's front wheel off the ground and make it spin, the spinning wheel is in rotational motion.

Rolling motion
Rolling is a combination of linear and rotational motion. As a wheel rolls, its axis moves in a line. Look at the motion of the axis in the picture below. As the wheel rolls, its axis moves in a straight line. The linear speed of a bicycle riding on the wheel is equal to the linear speed of the wheel's axis.

Linear distance equals circumference
The distance the bicycle moves depends on the wheel's size and angular speed. When the wheel makes one full rotation, the bicycle goes forward one circumference. The point that was contacting the ground at the beginning of the rotation travels once around the circle. The linear speed of the bicycle is therefore equal to the distance the point moves around the circle (the circumference) divided by the time taken for the wheel to rotate once.

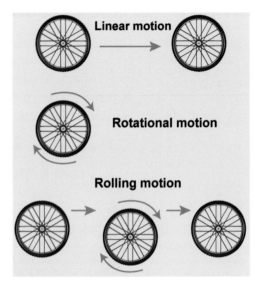

Figure 6.14: *Rolling is a combination of linear and rotational motion.*

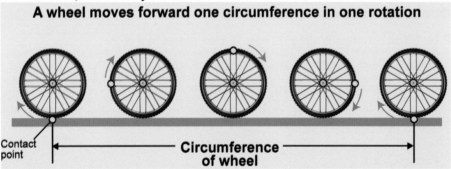

A wheel moves forward one circumference in one rotation

Contact point

Circumference of wheel

Speedometers

A bicycle speedometer uses a small magnet on the front wheel to measure speed. Before using it, you must enter in your wheel's circumference. The speedometer divides the circumference by the time for the magnet to revolve and displays the speed. It can also measure distance by counting rotations. A car's speedometer works in a similar way. It is programmed for tires of a certain size. If tires of the wrong radius are used, the speed and distance measurements will be inaccurate.

6.2 Section Review

1. Give your own examples of an object rotating and an object revolving.

2. List two units in which angular speed can be measured.

3. Several U.S. cities have rotating restaurants high atop buildings. Does every person in such a rotating restaurant have the same angular speed and linear speed? Explain.

6.3 Centripetal Force, Gravitation, and Satellites

Force is needed to accelerate an object. We usually think of acceleration as a change in speed, but it can also be a change in direction. An object moving in a circle is constantly changing direction, so a force must act on it. In this section you will learn how force can create circular motion. You will also learn about the force that keeps planets, moons, and satellites in orbit.

Centripetal force

Centripetal force causes circular motion
Any force that causes an object to move in a circle is called a **centripetal force**. Even though it is given its own name, centripetal force is not a new type of physical force. Any force can be a centripetal force if its action causes an object to move in a circle. For example, a car can move in a circle because friction provides the centripetal force. The lack of friction on an icy road is what makes it difficult for a car to turn.

The effect of a force depends on direction
Whether a force makes an object accelerate by changing its speed or by changing its direction depends on the direction of the force (Figure 6.15). A force in the same direction as the motion causes the object to speed up. A force exactly opposite the direction of motion makes the object slow down. A force *perpendicular* to the direction of motion causes the object to change its path from a line to a circle, without changing speed.

Centripetal force is toward the center
Centripetal force is always directed toward the center of the circle in which an object moves. Imagine tying a ball to the end of a string and twirling it in a circle over your head. The string exerts the centripetal force on the ball to move it in a circle. The direction of the pull is toward your hand at the center of the circle. Notice that the direction of the centripetal force changes as the object moves around you. If the ball is on your right, you pull to the left and vice versa. Centripetal forces change direction so they remain pointed toward the center of the circle.

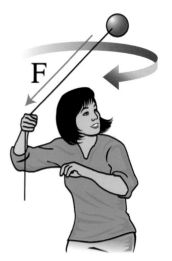

Vocabulary

centripetal force, centrifugal force, law of universal gravitation, gravitational constant, satellite, orbit, ellipse

Objectives

✓ Explain how a centripetal force causes circular motion
✓ List the factors that affect centripetal force
✓ Describe the relationship between gravitational force, mass, and distance
✓ Relate centripetal force to orbital motion

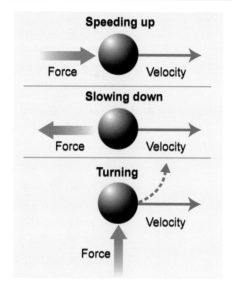

Figure 6.15: *The effect of a force depends on its direction.*

Centripetal force, inertia, and velocity

Inertia   Why doesn't centripetal force pull a revolving object toward the center of its circle? Inertia is the key to answering this question. Suppose you want to move a ball tied to a string in a circle on the top of a smooth table. You place the ball on the table, straighten out the string, and give it a hard pull along its length. Will the ball move in a circle? No! The ball will simply move straight toward your hand. The ball has a tendency to remain at rest, but the force of the string accelerates it toward your hand in the direction of the roll.

Getting circular motion started   Now suppose you hold the string with your right hand and use your left hand to toss the ball in a direction perpendicular to the string. As soon as the ball starts moving, you pull on the string. This time you can get the ball to move in a circle around your hand.

Centripetal force changes direction   Let's examine exactly what is happening. If you give the ball an initial velocity to the left at point A, it will try to keep moving straight to the left (Figure 6.16). But the centripetal force pulls the ball to the side. A short time later, the ball is at point B and its velocity is 90 degrees from what it was. But now the centripetal force pulls to the right. The ball's inertia makes it want to keep moving straight, but the centripetal force always pulls it towards the center. This process continues, moving the ball in a circle as long as you keep supplying the centripetal force.

Velocity and force are perpendicular   Notice that the velocity is always perpendicular to the string and therefore to the centripetal force. The centripetal force and velocity are perpendicular for any object moving in a circle. What happens if you release the string? Because there is nothing to provide the centripetal force, the ball stops moving in a circle. It moves in a straight line in the direction of the velocity the instant you let go. It flies away at a 90-degree angle from the string.

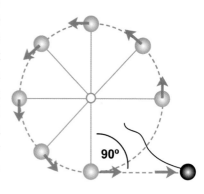

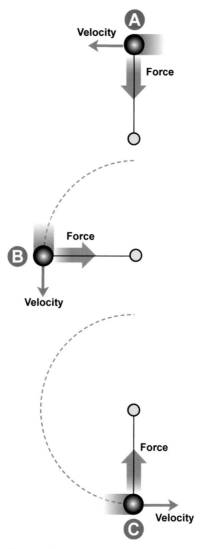

Figure 6.16: *The centripetal force changes direction so it is always perpendicular to the velocity.*

Newton's second law and circular motion

Acceleration   An object moving in a circle at a constant speed accelerates because its direction changes. The faster its change in direction, the greater its acceleration. How quickly an object changes direction depends on its speed and the radius of the circle. If an object gets faster, and stays moving in the same circle, its direction changes more quickly and its acceleration is greater. If an object stays at the same speed but the circle of its motion expands, the change in direction becomes more gradual and the acceleration is reduced. *Centripetal acceleration* increases with speed and decreases with radius.

Force, mass, and acceleration   Newton's second law relates force, mass, and acceleration. According to the law, more force is needed to cause a greater acceleration. More force is also needed when changing the motion of an object with a larger mass. The strength of centripetal force needed to move an object in a circle therefore depends on its mass, speed, and the radius of the circle (Figure 6.17).

1. Centripetal force is directly proportional to the mass. A two-kilogram object needs twice the force to have the same circular motion as a one-kilogram object.

2. Centripetal force is inversely proportional to the radius of its circle. The smaller the circle, the greater the force. An object moving in a one-half-meter circle needs twice the force it does when it moves in a one-meter circle at the same linear speed.

3. Centripetal force is directly proportional to the *square* of the object's linear speed. *Doubling* the speed requires *four* times the centripetal force. *Tripling* the speed requires *nine* times the centripetal force.

Driving around bends   The relationship between centripetal force and speed is especially important for automobile drivers to recognize. A car moves in a circle as it turns a corner. The friction between the tires and the road provides the centripetal force that keeps the car following the radius of the turn. This is why high-speed turns (on freeways) have a much larger radius than low-speed corners in town. You may have seen signs at highway ramps with sharp curves that warn drivers to reduce their speeds. Friction decreases when a road is wet or icy, and there may not be enough force to keep the car following the turn.

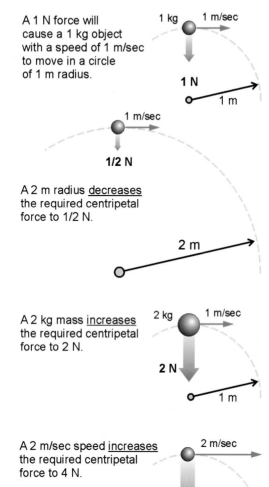

A 1 N force will cause a 1 kg object with a speed of 1 m/sec to move in a circle of 1 m radius.

A 2 m radius decreases the required centripetal force to 1/2 N.

A 2 kg mass increases the required centripetal force to 2 N.

A 2 m/sec speed increases the required centripetal force to 4 N.

Figure 6.17: *The centripetal force needed to move an object in a circle depends on its mass, speed, and the radius of the circle.*

Centrifugal force

A turning car Have you ever noticed that when a car makes a sharp turn, you are thrown toward the outside edge of the car? If the car turns to the right, you slide to the left. If the car turns to the left, you slide to the right. Although the centripetal force pushes the car toward the center of the circle, it seems as if there is a force pushing *you* to the *outside*. This apparent outward force is called **centrifugal force**. While it feels like there is a force acting on you, *centrifugal force is not a true force*.

Newton's first law According to Newton's first law, an object in motion tends to keep moving with the same speed and direction. Objects — including you — have inertia and the inertia resists any change in motion. When you are in a turning car, what seems like centrifugal force is actually your own inertia. Your body tries to keep moving in a straight line and therefore is flung toward the outer edge of the car. The car pushes back on you to force you into the turn, and that is the true *centripetal* force. This is one of many reasons why you should always wear a seat belt!

An example Figure 6.18 shows a view from above of what happens when a car turns a bend. Suppose a box is in the center of a smooth back seat as the car travels along a straight road. The box and the car are both moving in a straight line. If the car suddenly turns to the left, the box tries to keep moving in that same straight line. While it seems like the box is being thrown to the right side of the car, the car is actually turning under the box.

The role of friction The car is able to turn because of the friction between the road and the tires. However, the box is not touching the road, so this force does not act it. There is friction acting on the box from the seat, but this force may be too small if the seat is smooth. The box slides to the right until it is stopped by the door of the car.

A useful example *Centrifugal* force is an effect of inertia that you feel whenever your body is forced to move in a circle. Although not a force, the centrifugal effect is quite useful and is the basis of the centrifuge. Centrifuges are used to separate mixtures by density. A centrifuge spins a liquid mixture at high speed. The rapid spinning causes all the heavier particles in the mixture to move to the farthest point away from the center of rotation.

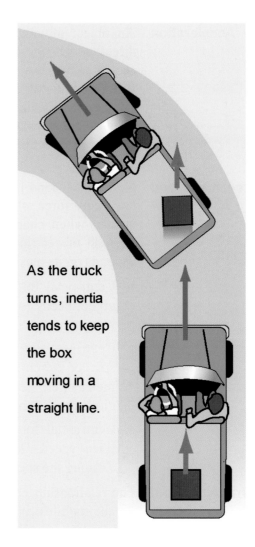

As the truck turns, inertia tends to keep the box moving in a straight line.

Figure 6.18: *As the car turns, the box keeps going straight ahead because of inertia.*

Gravitational force

Planets and moons
A centripetal force is needed to move any object in a circle. What is the force that makes Earth orbit the sun and the moon orbit Earth? Newton first realized that this force is the same force that causes objects to fall toward the ground. The force of gravity between Earth and the sun provides the centripetal force to keep Earth moving in a circle. The force of gravity between Earth and the moon keeps the moon in orbit (Figure 6.19).

The force of gravity between Earth and the sun keeps Earth in orbit.

Figure 6.19: *Gravitational force keeps the moon in orbit around Earth.*

Weight
Gravitational force exists between *all* objects that have mass. The strength of the force depends on the mass of the objects and the distance between them. Your *weight* is the force of gravity between you and Earth. It depends on your mass, the planet's mass, and your distance from the center of the planet. Until now you have used the equation $F_g=mg$ to calculate weight. Your mass is represented by *m*. The value of *g* depends on Earth's mass and the distance between its center and surface. If you travel to a planet with a different mass and/or radius, the value of *g* and your weight would change.

Gravitational force exists between all objects
You do not notice the attractive force between ordinary objects because gravity is a relatively weak force. It takes a great deal of mass to create gravitational forces that can be felt. For example, a gravitational force exists between you and your textbook, but you cannot feel it because both masses are small. You notice the force of gravity between you and Earth because the planet's mass is huge. Gravitational forces tend to be important only when one of the objects has an extremely large mass, such as a moon, star, or planet.

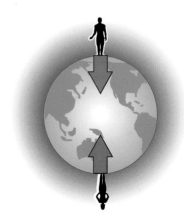

Figure 6.20: *The direction "down" is opposite on the north and south poles.*

Direction of the gravitational force
The force of gravity between two objects always lies along the line connecting their centers. As objects move, the direction of the force changes to stay pointed along the line between their centers. For example, the force between Earth and your body points from your center to the center of Earth. The direction of the planet's gravitational force is what we use to define "down." If you tell a person on the north pole and one on the south pole to point down, they will be pointing in opposite directions (Figure 6.20).

The gravitational force between objects

Mass and gravity The force of gravity between two objects is proportional to the mass of each object. If one object doubles in mass, then the gravitational force doubles. If both objects double in mass, then the force doubles twice, becoming four times as strong (Figure 6.21).

Distance and gravity The distance between objects, measured from center to center, is also important when calculating gravitational force. The closer objects are to each other, the greater the force between them. The farther apart, the weaker the force. The decrease in gravitational force is related to the square of the distance. Doubling the distance divides the force by four (2^2). If you are twice as far from an object, you feel one-fourth the gravitational force. Tripling the distance divides the force by nine ($9 = 3^2$). If you are three times as far away, the force is one-ninth as strong.

Changing elevation If you climb a hill or fly in an airplane, your distance from the center of Earth increases. The gravitational force on you, and therefore your weight, decreases. However, this change in distance is so small when compared with Earth's radius that the difference in your weight is not noticeable.

Measuring distance When calculating the force of Earth's gravity, distance is measured from the center of the object to the center of Earth. This is *not* because gravity "comes from" the center of the planet. Every part of Earth's mass contributes to the gravitational force. You measure the distance to the center because your distance from all the particles making up the planet varies. You are close to the mass under your feet but far from the mass on the other side of Earth. The distance used to calculate the force of gravity is the average distance between you and all the particles making up Earth's mass. This average distance is the distance to the planet's center.

Mass and the force of gravity

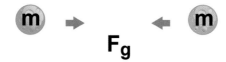

Figure 6.21: *Doubling one mass doubles the force of gravity. Doubling both quadruples the force of gravity.*

Newton's law of universal gravitation

The law of universal gravitation Newton's **law of universal gravitation** gives the relationship between gravitational force, mass, and distance. The **gravitational constant** (G) is the same everywhere in the universe (6.67×10^{-11} N·m²/kg²). Its small value shows why gravity is weak unless at least one mass is huge.

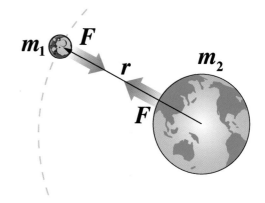

Figure 6.22: *The force on the moon is equal in strength to the force on Earth.*

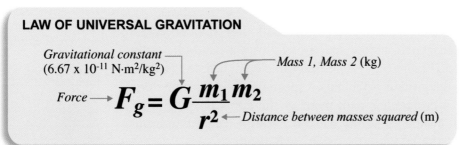

LAW OF UNIVERSAL GRAVITATION

Gravitational constant (6.67×10^{-11} N·m²/kg²)

Mass 1, Mass 2 (kg)

Force $\longrightarrow$ $$F_g = G \frac{m_1 m_2}{r^2}$$ $\longleftarrow$ Distance between masses squared (m)

The force on each object The force calculated using the law of universal gravitation is the force felt by *each* object (Figure 6.22). The gravitational force of Earth on the moon is the same strength as the gravitational force of the moon on Earth.

Calculating gravitational forces

Use the following information to calculate the force of gravity between Earth and the moon.
Mass of Earth: 5.97×10^{24} m   Mass of moon: 7.34×10^{22} kg   Distance between centers of Earth and moon: 3.84×10^8 m

1. Looking for: You are asked for the force of gravity between Earth and the moon.

2. Given: You are given their two masses in kilograms and the distance between their centers in meters.

3. Relationships: $$F_g = G \frac{m_1 m_2}{r^2}$$

3. Relationships:

$$F_g = (6.67 \times 10^{-11} \, \frac{\text{N} \cdot \text{m}^2}{\text{kg}^2}) \frac{(5.97 \times 10^{24} \text{ kg})(7.34 \times 10^{22} \text{ kg})}{(3.84 \times 10^8 \text{ m})^2}$$

$$F_g = (6.67 \times 10^{-11} \, \frac{\text{N} \cdot \text{m}^2}{\text{kg}^2}) \frac{(4.38 \times 10^{47} \text{ kg}^2)}{(1.47 \times 10^{17} \text{ m}^2)} = 1.99 \times 10^{20} \text{ N}$$

Your turn...

a. Calculate the force of gravity on a 50-kilogram person on Earth (6.38×10^6 m from its center). **Answer:** 489 N
b. Calculate the force of gravity on a 50-kilogram person on the moon (1.74×10^6 m from its center). **Answer:** 81 N

Orbital motion

Satellites A **satellite** is an object that circles around another object with gravity providing the centripetal force. Earth, its moon, and the other planets are examples of natural satellites. Artificial satellites that **orbit**, or move around Earth include the Hubble Space Telescope, the International Space Station, and satellites used for communications.

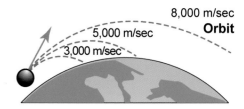

Figure 6.23: *A projectile launched fast enough from Earth becomes a satellite.*

Launching a satellite The motion of a satellite is closely related to projectile motion. If an object is launched above Earth's surface at a slow speed, it follows a parabolic path and falls back to the planet (Figure 6.23). The faster it is launched, the farther it travels before reaching the ground. At a launch speed of about 8 kilometers per second, the curve of a projectile's path matches the curvature of Earth. The object goes into orbit instead of falling back to Earth. A satellite in orbit *falls around Earth.* But as it falls, Earth curves away beneath it.

Elliptical orbits An orbit can be a circle or an oval shape called an **ellipse**. Any satellite launched above Earth at more than 8 kilometers per second will have an elliptical orbit. An object in an elliptical orbit does not move at a constant speed. It moves fastest when it is closest to the object it is orbiting because the force of gravity is strongest there.

Planets and comets All the planets' orbits are almost circular. Comets, however, orbit the sun in very long elliptical paths (Figure 6.24). Their paths bring them close to the sun and then out into space, often beyond Pluto. Some comets take only a few years to orbit the sun once, while others travel so far out that a solar orbit takes thousands of years.

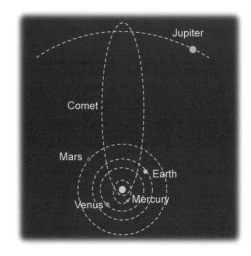

Figure 6.24: *The planets move in nearly circular orbits. Comets travel in elliptical orbits around the sun.*

6.3 Section Review

1. Draw a diagram of a ball at the end of a string moving in a clockwise circle. Draw vectors to show the direction of the centripetal force and velocity at three different locations on the circle.

2. Explain the difference between centrifugal force and centripetal force.

3. What factors affect the force of gravity between two objects?

4. What is the force that keeps Earth in orbit around the sun?

6.4 Center of Mass

Vocabulary

center of mass, center of gravity

Objectives

✓ Define center of mass and center of gravity

✓ Explain how to locate an object's center of mass and center of gravity

✓ Use the concept of center of gravity to explain toppling

The shape of an object and the way its mass is distributed affect the way it moves and balances. For example, a tall stool tips over much more easily than a low, wide chair. Wheels and other objects that spin are designed to rotate with as little effort as possible. In this section you will learn about the factors that affect an object's rotation.

Finding the center of mass

The motion of a tossed object
Earlier in this unit you learned that a ball thrown into the air at an angle moves in a parabola. But what if you hold the top of an empty soda bottle and toss it across a field? You will notice that the bottle rotates as it moves through the air. The rotation comes from the torque you exerted when throwing it. If you filmed the bottle and carefully looked at the film you would see that one point on the bottle moves in a perfect parabola. The bottle spins around this point as it moves.

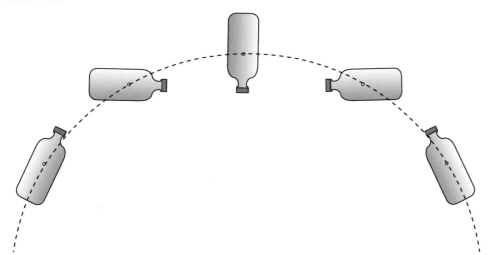

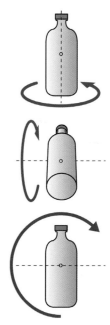

Figure 6.25: *An object naturally spins about three different axes.*

Defining center of mass
The point at which an object naturally spins is its **center of mass**. Since a solid object has length, width, and height, there are three different axes about which an object tends to spin. These three axes intersect at the center of mass (Figure 6.25). The center of mass is important because it is the average position of all the particles that make up the object's mass.

Finding the center of mass

The center of mass may not be "in" an object It is easy to find the center of mass for a symmetric object made of a single material such as a solid rubber ball or a wooden cube. The center of mass is located at the geometric center of the object. If an object is irregularly shaped, it can be found by spinning the object, as with the soda bottle on the previous page. The center of mass of some objects may not be inside the object. The center of mass of a doughnut is at its very center — where there is only space.

Finding the center of mass

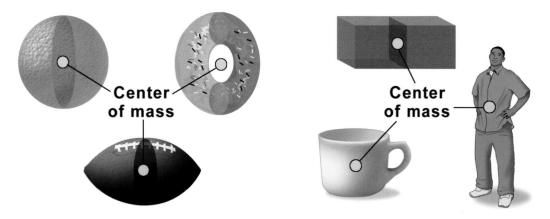

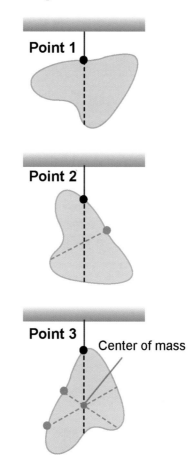

The center of gravity Closely related to the center of mass is the **center of gravity**, or the average position of an object's weight. If the acceleration due to gravity is the same at every point in an object, its centers of gravity and of mass are at the same point. This is the case for most objects, so the two terms are often used interchangeably. However, gravity toward the bottom of a skyscraper is slightly stronger than it is toward the top. The top half therefore weighs less than the bottom half, even when both halves have the same mass. The center of mass is halfway up the building, but the center of gravity is slightly lower.

Finding the center of gravity An object's center of mass can easily be found experimentally. When an object hangs from a point at its edge, the center of mass falls in the line directly below the point of suspension. If the object is hung from two or more points, the center of mass can be found by tracing the line below each point and finding the intersection of the lines (Figure 6.26).

Figure 6.26: *The center of mass of an irregularly shaped object can be found by suspending it from two or more points.*

Mass and the center of gravity

Balancing an object
To balance an object such as a book or a pencil on your finger, you must place your finger directly under the object's center of mass. The object balances because the torque caused by the force of the object's weight is equal on each side.

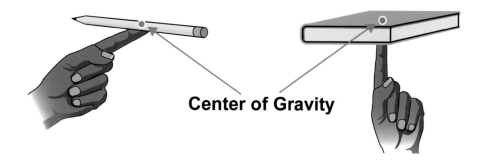

Center of Gravity

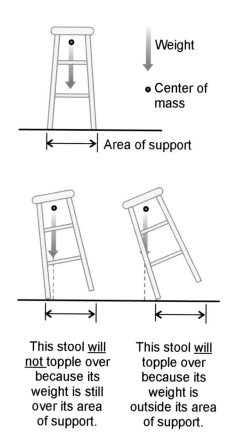

Figure 6.27: *A stool will topple if its weight vector is outside the area of support.*

The area of support
For an object to stay upright, its center of mass must be above its area of support. The area of support includes the entire region surrounded by the actual supports. For example, a stool's area of support is the entire rectangular area surrounded by its four legs. Your body's support area is not only where your feet touch the ground, but also the region between your feet. The larger the area of support, the less likely an object is to topple over.

When an object will topple over
An object will topple over if its center of mass is not above its area of support. A stool's center of mass is slightly below the center of the seat. A vector showing the force of gravity or the stool's weight points from the center of mass toward the center of Earth (Figure 6.27). If this vector passes through the area of support, the object will not topple over; if it passes outside that area, the object will topple. Tall stools topple over more easily than low ones for this reason.

6.4 Section Review

1. What is the difference between center of mass and center of gravity?
2. Explain how you can find an object's center of mass.
3. Is a pencil easier to balance on its sharp tip or on its eraser? Why?

History of the Helicopter

When we think of flying, we often imagine fixed-wing aircraft like airplanes. These flying machines are prominent in aviation history. However, helicopters were probably the first flight pondered by man. For example, the ancient Chinese played with a simple toy—feathers on a stick—that they would spin and release into flight.

In the 1400s, Leonardo Da Vinci (1452-1519) had a plan for a vertically flying machine that could lift a person. Da Vinci planned to use muscle power to revolve the rotor, but this was insufficient to lift his helicopter into the air. In the 1900s, the invention of the internal combustion engine provided adequate power, but not stability to the design.

In 1940, Igor Sikorsky (1889 - 1972) developed the first stable helicopter, named the VS-300. His design allowed stability at any speed, including a hover, and he could accelerate it in any direction!

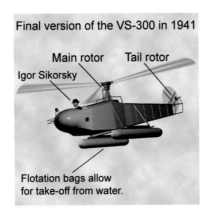

Final version of the VS-300 in 1941

Main rotor   Tail rotor
Igor Sikorsky

Flotation bags allow
for take-off from water.

Rotors and action-reaction forces

Today's helicopters retain much of Sikorsky's original design. The *main rotor*, is the large propeller on top that makes the "chop-chop" sound that gave helicopters the nickname "chopper." The main rotor is used to lift the helicopter straight up. However it can tilt in any direction to stabilize the helicopter in a hover.

Helicopters must be lightweight in order for them to be lifted. However, with such low inertia, a small net force can easily cause a helicopter to get out of control. A *tail rotor*, the propeller on the tail of the helicopter, provides a force that counteracts the tendency of the main rotor to spin the helicopter counterclockwise. In addition, the tail rotor is used to rotate the helicopter right or left in a hover. This tail rotor from Sikorsky's VS-300 is now considered to be part of the conventional design because it works so well.

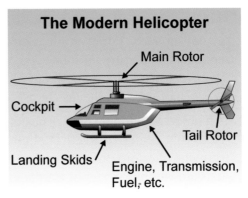

The Modern Helicopter

Main Rotor

Cockpit

Tail Rotor

Landing Skids

Engine, Transmission, Fuel, etc.

The helicopter tends to turn counterclockwise (a reaction force) because the helicopter engine turns the main rotor clockwise (an action force). The force provided by the tail rotor is a reaction force that counteracts the action force of the main rotor causing the helicopter to spin counterclockwise. This mechanism for how the helicopter works is an example of Newton's third law of motion.

Helicopter motion

Airplanes have propellers or jet engines to accelerate forward. In contrast, helicopters use the main rotor to accelerate.

Once the helicopter is moving forward, wind resistance (drag) increases until equilibrium is reached. Then, the helicopter moves at constant speed.

A lift force provided by the main rotor balances the weight of the helicopter so that it stays in the air. Also, the forward directing force of the lift (produced by the main rotor) balances the drag.

By tilting the main rotor, a helicopter pilot can increase the speed of the helicopter. The world's fastest helicopter can travel at 249 miles per hour, but most helicopters fly at 120 miles per hour. There are several limits to the maximum speed of a helicopter, but an obvious one is that if you tilt the main rotor of the helicopter too much, the lift force is large and occurs nearly parallel to the ground. Such a flying configuration causes the passengers and pilot of a helicopter to slide out of their seats!

As the speed of a helicopter increases, more lift is needed. Another role of the tail rotor is that it acts to balance the lift forces of the helicopter.

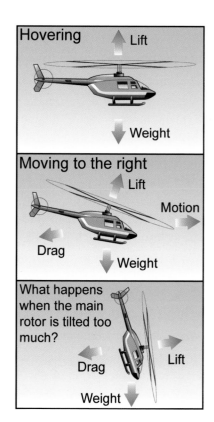

A helicopter mimics nature

If the engine of a helicopter failed, you might think that it would drop out of the sky like a rock. Fortunately, this does not happen. Instead, a helicopter with engine failure gently spins to the ground. This motion is similar to how a maple tree seed twirls to the ground when it falls from a tree. Helicopter pilots must practice and be able to perform this emergency landing maneuver in order to obtain a license.

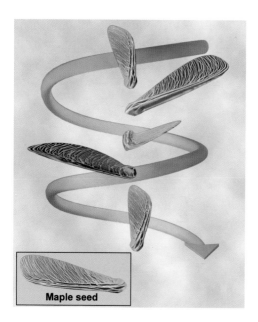

Maple seed

Questions:

1. What is the purpose of the main rotor?
2. Why is the tail rotor an important part of helicopter design?
3. Name two pairs of action-reaction forces that are involved in how a helicopter works.
4. In which directions can a helicopter move?
5. Helicopters are often used to transport seriously ill patients from one hospital to another. Given your answer to question (4), why are helicopters used instead of airplanes which can travel at faster speeds?

Chapter 6 Review

Understanding Vocabulary

Select the correct term to complete the sentences.

centripetal force	parabola	trajectory
range	revolves	center of mass
center of gravity	satellite	angular speed
rotates	projectile	law of universal gravitation
displacement		

Section 6.1

1. A _____ vector shows an object's change in position.

2. The path of a projectile is its _____.

3. A _____ is an object that moves through the air only affected by the force of gravity.

4. The mathematical shape of a projectile's trajectory is a _____.

5. The horizontal distance a projectile travels is its _____.

Section 6.2

6. An object _____ when it moves in a circle around an external axis.

7. A wheel _____ about an axis in its center.

8. _____ is the measure of how fast an object rotates or revolves.

Section 6.3

9. An inward _____ is needed to move an object in a circle.

10. The _____ describes the relationship between mass, distance, and gravitational force.

11. An object that orbits the earth is a _____.

Section 6.4

12. An object's _____ is the average position of all the particles that make up its mass.

13. You can balance an object on your finger if you support it at its _____.

Reviewing Concepts

Section 6.1

1. List the three ways to describe a displacement vector.

2. The directions north, south, east and west can be described using angles. List the angle for each of the four directions.

3. Explain how a vector diagram can be used to find an object's displacement.

4. A velocity vector tells you the object's _____ and _____ of motion.

5. State whether each of the following is a projectile.
    a. a diver who has jumped off a diving board
    b. a soccer ball flying toward the net
    c. a bird flying up toward its nest

6. What does it mean to say that the horizontal and vertical components of a projectile's velocity are independent of each other?

7. Is the horizontal velocity of a projectile constant? Is the vertical velocity of a projectile constant? Explain your answers.

8. Why does a projectile move in a curved path?

9. You kick a ball off the ground with a horizontal speed of 15 m/sec and a vertical speed of 19.6 m/sec. As it moves upward, its vertical speed _____ by _____ each second. It gets to its highest point _____ seconds after it is kicked. At the highest point, its vertical speed is _____ and its horizontal speed is _____. As it falls, its vertical speed _____ by _____ each second. It reaches the ground _____ seconds after it is kicked. Its horizontal speed is always _____.

10. At which angle should you kick a soccer ball if you want it to have the greatest range?

11. A ball kicked off the ground at an angle of 20 degrees and a ball kicked at an angle of _____ degrees have the same range.

Section 6.2

12. State whether each object is rotating or revolving.
    a. a satellite orbiting Earth
    b. a toy train moving on a circular track
    c. a fan blade

13. Which of the following units is appropriate for angular speed: rotations per second, meters per second, revolutions per minute.

14. How many degrees are in one revolution or rotation?

15. Two ants are sitting on a spinning record. One sits near the center and the other near the edge.
    a. How do their angular speeds compare?
    b. How do their linear speeds compare?

16. Rolling is a combination of _____ motion and _____ motion.

17. How far does the center of a wheel move in a line as the wheel rolls through one rotation?

Section 6.3

18. A force acts on a moving object. The force makes the object _____ if it acts in the same direction as the velocity. The force makes it _____ if it acts opposite the velocity. The force makes it _____ if it is perpendicular to the velocity.

19. A sports car moves around a sharp curve (small radius) at a speed of 50 mph. A four door family car moves around a wider curve (large radius) at the same speed. The cars have equal masses.
    a. Which car changes its direction more quickly?
    b. Which car has the greater acceleration?
    c. Which car has the greater centripetal force acting on it?
    d. What provides the centripetal force on each car?

20. A ball tied to a string is twirled around in a circle as shown. Copy the diagram and draw a vector showing the direction of the ball's velocity and the direction of the centripetal force on the ball at each of the three points.

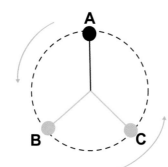

21. Explain how the centripetal force needed to move an object in a circle is related to its mass, speed, and the radius of the circle.

22. What is centrifugal force? Is it a real force?

23. What keeps the moon in orbit around the Earth?

24. Is there a gravitational force between you and your pencil? Do you notice this force? Explain.

25. You experience a gravitational force that attracts you to Earth. Does Earth also experience a force? Explain.

26. What is a satellite?

27. Do all satellites move in perfect circles?

Section 6.4

28. Explain how you can find the location of an object's center of mass.

29. What is the difference between the center of mass and the center of gravity?

30. Explain how you can find the location of an object's center of gravity.

31. Why is a tall SUV more likely than a car to roll over in an accident?

32. A force is needed to change an object's linear motion. What is needed to change its rotational motion?

33. Tightrope walkers often use long poles to help them balance. Explain why this makes sense.

34. Explain the relationship between velocity and centripetal force in creating circular motion.

Solving Problems

Section 6.1

1. Use a scaled drawing to find the displacement for each of the following. Then check your work with the Pythagorean theorem.
    a. an ant that walks 3 meters north and 3 meters east
    b. a cat who runs 6 meters west and 2 meters north
    c. a car that drives 8 km south and 6 km west
    d. a plane that flies 200 miles north, turns, and flies 200 miles south

2. Draw a vector to scale to represent each velocity. Specify your scale.°
    a. (20 m/sec, 60°)
    b. (40 mph, 150°)
    c. (500 km/h, 180°)

3. Calculate the speed of each velocity given in component form. Then draw the velocity vector to scale. State the scale you use.

   a. (5, 8) m/sec
   b. (60, 20) m/sec

4. You run straight off a high diving board at a speed of 6 m/sec. You hit the water 2 seconds later.

   a. How far did you travel horizontally during the 2 seconds?
   b. How far did you travel vertically during the 2 seconds?
   c. How fast were you moving horizontally when you hit the water?
   d. How fast were you moving vertically when you hit the water?

5. A monkey throws a banana horizontally from the top of a tree. The banana hits the ground 3 seconds later and lands 30 meters from the base of the tree.

   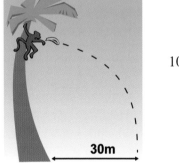

   a. How fast did the monkey throw the banana?
   b. How high is the tree?
   c. How fast was the banana moving horizontally as it hit the ground?
   d. How fast was the banana moving vertically as it hit the ground?
   e. What was the resultant velocity of the banana as it hit the ground?

6. A bowling ball rolls off a high cliff at 5 m/sec. Complete the chart that describes its motion during each second it is in the air.

Time (sec)	Horizontal velocity (m/s)	Vertical velocity (m/s)	Horizontal distance (m)	Vertical distance (m)
0	5	0	0	0
1				
2				
3				
4				

7. You kick a football off the ground with a horizontal velocity of 12 m/sec to the right and a vertical velocity of 29.4 m/sec upward. Draw a diagram showing the football's trajectory. Draw vectors showing its horizontal and vertical velocity at each second until it returns to the ground.

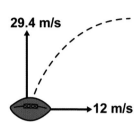

Section 6.2

8. Find the angular speed of a ferris wheel that makes 12 rotations during 3 minute ride. Express your answer in rotations per minute.

9. A wheel makes 10 rotations in 5 seconds.

   a. Find its angular speed in rotations per second.
   b. How many degrees does it turn during the 5 seconds?
   c. Find its angular speed in degrees per second.

10. You are sitting on a merry-go-round at a distance of 2 meters from its center. It spins 15 times in 3 minutes.

    a. What distance do you move as you make one revolution?
    b. What is your angular speed in RPM?
    c. What is your angular speed in degrees per minute?
    d. What is your linear speed in meters per minute?
    e. What is your linear speed in meters per second?

11. A car requires a centripetal force of 5,000 N to drive around a bend at 20 mph. What centripetal force is needed for it to drive around the bend at 40 mph? At 60 mph?

12. A 1000-kg car drives around a bend at 30 mph. A 2000-kg truck drives around the same bend at the same speed. How does the centripetal force on the car compare to the force on the truck?

13. What would happen to the force of gravity on you if you doubled your distance from the center of the Earth?

14. What would happen to the force of gravity on you if the Earth's mass suddenly doubled but the radius stayed the same?

15. Use Newton's law of universal gravitation to find the force of gravity between the Earth and a 60-kilogram person.

16. Use Newton's law of universal gravitation to find the force of gravity between the Earth and the Sun. Use the data inside the back cover of your book.

Section 6.3

17. Choose the point that is at the center of mass of each object.

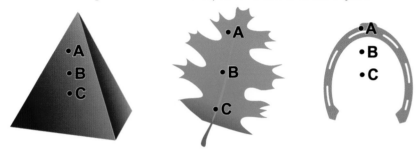

18. Which object(s) will topple? The center of gravity of each is marked.

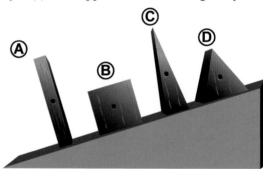

Applying Your Knowledge

Section 6.1

1. What is the mathematical equation for a parabola shaped like a projectile's trajectory? How is the equation for a parabola similar to the equations for projectile motion?

2. You want to throw a banana up to a monkey sitting in a tree. The banana is directed straight toward the monkey as you release it. While throwing it you make a sound that scares the monkey. He jumps down from the tree at the instant you let go of the banana. Will the monkey catch it as he falls through the air?

Section 6.2

3. Research to find out how the angular speeds of a music CDs and DVDs compare.

4. How are projectile motion and circular motion similar? How are they different?

Section 6.3

5. There are many satellites orbiting earth for communications, weather monitoring, navigation, and other purposes. Research one of the uses of satellites and prepare a poster summarizing your results.

6. A *geosynchronous* satellite makes one revolution around the Earth each day. If positioned above the equator, it is always over the same point on Earth. Geosynchronous satellites must be a distance of approximately 42,000 km from the center of the Earth (36,000 km above Earth's surface). Calculate the linear speed of a geosynchronous satellite in km/h.

7. The International Space Station is an Earth satellite. Research the history and purpose of this space station.

Section 6.4

8. The toy bird shown to the right can be easily balanced on a fingertip, and it sways side-to-side without falling if it is tapped. How do you think the bird balances this way?

UNIT 3

Matter and Energy

Temperature and

Pressure

Buoyancy......Density

Chapter 7

Temperature, Energy, and Matter

$$T_{Celsius} = \frac{5}{9}(T_{Fahrenheit} - 32)$$

$$T_{Fahrenheit} = \frac{9}{5}T_{Celsius} + 32$$

Have you ever imagined what it would be like to live in a atom-sized world? You may have seen movies where the characters are suddenly shrunk to the size of a flea or an even tinier animal. If you were that small, what would the matter around you look like? What if you were even smaller, say the size of an atom? In this world, even the air around you can be dangerous. Everywhere you looked, you would see atoms and molecules whizzing around at amazingly fast speeds and occasionally colliding with one another. Watch out! You might be hit by those particles!

If you were the size of an atom, you would notice that the particles that make up everything are in constant motion. In liquids, the particles slide over and around each other. In solids, the particles vibrate in place. In gases, the particles are moving around freely. Ordinary air would look like a crazy three-dimensional bumper-car ride where you are bombarded from all sides by giant beach balls. It will be helpful to imagine life as an atom as you study this chapter.

NASA photo

Key Questions

✓ How many atoms make up the thickness of a sheet of ordinary aluminum foil?

✓ Is it possible to melt a rock?

✓ Why does it take more energy to heat water than it does to heat steel or aluminum?

7.1 The Nature of Matter

Lying next to a tea cup, a sugar cube looks like a single piece of matter. But up close, you can tell it is made up of tiny, individual crystals of sugar fused together. Can those sugar crystals be broken into even smaller particles? What is the smallest particle of sugar that is still sugar?

Matter is made of tiny particles in constant motion

The idea of atoms
The idea that matter is made of tiny particles goes back to 430 BC. The Greek philosophers Democritus and Leucippus proposed that matter is made of tiny particles called *atoms*. For 2,300 years atoms were an idea that few believed. In 1803, John Dalton revived the idea of atoms, but lacked proof.

Brownian motion
In 1827, Robert Brown, a Scottish botanist, was looking through a microscope at tiny grains of pollen in water. He saw that the grains moved in an irregular, jerky way. After observing the same motion in tiny dust particles, he concluded that all tiny particles move in the same way. The irregular, jerky motion was named *Brownian motion* in Brown's honor.

Evidence for atoms
In 1905, Albert Einstein proposed that Brownian motion is caused by collisions between visible particles like pollen grains, and smaller, invisible particles. This was strong evidence that matter was indeed made of atoms.

A human-sized example
As a comparison, imagine throwing marbles at a car tire tube floating in the water. The impact of any single marble is much to small to make the tire tube move. However, if you throw enough marbles the tube will start moving slowly. The motion of the tire tube will appear smooth because the mass of a single marble is tiny compared to the mass of the tire tube (Figure 7.1).

Now imagine throwing marbles at a foam cup floating in the water. The cup's motion is not smooth at all. The motion is jerky, and the impact of individual marbles can be seen. The mass of the cup is not huge compared to the mass of a marble. A pollen grain suspended in water moves around in a jerky manner much like the foam cup. The irregular motion is caused by the impact of individual water molecules on the pollen grain. Like the cup, the mass of the pollen grain, while larger than a water molecule, is not *so* much larger that impacts are completely smoothed out.

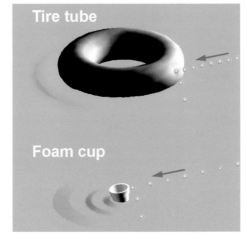

Tire tube

Foam cup

Figure 7.1: *Throwing marbles at a tire tube moves the tube smoothly. Throwing the same marbles at a foam cup moves the cup in a jerky way, like Brownian motion.*

Elements are the purest form of matter

Ancient Chinese ideas
In China, a collection of ancient texts compiled by Confucius (551-479 BC) discusses the basic "building blocks" of matter. Some of the writings in these texts were already a thousand years old when Confucius collected and preserved them in five volumes known as "The Five Classics." One volume contains a passage explaining that metal, wood, water, fire, and earth in different proportions make up all matter.

Ancient Indian ideas
In India, writings from the sixth century BC describe five elements — earth, water, fire, air, and ether — that make up the universe. The writings explain that all objects such as stones, gold, silver, and trees, are made up of the five elements. These elements can be rearranged in different proportions to make all of the other objects in the universe.

Ancient Greek ideas
The Greek philosopher Empedocles of Acragas (495-435 BC) also tried to answer questions about matter. He explained that everything we see is made up of four basic elements: fire, water, air, and earth. The different makeup of objects around us is due to differences in the ratio of these elements present in each object. Aristotle, another Greek philosopher, believed that Empedocles' explanation was the best way to understand why there are so many different types of matter.

Similar ideas about matter
While there are differences between the ancient Chinese, Indian, and Greek writings about matter, the similarities between these explanations is striking (Figure 7.2). Each culture concluded that everything we see is made of different proportions of a small number of basic building blocks, or *elements*. They also agreed that the diversity of matter on Earth is due to differences in the proportions of these elements everything contains.

What are elements?
An **element** is defined as a pure substance that cannot be broken down into simpler substances by physical or chemical means. For example, water is made from the elements hydrogen and oxygen. If you add energy, you can break water down into hydrogen and oxygen, but you cannot break the hydrogen and oxygen down into simpler substances (Figure 7.3). You will learn more about elements in chapter 9.

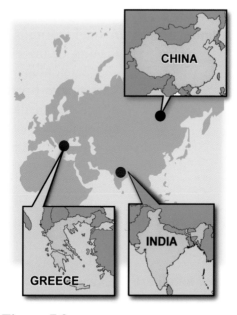

Figure 7.2: *Ancient cultures had similar ideas about the composition of matter.*

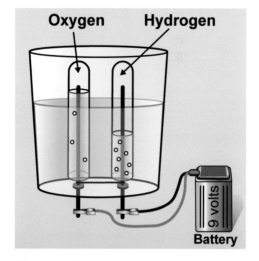

Figure 7.3: *You can break water down into oxygen and hydrogen by adding energy.*

Atoms are the smallest particles that make up elements

Defining atoms A single **atom** is the smallest particle of an element that retains the chemical identity of the element. For example, you can keep cutting a piece of the element gold into smaller and smaller pieces until you cannot cut it any more. That smallest particle you can divide it into is one atom. A single atom of gold is the smallest piece of gold you can have. If you split the atom, it will no longer be gold.

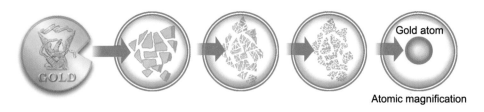

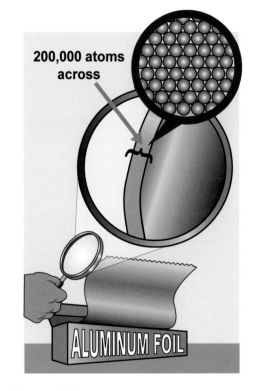

200,000 atoms across

How small are atoms? A single atom has a diameter of about 10^{-10} meters. This means that you can fit 10,000,000,000 (10^{10}) atoms side-by-side in a one-meter length. You may think a sheet of aluminum foil is thin, but it is actually more than 200,000 atoms thick (Figure 7.4).

Atoms of an element are similar to each other Each element has a unique type of atom. Carbon atoms are different from sodium atoms, sodium atoms from oxygen atoms. All atoms of a given element are similar to each other. If you could examine a million atoms of carbon you would find them all to be similar. You will find much more detail about atoms in chapter 9.

Figure 7.4: *A thin sheet of aluminum foil is 200,000 atoms thick.*

Sodium atom   Carbon atom   Aluminum atom   Oxygen atom

Compounds contain two or more elements

Compounds Sometimes elements are found in their pure form, but more often they are combined with other elements. Most substances contain several elements combined together. A **compound** is a substance that contains two or more different elements chemically joined and that has the same composition throughout. For example, water is a compound that is made from the elements hydrogen and oxygen. Figure 7.5 shows some familiar compounds.

Molecules If you could magnify a sample of pure water so you could see its atoms, you would notice that the hydrogen and oxygen atoms are joined together in groups of two hydrogen atoms to one oxygen atom. These groups are called molecules. A **molecule** is a group of two or more atoms joined together by *chemical bonds*. A compound is made up of only one type of molecule. Some compounds, like table salt (sodium chloride), are made of equal combinations of different atoms instead of individual molecules (Figure 7.6).

Mixtures Most of the things you see and use in everyday life are mixtures. A **mixture** contains more than one kind of atom, molecule, or compound. Cola is a mixture that contains water, carbon dioxide, corn syrup, caramel color, phosphoric acid, natural flavors, and caffeine.

COMPOUNDS contain more than one type of atom joined together

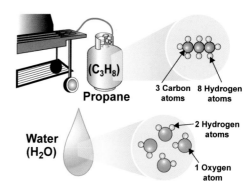

Figure 7.5: *Examples of compounds.*

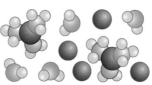

Element	**Compound**	**Mixture**
One single kind of atom	One type of molecule	Combination of different compounds and/or elements

Salt crystal

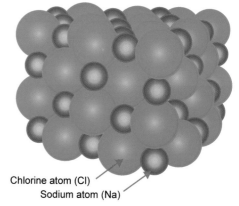

Chlorine atom (Cl)
Sodium atom (Na)

Figure 7.6: *Table salt is a compound made of equal numbers of sodium and chlorine atoms.*

7.1 Section Review

1. Explain why Brownian motion provides evidence for the existence of atoms and molecules.

2. Describe the difference between elements, compounds, and mixtures.

3. Give an example of each: element, compound, and mixture.

7.2 Temperature and the Phases of Matter

You will notice that on a hot day, a glass of iced tea (or any cold beverage) has water on the outside. The water does not come from inside the glass. The ice and cold liquid inside make the outside of the glass cold, too. This "outside" cold temperature causes water vapor in the air — a *gas,* remember — to condense into *liquid* water on the exterior of the glass. What is happening at the atomic level? Why can water take the form of solid, liquid, or gas?

Measuring temperature

Fahrenheit   There are two commonly used temperature scales. On the **Fahrenheit scale**, water freezes at 32 degrees and boils at 212 degrees (Figure 7.7). There are 180 Fahrenheit degrees between the freezing point and the boiling point of water. Temperature in the United States is commonly measured in Fahrenheit. For example, 72°F is a comfortable room temperature.

Celsius   The **Celsius scale** divides the difference between the freezing and boiling points of water into 100 degrees (instead of 180). Water freezes at 0°C and boils at 100°C. Most science and engineering temperature measurements are in Celsius because 0 and 100 are easier to remember than 32 and 212. Most other countries use the Celsius scale for all descriptions of temperature, including daily weather reports.

Converting between the scales   A weather report that says 21°C in London, England, predicts a pleasant day, suitable for shorts and a T-shirt. A weather report predicting 21°F in Minneapolis, Minnesota, means a heavy winter coat, gloves, and a hat. Because the United States is one of few countries that still use the Fahrenheit scale, it is useful to know how to convert between the two scales.

> ### CONVERTING BETWEEN FAHRENHEIT AND CELSIUS
>
> $$T_{Fahrenheit} = \frac{9}{5} T_{Celsius} + 32 \qquad T_{Celsius} = \frac{5}{9}(T_{Fahrenheit} - 32)$$

Vocabulary

Fahrenheit scale, Celsius scale, thermometer, solid, liquid, gas, intermolecular forces, evaporation, absolute zero, Kelvin, plasma

Objectives

✓ Convert between temperature scales.

✓ Explain the relationship between temperature and the movement of particles in a system.

✓ Describe the relationship between temperature and states of matter.

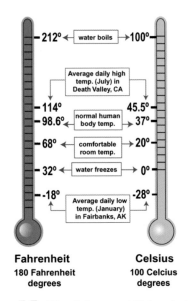

Figure 7.7: *The Celsius and Fahrenheit temperature scales.*

Thermometers

Thermometers Humans can sense warmth or cold, but not very accurately. Accurate measurement of temperature requires a **thermometer,** an instrument that measures temperature. The common alcohol thermometer uses the expansion of colored liquid alcohol as a gauge. As the temperature increases, the alcohol expands and rises up a long, thin tube. You tell the temperature by the height the alcohol rises. A small change in volume makes a large change in the height the alcohol rises up the thin tube (Figure 7.8).

How thermometers work There are many ways to make a thermometer. All thermometers are based on a physical property (such as color or volume) that changes with temperature. Some electronic thermometers sense temperature by measuring the resistance of a thermistor. A *thermistor* is a device that changes its electrical resistance as the temperature changes. A digital thermometer uses a thermistor to measure temperature. There are some chemicals that change color at different temperatures. These are used for aquarium "sticker" thermometers that are placed on the outside of the tank.

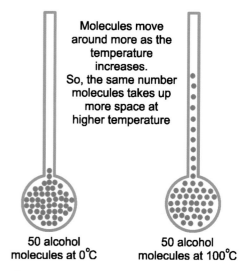

Molecules move around more as the temperature increases. So, the same number molecules takes up more space at higher temperature

50 alcohol molecules at 0°C

50 alcohol molecules at 100°C

Figure 7.8: *The expansion of the liquid in an alcohol thermometer is proportional to the increase in temperature.*

Converting between temperature scales

A friend in Paris sends you a recipe for a cake. The French recipe says to bake the cake at a temperature of 200°C for 45 minutes. At what temperature should you set your oven, which uses the Fahrenheit scale?

1. Looking for: You are asked for the temperature in degrees Fahrenheit.

2. Given: You are given the temperature in degrees Celsius.

3. Relationships: Use the conversion formula: $T_F = \frac{9}{5}T_C + 32$.

4. Solution: $T_F = (\frac{9}{5})(200) + 32 = 392\ °F.$

Your turn...

a. You are planning a trip to Iceland this summer. You find out that the average July temperature in Iceland is 11.2°C. What is the average July temperature in degrees Fahrenheit? **Answer:** 52.2°F

b. You are doing a science experiment with a Fahrenheit thermometer. Your data must be in degrees Celsius. If you measure a temperature of 125°F, what is this temperature in degrees Celsius? **Answer:** 51.7°C

What temperature really is

Temperature and energy Temperature is a measure of the kinetic energy of individual atoms. Imagine you had a microscope powerful enough to see individual atoms in a solid at room temperature. You would see that the atoms are in constant motion. The atoms in a solid material act like they are connected by springs (Figure 7.9). Each atom is free to move a small amount. When the temperature goes up, the energy of motion increases and the atoms jiggle around more vigorously.

Average motion If you throw a rock, the rock gets more kinetic energy, but the temperature of the rock does *not* go up. How can temperature measure kinetic energy then? We already know the relationship between motion and kinetic energy for a single object (or atom). For a collection of atoms, the situation is different. The kinetic energy of a collection has two parts. The kinetic energy you know comes from the average motion of the whole collection, like the motion of the whole rock. The kinetic energy that comes from the average motion of *all the atoms together* is *not* what temperature measures.

Random motion Each atom in the rock is also jiggling back and forth independently of the other atoms in the rock. This jiggling motion is *random*. Random motion is motion that is scattered equally in all directions. On average, there are as many atoms moving one way as there are moving the opposite way.

Temperature and random motion Each atom in the rock has kinetic energy from its random motion, as well as from the average motion of the whole rock. *Temperature measures the kinetic energy in just the random motion*. Temperature is not affected by any kinetic energy associated with average motion. That is why throwing a rock does not make it hotter (Figure 7.10). When you heat a rock with a torch, each atom jiggles back and forth with more energy but the whole rock stays in the same place.

Melting and boiling The higher the temperature, the higher the random kinetic energy of each atom. Hot atoms move faster than cold atoms. If you heat a rock with a torch long enough, the atoms get so much energy they start to break away from each other. The rock *melts*. If you keep heating even more the liquid rock will start to boil. In *boiling* some atoms have so much energy they leave the rock altogether and fly off into the atmosphere.

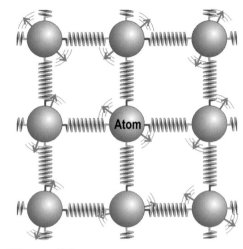

Figure 7.9: *Atoms in a solid are connected by bonds that act like springs. The atoms are never still, but are always jiggling back and forth in random directions around their positions.*

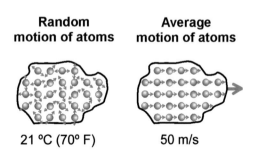

Random motion of atoms	Average motion of atoms
21 °C (70° F)	50 m/s

Figure 7.10: *A collection of atoms can have both average motion and random motion. That is why a thrown rock has both a velocity and a temperature.*

The phases of matter

Solid, liquid, and gas
Most of the matter you find around you is in one of three phases: solid, liquid, or gas. A **solid** holds its shape and does not flow. The molecules in a solid vibrate in place, but on average, don't move far from their places. A **liquid** holds its *volume*, but does not hold its shape — it flows. The molecules in a liquid are about as close together as they are in a solid, but have enough energy to exchange positions with their neighbors. Liquids flow because the molecules can move around. A **gas** flows like a liquid, but can also expand or contract to fill a container. A gas does not hold its volume. The molecules in a gas have enough energy to completely break away from each other and are much farther apart than molecules in a liquid or solid.

Intermolecular forces
When they are close together, molecules are attracted through *intermolecular forces*. These **intermolecular forces** have different strengths for different molecules. The strength of the intermolecular forces determines whether matter exists as a solid, liquid, or gas at any given temperature.

Temperature vs. intermolecular forces
Within all matter there is a constant competition between temperature and intermolecular forces. The kinetic energy from temperature tends to push molecules apart. When temperature wins the competition, molecules fly apart and you have a gas. The intermolecular forces tend to bring molecules together. When intermolecular forces win the competition, molecules clump tightly together and you have a solid. Liquid is somewhere in the middle. Molecules in a liquid are not stuck firmly together, but they cannot escape and fly away either.

Strength of intermolecular forces
Iron is a solid at room temperature. Water is a liquid at room temperature. This tells you that the intermolecular forces between iron atoms are stronger than those between water molecules. In fact, iron is used for building things because it so strong. The strength of solid iron is another effect of the strong intermolecular forces between iron atoms.

Temperature
As the temperature changes, the balance between temperature and intermolecular forces changes. At temperatures below 0°C, the intermolecular forces in water are strong enough to overcome temperature and water becomes solid (ice).

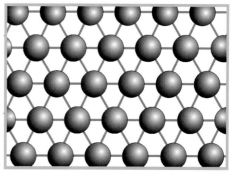

Solid

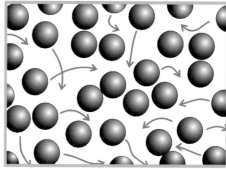

Liquid

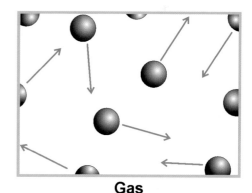

Gas

Figure 7.11: *Molecules (or atoms) in the solid, liquid, and gas phases.*

Changing phase

Melting point The *melting point* is the temperature at which a substance changes from a solid to a liquid. Different substances have different melting points. This is because the intermolecular forces between particles in each substance vary in their strength. Stronger intermolecular forces require more energy to break. Water melts at 0°C. Iron melts at a much higher temperature, about 1,500°C. The difference in melting points tells us that the forces between iron atoms are stronger than the forces between water molecules.

Boiling When enough energy is added, the intermolecular forces are completely pulled apart and the liquid becomes a gas. *Boiling* takes place within the liquid as bubbles of gas particles form and rise to the surface.

Changes in state require energy It takes energy to break the bonds created by intermolecular forces. This explains a peculiar thing that happens when you heat an ice cube. As you add heat energy, the temperature increases. Once it reaches 0°C, *the temperature stops increasing* as ice starts to melt and form liquid water. As you add more heat energy, more ice becomes liquid but the temperature stays the same. This is because the energy you are adding is being used to break the intermolecular forces and change solid into liquid. Once all the ice has become liquid, the temperature starts to rise again as more energy is added. The graph below shows the temperature in an experiment. When heat energy is added or subtracted from matter, either the temperature changes, or the phase changes, but usually not both at the same time.

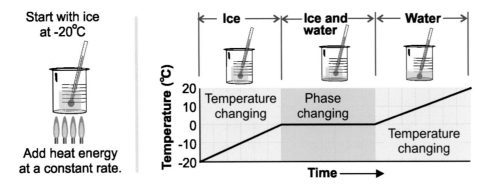

Evaporation

If you leave a pan of water in the room, eventually it drys out. How does this work? **Evaporation** occurs when molecules go from liquid to gas at temperatures below the boiling point. Evaporation happens because temperature measures the *average* random kinetic energy of molecules. Some have energy above the average and some below the average. Some of the highest energy molecules have enough energy to break bonds with their neighbors and become a gas if they are near the surface. Molecules with higher than average energy are the source of evaporation.

Evaporation takes energy away from a liquid. The molecules that escape are the ones with the most energy. The average energy of the molecules left behind is lowered. Evaporation cools the surface of a liquid because the fastest molecules escape and carry energy away. That is how your body cools off on a hot day. The evaporation of sweat from your skin cools your body.

Absolute zero

Absolute zero   There is a limit to how cold matter can get. As the temperature is reduced molecules move more and more slowly. When the temperature gets down to **absolute zero**, molecules have the lowest energy they can have and the temperature cannot get any lower. You can think of absolute zero as the temperature where molecules are completely frozen, like ice, with no motion. Technically, molecules never become absolutely motionless, but the kinetic energy is so small it might as well be truly zero. Absolute zero occurs at minus 273°C (-459°F). You cannot have a temperature lower than absolute zero.

The Kelvin scale   The **Kelvin** temperature scale is useful for many scientific calculations because it starts at absolute zero. For example, the pressure in a gas depends on how fast the atoms are moving. The Kelvin scale is used because it measures the actual energy of atoms. A temperature in Celsius measures only the *relative* energy, relative to zero Celsius.

Converting to Kelvin   The Kelvin (K) unit of temperature is the same size as the Celsius unit. Add 273 to the temperature in Celsius to get the temperature in Kelvins. For example, a temperature of 21°C is equal to 294 K (21 + 273).

High temperatures   Temperature can be raised almost indefinitely. As the temperature increases, exotic forms of matter appear. For example, at 10,000 °C atoms start to come apart and become a plasma. In a plasma the atoms themselves are broken apart into separate positive ions and negative electrons. Plasma conducts electricity and is formed in lightning and inside stars.

Plasma: A fourth state of matter

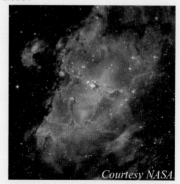

Courtesy NASA

At temperatures greater than 10,000 °C the atoms in a gas start to break apart. In the **plasma** state, matter becomes ionized as electrons are broken loose from atoms. Because the electrons are free to move independently, plasma can conduct electricity. Lightning is a good example of plasma, and the sun is another. In fact, most of the universe is plasma, including the Eagle nebula in the picture.

7.2 Section Review

1. A comfortable room temperature is 20 °C. What is this temperature in degrees Fahrenheit?

2. In which system are the molecules moving faster, a cold glass of tea or a hot cup of tea?

3. Describe what happens at the atomic level during melting.

4. Explain why particles in a gas are free to move far away from each other.

7.3 What Is Heat?

To change the temperature of a system you must add or subtract energy. For example, when it's cold outside, you turn up the *heat* in your house or apartment and the temperature goes up. You know that adding heat increases the temperature, but have you ever thought about exactly what "heat" is? What does "heat" have to do with the temperature?

Heat, temperature, and thermal energy

Thermal energy When you heat a pot of soup on a electric stove, *electrical energy* is converted into *thermal energy*. Thermal energy is related to temperature. Temperature measures the random kinetic energy of a single molecule or atom. **Thermal energy** is the *sum* of all the kinetic energy of the atoms or molecules added up together.

Thermal energy depends on mass and temperature The amount of thermal energy depends on the temperature and also on the *amount* of matter you have. Think about heating up two pots of water. One pot contains 1,000 grams of water and the other contains 2,000 grams of water. Both pots are heated to the same final temperature (Figure 7.12). Which takes more energy? Or, do both require the same amount of energy? The pot holding 2,000 grams of water takes twice as much energy as the pot with 1,000 grams, even though both start and finish at the same temperature. The two pots illustrate the difference between temperature and thermal energy. Thermal energy includes the energy of all the atoms in a sample of matter, and therefore depends on mass *and* temperature.

What is heat? What happens when you hold a chocolate bar in your hand? Thermal energy flows from your hand to the chocolate and it begins to melt. We call this flow of thermal energy **heat**. Heat is really just another word for thermal energy that is moving. In the scientific sense, heat flows any time there is a difference in temperature. Heat flows naturally from the warmer object (higher energy) to the cooler one (lower energy). In the case of the melting chocolate bar, the thermal energy lost by your hand is equal to the thermal energy gained by the chocolate bar.

Vocabulary

thermal energy, heat, calorie, specific heat

Objectives

✓ Explain the difference between temperature and thermal energy.
✓ Define heat.
✓ Calculate the heat required to raise the temperature of a material.

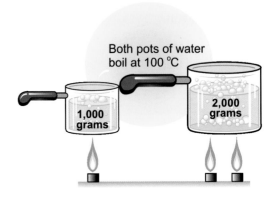

Both pots of water boil at 100 °C

1,000 grams

2,000 grams

Figure 7.12: *It takes twice as much energy to heat a 2,000-gram mass of water compared to a 1,000-gram mass.*

Units of heat and thermal energy

The joule There are three different units that are commonly used for heat and thermal energy. This is because people did not realize heat was energy for a long time. The metric unit for measuring heat is the *joule*. This is the same joule used to measure all forms of energy, not just heat. A joule is a small amount of heat. The average hair dryer puts out 1,200 joules of heat every second!

The calorie The **calorie** is defined as the quantity of heat needed to increase the temperature of 1 gram of water by 1 degree Celsius. One calorie is a little more than 4 joules (Figure 7.13). You may have noticed that most food packages list "Calories per serving." The unit used for measuring energy content of the food we eat is the kilocalorie, which equals 1,000 calories. The kilocalorie is often written as Calorie (with a capital C). If a candy bar contains 210 Calories, it contains 210,000 calories!

The British thermal unit Still another unit of heat energy you may encounter is the *British thermal unit*, or Btu. The Btu is often used to measure the heat produced by heating systems or heat removed by air-conditioning systems. A Btu is the quantity of heat it takes to increase the temperature of 1 pound of water by 1 degree Fahrenheit. One Btu is a little more than 1,000 joules. Figure 7.13 shows the conversion factors for units of heat.

Unit	Is Equal To
1 calorie	4.186 joules
1 kilocalorie	1,000 calories
1 Btu	1055 joules
1 Btu	252 calories

Figure 7.13: *Conversion table for units of heat.*

Heat and Work

Work can be done whenever heat flows from a higher temperature to a lower temperature. Many human inventions use heat to do work. The engine in your car uses the heat released by the burning of gasoline. Since heat flows from hot to cold, to get output work you need to maintain a temperature difference. In a car engine, the high temperature is inside the engine and comes from the burning gasoline. The low temperature is the air around the car. The output work produced by the engine is extracted from the flow of heat. Only a fraction of the heat is converted to work, and that is why a running car gives off so much heat through the radiator and exhaust.

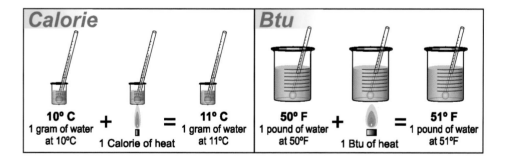

Why so many units? The calorie and Btu were being used to measure heat well before scientists knew what heat really was. They are still used because people give up familiar ways very slowly, even 100 years after heat was shown to be energy!

Specific heat

Temperature and mass

If you add heat to an object, how much will its temperature increase? It depends in part on the mass of the object. If you double the mass of the object you are going to heat, you need twice as much energy to increase the temperature.

Temperature and type of material

The amount of temperature increase also depends on the kind of material you are heating. It takes different amounts of energy to raise the temperature of different materials. You need to add 4,184 joules of heat to one kilogram of water to raise the temperature by 1°C. (Figure 7.14). You only need to add 470 joules to raise the temperature of a kilogram of steel by 1°C. It takes 9 times more energy to raise the temperature of water by 1°C than it does to raise the temperature of the same mass of steel by 1°C. Knowing how materials resist temperature change is important. For example, if you know that an apple pie's filling is much more resistant to temperature change than its crust, you might test the filling temperature before taking a bite!

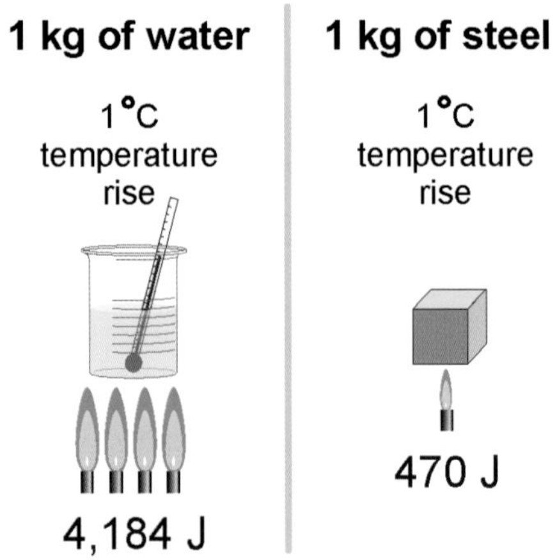

Specific heat

The **specific heat** is a property of a substance that tells us how much heat is needed to raise the temperature of one kilogram of a material by one degree Celsius. A large specific heat means you have to put in a lot of energy for each degree increase in temperature. Specific heat is measured in joules per kilogram per degree Celsius (joule/kg°C).

The specific heat is the amount of energy that will raise the temperature of one kilogram by one degree Celsius.

Uses for specific heat

Knowing the specific heat tells you how quickly the temperature of a material will change as it gains or loses energy. If the specific heat is *low* (like steel), then temperature will change relatively quickly because each degree of change takes less energy. If the specific heat is *high* (like water), then the temperature will change relatively slowly because each degree of change takes more energy. Hot apple pie filling stays hot for a long time because it is mostly water, and therefore has a large specific heat. Pie crust has a much lower specific heat and cools much more rapidly.

Figure 7.14: *It takes 4,184 joules to raise the temperature of 1 kg of water by 1 °C. The same temperature rise takes only 470 joules for a kilogram of steel.*

Calculating energy changes from heat

How could you figure out how much energy it would take to heat a swimming pool or boil a liter of water? The heat equation below tells you how much energy (E) it takes to change the temperature (T) of a mass (m) of a substance with a specific heat value (C_p). Figure 7.15 shows the specific heat values for some common materials.

Material	Specific heat (J/kg°C)
water	4,184
oil	1,900
wood	1,800
aluminum	900
concrete	880
glass	800
steel	470
silver	235
gold	129

HEAT EQUATION

Mass (kg) — Specific heat ($\frac{\text{joule}}{\text{kg °C}}$)

Heat energy (joules) $\longrightarrow E = mC_p (T_2 - T_1)$

Change in temperature (°C)

Figure 7.15: *Specific heat values of some common materials.*

Calculate the heat required to reach a temperature

How much heat is needed to raise the temperature of a 250-liter hot tub from 20°C to 40°C? The specific heat of water is 4,184 J/kg°C. (HINT: 1 liter of water has a mass of 1 kilogram.)

1. Looking for: You are looking for the amount of heat energy needed in joules.

2. Given: You are given the volume in liters, temperature change in °C, and specific heat of water in J/kg°C. You are also given a conversion factor for volume to mass of water.

3. Relationships: $E = mC_p(T_2 - T_1)$

4. Solution: $E = (250\,\text{L} \times 1\,\text{kg/L}) \times 4{,}184\ \text{J/kg°C}\ (40°C - 20°C) = 20{,}920{,}000$ joules.

Your turn...

a. How much heat energy is needed to raise the temperature of 2.0 kilograms of concrete from 10°C to 30°C? The specific heat of concrete is 880 J/kg°C. **Answer:** 35,200 joules

b. How much heat energy is needed to raise the temperature of 5.0 grams of gold from 20°C to 200°C? The specific heat of gold is 129 J/kg°C. **Answer:** 116.1 joules

Why is specific heat different for different materials?

Why specific heat varies In general, materials made up of heavy atoms or molecules have low specific heat compared with materials made up of lighter ones. This is because temperature measures the average kinetic energy *per particle*. Heavy particles mean fewer per kilogram. Energy that is divided between fewer particles means more energy per particle, and therefore more temperature change.

An example: silver and aluminum Suppose you add four joules of energy to a kilogram of silver and four joules to a kilogram of aluminum. Silver's specific heat is 235 J/kg°C and four joules is enough to raise the temperature of the silver by 17°C. Aluminum's specific heat is 900 J/kg°C, and four joules only raises the temperature of the aluminum by 4.4°C. The silver has fewer atoms than the aluminum because silver atoms are heavier than aluminum atoms. When energy is added, each atom of silver gets more energy than each atom of aluminum because there are fewer silver atoms in a kilogram. Because the energy per atom is greater, the temperature increase in the silver is also greater.

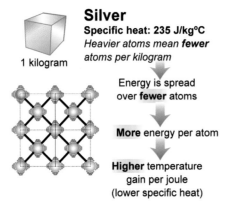

Silver
Specific heat: 235 J/kg°C
*Heavier atoms mean **fewer** atoms per kilogram*

1 kilogram

Energy is spread over **fewer** atoms

More energy per atom

Higher temperature gain per joule
(lower specific heat)

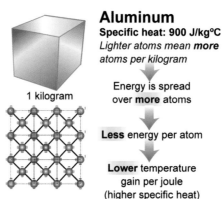

Aluminum
Specific heat: 900 J/kg°C
*Lighter atoms mean **more** atoms per kilogram*

1 kilogram

Energy is spread over **more** atoms

Less energy per atom

Lower temperature gain per joule
(higher specific heat)

The specific heat of water

Water has a higher specific heat than many other common materials. Its specific heat is more than four times greater than the specific heat of rocks and soil. The high specific heat of water is very important to our planet. Water covers about 75 percent of Earth's surface. One of the fundamental reasons our planet is habitable is that the huge amount of water on it helps regulate the temperature. Land, because it has a low specific heat, experiences large changes in temperature when it absorbs heat from the sun. Water tends to have smaller changes in temperature when it absorbs the same amount of heat. During the day, oceans help keep Earth cool, while at night, they keep Earth warm by slowing the rate at which heat is emitted back into space.

7.3 Section Review

1. What is the difference between temperature and thermal energy?

2. What conditions are necessary for heat to flow?

3. How much heat energy is required to raise the temperature of 20 kilograms of water from 0°C to 35°C?

7.4 Heat Transfer

Thermal energy flows from a material at a higher temperature to a material at a lower temperature. This process is called *heat transfer*. How is heat transferred from material to material, or from place to place? It turns out there are three ways heat flows. In this section, you will learn about *heat conduction*, *convection*, and *thermal radiation*.

Heat conduction

What is conduction? **Heat conduction** is the transfer of heat by the direct contact of particles of matter. If you have ever held a warm mug of hot cocoa, you have experienced conduction. Heat is transferred from the mug to your hand. Conduction only occurs between two materials at different temperatures and when they are touching each other. In conduction, heat can also be transferred *through* materials. If you stir hot cocoa with a metal spoon, heat is transferred *from* the cocoa, *through* the spoon, and *to* your hand.

> *Conduction is the transfer of heat by the direct contact of particles of matter.*

How does conduction work? Imagine placing a cold spoon into a mug of hot cocoa (Figure 7.16). The molecules in the cocoa have a higher average kinetic energy than those of the spoon. The molecules in the spoon exchange energy with the molecules in the cocoa through collisions. The molecules within the spoon itself spread the energy up the stem of the spoon through the intermolecular forces between them. Conduction works through both collisions and also through intermolecular forces between molecules.

Thermal equilibrium As collisions continue, the molecules of the hotter material (the cocoa) lose energy and the molecules of the cooler material (the spoon) gain energy. The kinetic energy of the hotter material is transferred, one collision at a time, to the cooler material. Eventually, both materials are at the same temperature. When this happens, they are in *thermal equilibrium*. Thermal equilibrium occurs when two bodies have the same temperature. No heat flows in thermal equilibrium because the temperatures are the same.

Flow of heat energy

Figure 7.16: *Heat flows by conduction from the hot cocoa into and up the spoon.*

Thermal conductors and insulators

Which state of matter conducts best?

Conduction can happen in solids, liquids, and gases. Solids make the best conductors because their particles are packed closely together. Because the particles in a gas are spread so far apart, relatively few collisions occur, making air, for instance, a poor conductor of heat. This explains why many materials used to keep things warm, such as fiberglass insulation and down jackets, contain air pockets (Figure 7.17).

Thermal conductors and insulators

Materials that conduct heat easily are called **thermal conductors** and those that conduct heat poorly are called **thermal insulators**. For example, metal is a thermal conductor, and a foam cup is a thermal insulator. The words *conductor* and *insulator* are also used to describe a material's ability to conduct electrical current. In general, good electrical conductors like silver, copper, gold, and aluminum are also good thermal conductors.

Figure 7.17: *Because air is a poor conductor of heat, a down jacket keeps you warm in the cold of winter.*

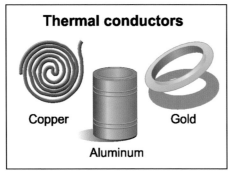

Thermal conductors

Copper
Aluminum
Gold

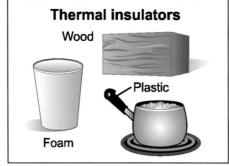

Thermal insulators

Wood
Foam
Plastic

Heat conduction cannot occur through a vacuum

Conduction happens only if there are particles available to collide with one another. For this reason, heat transfer by conduction cannot occur in the vacuum of space. One way to create an excellent thermal insulator on Earth is to make a vacuum. A thermos bottle keeps liquids hot for hours using a vacuum. A thermos is a container consisting of a bottle surrounded by a slightly larger bottle. Air molecules have been removed from the space between the bottles to create a vacuum. This prevents heat transfer by conduction. A small amount of heat is conducted through the cap and the glass (where the two walls meet), so eventually the contents will cool, only much slower than they would otherwise (Figure 7.18).

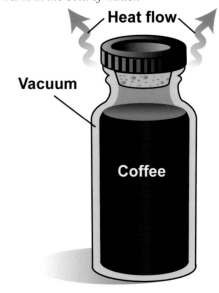

Heat flow

Vacuum

Coffee

Figure 7.18: *A thermos bottle uses a vacuum to prevent heat transfer by conduction and convection.*

Convection

What is convection? Have you ever watched water boil in a pot? Bubbles form on the bottom and rise to the top. Hot water near the bottom of the pan circulates up, forcing cooler water near the surface to sink. This circulation carries heat through the water (Figure 7.19). This heat transfer process is called **convection**. Convection is the transfer of heat through the motion of fluids such as air and water.

Natural convection Fluids expand when they heat up. Since expansion increases the volume, but not the mass, a warm fluid has a lower mass-to-volume ratio (called *density*) than the surrounding cooler fluid. In a container, warmer fluid floats to the top and cooler fluid sinks to the bottom. This is called *natural convection*.

Forced convection In many houses a boiler heats water and then pumps circulate the water to rooms. Since the heat is being carried by a moving fluid, this is another example of convection. However, since the fluid is *forced* to flow by the pumps, this is called forced convection.

Both natural and forced convection often occur at the same time. Forced convection transfers heat to a hot radiator. The heat from the hot radiator then warms the room air by natural convection. The warmer air rises and cooler air from the far side of the room replaces it. Then the cooler air is warmed and rises. The circulation distributes heat throughout the room.

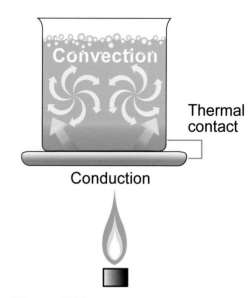

Figure 7.19: *Convection currents in water. The hot water at the bottom of the pot rises to the top and replaces the cold water.*

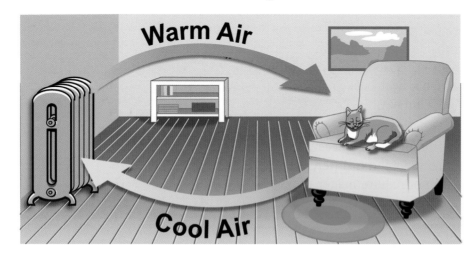

Thermal radiation

Definition of thermal radiation
If you stand in the sun on a cold, calm day, you will feel warmth from the sun. Heat from the sun is transferred to Earth by thermal radiation. **Thermal radiation** is electromagnetic waves (including light) produced by objects because of their temperature. All objects with a temperature above absolute zero (-273 °C or -459 °F) emit thermal radiation. To *emit* means to give off.

Thermal radiation is heat transfer in the form of electromagnetic waves, including light.

Thermal radiation comes from atoms
Thermal radiation comes from the thermal energy of atoms. The energy in thermal radiation increases with higher temperatures because the thermal energy of atoms increases with temperature (Figure 7.20). Because the sun is extremely hot, its atoms emit lots of thermal radiation.

Objects emit and absorb radiation
Thermal radiation is also *absorbed* by objects. An object constantly receives thermal radiation from everything else in its environment. Otherwise all objects would eventually cool down to absolute zero by radiating their energy away. The temperature of an object rises if more radiation is absorbed. The temperature falls if more radiation is given off. The temperature adjusts until there is a balance between radiation absorbed and radiation emitted.

Some surfaces absorb more energy than others
The amount of thermal radiation absorbed depends on the surface of a material. Black surfaces absorb almost all the thermal radiation that falls on them. For example, black asphalt pavement gets very hot in the summer sun because it effectively absorbs thermal radiation. A silver mirror surface reflects most thermal radiation, absorbing very little (Figure 7.21). A mirrored screen reflects the sun's heat back out your car window, helping your parked car stay cooler on a hot day.

Radiation can travel through space
Thermal radiation can travel through the vacuum of space. Conduction and convection cannot carry heat through space because both processes require matter to transfer heat. Thermal radiation is different because it is carried by electromagnetic waves that do not require matter to provide a path for heat flow. Thermal radiation also travels fast — at the speed of light.

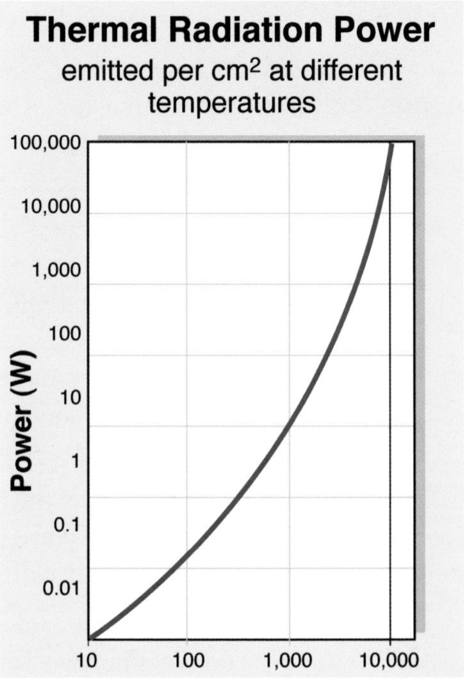

Thermal Radiation Power
emitted per cm² at different temperatures

Figure 7.20: *The higher the temperature of an object, the more thermal radiation it emits.*

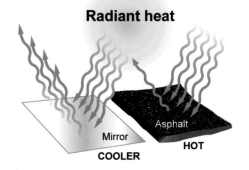

Figure 7.21: *Dark surfaces absorb most of the thermal radiation they receive. Silver or mirrored surfaces reflect most of the thermal radiation they receive.*

The rate of heat transfer

The cause of heat transfer In nature, heat transfer *always* occurs from hot to cold until thermal equilibrium is reached. The rate of heat transfer is proportional to the difference in temperature. If the temperature difference is large, heat flows faster than when the temperature difference is small.

Heat transfer in living things Heat flow is necessary for life. Biological processes release energy. Your body regulates its temperature through the constant flow of heat. The inside of your body averages 98.6°F. Humans are most comfortable when the air temperature is about 75°F because the rate of heat flow out of the body matches the rate at which the body generates heat internally. If the air is 50°F, you get cold because heat flows too rapidly from your skin to the air. If the air is 100°F, you feel hot partly because heat flows from the air to your body and partly because your body cannot get rid of its internal heat fast enough (Figure 7.22).

Heat transfer is everywhere All three forms of heat transfer are usually working at the same time to transfer energy from warmer objects to cooler objects. Heat flow continues as long as there is a temperature difference. If you look around you, you can see heat transfer virtually everywhere, between air and objects, between objects, and even between you and the environment!

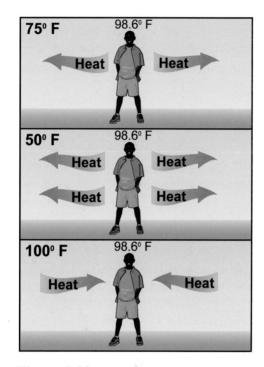

Figure 7.22: *Heat flow depends on temperature differences.*

7.4 Section Review

1. Name one example of heat transfer through conduction.
2. What is the primary type of heat transfer that occurs between a hot and cold fluid when they are mixed together?
3. Which object would you expect to emit more thermal radiation, a lamp that is turned on, or a rock at room temperature. Explain your answer.
4. In which direction will heat flow between an ice cube and the air on the room? Explain your answer.

Extraordinary Materials

Materials scientists spend their time learning about the properties of different materials, and also designing, creating, or discovering new materials to meet the demands of rapidly changing industries. Many materials you may be familiar with were discovered accidentally, while others were created in a laboratory with a particular application in mind.

Vulcanized Rubber

In the mid-1800's, rubber was used as it was found in nature - a form that becomes sticky when exposed to heat and cracks when frozen. Many inventors sought to discover a more durable form of rubber, knowing it could be used in a variety of products.

Perhaps none tried as hard as Charles Goodyear. He only discovered the secret to improving the properties of rubber after years of research and poverty. Though many historians consider his discovery an accident (an experimental rubber mixture he spilled on a hot stove turned out to be very durable), it was his attention to detail that made him realize that burned rubber was actually the substance he was looking for.

Goodyear's experimental mixture contained sulphur, and exposing the mixture to heat caused a chemical change. Natural rubber is comprised of many long molecules. Heating it in the presence of sulphur causes these molecules to bond together and prevents it from breaking down when exposed to hot or cold temperatures.

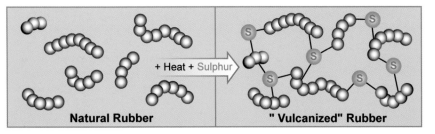

Natural Rubber   + Heat + Sulphur →   **" Vulcanized" Rubber**

Now that materials scientists better understand the interaction of the molecules in rubber, they've applied this knowledge to other materials to make a variety of plastics and synthetic rubber.

Carbon Nanotubes

Imagine a material so strong you could hang from a thread the thickness of a single hair! As amazing as it seems, this super-strong material really exists.

Scientists discovered that one form of carbon, called a nanotube, has some amazing properties, including very high tensile strength. Nanotubes are very narrow, tube-shaped molecules that form under special conditions.

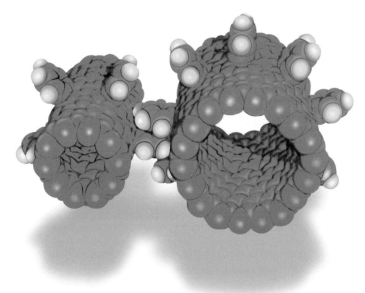

Because of their desirable properties including good conductance of heat, high strength, and potential use as very small wires in electronic devices, many scientists are trying to find out how to create and use these carbon nanotubes.

Memory Wire

Another material discovered "accidentally" is nitinol, commonly called memory wire. While searching for a metal resistant to rust or corrosion, a US Navy lab discovered that one of its test materials had the unique property of "remembering" its shape. After bending the material into a new shape, they exposed it to heat and it snapped back in to the original form. Of course the metal doesn't really "remember" the shape it started in. When deformed, the molecules in the material undergo a transition from an orderly, crystalline alignment to a more random form. Heating the material causes a transition back to the crystal form, returning the original shape. Some uses for nitinol include medical devices, eyeglass frames, temperature control devices, and cellular telephone antennas.

Aerogel

Would you believe that someone has made a solid material that has about the same density as air? If someone put a chunk of it your hand, you might not even notice. Silica aerogel is a foam that's like solidified smoke. Aerogel is mostly air and has remarkable thermal, optical and acoustical properties.

Aerogels are fantastic insulators. You could hold a flame under a chunk of the material and touch the top without being burned. Aerogels have the potential to replace a variety of materials in everyday life. If researchers could make a transparent version of an aerogel, it would almost certainly be used in double pane windows to keep heat inside your house in the winter and outside in the summer. Opaque aerogels are already being used as insulators. Aerogels have been put to use by NASA in several projects, including the Mars Pathfinder Soujourner Rover and the Stardust mission.

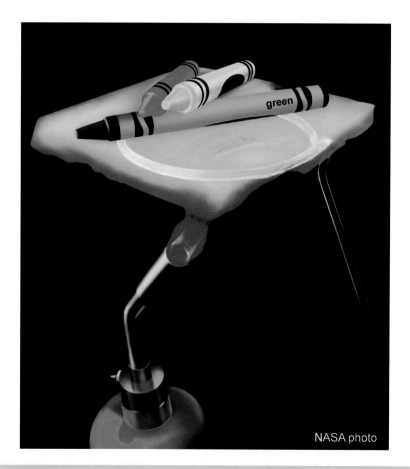

NASA photo

Questions:

1. Can you think of some new uses for vulcanized rubber? How about some uses for natural (sticky) rubber?
2. Can you think of some uses for carbon nanotubes if they could be easily manufactured? What existing materials could they replace? Why might one material be better than another?
3. Can you think of some uses for memory wire and aerogel?

Chapter 7 Review

Understanding Vocabulary

Select the correct term to complete the sentences.

specific heat	temperature	atom
heat conduction	liquid	compound
heat	gas	molecules
Celsius scale	convection	mixture
thermal radiation	thermal energy	

Section 7.1

1. A(n) _____ is made up of only one type of molecule.

2. A(n) _____ is a combination of different compounds and/or elements.

3. Each element has a unique type of _____.

4. Groups of atoms joined together by chemical bonds are called _____.

Section 7.2

5. On the _____, water boils at 100 degrees and freezes at 0 degrees.

6. _____ is a measure of the average kinetic energy of particles in a system.

7. A state of matter that has a definite volume and can flow is a(n) _____.

8. A state of matter that can expand or contract to fill a container is a(n) _____.

Section 7.3

9. _____ is the sum of all the kinetic energy of the particles of a system.

10. Oceans are able to help regulate the temperature of Earth due to the high _____ of water.

11. The flow of thermal energy is called _____.

Section 7.4

12. When you grab a hot mug of cocoa, heat is transferred from the mug to your hand by _____.

13. Heat transfer through currents in air or water is called _____.

14. Heat from the sun is transferred to Earth by _____.

Reviewing Concepts

Section 7.1

1. Describe the appearance of table salt at the macroscopic and atomic levels.

2. Explain the difference between an element and a compound and give one example of each.

3. Explain how a mixture is different than a compound.

4. Explain the difference between an atom and a molecule.

Section 7.2

5. At what temperature does water boil on the Celsius scale? On the Fahrenheit scale?

6. A student in Italy flies to visit a family in New York. He hears the pilot report the weather on arrival as "clear and sunny with temperatures in the low 20's." He changes on the plane into shorts and a T-shirt. Explain his behavior.

7. Describe the four states of matter.

8. Give an example for each of the following: a solid mixture, a liquid mixture, a mixture that is a gas.

9. What holds together the particles in a solid?

10. How is a plasma different from a gas?

11. What happens to the temperature of ice at its melting point while you add heat? While it is melting, does it gain or lose energy?

12. What happens during boiling at the macroscopic and atomic levels?

13. When water cools and changes to ice, does the surrounding air get cooler or warmer?

14. Absolute zero is the lower limit of temperature. Is there an upper limit of temperature? Explain your answer.

15. What is evaporation? How is it different than boiling?

Section 7.3

16. Explain the difference between temperature and thermal energy.

17. What is heat? How is heat related to temperature?

18. Which has higher thermal energy, a swimming pool of water at 70°F or a teacup of water at 80°F? Does higher thermal energy mean higher temperature?

19. Name three different units of energy used to measure heat and describe what type of situations each is usually used.

20. If you add the same amount of heat to a kilogram of water and a kilogram of gold, would they both be the same temperature? If not, which would be higher? Why? Assume that both start out at the same temperature.

21. Using the term *specific heat*, explain how oceans help regulate the temperature on Earth.

Section 7.4

22. Define the three main types of heat transfer.

23. Describe the flow of thermal energy when you hold a cold can of soda in your hand. What types of heat transfer are occurring?

24. Why do you think pots and pans for cooking are made out of metal?

25. What properties make a material a good thermal insulator? Give three examples of good thermal insulators.

26. Compare the ability of solids, liquids, and gases to conduct heat.

27. Why does hot air rise? What type of heat transfer is occurring?

28. Why doesn't convection occur in a solid material?

29. Name one property that increases an object's ability to absorb thermal radiation.

30. A blacktop road leads to a white sand beach. On a warm sunny day, which surface will heat up faster? Which will cool down faster at night? Explain why.

31. Explain, using your knowledge of heat transfer, why it is difficult to keep cool when it is 100°F outside.

Solving Problems

Section 7.1

1. Identify the following substances as an *element*, a *compound*, or a *mixture*.
   a. vanilla pudding
   b. oxygen gas
   c. table salt (sodium chloride)
   d. fruit salad

Section 7.2

2. What is a normal human body temperature, 98.6°F, on the Celsius scale?

3. Convert the Celsius temperature of the surface of the sun, which is 5,500°C, to degrees Fahrenheit.

4. If a recipe says to bake a pizza in a 250°C oven, at what temperature should you set your oven that uses the Fahrenheit scale?

5. Convert the Fahrenheit temperature at which paper burns, 451°F, to degrees Celsius.

6. As you know Earth is a watery planet. About 70 percent of Earth's surface is covered by water. There is water underground, and even in the atmosphere. What is water's state at each of the following temperatures?
   a. temperatures below 0°C
   b. temperatures between zero and 100°C
   c. temperatures above 100°C

7. You place 1 liter of a substance into a 2-liter bottle and tightly cover the bottle. The substance completely fills the bottle. What state is the substance in?

Section 7.3

8. How much heat is needed to raise the temperature of 10 kilograms of wood from 20°C to 25°C? The specific heat of wood is 2,500 J/kg°C.

9. A teapot contains 0.5 kilograms of water. Five thousand joules of heat are added to the teapot. What is the increase in the temperature of the water? The specific heat of water is 4,184 J/kg°C.

10. You add 47,000 joules of heat to 1 kilogram of steel. What is the temperature change in the steel? Steel's specific heat is 470 J/kg°C.

11. How much heat is needed to raise the temperature of 10 kilograms of aluminum from 10°C to 40°C? The specific heat of aluminum is 900 J/kg°C.

12. How many calories does it take to increase 1 gram of water by 20°C?

Section 7.4

13. Why does a chickadee fluff its feathers when it get cold outside?

14. You pour some hot water into a metal cup. After a minute, you notice that the handle of the cup has become hot. Explain, using your knowledge of heat transfer, why the handle of the cup heats up. How would you design the cup so the handle does not heat up?

15. What primary type of heat transfer occurs in the following situations?
    a. A cool breeze blows off the water when you are at the beach.
    b. You burn your hand on a hot pan.
    c. The sun warms your skin.
    d. Your feet feel cold on a tile floor.
    e. Smoke rises up a chimney.
    f. You feel warmer in a black T-shirt than a white T-shirt.

Applying Your Knowledge

Section 7.1

1. Design a poster to illustrate the classification of matter. Be sure to use the terms: *matter*, *element*, *compound*, and *mixture*. Provide examples of everyday objects that belong in each category.

2. Design a demonstration of Brownian motion for your class.

3. Research how a scanning tunneling electron microscope (STM) works. Prepare a short report of your findings.

Section 7.2

4. Research why plasmas, or ionized gases as they are sometimes called, are of great interest to scientists and manufacturers. Describe at least two current uses of plasmas, and describe one way scientists and engineers hope to use plasmas in the future.

5. Prepare a short report that describes how different types of thermometers work. Be sure to apply what you know about the behavior of atomic particles.

6. Imagine you are the size of an atom. Write a short story that describes what your life would be like as a solid, liquid, and a gas. Be creative in your descriptions.

Section 7.3

7. Research one or both of the following and write a short paper or give a presentation based on your findings.
    a. Scottish chemist Joseph Black (1728-1799) developed the theory of specific heat. Research his life and how he made this discovery.
    b. Lord Kelvin (1824-1907), a British Physicist, developed the idea of absolute zero, the coldest possible temperature. Research absolute zero, the Kelvin scale, and Lord Kelvin's life.

8. Explain, using your knowledge of specific heat, why coastal areas are often warmer at night and cooler in the day compared to inland areas.

Section 7.4

9. Describe the heating system in your home. What type or types of heat transfer does it use?

10. Find out how much insulation is recommended for homes in your community. Where is the most insulation recommended: in the ceiling, walls, or floors? Using what you know about heat transfer, explain why.

11. The diagram (right) shows an automobile engine cooling system. Describe, using your knowledge of heat transfer, how this system works.

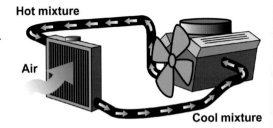

Hot mixture

Air

Cool mixture

Chapter 8

Physical Properties of Matter

In 1907, a Belgian-born New York chemist named Leo Baekeland (1863-1944) created a liquid substance that hardened rapidly and formed an exact replica of any container that held it. The new material would not burn, boil, melt, or dissolve in any commonly available acid or solvent. This meant that once it was hard, it would never change under normal circumstances. The new substance, which Baekeland called Bakelite, was the first useful plastic. Since then, many more plastics have been developed for many different uses. In fact, it is hard to imagine life without plastics.

The physical properties of plastics that make them useful come from the shape and arrangement of plastic molecules. Scientists can even "engineer" molecules so that they can be used for different purposes. In this chapter you will learn about the physical properties of matter and how those properties are directly related to the shape, arrangement, and behavior of atoms and molecules.

Key Questions

✓ What makes a material strong?
✓ Why does a steel boat float but a steel cube does not?
✓ Why does heating the air inside a balloon cause it to float in the air?

ncy.....Density

8.1 Properties of Solids

You have learned that matter is made up of tiny atoms and molecules. In a solid the atoms or molecules are closely packed, and stay in place. That is why solids hold their shape. In this section you will learn how the properties of solids result from the behavior of atoms and molecules.

Matter has physical and chemical properties

Characteristics of matter
Different types of matter have different characteristics. They melt and boil at different temperatures. They might be different colors or have different odors. Some can stretch without breaking, while others shatter easily. These and other properties help us distinguish one kind of matter from another. They also help us choose which kind of material to use for a specific purpose.

Physical properties
Characteristics that can you can see through direct observation are called **physical properties**. Physical properties include color, texture, density, brittleness, and state (solid, liquid, or gas). Substances can often be identified by their physical properties. For example, water is a colorless, odorless substance that exists as a liquid at room temperature. Gold is shiny, exists as a solid at room temperature, and can be pounded into very thin sheets.

Physical changes
A *physical change* is any change in the size, shape, or phase of matter in which the identity of a substance does not change. Physical changes are reversible. For example, when water is frozen, it changes from a liquid to a solid. This does not change the water into a new substance. It is still water, only in solid form. The change can easily be reversed by melting the water. Bending a steel bar is another physical change.

Chemical properties
Properties that can only be observed when one substance changes into a different substance are called **chemical properties**. For example, if you leave an iron nail outside, it will eventually rust. A chemical property of iron is that it reacts with oxygen in the air to form iron oxide (rust). Any change that transforms one substance into a different substance is called a *chemical change* (Figure 8.1). Chemical changes are not easily reversible. Rusted iron will not turn shiny again even if you take it away from oxygen in the air.

Vocabulary

physical properties, chemical properties, density, crystalline, amorphous, stress, tensile strength, elasticity, brittleness, thermal expansion

Objectives

✓ Distinguish between physical and chemical properties.
✓ Calculate the density of a substance.
✓ Calculate stress.
✓ Give examples of brittleness, elasticity, tensile strength, and thermal expansion.

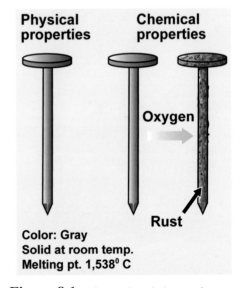

Physical properties **Chemical properties**

Oxygen

Rust

Color: Gray
Solid at room temp.
Melting pt. 1,538° C

Figure 8.1: *Physical and chemical properties of iron.*

Density is a physical property of matter

The definition of density

Density is the ratio of mass to volume. Density is a property of solids, liquids, and gases. To find the density of a material, you divide its mass by its volume. You can calculate volume if you know density and mass. You can calculate mass if you know density and volume. Physicists and engineers use units of kilograms per cubic meter for density. In classroom experiments, it is more convenient to use units of grams per cubic centimeter.

DENSITY

$$\text{Density } (\text{kg/m}^3 \text{ or g/cm}^3) \longrightarrow D = \frac{m}{V} \longleftarrow \begin{array}{l} \text{Mass (kg or g)} \\ \text{Volume (m}^3 \text{ or cm}^3) \end{array}$$

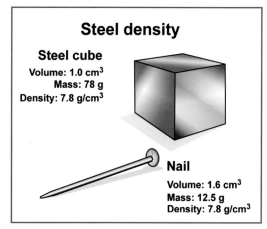

Steel density

Steel cube
Volume: 1.0 cm³
Mass: 78 g
Density: 7.8 g/cm³

Nail
Volume: 1.6 cm³
Mass: 12.5 g
Density: 7.8 g/cm³

Figure 8.2: *The density of a steel nail is the same as the density of a solid cube of steel.*

Density of homogeneous materials

The densities of a steel nail and a steel cube are the same. For example, a steel cube one meter on a side has a mass of 7,800 kilograms. A steel nail has a volume of 1.6 millionths of a cubic meter (1.6×10^{-6} m³) and a mass of 0.0125 kg. Although they have different size and mass, both objects have the same density of 7,800 kg/m³. Figure 8.2 shows the calculations in g/cm³. For a material that is the same throughout, the density is the same and does not depend on the amount of the material you have.

Solids have a wide range of density

Solids have a wide range of densities (Figure 8.3). One of the densest metals is platinum with a density of 21,500 kg/m³. Platinum is twice as dense as lead and almost three times as dense as steel. A ring made of platinum has three times as much mass as a ring of the exact same size made of steel. Rock has a lower density than metals, between 2,200 and 2,700 kg/m³. As you might expect, the density of wood is less than rock, ranging from 400 to 600 kg/m³.

Material	(kg/m³)	(g/cm³)
Platinum	21,500	21.5
Lead	11,300	11.3
Steel	7,800	7.8
Titanium	4,500	4.5
Aluminum	2,700	2.7
Glass	2,700	2.7
Granite	2,600	2.6
Concrete	2,300	2.3
Plastic	2,000	2.0
Rubber	1,200	1.2
Liquid water	1,000	1.0
Ice	920	0.92
Oak (wood)	600	0.60
Pine (wood)	440	0.44
Cork	120	0.12
Air (avg.)	0.9	0.0009

Figure 8.3: *The densities of some common materials.*

Density of liquids and gases

The density of water is 1,000 kg/m³ and many common liquids have densities between 500 and 1,500 kg/m³. The density of air and other gases is much lower. The air in your room has a density near 1 kg/m³. Gases have low density because the molecules in a gas are far from each other.

Why density varies

Atoms have different masses
The density of a material depends on two things. One is the individual mass of each atom or molecule. The other is how closely the atoms or molecules are packed together. Lead is a very dense metal compared to aluminum. One atom of lead has 7.7 times more mass than one atom of aluminum. Solid lead is denser than solid aluminum mostly because a single lead atom has more mass than an aluminum atom.

Atoms may be "packed" loose or tight
Density also depends on how tightly the atoms and molecules are "packed." Diamond is made of carbon atoms and has a density of 3,500 kg/m^3. The carbon atoms in diamond are relatively closely packed together. Paraffin wax is also mostly carbon but the density of paraffin is only 870 kg/m^3. The density of paraffin is low because the carbon atoms are mixed with hydrogen atoms in long molecules that take up a lot of space.

Solving density problems
Density problems usually ask you to find one of the three variables (mass, volume, density) given the other two. Figure 8.4 shows three forms of the density equation you can use. Which one you choose depends on what you are asked to find.

Use...	...if you know...	...and want to find...
$D = m \div V$	mass and volume	density
$m = D \times V$	volume and density	mass
$V = m \div D$	mass and density	volume

Figure 8.4: *Relationships to use when solving density problems.*

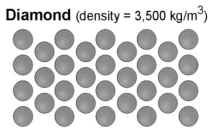

Diamond (density = 3,500 kg/m^3)

Paraffin (density = 870 kg/m^3)

● Carbon atom ○ Hydrogen atom
Molecule

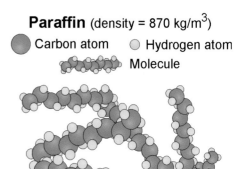

Figure 8.5: *The carbon atoms in diamond are packed relatively tightly while the carbon atoms in paraffin are part of long molecules that take up a lot of space.*

Using the density equation

Titanium has a density of 4.5 g/cm^3. What is the volume of a cube of titanium that has a mass of 4,500 g?

1. Looking for: You are looking for the volume of a solid.

2. Given: You are given the density and mass.

3. Relationships: $V = m \div D$

4. Solution: $V = 4{,}500 \text{ g} \div 4.5 \text{ g/cm}^3 = 1{,}000 \text{ cm}^3$

Your turn...

a. What is the density of a cork that has a mass of 0.24 g and a volume of 2.0 cm^3? **Answer:** 0.12 g/cm^3

b. What is the mass of an ice cube that has a volume of 8.0 cm^3? (The density of ice is 0.92 g/cm^3) **Answer:** 7.4 g

The arrangement of atoms and molecules in solids

Crystalline and amorphous solids

The atoms or molecules in a solid are arranged in two ways. If the particles are arranged in an orderly, repeating pattern, the solid is called **crystalline**. Examples of crystalline solids include salts, minerals, and metals. If the particles are arranged in a random way, the solid is **amorphous**. Examples of amorphous solids include rubber, wax, and glass.

Crystalline solids

Most solids on Earth are crystalline. Some materials, like salt, exist as single crystals and you can see the arrangement of atoms reflected in the shape of the crystal. If you look at a crystal of table salt under a microscope, you see that it is cubic in shape. If you could examine the arrangement of atoms, you would see that the shape of the crystal comes from the cubic arrangement of sodium and chlorine atoms (Figure 8.6). Metals are also crystalline. They don't look like "crystals" because solid metal is made from very tiny crystals fused together in a jumble of different orientations (Figure 8.7).

Amorphous solids

The word *amorphous* comes from the Greek for "without shape." Unlike crystals, amorphous solids do not have a repetitive pattern in the arrangement of molecules or atoms. The atoms or molecules are randomly arranged. While amorphous solids also hold their shape, they are often softer and more elastic than crystalline solids. This is because a molecule in an amorphous solid is not tightly connected to as many neighboring molecules as it would be in a crystalline solid. Glass is a common amorphous solid. Glass is hard and brittle because it is made from molten silica crystals that are cooled quickly, before they have time to re-crystallize. The rapid cooling leaves the silica molecules in a random arrangement. Plastic is another useful amorphous solid.

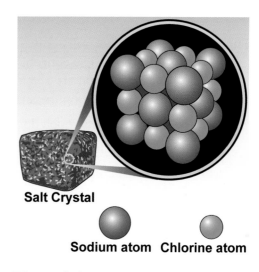

Salt Crystal

Sodium atom   Chlorine atom

Figure 8.6: *The shape of a salt crystal is due to the arrangement of sodium and chlorine atoms.*

Individual crystals

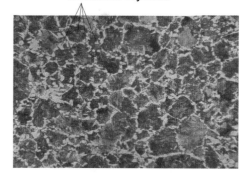

Figure 8.7: *Metallic crystals in steel. Single crystals are very small. This image is taken with an electron microscope at very high magnification.*

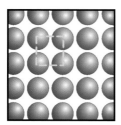

Cubic crystal

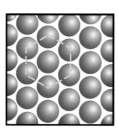

Hexagonal crystal

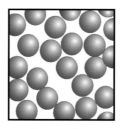

Amorphous

Solids vary in their strength

The meaning of "strength"
When you apply a force to an object, the object may change its size, shape, or both. The concept of physical "strength" means the ability of a solid object to maintain its shape even when force is applied. The strength of an object depends on the answers to two questions (Figure 8.8):

1. How much does the object bend or deform when force is applied?

2. How much force can the object take before it breaks?

Strength and design
The strength of an object can be broken down into *design* and *materials*. Design means size and shape. For example, think of two beams, thin and thick, made of oak, a strong wood. Both beams are the same material (oak) but have different strengths because of their design. A small force can break the thin beam. The thicker beam takes much more force to break (Figure 8.9). To properly assess the strength of oak as a *material*, we need to separate the effects of shape and size.

Force and stress
The strength of solid materials is described best in terms of *stress*, not force. **Stress** is the ratio of the force acting through the material divided by the cross-section area through which the force is carried. The cross-section area is the area perpendicular to the direction of the force. Dividing force by cross-section area (mostly) separates out the effects of size and shape from the strength properties of the material itself. The Greek letter sigma (σ) is used for stress. Stress (σ) is force (F) divided by the area (A) of the cross-section.

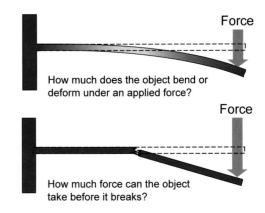

Figure 8.8: *Two questions that we use to define the physical strength of an object.*

STRESS

$$Stress\ (\text{N/m}^2) \longrightarrow \sigma = \frac{F \longleftarrow Force\ (\text{N})}{A \longleftarrow Area\ (\text{m}^2)}$$

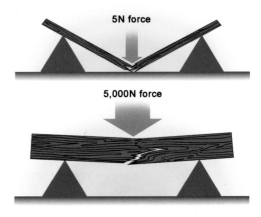

Figure 8.9: *It takes a much larger force to break a beam of oak than to break a thin stick.*

Solving problems with stress

Units for stress   The metric unit of stress is the *pascal* (Pa). One pascal is equal to one newton of force per square meter of area (1 N/m^2). Most stresses are much larger than one pascal. Strong materials like steel and aluminum can take stresses of 100 *million* pascals. The English unit for stress is pounds per square inch (psi). A stress of one psi is equivalent to one pound of force for each square inch of area (1 lb/in^2).

Tensile strength   **Tensile strength** is a measure of how much stress in pulling, or tension, a material can withstand before breaking (Figure 8.10). Strong materials like steel have high tensile strength. Weak materials like wax and rubber have low tensile strength. Brittle materials also have low tensile strength. Figure 8.11 lists the tensile strength of some common materials.

Stress problems   Materials break when the stress reaches or exceeds the tensile strength. In many problems you can find the force at which something will break by multiplying the tensile strength by the cross-section area.

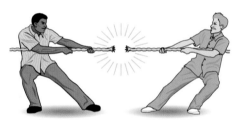

TENSILE STRENGTH

Figure 8.10: *Tensile strength measures how much pulling or tension a material can withstand before breaking.*

Calculating stress

20,000 newtons of force is applied to a steel beam with a cross-section area of 0.5 m^2. Calculate the stress on the steel beam.

1. **Looking for:**   You are looking for stress.

2. **Given:**   You are given the force applied in newtons and the cross section area in m^2.

3. **Relationships:**   Use the stress equation: $\sigma = F/A$

4. **Solution:** $\sigma = 20{,}000 \text{ N}/0.5\text{m}^2 = 40{,}000 \text{ N/m}^2$

Your turn...

a.   The maximum stress on a wooden beam with a cross-section area of 0.20 m^2 is 5,000 N/m^2. What is the maximum force that can be applied to the beam before it breaks? **Answer:** 1,000 N

b.   45 N is the amount of force that breaks a pencil with a cross-section area of 0.002 m^2. Calculate the maximum stress the pencil can take.
Answer: 22,500 N/m^2

Material	Tensile strength (MPa)
1 MPa = 1 million Pa	
Titanium	900
Steel (alloy)	825
Steel (type 1010)	400
Aluminum (alloy)	290
Aluminum (pure)	110
Oak (wood)	95
Pine (wood)	60
Nylon plastic	55
Rubber	14

Figure 8.11: *Tensile strength of some common materials.*

Elasticity, brittleness, and bending

What is elasticity?

If you pull on a rubber band, its shape changes. If you let it go, the rubber band returns to its original shape. Rubber bands can stretch many times their original length before breaking, a property called **elasticity**. Elasticity describes a solid's ability to be stretched and then return to its original size. This property also gives objects the ability to bounce and to withstand impact without breaking. Materials that do not return to their original shape are *inelastic*. Clay and soft metals like lead are inelastic. Clay or lead objects do not return to their original shape once they are squashed or bent.

Brittleness

Brittleness is defined as the tendency of a solid to crack or break when forces are applied. A brittle material breaks at a low value of stress. Glass is a good example of a brittle material. You cannot stretch glass even one-tenth of a percent (0.001) before it breaks. However, if you heat glass until it is almost melted, you can stretch it. This is because heating causes its particles to move faster, temporarily breaking the forces that hold them together.

Bending

You don't usually try and stretch a piece of wood. However, you might make a wooden deck and stand on the wood so that it bends. In a deck, pieces of wood (like 2-by-4s) experience *bending* instead of tension as they are walked on. Stress and tensile strength also describe how materials break in bending. Imagine you have a rubber bar. When you bend the bar, it stretches in *tension* on one side and squeezes together in *compression* on the other side. The bar breaks when the stress on the tension side reaches the tensile strength of the material. In a similar way, a 2-by-4 used in a deck will break when the stress on the lower side reaches the tensile strength.

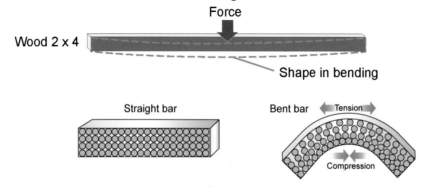

BRITTLENESS

Figure 8.12: *Brittleness is the tendency of a solid to crack when force is applied.*

Thermal expansion

Particles and thermal expansion

As the temperature increases, the kinetic energy in vibration of the atoms and molecules also increases. The increased vibration makes each particle take up a little more space, causing **thermal expansion**. Almost all solid materials expand as the temperature increases. Some materials (like plastic) expand a great deal. Other materials (like glass) expand only a little.

The coefficient of thermal expansion

The *coefficient of thermal expansion* describes how much a material expands for each degree change in temperature. A material with a thermal expansion coefficient of 10^{-4} per degree Celsius means each one degree Celsius rise in temperature causes an object to expand by 0.0001 times its original length. Figure 8.14 gives the thermal expansion coefficient for common materials.

Materials contract as well as expand

The thermal expansion coefficient works both ways. If the temperature *decreases*, objects *contract*. The amount of contraction or expansion is equal to the temperature change times the coefficient of thermal expansion.

Thermal stress

Very large stresses can develop if objects are prevented from expanding or contracting with temperature. Drop an ice cube in hot water and you can hear it crack from thermal stress. Thermal stresses can be great enough to cause cracks and failure in buildings and other structures. All bridges longer than a certain size have special joints that allow the bridge surface to expand and contract with the seasons (Figure 8.13). The bridge surface would crack without these expansion joints.

Expansion joint

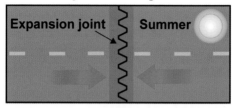

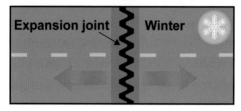

Figure 8.13: *Bridges have expansion joints to allow for thermal expansion of concrete.*

Material	Coefficient of thermal expansion ($\times 10^{-5}$ per °C)
Steel	1.2
Brass	1.8
Aluminum	2.4
Glass	2.0
Copper	1.7
Concrete	1
Nylon plastic	8
Rock	7
Rubber	16
Wood	3

Figure 8.14: *Thermal expansion coefficients for some materials.*

8.1 Section Review

1. Name one example of a physical change and one example of a chemical change.

2. Aluminum has a density of 2,700 kg/m^3. What is the mass of a cube of aluminum that measures 2.5 cm (0.025 m) on each side?

3. A man weighing 800 N is hanging from a 2 mm diameter titanium wire with a cross-section of 3×10^{-6} m^2. Will the wire break?

4. Name one example of a material for each set of properties:
   a. high elasticity and high tensile strength.
   b. amorphous and brittle.
   c. crystalline and brittle.
   d. crystalline and elastic.

8.2 Fluids

A **fluid** is defined as any matter that flows when force is applied. Liquids like water are one kind of fluid. Gases, like air, are also fluids. You may notice cool air flowing into a room when a window is opened, or the smell of someone's perfume drifting your way. These examples provide evidence that gases flow. What are some other properties of fluids?

Density of fluids

How could you find the density of *liquid* silver? A piece of pure silver in the shape of a candlestick has the same density as a pure silver coin. Size and shape do not change a material's density. But what if you heated the silver until it completely melted? Could you measure its density in liquid form? Would the density change?

Atoms in liquid form tend to take up more space The density of a liquid is the ratio of mass to volume, just like the density of a solid. The mass of the silver does not change when the candlestick is melted. The volume of the liquid silver, however, is greater than the volume of the solid silver. The particles in a solid, as you remember, are fixed in position. Although the silver atoms in a candlestick are constantly vibrating, they cannot switch places with other atoms. They are neatly stacked in a repeating pattern. The atoms in the liquid silver are less rigidly organized. They can slide over and around each other and take up a little more space.

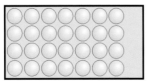
Solid silver

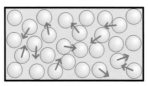
Liquid silver

Why liquids are less dense than solids The silver atoms in solid form can be compared to a brand-new box of children's wooden blocks. When you open the box, the blocks are tightly packed in an organized, repeating pattern. Now imagine that you empty the box of blocks into a large container, and then pour them back into their original box. Although the blocks are still touching one another, they do not fit entirely inside the box. The blocks now resemble the arrangement of silver atoms in liquid form (Figure 8.15).

Figure 8.15: *Neatly stacked toy blocks take up less space than blocks that are not as orderly.*

Comparing liquid and solid densities

The density of liquid silver
The density of silver is lower in its liquid state but not by as much as you might think. The table below gives some actual data. Liquid silver is about 13% less dense than solid silver. This ratio of liquid to solid densities is typical of metals.

Table 8.1: Density of solid and liquid silver

	Mass	Volume	Density
Candlestick (at 20°C)	1.30 kg	0.00012 m^3	10,833 kg/m^3
Melted candlestick (962°C)	1.30 kg	0.00014 m^3	9,286 kg/m^3

Temperature and solid density
The density of most solids decreases slightly as temperature increases because solids expand when heated. As the temperature of the solid silver increases, the volume increases slightly, even before the silver melts. This is due to the increased vibration of the silver atoms.

Water is *less dense* in solid form
Most materials are denser in their solid state than in their liquid state. Water is a notable exception. Solid water has a very open crystal structure that resembles a honeycomb where each water molecule forms intermolecular bonds with four other water molecules (Figure 8.16). This creates a six-sided arrangement of molecules. The six-sided crystal form explains six-way shapes you see when you examine snowflakes with a magnifying lens.

Decreasing density
As water freezes, molecules of water separate slightly from each other because of the honeycomb structure. This causes the volume to increase slightly, while the mass stays the same. As a result the density decreases. This explains why water expands when it is frozen and floats. The density of ice is 920 kg/m^3 whereas the density of liquid water is 1,000 kg/m^3.

Water's density and living organisms
Because ice is less dense than liquid water, it floats on the surface of lakes and ponds when they freeze over in winter. When this occurs, the temperature of the water below the ice layer remains above freezing. This is one factor that helps fish and other aquatic organisms to survive over long, cold winters (Figure 8.17).

Figure 8.16: *Water freezes in a rigid pattern that causes the molecules to separate slightly from each other.*

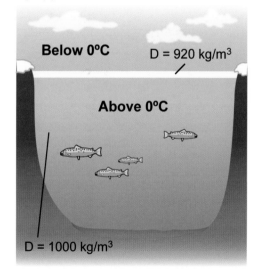

Figure 8.17: *Ice floats on the surface of a pond, keeping the pond water beneath it from reaching freezing temperatures.*

Buoyancy

What is buoyancy?
It is much easier to lift yourself in a swimming pool compared with lifting yourself on land. That's because the water is exerting an upward force on you. We call this force *buoyancy*. **Buoyancy** is a measure of the upward force a fluid exerts on an object that is immersed.

Demonstrating buoyancy
A simple experiment demonstrates the buoyancy force. A rock is weighed with a spring scale. The scale measures 2.25 newtons. Next, the rock is immersed in water, but not allowed to touch the bottom or sides of the container. Now the spring scale measures 1.8 newtons (Figure 8.18). The water has exerted a buoyancy force of 0.45 newtons on the rock.

Archimedes' principle
In the third century BC, a Greek mathematician named Archimedes realized the buoyancy force is equal to the weight of fluid displaced by an object. We call this relationship **Archimedes' principle**. Archimedes' principle tells us that the water displaced by the rock in the experiment above had a weight of 0.45 newtons. Archimedes' principle can be used to find the buoyant force in any liquid once you know the density.

Why objects sink and float
Buoyancy explains why some objects sink and others float. An object floats if the buoyant force is greater than its weight. If the buoyant force is less than its weight, then the object will sink. *Neutral buoyancy* occurs when the buoyant force is equal to the weight of the object. When an object is neutrally buoyant, it will stay immersed in the liquid at the level where it was placed. Scuba divers use weights and a buoyancy control device (or BCD) to help them maintain neutral buoyancy. When a scuba diver is neutrally buoyant he or she can swim and move underwater without rising or sinking.

Buoyancy and density
Buoyancy forces are created by differences in density. An object with the same density of water has neutral buoyancy because the weight of water displaced is the same as the weight of the object. An object with a density *greater* than 1,000 kg/m^3 sinks because the weight of water displaced is *less* than the weight of the object. An object with density *less* than 1,000 kg/m^3 floats because the weight of water displaced is *more* than the weight of the object.

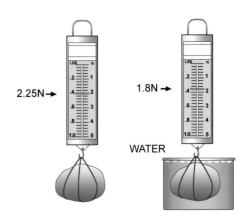

Figure 8.18: *Demonstrating the buoyant force of water on a rock. When the rock is suspended in air, it weighs 2.25 N. In water, the same rock has an apparent weight of 1.8 N.*

How can steel float?

Steel has a density of 7,800 kg/m^3 compared to water's 1,000 kg/m^3. Solid steel sinks because of the difference in density. To make steel float, its average density must be made less than that of water. In a boat, the steel is flattened and shaped so it takes up much more space than solid steel. One cubic meter of steel can easily make a boat with 10 cubic meters of volume. The average density of this boat is 780 kg/m^3. This is less dense than water so the boat floats.

Pressure

Force and fluids Think about what happens when you push down on a balloon. The downward force you apply creates forces that act sideways as well as down. This is very different from what happens when you push down on a solid bowling ball. The ball transmits the force directly down. Because fluids change shape, forces in fluids are more complicated than forces in solids.

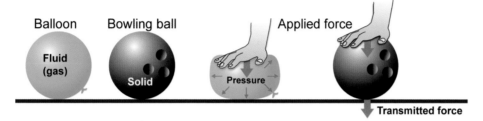

Pressure A force applied to a fluid creates **pressure** instead of stress. Like stress, pressure is a ratio of force per unit area. Unlike stress however, pressure acts in all directions, not just the direction of the applied force.

Pressure is an important concept The idea of pressure helps explain how fluids move and how they act on surfaces, such as containers. The motion of fluids depends on pressure and density in a similar way as the motion of solids depends on force and mass.

Units of pressure Pressure is force per unit area, like stress. A pressure of 1 N/m² means a force of one newton acts on each square meter of surface. The metric unit of pressure is the pascal (Pa). One pascal is one newton of force per square meter of area (1 Pa = 1 N/m²). The English unit of pressure is pounds per square inch (psi). One psi means one pound of force per square inch of area (lb/in²).

Pressure underwater Gravity creates pressure because fluids have weight. The pressure increases the deeper you go beneath the surface of the ocean because the weight of water above you increases with depth. One thousand meters beneath the ocean surface, the pressure is 9,800,000 Pa, almost 100 times the pressure of the air you are breathing (Figure 8.20)! Earth's atmosphere has a pressure due to the weight of air. The density of air is very low, but the atmosphere is more than 80,000 meters deep (Figure 8.19). Atmospheric pressure at ground level is about 100,000 Pa. We are not crushed by atmospheric pressure because the pressure of air inside our lungs is the same as the pressure outside.

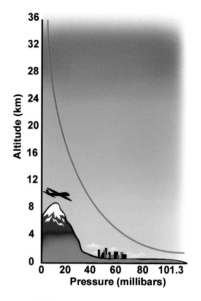

Figure 8.19: *The pressure of the atmosphere comes from the weight of air and decreases with altitude.*

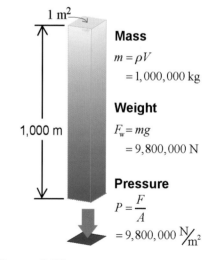

Figure 8.20: *The pressure in a liquid is created by the weight of liquid above.*

Pressure, energy, and force

The atomic level explanation
What causes pressure? On the atomic level, pressure comes from collisions between atoms and molecules. Molecules move around and bounce off each other and the walls of a container. It takes force to make a molecule reverse its direction and bounce the other way. The bouncing force is applied *to* the molecule *by* the inside surface of a jar. According to Newton's third law, an equal and opposite reaction force is exerted *by* the molecule *on* the jar (Figure 8.21). The reaction force is what creates the pressure acting on the inside surface of the jar. Trillions of molecules per second are constantly bouncing against every square millimeter of the inner surface of the jar. Pressure comes from the collisions of those many, many atoms.

Pressure creates forces on surfaces
Pressure exerts force on any surface touching a fluid. The force is the pressure multiplied by the area of contact. Submarines are built to withstand the tremendous pressure forces deep underwater. Your car tires hold up the car by exerting pressure on a small area contacting the road (Figure 8.22).

Pressure and energy are related. Remember, one property of energy is the ability to exert force and do work. Water in a jar has energy because any pressure created by the water pushes on the sides of the jar with forces that can do work. One joule of work is done when a pressure of one pascal pushes a surface of one square meter a distance of one meter.

Pressure is potential energy
Differences in pressure create potential energy in fluids just like differences in height create potential energy from gravity. A pressure difference of one newton per m^2 is equivalent to a potential energy of one joule per m^3.

We get useful work when we let a fluid under pressure expand. In an engine high pressure is created by an exploding gasoline-air mixture. This pressure pushes the cylinders of the engine down, doing work that moves the car.

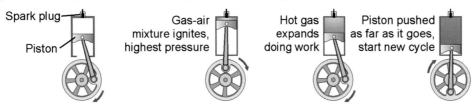

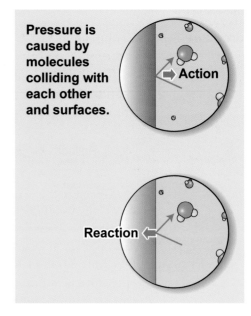

Figure 8.21: *The molecular explanation of pressure.*

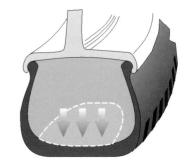

Figure 8.22: *The pressure inside your tire is what holds your car up. When your tire pressure is too low, your tire squashes down because more area is needed to get enough force to hold up the car.*

Energy conservation and Bernoulli's principle

Bernoulli's principle   Everything obeys the law of energy conservation. It just gets trickier when talking about a fluid (liquid or gas)! You still have potential and kinetic energy, but you also have pressure energy. If friction is neglected, the total energy stays constant for any particular sample of fluid. This relationship is known as **Bernoulli's principle**.

Streamlines   Streamlines are imaginary lines drawn to show the flow of fluid. We draw streamlines so that they are always parallel to the direction of flow. If water is coming out of a hole in a bucket the streamlines look like Figure 8.23. Bernoulli's principle tells us that the energy of any sample of fluid moving along a streamline is constant.

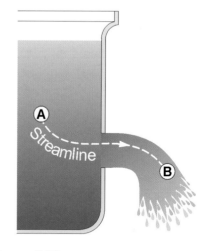

Figure 8.23: *A streamline is an imaginary line tracing the flow of a single particle of fluid.*

Bernoulli's principle

Form of energy	Potential energy	+	Kinetic energy	+	Pressure energy	= Constant
						Along any streamline in a fluid
Variable	*height*		*speed*		*pressure*	

The three variables   Bernoulli's principle says the three variables of height, pressure, and speed are related by energy conservation. Height is associated with potential energy, speed with kinetic energy, and pressure with pressure energy. If one variable increases along a streamline, *at least one of the other two must decrease.* For example, if speed goes up, pressure goes down.

Fluid at rest   If the kinetic energy is zero (fluid at rest) then Bernoulli's principle gives us the relation between pressure and depth. A bit of fluid that is low (deep) has higher pressure than one that is high (near the surface).

The airfoil   One of the most important applications of Bernoulli's principle is the airfoil shape of wings on a plane (Figure 8.24). The shape of an airfoil causes air flowing along the top (A) to move faster than air flowing along the bottom (B). According to Bernoulli's principle, if the speed goes up, the pressure goes down. When a plane is moving, the pressure on the top surface of the wings is lower than the pressure beneath the wings. The difference in pressure is what creates the lift force that supports the plane in the air.

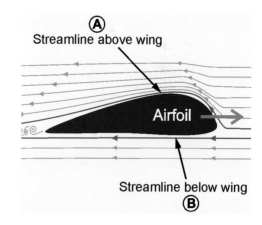

Figure 8.24: *Streamlines showing air moving around an airfoil (wing) that is moving from left to right.*

Viscosity

What is viscosity? **Viscosity** is the property of fluids that causes friction. High-viscosity fluids take longer to pour from their containers than low-viscosity fluids. Ketchup, for example, has a high viscosity and water has a low viscosity (Figure 8.25).

Viscosity and motor oils Viscosity is an important property of motor oils. If an oil is too thick, it may not flow quickly enough to parts of an engine. However, if an oil is too thin, it may not provide enough "cushion" to protect the engine from the effects of friction. A motor oil must function properly when the engine is started on a bitterly cold day, and when the engine is operating at high temperatures.

Viscosity and particles Viscosity is determined in large part by the shape and size of the particles in a liquid. If the particles are large and have bumpy surfaces, a great deal of friction will be created as they slide past each other. For instance, corn oil is made of large, chain-like molecules. Water is made of much smaller molecules. As a result, corn oil has greater viscosity than water.

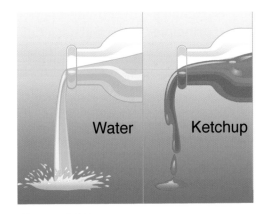

Figure 8.25: *Which liquid has greater viscosity?*

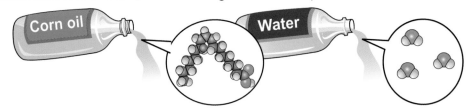

As a liquid gets warmer, its viscosity decreases As the temperature of a liquid is raised, the viscosity of the liquid decreases. In other words, warm liquids have less viscosity than cold liquids. Warmed maple syrup or hot fudge, for example, is much easier to pour than the same syrup chilled. Why does this happen? When temperature rises the jiggling of molecules increases. This allows molecules to slide past each other with greater ease. As a result, the viscosity decreases (Figure 8.26).

8.2 Section Review

1. Explain why liquid silver is less dense than solid silver.
2. A toy boat weighs 12 newtons. What is the weight of the water it displaces when it floats?
3. At the atomic level, what causes hot fudge to pour faster when it is heated?

Figure 8.26: *Heating fudge makes it much easier to pour.*

8.3 The Behavior of Gases

The air you breath is a gas, as is the carbon dioxide you exhale. While gases are fluids, they are different from liquids because the molecules in a gas are completely separated from each other. Because gas molecules act independently, gases are free to expand or contract. A gas will expand to completely fill its container.

Pressure, volume and density

Pressure and volume
When you squeeze a fixed quantity of gas into a smaller volume the pressure goes up. This rule is known as **Boyle's law**. The pressure increases because the same number of molecules are now squeezed into a smaller space. The molecules hit the walls more often because there are more of them per unit of area. The formula for Boyle's law relates the pressure and volume of gas. If the mass and temperature are kept constant, the product of pressure times volume stays the same (Figure 8.27).

BOYLE'S LAW

Initial volume ⟶   ⟵ New pressure
Initial pressure ⟶ $P_1 V_1 = P_2 V_2$ ⟵ New volume

Mass and temperature constant

Pressure and density
The density of a gas increases when the pressure increases. By increasing the pressure you are doing one of two things: squeezing the same amount of mass into a smaller volume, or squeezing more mass into the same volume. Either way, the density *usually* goes up. We say 'usually' because density and pressure are also affected by temperature. The density of a gas can change by a large amount. Air has a density of 0.9 kg/m^3 at atmospheric pressure. When compressed in a diving tank to 150 times higher pressure, the density is about 135 kg/m^3. The density of a gas can vary from near zero (in outer space) to greater than solids. This is very different from liquids or solids.

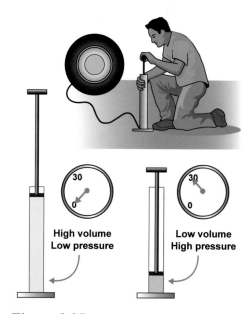

Figure 8.27: *Compressing the volume of air to increase the pressure.*

Pressure and temperature

Pressure and temperature The pressure of a gas is affected by temperature changes. If the mass and volume are kept constant, the pressure goes up when the temperature goes up, and down when the temperature goes down.

Why temperature affects pressure The pressure changes with temperature because the average kinetic energy of moving molecules is proportional to temperature. Hot molecules move faster than cold molecules. Faster molecules exert more force when they bounce off each other and the walls of their container (Figure 8.28).

Gay-Lussac's law The mathematical relationship between the temperature and pressure of a gas at constant volume and mass was discovered by Joseph Gay-Lussac in 1802.

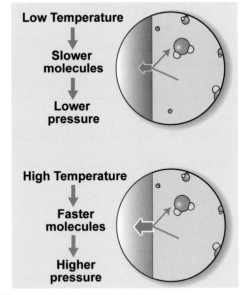

Figure 8.28: *Faster molecules create higher pressure because they exert larger forces as they collide with the sides of the container.*

PRESSURE-TEMPERATURE RELATIONSHIP

Initial pressure (N/m^2) → $$\frac{P_1}{T_1} = \frac{P_2}{T_2}$$ ← New pressure

Initial temperature (K) → ← New temperature

Volume and mass constant

Using Boyle's law

A balloon is filled with 500 cubic centimeters of helium at a pressure of one atmosphere. If the balloon reaches an altitude where the pressure is 0.5 atmospheres, what volume will the gas occupy? Assume that the temperature does not change.

1. Looking for: You are asked for volume in cm^3.

2. Given: You are given initial and final pressures in atmospheres, and initial volume in cm^3.

3. Relationships: Apply Boyle's law: $P_1 V_1 = P_2 V_2$.

4. Solution: $V_2 = (P_1 \times V_1) \div P_2 = (1\ atm \times 500\ cm^3) \div 0.5\ atm = 1{,}000\ cm^3$.

Your turn...

a. The air inside a tire pump occupies a volume of 135 cubic centimeters at a pressure of one atmosphere. If the volume is reduced by half, what is the pressure, in atmospheres, inside the pump? **Answer:** 2 atm

b. A gas occupies a volume of 24 cubic meters at 9,800 pascals. If the pressure is lowered to 5,750 pascals, what volume will the gas occupy? **Answer:** 40.90 m^3

Density and buoyancy

Sinking in a gas Like water, gases can create buoyancy forces. Because gas can flow and has a very low density, objects of higher density sink quickly. For example, if you drop a penny, it drops through the air quite easily. That is because the density of a penny is 9,000 times greater than the density of air.

Floating in a gas Objects of lower density can float on gas of higher density. A hot-air balloon floats because it is less dense than the surrounding air. What makes the air inside the balloon less dense? The word "hot" is important. To get their balloons to fly, balloonists use a torch to heat the air inside the balloon. The heated air in the balloon expands and lowers the overall density of the balloon to less than the density of the surrounding cooler air (Figure 8.29).

Charles' law The balloon example illustrates an important relationship, known as **Charles' law**, discovered by Jacques Charles (1746 - 1843) in 1787. According to Charles' law, the volume of a gas increases with increasing temperature. The volume decreases with decreasing temperature.

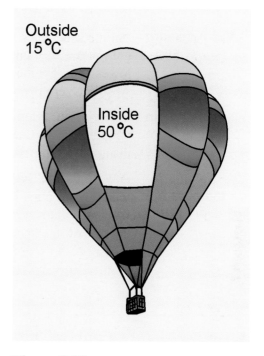

Outside 15°C

Inside 50°C

Figure 8.29: *A hot-air balloon floats because the air inside is less dense than the air outside.*

CHARLES' LAW

Initial volume (m³) ⟶ $\dfrac{V_1}{T_1} = \dfrac{V_2}{T_2}$ ⟵ New volume (m³)

Initial temperature (K) ⟶ ⟵ New temperature (K)

Pressure and mass constant

The buoyancy of hot air Charles' law explains why the air inside the balloon becomes less dense than the air outside the balloon. The volume increases as the temperature increases. Since there is the same total mass of air inside, the density decreases and the balloon floats. Stated another way, the weight of the air displaced by the balloon provides buoyant force to keep the balloon in flight.

Temperature and the Kelvin scale

Absolute zero In the last chapter you learned that *absolute zero* is as cold as any matter can get. When the temperature gets down to absolute zero, particles have the lowest energy they can have and the temperature cannot get any lower. Absolute zero occurs at - 273°C (- 459°F).

Kelvin temperature scale The Kelvin temperature scale starts at absolute zero. Add 273 to the temperature in Celsius to get the temperature in Kelvins (Figure 8.30). For example, a temperature of 21°C is equal to 294 K (21 + 273).

Use Kelvins for temperature problems Any time you see a temperature in a formula in this section (gases) the temperature must be in Kelvins. This is because only the Kelvin scale starts from absolute zero. A temperature in Kelvins expresses the true thermal energy of the gas above zero thermal energy. A temperature in Celsius measures only the *relative* energy, relative to zero Celsius. Remember, temperature must be in Kelvins for gas law problems!

> **CONVERTING CELSIUS TO KELVIN**
>
> $$T_{Kelvin} = T_{Celsius} + 273$$

Figure 8.30: *To convert degrees Celsius to Kelvins, simply add 273 to the Celsius temperature.*

Gases and temperature change problems

A can of hair spray has a pressure of 300 psi at room temperature (21°C = 294 K). The can is accidentally moved too close to a fire and its temperature increases to 295°C (568 K). What is the final pressure in the can (rounded to the nearest whole number)?

1. Looking for: You are asked for final pressure in psi.

2. Given: You are given initial pressure in psi, and initial and final temperatures in °C and Kelvins.

3. Relationships: Apply Gay-Lussac's law (pressure and temperature relationship): $P_1 \div T_1 = P_2 \div T_2$.

4. Solution: $P_2 = (P_1 \times T_2) \div T_1 = (300 \text{ psi} \times 568 \text{ K}) \div 294 = 580 \text{ psi}$.
NOTE: This is why you should NEVER put spray cans near heat. The pressure can increase so much that the can explodes.

Your turn...

a. A balloon filled with air occupies a volume of 0.50 cubic meters at 21°C (294 K). Assuming the pressure remains constant, what volume will the balloon occupy at 0°C (273 K)? **Answer:** 0.46 m^3

b. A tire contains 255 cubic inches of air at a temperature of 28°C (301 K). If the temperature drops to 1°C (274 K), what volume will the air in the tire occupy? Assume no change in pressure. **Answer:** 232 in^3

Earth's atmosphere

Air is a mixture of gases Air feels "light" because air is 1,000 times less dense than water. Earth's atmosphere is a mixture of nitrogen, oxygen, water vapor, and a few other gases such as argon and carbon dioxide (CO_2) (Figure 8.31). Molecules of nitrogen (N_2) and oxygen (O_2) account for 97.2 percent of the mass of air. The amount of water vapor depends on the temperature and relative humidity.

Relative humidity Water vapor is water in gas form. Ordinary air contains a small percentage of water vapor. Evaporation adds water vapor to the air. Condensation removes water vapor. The percentage of water vapor in the air is a balance between evaporation and condensation. The **relative humidity** tells how much water vapor is in the air compared to how much the air can hold. When the relative humidity is 100 percent, the air has as much water vapor as it can hold. That means any water vapor that evaporates from your skin is condensed right back again, which is why you feel hot and sticky when the humidity is high. The opposite is true in the dry air of desert climates. Hot desert air has a very low relative humidity, allowing water to evaporate rapidly. This is why dry heat feels more bearable than humid heat.

Air supports life The gases in air are very important to living things on Earth. Animals use oxygen in the air. Plants use carbon dioxide. As a tree grows, you don't see soil disappear to provide mass for the tree. After oxygen and hydrogen (water), the most abundant element in a tree is carbon. All of the carbon atoms in wood come from carbon dioxide in the air.

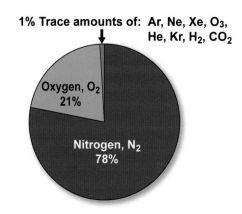

Composition of Earth's

1% Trace amounts of: Ar, Ne, Xe, O_3, He, Kr, H_2, CO_2

Figure 8.31: *Air is a mixture of gases.*

8.3 Section Review

1. Why does the pressure of a gas increase with a decrease in volume? (Assume the temperature does not change.)

2. Explain why the pressure of a gas increases with an increase in temperature. (Assume the volume does not change.)

3. Which gas law best explains why a hot-air balloon floats in the air?

The Deep Water Submarine Alvin

Imagine you are 4,500 meters (14,764 feet) below the ocean's surface, near an undersea volcanic vent. Because light from the sun cannot penetrate these depths, you are surrounded by total darkness. The pressure, 400 times greater than at the surface, is so great that it could crush an automobile. Surprisingly, you are surrounded by abundant and strange sea life including giant clams, tube worms, and spider crabs. The deep water submarine Alvin is a research vessel designed to take scientists into this environment.

Exploring the ocean depths requires courage and very sophisticated engineering. A typical eight-hour dive takes two scientists and a pilot as deep as 4,500 meters. When working at maximum depth, it takes about two hours for the Alvin submarine to reach the seafloor and another two to return to the surface. The four hours of working time on the bottom are crammed with carefully planned photography, sampling, and experiments.

Under pressure

At 4,500 meters, the water pressure is 44 million N/m^2. This extreme pressure is equivalent to the weight of a car supported on an area the size of your big toe! The Alvin submarine is 7.1 meters long and 3.7 meters tall, but the spherical pressure hull inside (where scientists work) is only two meters in diameter.

The hull is spherical because a sphere is the shape that best withstands the uniform pressure exerted by a fluid like seawater. Even with its sturdy shape, the hull needs to be made from a strong material. The titanium alloy used in Alvin's hull (only 4.9 centimeters thick) is one of the strongest materials ever developed. A hull of ordinary steel or aluminum would be crushed flat by the forces exerted by the ocean's enormous pressure.

Diving into the depths

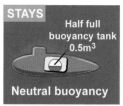
STAYS
Half full buoyancy tank 0.5m³
Neutral buoyancy

DIVES
Full buoyancy tank
Negative buoyancy

RISES
Empty buoyancy tank
Positive buoyancy

Alvin and other submarines control their depth by changing their buoyancy. Aboard the submarine is a chamber that is filled with different amounts of air and water. The amount of air and water is adjusted with pumps until the average density for the whole submarine is the same as the density of water. When the average densities are matched (neutral buoyancy), the submarine neither rises nor sinks. To dive, water is pumped into the tank and air is released. The average density becomes greater than the density of water and the submarine sinks (negative buoyancy). To rise, some water is pumped out of the tank and replaced with air. The average density decreases and the submarine rises (positive buoyancy).

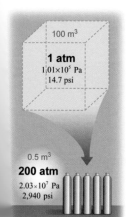
100 m³
1 atm
1.01×10⁵ Pa
14.7 psi
0.5 m³
200 atm
2.03×10⁷ Pa
2,940 psi

Breathing at the bottom of the ocean

At 20 breaths per minute (a normal rate), an average adult inhales 0.08 m³ of air each minute. The small volume of Alvin's hull means that the normal three-person crew would use up all of the oxygen in the air in just eight minutes without an additional supply. How can the crew survive a seven hour expedition?

Air for breathing is kept in tanks at very high pressure. A seven-hour mission with a crew of three requires at least 100 m³ of air at atmospheric pressure. This volume can be stored in a tank with a volume of 0.5 m³ by raising the pressure (Boyle's law) to 200 times atmospheric pressure. Air tanks for diving typically store air at pressures near or exceeding 200 atmospheres.

Amazing discoveries

The Alvin submarine has made more than 3,700 dives, and is considered the most productive research submarine in the world. Exploring undersea volcanoes and discovering strange new life forms are part of Alvin's long and successful career. The major discovery of an abundance of exotic animal life near undersea volcanic vents has led to new theories about the generation of life. Since no light can penetrate through the deep waters, scientists concluded that the animal chemistry there is based on chemosynthesis, not photosynthesis.

In addition to research, Alvin has participated in several exciting recovery missions. In 1966, Alvin located and recovered a nuclear weapon when the plane carrying it crashed into the ocean off the coast of Spain. In 1986, Alvin made a dozen dives to the Titanic, which in 1912 had sunk in 3,789 meters of water.

Questions:

1. What challenges face scientists when studying the deep ocean?
2. How is buoyancy involved in the operation of a submarine?
3. Explain how enough air is brought along on a mission for the crew to breathe.
4. Name two important discoveries made by the Alvin.

Chapter 8 Review

Understanding Vocabulary

Select the correct term to complete the sentences.

thermal expansion	pressure	density
viscosity	Archimedes' principle	tensile strength
pascal	Boyle's law	buoyancy
amorphous	stress	Charles' law
elastic		

Section 8.1

1. The metric unit used when measuring stress or pressure is the ____.

2. ____ is a measure of how much force a material can withstand per cross-section area.

3. Rubber is a more ____ material than steel.

4. Salt is crystalline and plastic is ____.

5. The ____ of a material is its mass divided by its volume.

6. The ____ of a material is the stress at which it breaks under tension.

7. Temperature increases cause ____ in almost all solid materials.

Section 8.2

8. ____ is a measure of the upward force a fluid exerts on an object that is immersed.

9. Maple syrup is a thick fluid that does not flow easily and has a high ____.

10. ____ states that the force exerted on an object by a liquid is equal to the weight of the fluid displaced by the object.

Section 8.3

11. As you pump more air into a bicycle tire, you increase the ____ inside the tire.

12. ____ states that the volume of a gas increases with increasing temperature.

13. ____ states that as the pressure of a gas increases, its volume decreases proportionally.

Reviewing Concepts

Section 8.1

1. How can you tell the difference between a physical property and a chemical property?

2. Which has greater density, a piece of copper wire, or the bar of copper from which the wire is made?

3. Which has more volume, one kilogram of glass or one kilogram of cork?

4. Platinum has a much higher density than aluminum. Which has more mass, 1 m^3 of platinum or 1 m^3 of aluminum?

5. Describe how the arrangement of the atoms and molecules in a sugar crystal differ from those in a piece of plastic.

6. Why is the strength of a material described in terms of stress instead of force?

7. If two steel wires made with different cross-section areas are tested under the same force, which would have the higher stress?

8. Rubber and steel are both elastic, yet engineers do not design bridges out of rubber. Explain why.

9. What is the difference between tension and compression?

10. What causes thermal expansion?

Section 8.2

11. How does the buoyant force of a rock submerged in water compare to the weight of the water displaced by the rock?

12. Why does ice float in a glass of water?

13. Would a cube of solid silver sink or float in liquid silver? How do you know?

14. When poured into water in a glass jar, oil floats to the top.
    a. How does the oil's density compare to the water's density?
    b. If an object floats in the oil, will it also float in the water?
    c. If an object floats in the water, will it also float in the oil?

15. Seawater has a higher density than freshwater. Would you find it easier to float in an ocean or in a freshwater lake? Give a reason for your answer.

16. Steel is more dense than water but steel ships float in water. Explain.

17. What is the relationship between density and buoyancy?

18. Explain how height, pressure, and speed are related by energy conservation in fluids.

19. How does the pressure compare at 5 cm below the surface of the water in your kitchen sink and 5 cm below the surface of the water in a lake?

20. What is the relationship between the pressure in a liquid and the depth of the liquid?

21. What is the relationship between the viscosity of a liquid and its temperature?

22. Honey is more viscous than water. How are they different at the atomic level?

Section 8.3

23. What does Boyle's law say about the relationship between the pressure and volume of a gas?

24. What does Charles' law say about the volume and temperature of a gas?

25. Explain why it is not possible to have a temperature lower than absolute zero.

26. How is the pressure of a gas affected by temperature changes?

27. What is relative humidity? Why do you feel hotter at the same temperature when the relative humidity is high compared to when it is low?

28. How does the density of a gas differ from the density of a liquid or solid?

Solving Problems

Section 8.1

1. For the following events, state whether a physical change or a chemical change has occurred:

   a. You notice that your grandmother's silver is very dark in places and needs polishing.
   b. Your cup of hot chocolate gives off steam.
   c. When you mix baking soda and vinegar, the resulting mixture fizzes and produces bubbles.
   d. An ice cube melts.
   e. You burn an oak log in a fireplace.
   f. You activate a heat pack to warm your hands.

2. The density of brick is 1,600 kg/m^3. What is the mass of a brick with a volume of 0.0006 m^3?

3. The density of pure gold is 19,300 kg/m^3. Calculate the mass of a pure gold bracelet if it displaces 2×10^{-6} m^3 of water.

4. Your teacher gives you two stainless steel ball bearings. The larger has a mass of 0.025 kg and a volume of 0.0032 m^3. The smaller has a mass of 0.010 kg. Calculate the volume of the smaller ball bearing.

5. The density of ice is 920 kg/m^3. What is the volume of 1 kilogram of ice? If one kilogram of ice completely melted, what would the volume of the water be? The density of water is 1,000 kg/m^3.

6. You are an engineer who must calculate the stress on a steel rod of cross-section area 0.05 m^2 under a force of 500 N. The rod is rated for a maximum of 12,000 N/m^2 of stress before breaking. What is the stress on the rod? Will the rod break?

7. A steel cable has a maximum safe stress of 3,000 N/m^2. What is the largest cross-section area of steel cable you can use under a 100 N force?

8. A solid cubic centimeter of platinum weighs 21.5 N. If this cube of platinum is placed under water, what volume of water is displaced? What weight of water is displaced?
(Hints: 1 cm^3 of water has a mass of 1 gram; 1 gram weighs 0.0098 N; density of platinum = 21.5 g/cm^3.)

9. On a cold morning, your pancake syrup is difficult to pour. How could you get your pancake syrup to pour faster?

Section 8.3

10. You pump 5 liters of air into a beach ball. If you pump the same amount of air into a basketball with *half* the volume of the beach ball, at constant temperature, which has the greater amount of pressure?

11. Suppose you pump 100 cm^3 of air at 10 psi into a bicycle tire. If the pressure in the tire is 30 psi, what is the volume of the tire?

12. If the pressure in a car tire is 33 psi on a 0°C (= 273 K) day, what is its pressure on a 25°C (= 298 K) day?

13. What are the freezing point and boiling point of water in Kelvins?

14. What is the new pressure of helium at 200 psi when it is cooled from 50°C (= 323 K) to 20°C (= 293 K) in a 1-liter tank?

15. Five liters of oxygen at 600 psi are pumped into a 1-liter tank. What is the pressure inside the tank, assuming that the temperature does not change?

16. A 100-liter hot air balloon is filled with 75 liters of air at 20°C (= 293 K). To what temperature does the air need to be heated in order to completely fill the balloon?

Applying Your Knowledge

Section 8.1

1. You can use the physical properties of matter to separate a mixture. Describe which physical property you would use and how you would take advantage of it to separate the following mixtures:
   a. a mixture of fine sawdust and iron shavings
   b. a mixture of gold and sand
   c. a mixture of cooking oil and sand

2. A large amount of the gold reserve for the United States is stored in the Fort Knox Bullion Depository vault in Kentucky. Much of it is in the form of bars with a dimension of 7 in × 3-5/8 in × 1^3/$_4$ in. The gold has a density of 19,300 kg/m^3. Calculate the mass of one gold bar. If you picked up this gold bar, would it be more like picking up a can of soda, a gallon of water, or a box of books?
(Hints: 1 inch = 2.54 cm; the volume of a rectangular bar equals its length × width × height.)

Section 8.2

3. Almost all fish have a swim bladder filled with gas in order to maintain a neutral buoyancy. Neutral buoyancy allows fish to conserve energy by not having to continuously swim to avoid sinking. Explain how a fish's swim bladder allows it to keep a neutral buoyancy.

4. Describe how the density of ice affects our daily lives. Explain why ice forms on the top of ponds and lakes, and not the bottom. Use the following terms in your explanation: *density, organized structure,* and *water molecules.* How does this property of water help support life in lakes and ponds?

5. Quite a number of studies have been done on the viscosity of lava from various volcanic eruptions around the world. Do some research to find out how scientists determine the viscosity of lava, and discover if there is much variation in the viscosity of different lava flows.

Section 8.3

6. Describe how your body makes use of Boyle's law in order to breathe.

7. SCUBA stands for self-contained underwater breathing apparatus. A number of inventors have contributed to developing the technology for scuba diving. The invention of the aqualung by Jacques-Yves Cousteau and Emile Gagnan in 1943 made scuba diving available to anyone who wanted to do underwater exploring. A standard sized scuba tank is filled with the equivalent of 80 cubic feet of air at 1 atm compressed into a 0.39-cubic foot space. What is the pressure within the tank?

.....Density

Chapter 9

The Atom

We know the planets in our solar system exist, but are there other planets orbiting other stars? Based on its size and the laws of probability, the odds are excellent that there are other planets in the universe. But finding one is another story. Astronomers estimate that there are over 200 billion stars in our galaxy and that there are at least 50 billion galaxies in the universe! The photo at right, taken by the Hubble Space Telescope, shows countless galaxies in a tiny speck of space.

Since 1995, some planets have been found. The first planets found around stars other than our sun have never been seen. Instead, astronomers discovered them *indirectly*, by observing the effects of the planet on its companion star. Even though a planet has a much smaller mass than the star it orbits, its gravitational force "tugs" on the star, causing it to wobble slightly. That wobble can be detected by analyzing the light given off by the star. Is it possible one of those planets has life? Maybe in your lifetime scientists will discover that we are not alone in the universe!

Finding out about atoms is much like searching for planets in the universe. Both endeavors rely on indirect evidence. In fact, atoms are so small that there are far more atoms in a drop of water than there are stars in our galaxy!

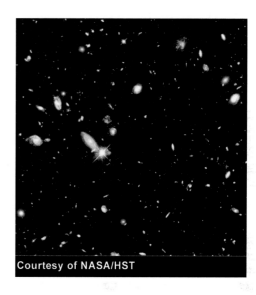

Courtesy of NASA/HST

Key Questions

- ✓ If you built a model of a single atom as large as a football stadium, what object could represent the nucleus in the center of the stadium?
- ✓ What is the strongest force in the universe? (Hint: it exists inside atoms!)
- ✓ What color of light has the highest energy?

9.1 Atomic Structure

You have read that atoms, by themselves or combined with other atoms in molecules, are the building blocks of every type of matter. Even though scientists have only recently been able to see atoms directly, they have been able to *infer* a model for atomic structure that is based on an enormous amount of evidence. Like good detective work, to infer is to draw a conclusion that is supported by all the available evidence (observations).

The atomic theory

What is the atomic theory? English scientist John Dalton (1766-1844) started experimenting with gases in the atmosphere in 1787. He found that water existed as a gas in the air. Since air and water could not occupy the same space at the same time, he concluded that they must be made of tiny particles that mixed. His careful measurements gave him repeatable evidence that matter is made up of *atoms*. In 1808, Dalton published a detailed **atomic theory** that contained the following statements:

1. Matter is composed of tiny, indivisible, and indestructible particles called *atoms*.

2. An *element* is composed entirely of one type of atom. The properties of all atoms of one element are identical and are different from those of any other element.

3. A *compound* contains atoms of two or more different elements. The relative number of atoms of each element in a particular compound is always the same.

4. Atoms do not change their identities in chemical reactions. They are just rearranged into different substances.

Exceptions to the atomic theory Dalton's theory has been amended as we learned more about the atom. Today we know that atoms are not indivisible, but are made of smaller particles. Atoms are not indestructible, but can be split. Not all of the atoms of a given element are *exactly* identical. In this section, you will learn about some changes to the first two statements of Dalton's atomic theory.

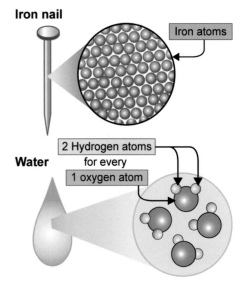

Figure 9.1: *An element is composed of one type of atom. A compound contains atoms of two or more elements in specific ratios.*

The puzzle of the inside of the atom

The electron identified

An English physicist named J. J. Thomson (1856-1940) observed that streams of particles could be made to come from different gases placed in tubes carrying electricity. Thomson identified a negatively charged particle he called the *electron*. These electrons must have come out of atoms. Thompson proposed that the atom was a positive sphere with negative electrons embedded in it "like raisins in a bun." (Figure 9.2).

The proton and the nucleus discovered

In 1911, Ernest Rutherford (1871-1937), Hans Geiger (1882-1945), and Ernest Marsden (1889-1970) did a clever experiment to test Thompson's theory. They launched fast, positively-charged helium ions at extremely thin pieces of gold foil. They expected a few helium ions to be deflected a small amount when they chanced to hit a gold atom and plowed through Thompson's "pudding." They found something else instead. Most of the helium ions passed straight through the foil (Figure 9.3). Even more surprising, a few bounced back in the direction they came! The unexpected result prompted Rutherford to remark, "*It was as if you fired an artillery shell at a piece of tissue paper and it came back and hit you in the head!*"

The nuclear model of the atom

The best way to explain the pass-through result was if the gold atoms were mostly empty space, allowing most of the helium ions to go through undeflected. The best way to explain the bounce-back result was if nearly all the mass of a gold atom were concentrated in a tiny, hard core at the center. Further experiments confirmed Rutherford's ideas and we know that every atom has a tiny *nucleus*, that contains more than 99% of the atom's mass. Electrons occupy the area between the nucleus and the atom's edge.

The neutron

The positively charged proton was soon discovered and located in the nucleus. But there still was a serious problem with the atomic model. Protons could only account for about half the observed mass. This problem was solved in 1932 by James Chadwick (1891-1974). Chadwick bombarded a thin sheet of beryllium with positively-charged particles. His experiment showed a third type of subatomic particle, about the same mass as the proton, called the *neutron*. The missing mass was now explained. The nucleus contains about equal numbers of protons and neutrons.

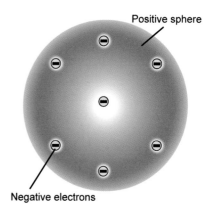

Figure 9.2: *Thomson's model of the atom.*

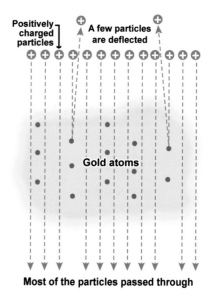

Figure 9.3: *Rutherford's famous experiment led to the discovery of the nucleus.*

Three subatomic particles make up an atom

Protons, neutrons, and electrons
Today we know that atoms are made of three tiny *subatomic particles*: protons, neutrons, and electrons. A **proton** is a particle with a positive charge. An **electron** is a particle with a negative charge. A **neutron** is a neutral particle and has a zero charge. The charge on one proton and one electron are exactly equal and opposite. A **charge** is an electrical property of particles that causes them to attract and repel each other. If you put a proton and an electron together, the total charge is zero. Atoms that have the same number of protons and electrons have a net charge of zero.

The nucleus
The protons and neutrons are grouped together in the **nucleus**, which is at the center of the atom. The mass of the nucleus determines the mass of an atom. This is because protons and neutrons are much larger and more massive than electrons. In fact, a proton is 1,837 times heavier than an electron. Electrons are found outside the nucleus (Figure 9.4). All atoms have protons and neutrons in their nuclei except the simplest type of hydrogen, which only has one proton and no neutrons. The chart below compares electrons, protons, and neutrons in terms of charge and mass.

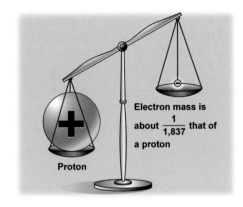

Figure 9.4: *The mass of at atom is mostly in the nucleus because protons and neutrons are much heavier than electrons.*

Electron mass is about $\frac{1}{1,837}$ that of a proton

	Occurrence	Charge	Mass (g)	Relative Mass
⊖ Electron	found outside of nucleus	-1	9.109×10^{-28}	1
⊕ Proton	found in all nuclei	+1	1.673×10^{-24}	1,837
Neutron	found in almost all nuclei (exception: most H nuclei)	0	1.675×10^{-24}	1,839

The volume of an atom
The size of an atom is determined by how far the electrons spread away from the nucleus. The electrons define a region called the *electron cloud*. The diameter of an atom is really the diameter of the electron cloud (10^{-10} m). The diameter of the nucleus is 100,000 times smaller than the diameter of the atom itself, about 10^{-15} meter (Figure 9.5). As a comparison, if an atom were the size of a football stadium, the nucleus would be the size of a pea, and the electrons would be equivalent to a few gnats flying around the stadium at high speed.

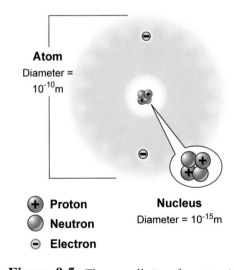

Size and Structure of the Atom

Atom
Diameter = 10^{-10} m

⊕ Proton
Neutron
⊖ Electron

Nucleus
Diameter = 10^{-15} m

Figure 9.5: *The overall size of an atom is the size of its electron cloud. The nucleus is much, much smaller.*

Forces inside atoms

Electromagnetic forces

Electrons are bound to the nucleus by **electromagnetic force**. This force is the attraction between the positive charge on protons and the negative charge on electrons. The electrons don't fall into the nucleus because they have momentum. The momentum of an electron causes it to move around the nucleus instead of falling in (Figure 9.6). A good analogy is Earth orbiting the sun. Gravity creates a force that pulls Earth toward the sun. Earth's momentum causes it to orbit the sun rather than fall straight in. While electrons don't move in orbits, the analogy is approximately correct.

Strong nuclear force

Because of electromagnetic force, all the positively charged protons in the nucleus *repel* each other. What holds the nucleus together? There is another force that is even stronger than the electromagnetic force. We call it the **strong nuclear force**. This force attracts neutrons and protons to each other and works only at extremely small distances (10^{-15} meter). If there are enough neutrons, the attraction from the strong nuclear force wins out over repulsion from the electromagnetic force and the nucleus stays together. In every atom heavier than helium there is at least one neutron for every proton in the nucleus. Even though it only acts over tiny distances, the strong nuclear force is the strongest force known to science (Figure 9.7).

Weak force

There is another nuclear force called the *weak force*. The weak force is weaker than both the electromagnetic force and the strong nuclear force. If you leave a single neutron outside the nucleus, the weak force eventually causes it to break down into a proton and an electron. The weak force does not play an important role in a stable atom, but comes into action in certain special cases when atoms break apart.

Gravity

The force of gravity inside the atom is much weaker even than the weak force. It takes a relatively large mass to create enough gravity to make a significant force. We know that particles inside an atom do not have enough mass for gravity to be an important force on the scale of atoms. But there are many unanswered questions. Understanding how gravity works inside atoms is an unsolved mystery in science.

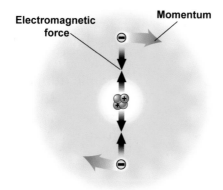

Figure 9.6: *The negative electrons are attracted to the positive protons in the nucleus, but their momentum keeps them from falling in.*

Figure 9.7: *When enough neutrons are present the strong nuclear force wins out over the repulsion between positively charged protons and pulls the nucleus together tightly. The strong nuclear force is the strongest force in the universe that we know.*

How are atoms of each element different?

Atomic number How is an atom of one element different from an atom of another element? The atoms of different elements contain different numbers of protons in the nucleus. Because the number of protons is so important, it is called the **atomic number.** The atomic number of an element is the number of protons in the nucleus of every atom of that element. Each element has a unique atomic number. An atom with only one proton in its nucleus is the element hydrogen. An atom with eight protons is the element oxygen.

Atoms of the same element always have the same number of protons.

Isotopes All atoms of the same element have the same number of protons in the nucleus. However, atoms of the same element may have different numbers of neutrons in the nucleus. **Isotopes** are atoms of the *same* element that have different numbers of neutrons. The number of protons in isotopes of an element is the same.

The isotopes of carbon Figure 9.9 shows three ways to make atoms of carbon. Most carbon atoms have six protons and six neutrons in the nucleus. However, some carbon atoms have seven or eight neutrons. They are all carbon atoms because they all contain six protons but they are different *isotopes* of carbon. The isotopes of carbon are called carbon-12, carbon-13, and carbon-14. The number after the name is called the mass number. The **mass number** of an isotope tells you the number of protons plus the number of neutrons.

Mass number = number of protons + number of neutrons

What if there are too many neutrons? Almost all elements have one or more isotopes that are *stable.* "Stable" means the nucleus stays together. For complex reasons the nucleus of an atom becomes unstable if it contains too many or too few neutrons compared to protons. If the nucleus is unstable it breaks apart. Carbon has two stable isotopes, carbon-12 and carbon-13. Carbon-14 is *radioactive* because it has an unstable nucleus. An atom of carbon-14 eventually changes itself into an atom of nitrogen-14. This process, called *radioactive decay*, is discussed further in chapter 11.

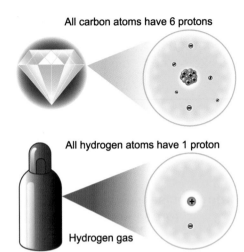

All carbon atoms have 6 protons

All hydrogen atoms have 1 proton

Hydrogen gas

Figure 9.8: *Atoms of the same element always have the same number of protons.*

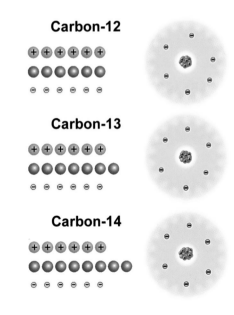

Carbon-12

Carbon-13

Carbon-14

Figure 9.9: *The isotopes of carbon.*

Atomic mass

Units of atomic mass

The atomic mass of an atom is usually given in atomic mass units (amu). One amu is 1.66×10^{-27} kg, which is one-twelfth (1/12) the mass of a carbon-12 atom. To determine the mass of a single atom, you multiply the atomic mass in amu by 1.66×10^{-27} kg/amu. For example, an "average" lithium atom has a mass of 1.15×10^{-26} kg ($6.94 \times 1.66 \times 10^{-27}$ kg/amu). This is a very small mass compared to the mass of every day objects!

Atomic mass

Elements in nature usually have a mixture of isotopes. For example, a standard table of elements lists an atomic mass of 6.94 for the element lithium. That does NOT mean there are 3 protons and 3.94 neutrons in a lithium atom! On average, 94 percent of lithium atoms are lithium-7 and 6 percent are lithium-6 (Figure 9.10). The average atomic mass of lithium is 6.94 because of the weighted average of the mixture of isotopes.

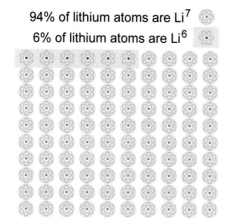

94% of lithium atoms are Li^7
6% of lithium atoms are Li^6

Figure 9.10: *Naturally occurring elements have a mixture of isotopes.*

Identifying the number of particles in a nucleus

How many neutrons are present in an aluminum atom that has an atomic number of 13 and a mass number of 27?

1. Looking for: You are asked to find the number of neutrons.

2. Given: You are given the atomic number and the mass.

3. Relationships: Use the formula: protons + neutrons = mass number.

4. Solution: Solve the equation for neutrons: neutrons = mass number - protons
Plug in and solve: neutrons = 27 - 13 = 14
The aluminum atom has 14 neutrons.

Your turn...

a. How many neutrons are present in a magnesium atom (atomic number 12) with a mass number of 25? **Answer:** 13
b. Find the number of neutrons in a calcium atom (atomic number 20) that has a mass number of 42. **Answer:** 22

9.1 Section Review

1. Name the three subatomic particles. Describe the location and charge of each particle.
2. What force holds an electron in an atom? What force holds the nucleus together?
3. One atom has 12 protons and 12 neutrons. Another has 13 protons and 12 neutrons. Are they the same or different elements?
4. Argon-36 has 18 protons. How many neutrons does it have?

9.2 Electrons and the Periodic Table

Before scientists understood how atoms were put together, they were able to identify elements by their chemical properties. In this section, you learn how the elements are organized in the *periodic table* and how an element's chemical properties are related to the arrangement of electrons.

The periodic table

How many elements are there? In the 18th through 20th centuries, scientists tried to find and catalog all the elements that make up our universe. To do so, they had to carefully observe substances in order to identify them, and then try to break them apart by any possible means. If a substance could be broken apart it could not be an element. Only a substance that could not be broken apart could truly be an element. As of this writing, scientists have identified 118 elements. Only 88 of these occur naturally. The others are made in laboratories.

The modern periodic table As chemists worked on determining which substances were elements, they noticed that some elements acted like other elements. The soft metals lithium, sodium, and potassium always combine with oxygen in a ratio of two atoms of metal per atom of oxygen (Figure 9.11). By keeping track of how each element combined with other elements, scientists began to recognize repeating patterns. From this data, they developed the first *periodic table of the elements*. The **periodic table** organizes the elements according to how they combine with other elements (chemical properties).

Organization of the periodic table The periodic table is organized in order of increasing atomic number. The lightest element (hydrogen) is at the upper left. The heaviest (#118) is on the lower right.

The periodic table is further divided into *periods* and *groups*. Each horizontal row is called a **period**. Across any period, the properties of the elements gradually change. Each vertical column is called a **group**. Groups of elements have similar properties. The *main group elements* are Groups 1-2 and 13-18 (the tall columns of the periodic table) Elements in Groups 3 through 12 are called the *transition elements*. The inner transition elements, called lanthanides and actinides, are usually put below to fit on a page.

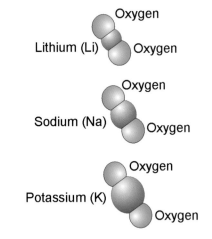

Figure 9.11: *The metals lithium, sodium, and potassium all form molecules with two atoms of oxygen. All the elements in group one of the periodic table form molecules with two oxygen atoms.*

Reading the periodic table

Metals, nonmetals, and metalloids

Most of the elements are metals. A **metal** is typically shiny, opaque, and a good conductor of heat and electricity as a pure element. Metals are also malleable, which means they can be hammered into different shapes or bent without breaking. With the exception of hydrogen, the nonmetals are on the right side of the periodic table. **Nonmetals** are poor conductors of heat and electricity. Solid nonmetals are brittle and appear dull. **Metalloids** have properties of both metals and nonmetals. They are weak conductors of electricity and are often used as semiconductors in computer circuits.

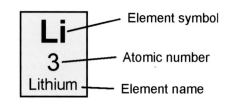

Figure 9.12: *Reading the periodic table.*

Periodic Table of the Elements

1																	**18**
H 1 hydrogen	**2**			Main Group Elements			Non metals				**13** **14** **15** **16** **17**						**He** 2 helium
Li 3 lithium	**Be** 4 beryllium			Transition Elements			Metals				**B** 5 boron	**C** 6 carbon	**N** 7 nitrogen	**O** 8 oxygen	**F** 9 fluorine		**Ne** 10 neon
Na 11 sodium	**Mg** 12 magnesium	**3**	**4**	**5**	**6**	**7**	**8**	**9**	**10**	**11**	**12** **Al** 13 aluminum	**Si** 14 silicon	**P** 15 phosphorus	**S** 16 sulfur	**Cl** 17 chlorine		**Ar** 18 argon
K 19 potassium	**Ca** 20 calcium	**Sc** 21 scandium	**Ti** 22 titanium	**V** 23 vanadium	**Cr** 24 chromium	**Mn** 25 manganese	**Fe** 26 iron	**Co** 27 cobalt	**Ni** 28 nickel	**Cu** 29 copper	**Zn** 30 zinc	**Ga** 31 gallium	**Ge** 32 germanium	**As** 33 arsenic	**Se** 34 selenium	**Br** 35 bromine	**Kr** 36 krypton
Rb 37 rubidium	**Sr** 38 strontium	**Y** 39 yttrium	**Zr** 40 zirconium	**Nb** 41 niobium	**Mo** 42 molybdenum	**Tc** 43 technetium	**Ru** 44 ruthenium	**Rh** 45 rhodium	**Pd** 46 palladium	**Ag** 47 silver	**Cd** 48 cadmium	**In** 49 indium	**Sn** 50 tin	**Sb** 51 antimony	**Te** 52 tellurium	**I** 53 iodine	**Xe** 54 xenon
Cs 55 cesium	**Ba** 56 barium		**Hf** 72 hafnium	**Ta** 73 tantalum	**W** 74 tungsten	**Re** 75 rhenium	**Os** 76 osmium	**Ir** 77 iridium	**Pt** 78 platinum	**Au** 79 gold	**Hg** 80 mercury	**Tl** 81 thallium	**Pb** 82 lead	**Bi** 83 bismuth	**Po** 84 polonium	**At** 85 astatine	**Rn** 86 radon
Fr 87 francium	**Ra** 88 radium		**Rf** 104 rutherfordium	**Db** 105 dubnium	**Sg** 106 seaborgium	**Bh** 107 bohrium	**Hs** 108 hassium	**Mt** 109 meitnerium	**Ds** 110 darmstadium	**Rg** 111 roentgenium	**Uub** 112 ununbium	**Uut** 113 ununtrium	**Uuq** 114 ununquadium	**Uup** 115 ununpentium	**Uuh** 116 ununhexium	**Uus** 117 ununseptium	**Uuh** 118 ununoctium

ROWS = PERIODS   COLUMNS = GROUPS

La 57 lanthanum	**Ce** 58 cerium	**Pr** 59 praseodymium	**Nd** 60 neodymium	**Pm** 61 promethium	**Sm** 62 samarium	**Eu** 63 europium	**Gd** 64 gadolinium	**Tb** 65 terbium	**Dy** 66 dysprosium	**Ho** 67 holmium	**Er** 68 erbium	**Tm** 69 thulium	**Yb** 70 ytterbium	**Lu** 71 lutetium
Ac 89 actinium	**Th** 90 thorium	**Pa** 91 protactinium	**U** 92 uranium	**Np** 93 neptunium	**Pu** 94 plutonium	**Am** 95 americium	**Cm** 96 curium	**Bk** 97 berkelium	**Cf** 98 californium	**Es** 99 einsteinium	**Fm** 100 fermium	**Md** 101 mendelevium	**No** 102 nobelium	**Lr** 103 lawrencium

Electrons in atoms

Electrons determine most properties

Why is pure gold a shiny yellow color? Why is iron hard? Why is oxygen important to life? What about atoms gives the elements their unique physical and chemical properties? The answer is the electrons. Electrons determine almost all the physical and chemical properties of matter, except for mass.

The electron cloud

Recall that electrons form the *electron cloud* outside the nucleus. Complete atoms have the same number of protons and electrons. A helium atom has 2 protons and 2 electrons. A silver atom has 47 protons and 47 electrons.

Quantum rules

The electrons in an atom obey an unusual set of rules that only allow them to have special values of energy and momentum. These rules are given by *quantum mechanics*, the branch of physics that deals with the world at the atomic scale. The two most important rules are:

1. The energy of any electron in an atom must match one of the energy levels in the atom.

2. Each energy level can hold only a certain number of electrons, and no more.

Energy levels

An **energy level** is a region in the electron cloud with a specific electron energy. The first (lowest) energy level holds up to 2 electrons and is closest to the nucleus. The second and third energy levels hold up to eight electrons each. The first four energy levels are shown in (Figure 9.13).

How electrons fill in the energy levels

Each energy level can hold only a fixed number of electrons. Electrons fill up the energy levels element-by-element, starting from the first. For example, a helium atom has two electrons. The two electrons completely fill up the first energy level (Figure 9.14). The next element is lithium with three electrons. Since the first energy level only holds two electrons, the third electron must go into the second energy level. Lithium starts the second row (period) of the periodic table because it is the first element with an electron in the second energy level.

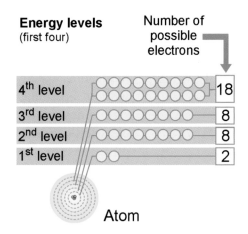

Figure 9.13: *Electrons occupy energy levels around the nucleus. The farther away an electron is from the nucleus, the higher the energy it possesses.*

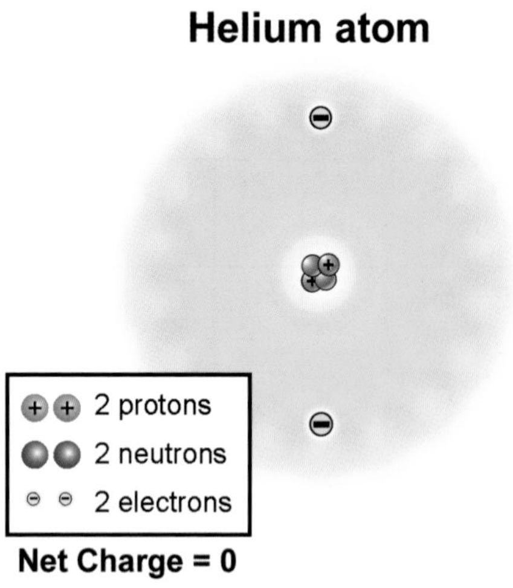

Helium atom

Net Charge = 0

Figure 9.14: *A helium atom has two protons in its nucleus and two electrons.*

Valence electrons and the periodic table

Period 2 elements
The picture below shows how the electrons in the elements in the second period (lithium to neon) fill the energy levels. Carbon has six electrons so the first energy level is full and four electrons go into the second level (Figure 9.15). Each element in the second period adds one more electron until all 8 spots in the second energy level are full at atomic number 10, which is neon.

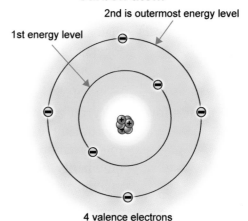

Carbon atom

1st energy level
2nd is outermost energy level

4 valence electrons

Figure 9.15: *A carbon atom has four valence electrons. The second energy level is its outermost level.*

	Li	Be	B	C	N	O	F	Ne
⊖ Total	3	4	5	6	7	8	9	10
⊖ In the outermost energy level	1	2	3	4	5	6	7	8

Valence electrons
Electrons in the highest energy level are called **valence electrons**. Think of the valence electrons as forming the outer edge of the atom. The inner core electrons and the nucleus do not interact with other atoms. Therefore, the valence electrons determine almost all the properties of an element.

Atoms combine by sharing or trading electrons
Atoms combine with other atoms by sharing or trading valence electrons. Shared electrons are how molecules are held together. That is why valence electrons are so important. The valence electrons determine how atoms of one element combine with atoms of other elements.

Atoms seek full or empty energy levels
Atoms share or trade electrons so they can have energy levels that are either completely filled or completely empty. Hydrogen has one valence electron and needs one more to fill its outer energy level. Oxygen has six valence electrons and needs two more to fill its outer energy level. So one oxygen atom shares electrons with *two* hydrogen atoms to make a water molecule (Figure 9.16).

Chemistry
Many mysteries in chemistry were explained when we finally understood how electrons in atoms behaved. Atoms combine with each other into molecules and compounds by sharing or trading valence electrons. Atoms combine in molecules so that each atom in the molecule has completely filled or completely empty energy levels.

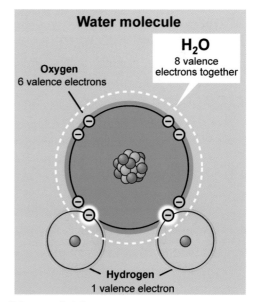

Water molecule

H_2O
8 valence electrons together

Oxygen
6 valence electrons

Hydrogen
1 valence electron

Figure 9.16: *The valence electrons in a water molecule.*

Energy and chemical bonds

Electrons form chemical bonds

A **chemical bond** forms when atoms trade or share electrons. Two atoms that are sharing one or more electrons are chemically bonded and move together. In a water molecule, each hydrogen atom shares its single electron with the oxygen atom at the center. Almost all elements form chemical bonds easily. Most matter on Earth is in the form of compounds not pure elements.

Why bonds form

Why do atoms form bonds with other atoms? Like many other physics questions, the answer involves energy. When an energy level is completely full (or empty) the total energy of the atom is lower than when the level is only partly filled. By combining with other atoms into molecules, each atom in a molecule is able to lower its energy.

Noble gases

Some atoms already have completely filled energy levels. The **noble gases** (helium, neon, argon,...) all have completely filled energy levels. These elements usually do not form chemical bonds with other elements and are found as pure elements in nature.

Energy is released as molecules form

When a molecule forms, energy is released. When pure hydrogen is mixed with pure oxygen, a tiny spark causes a huge explosion. The explosion comes from the energy released as hydrogen atoms combine with oxygen atoms to make water molecules. The space shuttle engines use pure hydrogen and oxygen for fuel because of the amount of energy released.

Chemical energy

Chemical energy is energy stored in chemical bonds between atoms. The energy is released when a molecule forms. You must supply energy to separate the atoms in a molecule.

9.2 Section Review

1. What is the atomic mass of manganese?
2. To which group of the periodic table does oxygen belong? List the other elements in the group.
3. Does argon combine with other elements to make compounds? Explain your answer.
4. Lithium and carbon have their valence electrons in the second energy level. In what level does each of the elements calcium, rubidium, iodine, and krypton have their valence electrons?

Dot diagrams

Valence electrons are often shown using *dot diagrams*. This system was developed in 1916 by G.N. Lewis, an American chemist. The symbol of the element in the diagram represents the nucleus of an atom and all of its electrons except for the valence electrons. The number of dots placed around the symbol of the element is equal to the number of valence electrons. Dots are shown in pairs around the four sides of the symbol as a reminder that valence electrons occur in pairs. Electrons begin to pair up only when no more single spaces are left. This is why the first four electrons are shown as single dots around the symbol, as in the diagram for carbon.

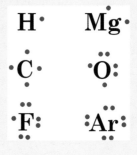

9.3 Quantum Theory and the Atom

Have you ever seen a neon light? Inside the glass tube there is an element in the gas phase, such as neon, argon or krypton. When the right amount of energy is added to the atoms, they emit light that we can see. Neon emits red light when energized. Other elements emit other colors. Each element emits a characteristic color of light. Why? In this section, you will learn how the colors of light given off by atoms tell scientists a lot about the inside of the atom.

The spectrum

The spectrum — Light is given off when electricity passes through a gas. This is how fluorescent bulbs and neon signs work. If you look through a prism at the light given off by a pure element you see that the light does not include all colors. Instead you see a few very specific colors, and the colors are different for different elements (Figure 9.17). The characteristic pattern of colors is called a **spectrum**. The colors of clothes, paint, and everything else around you come from this property of elements to emit or absorb light of only certain colors.

Spectrometers and spectral lines — Each individual color is called a **spectral line** because each color appears as a line in a **spectrometer**. A spectrometer is a device that spreads light into its different colors. The diagram below shows a spectrometer made with a prism. The spectral lines appear on the screen on the right.

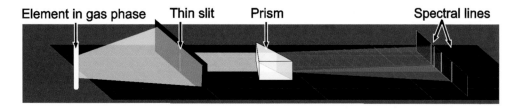

Energy and color — Light is a form of energy. The amount of energy depends on the color of the light. Red light has low energy and blue light has higher energy. Green and yellow light have energy between red and blue. The fact that atoms only emit certain colors of light tells us that something inside an atom can only have certain values of energy. Light is given off by electrons and this is how scientists first discovered the energy levels in an atom.

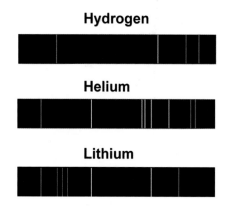

Figure 9.17: *When light from energized atoms is directed through a prism, spectral lines are observed. Each element has its own distinct pattern of spectral lines.*

Quantum theory and the Bohr atom

Neils Bohr   Light is emitted by electrons as they are accelerated, or as they change their energy. Danish physicist Neils Bohr (1885-1962) proposed the concept of energy levels to explain the spectrum. When an electron moves from one energy level to another the atom gives up the energy difference between the two levels. The energy comes out as different colors of light. The specific colors of the spectral lines correspond to the differences in energy between the energy levels. The energy in atoms changes in little jumps which Bohr called *quanta*. For electrons, it's an-all-or-nothing jump between energy levels that releases quantities of energy as colors of light.

Explaining spectral lines   When a hydrogen atom absorbs energy from electricity, an electron moves to a higher energy level (Figure 9.18). That is *how* the atom absorbs the energy, by promoting electrons to higher energy levels. The atom emits the energy when the electron falls back to a lower energy. The emitted energy comes out as light with a color proportional to the energy difference between the level where the electron started and where it ended up. The diagram below shows how the spectral lines of hydrogen come from electrons falling from the 3rd, 4th, 5th, and 6th energy levels down to the 2nd energy level.

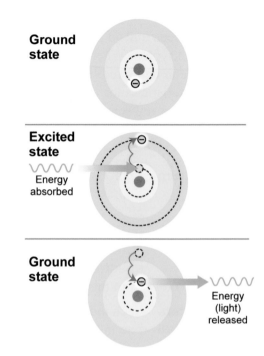

Figure 9.18: *When the right amount of energy is absorbed, an electron in a hydrogen atom jumps to a higher energy level—an excited state. When the electron falls back to lower energy—the ground state—it releases the same amount of energy it absorbed. The energy comes out of the atom as light of a specific color.*

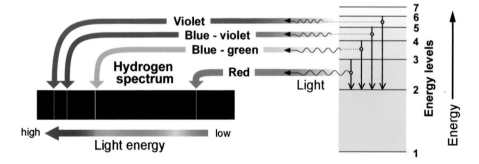

Light can be thought of as a particle   The Bohr atom led to a new way of thinking about energy in atomic systems. A *quanta* is a quantity of something that cannot be divided any smaller. One electron is a quanta of matter because you can't split an electron. **Quantum theory** says that when a particle (such as an electron) is confined to a small space (inside an atom) the energy, momentum, and other variables of the particle become quantized and can only have specific values.

The quantum model of the atom

Quantum theory and probability

Quantum theory says that when things get very small, on the size of atoms, matter and energy do *not* obey Newton's laws or other laws of *classical* physics. At least the classical laws are not obeyed in the same way as with larger objects, like a baseball.

The quantum model of the atom

In 1925, Erwin Schrödinger (1887-1961) proposed the quantum model of the atom we still use today. The quantum atom still has all the protons and neutrons in a tiny nucleus. However, instead of thinking about an electron as a particle moving around the nucleus, the electron dissolves into a fuzzy cloud of negative charge called a **quantum state**. The quantum state spreads the electron out into a three-dimensional cloud with a shape that depends on the electron's energy level and location within its energy level. The second energy level has 8 quantum states, one for each of the 8 electrons the level can hold. Figure 9.19 shows the shapes of these 8 quantum states. These shapes are important because they determine the shape of molecules the atom forms.

The Pauli exclusion principle

According to the quantum model, two electrons can never be in the same quantum state at the same time. This rule is known as the *Pauli exclusion principle* after Wolfgang Pauli (1900-1958). The exclusion principle is why an electron cannot fall to a lower energy level if it is already filled by other electrons. Once all the quantum states in the first energy level are occupied, the next electron has to go into a higher energy level.

Two electrons can never be in the same quantum state in the same atom at the same time.

Planck's constant

The "smearing out" of particles into fuzzy quantum states becomes important when size, momentum, energy or time become comparable in size to **Planck's constant**. Planck's constant (h) has the value 6.6×10^{-34} joule-seconds. The units are energy × time but are the same as distance × momentum. If you measure the momentum of an electron in a hydrogen atom, and multiply it by the size of the atom, the result is about 1×10^{-34} joule-seconds. This is comparable to Planck's constant and is why quantum theory must be used to describe this electron.

The directions x, y, and z in 3-D coordinates

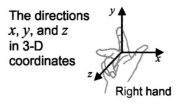

Right hand

The eight quantum states in the second energy level

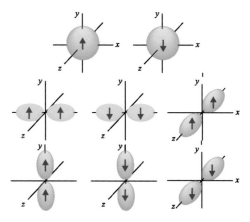

The quantum states of valence electrons determine the shape of molecules

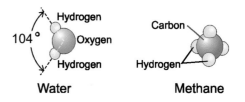

Water

Methane

Figure 9.19: *The 3-D shapes of the 8 quantum states in the second energy level.*

The uncertainty principle

The uncertainty principle
If an electron is spread out into a quantum state, how can you locate its exact position in an atom? You can't! The work of German physicist Werner Heisenberg (1901-1976) led to Heisenberg's **uncertainty principle.** According to the uncertainty principle, a particle's position, momentum, energy, and time can never be precisely known in a quantum system.

Understanding the uncertainty principle
The uncertainty principle arises because the quantum world is so small. In the quantum world light energy comes in little bundles called **photons**. When you see a car, your eye collects trillions of photons that bounce off the car. Photons are so small compared with a car that the car is not affected by your looking at it. To "see" an electron you also have to bounce a photon of light off it, or interact with the electron in some way (Figure 9.20). Because the electron is so small, even a single photon moves it and changes its motion. That means the moment you use a photon to locate an electron, you push it so you no longer know precisely how fast it is going. In fact, any process of observing in the quantum world changes the very system you are trying to observe. The uncertainty principle works because measuring any variable disturbs the others in an unpredictable way.

The meaning of the uncertainty principle
The uncertainty principle has some very strange implications. In the quantum world, anything that *can* happen, *does* happen. Put more strongly, unless something is specifically *forbidden* from happening, it *must* happen. For example, suppose you could create a particle out of nothing, then make it disappear again. Suppose you could do this so fast that it was within the energy and time limit of the uncertainty principle. You could break the law of conservation of energy if you did it quickly enough and in a very small space. *We believe this actually happens.* Physicists believe the so-called "vacuum" of space is not truly empty when we consider details so small the uncertainty principle prevents us from seeing them. There is considerable experimental evidence that supports the belief that particles of matter and antimatter are continually popping into existence and disappearing again, out of pure nothing. This implies that empty space (vacuum) may have energy of its own, even when there is absolutely no ordinary matter or energy present.

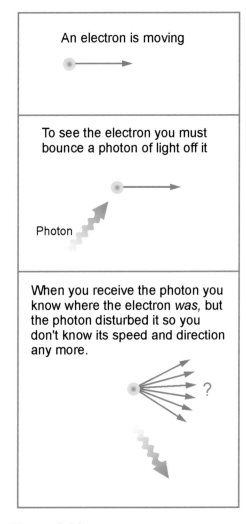

Figure 9.20: *The act of observing anything in the quantum world means disturbing in unpredictable ways the very system you are trying to measure.*

Probability and quantum theory

Predicting the behavior of particles in a system

According to Newton's laws, if you throw a ball, you can calculate exactly where the ball will be at every moment of its motion. Because electrons are so tiny, this type of calculation is not possible. Instead, quantum theory uses *probability* to predict the behavior of large numbers of particles in a system.

The meaning of probability

Probability describes the chance for getting each possible outcome of a system. If you toss a penny, there are two ways it can land, either heads up or tails up. With a single penny, there is a 50 percent probability of getting heads, and a 50 percent probability of getting tails. Suppose you flip 100 pennies and record the number of heads. You repeat this experiment 100 times and graph your results (Figure 9.21). The graph tells you that there is a 5.5% chance that you will get exactly 50 heads out of 100 coin tosses. If you repeated the experiment 1,000 times you would expect 55 experiments to come up with exactly 50 heads and 50 tails. While you can never accurately predict the outcome of one toss of the penny, you *can* make accurate predictions about a collection of many tosses.

The wave function

In quantum theory, each quantum of matter or energy is described by its *wave function*. The wave function mathematically describes how the probability for finding a particle is spread out in space (Figure 9.22). If you observe a trillion identical electrons, you can say with great precision how many will be found at that place. But quantum theory still cannot tell you where *any* single electron is. Because of its basis in probability, quantum theory can only make accurate predictions of the behavior of large systems with many particles.

Heads   Tails

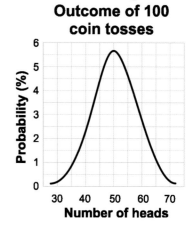

Figure 9.21: *The probability for the outcome of 100 tosses of a penny.*

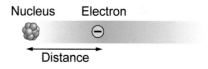
Nucleus   Electron
Distance

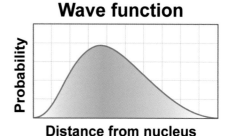

Figure 9.22: *The wave function describes how the probability of an electron is spread out in the space around the nucleus.*

9.3 Section Review

1. Describe how the colors in a spectrum from an atom are different from those in a rainbow.
2. Why does light from atoms show spectral lines?
3. How many electrons can fit in the same quantum state in the same atom?
4. Give an example of probability.

Indirect Evidence and Archaeology

Ernest Rutherford located the atom's nucleus through experiments—without ever seeing it directly. Using indirect evidence is also transforming the field of archaeology. Using remote sensing techniques, archaeologists can locate and describe features of ancient civilizations before a shovel ever touches the soil.

Searching for a lost city

American archaeologist Dr. Juris Zarins had long been fascinated by tales of a bustling ancient Arabian city called Ubar. The city is mentioned in Bedouin tales, in Greek and Roman histories, the *Arabian Knights*, and the Koran. Clues in these manuscripts led Dr. Zarins to believe that Ubar thrived for centuries as a crossroad for trade until its decline around 300 A.D.

Since then, all traces of the city had vanished, buried in 600-foot tall sand dunes that spread across an area the size of Texas in the southern Arabian peninsula. The area is known as "the empty quarter" and "the sandy sea." How could anyone possibly find a city buried in such a vast, featureless terrain?

Still, Zarins wanted to try. In 1987, he teamed up with American filmmaker and amateur archaeologist Nicholas Clapp to organize an expedition. Knowing it would take several lifetimes to excavate an area that large, they turned to NASA geologist Ron Blom for help. Could space shuttle or satellite imaging reveal anything that would narrow the search?

Hidden pathways revealed

Blom collected images of the region from a space shuttle mission and two satellites. The satellites, known as Landsat, make images from electromagnetic radiation reflected from Earth's surface. The sun also shines at light wavelengths slightly longer than the human eye can see, called "near infrared" wavelengths. Many landscape features are more distinct at these wavelengths, normally unseen by your eyes.

Centuries of foot travel and camel caravans packed down the desert floor so that 1,700 years later, they still reflected infrared radiation differently than the surrounding terrain. The roads, invisible to the naked eye, showed up clearly in the infrared images. The Landsat images covered a vast area: 30,000 square kilometers. Blom also used close-up images from a French satellite called SPOT to zoom in on the area where the caravan roads converged. The expedition team, equipped with the infrared "maps," began their search for Ubar at that convergence point— at the eastern edge of the "empty quarter," in the country of Oman.

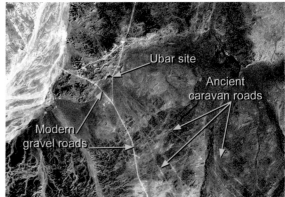

Ron Bloom/NASA/JPL

Ubar rediscovered

The excavation uncovered an octagon-shaped fortress with ten-foot walls and a tall tower at each corner. Pottery fragments from faraway places such as Greece, Rome, and Syria suggested that this had indeed been a major trading center. The city of Ubar, lost for seventeen centuries, was found with the help of some remarkable technology.

The Landsat and SPOT satellites Blom used are *remote sensing* devices. They collect information about Earth from a distant location, without coming into direct contact with the planet or disturbing it in any way.

The infrared images produced using the satellite data are a kind of indirect evidence. Just as nobody has actually seen the inside of an atom, nobody had actually seen the caravan roads to Ubar before the expedition began. Small differences in the way the desert surface reflected the infrared radiation provided clues to the roads' locations.

Juris Zarins photo

tombs, as well as ancient roads, farms and earthworks, because they are more resistant to current than the surrounding dirt. Microwave radar, used by both space shuttles and satellites, can detect stone walls and other features buried beneath the Earth's surface.

These new methods of gathering indirect evidence are providing archaeologists with something akin to X-ray vision: the ability to collect a wealth of information about a site without ever disturbing the soil.

These new methods save time and resources by narrowing in on the best sites to excavate, and in some places they can even take the place of excavation. Archaeologists can learn a great deal about a site using remote sensing devices. This allows sacred sites to remain untouched while respecting the cultures of other people.

Transforming archaeology

Other types of remote sensing continue to transform the field of archaeology. Ground-penetrating radar helped the Ubar team find structural features buried up to 20 feet below the surface.

Around the world, archaeologists are experimenting with new methods such as surveying the magnetic properties of the soil, which can help locate iron-containing items buried underneath. They also measure the electrical resistance of the soil. This technique can detect buried brick and stone walls, pavements, shaft

Questions:

1. What is *indirect evidence*?
2. How did a map showing infrared radiation reflected from the desert surface help Dr. Zarins and his team find the lost city of Ubar?
3. Name three benefits of using remote sensing in the field of archaeology.

Chapter 9 Review

Understanding Vocabulary

Select the correct term to complete the sentences

periodic table	energy level	spectral lines
atomic number	electron	isotopes
strong nuclear force	groups	uncertainty principle
probability	nucleus	metal
photons		

1. Protons and neutrons are found in the _____, at in the center of the atom.

2. A(n) _____ is a particle with a negative charge.

3. _____ are atoms of the same element with different numbers of neutrons.

4. The strongest force in the universe is known as the _____.

5. The number of protons in the nucleus in an atom is the element's _____.

Section 9.1

6. The _____ is a way of organizing the elements based on their chemical properties.

7. The first _____ of an electron cloud has the lowest energy and is closest to the nucleus.

8. The vertical columns of the periodic table are called _____.

9. A(n) _____ is a shiny, opaque element that is a good conductor.

Section 9.2

10. According to quantum theory, light energy comes in little bundles called _____.

11. Each element emits a characteristic pattern of _____.

12. Heisenberg's _____ states that you cannot precisely measure the location of an electron because it is so tiny.

13. If you toss a single penny, the _____ of getting heads is 50%.

Reviewing Concepts

Section 9.1

1. What did Ernest Rutherford discover about the atom with his gold foil experiment?

2. What particles make up the nucleus of the atom?

3. What takes up the most space in an atom, the nucleus or the electron cloud?

4. Which is the strongest of the four forces inside atoms?

5. Which is the weakest of the four forces inside atoms?

6. If the protons in the nucleus of an atom repel each other due to electromagnetic forces, why doesn't the nucleus just fly apart?

7. Compare electrons, protons, and neutrons in terms of size, mass, and charge.

8. What does the atomic number of an element tell you about its atom? What does it mass number tell you?

9. What is an isotope? Are the mass numbers of isotopes different? The atomic numbers?

10. Draw a model of an atom that has 5 protons, 5 neutrons, and 5 electrons. Label the charge of each particle. What element is this?

Section 9.2

11. Why don't atoms in group 18 usually form chemical bonds with other atoms?

12. What is a valence electron?

13. Why is most matter on Earth found in the form of molecules and not atoms?

Section 9.3

14. What is the evidence that electrons in atoms cannot have any amount of energy but instead are restricted to have only certain amounts of energy?

15. What is a photon?

16. How did Niels Bohr explain spectral lines?

7. Why does quantum theory use probability to predict the behavior of particles instead of exact calculations?

olving Problems

ection 9.1

An atom has 7 protons and 8 neutrons. What is this atom's atomic number? What is its mass number? What element is this atom?

How many neutrons are in a silicon atom with an atomic number of 14 and a mass number of 30?

Carbon-12 and carbon-14 have an atomic number of 6. How many protons and neutrons do carbon-12 and carbon-14 have?

Find the number of protons in an oxygen atom.

An atom has 20 protons and 24 neutrons.
a. What is this atom's mass number?
b. What is this atom's atomic number?
c. What element is this atom?

A common isotope of carbon has a mass number of 13. What is the total number of particles in its nucleus?

ection 9.2

Use the periodic table to give the following information for an atom of potassium with a mass number of 39.
a. Symbol
b. Atomic number
c. Number of protons
d. Number of neutrons
e. Number of electrons

Which element would you have if you added 4 protons and 4 neutrons to the nucleus of titanium (Ti)?

Which element is more likely to combine with other elements, calcium or xenon? How do you know?

Draw dot diagrams for the elements chlorine (7 valence electrons), sodium (1 valence electron), and neon (8 valence electrons).

Section 9.3

11. Atom A gains enough energy to promote an electron from the first energy level to the fourth energy level. Atom B gains enough energy to promote an electron from the third energy level to the fourth energy level. When both electrons fall back to their original energy levels, one atom emits a red photon and the other a green photon. Which atom emits the green photon? Explain your answer.

12. If you roll a dice once, what is the probability that you will roll a six? If you roll the dice 100 times, how many times would you expect to roll a six?

Applying Your Knowledge

Section 9.1

1. Make a poster illustrating models of the atom scientists have proposed since the 1800s. Explain how each model reflects the new knowledge that scientists gained through their experiments. When possible, comment on what they learned about charge, mass, and location of subatomic particles.

2. Research the Bohr model of the atom. Then, choose an atom and make a three-dimensional model of its structure. Choose different materials to represent protons, neutrons, and electrons. Attach a key to your model to explain what each material represents.

Section 9.2

3. Research alternative shapes for the periodic table. Make a poster of one of these alternatives and present the rationale for its shape to the class.

Section 9.3

4. The element helium is a light gas that is very rare on Earth. In fact, helium was not discovered on this planet. It was discovered in the sun, hence the name. In Greek, *helios* means "sun." Astronomers saw a series of spectral lines in the sun that did not match any known element on Earth. Helium was first identified from its spectrum of light from the sun. Researchers were then able to find it on Earth because they knew what to look for. Research and draw the visible spectrum for helium, labeling the wavelength of each spectral line. Rank the spectral lines from highest energy to lowest energy.

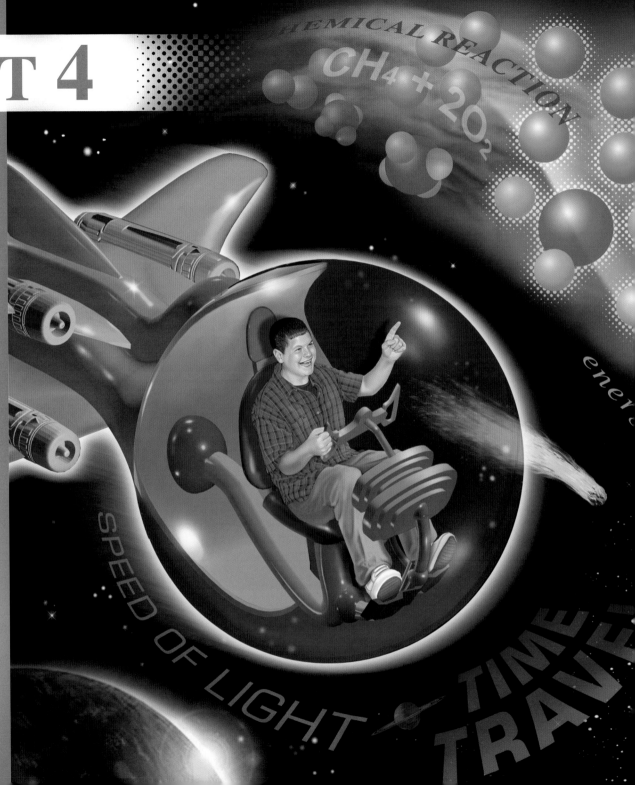

UNIT 4

Energy and Change

Chapter 10

Energy Flow and Systems

There is a country about the same size as the state of Virginia, that can be reached from London by airplane in about 3 hours. It is a country of contrasts often referred to as the land of fire and ice. Eleven percent of the country is covered by glaciers, yet there are many places where the Earth's molten rock, or magma, is very close to the surface. This magma heats underground reservoirs of water. Wells have been drilled to tap into the hot water that is available. This water is used in homes and in the generation of electricity.

Do you know the name of this country? As you study this chapter, you will become familiar with the many ways that energy is used in a variety of different systems. Energy flow diagrams, power in flowing energy, efficiency, and thermodynamics are topics that will be discussed in this chapter. These topics will help you recognize the role of energy and power in technology, nature, and living things. The country described above is Iceland. Did you guess correctly?

Think of all the different things you do each day that require energy. Where does all this energy come from? Which energy-converting systems are the most efficient? How does the efficiency of the energy flow in a natural system compare to the energy flow efficiency in human technology systems?

Key Questions

- ✓ Can a person lift a 1,000-kg car one meter off the ground? How about in a time period of ten seconds?
- ✓ Why can average automobiles only use about 13% of the energy available from the gasoline they burn?
- ✓ Why do natural systems have a much greater range of power than human technology?

10.1 Energy Flow

Looking at the big picture, our universe is matter and energy organized in *systems*. There are large systems, like our solar system composed of the sun, planets, asteroids, comets, smaller bits of matter, and lots of energy. There are smaller systems within the solar system, such as Earth. There are systems within systems ranging in scale from the solar system, to Earth, to a single animal, to a single cell in the animal, right down to the scale of a single atom. In every system energy flows, creating change.

Energy and systems

Energy as nature's "money"
Energy exists in many forms and can be changed from one form to another. You can think of energy as nature's money. It is spent and saved in a number of different ways. You can use energy to buy speed, height, temperature, mass, and other things. But you have to have some energy to start with, and what you spend decreases what you have left.

An example
The energy available to a system determines how much the system can change. We often use this line of thinking to tell whether something is possible or not. Consider the "Rube Goldberg" machine in Figure 10.1. The blue ball is dropped and makes things happen that are eventually supposed to swing the hammer and launch the green ball. How fast will the green ball be launched? Will it be launched at all? Can things be adjusted to launch the green ball at 1 m/sec? These are the questions that we can answer by looking at how the energy moves in the machine. This is a fun example, but thinking about it is very similar to how we analyze much more important systems, such as machines, planets, and even living bodies.

Possible or impossible?
You can only have as much "change" as you have energy to "pay for." By looking at how much energy there is in a system, and how much energy is used by the system, you can tell a lot about what kind of changes are possible. You can also tell what changes are impossible. The ideas in this chapter apply to much more than just physics. Plants and animals need energy to survive and grow. The number of plants and animals that can be supported depends partly on the amount of energy available in the right forms.

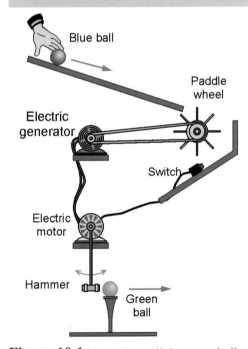

Figure 10.1: *How fast will the green ball be launched if the only source of energy is the falling blue ball?*

Energy exists in many different forms

Forms of energy
There are many forms of energy. Any form of energy can be converted into any other form. Most technology tries to find clever ways of converting one form of energy into another, like output work or electricity (Figure 10.2).

Mechanical energy
Mechanical energy is the energy an object has due to its *motion* or *position*. Kinetic and potential energy are both forms of mechanical energy. Work is also a form of mechanical energy and so is the energy in a stretched rubber band or a spring.

Radiant energy
Radiant energy is also known as *electromagnetic* energy. Light is made up of waves called electromagnetic waves. There are many different types of electromagnetic waves, including the light we see, ultraviolet light, x-rays, infrared radiation, radio waves, and microwaves.

Electrical energy
Electrical energy is carried by the flow of electric current. Batteries and electrical wall outlets are common sources of electrical energy. You will learn about electricity and electric circuits in Unit 5.

Chemical energy
Chemical energy is energy stored in the bonds that join atoms. Chemical energy can be released when atoms in a molecule are rearranged into different molecules. Gasoline and food are both common sources of chemical energy. Batteries change chemical energy into electrical energy.

Nuclear energy
Nuclear energy results from splitting up large atoms (like uranium) or combining small atoms (like hydrogen) to form larger ones. Nuclear energy from splitting uranium is converted to electrical energy in power plants. Nuclear energy from combining hydrogen atoms is the basic source for all other energy forms because it is how the sun and stars make energy.

Thermal energy
Heat is a form of thermal energy. You add thermal energy to a kettle of water to raise its temperature and to make the water boil. Thermal energy can be used to do work whenever there is a temperature difference. The combustion of gasoline and the splitting of uranium atoms release thermal energy at first. The thermal energy then becomes output work in a car or electricity in a power plant.

Pressure
The pressure in a fluid is a form of energy. If you blow up a balloon and let it go you can see **energy of pressure** converted to kinetic energy.

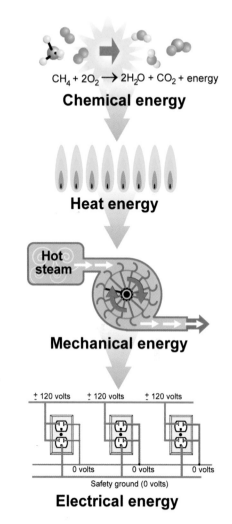

$CH_4 + 2O_2 \rightarrow 2H_2O + CO_2 + energy$
Chemical energy

Heat energy

Hot steam

Mechanical energy

± 120 volts   ± 120 volts   ± 120 volts

0 volts   0 volts   0 volts
Safety ground (0 volts)
Electrical energy

Figure 10.2: *Some of the forms energy takes on its way to your house or apartment.*

Solving a mystery in the laboratory

An experiment   Here is a mystery. Several groups of students are doing an experiment with a small car that rolls along a track. The track starts with a down-hill section then becomes flat. The car bounces off a rubber band at the bottom and the students measure the speed after the car bounces. One group measures a speed of 5 m/sec while all the other groups get an average speed of 2.5 m/sec (Figure 10.3). The group with the higher speed claims they did not push the car at the start, but the other groups are suspicious! Did the faster car get pushed or not? How can you tell?

The energy at the start   Some detective work with energy can solve the case. At the start, the only energy in the system should be the potential energy of the car. Remember, potential energy is given by: $E_p = mgh$, where m is the mass of the car (kg), g is the strength of gravity (9.8 N/kg), and h is the height (m). Using the values for the experiment the potential energy is 0.49 joules (Figure 10.4).

The kinetic energy   Let's calculate the kinetic energy if the car moves at 5 m/sec. The kinetic energy depends on mass and speed: $E_k = 1/2\ mv^2$ where v is the speed of the car (m/sec). Using a mass of 0.1 kg, the kinetic energy comes out to be 1.25 joules (Figure 10.4)! This is not possible. A system that starts with 0.49 J of energy cannot just "make" 0.76 joules *more* energy. The energy had to come from somewhere. The scientific evidence supports the conclusion that a student pushed the car at the start! That would explain the extra energy.

Analyzing energy   Using energy to investigate is a powerful tool because it does not matter what goes on between start and finish. Notice our detective analysis didn't mention the rubber band. As long as nothing adds energy to the system, there can never be more energy at the end than there was at the beginning. It does not matter what happens in between!

Friction   There *can* be less kinetic energy at the finish however. Friction steadily converts kinetic energy into heat. The kinetic energy is 0.31 joules when the speed of the car is 2.5 m/sec. Since the car started with 0.49 joules, the difference (0.18 J) is "lost" to friction.

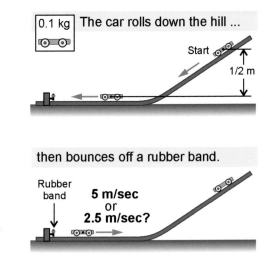

The car rolls down the hill ...

0.1 kg

Start

1/2 m

then bounces off a rubber band.

Rubber band

5 m/sec
or
2.5 m/sec?

Figure 10.3: *An experiment in energy conservation.*

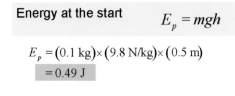

Energy at the start $E_p = mgh$

$E_p = (0.1\ \text{kg}) \times (9.8\ \text{N/kg}) \times (0.5\ \text{m})$

$= 0.49\ \text{J}$

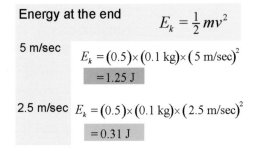

Energy at the end $E_k = \frac{1}{2} mv^2$

5 m/sec $E_k = (0.5) \times (0.1\ \text{kg}) \times (5\ \text{m/sec})^2$

$= 1.25\ \text{J}$

2.5 m/sec $E_k = (0.5) \times (0.1\ \text{kg}) \times (2.5\ \text{m/sec})^2$

$= 0.31\ \text{J}$

Figure 10.4: *Looking at the energy of the system solves the mystery.*

What happens to the energy "lost" from a system?

How can energy be lost in a system? Saying energy is "lost" really means it changes into a form you are not counting. Most often the "uncounted" energy is work done against friction. This work changes other forms of energy into heat and wear. If you could measure every form of energy, you would find that the tires of the car and the track became a little warmer. The air that the car pushed out of the way also became warmer. Some rubber was worn off the tires and some wood was worn off the track. Wear means grinding away molecules from surfaces. This means breaking bonds between molecules, which takes energy. If you could add it all up you would find that all the energy at the start is still there at the end, just in different forms.

Open and closed systems It would be easiest to study energy conservation in a *closed system*. A system is closed if *all* forms of energy and matter are counted and neither is allowed in or out of the system. In a closed system the total matter and energy stays the same forever. However, it is difficult to make a truly closed system. An *open system* is one that counts only *some* forms of matter or energy or allows either to go in or out of the system. Many physics problems are really open systems because you count only potential and kinetic energy and ignore heat.

Energy flow diagrams An **energy flow diagram** is a good way to show what happens to the energy in a system that is changing. To make an energy flow diagram, first write down the different forms that energy takes in the system. In the car experiment energy changes from potential to kinetic, to elastic (rubber band) and back to kinetic again. An energy flow diagram looks like Figure 10.5. Each place where energy changes form is called *conversion*. Like the car and track, systems change by converting energy from one form to another.

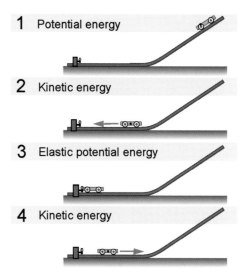

1 Potential energy

2 Kinetic energy

3 Elastic potential energy

4 Kinetic energy

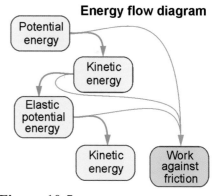

Energy flow diagram

Figure 10.5: *An energy flow diagram for the experiment with the car.*

10.1 Section Review

1. Use energy to explain why dropping a ball from a height of one meter will not make the ball go 30 m/sec (67 mph).

2. Name at least four forms that energy takes before becoming light from the electric lights in your classroom.

3. Draw an energy flow diagram showing the conversions of energy that occur as energy becomes light from the electric lights in your classroom.

10.2 Power

Can a single person lift a 1,000 kg car one meter in ten seconds using just their own muscles? In Chapter 4 you learned about simple machines that would easily allow a person to lift the car. The problem is the ten second time limit. Raising a 1,000 kg car 1 meter takes 9,800 joules of energy. Doing it in ten seconds requires a power output of 980 watts. This is more than a human can do. When doing detective work with energy you also need to think about how *fast* the energy flows. What power is involved? Lifting the car in five minutes would be no problem for one person. Spreading 9,800 J of energy over five minutes requires a power of only 32 watts. Even a small child could do this with the right system of ropes and pulleys!

Power doing work

How fast work is done Power is the rate of converting energy, or doing work. Suppose you drag a box with a force of 100 newtons for 10 meters in 10 seconds. Your power is 100 joules per second, or 100 *watts*. Your friend drags a similar box and takes 60 seconds. Your friend's power is only 16.7 watts even though the actual work done (force × distance) is the same as yours. However, your friend used 1/6th the power for 6 times longer.

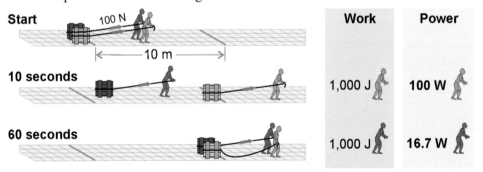

Power is the rate of doing work or using energy Power is the amount of energy changed (or work done) divided by the time it takes. Power is measured in watts, (W). One watt is one joule per second. When you see the word "power" you should think "energy used divided by time taken." This is similar to thinking about speed as "distance traveled divided by time taken." Doing 1,000 joules of work in 10 seconds equals a power of 100 watts (1,000 J ÷ 10 sec).

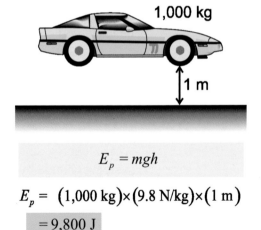

$$E_p = mgh$$

$$E_p = (1{,}000 \text{ kg}) \times (9.8 \text{ N/kg}) \times (1 \text{ m})$$
$$= 9{,}800 \text{ J}$$

Figure 10.6: *Lifting a 1,000 kg car a height of 1 meter takes (at least) 9,800 joules of energy.*

Vocabulary

thermodynamics, first law of thermodynamics, second law of thermodynamics

Objectives

✓ Calculate power given force, time, height, mass or other variables.

✓ Determine the efficiency of energy conversion in a system.

✓ Explain why heat engines can never be 100% efficient.

Power in flowing energy

Horsepower   Another unit of power commonly used is horsepower. One horsepower is 746 watts. The power output of car engines or electric motors is usually given in horsepower because it is a larger unit than a watt.

Three ways to look at power   Power is used to describe three kinds of similar situations. The first kind is work being done by a force. Power is the rate at which the work is done. The second situation is energy flowing from one place to another, such as electrical energy flowing through wires. The power is the rate at which energy flows. The third situation is when energy is converted from one form to another. Power is the rate at which energy is converted. In all three situations you calculate the power by dividing the energy or work by the time it takes for the energy to change or the work to be done.

Calculating power   Hoover Dam converts the potential energy of the flowing Colorado river into electricity. Each second, a mass of 700,000 kilograms of water drops 200 meters through huge tunnels in the dam. How much power could Hoover Dam produce? The change in potential energy (*mgh*) is 1.4 billion joules each second (Figure 10.7), making a power of 1.4 billion watts. This is about the same power used by a single medium-sized city. In reality, Hoover Dam makes less electrical power because the conversion from potential energy of the water to electrical energy is not 100% efficient.

700 m³/sec

$Energy = mgh$
$= (700,000 \text{ kg})$
$\times (9.8 \text{ N/kg})$
$\times (200 \text{ m})$
$\overline{= 1,372,000,000 \text{ J}}$

Figure 10.7: *The Colorado river flows at an average rate of 700 cubic meters per second. The density of water is 1,000 kg/m³ therefore the river moves 700,000 kg of water per second.*

Calculating the power in a system

A 2 kg owl gains 30 meters of height in 10 seconds. How much power does the owl use?

1. Looking for: You are asked for power.

2. Given: You are given the mass, height, and time.

3. Relationships: Power = energy ÷ time. Potential energy: $E_p = mgh$

4. Solution: $E_p = (2 \text{ kg})(9.8 \text{ N/kg})(30 \text{ m}) = 588$ joules
$P = 588 \text{ J} \div 10 \text{ sec} = 58.8$ watts, or about 1/2 the power of a 100W light bulb

Your turn...

a. A 50 gram frog leaps 1 meter in 0.5 seconds. Calculate the frog's power output. **Answer**: 0.98 watts

b. To go from zero to 60 mph in 5 seconds (0 - 27 m/sec) a sports car engine produces a force of 9,180 N. The car moves a distance of 67.5 meters in the 5 seconds it is accelerating. Calculate the power. **Answer**: 123,930 W or 166 horsepower.

Efficiency

Energy use in a typical car

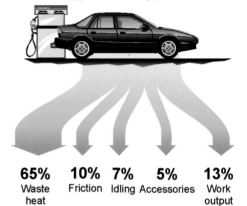

Efficiency The *efficiency* of a process describes how well energy or power is converted from one form into another. Efficiency is the ratio of output energy or power divided by input energy or power. Because of friction the efficiency of any process that uses power or energy is *always* less than 100 percent. Some machines (like a car) have efficiencies a *lot* lower than 100% (Figure 10.8).

Efficiencies always add up to 100% It is important to remember that, in any system, all of the energy goes *somewhere*. For example, rivers flow downhill. Most of the potential energy lost by water moving downhill becomes kinetic energy in motion of the water. Erosion takes some of the energy and slowly changes the land by wearing away rocks and dirt. Friction takes some of the energy and heats up the water. If you could add up the efficiencies for *every single process*, in a system that total would be 100 percent.

65%	10%	7%	5%	13%
Waste heat	Friction	Idling	Accessories	Work output

Figure 10.8: *The average car converts 13% of the energy in gasoline to output work.*

Calculating the efficiency of a process

A 12-gram paper airplane is launched at a speed of 6.5 m/sec with a rubber band. The rubber band is stretched with a force of 10 N for a distance of 15 cm. Calculate the efficiency of the process of launching the plane.

1. Looking for: You are asked for the efficiency.

2. Given: You are given the input force (N) and distance (cm) and the output mass (g) and speed (m/sec).

3. Relationships: Efficiency = output energy/input energy;
Input energy is work = $F \times d$;
Output energy $(E_k) = 1/2\ mv^2$

4. Solution: $e = [(0.5)(0.012\ \text{kg})(6.5\ \text{m/sec})^2]/[(10\ \text{N})(0.15\ \text{m})]$
= 0.17 or 17%

15 cm

Input work 10 N

Output energy 12 g 6.5 m/sec

Your turn...

a. A sled drops 50 meters in height on a hill. The mass of the sled and rider is 70 kg and the sled is going 10 m/sec at the bottom of the hill. What is the efficiency of energy conversion from potential to kinetic? **Answer**: 10%

b. A car engine has an efficiency of 15%. How much power must go into the engine to produce 75,000 watts of output power (100 hp)? **Answer**: 500,000 watts or 670 horsepower

Thermodynamics

Technology and thermodynamics
95% of the power used by human technology is converted from either fossil fuels (coal, gas, oil) or nuclear energy (Figure 10.9). A fraction (5%) comes from hydroelectric, solar, wind, and other renewable resources. Both fossil fuels and nuclear power first convert chemical energy to heat, and then use the heat to drive machines such as cars or electric generators. **Thermodynamics** is the physics of heat. Since so much of our technology depends on heat, it is important to understand thermodynamics.

The first law
The law of conservation of energy is also called the **first law of thermodynamics**. It says that energy cannot be created or destroyed, only converted from one form into another.

The second law
The **second law of thermodynamics** says that when work is done by heat flowing, the output work is always *less* than the amount of heat that flows. A car engine is a good example. From the physics point of view, an engine produces output work from the flow of heat. In Chapter 7 you learned that the rate of heat flow depends on the difference between high and low temperatures. Gasoline burns very hot. By comparison, the outside air is cold. Heat from the gasoline does work as it moves from hot to cold.

The efficiency of a heat engine
The *best* efficiency you can *ever* have in any heat engine is $1 - T_c/T_h$ where T_h and T_c are the hot and cold temperatures (in Kelvins) that the engine operates between. A typical engine has a combustion temperature of 400°C (673K). When the outside air is 21 °C (294K) the efficiency is $1 - (294 K \div 673 K) = 56\%$. Because the heat does not flow all the way to absolute zero, not all of its energy is available to do work. This lowers efficiency even *without any friction*! Friction takes another 20% leaving the overall efficiency at only 36%. That means almost 2/3 (64%) of the energy in gasoline flows out the car's tailpipe and radiator as waste heat.

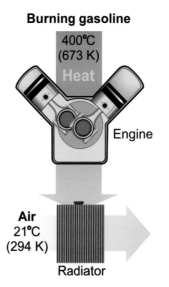

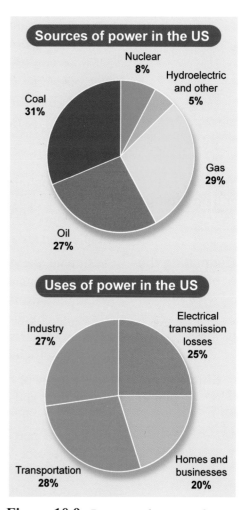

Figure 10.9: *Power production and usage in the US in the 1990's.*

How energy efficient are living things?

Calories in food   Living things convert chemical energy in food to work done by muscles, heat, reproduction, and other processes. The energy in foods is measured in *kilocalories*, also called *food* Calories. A Calorie is equal to 4,187 joules. Next time you eat a pint of ice cream, consider that it represents 4 million joules of energy (Figure 10.10). By comparison, you do one joule of work equivalent by lifting that pint of ice cream 21 centimeters.

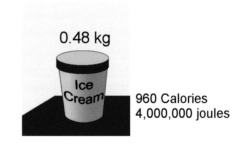

0.48 kg

Ice Cream

960 Calories
4,000,000 joules

$$1\ kilocalorie\ (food\ calorie) = 1,000\ calories = 4,187\ joules$$

Efficiency is low for living things   In terms of output work, the energy efficiency of living things is quite low. Most of the energy in the food you eat becomes heat; very little becomes physical work. Of course, you do much more than just physical work. For example, you are reading this book. Thinking takes energy too!

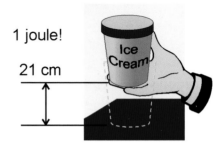

1 joule!

21 cm

Ice Cream

Estimating the efficiency of a human   To estimate the efficiency of a person at doing physical work, consider climbing a mountain 1,000 meters high. For the average person with a mass of 70 kilograms, the increase in potential energy is 686,000 joules. A human body doing strenuous exercise uses about 660 kilocalories per hour. If it takes three hours to climb the mountain, the body uses 1,980 calories (8,300,000 J). The energy efficiency is about 8 percent (Figure 10.11).

Figure 10.10: *A pint of ice cream is the equivalent of 4 million joules of work!*

Efficiency of plants   The efficiency of plants is similar. Photosynthesis in plants takes input energy from sunlight and creates sugar, a form of chemical energy. To an animal, the output of a plant is the energy stored in sugar, which can be eaten. The efficiency of pure photosynthesis is 26 percent, meaning 26 percent of the sunlight absorbed by a leaf is stored as chemical energy. As a system however, plants are 1 to 3 percent efficient *at making sugar* because some energy goes into reproduction, growth and other plant functions.

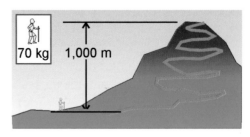

70 kg   1,000 m

10.2 Section Review

1. Which is greater, the power output of a human or that of an electric light bulb (100 W)?

2. What is your efficiency if you eat 1 million joules of food energy to do 1,000 joules of work?

3. What is thermodynamics and how does it relate to energy?

$E_p = mgh$

$= (70\ kg)(9.8\ N/kg)(1,000\ m)$

$= 686,000\ J$

Figure 10.11: *The (output) work done against gravity when climbing a mountain.*

10.3 Systems in Technology and Nature

You use energy conversion every day and you live in a universe where energy conversion is constantly occurring. The concepts of this chapter apply to systems of living organisms, planets, forests, and even single atoms as well as systems of human technology. Energy and power are important from the size of atoms to the scale of the entire universe, and everything in between.

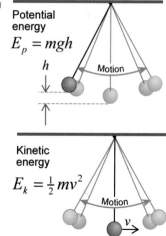

Vocabulary

energy conversions, steady state, food chain

Objectives

✓ Draw energy flow diagrams for systems.

✓ Recognize the role of energy and power in technology, nature, and living things.

Energy flow

The energy flow in a pendulum   A pendulum is a mechanical system in which a mass swings back and forth on a string. At its highest point, a pendulum has only potential energy, because it is not moving. At its lowest point, a pendulum has kinetic energy. Kinetic energy and potential energy are the two main forms of energy in this system. As the pendulum swings back and forth, the energy flows back and forth between potential and kinetic, with a little lost as heat from friction.

Energy conversion   The flow of energy almost always involves **energy conversion**. In a pendulum, the main conversion is between potential and kinetic energy. A smaller conversion is between kinetic energy and other forms of energy created by friction, such as heat and wearing away of the string.

Another example   Let's try making an energy flow diagram for an electric drill. Chemical energy, stored in the battery, is converted to electrical energy flowing through wires. The motor converts electrical energy to mechanical energy. The rotation of the motor is transferred to the drill bit by gears. The output work of the drill is the force turning the drill bit and cutting wood.

Pendulum

Potential energy

$E_p = mgh$

Kinetic energy

$E_k = \frac{1}{2}mv^2$

Energy flow diagram

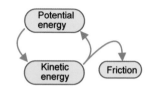

Figure 10.12: *In a pendulum, the energy mostly flows back and forth between potential energy and kinetic energy. Some energy is lost to friction on every swing.*

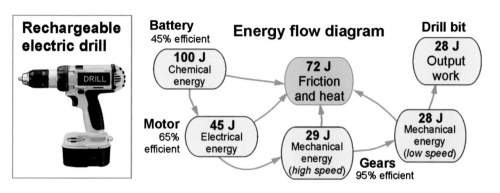

Rechargeable electric drill

Energy flow diagram

Battery 45% efficient
100 J Chemical energy

Motor 65% efficient
45 J Electrical energy

72 J Friction and heat

29 J Mechanical energy *(high speed)*

Gears 95% efficient

28 J Mechanical energy *(low speed)*

Drill bit
28 J Output work

Power in human technology

Ranges of power An average person generates about 150 watts of work and generates about the same amount of heat. You probably use inventions with both more and less power every day. On the high end of the power scale are cars and trucks. A typical small car engine makes an output power of 150 horsepower (hp), which is 112,000 watts (W). This power is delivered in the form of work done by the wheels. Moderate power devices include appliances such as washing machines, fans, and blenders. Many household machines have electric motors that do work and all use power.

Machine	Power used (W)
Small car	112,000
Lawn mower	2,500
Refrigerator	700
Washing machine	400
Computer	200
Electric drill	200
Television	100
Desk lamp	100
Small fan	50

Figure 10.13: *Power used by common machines.*

Motors Electric motors found around the house range from 1 horsepower (746 watts) down to 1/20th of a horsepower (37 watts). Many appliances have "power ratings" that indicate their power. For example, an electric blender might say it uses 1/3 hp, indicating a power of about 250 watts. Gasoline engines make much more power for their weight than electric motors. That is why gas engines are used for lawn mowers, tractors, cars and other inventions that need more power. Figure 10.13 lists the power used by some everyday machines.

Estimating power requirements You can calculate the power required if you know the force you need and the rate at which things have to move. For example, suppose your job is to choose a motor for an elevator. The elevator must lift 10 people, each with a mass of 70 kilograms. The elevator car itself has a mass of 800 kg. The plans for the elevator say it must move 3 meters between floors in 3 seconds.

The elevator needs a 60 hp motor This is work done against gravity so the energy required is $E_p = mgh$. Substituting the numbers gives a value of 44,100 J (Figure 10.14). This amount of energy is used in 3 seconds, so the power required is 44,100 J ÷ 3 seconds = 14,700 W. Motors are rated by horsepower, so divide again by 746 W/hp to get 19.7 hp. The smallest motor that would do the job is 19.6 hp. The actual motor required would be about 3 times larger (60 hp) because our calculation did not include any friction and assumed an efficiency of 100%. Engineers do calculations like this all the time as they design buildings, cars, and other inventions that use power.

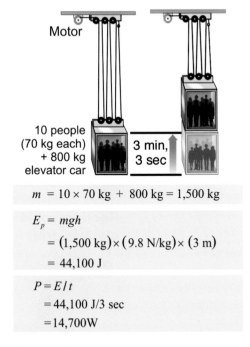

Motor

10 people (70 kg each) + 800 kg elevator car

3 min, 3 sec

$m = 10 \times 70 \text{ kg} + 800 \text{ kg} = 1,500 \text{ kg}$

$E_p = mgh$

$= (1,500 \text{ kg}) \times (9.8 \text{ N/kg}) \times (3 \text{ m})$

$= 44,100 \text{ J}$

$P = E/t$

$= 44,100 \text{ J/3 sec}$

$= 14,700 \text{W}$

Figure 10.14: *Calculating the power of an elevator.*

Energy flow in natural systems

Steady state energy balance
Unlike mechanical systems, energy flow in natural systems tends to be in a steady state. **Steady state** means there is a balance between energy in and energy out so that the total energy remains the same. For example, on Earth, radiant energy from the sun is *energy input*. That energy is converted into many different forms through different processes. However, the average energy of the Earth stays about the same because energy input is balanced by energy radiated back into space (*energy output*) as shown in Figure 10.15.

Natural systems work in cycles
Much of the energy from the sun is absorbed by oceans and lakes and used to drive the *water cycle*. Some water evaporates into the air, carrying energy from the warm water into the atmosphere. The water vapor goes up into the atmosphere and cools, releasing its energy to the air. The cooled water condenses into droplets as precipitation, which falls back to the ground. Eventually, the rainwater makes its way back to the ocean through rivers and groundwater and the cycle begins again. The water cycle moves energy from the oceans into the atmosphere and creates weather (Figure 10.16).

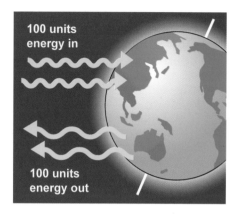

Figure 10.15: *The total energy of the Earth stays relatively steady because the energy input from the sun equals the energy radiated back into space.*

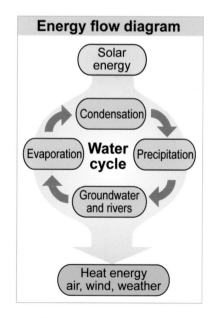

Figure 10.16: *An energy flow diagram for the water cycle.*

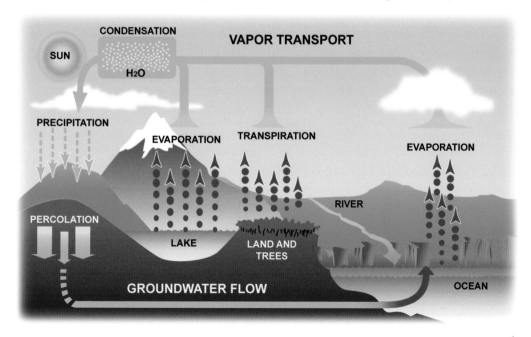

Power in natural systems

Stars and supernovae
Natural systems have a huge range of power, much greater than human technology. At the top of the power scale are stars. The sun has a power output of 3.8×10^{26} watts. This is tremendous power, especially considering the sun has been shining continuously for more than 4 billion years. A supernova is the explosion of an old star at the end of its normal life. These explosions are among the most powerful events in the known universe, releasing 10 billion times the power of the sun. Fortunately, supernovae are rare, occurring about once every 75 years in the Milky Way galaxy.

Energy from the sun
Almost all of the sun's power comes to the Earth as radiant energy, including light. The top of the Earth's atmosphere receives an average of 1,373 watts per square meter. In the summer at northern latitudes in the United States, about half that power (660 W/m²) makes it to the surface of the Earth. The rest is absorbed by the atmosphere or reflected back into space. In the winter, the solar power reaching the surface drops to 350 W/m². About half of the power reaching the Earth's surface is in the form of visible light. The remaining power is mostly infrared and ultraviolet light.

Estimating the mass of a gust of wind
The power received from the sun is what drives the weather on Earth. To get an idea of the power involved in weather, suppose we estimate the power in a gust of wind. A moderate wind pattern covers 1 square kilometer and involves air up to 200 meters high (Figure 10.17). This represents a volume of 200 million cubic meters (2×10^8 m³). The density of air is close to 1 kg/m³, so the mass of this volume of air is 200 million kilograms.

Estimating the power
Assume the wind is moving at 10 m/sec (22 mph) and it takes 3 minutes to get going. The power required to start the wind blowing is the kinetic energy of the moving air divided by 180 seconds (3 minutes). The result is 56 million watts, nearly the power to light all the lights in a town of 60,000 people. Compared with what people use, 56 million watts is a lot of power. But 1 square kilometer receives 1.3 *billion* watts of solar power. A 10 m/sec wind gust represents only 4 percent of the available solar power. A storm delivers much more power than 56 million watts because much more air is moving (Figure 10.18).

Estimating the power of a gust of wind

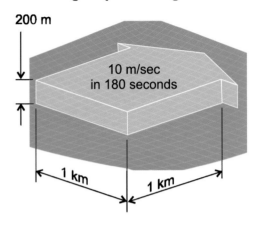

Figure 10.17: *Estimating the power in a gust of wind*

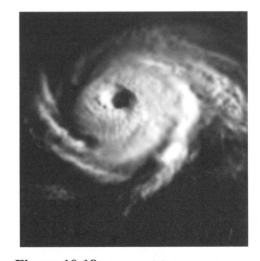

Figure 10.18: *A powerful storm system like this hurricane has a power of billions of watts. Photo courtesy NASA.*

Energy flow in living systems

Producers and food chains

A **food chain** is a way of describing the flow of energy between living things (Figure 10.19). Organisms at the bottom of the food chain are *producers*. A producer is a plant or one-celled organism that converts energy from the sun into chemical energy in molecules like sugar. Grass and trees are producers, as are corn, wheat, and all the crops we grow for food.

Herbivores

Next up on the food chain are the *herbivores*. An herbivore gets energy by eating plants. Herbivores include rabbits, most insects, and many land and sea animals. Herbivores concentrate energy from plants into complex molecules but they also use energy for living. It takes many producers to support one herbivore. Think of how many blades of grass a single rabbit can eat!

Carnivores

Carnivores get their energy by eating herbivores or other carnivores. A *primary* carnivore eats herbivores. A hawk is an example of a primary carnivore. Hawks eat mice and other small herbivores. *Secondary* carnivores eat other carnivores as well as herbivores. A shark is an example of a secondary carnivore. The food chain is often drawn as a pyramid to show that producers are the basis for all other life and also the most abundant.

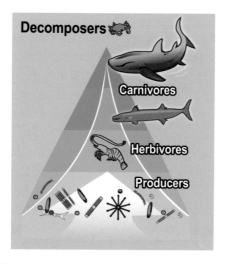

Figure 10.19: *The energy pyramid is a good way to show how energy moves through an ecosystem.*

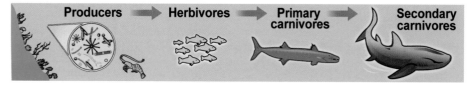

Decomposers

The last important group in the food chain are *decomposers*. Decomposers break down waste and bodies of other animals into simple molecules that can be used by plants. Earthworms, fungi, and many bacteria are examples of decomposers. You can think of decomposers as *recycling* raw materials such as carbon and nitrogen so they can be used by producers again.

10.3 Section Review

1. Draw an energy flow diagram for a person who eats then runs a race.
2. Describe at least three examples of energy and power in a natural system.
3. What categories of plants and animals make up a food chain?

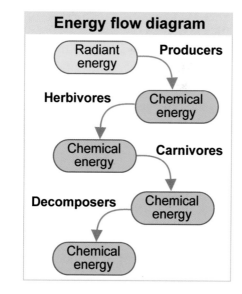

Figure 10.20: *Energy flow in an ecosystem.*

Energy in the Ocean

Governments and engineering companies are heading to the beach in large numbers. With them they bring millions of dollars in the hopes of being able to harvest the renewable energy of the moving ocean. In theory it is simple; use the moving water found in currents, waves, and tides to turn electrical generating turbines. Most believe that those who are successful will be able to provide a significant portion of the energy demands of the future. Scientists estimate that the kinetic energy of waves crashing on the shores of the world each day release enough energy to power the world many times over.

The race is on

The race is indeed on and the stakes are very, very high! Companies around the world are offering their engineers the opportunity to develop new and more futuristic machines to harness the renewable energy of the moving ocean. Looking to the ocean as a renewable source of energy makes sense because oceans cover roughly 71% of Earth's surface. The gravitational pull of the sun and the moon do the hard work! The challenge is to be able to develop the technology that harnesses this energy safely, efficiently at or below the current cost of producing electricity, and without harming the environment.

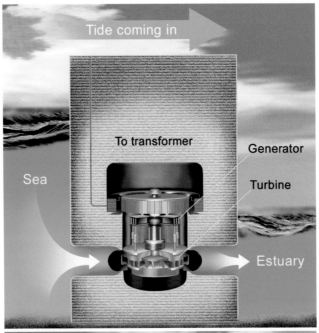

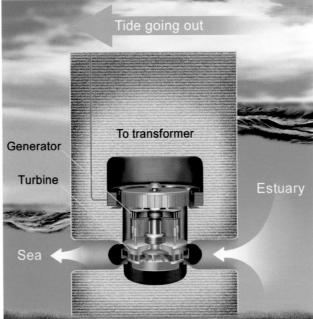

Tidal power

Most hydroelectric generators use a dam built across a river or stream. Flowing water spins a turbine that in turn spins a generator to produce electricity. But how do you capture the energy of tides which ebb and flow in a rhythm instead of flowing in one direction only?

Tidal power uses a huge dam (called a "barrage") built across a river estuary. When the tide goes in and out, the water flows through tunnels in the dam. The ebb and flow of the tides turns a turbine. Large lock gates, like the ones used on canals, allow ships to pass.

Wave power

On the Scottish Isle of Islay, there is a unit called a Land Installed Marine Powered Energy Transformer (LIMPET). The LIMPET is installed onshore with a chamber that extends into the sea. As a wave approaches, it forces captured air in the chamber through a turbine. As the wave retreats, the pressure inside the chamber drops and air is drawn through the turbine in the opposite direction. The turbine generates electricity as the wave approaches and when it retreats (picture shown on the facing page.)

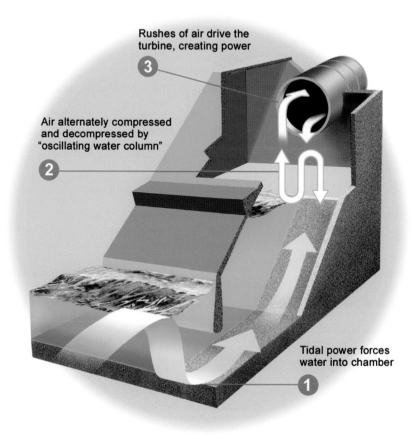

3 Rushes of air drive the turbine, creating power

2 Air alternately compressed and decompressed by "oscillating water column"

Tidal power forces water into chamber **1**

Engineers are pleased since the movement of the water is very predictable, unlike solar and wind energy, so they can depend on the generation of the needed electricity.

Clean energy for the future

One of the difficult lessons learned from our production of electricity by nuclear and fossil fuels is that we cannot trade a perfectly clean environment for electrical power. Initial studies show that careful planning might be able to utilize the movement of the oceans to generate electricity without harming the environment. Environmental scientists are working very closely with today's engineers as they develop new and exciting ways to harness the energy of our oceans.

Undersea currents

In September 2003, an undersea "windmill" with 10 meter diameter blades began sending electricity to the tiny town of Hammerfest, Norway. The windmill is deep enough not to disturb shipping in the area and the company believes that the blades turn slowly enough so as not to disturb the local sea life. When completed there will be a field of as many as 20 such windmills generating power for the town. The current of the channel travels around 3 m/sec, and the windmills are able to rotate in order to follow the current.

Questions:

1. Make an energy flow diagram that traces the energy flow in hydroelectric power.
2. Make a table that summarizes three ways to harness the energy of the moving ocean.
3. What are the positive and negative aspects of generating electricity in the oceans?

Chapter 10 Review

Understanding Vocabulary

Select the correct term to complete the sentences.

chemical energy	electrical energy	thermal energy
nuclear energy	power	second law of thermody-
horsepower	efficiency	namics
watt	energy conversion	food chain
joule	steady state	radiant energy
mechanical energy		

Section 10.1

1. Light is a form of ____.

2. ____ results from splitting or fusing atoms.

3. Energy stored in a candy bar is an example of ____.

4. ____ can be used to do work whenever there is a temperature difference.

5. Kinetic and potential energy are both forms of ____.

Section 10.2

6. ____ is the amount of energy changed divided by the time it takes.

7. One ____ is equal to one joule per second.

8. One ____ is equal to 746 watts.

9. When work is done by heat flowing, the output work is always less than the amount of heat that flows. This is a statement of the ____.

Section 10.3

10. The flow of energy almost always involves ____.

11. ____ means there is a balance between energy in and energy out so the total energy remains the same.

12. A ____ is a way of describing the flow of energy between living things.

Reviewing Concepts

Section 10.1

1. Why can energy be thought of as "nature's money?"

2. Chemical energy is sometimes thought of as a form of potential energy. Explain this statement.

3. Explain what is meant by the "energy of pressure."

4. Is a stretched rubber band a form of potential or kinetic energy? Explain.

5. Why is work done against friction "lost" to a system?

Section 10.2

6. Describe the meaning of power and how it is calculated.

7. Name two units of power and an application for each.

8. List two different ways to describe power.

9. What is efficiency and how is it calculated?

10. Use the example of a car engine to explain the meaning of the second law of thermodynamics.

11. Explain, in terms of work output, why the efficiency of living things is quite low.

12. Would the efficiency of a motorcycle be higher or lower than the efficiency of a bicycle? Explain your answer.

Section 10.3

13. Describe the energy conversions that happen in a swinging pendulum.

14. List two examples of technology you use each day that have a high power rating, and two examples of technology that have a relatively low power rating. Explain why these particular examples have high and low power ratings.

15. What is the primary energy input on Earth? What happens to that energy once it gets to Earth?

16. Why are herbivores more abundant than carnivores?

17. What are decomposers and what is their role in energy transfer?

Solving Problems

Section 10.1

1. A 1.0-kilogram ball rolls down a 1.0-meter high hill and reaches a speed of 20.0 meters per second at the bottom. Was the ball pushed by someone? Explain your answer using calculations of potential and kinetic energy.

2. A ball at the top of a hill has 12.5 joules of energy. After it rolls down, it converts 11.6 joules to kinetic energy. How much energy is "lost" to the system? Where did that energy go?

3. Use the diagram below to answer questions a through d.

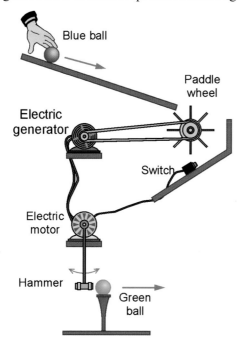

a. Where does the initial energy come from in the apparatus?
b. What forms of energy are involved in the operation of the apparatus?
c. Draw an energy flow diagram.
d. Do you think the apparatus will work? Why or why not?

Section 10.2

4. Michelle takes her 75 kilogram body up a 3.0 meter staircase in 3.0 seconds.
   a. What is her power in watts?
   b. What is her power in horsepower?
   c. How many joules of work did she do?
   d. If Michelle uses 10 food Calories to do the work, what is her efficiency?

5. A motor pushes a car with a force of 35 newtons for a distance of 350 meters in 6 seconds.
   a. How much work has the motor accomplished?
   b. How powerful is the motor in watts?
   c. How powerful is the motor in horsepower?

6. How much power is required to do 55 joules of work in 55 seconds?

7. The manufacturer of a machine says that it is 86 percent efficient. If you use 70 joules of energy to run the machine, how much output work will it produce?

8. Carmen uses 800 joules of energy on a jack that is 85 percent efficient to raise her car to change a flat tire.
   a. How much energy is available to raise the car?
   b. If the car weighs 13,600 newtons, how high off the ground can she raise the car?

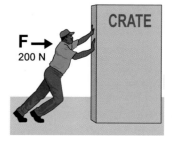

9. Suppose you exert 200 newtons of force to push a heavy box across the floor at a constant speed of 2.0 meters per second.
   a. What is your power in watts?
   b. What would happen to your power if you used the same force to push the box at a constant speed of 1.0 meters per second?

10. Suppose your job is to choose a motor for an escalator. The escalator must be able to lift 20 people at a time, each with a mass of 70 kilograms. The escalator must move between two floors, 5 meters apart in 5 seconds.

    a. What energy is required to do this work?

    b. What is the power rating of the required motor, in horsepower?

11. Fill in the joules of energy for each box below. Compute the output work and total wasted energy. What is the overall efficiency of the model solar car?

Energy Flow Diagram for Model Solar Car

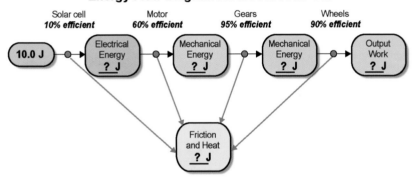

Applying Your Knowledge

Section 10.1

1. Solar cells (also called photo voltaic cells) are used to power satellites in outer space, yet they are not as commonly used to power households on Earth. Conduct Internet research on the use of solar cells to generate electricity for homes. Prepare a short report that answers the following questions:

    a. Why is it more difficult to use solar cells on the surface of the Earth as opposed to outer space?

    b. What are the advantages and disadvantages to using solar cells to power homes?

    c. What current percentage of homes in the United States use solar cells to generate some of their power? Is this number on the rise or decline?

    d. Which state currently leads the nation in using solar cells to power homes? What are the reasons?

Section 10.2

2. A typical car is about 13 percent efficient at converting energy from gasoline to energy of motion. The average car today gets about 25 miles for each gallon of gasoline.

    a. Name at least four energy transformations that occur in a car.

    b. Name three things that contribute to lost energy and prevent a car from ever being 100 percent efficient.

    c. If a car that currently gets 25 miles per gallon was 100 percent efficient, what would be its miles per gallon?

3. Two mountain lions run up a steep hillside. One animal is twice as massive as the other, yet the smaller animal got to the top of the hill in half the time. Which animal did the most work? Which delivered the most power?

4. Steve lifts a toolbox 0.5 meters off the ground in one second. If he does the same thing on the moon, does he have to use more power, less power, or the same amount of power? Explain your answer.

Section 10.3

5. At each level of the food pyramid, about 90 percent of the usable energy is lost in the form of heat.

    a. Which level requires the most overall input of energy to meet its energy needs?

    b. Use the diagram to explain why a pound of steak costs more than a pound of corn.

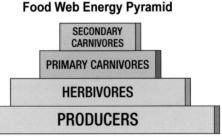

Food Web Energy Pyramid

Chapter 11

Changes in Matter

What does the word "chemical" mean to you? Does it make you think of strange, bubbling concoctions in test tubes, mixed by a scientist in a white lab coat? You might have heard or read about a "hazardous chemical spill", or you might have experimented with chemicals in a science lab. Would it surprise you to know that YOU are a mixture of chemicals? So is a block of wood or a glass of orange juice. In fact, the word chemical is used to describe any substance that is composed of atoms bonded together. Water (H_2O) is a chemical. Sodium chloride (NaCl) is a chemical. Your body contains thousands of different chemicals. Not all chemicals are hazardous to your health! Many chemicals are necessary for growth and survival.

All of the millions upon millions of different chemicals are made of only 92 elements combined in different ways. Just as you can spell thousands of words with the same 26 letters, you can make all the variety of chemicals from 92 elements.

By rearranging atoms you can turn wood into ashes or iron and air into rust. By rearranging particles inside the atom, you can even turn lead into gold!

Key Questions

✓ How can you predict how certain atoms will combine to form compounds?
✓ Why do nuclear reactions involve HUGE amounts of energy?
✓ Are all forms of radiation dangerous?

11.1 Chemical Bonds

Most matter is in the form of compounds. You learned in the last unit that water (H_2O) is a compound made of hydrogen and oxygen atoms. If a substance is made of a pure element, chances are it will eventually combine with other elements to make a compound. For example, an iron nail combines with oxygen in water or air to make a compound called iron oxide, better known as rust. Why do atoms tend to combine with other atoms?

Vocabulary

ionic bond, covalent bond, ion

Objectives

✓ Explain why most atoms combine with other atoms to make compounds.

✓ Predict whether a chemical bond is ionic or covalent.

✓ Describe the differences between ionic and covalent bonds.

What are chemical bonds?

Electrons form chemical bonds
When atoms combine, they form chemical bonds. A chemical bond forms when atoms transfer or share electrons. Two atoms that are sharing one or more electrons are chemically bonded and move together. In a water molecule, each hydrogen atom shares its single electron with the oxygen atom at the center. Almost all the elements form chemical bonds easily. This is why most of the matter you experience is in the form of compounds.

A chemical bond forms when atoms transfer or share electrons.

Chemical bonds determine chemical properties
The chemical properties of a substance come from how it forms chemical bonds with other substances. For example, the nonstick coating on cooking pans is "non-stick" because it does *not* form chemical bonds with substances in food. The active ingredient in aspirin works because it bonds with chemicals in the body called *prostaglandins* and prevents them from creating swelling that causes pain.

The importance of the molecule
The properties of a material depend *much* more on the molecule than on the elements of which the molecule is made. Aspirin is made from carbon, hydrogen, and oxygen. By themselves, these elements do not have the property of reducing pain. Other molecules formed from the same elements have different properties than aspirin. For example, polyethylene plastic wrap and sugar are also made from carbon, oxygen, and hydrogen. The pain-relieving properties of aspirin come from the way the atoms bond together and the particular shape of the aspirin molecule (Figure 11.1).

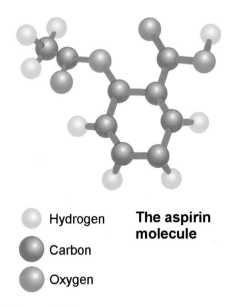

○ Hydrogen

● Carbon

● Oxygen

The aspirin molecule

Figure 11.1: *An aspirin molecule.*

Chemical bonds

Atoms form bonds to reach lower energy

Chemical bonds release energy when they form. Imagine pulling adhesive tape off a surface. It takes energy to separate atoms that are bonded together just like it takes energy to pull tape off a surface. If it takes energy to separate bonded atoms, then the same energy must be released when the bond is formed. Energy is released when atoms form chemical bonds because chemically bonded atoms have lower energy than free atoms. Like a ball rolling downhill, atoms collect into molecules because the atoms have lower energy when they are together in molecules (Figure 11.2).

Valence electrons

Valence electrons form chemical bonds. In Chapter 9 you learned that the outer electrons (valence electrons) in an atom form chemical bonds. For example, carbon has four valence electrons and can make up to four chemical bonds with other atoms. Oxygen *needs* 2 valence electrons and therefore can form bonds with up to two atoms.

Two types of chemical bonds

Most chemical bonds fall into two categories, depending on whether the valence electrons are transferred or shared. Electrons in an **ionic bond** are transferred from one atom to another. In a **covalent bond** the electrons are shared between atoms.

Ionic bonds

An **ion** is an atom or molecule that has a net positive or negative electric charge. Atoms that either gain or lose an electron become ions. In an ionic bond, the atoms that give up electrons become positive. The atoms that take electrons become negative. The positive and negative ions are attracted to each other, making the ionic bond.

Alkali metals tend to form ionic bonds

The *alkali metals* with one valence electron have a tendency to *give up* one electron. The *halogens* with seven valence electrons have a tendency to *take* one electron (Figure 11.3). If you put an alkali metal (Na) with a halogen (Cl), you get an ionic bond because one atom has a strong tendency to lose an electron and the other has a strong tendency to gain one.

Multiple ionic bonds

Ionic bonds tend to form between more than one pair of atoms at a time. The bond between sodium (Na) and chlorine (Cl) in sodium chloride (salt) is a good example of an ionic bond. In a crystal of salt each sodium ion is attracted to all the neighboring chlorine ions.

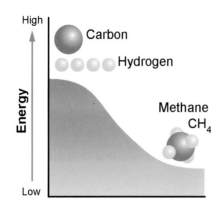

Figure 11.2: *The methane (CH$_4$) molecule has lower total energy than four separate hydrogen and one separate carbon atom.*

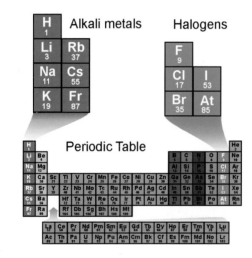

Figure 11.3: *The alkali metals have one valence electron and transfer it readily. The halogens have 7 valence electrons and accept electrons easily. An alkali and a halogen atom form an ionic bond with each other.*

Covalent bonds

How covalent bonds form

In a covalent bond, valence electrons are *shared* between atoms, not transferred. The bonds between hydrogen and oxygen in a water molecule are an example of covalent bonds. The oxygen atom in the molecule needs two electrons to have eight valence electrons. Hydrogen atoms need only one electron to have two valence electrons, also a stable number. When a hydrogen atom bonds to an oxygen atom, the electrons act like ties between the two atoms (Figure 11.4).

Examples of covalent bonds

Elements in groups 13 to 17 tend to form covalent bonds with each other since the tendency to take or receive electrons is nearly evenly matched. For example, all the bonds in silicon dioxide (glass) are covalent bonds between silicon and oxygen atoms. Diamonds are the hardest substance known. A diamond is a pure carbon crystal in which every carbon atom is joined to four other carbon atoms by a covalent bond (Figure 11.5). The hardness of diamonds is due to the fact that four covalent bonds must be broken to move each carbon atom.

How are covalent and ionic bonds different?

An important difference between covalent and ionic bonds is that covalent bonds act only between the atoms in a single molecule, while ionic bonds act between all adjacent atoms (ions). Molecules joined by covalent bonds tend to be much harder to separate into their individual atoms. Ionic compounds do not exist as individual molecules, but as groups of oppositely charged ions. Many ionic compounds separate into individual ions when dissolved in water.

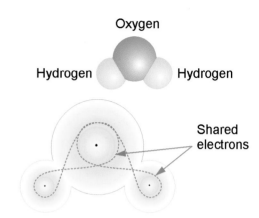

Figure 11.4: *In a covalent bond the shared electrons act like ties that hold a molecule together.*

11.1 Section Review

1. Explain why a hydrogen atom is more likely to combine with other atoms than a helium atom.

2. Our atmosphere consists of 21 percent oxygen in the form of O_2 molecules. Is the chemical bond between two oxygen atoms ionic or covalent? Explain your answer.

3. Lithium atoms easily combine with fluorine atoms. Is this an ionic or covalent bond? Explain your answer.

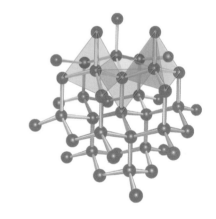

Figure 11.5: *Diamond is the hardest substance known because each carbon atom is bonded to its four neighbors by strong covalent bonds.*

11.2 Chemical Reactions

Chemical reactions rearrange atoms into different substances by breaking and reforming chemical bonds. If you leave an iron nail out in the rain, the gray surface soon turns reddish-brown with rust. Rust forms through a chemical reaction between iron in the nail and oxygen. Chemical reactions are the process through which chemical changes happen, like iron turning to rust.

Chemical changes rearrange chemical bonds

Chemical change
Ice melting is an example of a *physical change*. During a physical change, a substance changes its form but remains the same substance. A *chemical change* turns one or more substances into a different substance that has different properties. An example of chemical change is burning wood into carbon dioxide, water, and ashes.

Using chemical changes
We use chemical changes to create materials with properties that are useful. The rubber in car tires is an example of a material that has been modified by chemical changes. A chemical change called *vulcanization* inserts pairs of sulfur atoms into the long chain molecules of natural rubber. The sulfur ties adjacent molecules together like rungs on a ladder and makes vulcanized rubber much harder and more durable.

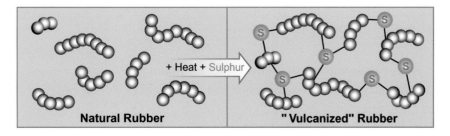

+ Heat + Sulphur

Natural Rubber   **"Vulcanized" Rubber**

Recognizing chemical change
A **chemical reaction** is a system of chemical changes that involves the breaking and reforming of chemical bonds to create new substances. A chemical reaction occurs when you mix baking soda with vinegar. The mixture bubbles violently as carbon dioxide gas, a new substance, is formed. The temperature of the mixture also gets noticeably colder. Bubbling, new substances, and temperature change, are all evidence of chemical change (Figure 11.6).

Vocabulary

chemical reaction, reactant, product, chemical equation, activation energy, exothermic, endothermic, photosynthesis, respiration

Objectives

✓ Recognize the signs of chemical change
✓ Explain how energy is used or released by chemical reactions
✓ Write an equation for a chemical reaction

Evidence of chemical change

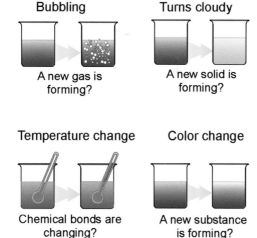

Bubbling
A new gas is forming?

Turns cloudy
A new solid is forming?

Temperature change
Chemical bonds are changing?

Color change
A new substance is forming?

Figure 11.6: *Four observations that are evidence of chemical change.*

Chemical equations are recipes for chemical reactions

What are chemical reactions? *A chemical reaction rearranges atoms in one or more substances into one or more new substances.* Hydrogen reacts with oxygen to produce water and energy. Because so much energy is produced, hydrogen is used as fuel for rockets and may eventually replace gasoline in automobiles.

Products and reactants in chemistry How do we show the chemical reaction between hydrogen and oxygen to produce water and energy? In cooking you start with *ingredients* that are combined to make different *foods*. In chemical reactions you start with **reactants** that are combined to make **products**. The reactants and products may include atoms, molecules, and energy. When hydrogen is used for fuel, two hydrogen molecules combine with one oxygen molecule to make two water molecules. Hydrogen and oxygen are the reactants. Water and energy are the products.

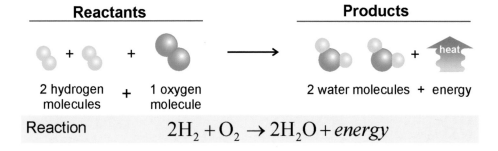

Reactants		**Products**
2 hydrogen molecules + 1 oxygen molecule	→	2 water molecules + energy
Reaction		$2H_2 + O_2 \rightarrow 2H_2O + energy$

Writing chemical reactions A **chemical equation** is an abbreviated way to show the exact numbers of atoms and molecules in a chemical reaction. In the equation above, H_2 represents a hydrogen molecule, O_2 represents an oxygen molecule, and H_2O is a water molecule. The little numbers (subscripts) tell you how many atoms of each element there are in *one molecule*. For example, the subscript 2 in H_2O means there are two hydrogen atoms in a water molecule. The large number 2 in "$2H_2O$" tells you there are *two molecules* of H_2O in the reaction. To keep the numbers straight remember that the little numbers (subscripts) tell you how many atoms are in one molecule. The larger numbers (called *coefficients*) tell you how many molecules are in the reaction. If a number is not written it is understood to be "1."

Balancing a chemical equation

A balanced equation means that the same number of atoms of each element appear in the products and in the reactants.

Step 1: Make sure that you have the correct chemical formula for each molecule that appears as a reactant or product.

Step 2: Write down the equation for the reaction.

Step 3: Count the number of atoms of each element in the reactants. Also, count the number of atoms of each element in the products.

Step 4: Adjust the coefficient of each reactant or product until the total number of each type of atom is the same on both sides of the equation. This is done by trial and error.

Important reminder

You can *never* change subscripts in order to balance an equation. For example, calcium chloride has the chemical formula, $CaCl_2$. You cannot change the subscript on Cl from 2 to 3 and make $CaCl_3$ to get an extra chlorine atom. Changing subscripts creates a totally different molecule. You can only change coefficients to balance equations.

Conservation of mass and energy

Conservation of mass
Chemical reactions do not create new atoms; they rearrange existing atoms to make new substances. *This means that the mass of the reactants must be equal to the mass of the products.* That is why chemical equations must be balanced. A balanced chemical equation conserves mass because the same number of atoms of each element appear on both sides of the equation.

Energy is involved in two ways
During a chemical reaction, the bonds in the reactants must be broken so that atoms are available to form new bonds. Energy is involved in chemical reactions in two ways: (1) energy is used to break the bonds in the reactants, and (2) energy is released when new bonds form.

Activation energy
The energy needed to break chemical bonds in the reactants is called the **activation energy** of the reaction. If you put pure hydrogen and oxygen together nothing happens until you make a spark (Figure 11.7). The spark supplies the activation energy to start the reaction.

Reaction: $2H_2 + O_2 \rightarrow 2H_2O + energy$

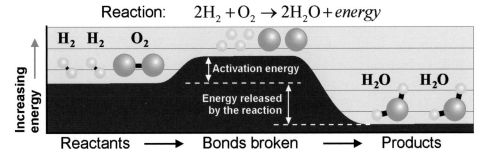

Exothermic reactions
If forming new bonds releases *more* energy than it took to break the old bonds, the reaction is said to be **exothermic**. *Exothermic reactions release the excess energy.* Once started, exothermic reactions tend to keep going because each reaction releases enough activation energy to start the reaction in neighboring molecules. The reaction above is exothermic.

Endothermic reactions
If forming new bonds in the products releases *less* energy than it took to break the original bonds in the reactants, the reaction is **endothermic**. *Endothermic reactions absorb energy.* These reactions do not usually keep going unless energy is supplied. For example, if you make a spark in water, a few molecules might react but reactions do not occur in the rest of the water.

Start

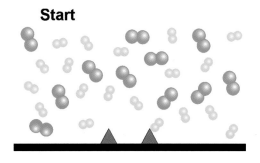

Energy from a spark splits a few nearby molecules

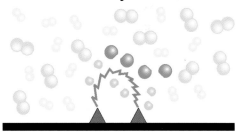

Energy released from the reaction splits more molecules and the reaction grows

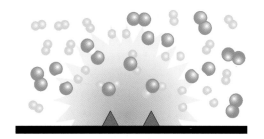

Figure 11.7: *Energy from a spark breaks the initial bonds to start an exothermic reaction in which hydrogen molecules combine with oxygen molecules (burn) to become water.*

Photosynthesis is an important chemical reaction

The importance of photosynthesis
The energy that supports life on Earth starts with a reaction that takes energy from sunlight and stores it as chemical bonds in molecules of *glucose*. This reaction is called **photosynthesis** (Figure 11.8). Photosynthesis occurs mostly in plants and in some types of bacteria. Animals (including ourselves) also get energy from photosynthesis, because we eat plants or other animals that eat plants. Nearly all the energy in living things can be traced to this important reaction.

Photosynthesis releases oxygen
Photosynthesis also produces the oxygen in our atmosphere. Without plants, Earth's atmosphere would have no oxygen, and could not support life. Although oxygen is a very common element, it is usually trapped by rocks and minerals in compounds like calcium carbonate ($CaCO_3$).

Photosynthesis removes CO_2
Photosynthesis removes carbon dioxide from the atmosphere. For every glucose molecule produced, six molecules of carbon dioxide are removed from the air, and six molecules of oxygen are produced. Carbon dioxide absorbs infrared radiation and therefore traps heat in the atmosphere. If too much carbon dioxide is present, the Earth cannot cool itself by radiating energy into space. Higher levels of carbon dioxide may be responsible for the warming of our planet by several degrees over the past 200 years. Can you think of ways to stabilize carbon dioxide levels?

Respiration
Animals who eat plants get energy by breaking up glucose molecules. This process is called **respiration**. The reactions of respiration proceed in many steps, but the end result is that glucose and oxygen are used up and carbon dioxide and water are produced. Respiration is almost the reverse of photosynthesis. It releases the energy that originally came from the sun.

The photosynthesis reaction

$$6\,CO_2 + 6\,H_2O + \text{energy}$$
Carbon dioxide   Water

$$\rightarrow \quad C_6H_{12}O_6 + 6\,O_2$$
Glucose   Oxygen

Carbon dioxide, water and energy are reactants in photosynthesis.

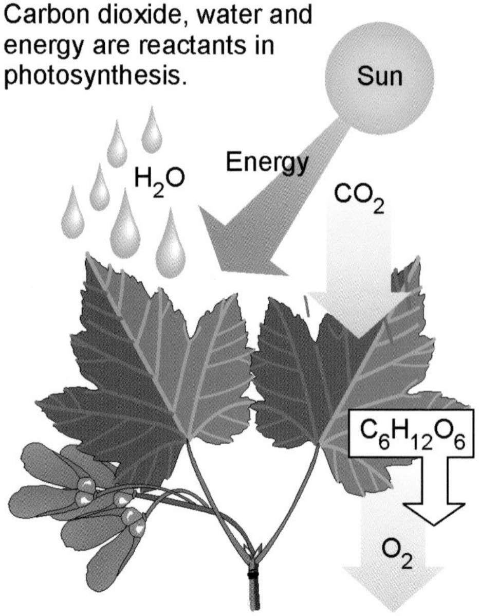

Sun

H_2O Energy CO_2

$C_6H_{12}O_6$

O_2

Glucose and oxygen are products of the photosynthesis reaction.

Figure 11.8: *Photosynthesis is a chemical reaction that is the basis for the food chain on Earth.*

11.2 Section Review

1. Give four observations that are evidence of chemical change.
2. Write a balanced chemical equation for burning hydrogen in oxygen to make water.
3. Explain why a balanced chemical equation conserves mass.
4. Explain how activation energy relates to the energy used or produced by a chemical reaction.

11.3 Nuclear Reactions

You would be very surprised if you saw a bus turn itself into two cars and a van! A radioactive atom does something almost as strange. If left alone, an atom of uranium eventually turns into an atom of lead! This radioactive decay is one example of a **nuclear reaction.** Nuclear reactions change the nucleus of an atom. Until just 100 years ago people looked for a way to turn lead into gold. With today's understanding of nuclear reactions, it is now possible. However, we don't do it very often because the process is much more expensive than the gold it produces!

Nuclear reactions are different than chemical reactions

Nuclear versus chemical
Because they affect the nucleus itself, nuclear reactions can change one element into a different element. Nuclear reactions can also change an isotope into a different isotope of the same element. Remember, isotopes of the same element have the same number of protons but different numbers of neutrons in the nucleus. By comparison, chemical reactions do *not* change the types of atoms. Chemical reactions only rearrange atoms into different compounds.

Nuclear reactions involve more energy
Nuclear reactions involve much more energy than chemical reactions. The energy in a nuclear reaction is much greater because nuclear reactions involve the strong nuclear force, the strongest force in the universe. Chemical reactions involve electrical forces. The electrical force acting on an electron far from the nucleus is much smaller than the strong force acting on a proton or neutron *inside* the nucleus. The difference in strength between the forces involved is the reason nuclear reactions are so much more energetic than chemical reactions (Figure 11.9).

Mass and energy in nuclear reactions
Mass and energy are conserved together but *not* separately in nuclear reactions. This is because nuclear reactions can convert mass into energy. If you could take apart a nucleus and separate all of its protons and neutrons, the separated protons and neutrons would have more mass than the nucleus does all together. This bizarre fact is explained by Einstein's formula ($E = mc^2$), which tells us that mass (m) can be converted to energy (E), when multiplied by the speed of light (c) squared. The mass of a nucleus is reduced by the energy that is released when the nucleus comes together. You'll learn more about this important relationship in Chapter 12.

Vocabulary

nuclear reaction, chain reaction, radioactive, radioactive decay, alpha decay, beta decay, gamma decay, half-life

Objectives

✓ Compare and contrast nuclear reactions and chemical reactions.

✓ Explain the difference between fusion and fission reactions.

✓ Describe what happens during radioactive decay.

Chemical reactions	Nuclear reactions
What part of the atom is involved?	
Outer electrons	Nucleus (protons and neutrons)
What changes?	
Atoms are rearranged into new molecules but the atoms stay the same	Atoms may change into atoms of a different element
How much energy is involved?	
A small amount	A huge amount

Figure 11.9: *Comparing nuclear and chemical reactions.*

Nuclear reactions and energy

Energy of the nucleus

When separate protons and neutrons come together in a nucleus, energy is released. Think about many balls rolling downhill (Figure 11.10). The balls roll down under the force of gravity and potential energy is released. Protons and neutrons are attracted by the strong nuclear force and also release energy as they come together. The more energy that is released, the lower the energy of the final nucleus. The energy of the nucleus depends on the mass and atomic number. The nucleus with the lowest energy is iron-56 with 26 protons and 30 neutrons (the low point on the graph below). Protons and neutrons assembled into nuclei of carbon or uranium have higher energy so appear higher on the graph.

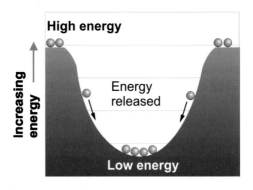

Figure 11.10: *Energy is released when balls roll downhill, to a lower energy level.*

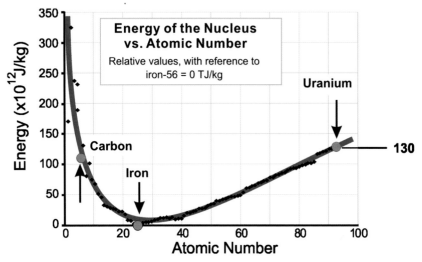

Nuclear energies are very large

The graph compares the energy of the nucleus in one kilogram of matter for elements 2 (helium) through 92 (uranium). The units of energy are hundreds of trillions (10^{12}) of joules per kilogram of material! Nuclear reactions often involve huge amounts of energy as protons and neutrons are rearranged to form different nuclei. A nuclear reaction *releases* energy when it rearranges protons and neutrons to make a new nucleus that is lower in energy on the graph (Figure 11.11). A nuclear reaction *uses* energy when the protons and neutrons form a nucleus that is higher in energy on the graph.

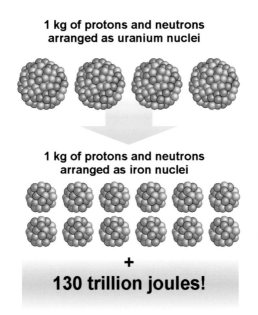

Figure 11.11: *A nuclear reaction that changed 1 kilogram of uranium into 1 kg of iron would release 130 trillion joules of energy.*

Fusion reactions

Writing nuclear reactions

Nuclear reactions are written using symbols for the elements, like chemical reactions. The difference is that the mass number is important in nuclear reactions. Remember from Chapter 9, the mass number is the total number of protons plus neutrons in the nucleus. In a nuclear reaction, each atom is written with a superscript to indicate the mass number. In an equation for a nuclear reaction, the isotope carbon-12 is written C^{12}.

Fusion reactions

Fusion reactions release energy if the final nucleus has lower energy than the initial nuclei (Figure 11.12). A kilogram of C^{12} contains 104 trillion joules (TJ) of nuclear energy according to the graph. A kilogram of Mg^{24} has 48 TJ of nuclear energy. An astounding 56 trillion joules are released if the protons and neutrons in one kilogram of C^{12} are rearranged to make one kilogram of Mg^{24} nucleus. The fusion reaction to make magnesium from carbon would actually go through a series of steps, but the end result would be the same release of energy.

Fusion reactions need very high temperatures

Positively charged nuclei repel each other. Two nuclei must get very close for the attractive strong nuclear force to overcome the repulsive electric force. One way to make two nuclei get close is to make the temperature very high. At very high temperatures, kinetic energy slams two nuclei together with enough force to almost touch, allowing the strong force to take over and initiate a fusion reaction. The hydrogen fusion reactions in the core of the sun occur at a temperature of about 15 million degrees Celsius.

Density and fusion power

A single fusion reaction makes a lot of energy for a single atom. But a single atom is tiny. To produce enough power to light a single 100-watt bulb requires 10^{14} fusion reactions per second. The density of atoms must be large enough to get a high rate of fusion reactions.

Fusion in the sun

Stars like the sun make energy from fusion reactions because the core of a star is both hot and very dense. The density at the core of the sun is so high that a tablespoon of material weighs more than a ton. The primary fusion reaction that happens in the sun combines hydrogen nuclei to make helium, converting two protons and two electrons into two neutrons along the way. All of the energy reaching Earth from the sun comes ultimately from these fusion reactions in the sun's core.

Energy release by a fusion reaction

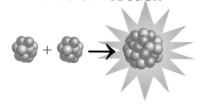

$$C^{12} + C^{12} \rightarrow Mg^{24} + \text{energy}$$

Energy of Nucleus vs. Atomic Number

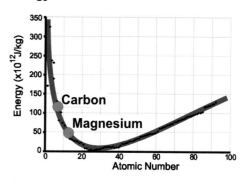

+104 TJ Energy of carbon (C) nucleus

−48 TJ Energy of magnesium (Mg) nucleus

───────

+56 TJ Energy released by fusion of carbon into magnesium.

Figure 11.12: *A fusion reaction releases energy if the product nucleus is lower on the energy graph. The energy released is the difference between the energies of the starting and ending nuclei.*

Fission reactions

Fission reactions For elements heavier than iron, breaking the nucleus up into smaller pieces (fission) releases nuclear energy (Figure 11.13). For example, a kilogram of uranium-235 (atomic number 92) has about 123 trillion joules (TJ) of nuclear energy. A fission reaction splits the uranium nucleus into two pieces. Both pieces have a lower atomic number, and are lower on the energy of the nucleus graph. The fission of a kilogram of uranium into the isotopes molybdenum-99 and tin-135 releases 98 trillion joules. This amount of energy from a golf-ball-sized piece of uranium is enough to drive an average car 19 million miles!

Fission is triggered by neutrons A fission reaction typically starts when a neutron hits a nucleus with enough energy to make the nucleus unstable. Fission breaks the nucleus into two smaller pieces and often releases one or more extra neutrons. Some of the energy released by the reaction appears as gamma rays and some as kinetic energy of the smaller nuclei and the extra neutrons.

Chain reactions A **chain reaction** occurs when the fission of one nucleus triggers fission of many other nuclei. In a chain reaction, the first fission reaction releases two (or more) neutrons. The two neutrons hit two other nuclei and cause fission reactions that release four neutrons. The four neutrons hit four new nuclei and cause fission reactions that release eight neutrons. The number of neutrons increases rapidly. The increasing number of neutrons causes more nuclei to have fission reactions and enormous energy is released. The fission chain reaction of uranium is how nuclear power plants release nuclear energy.

Radioactive materials The products of fission usually have too many neutrons to be stable and are **radioactive**. Radioactive means the nucleus continues to change by ejecting protons, neutrons, or other particles. A radioactive nucleus may also change a neutron into a proton and an electron, or vice-versa. Both Mo^{99} and Sn^{135} are radioactive. Radioactive atoms may be dangerous because they continue to give off energy, some for a long time. The term *nuclear waste* includes used fuel from nuclear reactors that contains radioactive isotopes such as molybdenum-99 and tin-135.

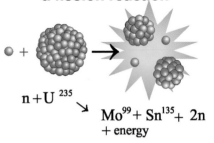

Energy release by a fission reaction

$$n + U^{235}$$
$$\searrow$$
$$Mo^{99} + Sn^{135} + 2n$$
$$+ \text{ energy}$$

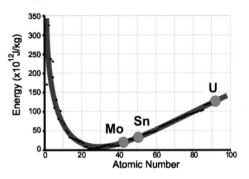

Energy of Nucleus vs. Atomic Number

+123 TJ	Energy of uranium (**U**) nucleus.
-25 TJ	Average energy of nuclei of molybdenum (**Mo**) and Tin (**Sn**)
+98 TJ	Energy released by fission of uranium into molybdenum and tin.

Figure 11.13: *Fission releases energy because the uranium nucleus is higher in energy than tin (Sn) or molybdenum (Mo).*

Radioactivity and radiation

Radioactive decay
If an atomic nucleus is unstable for any reason, the atom undergoes a type of nuclear reaction called **radioactive decay**. The word *decay* means to *break down*. In radioactive decay, the nucleus of an atom spontaneously breaks down and emits subatomic particles and/or radiation. The three most common types of radioactive decay are: alpha decay, beta decay, and gamma decay.

Alpha decay
In **alpha decay**, the nucleus ejects two protons and two neutrons. Check the periodic table and you can quickly show that two protons and two neutrons are the nucleus of a helium-4 (He^4) atom. Alpha radiation is actually fast-moving He^4 nuclei. When alpha decay occurs, the atomic number is reduced by two because two protons are removed. The atomic mass is reduced by four because two neutrons go along with the two protons. For example, uranium-238 undergoes alpha decay to become thorium-234.

Beta decay
Beta decay occurs when a neutron in the nucleus splits into a proton and an electron. The proton stays in the nucleus, but the high energy electron is ejected and is called beta radiation. During beta decay the atomic number increases by one because one new proton is created. The mass number stays the same because neutrons and protons both have a mass number of 1.

Gamma decay
Gamma decay is how the nucleus gets rid of excess energy. In gamma decay the nucleus emits a high-energy photon (electromagnetic radiation), but the number of protons and neutrons stays the same. The nucleus decays from a state of high energy to a state of lower energy. Gamma ray photons are energetic enough to break apart other atoms, making them dangerous to living things. Gamma rays require heavy shielding to stop. Alpha and beta decay are often accompanied by gamma radiation from the same nucleus.

Radiation
The word radiation means the flow of energy through space. There are many forms of radiation. Light, radio waves, microwaves, and x-rays are forms of electromagnetic radiation. The energy in alpha and beta radiation comes from moving particles. Radiation is dangerous when it has enough energy to break chemical bonds in molecules. Ultraviolet light, gamma rays and x-rays are some forms of radiation that can be harmful to living things in large quantities.

Alpha decay
Nucleus ejects a helium-4 nucleus

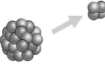

Protons	Decrease by 2
Neutrons	Decrease by 2
Atomic number	Decrease by 2
Mass number	Decrease by 4

Beta decay
Nucleus converts a neutron to a proton and electron, ejecting the electron.

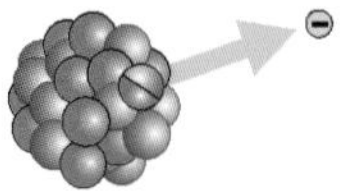

Protons	Increase by 1
Neutrons	Decrease by 1
Atomic number	Increase by 1
Mass number	Stays the same

Gamma decay
Nucleus emits gamma radiation and lowers its energy.

Gamma ray

Protons	Stays the same
Neutrons	Stays the same
Atomic number	Stays the same
Mass number	Stays the same

Figure 11.14: *The three most common radioactive decay reactions.*

Half-life

Chance and radioactivity

Americium-241 is a radioactive isotope used in household smoke detectors. If you were looking at an individual americium-241 atom, it would be impossible to predict when it would decay. However, if you have a large collection of americium atoms, then the *rate* of decay becomes predictable. For americium-241, it is known that half of the atoms in the sample decay in 458 years. Therefore, 458 years is the *half-life* of americium-241. The **half-life** is the time it takes for one half of the atoms in any sample to decay.

The half-life of carbon-14

Every radioactive element has a different half-life, ranging from fractions of a second to millions of years, depending on the specific isotope. For example, the half-life of carbon-14 is about 5,700 years. If you start out with 200 grams of C^{14}, 5,700 years later only 100 grams will still be carbon-14. The rest will have decayed to nitrogen-14 (Figure 11.15). If you wait another 5,700 years, half of your 100 remaining grams of carbon-14 will decay, leaving 50 grams of carbon-14 and 150 grams of nitrogen-14. Wait a third interval of 5,700 years, and you will be down to 25 grams of carbon-14. *One half of the atoms decay during every time interval of one half-life.*

The half-life of different isotopes varies greatly

Uranium-238 has a half-life of 4.5 billion years. It was created in the nuclear reactions of exploding stars, the remains of which condensed to form the solar system. We can still find uranium-238 on Earth because the half-life is so long. The isotope fluorine-18 has a half-life of 1 hour, 50 minutes. This isotope is used in medicine. Hospitals have to make it when they need it because it decays so quickly. Any natural fluorine-18 decayed billions of years ago. Carbon-15 has a half-life of 2.3 seconds. Scientists who make carbon-15 in a laboratory have to use it immediately.

Radioactive decay series

Most radioactive materials decay in a series of reactions. For example, radon gas comes from the decay of naturally occurring uranium in the soil (Figure 11.16). Radon itself decays into lead in a chain of three alpha decays and two beta decays. Radon is a source of indoor air pollution in some houses that do not have adequate ventilation. Many people test for radon before buying a house.

Radioactive decay of C^{14}

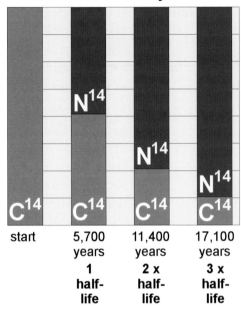

Figure 11.15: *Half the carbon-14 turns into nitrogen-14 every half-life. The half-life of C^{14} is 5,700 years.*

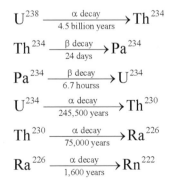

Figure 11.16: *Radon gas (Rn^{222}) is created by a chain of radioactive decay reactions starting with uranium.*

Carbon dating

Carbon dating Living things contain a large amount of carbon. The isotope carbon-14 is used by archeologists to determine age. We find this isotope in the environment because it is constantly being produced in the upper atmosphere by cosmic rays—high energy particles from the sun and elsewhere in the universe. The ratio of carbon-14 to carbon-12 in the environment is a constant, determined by the balance between production and decay of carbon-14. As long as an organism is alive, it constantly exchanges carbon with the environment. Therefore, the ratio of carbon-14 to carbon-12 in the organism stays the same as in the environment.

How carbon dating works

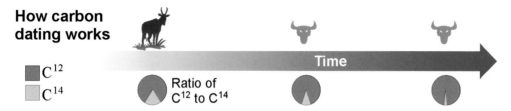

Time

■ C^{12}
■ C^{14}

Ratio of C^{12} to C^{14}

Why carbon dating works When a living organism dies it stops exchanging carbon with the environment. All the carbon-12 in the organism remains because it is a stable isotope. Almost no new carbon-14 is created because most cosmic rays do not reach the ground. As the carbon-14 decays, the ratio of carbon-14 to carbon-12 slowly gets smaller with age. By measuring this ratio, an archeologist can tell how long it has been since the material was alive. Carbon dating works reliably up to about 10 times the half-life, or 57,000 years. After 10 half-lives there is not enough carbon-14 left to measure accurately. Carbon dating only works on material that has once been living, such as bone or wood.

How a smoke detector works

Smoke detectors contain a tiny amount of americium-241, a radioactive isotope that emits alpha radiation. When an alpha particle hits a molecule of air, it knocks off an electron, making the air ionized. The positive ion and negative electron are collected by positive- and negative-charged metal plates attached to the battery in the smoke detector. The flow of ions and electrons creates a tiny electric current that is measured by the electronics of the smoke detector.

When smoke is in the air, particles of smoke interrupt the flow of ions and electrons. The electric current collected by the metal plates drops. The circuit in the smoke detector senses the drop in current and sounds the alarm.

11.3 Section Review

1. Sketch a graph showing the energy of the nucleus versus the atomic number and use the graph to explain what kinds of nuclear reactions release energy.

2. Write the nuclear reaction that represents the alpha decay of uranium-238.

3. If Americium-241 has a half life of 458 years, how long do you need to wait until only 1/4 of a sample of Am^{241} is left?

CONNECTIONS

Cook or Chemist?

Measure accurately, stir, heat, carefully judge for reaction completion, and don't stick your finger in anything. If you're thinking about a scientist in the lab, well, that's one possibility. This also accurately describes the action of a chef in the kitchen. A chef is very much like a scientist. Precise mixing and temperature control lead to accurate, reproducible results in both situations. New ideas based on sound principles and trial-and-error produce new products for both the chemist and the chef.

What's food made of?

Look at the label of any packaged food in a supermarket and you'll find a table giving the Nutritional Facts for it. Along with a few other items, all such tables give the total amounts of fat, carbohydrates, and protein that the item contains. In fact, with few exceptions (vitamins and minerals being among them) all food is made of these three groups of molecules in varying proportions.

Cooking transforms food

What happens to food during cooking is due to changes in carbohydrate, fat, and protein molecules. Heat is thermal energy that manifests itself as the kinetic energy of molecules vibrating and moving. Cooking transforms food by the transfer of thermal energy to the food molecules. The transferred energy is used to rearrange molecules, break existing bonds and form new ones. These changes in the microscopic structure result in both microscopic and macroscopic changes in food.

Have you ever tried to "uncook" an egg? It's not just difficult, it's impossible. In fact, it's impossible to "uncook" just about everything. Cooking transforms food irreversibly. One of the interesting features of the molecules that make up food is how they are delicately balanced in higher energy states. Food molecules originate in plants that harness energy from the sun into high-energy molecules through a chemical reaction called photosynthesis.

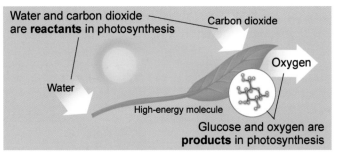

Water and carbon dioxide are **reactants** in photosynthesis — Carbon dioxide — Oxygen — Water — High-energy molecule — Glucose and oxygen are **products** in photosynthesis

Simple molecules link together through other reactions inside plants to form the molecules that make up foods. The energy supplied in cooking tips those molecules over the edge irreversibly to a lower energy state from which they never return.

Eggs - a mass of proteins

Eggs have three parts: the white (90% water, 10% protein), the yolk (50% water, 34% fats, 16% protein) and the shell (calcium carbonate). Cooking an egg transforms the proteins. Proteins are very large, very long chains of amino acids linked together. Amino acids are the building blocks of all proteins, including the ones that make up our bodies.

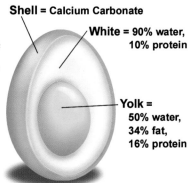

Shell = Calcium Carbonate

White = 90% water, 10% protein

Yolk = 50% water, 34% fat, 16% protein

Hard-boiled eggs

The reshaping of proteins from their natural shape is called *denaturing*. An egg's protein molecules in their natural, uncooked state are loosely coiled in individual "globs" held together by weak bonds between different parts of the amino acid chain. Because the molecules are able to move around, the egg white and yolk remain liquid. Heat gives the proteins enough energy to break those bonds and each protein strand begins to straighten out. If enough heat is added, the ends of each protein molecule join together in bridge-like bonds. Other links form at points along the protein strands. The network of bonds prevent individual molecules from moving around and the egg becomes solid.

Uncooked - coiled individual molecules

During heating - protein strands unravel

Cooked - bridge structure

Carbohydrates: The sweet life

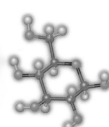

Carbohydrates, made mostly of carbon and hydrogen atoms, are much simpler than proteins. Small carbohydrate molecules are called sugars, because they are generally sweet. Sugars are "simple carbohydrates." Sucrose (table sugar) and glucose are examples of simple carbohydrates. When simple sugars are linked together in long chains, "complex carbohydrates" are formed.

When sugars are cooked, a number of chemical reactions occur. As sugars cook, water is released and caramelization takes place. This gives us the characteristic aroma of cooking. Baking bread causes a browning reaction to take place causing carbohydrates to react with the amino acids of proteins. This reaction is responsible for the wonderful browning of bread and contributes to the aroma and flavor of roasted coffee beans and chocolate.

Fats: A stable ingredient

Fats are also made mostly of carbon and hydrogen atoms. The lower the ratio of hydrogen to carbon, the more "unsaturated" the fat. Aside from providing energy, fats help transport molecules in and out of cells and are an important part of many hormones. Fats are very stable to heat, making them useful in cooking. Cooking oils, butter and margarine are part of this group. Along with providing flavor, cooking with fats is fast.

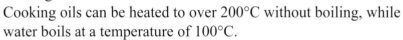

Cooking oils can be heated to over 200°C without boiling, while water boils at a temperature of 100°C.

Questions:

1. List some microscopic changes in foods that occur when they are cooked.
2. Why is cooking an irreversible process?
3. Describe what happens to egg protein when it is cooked.
4. Is a completely fat free diet healthy? Explain your answer.

Chapter 11 Review

Understanding Vocabulary

Select the correct term to complete the sentences.

ion	covalent	ionic
chemical reaction	half-life	nuclear reaction
chain reaction	beta decay	alpha decay
activation energy	endothermic	gamma decay
exothermic	reactant	product

Section 11.1

1. Electrons in a(n) _____ bond are transferred from one atom to another.

2. Electrons in a(n) _____ bond are shared between atoms.

3. An atom that has lost or gained an electron is called a(n) _____.

Section 11.2

4. Mixing baking soda and vinegar is an example of a(n) _____.

5. A chemical reaction that gets hot is _____.

6. In a chemical reaction, you start with _____ that are combined to make _____.

7. A chemical reaction that gets colder is _____.

8. To make water from hydrogen and oxygen, a spark provides the _____ needed to make the reaction happen.

Section 11.3

9. _____ can change one element into another element.

10. A(n) _____ occurs when the fission of one nucleus triggers the fission of many other nuclei.

11. In _____ an atomic nucleus ejects two protons and two neutrons.

12. In _____ a neutron in a nucleus splits into a proton and an electron.

13. In _____ the nucleus of an atom emits a high-energy photon but the number of protons and neutrons stays the same.

Reviewing Concepts

Section 11.1

1. Aspirin and plastic wrap are both made from carbon, hydrogen, and oxygen. Why are their properties so different?

2. Explain how energy is involved in the formation and breaking of chemical bonds.

3. What are the major difference between ionic and covalent bonds?

4. What makes a diamond one of the hardest materials on Earth?

5. Are the bonds in a water molecule covalent or ionic? Explain.

Section 11.2

6. Explain how a physical change is different from a chemical change and give one example of each.

7. How can you tell when a chemical change has occurred?

8. What happens to chemical bonds during a chemical reaction?

9. Explain how mass is conserved in a chemical reaction.

10. What is the activation energy of a chemical reaction?

11. In terms of energy and chemical bonds, how are exothermic and endothermic reactions different?

12. How does photosynthesis harness energy from the sun for animals to use?

Section 11.3

13. In what ways are chemical reactions similar to nuclear reactions? In what ways are they different?

14. How is a fusion reaction different from a fission reaction? Which reaction is responsible for all of the energy reaching Earth from the sun?

15. In a chemical reaction, balanced equations are written using the law of conservation of mass. Can this same law be applied to nuclear reactions? Explain your answer.

16. Why is the energy released from a nuclear reaction so much greater than the energy from a chemical reaction?

17. Summarize the three kinds of radioactive decay in the chart below.

Decay	Proton #change	Neutron #change	Ejected particle
Alpha			
Beta			
Gamma			

Solving Problems

Section 11.1

1. For each of the following decide the type of change indicated and label the event as a physical (P) or chemical (C) change.

    a. Hot, molten lead for making black-powder shot hardens in the mold.

    b. Steam rises from a cup of hot water.

    c. Lead nitrate solution added to sodium iodide solution produces a yellow solid.

    d. A "cold pack" used to treat injuries uses ammonium nitrate mixed with water. When activated, the pack gets very cold.

    e. When calcium carbonate is added to hydrochloric acid, bubbles of gas rise.

    f. Chewing food breaks it up into smaller pieces to prepare it for digestion.

    g. Pepsin, an enzyme in the stomach, breaks protein into smaller molecules.

2. With which elements would sodium most likely form a chemical bond? (Hint: more than one answer is possible)

    a. francium

    b. bromine

    c. hydrogen

    d. argon

    e. oxygen

3. Which elements would form a covalent bond?

    a. carbon and hydrogen

    b. sodium and fluorine

Section 11.2

4. Calcium carbonate antacids neutralize acids in your stomach. In the reaction, hydrochloric acid reacts with calcium carbonate to produce carbon dioxide and water. Use the balanced equation for the reaction to answer questions a through f.

$$2HCl + CaCO_3 \rightarrow CaCl_2 + CO_2 + H_2O$$

    a. What are the reactants in the equation?

    b. What are the products in the equation?

    c. How many HCl molecules are used in the reaction?

    d. How many CO_2 molecules are produced?

    e. How many atoms of oxygen are found in the reactants? How many are found in the products?

    f. How many hydrogen atoms are found in the reactants? How many hydrogen atoms are found in the products?

5. Use the chemical reaction below to answer questions a through d.

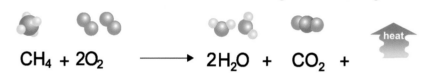

$$CH_4 + 2O_2 \longrightarrow 2H_2O + CO_2 +$$

methane + oxygen $\longrightarrow$ water + carbon dioxide + energy

    a. List the products and reactants in the equation.

    b. How many oxygen molecules react with methane to make the products?

    c. Suppose the amount of methane was doubled. How many oxygen molecules would be required? How many water molecules would be produced?

    d. Is the reaction above exothermic or endothermic?

6. Which of the following chemical equations are balanced?

    a. $CS_2 + 3O_2 \rightarrow CO_2 + SO_2$

    b. $2N_2O_5 + NO \rightarrow 4NO_2$

    c. $P_4 + 5O_2 \rightarrow P_2O_5$

    d. $Cl_2 + 2Br \rightarrow 2Cl + Br_2$

    e. $Na_2SO_4 + BaCl_2 \rightarrow BaSO_4 + NaCl$

7. Use the graph below and the "Periodic Table of the Elements on page 224 to number the elements in a through f in order of increasing energy of their nuclei.

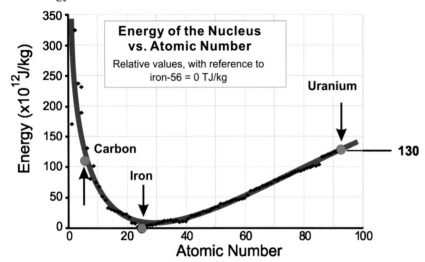

a. carbon (C)
b. iron (Fe)
c. magnesium (Mg)
d. lithium (Li)
e. Lead (Pb)
f. Krypton (Kr)

8. Use the graph in question 7 and your knowledge of nuclear reactions to indicate which pairs of atomic nuclei would be most likely to release energy by fission and which would release energy by fusion.

a. helium-4 and carbon-12
b. uranium-235 and strontium-135
c. carbon-12 and carbon-12

9. Radon has a half-life of 3.8 days. How long does it take for 16 grams of radon to be reduced to 2 grams of radon?

Applying Your Knowledge

Section 11.1

1. Rocks are the most common materials on Earth. The *rock cycle* is a group of changes that continuously recycles rocks. Research the rock cycle. Make a poster that illustrates the rock cycle. List the chemical and physical changes that rocks undergo for each phase of the cycle.

2. Around the world, over 5 million tires are discarded each day. Recycling scrap tires requires the use of physical and chemical changes. Research the recycling of scrap tires. Prepare a short report that answers the following questions:

   a. What are the challenges to recycling tires?
   b. What are the chemical and physical changes used in recycling tires?
   c. How are recycled tires used? What are the advantages and disadvantages for each use?

Section 11.2

3. Identify an industry in your community that uses chemical reactions. (It may be more difficult to find an industry that doesn't use them!) Examples of industries you may consider include: hospitals, sewage or water treatment plants, dry cleaners, photo developers and manufacturers of any product. Research the chemical reactions the facility uses. Write balanced chemical equations for each reaction you identify.

4. Global warming is a concern of scientists and other citizens around the world. Conduct research to find out the major global warming gases and the chemical reactions that produce them.

Section 11.3

5. Research the possibility of using nuclear fusion as an energy source. Prepare a short report that answers the following questions:

   a. What are the challenges to using nuclear fusion for power?
   b. What are the advantages of using nuclear fusion for power?
   c. What is magnetic confinement fusion and how does it work?

Chapter 12 Relativity

- In a black hole, time stops forever.

- Every particle of matter has an antimatter twin. When matter and antimatter meet, they annihilate each other in a flash of pure energy.

- The sun creates a warp in space near it. This space-warp results in what we feel as gravity.

The statements above are ideas put forth by Albert Einstein who lived from 1879 to 1955. His name is recognized around the world, and nearly everyone knows that he was a brilliant scientist. What did Albert Einstein discover? What were his greatest contributions to our understanding of science?

Einstein's remarkable discoveries changed our understanding of matter and energy. Once thought to be separate concepts, Einstein's theories show how matter and energy can be turned into one another! This chapter will introduce you to an understanding of Einstein's theory of special relativity and general relativity. You will study the speed of light, antimatter, strange particles, curved space-time, black holes, and the "big bang". Is this the stuff of science fiction? The science of Star Trek? Read this chapter to answer some interesting questions that probe our edge of understanding of how the universe works.

Key Questions

- ✓ What does $E = mc^2$ mean?
- ✓ What is the speed limit of the universe?
- ✓ What is a "black hole"?

12.1 The Relationship Between Matter and Energy

Up until Chapter 11, we discussed matter and energy as related, but separate things. This was how physicists viewed the universe before Einstein. Einstein's remarkable discoveries changed all that. Today we know that matter and energy can be turned into one another! In some ways you can think of matter as a form of extremely concentrated energy.

Einstein's formula

The meaning of Einstein's formula The formula $E = mc^2$ is probably the most widely recognized formula in the world, even though few people know how to actually *use* the formula. The formula tells you the amount of energy (E) that is released when a mass (m) is completely converted to energy. It also tells you how much mass (m) you can create out of an amount of energy (E).

EINSTEIN'S FORMULA

$$\text{Energy (joules)} \longrightarrow E = mc^2 \longleftarrow \text{Mass (kg)}$$
$$\text{Speed of light } (3 \times 10^8 \text{ m/sec})$$

Mass and energy In a nuclear reaction, some mass is converted to energy according to Einstein's formula. The c^2 means even a tiny amount of mass is equivalent to a huge amount of energy. The speed of light (c) is 3×10^8 m/sec so the speed of light squared (c^2) is 9×10^{16} m^2/sec^2. This means 1 kg of mass is equivalent to 9×10^{16} joules of energy. This is enough energy to drive a powerful sports car for 25,000 years, non-stop, 24 hours a day!

Energy in reactions Einstein's formula explains how nuclear (and chemical) reactions release energy. With nuclear reactions the amount of energy is large enough that there is a measurable mass difference between reactants and products (Figure 12.1). With chemical reactions, the energy released is so small that the difference in mass is too small to measure.

Objectives

✓ Describe how matter and energy are interchangeable.
✓ Describe the fastest speed in the universe.
✓ Explain the concept of antimatter.

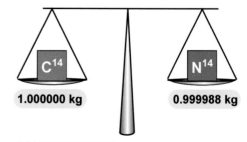

Mass difference

1.000000 kg
- 0.999988 kg
———————
0.000012 kg

Energy released

$E = mc^2$
$= (0.000012 \text{ kg})(3 \times 10^8 \text{ m/sec})^2$
$= 1.1 \times 10^{12}$ joules

Figure 12.1: *A tiny amount of mass is converted to energy by the radioactive decay of carbon-14.*

The speed of light

The ultimate speed limit   Einstein's theory of relativity says that nothing in the universe can travel faster than the speed of light. Even gravity travels at the speed of light. You may know that it takes light from the sun 8 minutes and 19 seconds to get to Earth. If the sun were to vanish, we would still see it in the sky for 8 minutes and 19 seconds. According to Einstein, Earth would also keep moving in its orbit for 8 minutes and 19 seconds too! Earth would not feel the loss of the sun's gravity until 8 minutes and 19 seconds has passed because the change in gravity moves at the speed of light (Figure 12.2).

Comparing the speeds of sound and light   Imagine shining a flashlight on a mirror that is far away. You don't see the light leave your flashlight, move to the mirror, then come back. But that is exactly what happens. You don't see light move because it happens so fast. If the mirror was 170 meters away the light travels there and back in about one-millionth of a second (0.000001 sec). Sound travels much slower than light. If you shout at a wall 170 m away, you will hear an echo one second later. Light travels almost a million times faster than sound.

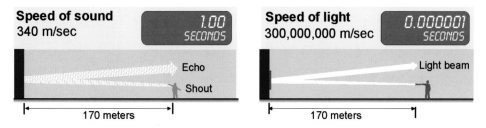

The speed of light, $c = 3 \times 10^8$ m/sec   The speed at which light travels through air is about 300 million meters per second. This is so fast it is hard to find a comparison. Light can travel around the entire Earth 7 $\frac{1}{2}$ times in 1 second. The **speed of light** is so important in physics that it is given its own symbol, a lower case c. When you see this symbol, remember that $c = 3 \times 10^8$ m/sec.

The sound of thunder lags the flash of lightning   The speed of light is so fast that when lightning strikes a few miles away, you hear the thunder several seconds after you see the lightning. At the point of the lightning strike, the thunder and lightning occur at the same time. But just a mile away from the lightning strike, the sound of the thunder is already about 5 seconds behind the flash of the lightning.

Sun disappears

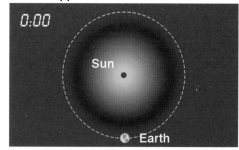

4 minutes later Earth still "sees" the sun and feels the sun's gravity.

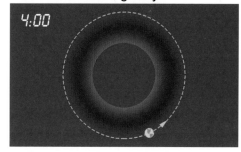

8 minutes and 19 seconds later Earth "sees" the sun go out and flies out of its orbit because sun's gravity stops.

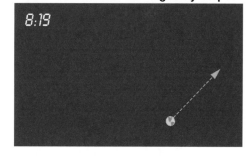

Figure 12.2: *If the sun were to vanish, Earth would not feel any change for 8 minutes and 19 seconds. This is the time it takes light to get from the sun to Earth.*

Antimatter

Other particles of matter

Up until the 1930's scientists were confident that they could explain all the elements with three subatomic particles: protons, neutrons, and electrons. This changed as new developments in technology allowed more sophisticated experiments. The first new thing they discovered was **antimatter**. Then they found other kinds of subatomic particles such as neutrinos. Finally, they discovered that there were *even smaller* particles *inside* protons and neutrons!

Matter and antimatter

Every particle of matter has an antimatter twin. Antimatter is the same as regular matter, except properties like electric charge are reversed. An antiproton is just like a normal proton except it has a negative charge. An anti electron (also called a *positron*) is like an ordinary electron except that it has positive charge. Some nuclear reactions create antimatter. When matter is created from pure energy equal quantities of matter and antimatter always appear together.

Figure 12.3: *Every particle of matter has an antimatter twin that has a reversed electric charge.*

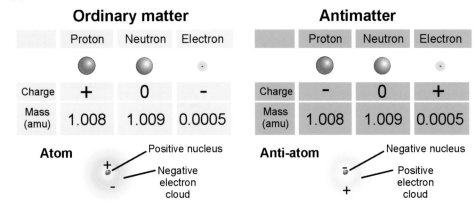

Ordinary matter				Antimatter		
	Proton	Neutron	Electron		Proton	Neutron	Electron
Charge	+	0	–	Charge	–	0	+
Mass (amu)	1.008	1.009	0.0005	Mass (amu)	1.008	1.009	0.0005

Atom — Positive nucleus / Negative electron cloud

Anti-atom — Negative nucleus / Positive electron cloud

Antimatter reactions

When antimatter meets an equal amount of normal matter, both the matter and antimatter are converted to pure energy. Antimatter reactions release thousands of times more energy than ordinary nuclear reactions. If a grain of sand weighing 0.002 kilogram made of ordinary matter were to collide and react with a grain of sand made from 0.002 kilogram of antimatter, the resulting explosion would release 400 trillion joules of energy, enough to power a small city for almost a week (Figure 12.4)!

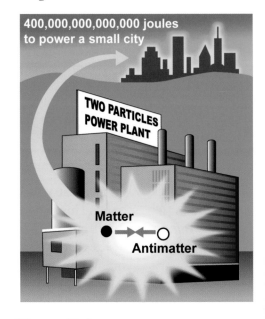

Figure 12.4: *A bit of antimatter the size of a grain of sand would release enough energy to power a small city for a week if it combined with an equal amount of normal matter.*

Strange particles

Neutrinos In Chapter 11 you learned about beta decay, where a neutron turns into a proton and an electron. Although we did not say it then, a *third* particle is also created. This particle is a type of *neutrino*. Neutrinos are lighter than electrons and are very difficult to detect.

Neutrinos are hard to see Huge numbers of neutrinos are created by nuclear reactions in the sun. Every second more than a trillion neutrinos pass right through your body! And you don't feel a thing. That is because neutrinos do not feel the electromagnetic force or the strong nuclear force. Neutrinos only feel the weak force. The weak force is so weak that most neutrinos pass right through all of Earth without interacting with a single atom. Physicists have built very special experiments to capture and study neutrinos.

Accelerators Other particles even heavier than the proton and neutron have also been found. We don't see these particles every day because regular protons and neutrons have lower energy that the other heavy particles. Since matter tends to find the lowest energy, ordinary matter tends to become protons and neutrons. Physicists use high-energy accelerators to produce the heavy particles so we can study them (Figure 12.5).

Quarks Today we believe that protons and neutrons are made of even smaller particles called quarks. Quarks come in different types and the lightest two are named the *up* quark and the *down* quark. A proton is made of two up quarks and one down quark (Figure 12.6). A neutron is made from two down quarks and one up quark. Today, we believe all the heavy particles are made of just six kinds of quarks named *up*, *down*, *strange*, *charm*, *top*, and *bottom*.

12.1 Section Review

1. Explain the symbols in Einstein's formula.
2. Calculate how far light would travel in one year. This distance is called a "light year."
3. Calculate the energy released by one kilogram of matter turning unto pure energy.
4. Give one difference between antimatter and normal matter.

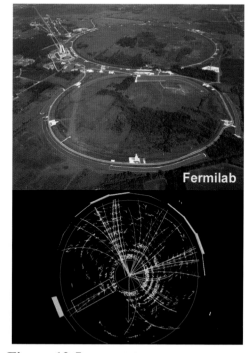

Figure 12.5: *Fermilab, near Chicago, is a high-energy particle accelerator. The ring-shaped building in the top photo is 4 miles in circumference! The lower image shows a high-energy collision between particles. Each colored track represents a particle.*

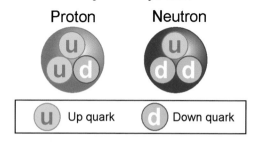

Figure 12.6: *Protons and neutrons are each made of 3 up and down quarks.*

12.2 Special Relativity

Science fiction writers love to invent "impossible" tricks like time travel. It may surprise you, but time travel into the future is actually possible. It just takes a lot more energy than we know how to control today. Albert Einstein's theory of special relativity makes a connection between time and space that depends on how fast you are moving.

Vocabulary

theory of special relativity, time dilation

Objectives

✓ Describe some consequences of special relativity.

What special relativity is about

The relationship between matter, energy, time, and space

The **theory of special relativity** describes what happens to matter, energy, time, and space at speeds close to the speed of light. The fact that light *always* travels at the same speed forces other things about the universe to change in surprising ways. Special relativity does not affect ordinary life because things need to be moving faster than 100 million m/sec before the effects of special relativity become obvious. However, these effects are seen and measured every day in physics labs. Some surprising effects of special relativity are shown in Figure 12.7.

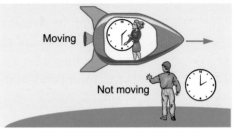

Time runs slower for moving objects

Time moves slower

1. Time moves more slowly for an object in motion than it does for objects that are not in motion. In practical terms, clocks run slower on moving spaceships compared with clocks on the ground. By moving very fast, it is possible for one year to pass on a spaceship while 100 years have passed on the ground. This effect is known as **time dilation**.

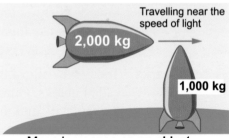

Mass increases as an object gets close to the speed of light

Mass increases

2. As objects move faster, their *mass increases*. The closer the speed of an object gets to the speed of light, the more of its kinetic energy becomes mass instead of motion. Matter can never exceed the speed of light because adding energy creates more mass instead of increasing an object's speed.

Distances contract

3. The length of an object measured by one person at rest will not be the same as the length measured by another person who is moving close to the speed of light. The object does not get smaller or larger, *space itself* gets smaller for an observer moving near the speed of light.

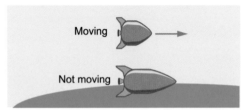

Space contracts in the direction of motion

Figure 12.7: *Three ways relativity changes the universe.*

The speed of light problem

How you can be moving and appear at rest

The theory of special relativity comes from thinking about light. Einstein wondered what light would look like if you could see it when it wasn't moving. Instead of making the light stop, Einstein thought about moving beside a beam of light at the same speed as light itself. Imagine you could move as fast as light and were traveling right next to the beam from a flashlight. If you looked over, you should see the light standing still, *relative to you*. A similar situation occurs when two people are driving on a road side-by-side at the same speed. The two people look at each other and appear (to each other) not to be moving because both are traveling at the same speed.

The way speed normally adds

Consider a girl on a railroad train moving at a constant speed of 10 m/sec. If you are standing on the track, the girl gets 10 meters closer to you every second. Now consider what happens if the girl on the train throws a ball at you at 10 m/sec. In one second, the ball moves forward on the train 10 meters. The train also moves toward you by 10 meters. Therefore, the ball moves toward you 20 meters in one second. The ball approaches you with a speed of *20 m/sec* as far as you are concerned (Figure 12.8).

How you expect light to behave

Einstein considered the same trick using light instead of a ball. If the girl on the train were to shine a flashlight toward you, you would expect the light to approach you faster. You would expect the light to come toward you at the speed of the train plus 3×10^8 m/sec.

The speed of light does not behave this way

That is *not* what happens (Figure 12.9). The light comes toward you at a speed of 3×10^8 m/sec *no matter how fast the train approaches you!* This experiment was done in 1887 by Albert A. Michelson and Edward W. Morley. They used Earth itself as the "train." Earth moves with an orbital speed of 29,800 m/sec. Michelson and Morley measured the speed of light parallel and perpendicular to Earth's orbital motion. They found the speed to be exactly the same! This result is not what they expected, and was confusing to everyone. Like all unexpected results, it forced people to rethink what they thought they already knew. Einstein's theory of special relativity was the result and it totally changed the way we understand space and time.

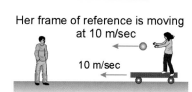

A girl throws a ball at 10 m/sec relative to her frame of reference

10 m/sec

Her frame of reference is moving at 10 m/sec

10 m/sec

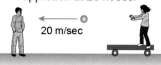

An observer at rest sees the ball approach at 20 m/sec.

20 m/sec

Figure 12.8: *A ball thrown from a moving train approaches you at the speed of the ball relative to the train plus the speed of the train relative to you.*

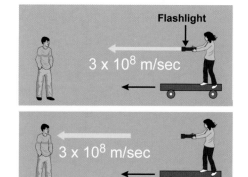

Flashlight

3×10^8 m/sec

3×10^8 m/sec

Figure 12.9: *The speed of light appears the same to all observers independent of their relative motion.*

Speed, time, and clocks

Einstein's thinking

With this new idea that the speed of light is the same for all observers, Einstein thought about what this meant for everything else in physics. One of the strangest results of special relativity is that time itself changes depending on the motion of an observer. Einstein's conclusion about the flow of time is totally revolutionary, and completely changed our understanding of how physics works.

A light clock on a spaceship

Einstein thought about a clock that measures time by counting the trips made by a beam of light going back and forth between two mirrors (Figure 12.10). The clock is on a moving spaceship. A person standing next to the clock sees the light go back and forth straight up and down. The time it takes to make one trip is the distance between the mirrors divided by the speed of light.

How the light clock appears on the ground

To someone who is not moving, the path of the light is not straight up and down. The light appears to make a zigzag because the mirrors move with the spaceship (Figure 12.11). The observer on the ground sees the light travel a longer path. This would not be a problem, *except that the speed of light must be the same to all observers, regardless of their motion.*

The paradox

Suppose it takes light one second to go between the mirrors. The speed of light must be the same for both people, yet the person on the ground sees the light move a longer distance! How can this be?

Time itself must be different for a moving object

The only way out is that *one second on the ground is not the same as one second on the spaceship.* The speed of light is the distance traveled divided by the time taken. If one second of "ship time" was longer than one second of "ground time," then the problem is resolved. Both people measure the same speed for light of 3×10^8 m/sec. The difference is that one second of "ship time" is *longer* than one second of "ground time."

Time slows down close to the speed of light

The consequence of the speed of light being constant is that *time slows down for objects in motion, including people.* If you move fast enough, the change in the flow of time is enormous. For a spaceship traveling at 99.9 percent of the speed of light, 22 years pass on Earth for every year that passes on the ship. The closer the spaceship's speed is to the speed of light, the slower time flows.

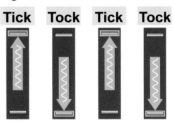

A light clock counts trips of light between two mirrors

Figure 12.10: *A light clock measures time by measuring the how long it takes a pulse of light to move between two parallel mirrors.*

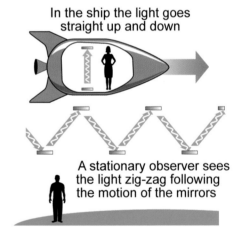

In the ship the light goes straight up and down

A stationary observer sees the light zig-zag following the motion of the mirrors

Figure 12.11: *A clock that counts ticks of light going back and forth in a spaceship. The light pulse of a light clock that is moving relative to an observe traces out a triangular path.*

The twin paradox

Proof of time dilation
The idea that moving clocks run slower is difficult to believe. Before Einstein's theory of special relativity, time was always considered a universal constant. One second was one second, no matter where you were or what you were doing. After Einstein, we realized this was not true. The rate of time passing for two people depends on their relative motion.

Atomic clocks
One of the most direct measurements of this effect was done in the early 1970s by synchronizing two precise atomic clocks. One was put on a plane and flown around the world. The other was left on the ground. When the flying clock returned home, the clocks were compared. The clock on the plane measured less time than the clock on the ground. The difference agreed precisely with special relativity.

The twin paradox
A *paradox* is a situation that does not seem to make sense. A well-known thought experiment in relativity is known as the *twin paradox*. The story goes like this: Two twins are born on Earth. They grow up to young adults and one of the twins becomes an astronaut. The other twin chooses a different career.

Traveling into the future
The astronaut twin goes on a mission into space. The space ship moves very fast, near the speed of light. Because of traveling at this high speed, the clocks on the ship, including the twin's biological clock, run much slower than the clocks on Earth. Upon returning from a two-year (ship time) trip, the astronaut is two years older than when she left. However her twin brother is 20 years older now! In essence, the astronaut twin has traveled 18 years into the future by moving near the speed of light (Figure 12.12).

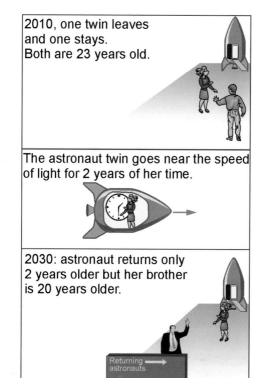

2010, one twin leaves and one stays. Both are 23 years old.

The astronaut twin goes near the speed of light for 2 years of her time.

2030: astronaut returns only 2 years older but her brother is 20 years older.

Returning astronauts

Figure 12.12: *Relativity allows time travel into the future, if you can move at speeds near the speed of light!*

12.2 Section Review

1. List at least three ways special relativity changes the universe.

2. Which person experiences a "longer second", a person who is in motion or a person who is standing still?

3. You are standing on the ground beside a train track. A person on the train throws a ball at you at a speed of 20 m/sec relative to the train. If the train is moving toward you at 30 m/sec, what is the speed of the ball relative to you?

4. Explain how you could travel into the future.

12.3 General Relativity

Einstein's theory of **general relativity** describes gravity in a very different way than does Newton's law of universal gravitation. According to Einstein, the presence of mass changes the shape of space-time itself. In general relativity, an object in orbit is moving in a straight line through curved space. The curvature of space itself causes a planet to move in an orbit. The force we call gravity is an effect created by the curvature of space and time.

The equivalence of acceleration and gravity

Different perspectives on the same motion
Imagine a boy and girl who jump into a bottomless canyon, where there is no air friction. On the way down, they play catch and throw a ball back and forth. If the girl looks at the boy, she sees the ball go straight to him. If the boy looks at the girl, he sees the ball go straight to her. However, an observer watching them fall sees the ball follow a curved zigzag path back and forth (Figure 12.13). Who is correct? What is the real path of the ball?

The boy and girl perceive no gravity
Both are correct from *their frame of reference*. Imagine enclosing the boy and girl in a windowless box falling with them. From inside their box, they see the ball go straight back and forth. To the boy and girl in the box, the ball follows the exact same path it would *if there were no gravity*.

The reverse situation
Next, imagine the boy and girl are in the same box throwing the ball back and forth in deep space, *where there is no gravity*. This time the box is accelerating upwards. When the boy throws the ball to the girl, the ball does not go straight to her, but drops in a parabola toward the floor. This happens because the floor is accelerating upward and pushing the girl with it. The girl moves up while the ball is moving toward her. But, from her perspective she sees the ball go down. To the girl the path of the ball is a parabola *exactly like it would be if there was a force of gravity pulling it downward*.

Reference frames
In physics, the box containing the boy and girl is called a **reference frame**. Everything they can do, measure, or see is inside their reference frame. *No experiment the boy or girl do inside the box can tell whether they are feeling the force of gravity or they are in a reference frame that is accelerating.*

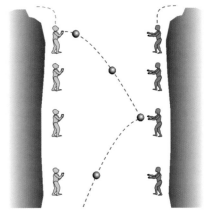

How it appears to an observer

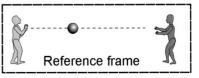

Reference frame

How things look in *their* reference frame

Figure 12.13: *How the path of the ball appears to an outside observer and in the accelerating reference frame of the boy and girl.*

Curved space-time

Light and the equivalence principle
Earlier in this Chapter we talked about special relativity, which says the speed of light is the same for all observers whether they are moving or not. The equivalence of acceleration and gravity must also be true for experiments that measure the speed of light. In order to meet both these conditions, Einstein deduced two strange things which must also be true.

1. Space itself must be curved.
2. The path of light must be deflected by gravity, even though light has no mass.

Flat space
To understand what we mean by curved space, consider rolling a ball along a sheet of graph paper. If the graph paper is flat the ball rolls along a straight line. A flat sheet of graph paper is like "flat space." In flat space, parallel lines never meet, all three angles of the triangle add up to 180 degrees, etc. Flat space is what you would consider "normal."

Curved space
A large mass, like a star, curves space nearby. Figure 12.14 shows an example of a graph paper made of rubber which has been stretched down in one point. If you roll a ball along this graph paper, it bends as it rolls near the "well" created by the stretch. From directly overhead, the graph paper still looks square. If you look straight down on the graph paper, the path of the ball appears to be deflected by a force pulling it toward the center. You might say the ball felt a force of gravity which deflected its motion. You would be right. The effect of curved space is identical to the force of gravity.

Orbits and curved space
In fact, close to a source of gravity, straight lines become circles. A planet moving in an orbit is actually moving in a straight line through curved space. This is a strange way to think, but all of the experimental evidence we have gathered tells us it is the right way to think. The event that made Einstein famous was his prediction that light from distant stars should be bent by the curvature of space near the sun. People were skeptical because, according to Newton's law of gravitation, light is not affected by gravity. In 1919 careful observations were made of a star near the sun during a solar eclipse. Einstein was proven to be right!

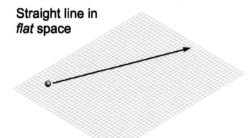

Straight line in *flat* space

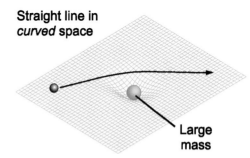

Straight line in *curved* space

Large mass

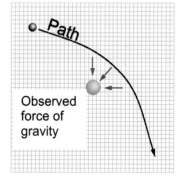

Figure 12.14: *Large amounts of mass cause space to become curved. An object following a straight path in curved space bends the same way as if it were acted on by a force we call gravity.*

Black holes

General relativity predicts black holes
One of the strangest predictions of general relativity is the existence of **black holes**. To understand a black hole, consider a rocket trying to leave Earth. If the rocket does not go fast enough, Earth's gravity pulls it back. The minimum speed a rocket needs to escape a planet's gravity is called the *escape velocity*. The stronger the force of gravity, the faster the escape velocity.

Figure 12.15: *On Earth, light travels in nearly straight lines because Earth's escape velocity is much less than the speed of light.*

The escape velocity of a black hole
If gravity becomes strong enough, the escape velocity can reach the speed of light. A *black hole* is an object with such strong gravity that its escape velocity equals or exceeds the speed of light. When the escape velocity equals the speed of light, nothing can get out because nothing can go faster than light. In fact, even light cannot get out. The name *black hole* comes from the fact that no light can get out, so the object appears "black" (Figure 12.16).

Black holes are extremely compact matter
To make a black hole, a very large mass must be squeezed into a very tiny space. For example, to make Earth into a black hole, you would have to squeeze the mass of the whole planet down to the size of a marble as wide as your thumb. For a long time, nobody took black holes seriously because they seemed so strange that they could not actually be real.

We see black holes by what is around them

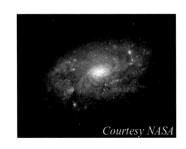

Courtesy NASA

But then astronomers started finding them! You might think it would be impossible to see a black hole—and it is. But, you *can see* what happens *around* a black hole. In Chapter 3, you learned that an object loses potential energy as it falls. When an object falls into a black hole, it loses so much energy that a fraction of its mass turns into energy. Any matter that falls into a black hole gives off so much energy it creates incredibly bright radiation as it falls in. Because they have observed this radiation, astronomers believe our own Milky Way Galaxy has a huge black hole at its very center. The Milky Way's central black hole is believed to have a mass more than a million times the mass of our sun.

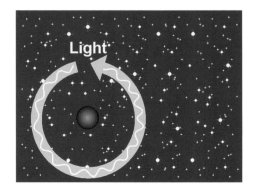

Figure 12.16: *Light from a black hole cannot escape because the escape velocity is higher than the speed of light.*

The big bang

Milky Way Galaxy When we look out into space with powerful telescopes, we see stars of our own Milky Way Galaxy. The Milky Way contains about 200 billion stars distributed in a gigantic spiral. Some of the stars are like the sun. Some are hotter, some are cooler, some older, some younger. Just recently we have discovered that many stars have planets like the planets in our solar system.

The universe Beyond our galaxy with its 200 billion stars are other galaxies. We can see billions of galaxies, many of them as full of stars as our own. This is the universe on its largest scale.

When we look at these distant galaxies we find an astounding fact. All the galaxies are moving away from each other! The farther away they are from us, the faster they are moving. *This means the entire universe is expanding.*

An expanding universe implies a beginning If the universe is expanding, then it must have been smaller in the past. It seems reasonable to ask how small was the early universe? And how long has it been since the universe was small? The best evidence indicates that the age of the universe is 13 billion years, plus or minus a few billion years (Figure 12.17). This is roughly three times older than the age of the sun. This age for the universe agrees with other estimates, such as the oldest stars we can see.

The big bang It also appears that the universe was once very small, possibly smaller than a single atom. Sixteen billion years ago a cataclysmic explosion occurred and the universe started growing from a tiny point into the incredible vastness we now see. In jest, someone called this beginning the "**big bang**" and the name stuck. We have no idea why the big bang happened or what came before the big bang. It is not clear these questions can even be answered by science.

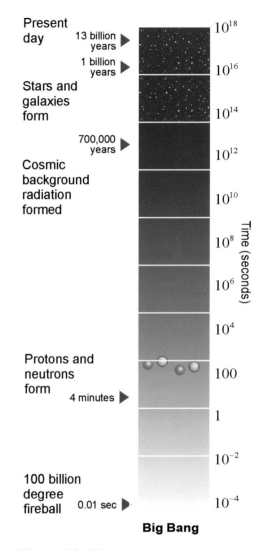

Figure 12.17: *A time line of the history of the universe.*

12.3 Section Review

1. How does general relativity explain gravity?
2. Describe your reference frame. Is it moving? If so, moving relative to what?
3. What is a black hole? What is the big bang?

Traveling Faster than Light

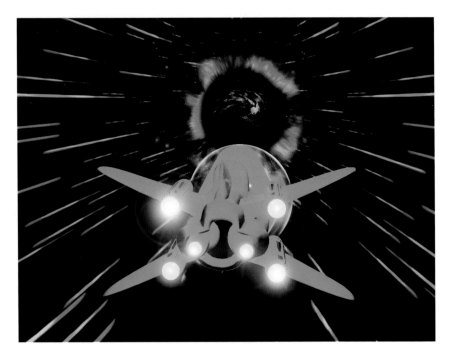

Have you ever watched a science fiction program and wondered how your heroes can travel from galaxy to galaxy, spanning the universe in mere days? Such a feat would require travel at speeds faster than the speed of light. However, a major assumption of special relativity is that matter cannot travel faster than the speed of light. Some physicists are looking for loopholes in the laws of physics in hopes that one day, science fiction may become reality.

A long, long way from home

Why do we need to travel faster than light to explore the universe in person? Consider that Alpha Centauri, the star closest to the sun, is 4.2 light years away—that's about 26 trillion miles.

The space shuttle travels at about 11,000 miles per hour. At that speed, it would take over 150,000 years to reach Alpha Centauri. At light speed with time dilation, it would take only about 2.3 years. As you can see, faster-than-light-speed travel has its benefits.

A shortcut through the universe

One idea being explored to bypass the light-speed barrier involves Einstein's concept that space can be distorted into structures called *wormholes*. A wormhole is a space-time distortion that is like a corridor connecting areas of space that are far away. Just as hallways in your school lessen the time needed to get to each of your classes, wormholes significantly reduce the amount of time needed to travel across the universe. Imagine walking through a wormhole in your classroom onto the surface of a planet in another galaxy!

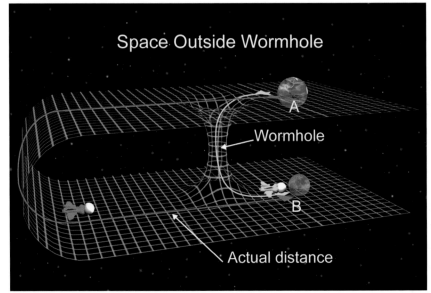

Although scientists predict that wormholes occur naturally, they are unsure about their stability and how to control them. Wormholes also present a particular concern to physicists. They require unheard of amounts of energy to create. Creating space-time distortions, like wormholes, also requires a very unusual form of energy called negative energy. It has been estimated that to produce even a tiny wormhole would require the same amount of negative energy as the entire energy output of a star over its 10 billion year life span.

What is negative energy?

Imagine removing all of the matter in your classroom. What's left? You would be in a vacuum containing only energy. You can imagine removing all the energy in the forms we know. Then you have truly nothing except "nothing." Well, according to some new theories in quantum mechanics, this "nothing" actually has some energy that is the energy of space-time itself. Negative energy means lower energy than the energy of empty space-time. Some recent evidence suggests negative energy may really exist.

A warped idea

Most theories that predict faster-than light travel involve negative energy, including *warp drive*. Warp drive is often compared with the moving sidewalks found in many airports. There is a limit to how fast you can walk, just like objects are not able to travel beyond light speed. However, you move faster if you are on a portion of the moving sidewalk because the floor itself moves. The warp drive concept is based on expanding space-time behind the spaceship and contracting it in front. The result is that a portion of space-time moves, pushing the spaceship forward.

A job for physicists

Physicists examine both the possibilities of exceeding light speed and the many challenges it presents. They use their extensive knowledge of the laws of physics to bring this dream closer to reality. Although they face many obstacles and uncertainties, scientists believe the possibilities of success create hope that future generations might solve many mysteries of our universe by actually going there!

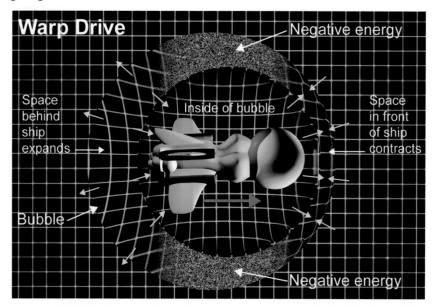

Warp Drive

Negative energy

Space behind ship expands

Inside of bubble

Space in front of ship contracts

Bubble

Negative energy

Questions:

1. Which theory predicts that faster-than-light travel is impossible?
2. What is the major obstacle to traveling faster than light?
3. What are some differences between wormholes and warp drive?
4. How is warp drive like a moving sidewalk?

Chapter 12 Review

Understanding Vocabulary

Select the correct term to complete the sentences.

speed of light	general relativity	antimatter
reference frame	big bang	time dilation
black hole	special relativity	

Section 12.1

1. Every particle of matter has a(n) _____ twin.

2. _____ is equal to 3×10^8 meters per second.

Section 12.2

3. _____ is a theory that describes what happens to matter, energy, time, and space at speeds close to the speed of light.

4. An effect known as _____ causes time to move more slowly for an object in motion than for one at rest.

Section 12.3

5. According to _____ the force we call gravity is an effect created by the curvature of space and time.

6. The perspective of an observer from which the position and motion of a system can be described is called a(n) _____.

7. A(n) _____ is an object with such a strong gravity that its escape velocity equals the speed of light.

8. According to the _____, the universe was once smaller than an atom and began to expand after a huge explosion.

Reviewing Concepts

Section 12.1

1. According to Einstein's formula, what is the relationship between mass, energy, and the speed of light?

2. What is the speed of light and why is it such an important concept in physics?

3. What is antimatter? What happens when antimatter meets an equal amount of normal matter?

4. What are quarks? In terms of quarks, what is the difference between a proton and a neutron?

Section 12.2

5. According to the theory of special relativity, why can't matter exceed the speed of light?

6. How is the speed of light coming toward you from a moving object different from the speed of a ball being thrown toward you from a moving object? Which theory did this difference lead scientists to?

7. Explain why time slows down at speeds close to the speed of light.

8. What is time dilation? How did scientists prove that it was true using atomic clocks?

9. Describe the twin paradox.

Section 12.3

10. How does the theory of general relativity describe the effects of gravity differently than the law of universal gravitation?

11. What are the effects of a large mass object, like a star, on space? What are its effects on the path of light?

12. How would you make a black hole?

13. According to the big bang, how did the universe begin? What is happening to the universe?

Solving Problems

Section 12.1

1. In a nuclear reaction, only a small fraction of mass is converted into energy. Suppose 0.1 kg of uranium is converted into energy in a nuclear reaction. How much energy is produced?

2. The sun produces 3.8×10^{26} joules of energy per second. How much mass does the sun lose each second?

3. Mars is 228 million kilometers from the sun. If the sun suddenly burned out, how long would it take for Martians to notice?

4. In 1969, Neil Armstrong and Buzz Aldrin were first to land a lunar module on the moon, 384,400 kilometers from Earth. You may have heard Armstrong's famous phrase, spoken when he stepped out of the module onto the moon's surface: "That's one small step for man, one giant leap for mankind." When he spoke, he was not heard immediately on Earth because of the moon's distance. How long did it take the radio waves to travel to Earth so that those words could be heard by millions of viewers? (HINT: Radio waves travel at the speed of light.)

Section 12.2

5. You are standing on a bicycle path. A person on a bike throws a ball at you at a speed of 10 m/sec relative to the bike. If the bike is moving toward you at 5 m/sec, what is the speed of the ball relative to you?

6. Two clocks are set at identical times. One is placed on a plane and travels around the world. The other remains on the ground, not moving. When the plane lands and the two clocks are compared, how would the times on the clocks compare?

7. Suppose you could travel to another galaxy and back at speeds near the speed of light. Why would it be risky to make a doctor's appointment for 9:00 am one month after your departure?

Section 12.3

8. Imagine looking down on a large star with an approaching light ray as shown below. Draw the path of the light ray as it travels past the star. Explain why the light ray follows the path you drew.

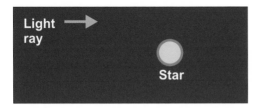

Applying Your Knowledge

Section 12.1

1. In 1989, the space probe Voyager II reached the planet Neptune and began sending images of the planet back to Earth. Assuming these radio waves had to travel 4.0×10^9 kilometers, how long did it take, in minutes, before astronomers received the signals from Voyager II?

2. How have our ideas about matter changed over the past 2,500 years?
   a. Use this book and the Internet to research how our ideas about matter have changed over the past 2,500 years.
   b. Create a timeline that shows the major discoveries and important events that have led to current theories about matter. Make a poster of your timeline with illustrations.
   c. Include dates, people and a brief description of each event.
   d. Make up a future event about matter that could change our ideas even more. Be creative!

Section 12.2

3. 1905 was a year that completely changed the field of physics. Many of the new theories and discoveries were made by Albert Einstein. Research the groundbreaking discoveries and theories made by Einstein in that year.

4. Explain each statement below.
   a. If a being on a planet that was billions and billions of miles from Earth had a super-powerful telescope, he or she would be able to observe events that happened long ago such as the ice age.
   b. Imagine that space travel at near-light-speed is possible. Space travelers could travel into Earth's future as far as they wished, but they could never travel back in time.

Section 12.3

5. The big bang is the dominant scientific theory about the origin of the universe. Research the scientific evidence for the big bang. Prepare a short report that describes the different pieces of evidence, who discovered them, and how they were discovered.

UNIT 5

Electricity

Chapter 13
Electric Circuits

Chapter 14
Electrical Systems

Chapter 15
Electrical Charges and Forces

Chapter 13 Electric Circuits

Suppose you had a stationary bicycle that was connected to a light bulb, so that when you pedal the bicycle, the energy from the turning wheels lights the bulb. How fast would you have to pedal the bicycle to generate enough electrical energy to light the bulb? You would be surprised at how hard you would have to pedal to do something as seemingly simple as lighting an ordinary household light bulb. Some science museums contain this type of exhibit to give everyone a good example of how much energy is needed to accomplish simple tasks in our daily lives.

What would your life be like without electricity? You can probably name at least a dozen aspects of your morning routine alone that would have to change if you didn't have electricity. Do you know how electrical circuits work? Do you know what the words voltage and current mean? This chapter will give you the opportunity to explore electricity, electrical circuits, and the nature of electrical energy. Electricity can be powerful and dangerous, but when you know some basic facts about how electricity works, you can use electricity safely with confidence.

Key Questions

✓ Are there electrical circuits in the human body? What about an electric eel?

✓ Why is the shock from a household outlet more dangerous to you if your skin is wet?

✓ What are semiconductors, and what common household items contain them?

13.1 Electric Circuits

Imagine your life without TV, radio, computers, refrigerators, or light bulbs. All of these things are possible because of electricity. The use of electricity has become so routine that most of us never stop to think about what happens when we switch on a light or turn on a motor. This section is about electricity and electric circuits. Circuits are usually made of wires that carry electricity and devices that use electricity.

Electricity

What is electricity? Electricity usually means the flow of **electric current** in wires, motors, light bulbs, and other inventions. Electric current is what makes an electric motor turn or an electric stove heat up. Electric current is almost always invisible and comes from the motion of electrons or other charged particles. This chapter and the next will teach you the practical use of electricity. Chapter 15 will deal with electricity at the atomic level.

Electric current Electric current is similar to a current of water, but electric current is not visible because it usually flows inside solid metal wires. Electric current can carry energy and do work just as a current of water can. For example, a waterwheel turns when a current of water exerts a force on it (Figure 13.1). A waterwheel can be connected to a machine such as a loom for making cloth, or to a millstone for grinding wheat into flour. Before electricity was available, waterwheels were used to supply energy to many machines. Today, the same tasks are done using energy from electric current. Look around you right now and probably you see wires carrying electric current into buildings.

Electricity can be powerful and dangerous Electric current can carry great deal of energy. For example, an electric saw can cut wood much faster than a hand saw. An electric motor the size of a basketball can do as much work as five big horses or fifteen strong people. Electric current also can be dangerous. Touching a live electric wire can result in serious injury. The more you know about electricity, the easier it is to use it safely.

Figure 13.1: *A waterwheel uses the force of flowing water to run machines.*

Electric circuits

Electricity travels in circuits
An **electric circuit** is a complete path through which electricity travels. A good example of a circuit is the one in an electric toaster. Bread is toasted by heaters that convert electrical energy to heat. The circuit has a switch that turns on when the lever on the side of the toaster is pulled down. With the switch on, electric current enters through one side of the plug from the socket in the wall, and goes through the toaster and out the other side of the plug.

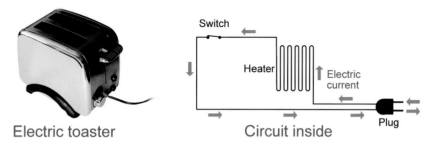

Electric toaster   Circuit inside

Wires are like pipes for electricity
Wires in electric circuits are similar in some ways to pipes and hoses that carry water (Figure 13.2). Wires act like pipes for electric current. Current enters the house on the supply wire and leaves on the return wire. The big difference between wires and water pipes is that you cannot get electricity to leave a wire the way water leaves a pipe. If you cut a water pipe, the water flows out. If you cut a wire, the electric current stops immediately.

Examples of circuits in nature
Circuits are not confined to appliances, wires, and devices built by people. The first experience humans had with electricity was in the natural world. These are some examples of natural circuits:

- The nerves in your body are an electrical circuit that carries messages from your brain to your muscles.
- The tail of an electric eel makes a circuit when it stuns a fish with a jolt of electricity.
- The Earth makes a gigantic circuit when lightning carries electric current between the clouds and the ground.

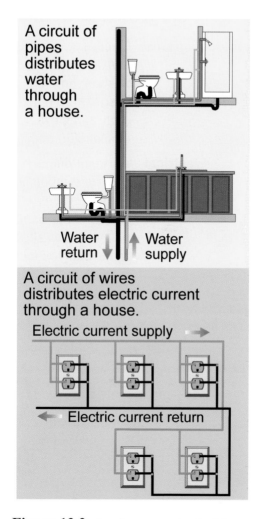

Figure 13.2: *In a house or other building, we use pipes to carry water and wires to carry electric current.*

Circuit diagrams and electrical symbols

Circuit diagrams Circuits are made up of wires and electrical parts such as *batteries*, *light bulbs*, *motors*, and *switches*. When designing a circuit people make drawings to show how the parts are connected. Electrical drawings are called **circuit diagrams**. When drawing a circuit diagram, symbols are used to represent each part of the circuit. These **electrical symbols** make drawing circuits quicker and easier than drawing realistic pictures.

Electrical symbols A circuit diagram is a shorthand method of describing a working circuit. The electric symbols used in circuit diagrams are standard so that anyone familiar with electricity can build the circuit by looking at the diagram. Figure 13.3 shows some common parts of a circuit and their electrical symbols. The picture below shows an actual circuit on the left and its circuit diagram on the right. Can you identify the real parts with their symbols? Note that the switch is open in the circuit diagram, but closed in the photograph. Closing the switch completes the circuit so the light bulb lights up.

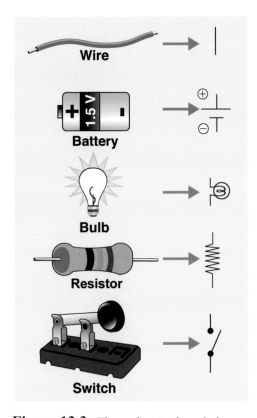

Figure 13.3: *These electrical symbols are used when drawing circuit diagrams.*

 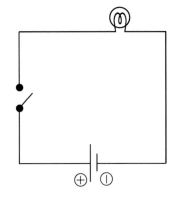

Resistors A **resistor** is an electrical device that uses the energy carried by electric current in a specific way. In many circuit diagrams any electrical device that uses energy is shown with a resistor symbol. A light bulb, heating element, speaker, or motor can be drawn with a resistor symbol. When you analyze a circuit, many electrical devices may be treated as resistors when figuring out how much current is in the circuit.

Open and closed circuits

Batteries All electric circuits must have a source of energy. Circuits in your home get their energy from power plants that generate electricity. Circuits in flashlights, cell phones, and portable radios get their energy from batteries. Some calculators have solar cells that convert energy from the sun or other lights into electrical energy. Of all the types of circuits, those with batteries are the easiest to learn. We will focus on battery circuits for now and will eventually learn how circuits in buildings work.

Open and closed circuits It is necessary to turn off light bulbs, radios, and most other devices in circuits. One way to turn off a device is to stop the current by "breaking" the circuit. Electric current can only flow when there is a complete and unbroken path from one end of the battery to the other. A circuit with no breaks is called a **closed circuit** (Figure 13.4). A light bulb will light only when it is part of a closed circuit. Opening a switch or disconnecting a wire creates a break in the circuit and stops the current. A circuit with any break in it is called an **open circuit**.

Switches **Switches** are used to turn electricity on and off. Flipping a switch to the "off" position creates an open circuit by making a break in the wire. The break stops the current because electricity cannot normally travel through air. Flipping a switch to the "on" position closes the break and allows the current to flow again, to supply energy to the bulb or radio or other device.

Breaks in circuits A switch is not the only way to make a break in a circuit. A light bulb burns out when the thin wire that glows inside it breaks. This also creates an open circuit and explains why a "burned out" bulb cannot light.

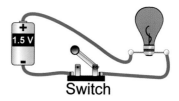

Open circuit

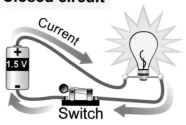

Closed circuit

Figure 13.4: *There is current in a closed circuit but not in an open circuit.*

13.1 Section Review

1. List one way electric current is similar to water current and one way it is different.
2. Draw a circuit diagram for the circuit shown in Figure 13.5.
3. What is the difference between an open circuit and a closed circuit?

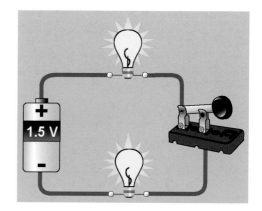

Figure 13.5: *What does the circuit diagram for this circuit look like?*

13.2 Current and Voltage

Current is what carries energy in a circuit. Like water current, electric current only flows when there is a difference in energy between two locations that are connected. Water flows downhill from high gravitational potential energy to low. Electric current flows from high electrical potential energy to low. Electrical *voltage* measures the difference in electrical potential energy between two places in a circuit. Differences in voltage are what cause electric currents to flow.

Current

Measuring electric current Electric current is measured in units called **amperes (A)**, or amps, for short. The unit is named in honor of Andre-Marie Ampere (1775-1836), a French physicist who studied electricity and magnetism. A small battery-powered flashlight bulb uses about 1/2 amp of electric current.

Current flows from positive to negative Examine a battery and you will find a positive and a negative end. The positive end on a AA, C, or D battery has a raised bump, and the negative end is flat. A battery's electrical symbol uses a long line to show the positive end and a short line to show the negative end.

Current in equals current out Electric current from a battery flows out of the positive end and returns back into the negative end. An arrow is sometimes used to show the direction of current on a circuit diagram (Figure 13.6). The amount of electric current coming out of the positive end of the battery must always be the same as the amount of current flowing into the negative end. You can picture this rule in your mind with steel balls flowing through a tube. When you push one in, one comes out. The rate at which the balls flow in equals the rate at which they flow out.

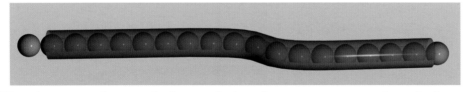

Current doesn't leak out Electric current does not leak out of wires the way water sometimes leaks out of a hose or pipe. Electrical forces are so strong that current stops immediately if a circuit is broken.

Objectives
- ✓ List the units used to measure current and voltage.
- ✓ Describe how to measure current and voltage in a circuit.
- ✓ Explain the function of a battery in a circuit.

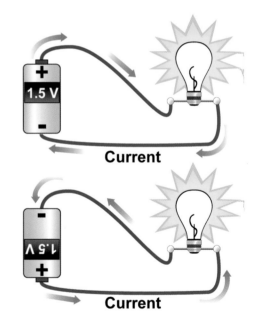

Figure 13.6: *Electric current flows in a circuit from the positive end of a battery and returns toward the negative end.*

Voltage

Energy and voltage

Voltage is a measure of electric potential energy, just like height is a measure of gravitational potential energy. Voltage is measured in **volts** (V). Like other forms of potential energy, a voltage difference means there is energy that can be used to do work. With electricity, the energy becomes useful when we let the voltage difference cause current to flow through a circuit. Current is what actually flows and does work. A difference in voltage provides the energy that causes current to flow.

What voltage means

A voltage difference of 1 volt means 1 amp of current does 1 joule of work in 1 second. Since 1 joule per second is a watt (power), *voltage is the power per amp of current that flows*. Every amp of current flowing out of a 1.5 V battery carries 1.5 watts of power. The voltage in your home electrical system is 120 volts, which means each amp of current carries 120 watts of power. The higher the voltage, the more power is carried by each amp of electric current.

Using a meter to measure voltage

Humans cannot see voltage, so we use an electrical meter to find the voltage in a circuit. A **voltmeter** measures voltage. A more useful meter is a **multimeter**, which can measure voltage or current. To measure voltage, the meter's probes are touched to two places in a circuit or across a battery. The meter shows the difference in voltage between the two places.

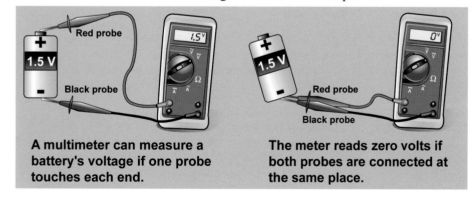

A multimeter can measure a battery's voltage if one probe touches each end.

The meter reads zero volts if both probes are connected at the same place.

Meters measure voltage difference

The meter reads *positive* voltage if the red (positive) probe is at a higher voltage than the black probe. The meter reads negative when the black probe is at the higher voltage. The meter reads voltage *differences* between its probes. If both probes are connected to the same place the meter reads zero.

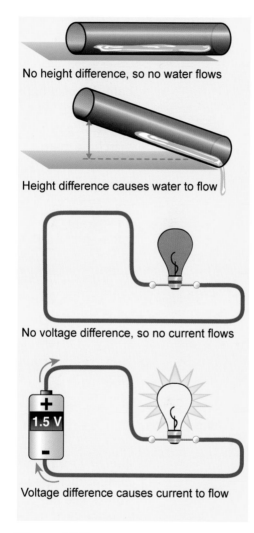

No height difference, so no water flows

Height difference causes water to flow

No voltage difference, so no current flows

Voltage difference causes current to flow

Figure 13.7: *A change in height causes water to flow in a pipe. Current flows in a circuit because a battery creates a voltage difference.*

Batteries

Batteries A **battery** uses chemical energy to create a voltage difference between its two terminals. When current leaves a battery, it carries energy. The current gives up its energy as it passes through an electrical device such as a light bulb. When a bulb is lit, the electrical energy is taken from the current and is transformed into light and heat energy. The current returns to the battery, where it gets more energy. Y4ou can think of the current as a stream of marching particles each carrying a bucket of energy (diagram below). A 1.5 volt battery means the marchers carry 1.5 joules out of the battery every second (1.5 watts).

A pump is like a battery because it brings water from a position of low energy to high energy.

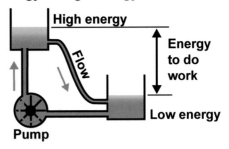

Figure 13.8: *A battery acts like a pump to give energy to flowing electrical current.*

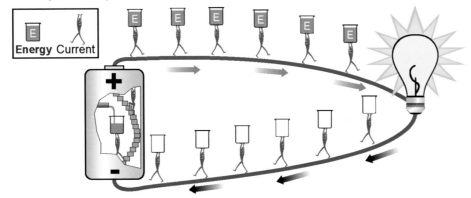

Batteries are like pumps Two water tanks connected with a pump make a good analogy for a battery in a circuit (Figure 13.8). The pump raises up the water, increasing its potential energy. As the water flows down, its potential energy is converted into kinetic energy. In a battery, chemical reactions provide the energy to the current. The current then flows through the circuit carrying the energy to any motors or bulbs. The current gets a "refill" of energy each time it passes through the battery, for as long as the battery's stored energy lasts.

Battery voltage The voltage of a battery depends on how the battery is made. Household zinc-carbon batteries are 1.5 volts each. Lead acid batteries, like those used in cars, are usually 12 volts. Different voltages can also be made by combining multiple batteries. A flashlight that needs 4.5 volts to light its bulb uses three 1.5 volt batteries (Figure 13.9).

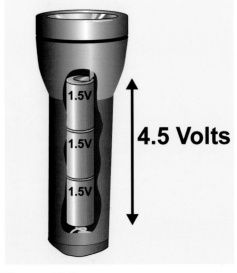

Figure 13.9: *Three 1.5-volt batteries can be stacked to make a total voltage of 4.5 volts c in a flashlight.*

Measuring current in a circuit

Measuring current with a meter
Electric current can be measured with a multimeter. However, if you want to measure current you must force the current to pass *through* the meter. That usually means you must break your circuit somewhere and rearrange wires so that the current must flow through the meter. For example, Figure 13.10 shows a circuit with a battery and bulb. The meter has been inserted into the circuit to measure current. If you trace the wires, the current comes out of the positive end of the battery, through the light bulb, *through the meter*, and back to the battery. The meter in the diagram measures 0.37 amps of current. Some electrical meters, called **ammeters**, are designed specifically to measure only current.

Setting up the meter
If you use a multimeter, you also must remember to set its dial to measure the type of current in your circuit. Multimeters can measure two types of electric current, called alternating current (AC) and direct current (DC). You will learn about the difference between alternating and direct current in Chapter 14. For circuits with light bulbs and batteries, you must set your meter to read direct current, or DC.

Be careful measuring current
The last important thing about measuring current is that the meter itself can be damaged if too much current passes through it. Your meter may contain a *circuit breaker* or *fuse*. Circuit breakers and fuses are two kinds of devices that protect circuits from too much current by making a break that stops the current. A circuit breaker can be reset the way a switch can be flipped. A broken fuse, however, is similar to a burned out light bulb and must be replaced for the meter to work again.

Measuring current

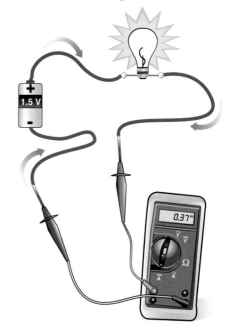

Figure 13.10: *Current must pass through the meter when it is being measured.*

13.2 Section Review

1. List the units for measuring current and voltage.
2. Why does a voltmeter display a reading of zero volts when both of its probes are touched to the same end of a battery?
3. What does a 1.5 V battery give to each amp of current in a circuit?
4. Draw a diagram showing how a meter is connected in a circuit to measure current.

13.3 Resistance and Ohm's Law

You can apply the same voltage to different circuits and different amounts of current will flow. For example, when you plug in a desk lamp, the current through it is 1 amp. If a hair dryer is plugged into the same outlet (with the same voltage) the current is 10 amps. For a given voltage, the amount of current that flows depends on the *resistance* of the circuit.

Electrical resistance

Current and resistance **Resistance** is the measure of how strongly a wire or other object resists current flowing through it. A device with low resistance, such as a copper wire, can easily carry a large current. An object with a high resistance, such as a rubber band, will only carry a current so tiny it can hardly be measured.

A water analogy The relationship between electric current and resistance can be compared with water flowing from the open end of a bottle (Figure 13.11). If the opening is large, the resistance is low and lots of water flows out quickly. If the opening is small, the resistance is greater and the water flow is slow.

Circuits The total amount of resistance in a circuit determines the amount of current in the circuit for a given voltage. Every device that uses electrical energy adds resistance to a circuit. The more resistance the circuit has, the less the current. For example, if you string several light bulbs together, the resistance in the circuit increases and the current decreases, making each bulb dimmer than a single bulb would be.

Vocabulary

resistance, ohm, Ohm's law, conductor, insulator, semiconductor, potentiometer

Objectives

✓ Explain the relationships between current, voltage, and resistance.
✓ Use Ohm's law to calculate current, resistance, or voltage.
✓ Distinguish between conductors and insulators.

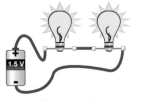
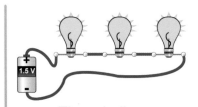

One bulb	Two bulbs	Three bulbs
Single resistance	Twice the resistance	Three times the resistance
Full current	Half the current	One-third the current

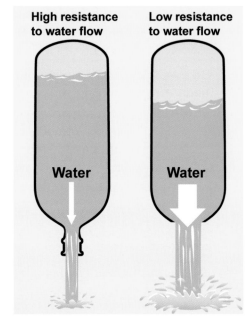

Figure 13.11: *The current is less when the resistance is great.*

Measuring resistance

The ohm Electrical resistance is measured in units called **ohms**. This unit is abbreviated with the Greek letter *omega* (Ω). When you see Ω in a sentence, think or read "ohms." For a given voltage, the greater the resistance, the lesser the current. If a circuit has a resistance of one ohm, then a voltage of one volt causes a current of one ampere to flow.

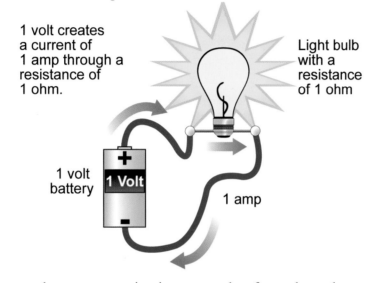

1 volt creates a current of 1 amp through a resistance of 1 ohm.

Light bulb with a resistance of 1 ohm

1 volt battery

1 amp

Figure 13.12: *A multimeter can be used to measure resistance of a device that has been completely removed from the circuit.*

How a multimeter measures resistance

A multimeter measures resistance by forcing a precise amount of current to flow through a electrical device. The meter then measures the voltage across the device. The resistance is calculated from the voltage and current. The currents used to measure resistance are typically small, 0.001 amps or less. Any other current through the device interferes with the meter's readings, and that is why a device must be removed from the circuit to measure its resistance.

Resistance of wires The wires used to connect circuits are made of metals such as copper or aluminum that have low resistance. The resistance of wires is usually so low compared with other devices in a circuit that you can ignore wire resistances when measuring or calculating the total resistance. The exception is when there are large currents. If the current is large, the resistance of wires may be important.

Measuring resistance You can use a multimeter to measure the resistance of wires, light bulbs, and other devices (Figure 13.12). You must first remove the device from the circuit. Then set the dial on the multimeter to the resistance setting and touch the probes to each end of the device. The meter will display the resistance in ohms (Ω), kilo-ohms (×1,000 Ω), or mega-ohms (×1,000,000 Ω).

Ohm's law

Ohm's law   The current in a circuit depends on the battery's voltage and the circuit's resistance. Voltage and current are *directly* related. Doubling the voltage doubles the current. Resistance and current are *inversely* related. Doubling the resistance cuts the current in half. These two relationships form **Ohm's law**. The law relates current, voltage, and resistance with one formula. If you know two of the three quantities, you can use Ohm's law to find the third.

Equation	... gives you ...	... if you know ...
$I = V \div R$	current (I)	voltage and resistance
$V = I \times R$	voltage (V)	current and resistance
$R = V \div I$	resistance (R)	voltage and current

Ohm's law

$$\text{Current (amps, A)} \to I = \frac{V}{R} \begin{matrix} \nearrow \;\; \textit{Voltage (volts, V)} \\ \searrow \;\; \textit{Resistance (ohms, } \Omega\text{)} \end{matrix}$$

Using Ohm's law

A toaster oven has a resistance of 12 ohms and is plugged into a 120-volt outlet. How much current does it draw?

1. Looking for: You are asked for the current in amperes.

2. Given: You are given the resistance in ohms and voltage in volts.

3. Relationships: Ohm's law: $I = \dfrac{V}{R}$

4. Solution: Plug in the values for V and R: $I = \dfrac{120\,\text{V}}{12\,\Omega} = 10\,\text{A}$

a. A laptop computer runs on a 24-volt battery. If the resistance of the circuit inside is 16 ohms, how much current does it use? **Answer:** 1.5 A

b. A motor in a toy car needs 2 amps of current to work properly. If the car runs on four 1.5-volt batteries, what is the motor's resistance? **Answer:** 3 ohms

The resistance of common objects

Resistance of common devices

The resistance of electrical devices ranges from small (0.001 Ω) to large (10×10^6 Ω). Every electrical device is designed with a resistance that causes the right amount of current to flow when the device is connected to the proper voltage. For example, a 60 watt light bulb has a resistance of 240 ohms. When connected to 120 volts from a wall socket, the current is 0.5 amps and the bulb lights (Figure 13.13).

Resistances match operating voltage

If you connect the same light bulb to a 1.5-volt battery it will not light because not enough current flows. According to Ohm's law, the current is only 0.00625 amps when 1.5 volts is applied to a resistance of 240 Ω This amount of current at 1.5 volts does not carry enough power to make the bulb light. All electrical devices are designed to operate correctly at a certain voltage.

The resistance of skin

Electrical outlets are dangerous because you can get a fatal shock by touching the wires inside. So why can you safely handle a 9 V battery? The reason is Ohm's law. Remember, current is what flows and carries power. The typical resistance of dry skin is 100,000 ohms or more. According to Ohm's law, 9 V ÷ 100,000 Ω is only 0.00009 amps. This is not enough current to be harmful. On average, nerves in the skin can feel a current of around 0.0005 amps. You can get a dangerous shock from 120 volts from a wall socket because that is enough voltage to force 0.0012 amps (120 V ÷ 100,000 Ω) through your skin, more than twice the amount you can feel.

Water lowers skin resistance

Wet skin has much lower resistance than dry skin. Because of the lower resistance, the same voltage will cause more current to pass through your body when your skin is wet. The combination of water and 120-volt electricity is especially dangerous because the high voltage and lower resistance make it possible for large (possibly fatal) currents to flow.

Changing resistance

The resistance of many electrical devices varies with temperature and current. For example, a light bulb's resistance increases when there is more current through the bulb. This change occurs because the bulb gets hotter when more current passes through it. The resistance of many materials, including those in light bulbs, increases as temperature increases.

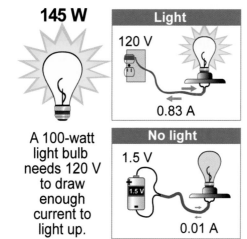

Figure 13.13: *A light bulb designed for use in a 120-volt household circuit does not light when connected to a 1.5-volt battery.*

Conductors and insulators

Conductors   Current passes easily through some materials, such as copper, which are called conductors. A **conductor** can *conduct*, or carry, electric current. The electrical resistance of wires made from conductors is low. Most metals are good conductors.

Insulators   Other materials, such as rubber, glass, and wood, do not allow current to easily pass through them. These materials are called **insulators,** because they insulate against, or block, the flow of current.

Semiconductors   Some materials are in between conductors and insulators. These materials are called **semiconductors** because their ability to carry current is higher than an insulator but lower than a conductor. Computer chips, televisions, and portable radios are among the many devices that use semiconductors. You may have heard of a region in California called "Silicon Valley." Silicon is a semiconductor commonly used in computer chips. An area south of San Francisco is called Silicon Valley because there are many semiconductor and computer companies located there.

Comparing materials   No material is a perfect conductor or insulator. Some amount of current will always flow in any material if a voltage is applied. Even copper (a good conductor) has some resistance. Figure 13.14 shows how the resistances of various conductors, semiconductors, and insulators compare.

Applications of conductors and insulators   Both conductors and insulators are necessary materials in human technology. For example, a wire has one or more conductors on the inside and an insulator on the outside. An electrical cable may have twenty or more conductors, each separated from the others by a thin layer of insulator. The insulating layer prevents the other wires or other objects from being exposed to the current and voltage carried by the conducting core of the wire.

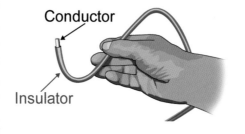

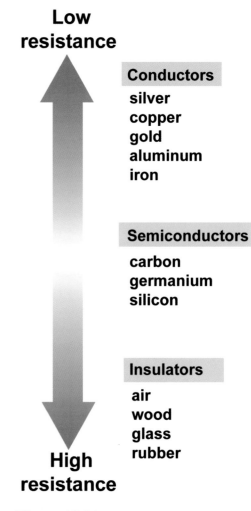

Figure 13.14: *Comparing the resistances of materials.*

Resistors

Resistors are used to control current Resistors are electrical components that are designed to have a specific resistance that remains the same over a wide range of currents. Resistors are used to control the current in circuits. They are found in many common electronic devices such as computers, televisions, telephones, and stereos.

Fixed resistors There are two main types of resistors, fixed and variable. Fixed resistors have a resistance that cannot be changed. If you have ever looked at a circuit board inside a computer or other electrical device, you have seen fixed resistors. They are small skinny cylinders or rectangles with colored stripes on them. Because resistors are so tiny, it is impossible to label each one with the value of its resistance in numbers. Instead, the colored stripes are a code that tells you the resistance (Figure 13.15).

Variable resistors Variable resistors, also called **potentiometers**, can be adjusted to have a resistance within a certain range. If you have ever turned a dimmer switch or volume control, you have used a potentiometer. When the resistance of a dimmer switch increases, the current decreases, and the bulb gets dimmer. Inside a potentiometer is a circular resistor and a little sliding contact called a wiper (Figure 13.16). If the circuit is connected at A and C, the resistance is always 10 Ω. But if the circuit is connected at A and B, the resistance can vary from 0 Ω to 10 Ω. Turning the dial changes the resistance between A and B and also changes the current (or voltage) in the circuit.

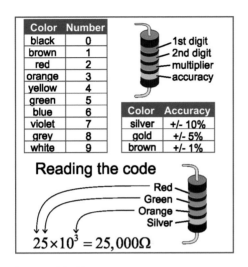

Color	Number
black	0
brown	1
red	2
orange	3
yellow	4
green	5
blue	6
violet	7
grey	8
white	9

Color	Accuracy
silver	+/- 10%
gold	+/- 5%
brown	+/- 1%

Figure 13.15: *The color code for resistors.*

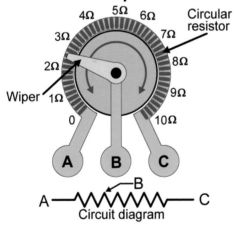

Figure 13.16: *The resistance of this potentiometer can vary from 0 Ω to 10 Ω.*

13.3 Section Review

1. What happens to the current if a circuit's resistance increases? What if the voltage increases instead?

2. List the units used to measure resistance, voltage, and current. Then give the abbreviation for each unit.

3. Classify as a conductor, semiconductor, or insulator each of the following: air, gold, silicon, rubber, aluminum.

Electric Circuits in Your Body

Imagine you're relaxing on the couch, watching your favorite television show. You're so absorbed in the action that you fail to notice your younger sister sneaking up behind you. Suddenly she reaches over the back of the couch and touches the back of your neck with a wet, frosty ice cube.

Before you even have a chance to think "who did that?" your body springs into action. The ice cube triggers a *withdrawal reflex* that happens automatically, without a conscious decision on your part.

A withdrawal reflex happens because electrical signals are sent through "circuits" in your body. When an ice cube touches the back of your neck, an electrical signal is sent through wire-like nerve fibers to your spinal cord. In the spinal cord, the signal is transferred to nerve fibers that control the muscles in your neck and shoulders, causing them to contract, jerking your body away from the ice cube. All of this happens in a split second!

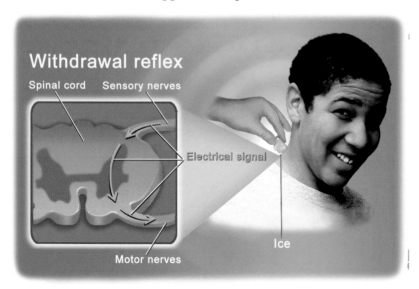

Your body sends electrical signals using specialized cells called neurons. A neuron has three basic parts: the cell body, a long stalk called the axon, and finger-like projections called dendrites.

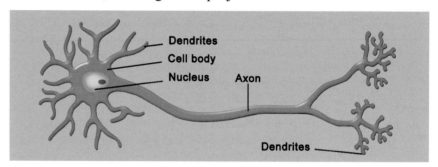

Unlike the components of a wire-and-battery circuit, most neurons don't touch one another. Instead, as the electrical signal reaches the end of the axon, a chemical is released. The chemical is picked up by receptors on another cell's dendrite. The dendrite then activates its own cell body to continue sending the signal through its axon.

Nerve impulse: a wave of electrical changes

A withdrawal reflex starts when sensory neurons in your skin receive some kind of stimulus from outside the body. In our example, the stimulus is a change in temperature caused by the ice cube. That stimulus starts a wave of electrical change called a nerve impulse along the cell membrane.

When a neuron is at rest, the inside of the cell membrane is electrically negative compared with the outside. A nerve impulse works like this:

1. The outside stimulus causes the cell membrane to open tiny channels that let positively-charged ions into the cell. The inside of the cell becomes positively charged relative to the outside.

2. Other channels open and let positively-charged ions out of the cell. As the ions leave, the inside the cell membrane once again becomes negatively-charged compared with the outside.

3. The nerve impulse travels down the axon like dominoes falling. When the impulse reaches the end of the axon, chemicals are released and picked up by an adjacent neuron, causing the nerve impulse to continue.

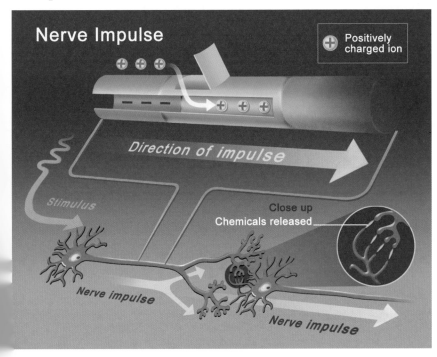

It's unlikely, however, that the withdrawal reflex would be your only response to the ice cube. Sensory neurons located in your eyes and ears would send messages to your brain as you turn to see and hear your sister scamper away. Your brain processes these in milliseconds, and billions of neurons there are activated as you decide how best to respond. Maybe you feel annoyed and chase after her with an ice cube of your own. Or you might just laugh at the clever way she "paid you back" for an earlier prank.

Your emotions, decisions, and physical actions all happen through nerve impulses sending electrical signals through neurons in your brain, spinal cord and body. A single neuron can have up to ten thousand dendrites connecting to other neurons, and it is estimated that just one cubic millimeter of brain tissue contains a billion connections between cells. Each second, your body fires off about five trillion nerve impulses, making possible all the things that make us human: thoughts, memories, decisions, emotions, and actions.

The nervous system

Your complex nervous system

The withdrawal reflex takes only a fraction of a second. In fact, the signal travels from the sensory nerve to the spinal cord and out to the nerves that control your muscles at about 250 miles per hour!

Questions:

1. Describe the similarities and differences between an electric circuit and the human nervous system.
2. How is an electrical signal sent in a nerve impulse?
3. Why are chemical signals necessary to keep a nerve impulse traveling through nerve fibers?

Chapter 13 Review

Understanding Vocabulary

Select the correct term to complete the sentences.

ohm	electric current	conductor
closed circuit	voltage	electrical symbols
resistance	potentiometer	battery
ampere	resistor	Ohm's law
switch	volt	open circuit

Section 13.1

1. _____ is what flows and carries power in a circuit.
2. _____ are used when drawing circuit diagrams.
3. A _____ is used to create a break in a circuit.
4. A(n) _____ has a break it, so there is no current.
5. A _____ has a complete path for the current and contains no breaks.
6. A light bulb, motor, or speaker acts as a _____ in a circuit.

Section 13.2

7. The unit for current is the _____.
8. A _____ provides voltage to a circuit.
9. _____ is the difference in the amount of energy carried by current at two points in a circuit.
10. The _____ is the unit for measuring voltage.

Section 13.3

11. The _____ is the unit for measuring resistance.
12. _____ explains the relationship between current, voltage, and resistance in a circuit.
13. _____ is the measure of how strongly a material resists current.
14. A _____ has a resistance that can be changed.
15. Wires in a circuit are made of a material that is a _____, such as copper.

Reviewing Concepts

Section 13.1

1. How are electric circuits and systems for carrying water in buildings similar?
2. Give one example of a circuit found in nature and one example of a circuit created by people.
3. Why are symbols used in circuit diagrams?
4. Draw the electrical symbol for each of the following devices.
   a. battery
   b. resistor
   c. switch
   d. wire
5. List three devices that could be a resistor in a circuit.
6. List two sources of energy that a circuit might use and give an example of a circuit that uses each type.
7. Will a bulb light if it is in an open circuit? Why?
8. Is flipping a switch the only way to create an open circuit? Explain.

Section 13.2

9. The direction of electric current in a circuit is away from the _____ end of the battery and toward the _____ end.
10. How are voltage and energy related?
11. A voltage of one volt means one _____ of _____ does one _____ of work in one second.
12. Explain how a battery in a circuit is similar to a water pump.
13. What are the differences between a multimeter, a voltmeter, and an ammeter?
14. Suppose you have a closed circuit containing a battery that is lighting a bulb. Why must you first create a break in the circuit before using an ammeter to measure the current?

Section 13.3

15. The greater the resistance in a circuit, the less the _____.

16. A circuit contains one light bulb and a battery. What happens to the total resistance in the circuit if you replace the one light bulb with a string of four identical bulbs? Why?

17. What is the unit for resistance? What symbol is used to represent this unit?

18. What does is mean to say that current and resistance in a circuit are inversely related?

19. What does it mean to say that current and voltage in a circuit are directly related?

20. According to Ohm's law, the current in a circuit increases if the _____ increases. The current decreases if the _____ increases.

21. A battery is connected to a light bulb, creating a simple circuit. Explain what will happen to the current in the circuit if

    a.   the bulb is replaced with a bulb having a higher resistance.
    b.   the bulb is replaced with a bulb having a lower resistance.
    c.   the battery is replaced with a battery having a greater voltage.

22. Why does a light bulb's resistance increase if it is left on for a period of time?

23. Why can you safely handle a 1.5-V battery without being electrocuted?

24. What is the difference between a conductor and an insulator?

25. Why is it important to always have dry hands when working with electric circuits?

26. Explain why electrical wires are made of copper covered in a layer of plastic.

27. What is a semiconductor?

28. Classify each of the following as a conductor, semiconductor, or insulator.

    a.   copper
    b.   plastic
    c.   rubber
    d.   silicon
    e.   iron
    f.   glass

29. What is the difference between a fixed resistor and a variable resistor?

30. What is another name for a variable resistor?

Solving Problems

Section 13.1

1.   Draw a circuit diagram of a circuit with a battery, three wires, a light bulb, and a switch.

Section 13.2

2.   What voltage would the electrical meter show in each of the diagrams below?

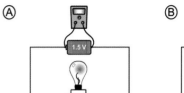
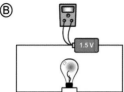

3.   Which of the following diagrams shows the correct way to measure current in a circuit?

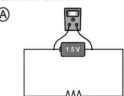
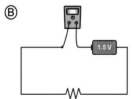

4.   A portable radio that runs on AA batteries needs 6 volts to work properly. How many batteries does it use?

5. What happens to the current in a circuit if the resistance doubles? What if the resistance triples?

6. What happens to the current in a circuit if the voltage doubles? What if it triples?

7. A hair dryer draws a current of 10 A when plugged into a 120 V outlet. What is the resistance of the hair dryer?

8. A television runs on 120 volts and has a resistance of 60 ohms. What current does it draw?

9. A digital camera uses one 6 V battery. The circuit that runs the flash and takes the pictures has a resistance of 3 ohms. What is the current in the circuit?

10. The motor in a toy car has a resistance of 3 ohms and needs 1.5 amperes of current to run properly.
    a. What battery voltage is needed?
    b. How many AA batteries would the car require?

11. Find the current in each of the circuits shown below.

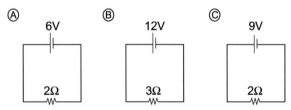

12. Household circuits in the United States run on 120 volts of electricity. Circuit breakers commonly break a circuit if the current is greater than 15 amperes. What is the minimum amount of resistance needed in a circuit to prevent the circuit breaker from activating?

13. A flashlight bulb has a resistance of approximately 6 ohms. It works in a flashlight with two C batteries. How much current is in the flashlight's circuit when the bulb is lit?

Applying Your Knowledge

Section 13.1

1. Write a paragraph explaining how your life would be different if electricity didn't exist.

2. Research Benjamin Franklin's experiments with electricity. Make a poster that describes one of his experiments.

Section 13.2

3. Brain and nerve cells communicate through the movement of charged chemicals that create electrical currents. Some conditions, such as epilepsy, occur because these currents are sometimes present when they shouldn't be. Research electrical currents in the body and problems that occur when the body's circuits don't work properly.

4. Ask an adult to show you the circuit breaker box in your home. Does it contain switches or fuses? How many?

5. There are many different kinds of batteries in use today. Research to answer following questions.
    a. Are all 1.5 volt household batteries the same on the inside?
    b. Why can some 1.5 batteries be recharged and used over and over again?
    c. Which type of batteries is used in portable electronics such as cell phones and laptop computers?

6. Do an experiment in which you determine whether more expensive household batteries last longer than cheaper ones. Why is it important to test the batteries in the same electrical device and to use it in the same way each time?

Section 13.3

7. Look on the back or underside of different appliances in your home to find information about the current and voltage each uses. Find two appliances that list the current and voltage. Calculate the resistance of each.

Chapter 14

Electrical Systems

You may recognize the abbreviations AC and DC. There is a classic rock music group called AC/DC that has helped to make the acronym famous. Did you know that in the late 1800's, a major disagreement over the use of AC and DC methods for transmitting electricity erupted between two famous inventors?

Thomas Edison favored the direct current (DC) method of moving electrical energy from electrical generation stations to homes and buildings. George Westinghouse argued that the alternating current (AC) method worked better. The feud became quite public, as each inventor tried to win support. The DC method works well over short distances, as between buildings in a densely populated city. AC works well over long distances but uses higher voltages than DC technology. Edison used some morbid methods for demonstrating his views of the danger involved with high voltage electrical transmission through his opponent's AC method.

Which inventor won the AC/DC debate? Does the United States rely on AC or DC technology for transmitting electrical energy? In this chapter, you will find out how our country distributes electricity, what the difference is between AC and DC current. You will also learn how electricity is "purchased" and paid for, as well as how simple electrical circuits are constructed and how they work.

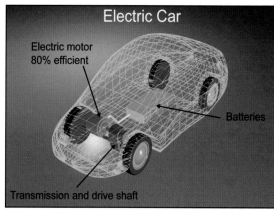

Electric Car

Electric motor 80% efficient

Batteries

Transmission and drive shaft

Key Questions

✓ Why does a string of inexpensive holiday lights stop working when one bulb burns out?

✓ What is a "short circuit", and why can it be dangerous?

✓ How is electricity generated, and how does it get to your house?

14.1 Series Circuits

We use electric circuits for thousands of things from flashlights to computers to cars to satellites. There are two basic ways circuits can be built to connect different devices. These two types of circuits are called *series* and *parallel*. Series circuits have only one path for the current. Parallel circuits have branching points and multiple paths for the current. This section discusses series circuits. You will learn about parallel circuits in the next section.

What is a series circuit?

A series circuit has one path A **series circuit** contains only one path for electric current to flow. That means the current is the same at all points in the circuit. All the circuits you have studied so far have been series circuits. For example, a battery, three bulbs, and a switch connected in a loop form a series circuit because there is only one path through the circuit (Figure 14.1). The current is the same in each bulb, so they are equally bright.

A series circuit has only one path for the current so the current is the same at any point in the circuit.

Stopping the current If there is a break at any point in a series circuit, the current will stop everywhere in the circuit. Inexpensive strings of holiday lights are wired with the bulbs in series. When one bulb burns out, the current stops and none of the bulbs will light until the bad bulb is replaced. The lights are connected this way because it requires the least amount of wire and therefore costs the least to manufacture.

Using series circuits There are times when devices are connected in series for specific purposes. On-off switches are placed in series with the other components in most electrical devices. When a switch is turned to the off position, it breaks the circuit and stops current from reaching all of the components in series with the switch. Dimmer switches placed in series with light bulbs adjust the brightness by changing the amount of current in the circuit.

Vocabulary

series circuit, voltage drop, Kirchhoff's voltage law

Objectives

✓ Describe a series circuit.
✓ Calculate the resistance and current in a series circuit.
✓ Explain how the voltage changes across each resistor in a series circuit.

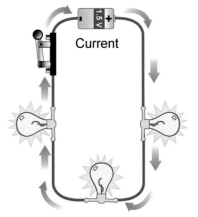

Series circuit

Current

Figure 14.1: *Three bulbs, a battery, and a switch are connected in series.*

Current and resistance in a series circuit

Use Ohm's law   You can use Ohm's law to calculate the current in a circuit if you know the voltage and resistance. If you are using a battery you know the voltage from the battery. If you know the resistance of each device, you can find the total resistance of the circuit by adding up the resistance of each device.

Adding resistances   You can think of adding resistances like adding pinches to a hose (Figure 14.2). Each pinch adds some resistance. The total resistance is the sum of the resistances from each pinch. To find the total resistance in a series circuit, you add the individual resistances.

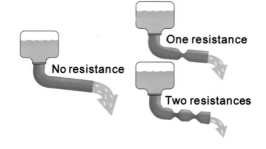

Figure 14.2: *Adding resistors in a circuit is like adding pinches in a hose. The greater the number of pinches or resistors, the greater the resistance to current.*

ADDING RESISTANCES IN SERIES

$$R_{total} = R_1 + R_2 + R_3 + \cdots$$

Total resistance (Ω)   *Individual resistances (Ω)*

Ignoring resistances   Everything has some resistance, even wires. However, the resistance of a wire is usually so small compared with the resistance of light bulbs and other devices that we can ignore the resistance of the wire.

Calculating current

A series circuit contains a 12-V battery and three bulbs with resistances of 1Ω, 2 Ω, and 3 Ω. What is the current in the circuit?

1. Looking for: You are asked for the current in amps.

2. Given: You are given the voltage in volts and resistances in ohms.

3. Relationships: $R_{tot} = R_1 + R_2 + R_3$ Ohm's law: $I = V/R$

4. Solution: $R_{tot} = 1\ \Omega + 2\ \Omega + 3\ \Omega = 6\ \Omega$ $I = (12\ \text{V})/(6\ \Omega) = 2\ \text{A}$

Your turn...

a. A string of 5 lights runs on a 9-V battery. If each bulb has a resistance of 2 Ω, what is the current? **Answer:** 0.9 A

b. A series circuit operates on a 6-V battery and has two 1 Ω resistors. What is the current? **Answer:** 3 A

Energy and voltage in a series circuit

Energy changes forms
Energy cannot be created or destroyed. The devices in a circuit convert electrical energy carried by the current into other forms of energy. As each device uses power, the power carried by the current is reduced. As a result, the *voltage gets lower after each device that uses power*. This is known as the **voltage drop**. The voltage drop is the difference in voltage across an electrical device that has current flowing through it.

Charges lose their energy
Consider a circuit with three bulbs and two batteries. The voltage is 3 V so each amp of current leaves the battery carrying 3 watts. As the current flows through the circuit, each bulb changes 1/3 of the power into light and heat. Because the first bulb uses 1 watt, the voltage drops from 3 V to 2 V as the current flows through the first bulb. Remember, the current in a series circuit is the same everywhere! As power gets used, the voltage gets lower.

Voltage
If the three bulbs are identical, each gives off the same amount of light and heat. Each uses the same amount of power. A meter will show the voltage drop from 3 volts to 2 volts to 1 volt, and finally down to zero volts after the last bulb. After passing through the last bulb, the current returns to the battery where it is given more power and the cycle starts over.

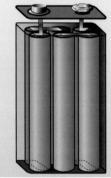
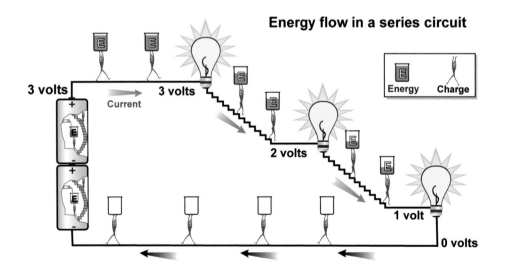

Energy flow in a series circuit

3 volts

Current

3 volts

2 volts

Energy   Charge

1 volt

0 volts

Voltage drops and Ohm's law

Voltage drops Each separate bulb or resistor creates a voltage drop. The voltage drop across a bulb is measured by connecting an electrical meter's leads at each side of the bulb (Figure 14.3). The greater the voltage drop, the greater the amount of power being used per amp of current flowing through the bulb.

Ohm's law The voltage drop across a resistance is determined by Ohm's law in the form $V = IR$. The voltage drop (V) equals the current (I) multiplied by the resistance (R) of the device. In a series circuit, the current is the same at all points, but devices may have different resistances. In the circuit below each bulb has a resistance of 1 ohm, so each has a voltage drop of 1 volt when 1 amp flows through the circuit.

Applying Kirchhoff's law In the circuit below, three identical bulbs are connected in series to two 1.5-volt batteries. The total resistance of the circuit is 3Ω The current flowing in the circuit is 1 amp ($I = 3V \div 3\Omega$). Each bulb creates a voltage drop of 1 volt ($V = IR = 1 A \times 1\Omega$). The total of all the voltage drops is 3 V, which is the same as the voltage of the battery.

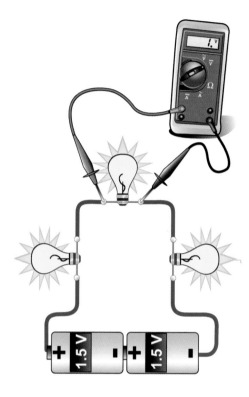

Figure 14.3: *Using a multimeter to measure the voltage drop across a bulb in a circuit.*

Each resistance drops the voltage

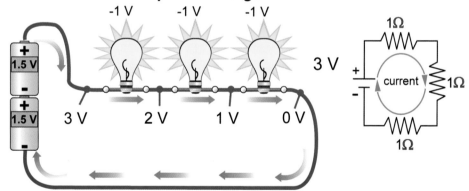

Energy conservation The law of conservation of energy also applies to a circuit. Over the entire circuit, the power used by all the bulbs must equal the power supplied by the battery. This means the total of all the voltage drops must add up to the battery's voltage. This rule is known as **Kirchhoff's voltage law**, after German physicist Gustav Robert Kirchhoff (1824-87).

Solving series circuit problems

Unequal resistances   Ohm's law is especially useful in series circuits where the devices do *not* have the same resistance. A device with a larger resistance has a greater voltage drop. However, the sum of all the voltage drops must still add up to the battery's voltage. The example below shows how to find the voltage drops in a circuit with two different light bulbs.

Calculating voltage drops

The circuit shown at right contains a 9-volt battery, 1-ohm bulb, and a 2-ohm bulb. Calculate the circuit's total resistance and current. Then find each bulb's voltage drop.

1. Looking for: You are asked for the total resistance, current, and voltage drops.

2. Given: You are given the battery's voltage and the resistance of each bulb.

3. Relationships: Total resistance in a series circuit: $R_{tot} = R_1 + R_2$
Ohm's law: $I = V/R$ or $V = IR$

4. Solution: Calculate the total resistance: $R_{tot} = 1\,\Omega + 2\,\Omega = 3\,\Omega$
Use Ohm's law to calculate the current:
$I = (9\ \text{V})/(3\,\Omega) = 3\ \text{A}$
Use Ohm's law to find the voltage across the 1 Ω bulb:
$V = (3\ \text{A})(1\,\Omega) = 3\ \text{V}$
Use Ohm's law to find the voltage across the 2 Ω bulb:
$V = (3\ \text{A})(3\,\Omega) = 6\ \text{V}$

Your turn...

a. The battery in the circuit above is replaced with a 12-volt battery. Calculate the new current and bulb voltages.
   Answer: 4 A, 4 V across 1 Ω bulb, 8 V across 2 Ω bulb

b. A 12-volt battery is connected in series to 1 Ω and 5 Ω bulbs. What is the voltage across each bulb? **Answer:** 2 V, 10 V

14.1 Section Review

1. What do you know about the current at different points in a series circuit?

2. Three bulbs are connected in series with a battery and a switch. Do all of the bulbs go out when the switch is opened? Explain.

3. What happens to a circuit's resistance as more resistors are added in series?

4. A series circuit contains a 9-volt battery and three identical bulbs. What is the voltage drop across each bulb?

14.2 Parallel Circuits

It would be a real problem if your refrigerator went off when you turned out the light! That is why houses are wired with parallel circuits instead of series circuits. Parallel circuits provide each device with a separate path back to the power source. This means each device can be turned on and off independently from the others. It also means that each device sees the full voltage of the power source without voltage drops from other devices.

What is a parallel circuit?

Parallel branches
A **parallel circuit** is a circuit with more than one path for the current. Each path in the circuit is sometimes called a *branch*. The current through a branch is also called the *branch current*. The current supplied by the battery in a parallel circuit splits at one or more branch points.

Example: three bulbs in parallel
All of the current entering a branch point must exit again. This rule is known as **Kirchhoff's current law** (Figure 14.4). For example, suppose you have three identical light bulbs connected in parallel as shown below. The circuit has two branch points where the current splits (red dots). There are also two branch points where the current comes back together (yellow dots). You measure the branch currents and find each to be 1 amp. The current supplied by the battery is the sum of the three branch currents, or 3 amps. At each branch point, the current entering is the same as the current leaving.

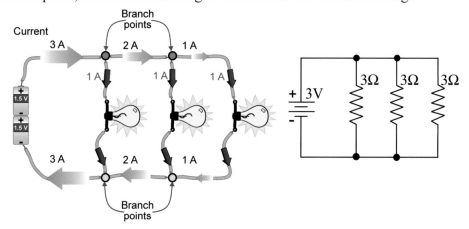

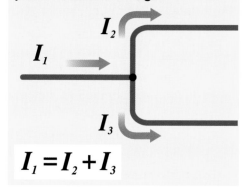

Kirchhoff's current law
All current flowing into a branch point must flow out again

$$I_1 = I_2 + I_3$$

Figure 14.4: *All the current entering a branch point in a circuit must also exit the point.*

Voltage and current in a parallel circuit

Each branch has the same voltage

The voltage is the same anywhere along the same wire. This is true as long as the resistance of the wire itself is very small compared to the rest of the circuit. If the voltage is the same along a wire, then the *same voltage appears across each branch of a parallel circuit.* This is true even when the branches have different resistances (Figure 14.5). Both bulbs in this circuit see 3 V from the battery since each is connected back to the battery by wires without any other electrical devices in the way.

The voltage is the same across each branch of a parallel circuit.

Parallel circuits have two big advantages over series circuits.

1. Each device in the circuit has a voltage drop equal to the full battery voltage.

2. Each device in the circuit may be turned off independently without stopping the current in the other devices in the circuit.

Parallel circuits in homes

Parallel circuits need more wires to connect, but are used for most of the wiring in homes and other buildings. Parallel circuits allow you to turn off one lamp without all of the other lights in your home going out. They also allow you to use many appliances at once, each at full power.

Current in branches

Because each branch in a parallel circuit has the same voltage, the current in a branch is determined by the branch resistance and Ohm's law, $I = V/R$ (Figure 14.6). The greater the resistance of a branch, the smaller the current. Each branch works independently so the current in one branch does not depend on what happens in other branches

Total current

The total current in a parallel circuit is the sum of the currents in each branch. The only time branches have an effect on each other is when the total current is more than the battery or wall outlet can supply. A battery has a maximum amount of current it can supply at one time. If the branches in a circuit try to draw too much current the battery voltage will drop and less current will flow.

Parallel circuit of two bulbs with different resistances

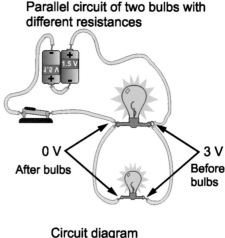

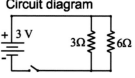

Figure 14.5: *The voltage across each branch of a parallel circuit is the same.*

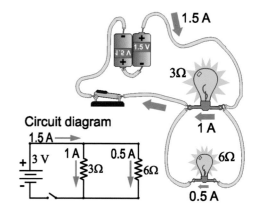

Figure 14.6: *The current in each branch depends on the branch resistance. The current may be different for each branch.*

Calculating current and resistance in a parallel circuit

More branches mean less resistance In series circuits, adding an extra resistor increases the total resistance of the circuit. The opposite is true in parallel circuits. Adding a resistor in a parallel circuit provides another independent path for current. More current flows for the same voltage so the total resistance is *less*.

Example of a parallel circuit Figure 14.7 compares a series circuit with a parallel circuit. In the series circuit, the current is 6 amps ($I = V/R = 12V \div 2\Omega$). In the parallel circuit, the current is 6 amps *in each branch*. The total current is 12 amps. So what is the total resistance of the parallel circuit? Ohm's law solved for resistance is $R = V \div I$. The total resistance of the parallel circuit is the voltage (12 V) divided by the total current (12 A) or 1 ohm. The resistance of the parallel circuit is *half* that of the series circuit.

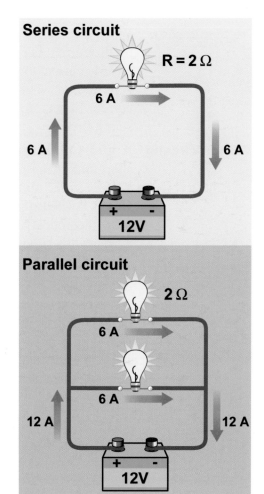

Figure 14.7: *The parallel circuit has twice the current and half the total resistance of the series circuit.*

Current in parallel circuits

All of the electrical outlets in Jonah's living room are on one parallel circuit. The circuit breaker cuts off the current if it exceeds 15 amps. Will the breaker trip if he uses a light (240 Ω), stereo (150 Ω), and an air conditioner (10 Ω)?

1. Looking for: You are asked whether the current will exceed 15 amps.

2. Given: You are given the resistance of each branch and the circuit breaker's maximum current.

3. Relationships: Ohm's law: $I = V/R$

4. Solution: Because the devices are plugged into electrical outlets, the voltage is 120 volts for each.
$I_{light} = (120\ V)/(240\ \Omega) = 0.5\ A$
$I_{stereo} = (120\ V)/(150\ \Omega) = 0.8\ A$
$I_{AC} = (120\ V)/(10\ \Omega) = 12\ A$
The total is 13.3 A, so the circuit breaker will not trip.

Your turn...

a. Will the circuit breaker trip if Jonah also turns on a computer ($R = 60\ \Omega$)? **Answer:** Yes. The additional current is 2 A, so the total is 15.3 A.

b. What is the total current in a parallel circuit containing a 12-V battery, a 2 Ω resistor, and a 4 Ω resistor? **Answer:** 9 A

Short circuits, circuit breakers, and fuses

Heat and wires When electric current flows through a resistance, some of the power carried by the current becomes heat. Toasters and electric stoves are designed to use electric current to make heat. Although the resistance of wires is low, it is not zero and so wires heat up when current flows through them. If too much current flows through too small a wire, the wire overheats and may melt or start a fire.

Short circuits A **short circuit** is a parallel path in a circuit with very low resistance. A short circuit can be created accidentally by making a parallel branch with a wire (Figure 14.8). A plain wire may have a resistance as low as 0.001Ω. Ohm's law tells us that with a resistance this low, 1.5 V from a battery results in a (theoretical) current of 1,500 A! A short circuit is dangerous because currents this large melt wires and burn anyone working with the circuit.

Parallel circuits in homes Appliances and electrical outlets in homes are connected in many parallel circuits. Each circuit has its own fuse or circuit breaker that stops the current if it exceeds the safe amount, usually 15 or 20 amps (Figure 14.9). If you turn on too many appliances in one circuit at the same time, the circuit breaker or fuse cuts off the current. To restore the current, you must first disconnect some or all of the appliances. Then, either flip the tripped circuit breaker (in newer homes) or replace the blown fuse (in older homes). Fuses are also used in car electrical systems and in electrical devices such as televisions.

14.2 Section Review

1. Is the voltage across each branch of a parallel circuit the same? Is the current in each branch the same?

2. Why do home electrical systems use parallel wiring?

3. What happens to the total current in a parallel circuit as more branches are added? Why?

4. What is the total resistance of two 12-ohm resistors in parallel? What is the total for three 12-ohm resistors in parallel?

Short circuit, a large amount of current passes through the short circuit branch. Almost no current is through the bulb.

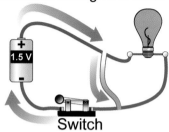

Figure 14.8: *A short circuit is created when there is a parallel branch of very low resistance. The current in this branch can be dangerously large.*

Circuit breaker

Fuse

Figure 14.9: *Houses and other buildings use either circuit breakers or fuses to cut off the current if it gets too high.*

14.3 Electrical Power, AC, and DC Electricity

If you look at a stereo, hair dryer, or other household appliance, you may find a label giving its power in watts. In this section you will learn what the power ratings on appliances mean, and how to figure out the electricity costs of using various appliances.

Electric power

A watt is a unit of power Electrical power is measured in watts, just like mechanical power you learned about in Chapter 4. Electrical power is the rate at which electrical energy is changed into other forms of energy such as heat, sound, or light. Anything that "uses" electricity is actually converting electrical energy into some other type of energy. The watt is an abbreviation for one joule per second. A 100-watt light bulb uses 100 joules of energy *every second* (Figure 14.10).

The three electrical quantities We have now learned three important electrical quantities:

Current (I)	Current is what carries power in a circuit. Current is measured in amperes (A).
Voltage (V)	Voltage measures the difference in energy carried by charges at two points in a circuit. A difference in voltage causes current to flow. Voltage is measured in volts (V). One volt is one watt per amp of current.
Resistance (R)	Resistance measures the ability to resist current. Resistance is measured in ohms (Ω). One amp of current flows if a voltage of 1 V is applied across a resistance of 1 Ω

Paying for electricity Electric bills sent out by utility companies don't charge by the volt, the amp, or the ohm. Electrical appliances in your home usually include another unit – the *watt*. Most appliances have a label that lists the number of watts or kilowatts. You may have purchased 60-watt light bulbs, a 1000-watt hair dryer, or a 1200-watt toaster oven. Electric companies charge for the energy you use, which depends on how many watts each appliance consumes and the amount of time each is used during the month.

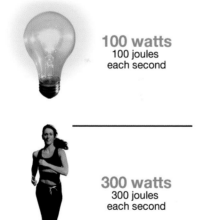

100 watts
100 joules each second

300 watts
300 joules each second

Figure 14.10: *One watt equals one joule per second.*

Calculating power in a circuit

Calculating power
Since one volt is a watt per amp, to calculate power in an electric circuit you multiply the voltage by the current. To calculate the power of a device in a circuit, multiply the voltage drop across the device by the current.

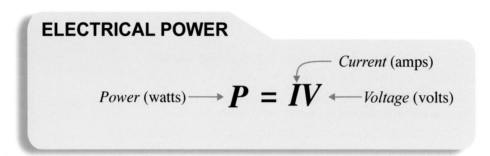

ELECTRICAL POWER

$$P = IV$$

Power (watts) → $P = IV$ ← Current (amps), Voltage (volts)

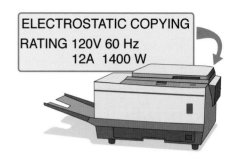

Figure 14.11: *Most appliances have a label that lists the power in watts.*

Watts and kilowatts
Most electrical appliances have a label that lists the power in watts (Figure 14.11) or kilowatts (kW). The **kilowatt** is used for large amounts of power. One kilowatt (kW) equals 1,000 watts. Another common unit of power, especially on electric motors, is the horsepower. One horsepower is 746 watts. The range in power for common electric motors is from 1/25th of a horsepower (30 watts) for a small electric fan to 1 horsepower (746 watts) for a garbage disposal.

Equation	...gives you ...	...if you know ...
$P = I \times V$	power (P)	current and voltage
$I = P \div V$	current (I)	power and voltage
$V = P \div I$	voltage (V)	power and current

Calculating power

A 12-volt battery is connected in series to two identical light bulbs. The current in the circuit is 3 amps. Calculate the power output of the battery.

1. Looking for: You are asked for the power in watts supplied by the battery.

2. Given: You are given the battery voltage in volts and current in amps.

3. Relationships: Power: $P=IV$

4. Solution: Battery: $P = (3 \text{ A})(12 \text{ V}) = 36 \text{ W}$

Your turn...

a. A 12-volt battery is connected in parallel to the same identical light bulbs as used in the example. The current through each bulb is now 6 amps. Calculate the power output of the battery. **Answer:** 144 W for battery

b. The label on the back of a television states that it uses 300 watts of power. How much current does it draw when plugged into a 120-volt outlet? **Answer:** 2.5 amps

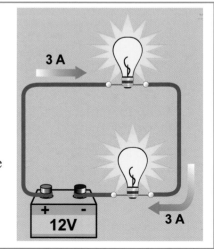

Buying electricity

Kilowatt-hours

Utility companies charge customers for the number of **kilowatt-hours** (abbreviated kWh) used each month. One kilowatt-hour means that a kilowatt of power has been used for one hour. A kilowatt-hour is not a unit of power but a unit of *energy*. A kilowatt-hour is a relatively large amount of energy, equal to 3.6 million joules. If you leave a 1,000-watt hair dryer on for one hour, you have used one kilowatt-hour of energy. You could also use 1 kilowatt-hour by using a 100-watt light bulb for 10 hours. The number of kilowatt-hours used equals the number of kilowatts multiplied by the number of hours the appliance was turned on.

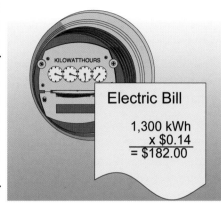

Electric Bill

1,300 kWh
x $0.14
= $182.00

Appliance	Power (watts)
Electric stove	3,000
Electric heater	1,500
Toaster	1,200
Hair dryer	1,000
Iron	800
Washing machine	750
Television	300
Light	100
Small fan	50
Clock radio	10

Figure 14.12: *Typical power usage of some common appliances.*

You pay for kilowatt-hours

Electric companies charge for kilowatt-hours used during a period of time, often a month. Your home is connected to a meter that counts up total number of kilowatt-hours used and a person comes to read the meter once a month. If you know the cost per kilowatt-hour the utility company charges, you can estimate the cost of operating any electrical appliance.

Electricity costs

How much does it cost to run an electric stove for 2 hours? Use the power in Figure 14.12 and a cost of $0.15 per kilowatt-hour.

1. Looking for: You are asked for the cost to run a stove for 2 hours.

2. Given: You are given the time, the power, and the price per kilowatt-hour.

3. Relationships: 1 kilowatt = 1000 watts   number of kilowatt-hours = (# of kilowatts) x (hours appliance is used)

4. Solution:

$$3000 \text{ W} = 3 \text{ kW} \qquad 3 \text{ kW} \times 2 \text{ hr} = 6 \text{ kWh} \qquad 6 \text{ kWh} \times \frac{\$0.15}{\text{kWh}} = \$0.90$$

Your turn...

a. At $0.15 per kilowatt-hour, what is the cost of running an electric heater for 4 hours? **Answer:** $0.90

b. At $0.15 per kilowatt-hour, what is the cost of running a clock radio for 24 hours? **Answer:** $0.04 (rounded to nearest cent)

Alternating (AC) and direct (DC) current

Direct current The current from a battery is always in the same direction, from the positive to the negative end of the battery. This type of current is called **direct current** or DC. Although the letters "DC" stand for "direct current" the abbreviation "DC" is used to describe both voltage and current. A DC voltage is one that stays the same sign over time. The terminal that is positive stays positive and the terminal that is negative stays negative. Your experiments in the lab use DC since they use batteries.

Alternating current The electrical system in your house uses **alternating current** or AC. Alternating current constantly switches direction. You can theoretically create alternating current with a battery if you keep reversing the way it is connected in a circuit (Figure 14.13). In the electrical system used in the United States, the current reverses direction 60 times per second. It would be hard to flip a battery this fast!

A DC current or voltage keeps the same sign over time.

An AC current or voltage reverses sign, usually 60 times per second in the US.

Electricity in other countries For large amounts of electricity, we use alternating current because it is easier to generate and to transmit over long distances. All the power lines you see overhead carry alternating current. Other countries also use alternating current. However, in many other countries, the current reverses itself 50 times per second rather than 60, and wall sockets are at a different voltage. When visiting Asia, Africa, or Europe, you need special adapters to use electrical appliances you bring with you from the United States.

Peak and average voltages The 120 volt AC (VAC) electricity used in homes and businesses alternates between peak values of +170 V and -170 V (Figure 14.14). This kind of electricity is called 120 VAC because +120V is the *average* positive voltage and -120V is the *average* negative voltage. AC electricity is usually described by the average voltage, not the peak voltage.

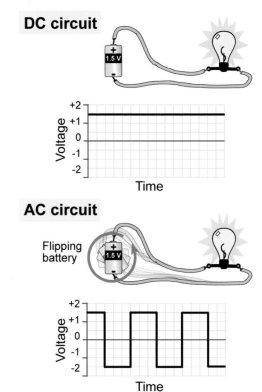

Figure 14.13: *Direct current is in one direction, but alternating current reverses.*

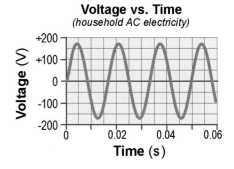

Figure 14.14: *The voltage in your wall outlets goes from +170 V to -170 V.*

Electricity, power, and heat

How do you get more power? How do you get more power when you need it? From the power formula, we can see that increasing voltage or current will increase power. The problem with raising voltage is that the electricity in a standard wall outlet is 120 volts and it is hard to change. While certain appliances use 240 volts, the higher voltage is more dangerous so 120 volts is used for most electrical appliances.

Higher power usually means more current The most common way to get higher power is to use more current. However, heat becomes a problem when wires carry large currents. A wire's voltage drop (from Ohm's law) equals the current multiplied by the wire's resistance. Because a wire's resistance is small, the voltage drop is usually small enough to be ignored. But if there is a large current, there can be a significant voltage drop. Remember, power is voltage drop multiplied by current. In a wire, this power is converted into heat. A small amount of heat can safely be transferred away from the wire by conduction or convection. Too much heat could melt the wire or start a fire.

Reducing heat in electrical wires Wires are made in different sizes to carry different amounts of current. A large diameter wire has less resistance and can safely carry more current than a smaller, thinner wire. A 12-gauge wire is thicker than a 14-gauge wire and can carry more current (Figure 14.15). You should always use the right wire for the current that is flowing. This includes extension cords, which you may use without thinking about whether they are safe or not. Extension cords are made with 18-gauge wire, 16-gauge, 14-gauge, and 12-gauge wire.

Length and resistance The length of a wire also affects its resistance. The longer a wire is, the more resistance it has. Think about moving around your school and how you can get through a short, crowded hallway quickly. But it takes a long time to get down a long, crowded hallway.

Check your extension cords for safety All extension cords are rated for how many amps of current they can carry safely. *Always* check to see if the extension cord can carry *at least* as much current as the device you are using requires. For powerful tools, such as a saw, you should use a 14-gauge or 12-gauge heavy-duty extension cord that is rated to carry 15-20 amps. Many fires have been caused by using the wrong extension cord.

Extension cords are made from multiple wires woven together

12-gauge wire

14-gauge wire

16-gauge wire

18-gauge wire

Wire gauge	Maximum current (amps)
12	20
14	15
16	10

Figure 14.15: *The larger the gauge of a wire, the smaller its diameter, and the smaller the amount of current the wire can safely carry.*

Electricity in homes and buildings

Circuit breaker panel
The 120 VAC electricity comes into a normal home or building through a circuit breaker panel. The circuit breakers protect against wires overheating and causing fires. Each circuit breaker protects one parallel circuit which may connect many wall outlets, lights, switches, or other appliances.

Parallel wiring of electrical outlets

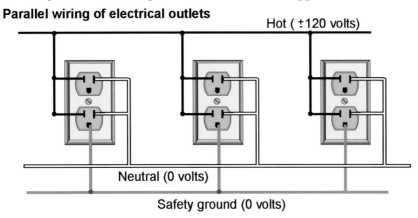

Hot (±120 volts)

Neutral (0 volts)

Safety ground (0 volts)

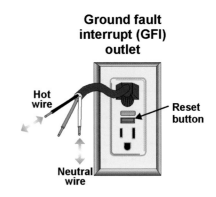

Ground fault interrupt (GFI) outlet

Hot wire

Reset button

Neutral wire

Figure 14.16: *A ground fault interrupt outlet might be found in bathrooms and kitchens where water may be near electricity.*

Hot, neutral, and ground wires
Each wall socket has three wires feeding it. The hot wire carries 120 volts AC. The neutral wire stays at zero volts. When you plug something in, current flows in and out of the hot wire, through your appliance (doing work) and back through the neutral wire. The ground wire is for safety and is connected to the ground (0 V) near your house. If there is a short circuit in your appliance, the current flows through the ground wire rather than through you.

Ground fault interrupt (GFI) outlets
Electrical outlets in bathrooms, kitchens, or outdoors are now required to have ground fault interrupt (GFI) outlets installed (Figure 14.16). A GFI outlet contains a circuit that compares the current flowing out on the hot wire and back on the neutral wire. If everything is working properly, the two currents should be exactly the same. If they are different, some current must be flowing to ground through another path, such as through your hand. The ground fault interrupter detects any difference in current and immediately breaks the circuit. GFI outlets are excellent protection against electric shocks, especially in wet locations.

Too many plugs!

If you plug too many appliances into the same circuit or outlet, you will eventually use more current than the wires can carry without overheating. Your circuit breaker will click open and stop the current. You should unplug things to reduce the current in the circuit before resetting the circuit breaker.

Distributing electricity

Why electricity is valuable Electricity is a valuable form of energy because electrical power can be moved easily over large distances. You would not want a large power plant in your backyard! One large power plant converts millions of watts of chemical or nuclear energy into electricity. The transmission lines carry the electricity to homes and businesses, often hundreds of miles away.

Power transmission lines Overhead power lines use a much higher voltage than 120V. That is because the losses due to the resistance of wires depend on the current. At 100,000 volts each amp of current carries 100,000 watts of power, compared to the 120 watts per amp of household electricity. Big electrical transmission lines operate at very high voltages for this reason (Figure 14.17). The wires are supported high on towers because voltages this high are *very dangerous*. Air can become a conductor over distances of a meter at high voltages. *Never* go near a power line that has fallen on the ground in a storm or other accident.

Transformers A device called a **transformer** converts high-voltage electricity to lower voltage electricity. Within a few kilometers of your home or school the voltage is lowered to 13,800 V or less. Right near your home or school the voltage is lowered again to the 120 V or 240 V that actually come into the circuits connecting your wall outlets and appliances.

Changing AC to DC Many electronic devices, like cell phones or laptop computers, use DC electricity inside, but also can be plugged into the AC electricity from a wall outlet with an *AC adapter* (Figure 14.18). An "AC adapter" is a device that changes the AC voltage from the wall outlet into DC voltage for the device. The adapter also steps the voltage down from 120 volts to the battery voltage, which is usually between 6 and 20 volts.

Figure 14.17: *Electrical power lines may operate at voltages of 100,000 volts or greater.*

14.3 Section Review

1. How is an appliance's power related to the amount of energy it uses?
2. How many watts or joules are a horsepower, kilowatt, and kilowatt-hour.
3. What does the electric utility company charge you for each month?
4. What is the difference between direct current and alternating current?

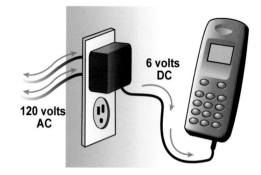

Figure 14.18: *Special adapters can change AC into DC and lower the voltage.*

CONNECTIONS

How do Hybrid Cars Work?

Gas-electric hybrid cars look and drive about like any other car, but use 20-30% less gas than their non-hybrid counterparts. For example, a hybrid car's gas mileage is about 50 miles per gallon. The gas mileage for standard cars ranges from 10 to 30 miles per gallon. To understand how hybrid cars get better gas mileage, we have to look at the engines.

Cars powered by gasoline

The efficiency of a gasoline engine is about 13%. This means that when the car is in motion, it only uses about 13% of the available energy from a tank of gas. The rest of the available energy from a tank of gas is lost as heat. The more energy that is lost as heat, the less efficient an engine or any system is.

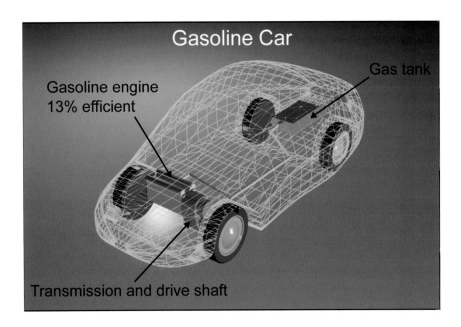

Gasoline Car

Gasoline engine 13% efficient

Gas tank

Transmission and drive shaft

Although the combustion of a gasoline engine produces many pollutants, gasoline is very energy-rich and easy for a car to carry. These two features have made the gasoline engine so easily adopted when oil was inexpensive and there was less concern for the impact of cars on the global environment.

Cars powered by electricity

Compared to gasoline-powered cars, electric motors are very efficient — 80% from batteries — and they produce no pollutants.

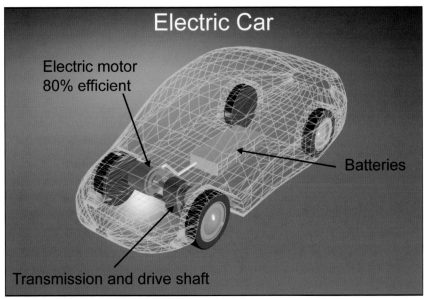

Electric Car

Electric motor 80% efficient

Batteries

Transmission and drive shaft

To run an electric car, the batteries need to be charged, often this is done by plugging in the car during the night. Unfortunately, batteries are heavy and don't have as much energy as gasoline. For instance, the available energy in a typical car battery is equivalent to about a small cupful of gasoline. Until there is a better electrical storage system, cars powered by electricity from a battery must be small and only used to travel short distances.

The best of both technologies

A hybrid car uses the best of both worlds—a gasoline-powered engine and an electric motor. By combining technologies, the efficiency is improved to about 26%. The electric motor helps the gas-powered system be more efficient by using electricity to transfer energy within the system.

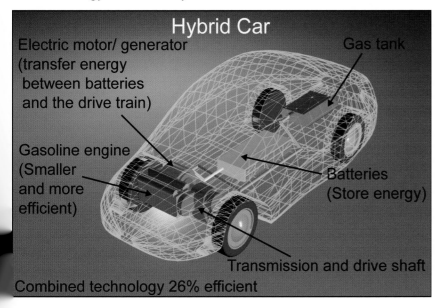

Hybrid Car

Electric motor/ generator
(transfer energy
between batteries
and the drive train)

Gas tank

Gasoline engine
(Smaller
and more
efficient)

Batteries
(Store energy)

Transmission and drive shaft

Combined technology 26% efficient

How do hybrids compare?

In a hybrid car, the gasoline engine and electric motor work together to accelerate the car. This allows the gasoline engine to be smaller and more efficient. Every time a standard car slows down, kinetic energy is lost as the brakes heat up. In contrast, the hybrid's electric motor operates as a generator during braking. When the car slows down, kinetic energy is converted to electrical energy that charges the batteries. Then, to speed up the car, the stored energy in the batteries is converted into useful kinetic energy by the motor.

In addition to getting great gas mileage, hybrid cars are rated as ulta-low emissions vehicles (ULEVs). This means that they do not produce as many pollutants as standard cars. Hybrid cars produce less pollution because the engine is smaller and simply uses less gasoline. Also, when a hybrid car comes to a stop, the engine automatically shuts off to save gas. When it is time to go again, the car turns on instantly. At very low speeds, as when you are driving in a city, the electric motor runs the car instead of the gasoline engine. When the electric motor is used, there is less pollution.

Hybrid technology is just a beginning

The gas-electric hybrid is only one of the many types of more efficient motor-powered vehicles that are being developed today. Driving this development is an interest in decreasing our use of fossil fuels for transportation. Interest in developing alternative transportation technologies will continue because they are potentially more efficient and less polluting.

In the meantime, since we all need to travel and often use gasoline-powered vehicles, how can you reduce your use a fossil fuels so that you save money and reduce pollution? Here are some options: share rides, take public transportation, and drive a medium-sized or small car that has high gas mileage.

Questions:

1. If you only need to drive two miles per day, which kind of car would be the best to use? Justify your answer.
2. Why is the efficiency of gasoline-powered cars so low?
3. Hybrid cars are better for driving in cities but not as efficient for highway driving? Why?
4. Some hybrid cars have efficiency meters—a gauge that shows your miles per gallon—so you can monitor and improve your driving habits. Make a list of driving habits that help you save gas.

Chapter 14 Review

Understanding Vocabulary

Select the correct term to complete the sentences.

parallel circuit	kilowatt-hour	electrical power
horsepower	series circuit	short circuit
transformer	direct	Kirchhoff's voltage law
Kirchhoff's current law	kilowatt	voltage drop
alternating		

Section 14.1

1. A _____ contains only one path for the current.

2. According to _____, if a circuit contains a 3-volt battery, the voltage drops around the complete circuit must add to 3 volts.

3. There is a _____ across each resistor in a circuit when current is flowing.

Section 14.2

4. _____ states that all the current entering a point in a circuit must also leave that point.

5. A _____ is created when a circuit contains one branch with very little or no resistance.

6. A _____ contains multiple paths or branches for the current.

Section 14.3

7. One _____ equals 1000 watts.

8. The rate of converting electrical energy into another form of energy is called _____.

9. The _____ is a unit used by electric utility companies to measure the electrical energy your home uses each month.

10. One _____ is equal to 746 watts.

11. A battery creates _____ current.

12. Electrical appliances in your home use _____ current.

13. A _____ converts high-voltage electricity to lower voltage electricity.

Reviewing Concepts

Section 14.1

1. Draw a circuit diagram for a circuit containing a battery and two bulbs in series.

2. Is the current at every point in a series circuit the same?

3. One of the bulbs burns out in a string of lights. What happens to the current in the circuit? What happens to the other bulbs?

4. Explain how to calculate the total resistance of a series circuit.

5. As more bulbs are added to a series circuit, what happens to the resistance of the circuit? What happens to the brightness of the bulbs?

6. Explain Kirchhoff's voltage law.

Section 14.2

7. What is a parallel circuit?

8. Draw the circuit diagram for a circuit containing two bulbs in parallel.

9. What does Kirchhoff's current law say about the current entering any point in a circuit?

10. Each branch in a parallel circuit has the same _____.

11. List two advantages of parallel circuits over series circuits.

12. Does the wiring in your home connect the appliances in series or parallel? How could you prove this?

13. What happens to the total resistance of a parallel circuit as more branches are added? Why?

14. How do you calculate the total resistance of two parallel resistors?

15. What is a short circuit?

16. Why can short circuits be dangerous?

Section 14.3

17. A light bulb has a power of 60 watts. Explain what this means in terms of energy and time.

18. Explain how to calculate the power of an electrical appliance.

19. What is the meaning of the kilowatt-hour?

20. What is the difference between direct current and alternating current?

21. How frequently does the alternating current used in the United States reverse direction?

22. Do thinner or thicker wires have more resistance?

23. Do longer or shorter wires have more resistance?

24. Why is it dangerous to connect several extension cords to make one long cord?

25. What is the purpose of the AC adapter on the end of the cord used for cell phones?

Solving Problems

Section 14.1

1. A circuit contains 5-ohm, 3-ohm, and 8-ohm resistors in series. What is the total resistance of the circuit?

2. A circuit contains a 9 volt battery and two identical bulbs. What is the voltage drop across each?

3. A circuit contains a 12 volt battery and two 3-ohm bulbs in series. Draw a circuit diagram and use it to find the current in the circuit and the voltage drop across each bulb.

4. A circuit contains a 12 volt battery and three 1-ohm bulbs in series. Draw the circuit diagram and find the current in the circuit.

5. Calculate the total resistance of each circuit shown below. Then calculate the current in each.

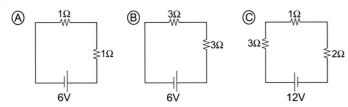

6. A circuit contains two 1-ohm bulbs in series. The current in the circuit is 1.5 amperes. What is the voltage provided by the batteries?

7. A circuit contains two identical resistors in series. The current is 3 amperes, and the batteries have a total voltage of 24 volts. What is the total resistance of the circuit? What is the resistance of each resistor?

Section 14.2

8. Find the amount and direction of the current through point P in each of the circuits shown below.

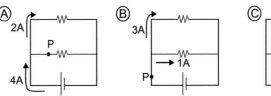 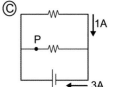

9. Do the following for each of the three circuits shown below.
   a. Find the voltage across each resistor.
   b. Use Ohm's law to find the current through each resistor.
   c. Find the total current in the circuit.
   d. Find the total resistance of the circuit.

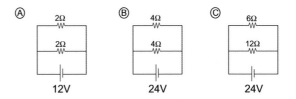

10. A parallel circuit contains a 6-volt battery and two 6-ohm bulbs.
    a. Draw the circuit diagram for this circuit.
    b. Calculate the current through each branch.
    c. Calculate the total current.
    d. Use Ohm's law to calculate the total resistance of the circuit.
    e. Use the formula for combining parallel resistors to calculate the total resistance of the circuit.

11. A parallel circuit contains a 24 V battery, 4 Ω bulb and a 12 Ω bulb.
    a. Draw the circuit diagram for this circuit.
    b. Calculate the current through each branch.
    c. Calculate the total current in the circuit.
    d. Use Ohm's law to calculate the total resistance of the circuit.
    e. Use the formula for combining parallel resistors to calculate the total resistance of the circuit.

12. Find the unknown quantity in each of the circuits below.

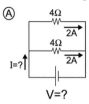 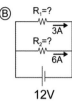 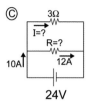

Section 14.3

13. Calculate the power of each of the following appliances when plugged into a 120-volt outlet.
    a. an iron that draws 10 A of current
    b. a stereo that draws 2 A of current
    c. a light bulb that draws 0.5 A of current

14. Calculate the current each of the following appliances draws when plugged into a 120-volt outlet.
    a. a 100 watt computer
    b. a 1200 watt microwave
    c. a 30 watt radio

15. A portable MP3 player requires 1.5 A of current and has a power of 15 watts. What is the voltage of the rechargeable battery it uses?

16. A flashlight contains a 6-watt bulb that draws 2 A of current. How many 1.5-volt batteries does it use?

17. Alex uses a 1000 watt heater to heat his room.
    a. What is the heater's power in kilowatts?
    b. How many kilowatt-hours of electricity does Alex use if he runs the heater for 8 hours?
    c. If the utility company charges $0.15 per kilowatt-hour, how much does it cost to run the heater for 8 hours?

18. You watch a 300-watt television for two hours while you watch a movie.
    a. What is the television's power in kilowatts?
    b. How many kilowatt-hours of electricity did you use?
    c. If the utility company charges $0.15 per kilowatt-hour, how much did it cost you to watch the movie?

Applying Your Knowledge

Section 14.1

1. Some appliances contain components that are connected in series. For example, many microwave ovens have a light that turns on while the microwave is running. Look around your house and see how many appliances you can find that use series circuits.

Section 14.2

2. A car contains a warning bell that turns on if you open the door while the key is in the ignition. The bell also turns on if you open the door while the headlights are on. A single circuit with three switches and a a bell can be built to ring in both cases. Figure out how the circuit is designed. Draw a circuit diagram that shows your solution.

3. Many circuits contain resistors in series and in parallel. Apply what you have learned about circuits to find the total resistance of each of the sets of resistors below.

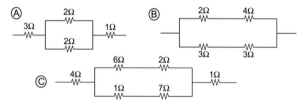

Section 14.3

4. Look at the back or underside of appliances in your home. Find the power of three appliances. Calculate the amount of current each draws when plugged into a 120-volt outlet.

5. Choose an appliance with a known power that you use frequently, such as a clock radio, stereo, or light.
    a. Calculate the power in kilowatts.
    b. Determine the amount of time you use the appliance in one day.
    c. Calculate the number of kilowatt-hours of energy the appliance uses in one day.
    d. Calculate the number of kilowatt-hours of energy it uses in one year.
    e. Find out the cost of electricity in your home.
    f. Calculate the cost of running the appliance for one year.

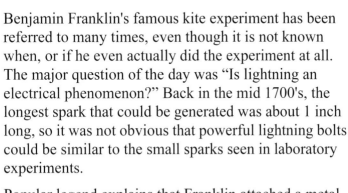

Chapter 15

Electrical Charges and Forces

Benjamin Franklin's famous kite experiment has been referred to many times, even though it is not known when, or if he even actually did the experiment at all. The major question of the day was "Is lightning an electrical phenomenon?" Back in the mid 1700's, the longest spark that could be generated was about 1 inch long, so it was not obvious that powerful lightning bolts could be similar to the small sparks seen in laboratory experiments.

Popular legend explains that Franklin attached a metal key to the end of a kite string and flew the kite in a raging lightning storm. Because he knew the experiment would be dangerous, he most likely attached a second silk string to the key that insulated him from the electrical charges, and held onto that string. He did not do his experiments during the peak of the storm, but chose to fly the kite as the storm was beginning to form. He noticed, according to an account written several years later, that he did receive a shock when he touched his knuckle to the metal key. He determined that lightning exhibited the same properties as small static electricity sparks, and he was correct!

In this chapter, you will study how atoms are ultimately responsible for electrical charges. You learned in an earlier chapter that all atoms contain positive and negative charges, and now you will see that these charges are the very same ones that allow us to benefit from generating, conducting, and using electricity.

Key Questions

✓ What is the actual source of current in a household electrical system?

✓ After you rub a balloon on your hair, why can you then stick the balloon to a wall but not to a metal doorknob?

✓ How does a defibrillator work, and what does it have to do with electricity?

15.1 Electric Charge and Current

In chapters 13 and 14 we looked at how electricity is used and measured. Amps, volts, and ohms describe most of what you need to know to use electricity safely. However, we did really discuss what electricity *is* on the atomic level. What is current? What sort of thing can flow through solid metal? Why can a little electric motor do the work of two horses?

Positive and negative charge

The true cause of electric current
Virtually all the matter around you has electric charge because atoms are made of electrons and protons (and neutrons). Electrons have negative charge and protons have positive charge. The electrons and protons are usually stuck together in atoms and are unable to separate from each other. However, in electrical conductors (like copper) a few electrons are not stuck to their atoms, but are free to move around. These mobile electrons are the real cause of electric current!

Like charges repel and unlike charges attract
Whether two charges attract or repel depends on whether they have the same or opposite sign. A positive and a negative charge will attract each other. Two positive charges will repel each other. Two negative charges will also repel each other. The force between charges is shown in Figure 15.1.

Charge is measured in coulombs
The unit of charge is the **coulomb (C)**. The name was chosen in honor of Charles Augustin de Coulomb (1736-1806), the French physicist who performed the first accurate measurements of the force between charges. One coulomb is a *huge* amount of charge. A single proton has a charge of 1.602×10^{-19} coulomb (Figure 15.1). An electron has the exact same charge, only negative. The charge of an electron -1.602×10^{-19} coulomb.

Two types of charge
Electric charge, like mass, is a fundamental property of matter. An important difference between mass and charge is that there are two types of charge, which we call positive and negative. We know there are two kinds because electric charges can attract or repel each other. As far as we know, there is only one type of mass. All masses *attract* each other through gravity. We have never found masses that repel each other.

Vocabulary

coulomb, electrically neutral, charged, static electricity, Coulomb's law, electroscope, charging by contact, charging by friction, polarized, charging by induction

Objectives

✓ Distinguish between a positive and negative net charge.
✓ Explain the meaning of Coulomb's law.
✓ Describe different ways of charging an electroscope.

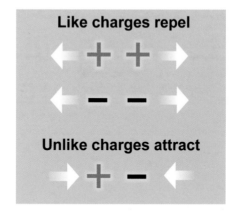

Figure 15.1: *The direction of the forces on charges depends on whether they have the same or opposite charges.*

Static electricity

Neutral objects
Matter contains trillions and trillions of charged electrons and protons because matter is made of atoms. Neutral atoms have the same number of electrons and protons. Therefore, the charge of an atom is *exactly zero*. Similarly, there is perfect cancellation between positive and negative in matter leaving a *net charge* of precisely zero. An object with a net charge of zero is described as being **electrically neutral**. Your pencil, your textbook, even your body are electrically neutral, at least most of the time.

Charged objects
An object is **charged** when its net charge is *not* zero. If you have ever felt a shock when you have touched a doorknob or removed clothes from a dryer, you have experienced a charged object. An object with more negative than positive charge has a net negative charge overall (Figure 15.2). If it has more positive than negative charge, the object has a positive net charge. The net charge is also sometimes called *excess* charge because a charged object has an excess of either positive or negative charges.

Static electricity and charge
A tiny imbalance in either positive or negative charge on an object is the cause of **static electricity**. If two neutral objects are rubbed together, the friction often pulls some electrons off one object and puts them temporarily on the other. This is what happens to clothes in the dryer and to your socks when you walk on a carpet. The static electricity you feel when taking clothes from a dryer or scuffing your socks on a carpet typically results from an excess charge of less than one-millionth of a *coulomb*, the unit of charge.

What causes shocks
You get a shock because excess of charge of one sign strongly attracts charge of the other sign and repels charge of the same sign. When you walk across a carpet on a dry day, your body picks up excess negative charge. If you touch a neutral door knob some of your excess negative charge moves to the door knob. Because the door knob is a conductor, the charge flows *quickly*. The moving charge makes a brief, intense electric current between you and the door knob. The shock you feel is the electric current as some of your excess negative charge transfers to the door knob (Figure 15.3).

This object is neutral

positive charge	+8
negative charge	-8
total	0

This object is charged

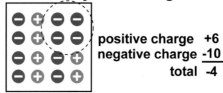

positive charge	+6
negative charge	-10
total	-4

Figure 15.2: *An object is neutral if it has an equal number of positive and negative charges.*

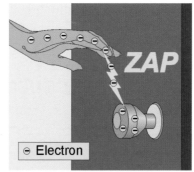

Static electricity

Figure 15.3: *The shock you get from touching a door knob on a dry day comes from moving charge.*

Coulomb's law

The force between charges is very strong

Electric forces are so strong it is hard to imagine. A millimeter cube of carbon the size of a pencil point contains about 77 coulombs of positive charge and the same amount of negative charge. If you could separate all the positive and negative charges by a distance of one meter, the attractive force between them would be 50 thousand billion newtons. This is the weight of three thousand, *million* cars. From the charge in a pencil point (Figure 15.4)! The huge forces between charges are the reason objects are electrically neutral.

More charge means more force

The force between two charges depends on the charge and the distance. The force is directly proportional to the charge of each object. The greater the charge, the stronger the force. Doubling the charge of one object doubles the force. Doubling the charge of both objects quadruples the force.

Less distance means more force

The force is inversely proportional to the square of the distance between the charges (Figure 15.5). Electric forces get stronger as charges move closer and weaker as they move farther apart. Doubling the distance makes the force 1/4 as strong ($1 \div 2^2$). The force is $^1/_9$ as strong ($1 \div 3^2$) at triple the distance.

Coulomb's law

Coulomb's law explains the relationship between the amount of each charge (q_1 and q_2), the distance between their centers (r), and the electrical force (F_E). The constant k relates the distance and charges to the force. Coulomb's law is very similar to Newton's law of gravitation (chapter 6).

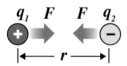

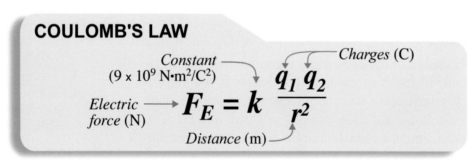

COULOMB'S LAW

$$F_E = k \frac{q_1 q_2}{r^2}$$

Constant $(9 \times 10^9 \text{ N·m}^2/\text{C}^2)$ — Charges (C)

Electric force (N) — Distance (m)

Action-reaction pairs

The force between two charges acts along a line joining their centers. As required by Newton's third law of motion, the forces on each charge make an action-reaction pair. They are equal in strength and opposite in direction.

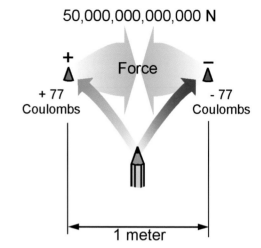

Figure 15.4: *If you could separate the positive and negative charge in a pencil point by one meter, the force between the charges would be 50 thousand, billion newtons!*

50,000,000,000,000 N

Force

+ 77 Coulombs   - 77 Coulombs

1 meter

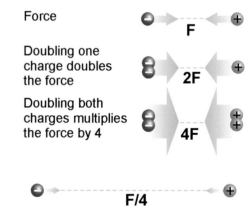

Force

Doubling one charge doubles the force

Doubling both charges multiplies the force by 4

Doubling the distance reduces the force to 1/4 its original strength

Figure 15.5: *How the electric force changes with charge and distance in Coulomb's law.*

Electrostatics

What is electrostatics? Electrostatics is the part of physics that deals with the forces created by unmoving charges. A conventional television uses electrostatics to create pictures. The tiny transistors inside a computer also work on electrostatics.

The picture tube and electron guns The working part of a television is the picture tube. At the back of the picture tube are three electron guns which make beams of electrons. The beams of electrons go back and forth across the front of the picture tube drawing the picture by lighting up colored dots called *phosphors*. An electron gun has three key parts: an emitter of electrons, a control grid, and an accelerator. The emitter is heated to a high temperature so electrons "boil off" its surface. The accelerator uses electric force to attract the electrons from the emitter.

Acceleration by electric fields in the electron gun The accelerator is kept at a high positive charge relative to the emitter. The electric force accelerates the negatively charged electrons from the emitter towards the accelerator. The beam is created by the electrons that pass through a small hole in the accelerator. Of course, some of the electrons also hit the accelerator plate itself and go back through the circuit. In a true electron gun, the shape of the accelerator steers most of the electrons through the hole and not into the plate (Figure 15.7).

Television picture tube

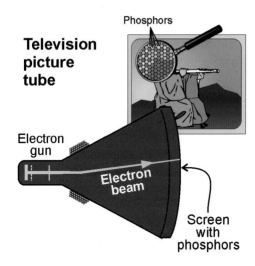

Phosphors

Electron gun

Electron beam

Screen with phosphors

Figure 15.6: *The working parts of a conventional television.*

Parts of an electron gun

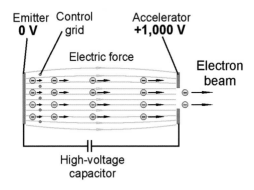

Figure 15.7: *An electron gun uses the attraction from a positively charged plate (accelerator) to create a beam of moving electrons.*

Using Coulomb's law

Two steel marbles are each given a net charge of one thousandth (0.001) of a coulomb. Calculate the size of the force on the marbles if they are held 2 meters apart.

1. ***Looking for:*** You are asked for the electric force in newtons.

2. ***Given:*** Two charges (0.001 C each) and the distance in meters.

3. ***Relationships:*** $F_E = k\dfrac{q_1 q_2}{r^2}$

4. ***Solution:*** $F_E = (9 \times 10^9 \text{ N} \cdot \text{m}^2/\text{C}^2)\dfrac{(0.001\,\text{C})(0.001\,\text{C})}{(2\,\text{m})^2} = 2250 \text{ N}$

Your turn...

a. Calculate the size of the force if the marbles are held 4 m apart. **Answer:** 563 N

b. Calculate the size of the force between 3 C and 4 C charges 500 m apart. **Answer:** 432,000 N

The electroscope

Electrons and static electricity

Electric forces are so strong that a "charged" object is really almost completely neutral. A tiny excess of charge, smaller than 1 part in a million, is enough to cause the "static electricity" effects we observe. Since electrons are small, light, and on the outside of atoms, almost all electrical effects are caused by moving electrons. A negatively charged object has an excess of electrons. A positively charged object is missing some electrons.

Charge spreads out in a conductor

Electrons in a conductor are free to move around. If a conductor has an excess of electrons, they repel each other with strong forces. The repelling forces cause the electrons to move as far away from each other as they can get. That means excess electrons spread out evenly over the surface of any conductor and flow along the conductor wherever they can get farther away from each other.

Electroscopes

The force between charges can be observed with an **electroscope**. An electroscope is an instrument that contains two very thin leaves of metal that can swing from a central rod (Figure 15.8) which may have a ball on it. Electrons can flow freely between the leaves, ball, and rod.

Observing electric forces

Suppose a negatively charged rod is held above (but not touching) a neutral electroscope. Free electrons in the electroscope are repelled by the rod and move from the ball down into the leaves. The leaves now have an excess of electrons. This gives the leaves a net negative charge and they repel each other. If the rod is pulled away, the excess electrons return to the ball, making the leaves neutral again.

Testing for positive or negative

If the rod touches the metal ball, some electrons are transferred to the electroscope. This is called **charging by contact**. The electroscope now has excess electrons all over it, so both leaves are negative and they repel. A charged electroscope can be used to test other charged objects. If a negative rod is brought close to the electroscope, the excess electrons in the ball move down to the leaves and they spread farther apart. But if a positive rod is held near the electroscope, electrons are attracted to the rod. They move away from the leaves and into the ball. Because the leaves have lost some excess electrons, they do not repel as strongly and fall toward each other.

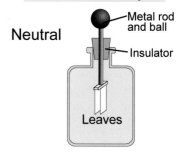

The electroscope

Neutral

Metal rod and ball

Insulator

Leaves

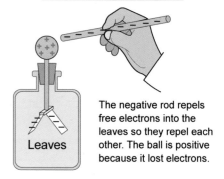

Separating charges

The negative rod repels free electrons into the leaves so they repel each other. The ball is positive because it lost electrons.

Leaves

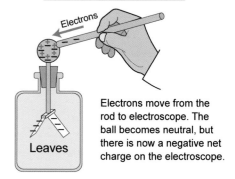

Charging by contact

Electrons

Electrons move from the rod to electroscope. The ball becomes neutral, but there is now a negative net charge on the electroscope.

Leaves

Figure 15.8: *You can use an electroscope to observe electric forces.*

Static electricity, charge polarization, and induction

Charging by friction If you rub a balloon on your hair, you can make it stick to a wall but not to a metal doorknob. When the balloon and your hair are rubbed together, electrons are transferred from your hair to the balloon. This is called **charging by friction**. Because the balloon gains electrons, it has a negative net charge. Your hair loses electrons, so it has a net positive charge.

Polarization When the balloon is brought near the wall, electrons inside atoms near the wall's surface are slightly repelled toward the far side of the atom. The wall's atoms become **polarized** — one end positive, the other negative (Figure 15.9). The balloon is both attracted to the positive side of each atom and repelled by the negative side. The attractive force is stronger because the positive side of each atom is closer to the balloon than the negative side.

Conductors If the balloon is brought toward a doorknob or other conductor, it doesn't stick. Because electrons in the doorknob can move freely, they repel to the opposite side of the doorknob as the balloon approaches. The side of the doorknob near the balloon becomes positively charged. The balloon first attracts the doorknob. But when the two touch, some of the balloon's excess electrons move onto the doorknob because it is a conductor. When the doorknob gains electrons, it becomes negative like the balloon and they repel.

Charging by induction **Charging by induction** is a method of using one object to charge another without changing the net charge on the first (Figure 15.10). Suppose you hold a negative balloon close to an electroscope. The balloon repels the electroscope's electrons, so they move down into the leaves. If you touch the ball (*grounding* the electroscope), electrons are repelled onto your finger. If you remove your finger, the electroscope is left with a net positive charge.

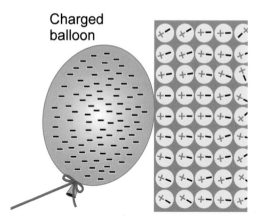

Figure 15.9: *A negative balloon sticks to a neutral wall.*

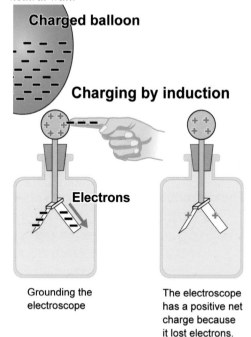

Grounding the electroscope

The electroscope has a positive net charge because it lost electrons.

Figure 15.10: *When a balloon charges the electroscope through induction, the charge on the balloon is not disturbed.*

15.1 Section Review

1. Explain how there can be charge inside matter yet the matter is electrically neutral.
2. Write down Coulomb's law and explain what the symbols mean.
3. Explain the difference between an electrically charged and a neutral object.
4. Explain two ways to charge an electroscope.

15.2 Electric Current, Resistance, and Voltage

In Chapter 13 we said electric current was what flowed and could do work. We can now say current is the *movement* of electric charge. Electric charge is always there, but it may not be moving. Current flows when charges move. One ampere is a flow of one coulomb per second. Higher current means more charge flows per second. For example, a current of 10 amperes means that 10 coulombs of charge flow every second.

Charge and current

Current is the flow of charge

Electric current is the flow of charge. If the current in a wire is one ampere, one coulomb of charge passes by a point in the wire in one second. The unit ampere is a shorter way of saying "coulomb per second."

If the current in a wire is one ampere, one coulomb of charge passes by a point in the wire in one second.

Positive and negative

Benjamin Franklin first used the terms "positive" and "negative" to describe charge. He believed electricity was a type of fluid. He thought positive objects had too much and negative objects had too little of the fluid. According to Franklin's theory, a positive object's extra fluid naturally flowed toward a negative object. The flow would stop when each had the right amount and became neutral.

The direction of current

Because of Franklin's work, the direction of electric current is defined as going *from positive to negative*. Long after Franklin's work, scientists discovered that current in wires is the flow of *electrons*. The direction in which electrons move in a circuit is *from negative to positive*, opposite the way current was defined earlier (Figure 15.11).

Current is from positive to negative

We still define current as going from positive to negative. For ordinary electric circuits it does not matter that negative electrons are really moving the other way. In a conductive liquid such as salt water, both positive and negative charges can move to create current. No matter what the sign of the moving charges, current is always defined as flowing from positive voltage to negative voltage.

Objectives

✓ Describe the relationship between electrons and current.
✓ Explain, at the atomic level, the difference between insulators, semiconductors, conductors.
✓ Identify how voltage and charge are related.

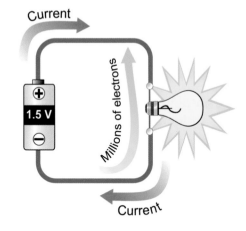

Figure 15.11: *Electrons move from negative to positive, but the conventional direction of current is from positive to negative.*

The source of current

Electron motion When atoms of a metal (like copper) are together they all bond together by sharing electrons. In some ways a solid piece of copper acts like a single huge molecule. Some *valence electrons* can move freely anywhere within the copper. The copper atoms (⊕) with the remaining electrons are bonded together and stay fixed in place.

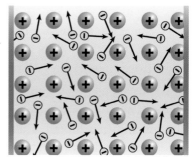

If a copper wire is not connected to a battery, the free electrons bounce around at high speeds. They have no average motion because as many are going one way as the other way. However, the free electrons move energy very effectively, so metals are good conductors of *heat* as well as electricity.

Drift velocity If a battery is connected across a copper wire, the free electrons are attracted to the positive terminal and repelled by the negative terminal. However, the electrons do not move directly from one end of the wire to the other because the copper atoms are in the way. Instead, the electrons bounce off the atoms while slowly making their way toward the positive end of the battery. The electric force created by the battery voltage creates a slow drift velocity in one direction on top of the electron's random bouncing (Figure 15.12). This slow *drift velocity* is what creates electrical current. The bouncing transfers some energy from the drift motion to the copper atoms. This explains how wires heat up when current is passed through them.

The source of current carrying electrons With a 1.5 volt battery the drift velocity is slower than a turtle, a few millimeters per second. So why does the bulb light up instantly? The electrons carrying current in a wire *do not come from the battery*. Current flows because the voltage from a battery makes electrons move that are *already in the wire*. This is why a light bulb goes on as soon as you flip the switch. A copper wire contains many electrons bouncing randomly around. Without an applied voltage, as many electrons bounce one way as the other. There is no net flow of electrons and no electrical current. When a voltage is applied all the free electrons in the wire start drifting because of the electric force.

⊕ Fixed atom   ←⊸ Mobile electron

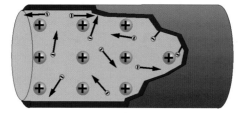

No voltage
electrons have only random motion
no average current

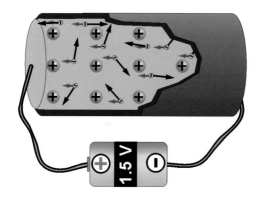

Applied voltage
electrons have random motion plus
small drift velocity
current flows

Figure 15.12: *When a voltage is applied across a wire, electrons slowly drift while randomly colliding with atoms in the wire.*

Conductors, insulators, and resistance

Insulators
The electrons in insulators are not free to move — they are tightly bound inside atoms (Figure 15.13). Since the atoms are fixed in place, the electrons in insulators are also fixed in place. Insulators have very high resistance because there are no free electrons to carry any current.

Semiconductors
A semiconductor has some free electrons, but not nearly as many as a conductor has. Semiconductors have a resistance in between conductors and insulators. The diagram below shows a model of the atoms and electrons in conductors, insulators, and semiconductors. The arrows on the electrons show the direction of their drift velocity (but not of their random bouncing).

Moving electron

Electrical current is made of moving electrons; atoms stay fixed in place.

Atom in an insulator — **Bound electron**

In an insulator, the electrons are tightly bound to atoms and cannot move.

Atom in a conductor — **Moving electron**

In a conductor, some electrons come free and can move to create electrical current. Since electrons are negative, they move in a direction opposite the (positive) current.

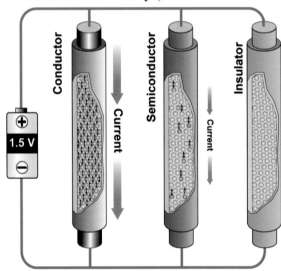

Figure 15.13: *In a conductor, some of an atom's electrons are free to move. In an insulator, all of the electrons are tightly bound to their atoms.*

Super-conductors
Certain materials become **superconductors** when they are cooled to very low temperatures. For example, the metal alloy niobium-zirconium becomes a superconductor at -262°C. A superconductor carries electrical current with *zero resistance*. A current in a loop of superconducting wire will keep flowing forever, even without a battery! An electric motor made with superconducting wires would be far more efficient than one made with copper wires. Many researchers are searching for superconductors that work at normal temperatures.

Voltage and charge

Current and voltage

In chapter 13 you learned that current flows in response to differences in voltage. If one point in a circuit is at 3 volts and another is at zero volts, current will flow toward the point at zero volts and away from the point at 3 volts. We now know current is moving charge. How do we understand voltage in terms of charges?

A volt is a joule per coulomb

Voltage measures electrical potential energy *per unit of charge*. One volt is one joule per coulomb. That means one coulomb of charge that moves through a difference of one volt gains or loses one joule of potential energy. The charge *loses* one joule if it goes from higher voltage to lower voltage. This is what happens in a device that uses energy, like a light bulb. The charge *gains* one joule if it moves from lower voltage to higher voltage. This is what happens inside a battery. A battery transforms chemical energy to electrical energy.

Joules or watts?

This new definition of a volt is really the same as our old one. In terms of charge, one volt is a joule per coulomb. One amp is a coulomb per second, and a watt is a joule per second. If you work the units out you can prove to yourself that a joule per coulomb (charge) is exactly the same as a watt per amp (current).

$$\text{Volt} = \frac{\text{Watt}}{\text{Amp}} = \frac{\left(\frac{\text{Joule}}{\text{Second}}\right)}{\left(\frac{\text{Coulomb}}{\text{Second}}\right)} = \frac{\left(\frac{\text{Joule}}{\text{Second}}\right)}{\left(\frac{\text{Coulomb}}{\text{Second}}\right)} = \frac{\text{Joule}}{\text{Coulomb}}$$

A charge <u>does</u> work, and <u>loses</u> potential energy when it moves <u>in</u> the direction of the electric force

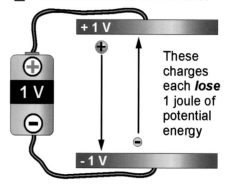

These charges each *lose* 1 joule of potential energy

Work must be done <u>on</u> a charge to move it <u>against</u> the direction of the electric force, so the charge <u>gains</u> potential energy.

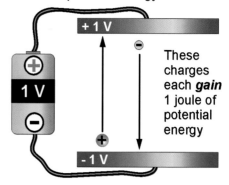

These charges each *gain* 1 joule of potential energy

Figure 15.14: *A charge of 1 coulomb can either gain or lose 1 joule of energy by moving across a voltage difference of 1 volt.*

15.2 Section Review

1. Explain what it means to say an object has a positive net charge.
2. What flows when there is a current in a wire?
3. How can charges in a circuit move at high speeds while having a slow drift velocity?
4. Why is it easy to create a current in a conductor and not in an insulator?

15.3 Capacitors

The circuits you have studied so far contained only wires, batteries, switches, and resistors such as bulbs. In these circuits, the current stops immediately when the source of voltage is removed. This section discusses a device called a *capacitor* which stores charge. If the voltage is removed from a circuit containing a capacitor, the current keeps going for a while, until all the capacitor's stored charge has flowed out. Almost all electric appliances, including televisions, cameras, and computers, use capacitors in their circuits. Capacitors are also a useful tool for investigating the relationship between electric charge, voltage, and current.

A capacitor is an energy storage device

A capacitor stores energy
A **capacitor** is a device that stores electrical energy by keeping positive and negative charges separated. The simplest type of capacitor is made of two parallel plates with an insulator between them. Both plates of the capacitor start out neutral. Energy is stored in the capacitor by transferring electrons from one plate to the other. The greater the number of electrons transferred, the greater the amount of stored energy. The plate that gains electrons gets a negative net charge, and the one that loses electrons gets an equal but opposite positive net charge.

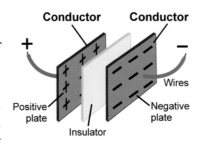

Using a capacitor's stored energy
Once a capacitor's plates are charged, it has a voltage and can drive current in a circuit. A capacitor is connected just like a battery (Figure 15.15). The positive plate attracts free electrons, and the negative plate repels them. This creates a voltage and current flows out of the capacitor from positive to negative just as it would be with a battery. Eventually the positive plate has gained enough electrons for it to be neutral and the negative plate has lost all its excess electrons. The current stops and the voltage of the capacitor drops to zero. A camera flash uses a capacitor in this way. When you press the button to take a picture, you close the circuit between the flash and a charged capacitor. The current is large, so the capacitor's energy is converted very quickly into the light you see.

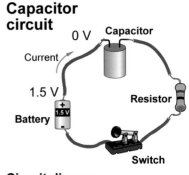

Figure 15.15: *A charged capacitor can create current in a circuit.*

Charging a capacitor

Equal and opposite charges
We say a capacitor is *charged* when one of its plates has a positive net charge and the other has a net negative charge. The amount of charge on each plate is the same but opposite in sign. Suppose one plate has a charge of +2 coulombs and the other has a charge of -2 coulombs. We say this capacitor's charge is 2 coulombs. However, the net charge on the *whole* capacitor is zero no matter how many electrons are transferred between the plates.

A battery can charge a capacitor
A capacitor can be charged by connecting it to a battery or any other source of voltage. In Figure 15.16, a capacitor, bulb, battery, and switch are connected in series. The capacitor's starts with zero charge and has zero voltage across its terminals. When the switch is closed, current flows and the capacitor builds up a charge separation on its plates. As the capacitor charges, a voltage develops across its terminals. The voltage keeps increasing until the capacitor has the same voltage as the battery. At this point, the capacitor has stored as much charge as it can for the voltage of the battery.

Current
The bulb is very bright at first, but gradually it becomes dim and eventually it goes out. The current starts out large and finally decreases to zero when the capacitor is fully charged (Figure 15.17). The amount of current and the time for the capacitor to charge is determined by the amount of resistance in the circuit. The greater the resistance, the smaller the current, and the longer the time needed to charge.

Voltage
The voltage of the capacitor starts at zero when no charge is stored. As the charge increases, the voltage also increases. The energy stored in the capacitor also increases with its voltage.

Electrons enter one plate
Think about what happens on the capacitor's plates. One plate (which was neutral) gradually has electrons added to it. The excess electrons repel the new electrons trying to get on by increasing the capacitor's voltage. This is similar to what happens when people climb onto a bus. If the bus is empty, it is very easy for people to get on. As the bus fills up, it becomes more and more difficult for each additional person to get on. The current decreases because each new electron has to fight a higher repulsive voltage to get on. Eventually, the voltage reaches the battery voltage and current stops.

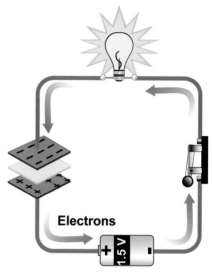

Electrons

Figure 15.16: *A battery can be used to charge a capacitor.*

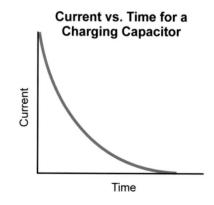

Current vs. Time for a Charging Capacitor

Current

Time

Figure 15.17: *The current starts out large but decreases as the capacitor charges*

Capacitance

Voltage and charge The amount of charge a capacitor will hold before the current stops depends on the voltage of the battery (or other source) that charges it. Voltage is what pushes the electrons onto the negative plate and pulls them from the positive plate. The higher the voltage, the greater the amount of charge on the capacitor when the current stops.

Measuring capacitance The amount of charge a capacitor will hold also depends on its **capacitance**. Capacitance is the measure of a capacitor's ability to store charge. It is measured in **farads (F)**. A one-farad capacitor attached to a   1-volt battery holds 1 coulomb of charge. A two-farad capacitor attached to the same battery holds 2 coulombs of charge.

Microfarads A coulomb is a huge amount of charge. Most capacitors hold much less than a coulomb of charge, and they have capacitances that are only a fraction of a farad. For this reason, capacitances are often measured in microfarads. One microfarad is 1×10^{-6} farad. A capacitor that supplies energy to a flash in a disposable camera is only about 200 microfarads and holds 0.02 coulombs of charge.

Factors determining capacitance The capacitance of a capacitor depends on three factors (Figure 15.18):

1. The greater the area of a capacitor's plates, the more charge it can hold, and the larger the capacitance.

2. The insulating material between the plates affects how much charge can be stored in a capacitor.

3. The smaller the separation distance between the plates, the greater the capacitance.

Parallel plates are not practical Parallel plate capacitors are not practical to use in most devices because they must be large to store enough charge to be useful. If a capacitor's plates and insulating material are made of a flexible material, it can be rolled into the shape of a cylinder (Figure 15.19). This allows each plate to have a large area while the capacitor fits into a small space.

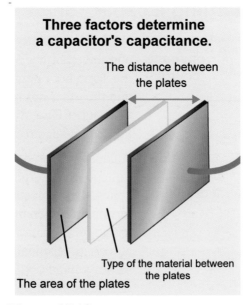

Three factors determine a capacitor's capacitance.

The distance between the plates

Type of the material between the plates

The area of the plates

Figure 15.18: *Three factors determine a capacitor's capacitance.*

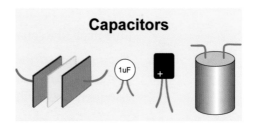

Capacitors

Figure 15.19: *There are many types of capacitors.*

Discharging a capacitor

Discharging a capacitor
A capacitor can be discharged by connecting it to any closed circuit that allows current to flow. A low-resistance circuit discharges the capacitor more quickly because the current is higher. Electrons are quickly removed from the negative plate and added to the positive plate. A capacitor is fully discharged when the two plates are both neutral and the voltage is zero.

Designing circuits
When using a capacitor that will be charged and discharged, the circuit can be designed to change from charging to discharging with the flip of a switch. In the circuit shown at right, the capacitor charges when the switch is at position A. When it is flipped to position B, the battery is cut off and the capacitor discharges.

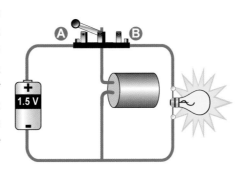

Capacitor safety
If connected in a circuit with little resistance, a capacitor can discharge very quickly, creating a large amount of current. For this reason, capacitors can be very dangerous. When working with a capacitor, never hold it by its terminals. It is also important to always fully discharge a capacitor when you finish working with it.

Defibrillators

If you have ever seen doctors working in an emergency room on television or in a movie, you have probably seen a device called a *defibrillator*. A defibrillator uses an electric current to make a patient's heart start beating again after a heart attack or other trauma.

A defibrillator uses a capacitor to create a very quick but large current. Before using a defibrillator, doctors must wait a few seconds for the capacitor to charge. If a patient's heart doesn't start after one attempt, the voltage across the capacitor is increased. This provides more current to stimulate the heart.

Small portable defibrillators are being placed in schools, airports, and other public buildings. These devices have saved many lives by allowing trained people to help heart attack victims even before paramedics arrive.

15.3 Section Review

1. Traditionally, we say that current flows from positive to negative. Why is it more correct to say that current flows from negative to positive?

2. Explain, using electrons, why current flows.

3. Why does an insulator have high resistance? Why does a conductor allow current to flow? (Hint: use electrons to explain your answer)

Lightning

Have you ever scuffed your feet across a carpeted floor and then touched a metal doorknob?—Zap! You feel a static electric shock, and if the room is dark, you can see a quick flash of light.

The zap happens because contact between your shoes and the carpet transfers some of the carpet atoms' electrons to your feet. Your body acquires an excess negative charge. When you touch a conducting object like the doorknob, the excess charge moves from your hand to the metal in a flash.

Believe it or not, the same process that caused you to get zapped when you touched the doorknob creates the spectacular lightning displays you see on a stormy evening.

How does lightning get started?

Lightning originates in towering, dark storm clouds. Inside these clouds, charges begin to separate. Scientists still don't really understand how this happens. Some think that collisions between hailstones and ice crystals are responsible, while others speculate that friction between particles of ice and raindrops causes electrons to be ripped from some of the atoms.

While the mechanism is still a mystery, we do know that the bottom of the cloud acquires an excess negative charge (like your feet after you scuff them on the carpet). Warm updrafts carry the positively charged particles to the cloud's top.

The buildup of negative charges at the bottom of the cloud repels negative charges in the ground and attracts positive charges. The positively charged ground surface pulls the cloud's freed electrons downward. On their way down, these electrons crash into air molecules, knocking even more electrons out of place. All of these electrons would continue hurtling snowball-like toward the earth, if it weren't for a tug-of-war that begins with the positively charged particles in the top of the cloud.

The stepped leader

Those positive charges at the top of the cloud tend to pull slower-moving electrons back upward. But remember, as the storm develops, more charges separate in the cloud. Newly freed electrons pull the slow

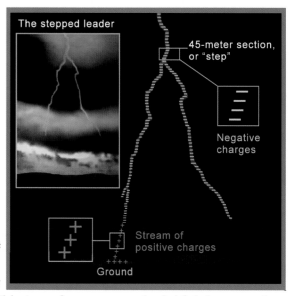

movers down again. This tug-of-war causes the initial downward path of electrons to move toward the ground in jerky 45-meter sections, or steps. This pathway is called the stepped leader.

Sometimes the stepped leader continues all the way down to the ground, but at other times, it will pull a stream of positive charges up to meet it about 100 meters above the ground. The stepped leader moves at about 390 kilometers per second, and takes about 5/1000 of a second to reach the ground. You can't see the stepped leader without using a special camera, because it moves so quickly and doesn't produce a lot of light.

A wire of plasma

The stepped leader is created as electrons knock other electrons off of air molecules. When these air molecules break apart, you end up with a pathway made of positive ions surrounded by a "sea" of electrons. That's a bit like what you find in a wire made of metal. The stepped leader creates a "wire" of *plasma* (a separate state of matter made up of ionized gas) in the atmosphere. This plasma wire, with all its freed electrons, conducts electricity extremely well.

The return stroke

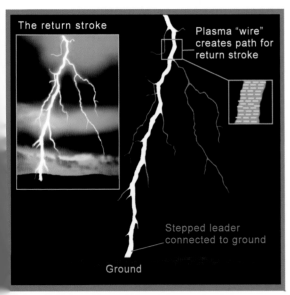

Once the stepped leader is connected to the ground, an amazing surge of electrons moves along the plasma wire from cloud to ground, traveling 98,000 kilometers per second! The air glows like a super-bright fluorescent light. This "return stroke" is the lightning you see.

The return stroke drains the cloud of its freed electrons, but more charges are continually being separated in the cloud. As a result, an average of four lightning bolts in a row zing along a single path. That's why lightning sometimes seems to flicker.

Volts, amps, and lightning

Lightning bolts can deliver between 15,000,000 and 1,000,000,000 volts of electricity. Although the flow of charge is very brief, the current has been estimated at about 50,000 amps. That much current can cause a great deal of damage. If a lightning bolt strikes a tree, the sap may boil, and the buildup of vapor pressure can cause the tree to explode.

Questions:

1. Name two ways a lightning bolt is like a static shock.
2. How does the stepped leader create a "plasma wire" in the atmosphere?
3. Find out how to stay safe during a lightning storm. Create a poster with lightning safety tips.

Chapter 15 Review

Understanding Vocabulary

Select the correct term to complete the sentences.

electric field	coulomb	polarized
electrically neutral	field lines	capacitor
electroscope	friction	static electricity
farads	induction	Coulomb's law

Section 15.1

1. The unit in which charge is measured is the _____.

2. An object is _____ when it has equal numbers of positive and negative charges.

3. _____ exists when there is an excess of one type of charge on an object.

4. _____ explains the relationship between electric force, charge, and distance.

5. Charging by _____ occurs when clothes brush against each other in the dryer.

6. A(n) _____ can be used to tell whether an object has a net charge.

7. If you use a charged balloon to charge a metal ball through _____, the balloon's net charge does not change.

Section 15.2

8. _____ are drawn to show the direction of the electric field.

9. An object is _____ if has a net positive charge on one side and a net negative charge on the other side.

10. There is a(n) _____ in the region around any charge.

Section 15.3

11. A _____ is used to store electrical energy by separating charge.

12. Capacitance is measured in _____.

Reviewing Concepts

Section 15.1

1. Protons are _____ charged, and electrons are _____ charged.

2. Like charges _____, and opposite charges _____.

3. What does it mean to say an object is electrically neutral?

4. In an object's net charge positive or negative if it loses electrons?

5. How many protons are needed to make one coulomb of charge?

6. How does the charge of an electron compare to the charge of a proton?

7. Why don't you usually notice electric forces between objects?

8. What two factors determine the amount of electric force between two objects?

9. What happens to the force between two charges as they are moved closer together?

10. Explain what happens to the force between two protons if each of the following occurs (consider each individually).
    a. The distance between them is cut in half.
    b. The distance between is doubled.
    c. The distance between them is tripled.
    d. One of the protons is replaced with an electron.
    e. One of the protons is replaced with two electrons.

11. Compare Coulomb's law to Newtons' law of gravitation.

12. Explain what happens inside an electroscope if a positively charged object is held above it without touching.

13. Explain how to charge an electroscope negatively through contact.

14. What happens to the charges in your hair and a balloon if you rub them together? What is this called?

15. Explain how to charge an electroscope positively through induction.

Section 15.2

16. How are the units *ampere* and *coulomb* related?

17. Ben Franklin defined current as going from _____ to _____. Now we know that electrons in a circuit move from _____ to _____.

18. Do all the electrons in a wire move to make the current in a circuit?

19. Does a battery supply the electrons to a circuit that create current in a circuit? Explain.

20. Why can current easily be created in a conductor but not in an insulator?

21. One volt equals one _____ of energy per _____ of charge. A volt is also equal to one _____ of power per _____ of current.

Section 15.3

22. What is a capacitor? What use do capacitors have?

23. What does it mean to say a capacitor is charged?

24. What happens to the current in a circuit as a capacitor charges? Why?

25. Which three factors affect a capacitor's capacitance?

Solving Problems

Section 15.1

1. What is the charge of 1000 electrons, measured in coulombs?

2. Find the net charge of an atom that contains
   a. 5 protons and 3 electrons
   b. 7 electrons and 6 protons
   c. 8 electrons and 8 protons

3. Six coulombs of charge pass through a wire in a time of two seconds. What is the current in the wire?

4. A wire carries a current of two amperes. How many coulombs of charge pass through the wire in 10 seconds?

Section 15.2

1. A circuit contains a 3 volt battery and a 2 ohm resistor.
   a. Calculate the current in the circuit.
   b. How many coulombs of charge pass by any point in the circuit in one second?
   c. How many coulombs of charge pass by any point in 2 seconds?

6. A battery provides 2 amperes of current in a circuit at a power of 6 watts. What is the battery's voltage?

7. A battery provides 6 joules of energy to 2 coulombs of charge in a circuit. What is the battery's voltage?

Section 15.3

8. How much charge does a 3 farad capacitor hold when charged with a 1.5 volt battery?

9. How much charge will a 6 farad capacitor hold if charged with a 1.5 volt battery?

10. How much charge will a 6 farad capacitor hold if charged with a 3 volt battery?

Applying Your Knowledge

Section 15.1

1. Static cling causes clothes to stick together when they come out of the dryer. What kinds of materials seem to stick together the most?

2. Static electricity is more often observed in dry weather than in damp weather. Why do you think this is?

3. How did Coulomb measure the force between electric charges? Research to find out the answer.

4. Conduct an experiment at home in which you charge an object by friction. You might use a balloon and hair or fleece, styrofoam and wool, or plastic and a tissue. Turn on a faucet so a narrow stream of water is created. Hold the charged object near the stream of water. What happens? What do you think is going on? Hint: water molecules are naturally polarized.

Section 15.2

5. Research superconductivity. Find out what it is and what applications it may have in the future.

Section 15.3

6. Research capacitors to find out how they are used in different electrical devices.

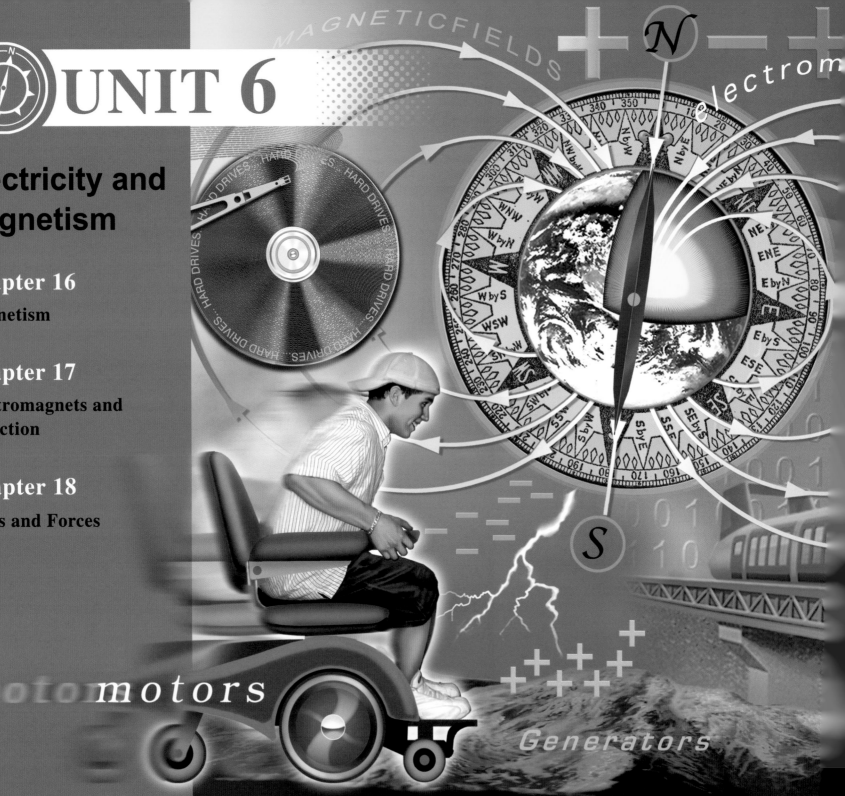

UNIT 6

Electricity and Magnetism

Chapter 16

16

Magnetism

Have you ever used a compass? A compass is very handy when you are on an open body of water with no land in sight, and you are trying to make sure you are headed in the right direction. It is also a good idea to have a compass with you if you are hiking. Some automobiles now come equipped with a built-in compass, and some even use more sophisticated global positioning system technology, which uses satellites rather than magnetic fields to determine direction.

How does a compass work? A simple compass is really nothing more than a lightweight magnet, in the shape of a pointer, that is mounted on a very low-friction pivot point. Earth, with its molten iron and nickel core, acts as though a giant magnet was buried deep inside, with the south pole end of the magnet located at the geographic North Pole. When you hold a compass in your hand, (and there is no other magnet nearby), the small pivoting magnet in the compass will be attracted by the geographic North Pole of Earth, and it will "point" north.

In this chapter, you will learn how magnets and magnetic fields work, and you will explore the source of magnetism. As with electricity, the source of magnetism can be traced back to atoms!

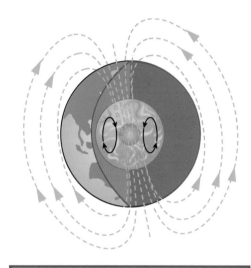

Key Questions
- ✓ How can a magnet be strong enough to lift a car?
- ✓ What is the biggest magnet on Earth?
- ✓ How does a compass work?

359

16.1 Properties of Magnets

Magnetism has fascinated people since the earliest times. We know that magnets stick to refrigerators and pick up paper clips or pins. They are also found in electric motors, computer disk drives, burglar alarm systems, and many other common devices. This chapter explains some of the properties of magnets and magnetic materials.

What is a magnet?

Magnets and magnetic materials
If a material is **magnetic**, it has the ability to exert forces on magnets or other magnetic materials. A magnet on a refrigerator is attracted to the steel in the refrigerator's door. A *magnet* is a material that can create magnetic effects by itself. *Magnetic materials* are affected by magnets but do not actively create their own magnetism. Iron and steel are magnetic materials that can also be magnets.

Permanent magnets
A **permanent magnet** is a material that keeps its magnetic properties, even when it is not close to other magnets. Bar magnets, refrigerator magnets, and horseshoe magnets are good examples of permanent magnets.

Bar magnet

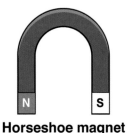
Horseshoe magnet

Magnetic materials

Poles
All magnets have two opposite **magnetic poles**, called the north pole and south pole. If a magnet is cut in half, each half will have its own north and south poles (Figure 16.1). It is impossible to have only a north or south pole by itself. The north and south poles are like the two sides of a coin. You cannot have a one-sided coin, and you cannot have a north magnetic pole without a south pole.

Vocabulary

magnetic, permanent magnet, magnetic poles, magnetic field, magnetic field lines

Objectives

✓ Recognize that magnetic poles always exist in pairs.

✓ Decide whether two magnetic poles will attract or repel.

✓ Describe the magnetic field and forces around a permanent magnet.

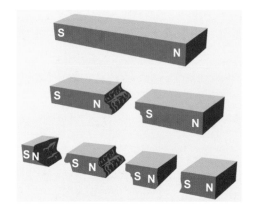

Figure 16.1: *If a magnet is cut in half, each half will have both a north pole and a south pole.*

The magnetic force

Attraction and repulsion

When near each other, magnets exert forces. Two magnets can either attract or repel. Whether the force between two magnets is attractive or repulsive depends on which poles face each other. If two opposite poles face each other, the magnets attract. If two of the same poles face each other, the magnets repel.

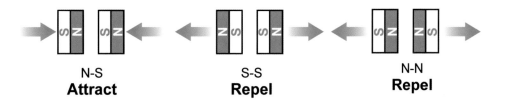

The three interactions between two magnets

N-S
Attract

S-S
Repel

N-N
Repel

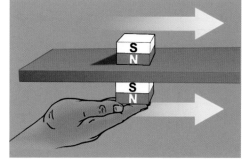

Figure 16.2: *The force between two magnets depends on how the poles are aligned.*

Most materials are transparent to magnetic forces

Magnetic forces can pass through many materials with no apparent decrease in strength. For example, one magnet can drag another magnet even when there is a piece of wood between them (Figure 16.2). Plastics, wood, and most insulating materials are transparent to magnetic forces. Conducting metals, such as aluminum, also allow magnetic forces to pass through, but may change the forces. Iron and a few metals near it on the periodic table have strong magnetic properties. Iron and iron-like metals can block magnetic forces and are discussed later in this chapter.

Using magnetic forces

Magnetic forces are used in many applications because they are relatively easy to create and can be very strong. There are large magnets that create forces strong enough to lift a car or even a moving train (Figure 16.3). Small magnets are everywhere; for example, some doors are sealed with magnetic weatherstripping that blocks out drafts. There are several patents for magnetic zippers and many handbags, briefcases, and cabinet doors close with magnetic latches. Many everyday devices rely on magnetic forces to make objects attract or repel one another. You could also use electric forces, but large-scale electric forces are harder to create and control than magnetic forces. Electrical forces tend to be much more important on the atomic level.

Figure 16.3: *Powerful magnets are used to lift discarded cars in a junkyard.*

The magnetic field

How to describe magnetic forces? Two magnets create forces on each other at a distance much larger than the size of the magnets. How do you describe the force everywhere around a magnet? One way is with a formula, like Newton's Law of Universal Gravitation. Unfortunately, magnetic forces are more complex than gravity because magnets can attract and repel. Gravity can only attract. Also, magnets all have two poles. That means part of the same magnet feels an attracting force and part feels a repelling force. While there *are* formulas for the magnetic force, they are complicated and usually used with computers.

The test magnet A convenient way to show the magnetic force around a magnet is with a drawing. The standard drawing shows the force acting on the north pole of an imaginary test magnet. The test magnet is so small that it does not affect the magnetic force. Also, since the test magnet is imaginary, we can let it have only a north pole. Having only one pole makes it easier to visualize the direction of the magnetic force (Figure 16.4).

Drawing the force The diagram shows a drawing of the magnetic force around a magnet. The force points away from the north pole because a north pole would be repelled from a north pole. The force points toward the south pole because a north pole magnet would be attracted.

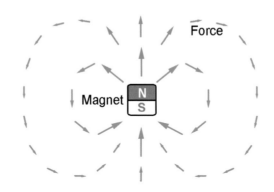

The magnetic field The drawing shows what physicists call the **magnetic field**. A *field* in physics is a quantity that has a value at all points in space. A magnet creates a field because it creates a force on other magnets at all points around itself. The interaction between two magnets really occurs in two steps. First, a magnet creates a magnetic field. Then the magnetic field creates forces on other magnets. In the drawing the field is represented by the arrows.

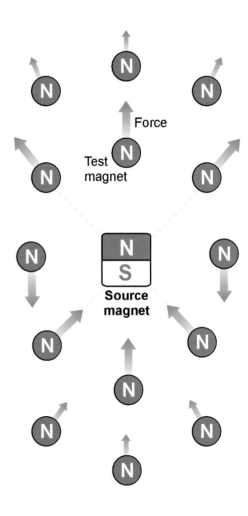

Figure 16.4: *The force on an imaginary north magnetic pole (test magnet) near a source magnet.*

Drawing the magnetic field

Drawing a magnetic field

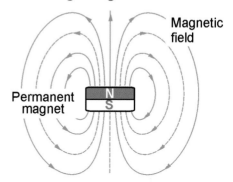

Describing magnetic force

The magnetic field is a *force field*, because it represents a force at all points in space. Every magnet creates a magnetic field in the space around it. The magnetic field then creates forces on other magnets. The idea of fields is relatively new and very important in physics. In chapter 18 you learn about other kinds of fields.

Field lines

The magnet that creates a field is called the *source magnet*. In the standard drawing of a magnetic field, the arrows we drew on the previous page are connected together into **magnetic field lines**. Magnetic field lines point in the direction of the force on an imaginary north pole test magnet. Magnetic field lines always point away from a north pole and toward a south pole.

Magnetic field lines always point away from a magnet's north pole and toward its south pole.

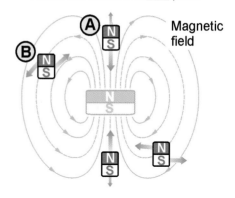

Reading a magnetic field
Forces are exerted on <u>both</u> poles

Understanding magnetic field lines

A field line must start on a north pole and finish on a south pole. You cannot just "stop" a field line anywhere. In the drawing in Figure 16.5 notice that the field lines spread out as they get farther away from the source magnet. If field lines are close together, the force is stronger. If field lines are farther apart, the force is weaker. The field lines spread out because the force from a magnet gets weaker as distance from the magnet increases.

Reading a magnetic field drawing

Figure 16.5 shows you how to "read" a magnetic field drawing. Magnet A will feel a net attracting force toward the source magnet. The north pole of magnet A feels a repelling force, but is farther away than the south pole. Since the south pole of magnet A is closest, the net force is attracting. Magnet B feels a twisting (torque) force because its north pole is repelled and its south pole is attracted with approximately the same strength.

Figure 16.5: *The magnetic field is defined in terms of the force exerted on the north pole of another magnet.*

16.1 Section Review

1. Is it possible to have a magnetic south pole without a north pole? Explain your answer.

2. Describe the interaction between each set of magnetic poles: two north poles; a north and south pole; two south poles.

3. What does the direction of magnetic field lines tell you?

16.2 The Source of Magnetism

It seems strange that magnets can attract and repel each other but can only *attract* objects such as steel paper clips and nails. The explanation for this lies inside atoms. Magnetism is created by moving charges, either in an electric current or in the atoms that make up a material. This section takes a closer look at how magnetism is created.

Electromagnets

A coil of wire   **Electromagnets** are magnets created by electric current flowing in wires. A simple electromagnet is a coil of wire wrapped around an iron core (Figure 16.6). When the coil is connected to a battery, current flows and a magnetic field appears around the coil, just as if the coil were a permanent magnet. The iron core concentrates and amplifies the magnetic field created by the current in the coil.

The poles of an electromagnet   The north and south poles of an electromagnet are at each end of the coil. Which end is the north pole depends on the direction of the electric current. When the fingers of your right hand curl in the direction of current, your thumb points toward the magnet's north pole. This method of finding the magnetic poles is called the **right-hand rule**.

Advantages of electromagnets   Electromagnets have some big advantages over permanent magnets. You can switch an electromagnet on and off by switching the current on and off. You can switch an electromagnet's north and south poles by reversing the direction of the current in the coil. The strength of an electromagnet's field can be changed by changing the amount of current in the coil. Electromagnets can also be much stronger than permanent magnets because they can use large currents.

One use for an electromagnet   Electromagnets are used in many devices around your house. One example is a toaster. The switch you press down both turns on the heating circuit and sends current to an electromagnet. The electromagnet attracts a spring-loaded metal tray to the bottom of the toaster. When a timer signals that the bread is done toasting, the electromagnet's current is cut off. This releases the spring-loaded tray, which pops the bread out of the toaster.

Objectives

- ✓ Learn how to build a simple electromagnet and change its strength.
- ✓ Use the right-hand rule to locate an electromagnet's poles.
- ✓ Explain the source of magnetism in materials.

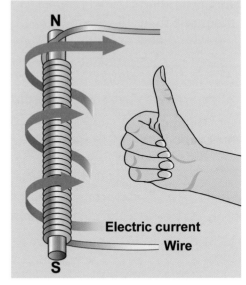

Figure 16.6: *If the fingers of your right hand curl in the direction of the current, your thumb points toward the north pole.*

Building an electromagnet

Wire and a nail
You can easily build an electromagnet from a piece of wire and an iron nail. Wrap the wire snugly around the nail many times and connect a battery as shown in Figure 16.7. When there is current in the wire, the nail and coil become magnetic. Use the right-hand rule to figure out which end of the nail is the north pole and which is the south pole. To switch the poles, reverse the connection to the battery, making the current go the opposite direction.

Increase the electromagnet's strength
There are two ways you can make the electromagnet's field stronger:

1. You can add a second battery to increase the current.
2. You can add more turns of wire around the nail.

Field is proportional to current
The strength of the magnetic field is directly proportional to the amount of current flowing around the nail. If you double the current, the strength of the magnetic field doubles.

Why adding turns of wire works
Adding turns of wire increases the field because the magnetism in your electromagnet comes from the *total* amount of current flowing *around* the nail (Figure 16.8). If there is 1 ampere of current in the wire, each loop of wire adds 1 ampere to the total amount of current flowing around the nail. Ten loops of 1 ampere each make 10 total amperes. By adding more turns, you use the same current over and over to create more magnetism.

Resistance
Of course, every gain has its cost. By adding more turns in order to strengthen the magnetism, you also increase the resistance of your coil. Increasing the resistance lowers the current a little and generates more heat. A good electromagnet design is a balance between having enough turns to make the magnet strong and not making the resistance too high.

Factors affecting the field
The magnetic field of a simple electromagnet depends on three factors:

- The amount of electric current in the wire.
- The amount and type of material in the electromagnet's core.
- The number of turns in the coil.

In more sophisticated electromagnets, the shape, size, and material of the core, and the winding pattern of the coil are specially designed to control the strength and shape of the magnetic field.

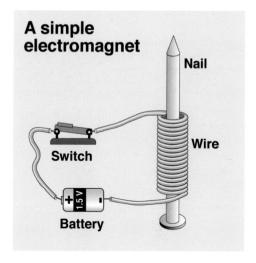

Figure 16.7: *Making an electromagnet from a nail, wire, and a battery.*

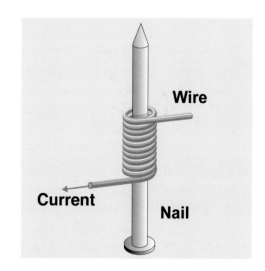

Figure 16.8: *Adding turns of wire increases the total current flowing around the electromagnet. The total current in all the turns is what determines the strength of the electromagnet.*

Magnetism in materials

Electric currents cause all magnetism
Once scientists discovered that electric current can make magnetism, they soon realized that *all magnetism comes from electric currents*. Each electron in an atom behaves like a small loop of current forming its own miniature electromagnet. All atoms have electrons, so you might think that all materials would be magnetic. In reality, we find great variability in the magnetic properties of materials. That variability comes from the arrangement of electrons in different atoms.

Diamagnetic materials
In many elements the magnetic fields of individual electrons in each atom cancel with each other. This leaves the whole atom with zero net magnetic field. Materials made of these kinds of atoms are called **diamagnetic**. Lead and diamond are examples of diamagnetic materials. Holding a magnet up to lead or diamond produces no effect. If you try hard enough, you can see magnetic effects in diamagnetic materials but it takes either a *very strong* magnetic field or very sensitive instruments.

Paramagnetic materials
Aluminum is an example of a **paramagnetic** material. In an atom of aluminum the magnetism of individual electrons does not cancel completely. This makes each aluminum atom into a tiny magnet with a north and a south pole. However, the atoms in a piece of aluminum are randomly arranged, so the alignment of the north and south poles changes from one atom to the next. Even a tiny piece of aluminum has trillions of atoms. Solid aluminum is "nonmagnetic" because the total magnetic field averages to zero over many atoms (top of Figure 16.9).

Magnetic fields in paramagnetic materials
We classify paramagnetic materials as "nonmagnetic." However, they do show weak magnetic activity that can be detected using sensitive instruments. If you hold the north pole of a permanent magnet near aluminum, it attracts the south poles of aluminum atoms nearby. Some atoms change their alignments (Figure 16.9). A weak overall magnetic field is created in the aluminum, so it weakly attracts the external magnet. When the permanent magnet is pulled away, the atoms go back to their random arrangement and the magnetic field disappears.

 **Atom**

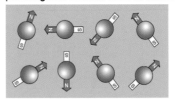

Each atom is a tiny weak magnet in a paramagnetic material such as aluminum.

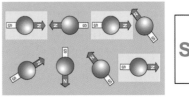

A permanent magnet causes some atoms to change their alignments.

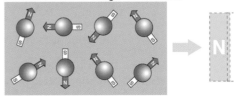

The atoms go back to their original directions when the magnet is removed.

Figure 16.9: *Atoms in a paramagnetic material such as aluminum are tiny magnets. A piece of aluminum is not magnetic because the atoms are arranged in random directions. However, weak magnetic effects can be created because a permanent magnet can temporarily change the orientation of the atom-size magnets near the surface.*

Ferromagnetic materials

Ferromagnetism
A small group of **ferromagnetic** metals have very strong magnetic properties. The best examples of ferromagnetic materials are iron, nickel, and cobalt. Like paramagnetic atoms, the electrons in a ferromagnetic atom do not cancel each other's magnetic fields completely. Each atom is therefore a tiny magnet. The difference is that individual atoms of ferromagnetic materials do *not* act randomly like atoms in paramagnetic materials. Instead, atoms align themselves with neighboring atoms in groups called **magnetic domains**. Because atoms in a domain are aligned with each other the magnetic fields of individual atoms add up. This gives each magnetic domain a relatively strong overall magnetic field.

Why all steel is not magnets
Each domain may contain millions of atoms but the overall size of a domain still small by normal standards. There are hundreds of domains in a steel paper clip. The domains in a steel paper clip are randomly arranged, so their magnetic fields cancel each other out (top of Figure 16.10). That is why a paper clip does not produce a magnetic field all the time.

Aligning domains
Ferromagnetic materials have strong magnetism because domains can grow very quickly by "adopting" atoms from neighboring domains. When a magnet is brought near a steel paper clip, magnetic domains that attract the magnet grow and domains that repel the magnet shrink. The paper clip quickly builds a magnetic field that attracts the magnet, no matter which pole is used (Figure 16.10). When the magnet is pulled away the domains tend to go back to their random orientation and the magnetism goes away.

Hard and soft magnets
Permanent magnets are created when the magnetic domains become so well aligned that they stay aligned even after the external magnet is removed. A steel paper clip can be *magnetized* (aligned magnetic domains) to make a weak permanent magnet by rubbing it with another magnet or with a strong magnetic field. Steel is a **soft magnet** because it is easy to magnetize but loses its magnetization easily too. Heat, shock, and other magnets can demagnetize steel. Materials that make better permanent magnets are called **hard magnets**. The domains in hard magnets tend to remain aligned for a long time. Strong electromagnets are used to magnetize hard magnets.

Unmagnetized
magnetic domains

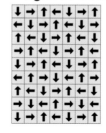

 North / South

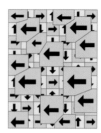

Magnetization
by a north pole

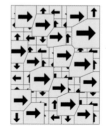

Magnetization
by a south pole

Figure 16.10: *A permanent magnet temporarily magnetizes a section of a paper clip.*

Magnetism in solids

High temperature destroys magnetism Permanent magnets are created when atoms arrange themselves so they are magnetically aligned with each other. Anything that breaks the alignment destroys the magnetism, so "permanent" magnets are not necessarily permanent. In chapter 7 you learned that atoms are always moving due to temperature. Temperature is the enemy of magnetism because temperature creates disorder between atoms. All permanent magnets become demagnetized if the temperature gets too hot. The best magnetic materials are able to retain their magnetism only up to a few hundred degrees Celsius. A permanent magnet can also be demagnetized by strong shocks or other (stronger) magnets.

Liquids and gases Permanent magnetism only exists in solids. There are no liquid or gaseous permanent magnets. Liquids or gases cannot be permanent magnets because the atoms have too much thermal energy to stay aligned with each other.

Materials for permanent magnets The strongest permanent magnets are made from ceramics containing nickel and cobalt, or the rare earth metal neodymium. Using these materials, it is possible to manufacture magnets that are very small but also very strong and harder to demagnetize than steel magnets.

Soft magnets Soft magnets are easy to magnetize with other magnets. You can see both the magnetization and demagnetization of paper clips or small iron nails using a magnet (Figure 16.11). If you use the north end of a bar magnet to pick up a nail, the nail becomes magnetized with its south pole toward the magnet. Because the nail itself becomes a magnet, it can be used to pick up other nails. If you separate that first nail from the bar magnet, the entire chain demagnetizes and falls apart.

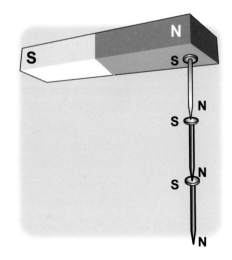

Figure 16.11: *Iron nails become temporarily magnetized when placed near a magnet.*

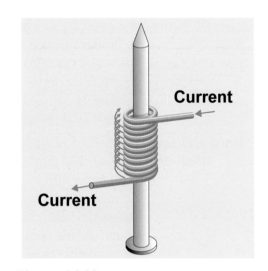

Figure 16.12: *Can you determine the location of the north and south poles of this electromagnet?*

16.2 Section Review

1. Use the right-hand rule to find the north and south poles in Figure 16.12.

2. List two ways to increase the strength of the electromagnet in Figure 16.12.

3. How is magnetism in an electromagnet related to magnetism in a permanent magnet?

4. Explain what happens when a ferromagnetic material is made into a permanent magnet.

5. Are permanent magnets truly permanent? Explain.

16.3 Earth's Magnetic Field

The biggest magnet on Earth is the planet itself. Earth has a magnetic field that has been useful to travelers for thousands of years. Compasses, which contain small magnets, interact with the Earth's magnetic field to indicate direction. Certain animals, including migratory birds, can feel the magnetic field of Earth and use their magnetic sense to tell which direction is north or south.

Discovering and using magnetism

Lodestone
As early as 500 B.C. people discovered that some naturally occurring materials had magnetic properties. The Greeks observed that one end of a suspended piece of *lodestone* pointed north and the other end pointed south, helping sailors and travelers find their way. This discovery led to the first important application of magnetism: the **compass** (Figure 16.13).

The Chinese "south pointer"
The invention of the compass was also recorded in China in 220 B.C. Writings from the Zheng dynasty tell stories of how people would use a "south pointer" when they went out to search for jade, so that they wouldn't lose their way home. The pointer was made of lodestone. It looked like a large spoon with a short, skinny handle. When balanced on a plate, the "handle" aligned with magnetic south.

The first iron needle compass
By 1088 A.D., iron refining had developed to the point that the Chinese were making a small needlelike compass. Shen Kua recorded that a needle-shaped magnet was placed on a reed floating in a bowl of water. Chinese inventors also suspended a long, thin magnet in the air, realizing that the magnet ends were aligned with geographic north and south. Explorers from the Sung dynasty sailed their trading ships all the way to Saudi Arabia using compasses among their navigational tools. About 100 years later a similar design appeared in Europe and soon spread through the civilized world.

Compasses and exploration
By 1200, explorers from Italy were using a compass to guide ocean voyages beyond the sight of land. The Chinese also continued exploring with compasses, and by the 1400s were traveling to the east coast of Africa. The compass, and the voyages it made possible, led to many interactions among cultures.

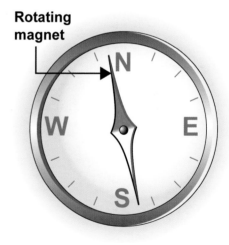

Rotating magnet

Figure 16.13: *A compass is made of a small bar magnet that is able to rotate.*

How does a compass work?

A compass is a magnet
A compass needle is a magnet that is free to spin. The needle spins until it lines up with any magnetic field that is present. (Figure 16.14). The north pole of a compass needle always points toward the south pole of a permanent magnet. This is in the direction of the magnetic field lines. Because the needle aligns with the local magnetic field, a compass is a great way to "see" magnetic field lines.

North and south poles
The origin of the terms "north pole" and "south pole" of a magnet comes from the direction that a magnetized compass needle points. The end of the magnet that pointed toward geographic north was called the magnet's north pole and the opposite pole was called south. The names were decided long before people truly understood how a compass needle worked.

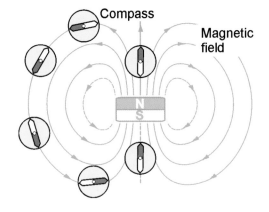

Figure 16.14: *A compass needle lines up with a magnetic field.*

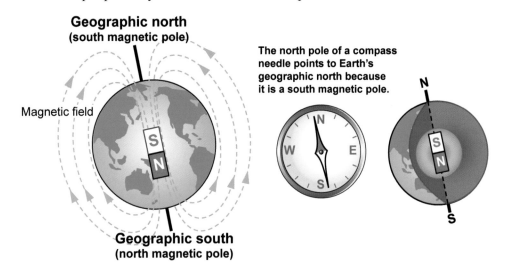

Geographic north
(south magnetic pole)

Magnetic field

The north pole of a compass needle points to Earth's geographic north because it is a south magnetic pole.

Geographic south
(north magnetic pole)

Geographic and magnetic poles
The true *geographic* north and south poles are where the Earth's axis of rotation intersects its surface. Earth's *magnetic* poles are defined by the planet's magnetic field. When you use a compass, the north-pointing end of the needle points toward a spot near (but not exactly at) Earth's geographic north pole. That means the *south magnetic pole* of the planet is near the north geographic pole. The Earth has a planetary magnetic field that acts as if the core of the planet contained a giant magnet oriented like the diagram above.

Some animals have biological compasses

Many animals, including species of birds, frogs, fish, turtles, and bacteria, can sense the planet's magnetic field. Migratory birds are the best known examples. Magnetite, a magnetic mineral made of iron oxide, has been found in bacteria and in the brains of birds. Tiny crystals of magnetite may act like compasses and allow these organisms to sense the small magnetic field of Earth. Samples of magnetite are common in rock collections or kits.

Magnetic declination and "true north"

Magnetic declination

Because Earth's geographic north pole (true north) and magnetic south pole are not located at the exact same place, a compass will not point *directly* to the geographic north pole. Depending on where you are, a compass will point slightly east or west of true north. The difference between the direction a compass points and the direction of true north is called **magnetic declination**. Magnetic declination is measured in degrees and is indicated on topographical maps.

Finding true north with a compass

Most good compasses contain an adjustable ring with a degree scale and an arrow that can be turned to point toward the destination on a map (Figure 16.15). The ring is turned the appropriate number of degrees to compensate for the declination. Suppose you are using a compass and the map shown below and you want to travel directly north. You do not simply walk in the direction of the compass needle. To go north, you must walk in a direction 16 degrees west of the way the needle points.

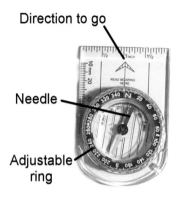

Figure 16.15: *Most compasses have an adjustable ring with a degree scale and an arrow that can be turned to a point toward the destination on a map.*

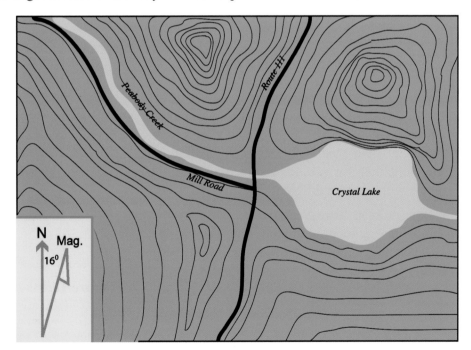

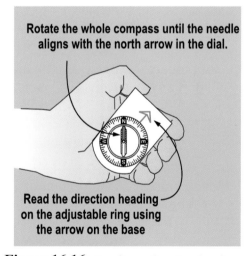

Figure 16.16: *Reading a direction heading (angle) from a compass*

The source of the Earth's magnetism

Earth's magnetic core
While Earth's core is magnetic, we know it is not a solid permanent magnet. Studies of earthquake waves reveal that the Earth's core is made of hot, dense molten iron, nickel, and possibly other metals that slowly circulate around a solid inner core (Figure 16.17). Huge electric currents flowing in the molten iron produce the Earth's magnetic field, much like a giant electromagnet.

The strength of Earth's magnetic field
The magnetic field of Earth is weak compared to the field near the ceramic magnets you have in your classroom. For this reason you cannot trust a compass to point north if any other magnets are close by. The **gauss** is a unit used to measure the strength of a magnetic field. A small ceramic permanent magnet has a field between 300 and 1,000 gauss at its surface. By contrast, the magnetic field averages about 0.5 gauss at Earth's surface.

Reversing poles
Historical data shows that both the strength of the planet's magnetic field and the location of the north and south magnetic poles change over time. Studies of magnetized rocks in Earth's crust provide evidence that the poles have reversed many times over the last tens of millions of years. The reversal has happened every 500,000 years on average. The last field reversal occurred roughly 750,000 years ago so Earth is overdue for another switch of the planet's north and south magnetic poles.

The next reversal
Today, Earth's magnetic field is losing approximately 7 percent of its strength every 100 years. We do not know whether this trend will continue, but if it does, the magnetic poles will reverse sometime in the next 2,000 years. During a reversal, Earth's magnetic field would not completely disappear. However, the main magnetic field that we use for navigation would be replaced by several smaller fields with poles in different locations.

Movements of the magnetic poles
The location of Earth's magnetic poles is always changing—slowly—even between full reversals. Currently, the magnetic south pole (to which the north end of a compass points) is located about 1,000 kilometers (600 miles) from the geographic north pole (Figure 16.18).

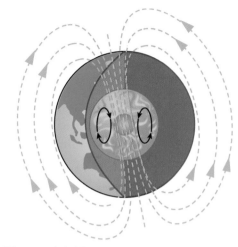

Figure 16.17: *Scientists believe moving charges in the molten core create Earth's magnetic field.*

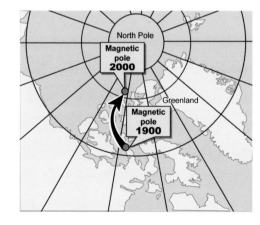

Figure 16.18: *The location of magnetic north changes over time. Magnetic north is where a compass needle points, and is actually Earth's magnetic south pole.*

Magnetism in stars and planets

Planets and moons

Magnetism is created by moving electric charge. Like the Earth, other planets in the Solar System also have magnetic fields. In the case of Jupiter the magnetic field is very strong and was mapped by the Cassini spacecraft Smaller bodies like the Moon do not have much magnetic field. The Moon is too small and cold to have a hot, liquid core.

The sun's magnetic field

Even stars have magnetic fields. Our most important star, the sun, has a strong magnetic field. Like Earth, the sun also rotates with a "day" of about 25 Earth days. Because the sun is not solid, different parts of the sun rotate at different rates. The sun rotates once every 25 days at its "equator" but takes 35 days to rotate once near its poles. The sun's uneven rotation twists the magnetic field lines. Every so often, the magnetic field lines become so twisted they "snap" and reconnect themselves. This sudden change causes huge solar storms where great eruptions of hot gas flare up from the sun's surface (Figure 16.19). The energy released by the sun's magnetic storms is great enough to disrupt radio and cell phone signals here on Earth. Magnetism also causes sunspots, regions of relative darkness on the sun's surface.

Energy for the Earth's field

The electrical currents that create Earth's magnetic field would quickly stop flowing if energy were not constantly being added. As the Earth moves in its orbit around the sun, its magnetic field acts like a giant net, sweeping up free electrons and protons flowing out from the sun. These charged particles create an electrical current that flows in and out through the planet's poles. This current in turn feeds energy into the planet's core, driving the currents that maintain the Earth's magnetic field.

The sun rotates faster at its equator than at its poles.

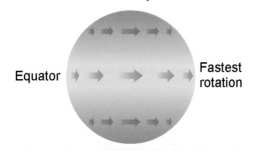

Equator — Fastest rotation

Courtesy NASA

Figure 16.19: *The sun rotates unevenly because it is not solid, but a ball of hot gas. This twists the sun's magnetic field resulting in both sunspots and also huge magnetic storms (lower photo).*

16.3 Section Review

1. Describe one of the early compasses people used to indicate direction.
2. How does a compass respond when it is placed in the magnetic field of a bar magnet?
3. What is the cause of Earth's magnetism?
4. Is Earth's magnetic north pole at the same location as the geographic north pole?

What is an MRI Scanner?

Has anyone ever told you that you have a magnetic personality? Well, here's a machine with one—an MRI scanner. MRI stands for Magnetic Resonance Imaging—a device that uses magnetism and radio waves to scan all or part of a body that may be sick or injured.

Unlike X rays, which have been around for over 100 years, the MRI scanner is a relatively new medical diagnostic tool, having first been used in 1977. The first MRI scanners were very large and intimidating, extremely loud, and slow with a single scan taking several hours. Fortunately, these machines have come a long way. Although they still are still large and loud, they are faster, and produce better results in diagnosing illness and injury.

MRIs are especially valuable as diagnostic tools because they are non-invasive. In other words, information about a person's body can be obtained without probes or cutting tissue. You may be wondering how an MRI "sees" inside a sick or injured body. This device uses magnetism, radio waves, and a lot of computer power to create images. To understand how the MRI works, let's examine each concept represented in the name of this technology—magnetism, resonance, and imaging.

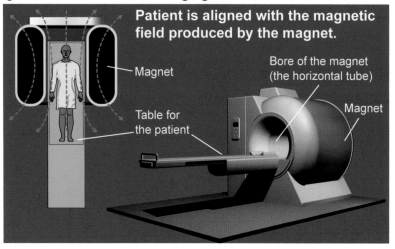

Patient is aligned with the magnetic field produced by the magnet.

Magnet

Bore of the magnet (the horizontal tube)

Magnet

Table for the patient

The role of magnetism

MRIs contain powerful magnets. The strength of common magnets such as ones found in motors or sound speakers ranges from a few hundred to a few thousand gauss. A *gauss* is a unit used to measure the strength of a magnetic field. The magnets in MRIs range from 5,000 to 20,000 gauss. Since 10,000 gauss equals 1 tesla, this translates to 0.5 to 2.0 tesla. In comparison, the strength of Earth's magnetic field is 0.3 to 0.5 gauss or 3×10^{-4} to 5×10^{-4} tesla.

There are two kinds of magnets used in an MRI. The main magnet creates a very strong magnetic field. The gradient magnets create a changing magnetic field.

The main magnet is used to temporarily "polarize" the nuclei of certain atoms in parts of the body. These atoms become tiny magnets in the body with a north and south pole. This process is similar to how an iron nail can be

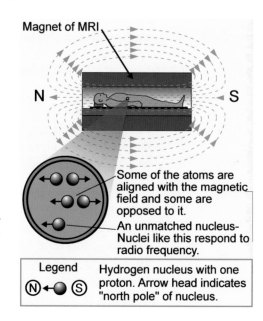

Magnet of MRI

N

S

Some of the atoms are aligned with the magnetic field and some are opposed to it.

An unmatched nucleus- Nuclei like this respond to radio frequency.

Legend — Hydrogen nucleus with one proton. Arrow head indicates "north pole" of nucleus.

$(N) \leftarrow \bullet (S)$

"magnetized" by rubbing a magnet along its length in one direction. Actually, all substances are capable of becoming internally "polarized" to some extent under the right conditions. This phenomenon is what makes an MRI work.

Some of the nuclei in a certain part of the body line up with the MRI magnetic field and some oppose it. Aligned and opposing nuclei cancel each other. Nuclei that are not cancelled are used to create the MRI image.

The role of the gradient magnets within the main magnet is to locate a particular area of the body to be imaged. The gradient magnets turn on and off quickly and cause changes in the magnetic field where a specific part of the body or a specific plane or "slice" of the body occurs. Unlike an X ray or CT scanner, which can only take scans of one plane at a time, the gradient magnets can take slices at virtually any angle. This not only produces a detailed picture of that slice, but image slices can be combined to form a two-dimensional (2-D) or three-dimensional (3-D) images.

The role of resonance

The effects of the main magnet and the gradient magnets set up conditions for creating an MRI scanner image using resonance. Resonance describes how an object responds when it receives a pulse of energy at its natural frequency. At its natural frequency, the object oscillates easily or "resonates." For example, if you speak into the sound box of a piano, some of the frequencies that make up your voice will match the natural frequencies of some of the strings, and set them oscillating!

For an MRI, radio waves, oscillating at thousands or even millions of cycles per second, are first produced by the on/off oscillations of an electrical current through a series of coils. The frequency of these oscillations (in the radio frequency part of the electromagnetic spectrum, or RF) is set to match the natural frequency of the nuclei of common elements found in the body, like hydrogen, carbon, or calcium. When the nuclei of atoms in the body absorb this specific energy, they too (like the strings in the piano) vibrate as they absorb and release energy.

The nuclei that respond to the RF are unmatched. The energy they absorb causes them to resonate and change their alignment in the magnetic field. When the RF is turned off, the unmatched nuclei return to their positions and give off energy which is captured by the MRI and used to make the final image.

Making images

Energy signals that are released by the unmatched nuclei are received by the coils are recorded as bits of mathematical data. This data is used to map the density of the particular atoms responding to the RF signal. A computer assembles the data and creates such a map and sends it to either a screen or film. The result is a clear, detailed picture of a part or "slice" of the body.

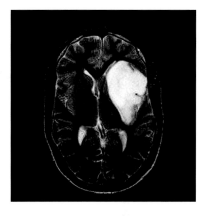

MRIs are commonly used to visualize, diagnose, and evaluate many abnormalities anywhere in the body due to disease or injury. As MRIs become more advanced, we will be able to use this wonderful application of physics to learn more about how the brain functions, how serious diseases develop and grow within the body, and how best to treat injured bone, tissue, and cartilage.

Questions:

1. What is the role of the main magnet in an MRI? What is the role of the gradient magnets?
2. In MRI technology what is it that resonates with radio waves that helps produce an MRI scanner image?
3. Imagine you had a choice of getting an MRI, a CAT scan, or an X ray. Research and describe what each procedure involves. List the pros and cons of each procedure. Which is the least expensive? Which is the most expensive?
4. MRI scanners are very safe devices. However, they do produce very strong magnetic fields that powerfully attract metal objects. Research the precautions that MRI facilities use when the strong magnetic field is turned on.

Chapter 16 Review

Understanding Vocabulary

Select the correct term to complete the sentences.

electromagnet	magnetic field	magnetic poles
right-hand rule	magnetic domains	diamagnetic
compass	magnetic declination	paramagnetic
soft magnet	permanent magnet	ferromagnetic
gauss		

Section 16.1

1. A _____ keeps its magnetic properties even when it is not near other magnets.

2. Every magnet has two _____.

3. A _____ is present in the region around a magnet.

Section 16.2

4. A(n) _____ is a magnet created by electric current in a wire.

5. You can use the _____ to figure out the locations of an electromagnet's poles.

6. A material that is _____ has the same number of electrons spinning in each direction, so there is no overall magnetic field.

7. In ferromagnetic materials, groups of atoms with the same magnetic alignment create _____.

8. _____ materials such as iron can create permanent magnets.

9. _____ materials are very weakly magnetic because electrons are randomly arranged.

10. A _____ quickly loses its magnetism when taken out of a magnetic field.

Section 16.3

11. The _____ is a unit used to measure the strength of magnetic fields.

12. A _____ is simply a permanent magnet that is free to spin.

13. The difference between the way a compass points and the direction of true north is called _____.

Reviewing Concepts

Section 16.1

1. What is a magnetic material able to do?

2. Suppose you stick a magnet on the door of your refrigerator. Is the magnet a magnetic material or a permanent magnet? Is the refrigerator door a magnetic material or permanent magnet? Explain.

3. Is it possible to have a south pole without a north pole or a north pole without a south pole? Explain.

4. What happens to a magnet if it is cut in half?

5. Two magnetic north poles _____ each other. Two south poles _____ each other. A north pole and a south pole _____ each other.

6. Can magnetic forces pass through non-magnetic materials?

7. List three uses for magnetism.

8. What describes the magnetic force in the space around a magnet?

9. Draw a bar magnet and sketch the magnetic field lines around it. Include arrows to show the direction of the lines.

10. Magnetic field lines outside a magnet point away from its _____ pole and toward its _____ pole.

11. What information can you get by looking at the spacing of magnetic field lines?

12. What happens to the strength of the magnetic field as you move away from a magnet?

Section 16.2

13. Explain the design of a simple electromagnet.

14. What is the purpose of the core of an electromagnet?

15. Explain how you can use the right-hand rule to determine the location of an electromagnet's poles.

16. What happens to an electromagnet's field if the current is increased?

17. What happens to an electromagnet's field if the direction of the current is reversed?

18. Describe two ways you could increase the strength of an electromagnet without increasing the current.

19. Why is it not always the best idea to increase an electromagnet's strength by simply increasing the current?

20. What advantages do electromagnets have over permanent magnets when used in machines?

21. Are diamagnetic materials magnetic? Why or why not?

22. Are paramagnetic materials magnetic? Why or why not?

23. What happens inside a paramagnetic material if a permanent magnet is brought close to it? What happens when the permanent magnet is removed?

24. List three ferromagnetic materials.

25. What are magnetic domains?

26. Which materials are more strongly magnetic, ferromagnetic or paramagnetic? Why?

27. Describe how to create a permanent magnet from a ferromagnetic material.

28. What is the difference between hard magnets and soft magnets?

29. Which is easier to magnetize, a hard magnet or a soft magnet? Once magnetized, which is easier to demagnetize?

30. List several ways to demagnetize a permanent magnet.

Section 16.3

31. For what purpose did people first use magnetism?

32. Describe the design of two early compasses.

33. Explain why the two ends of a magnet are called "north pole" and "south pole."

34. Is Earth's magnetic north pole at its geographic north pole? Explain.

35. Why does a compass point north?

36. Why is it important to know the magnetic declination in a region where you are using a compass to navigate?

37. How does the strength of Earth's field compare to the strength of the field of average permanent magnets?

38. What material is at the core of Earth?

39. What do scientists believe is the source of Earth's magnetism?

40. What has happened to the strength and location of Earth's magnetic field in the past?

41. If the current trend continues, how long do scientists think it will take for Earth's magnetic poles to reverse again?

Solving Problems

Section 16.1

1. A student knocked a ceramic permanent magnet off her desk, and it shattered when it hit the floor. Copy the broken pieces and label the north and south poles on each one.

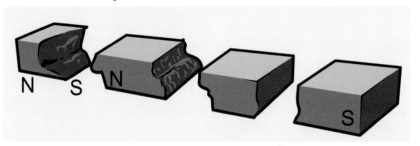

2. The diagram below shows the magnetic field in a region. The source of the field is not shown. At which of the labeled points in the diagram below is the magnetic field the strongest? At which point is it the weakest? Explain how you figured out your answers.

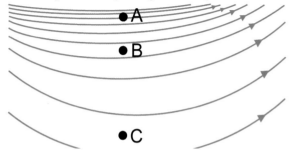

3. A horseshoe magnet is shown to the right. Copy the picture of the magnet and draw the magnetic field lines around it.

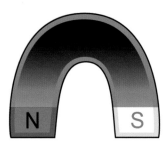

Section 16.2

4. Which picture below shows the correct location of the north and south poles of the electromagnet? Choose A or B and explain how you arrived at your choice.

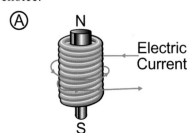

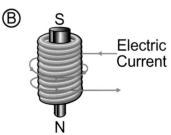

5. A permanent magnet attracts a steel pin as shown to the right. The pin has become a soft magnet. Copy the picture and then use what you know about magnetism to label the north and south poles of the pin.

6. A strong permanent magnet is brought near a piece of iron. Magnetic domains are created as shown below. Which pole of the permanent magnet is closest to the iron?

Iron   Permanent Magnet

Section 16.3

7. Suppose Earth's magnetic field were to change so it looks like the picture to the right. If you stand at the marked point, in which direction will your compass needle point? What is the approximate magnetic declination at this point?

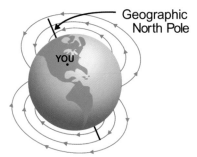

Applying Your Knowledge

Section 16.1

1. A story dating back 2,300 years describes Ptolemy Philadelphos' attempt at using magnetism. He had the dome of a temple at Alexandria made of magnetite and tried to suspend a statue of himself in midair. The experiment failed. However, you can use magnetism to suspend a small magnet by building a device like the one shown here. The upper magnet is fixed to a shelf or table. The lower one is held down with a thread. See how far apart you can position the magnets and still have the lower one levitate.

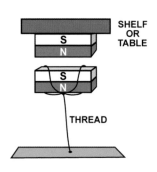

Section 16.2

2. Magnetically levitated or "maglev" trains use electromagnets to raise the train cars above the tracks to reduce friction. Research to find out where maglev trains are used and how they work.

Section 16.3

3. You can easily build your own compass using a sewing needle, permanent magnet, piece of cork or styrofoam, and dish of water. Run the magnet many times along the length of the needle, always in the same direction. Float a piece of cork or styrofoam in a cup of water. Place the needle on top of it and give it a gentle spin. When it stops, it will be lined up with Earth's magnetic field.

4. Find out the magnetic declination where you live.

Chapter 17

Electromagnets and Induction

Electricity and magnetism may not seem very similar. You don't get a shock from picking up a magnet! However, you can create magnetism with electric current in an electromagnet. Why does electric current create magnetism?

In 1819, a teacher named Hans Christian Øersted tried an experiment in front of his students for the first time. He passed electric current through a wire near a compass. To his surprise, the compass needle moved! A few years later Michael Faraday built the first electric motor. Today we know electricity and magnetism are two faces of the same basic force: the force between charges. In this chapter you will see how our knowledge of electricity and magnetism allows us to build both an electric motor and also an electric generator. It would be hard to imagine today's world without either of these important inventions.

As you read this chapter, you will see that our study of the atom, electricity, and magnetism has come full circle! This chapter will help you understand exactly how the electricity that we use in our homes, schools, and offices is generated. It is actually all about magnets! Isn't that amazing?

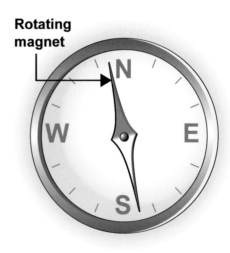

Rotating magnet

Key Questions

✓ Why are there magnets in an electric motor?
✓ How is the electricity that powers all of the appliances in your home generated?
✓ What is the purpose of a transformer on a power line?

17.1 Electric Current and Magnetism

For a long time, people believed electricity and magnetism were unrelated. As scientists began to understand electricity better, they searched for relationships between electricity and magnetism. In 1819, Hans Christian Øersted, a Danish physicist and chemist, placed a compass needle near a wire in a circuit. When a switch in the circuit was closed, the compass needle moved just as if the wire were a magnet. We now know that magnetism is created by the motion of electric charge and that electricity and magnetism are two forms of the same basic force.

The effect of current on a compass

An experiment with a wire and compasses   Magnetism is created by moving charges. Electric current is made of moving charges (electrons), so there is a magnetic field around a wire that carries current. Consider the following experiment. A long straight wire is connected to a battery and a switch. The wire passes through a board with a hole in it. Around the hole are many compasses that can detect any magnetic field.

Magnetism is created by moving charges.

Compasses react to electric current   When the switch is off, the compasses all point north (Figure 17.1). As soon as the switch is closed, current flows, and the compasses point in a circle (see graphic below). The compasses point in a circle as long as there is current in the wire. If the current stops, the compasses return to pointing north again. If the current is reversed in the wire, the compasses again point in a circle, but in the opposite direction.

Vocabulary
coil, solenoid
Objectives
✓ Describe the effect an electric current in a wire has on a compass.
✓ Explain how to change the strength and direction of a wire's magnetic field.
✓ Determine whether two wires or coils will attract or repel.

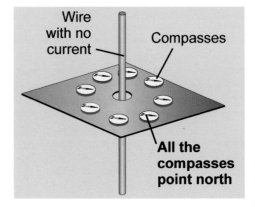

Figure 17.1: *When there is no current in a wire, all of the compasses point north.*

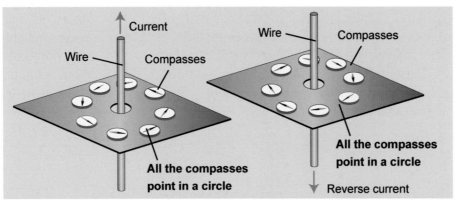

The magnetic field of a straight wire

The magnetic field of a wire

The experiment with the compasses shows that a wire carrying electric current makes a magnetic field around it. The magnetic field lines are concentric circles with the wire at the center. As you may have guessed, the direction of the field depends on the direction of the current in the wire. The *right-hand rule* can be used to tell how the magnetic field lines point. When your thumb is in the direction of the current, the fingers of your right hand wrap in the direction of the magnetic field.

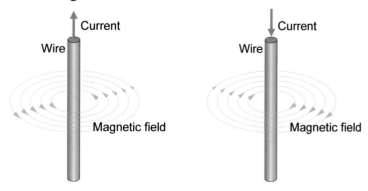

The strength of the field

The strength of the magnetic field near the wire depends on two factors:

1. The strength is directly proportional to the current, so doubling the current doubles the strength of the field.

2. The field strength is inversely proportional to the distance from the wire. The field gets stronger as you move closer to the wire. Decreasing the distance to the wire by half doubles the strength of the field.

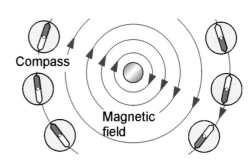

Near a straight wire, the north pole of a compass needle feels a force in the direction of the field lines. The south pole feels a force in the opposite direction. As a result, the needle twists to align its north-south axis along the circular field lines.

Electrical wiring

There is a magnetic field around all wires that carry current. So why don't you notice magnetic fields created by electrical wiring in your house?

The reason is that the wires in your home are actually made of two parallel wires. If you look at an appliance wire, you will notice the two wires inside the plastic covering. At any instant, the current in one wire is opposite the current in the other wire. Each creates a magnetic field, but the fields are in opposite directions so they cancel each other out. Because the wires are not at exactly the same location, and field strength depends on distance, the fields do not completely cancel each other very close to the wire, but quickly fall off to nothing only a short distance away.

The magnetic field of loops and coils

Making a strong magnetic field from current
The magnetic field around a single ordinary wire carrying a safe amount of current is too small to be of much use. However, there are two clever ways to make strong magnetic fields from reasonable currents in small wires.

1. Parallel wires placed side-by-side can be bundled together. Ten wires, each carrying 1 amp of current, create ten times as strong a magnetic field as one wire carrying 1 amp.

2. A single wire can be looped into a **coil,** concentrating the magnetic field at the coil's center. The magnetic field of a coil has the same shape as the field of a circular permanent magnet (Figure 17.2).

Coiling wires
When a wire is made into a coil, the total magnetic field is the sum of the fields created by the current in each individual loop. By wrapping a wire around into a coil, current can be "reused" as many times as there are turns in the coil. A coil with 50 turns of wire carrying 1 amp creates the same magnetic field as a single-wire loop with 50 amps of current. Virtually all electrical machines use coils because it is much easier and safer to work with 1 amp of current than to work with 50 amps of current.

Coils and solenoids
A coil concentrates the magnetic field at its center. When a wire is bent into a circular loop, field lines on the inside of the loop squeeze together. Field lines that are closer together indicate a higher magnetic field. Field lines on the outside of the coil spread apart, making the average field lower outside the coil than inside. The most common form of electromagnetic device is a coil with many turns (Figure 17.3) called a **solenoid.**

Where coils are used
The simple electromagnet made of a nail with wire wrapped around it (see Section 16.2) is one example of a solenoid. Solenoids and other coils are also used in speakers, electric motors, electric guitars, and almost every kind of electric appliance that has moving parts. Coils are the most efficient way to make a strong magnetic field with the least amount of current, which is why coils are found in so many electric appliances.

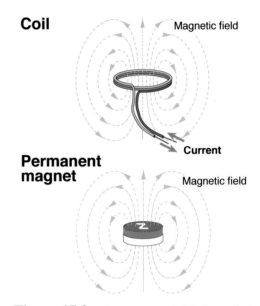

Figure 17.2: *The magnetic field of a coil of wire carrying a current resembles the magnetic field of a permanent magnet.*

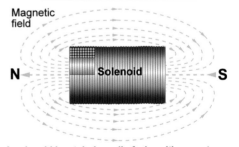

Figure 17.3: *A solenoid is a tubular coil of wire with many turns. The upper left corner of the solenoid in the diagram has been cut away to show the arrangement of wires.*

Magnetic forces and electric currents

The force between two coils
Two coils carrying electric current exert forces on each other, just as magnets do. The forces can be attractive or repulsive depending on the direction of current in the coils (Figure 17.4). If the current is in the same direction in both coils, they attract. If the currents are in opposite directions, they repel.

Observing the force between wires
Two straight wires have a similar effect on each other. When the current is in the same direction in both wires, they attract each other. If the currents go in opposite directions, the wires repel each other. For the amount of current in most electric circuits, the forces are small but can be detected. For example, if the wires are one meter long and each carries 100 amps of current (a lot), the force between them is 0.1 newton when they are one centimeter apart.

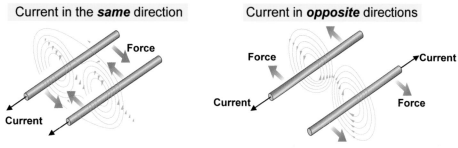

Permanent magnets
The force between wires comes from the interaction of the magnetic field with moving current in the wire. A similar effect can be seen with a wire in the magnetic field created by a permanent magnet. A wire can attract or repel a permanent magnet just as it can attract or repel another wire.

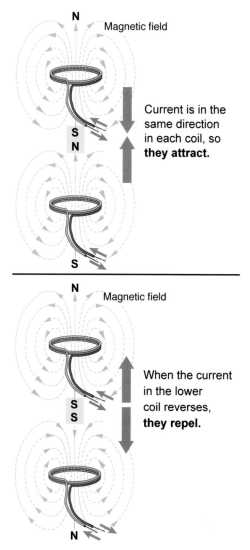

Figure 17.4: *Two coils attract if their currents are in the same direction. They repel if their currents are in opposite directions.*

17.1 Section Review

1. Why does a compass change direction when it is near a current-carrying wire?
2. What is the shape of the magnetic field created by a current-carrying wire?
3. How can you increase the magnetic field created by a wire? How can you change the direction of the field?
4. Do the two wires inside an appliance cord attract or repel each other?

17.2 Electric Motors

Permanent magnets and electromagnets work together to make electric motors and generators. In this section you will learn about how an electric motor works. The secret is in the ability of an electromagnet to reverse its north and south poles. By changing the direction of electric current, the electromagnet attracts and repels other magnets in the motor, causing the motor to spin. **Electric motors** convert electrical energy into mechanical energy.

Using magnets to spin a disk

Imagine a spinning disk with magnets
Imagine you have a disk that can spin on an axis at its center. Around the edge of the disk are several magnets. You have cleverly arranged the magnets so they have alternating north and south poles facing out. Figure 17.5 shows a picture of your rotating disk.

Making the disk spin
You also have another magnet which is not attached to the disk. To make the disk spin, you bring your other magnet close to its edge. The magnet attracts one of the magnets in the disk and repels the next one. These attract and repel forces make the disk spin a little way around.

Reversing the magnet is the key
To keep the disk spinning, you need to reverse the magnet in your fingers as soon as the magnet that was attracted passes by. This way you first attract the magnet, and then reverse your magnet to repel that magnet and attract the next one around the rotor. You make the disk spin by using your magnet to alternately attract and repel the magnets on the disk.

Knowing when to reverse the magnet
The disk is called the **rotor** because it can rotate. The key to making the rotor spin smoothly is to reverse your magnet when the disk is at the right place. You want the reversal to happen just as each magnet in the rotor passes by. If you reverse too early, you will repel the magnet in the rotor backward before it reaches your magnet. If you reverse too late, you attract the magnet backward after it has passed. For it to work best, you need to change your magnet from north to south just as each magnet on the rotor passes by.

Using a magnet to spin a rotor

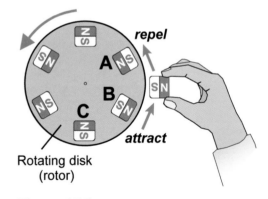

Rotating disk (rotor)

Figure 17.5: *Using a single magnet to spin a disk of magnets. Reversing the magnet in your fingers attracts and repels the magnets in the rotor, making it spin.*

How the electromagnets in a motor operate

How electromagnets are used in electric motors
In a working electric motor, an electromagnet replaces the magnet you reversed with your fingers. The switch from north to south is done by reversing the electric current in the electromagnet. The sketch below shows how an electromagnet switches its poles to make the rotor keep turning.

The three main parts of an electric motor

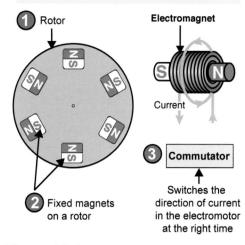

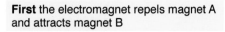

First the electromagnet repels magnet A and attracts magnet B

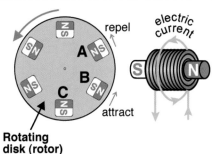

Then the electromagnet switches so it repels magnet B and attracts magnet C.

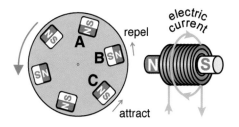

Figure 17.6: *An electric motor has three main parts.*

The commutator is a kind of switch
Just as with the magnet you flipped, the electromagnet must switch from north to south as each rotor magnet passes by to keep the rotor turning. The device that makes this happen is called a **commutator**. As the rotor spins, the commutator reverses the direction of the current in the electromagnet. This makes the electromagnet's side facing the disk change from north to south, and then back again. The electromagnet attracts and repels the magnets in the rotor, and the motor turns.

Three things you need to make a motor
All types of electric motors must have three parts (Figure 17.6). They are:

1 A rotating part (rotor) with magnets that alternate.
2 One or more fixed magnets around the rotor.
3 A commutator that switches the direction of current in the electromagnets back and forth in the right sequence to keep the rotor spinning.

AC motors
Motors that run on AC electricity are easier to make because the current switches direction all by itself. Almost all household, industrial, and power tool motors are AC motors. These motors use electromagnets for both the rotating and fixed magnets (Figure 17.7)

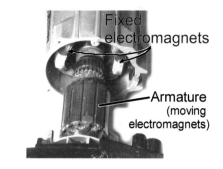

Figure 17.7: *The working parts of an AC motor. Electromagnets are used for both the rotating and non-rotating parts of the motor. There are no permanent magnets.*

How a battery-powered electric motor works

Inside a small electric motor   If you take apart an electric motor that runs on batteries, it doesn't look like the motor on the previous page. But those same three essential mechanisms are there. The difference is in the arrangement of the electromagnets and permanent magnets. The picture below shows a small battery-powered electric motor and what it looks like inside with one end of the case removed. The permanent magnets are on the outside, and they stay fixed in place.

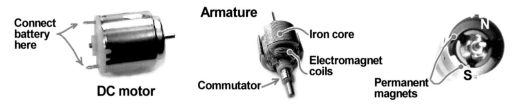

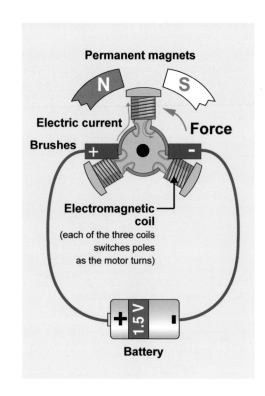

Figure 17.8: *A simple battery-powered motor has three electromagnets.*

Electromagnets and the armature   The electromagnets are in the rotor, and they turn. The rotating part of the motor, including the electromagnets, is called the **armature**. The armature (see picture above) has three electromagnets corresponding to the three coils you see in Figure 17.8.

How the switching happens   The wires from each of the three coils are attached to three metal plates (commutator) at the end of the armature. As the rotor spins, the three plates come into contact with the positive and negative **brushes**. Electric current passes through the brushes into the coils. As the motor turns, the plates rotate past the brushes, switching the electromagnets from north to south by reversing the positive and negative connections to the coils. The turning electromagnets are attracted and repelled by the permanent magnets and the motor turns.

17.2 Section Review

1. Explain how you can use a permanent magnet to make a rotor spin.
2. How do the magnetic poles in an electromagnet reverse?
3. List the three main parts every electric motor must have.

17.3 Electric Generators and Transformers

Motors transform electrical energy into mechanical energy. Electric *generators* do the opposite. They transform mechanical energy into electrical energy. Generators are used to create the electricity that powers all of the appliances in your home. In this section you will learn how generators produce electricity.

Electromagnetic induction

Magnetism and electricity
An electric current in a wire creates a magnetic field. The reverse is also true. If you move a magnet near a coil of wire, an electric current (or voltage) is *induced* in the coil. The word "induce" means "to cause to happen." The process of using a moving magnet to create electric current or voltage is called **electromagnetic induction**. A moving magnet *induces* electric current to flow in a circuit.

Symmetry in physics
Many laws in physics display *symmetry*. In physics, symmetry means a process works in both directions. Earlier in this chapter you learned that moving electric charges create magnetism. The symmetry is that changing magnetic fields also cause electric charges to move. Nearly all physical laws display symmetry of one form or another.

Making current flow
Figure 17.9 shows an experiment demonstrating electromagnetic induction. In the experiment, a magnet can move in and out of a coil of wire. The coil is attached to a meter that measures the electric current. When the magnet moves into the coil of wire, *as the magnet is moving,* electric current is induced in the coil and the meter swings to the left. The current stops if the magnet stops moving.

Reversing the current
When the magnet is pulled back out again, *as the magnet is moving,* current is induced in the opposite direction. The meter swings to the right as the magnet moves out. Again, if the magnet stops moving, the current also stops.

Current flows only when the magnet is moving
Current is produced only if the magnet is moving, because a *changing* magnetic field is what creates current. Moving magnets induce current because they create changing magnetic fields. If the magnetic field is not changing, such as when the magnet is stationary, the current is zero.

Vocabulary

electromagnetic induction, Faraday's law of induction, generator

Objectives

✓ Explain how a magnet can be used to produce current in a coil.

✓ Describe the design of a simple generator.

✓ Calculate the number of turns or voltage of a coil in a transformer.

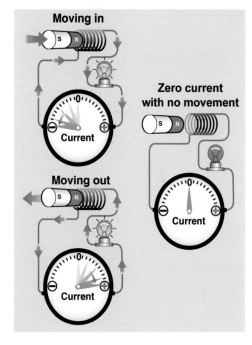

Figure 17.9: *A moving magnet produces a current in a coil of wire.*

Faraday's law of induction

When current is induced
Do you think a big current will flow in a coil if you wave a magnet around far away from the coil? If you guessed no, you are right. The coil has to be close to the magnet for any current to be induced. How close? Close enough that the magnetic field from the magnet passes *through* the coil (Figure 17.10). The induced current depends on the amount of magnetic field actually passing through the coil. Adding an iron core helps because iron amplifies the magnetic field and directs it through the coil.

Induced voltage
Current flows because a voltage difference is created between the ends of the coil. A moving magnet like the one in Figure 17.10 induces a voltage difference between the ends of the wires that make the coil. If the wires were connected, current *would* flow. When the wires are disconnected you see the voltage difference instead. Because the currents can be quite small, in experiments it is easier to measure the induced voltage instead of the current.

Faraday's law
The induced voltage or current depends on how *fast* the magnetic field through the coil changes. Michael Faraday (1791-1867), an English physicist and chemist, was first to explain it. He experimented with moving magnets and coils and discovered **Faraday's law of induction**. Faraday's law says the induced voltage is proportional to the *rate of change* of the magnetic field through the coil. If the magnetic field does not change, no voltage is produced even if the field is very strong.

The voltage induced in a coil is proportional to the rate of change of the magnetic field through the coil.

Induced current, work, and energy
As a magnet is pushed through a coil of wire, current is induced to flow and voltage develops. The induced current in the coil makes its own magnetic field that tries to push your magnet back out again. If you push a north pole into a coil, the coil itself will develop a repelling north pole from the induced current. If you pull the magnet back out again, the coil will reverse its current, making a south pole that attracts your magnet. Either way, you have to *push* the magnet in or out, doing work, to supply the energy that makes current flow (Figure 17.11). This is another example of conservation of energy.

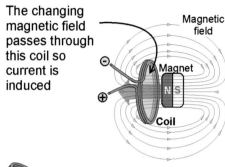

The changing magnetic field passes through this coil so current is induced

No magnetic field passes through this coil. No current is induced.

Figure 17.10: *The induced current depends on the magnetic field actually passing through the coil.*

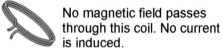

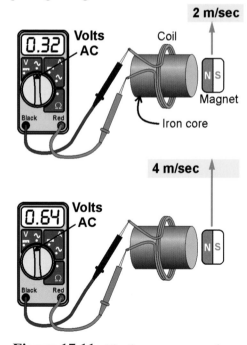

Figure 17.11: *The faster you move the magnet, the greater the induced current.*

Generating electricity

A simple generator
A **generator** converts mechanical energy into electrical energy using the law of induction. Most large generators use some form of rotating coil in a magnetic field (Figure 17.12). You can also make a generator by rotating magnets past a stationary coil (diagram below). As the disk rotates, first a north pole and then a south pole pass the coil. When a north pole is approaching, the current is in one direction. After the north pole passes and a south pole approaches, the current is in the other direction. As long as the disk is spinning, there is a changing magnetic field through the coil and electric current is created.

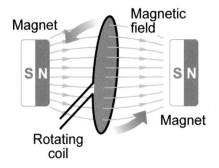

Figure 17.12: *Current is created when a coil rotates in a magnetic field.*

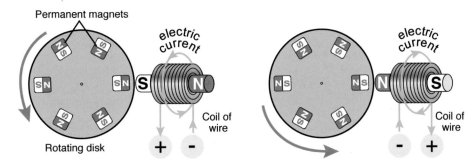

Alternating current
The generator shown above makes AC electricity. The direction of current is one way when the magnetic field is becoming "more north" and the opposite way when the field is becoming "less north". It is impossible to make a situation where the magnetic field keeps increasing (becoming more north) forever. Eventually the field must stop increasing and start decreasing. Therefore the current or voltage always alternates. The electricity in your home is produced by AC generators.

Energy for generators
The electrical energy created by a generator is not created from nothing. Energy must continually be supplied to keep the rotating coil (or magnetic disk) turning. In hydroelectric generator, falling water turns a *turbine* which spins the generator and generates electricity. Windmills can generate electricity in a similar way. Other power plants use gas, oil, or coal to heat steam to high pressures. The steam then spins turbines that convert the chemical energy stored in the fuels into electrical energy (Figure 17.13).

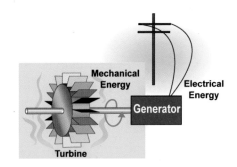

Figure 17.13: *A power plant generator contains a turbine that turns magnets inside loops of wire, generating electricity. Some other form of energy must be continually supplied to turn the turbine.*

Transformers

Electricity is transmitted at high voltage

From the perspective of physics, it makes sense to distribute electricity from a generator to homes using high voltage. For example, the main power lines on a city street carry AC current at 13,800 volts. Since power is current times voltage, each amp of current provides 13,800 watts of power. The problem is that you would *not* want your wall outlets to be at 13,800 volts! With a voltage this high, it would be dangerous to even plug in your appliances.

Electric power transformers

The voltage in your wall outlet is 120 volts. A transformer steps down the high voltage from the main power lines to the low voltage your appliances use. Transformers are useful because they efficiently change voltage and current with very little loss of power. A transformer can take one amp at 13,800 volts from the power lines outside and convert it to 115 amps at 120 volts (Figure 17.14). The total electrical power remains the same because 13,800 V × 1 A = 120 V × 115 A.

Transformers operate on electromagnetic induction

A transformer uses electromagnetic induction, similar to a generator. Figure 17.15 shows what a transformer looks like inside its protective box. You may have seen one inside a doorbell or an AC adapter. The two coils are called the *primary* and *secondary* coils. The input to the transformer is connected to the primary coil. The output of the transformer is connected to the secondary coil. The two coils are wound around an iron core. The core concentrates the magnetic field lines through the centers of the coils.

How a transformer works

Consider the transformer between the outside power lines and your house:

1. The primary coil is connected to outside power lines. Current in the primary coil creates a magnetic field through the secondary coil. The primary coil's field is shown by the magnetic field lines in Figure 17.15.

2. The current in the primary coil changes constantly because it is *alternating current*.

3. As the current changes, so does the strength and direction of the magnetic field through the secondary coil.

4. The changing magnetic field through the secondary coil induces current in the secondary coil. The secondary coil connects to your home's wiring.

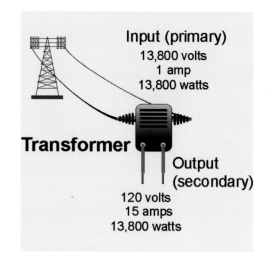

Figure 17.14: *A high power transformer can reduce the voltage keeping the power constant.*

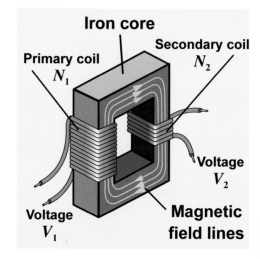

Figure 17.15: *A transformer contains coils wound around an iron core.*

Voltage relationships for a transformer

The number of turns is important
Transformers work because there are different number of turns in the primary and secondary coils. The strength of an electromagnet's magnetic field, induced voltage, and induced current all depend on the number of turns (Figure 17.16). In the same changing magnetic field, a coil with 100 turns produces ten times the induced voltage or current as a coil with 10 turns.

Voltage and current
With fewer turns than the primary coil, the secondary coil also has lower induced voltage than the voltage applied to the primary coil. In this case, voltage is *stepped down*. With more turns than the primary coil, the secondary coil has greater induced voltage than the voltage applied to the primary coil and the voltage is *stepped up*. Because of energy conservation, the power (voltage × current) is the same for both coils (neglecting resistance).

TRANSFORMER

Primary voltage (V)　　　Turns in primary coil

$$\frac{V_1}{V_2} = \frac{N_1}{N_2}$$

Secondary voltage (V)　　Turns in secondary coil

Figure 17.16: *The relationship between voltage and number of turns in a transformer.*

Changing voltage with a transformer

When you plug in a cell phone, a transformer on the plug changes the outlet's 120 volts to the 6 volts needed by the battery. If the primary coil has 240 turns, how many turns must the secondary coil have?

1. Looking for:　　You are asked for the number of turns of the secondary coil.

2. Given:　　You are given the voltage of each coil and the number of turns of the primary coil.

3. Relationships:　　$\dfrac{V_1}{V_2} = \dfrac{N_1}{N_2}$

4. Solution:　　$\dfrac{120\text{ V}}{6\text{ V}} = \dfrac{240\text{ turns}}{N_2}$　　$N_2 = 12$ turns

Your turn...

a. A transformer has 20 turns on the secondary coil and 200 turns on the primary. What is the secondary voltage if the primary voltage is 120 volts? **Answer:** 12 volts

b. How many turns must the primary coil have if it steps down 13,800 volts to 120 volts with 112 turns? **Answer:** 12,880 turns

---

17.3 Section Review

1. You hold a strong permanent magnet in place at the center of a coil. Is there a current induced in the coil? Why or why not?

2. Explain Faraday's law of induction.

3. What is the purpose of a transformer?

Does a Computer Ever Forget?

Many aspects of your life are bound to computers. Almost every piece of electronic equipment, from VCRs to cell phones, to microwave ovens, has at a tiny computer called a microcontroller. Like you, computers have a memory that allows them to store information. Computer memory and quick access to the information in memory are part of why computers are so useful.

It's all about information

The working of a computer can be broken down into three basic steps—putting information in, processing information, and sending information back out. Early computers required people to flip switches to enter information. Today there are many ways to input information: the mouse and keyboard, digital cameras, scanners, microphones, touch screens, and bar code readers. The list of these input devices grows each year. Familiar output devices include your monitor, printer, speakers. Other important outputs are connections to other computers through cables or wireless radio.

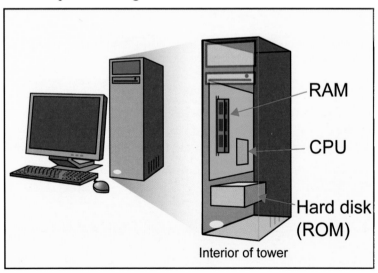

RAM

CPU

Hard disk (ROM)

Interior of tower

The long and the short of it

The two basic types of computer memory are short-term and long-term. Short-term memory is erased when the power is turned off. Long-term memory retains its information even with no power. Long-term memory is used for things that the computer uses many times such as *programs* that tell the computer what to do with the information in its memory. Programs use various languages such as C++ or Java to create complex lists of instructions that tell the computer how to accomplish tasks with information in memory.

Short-term or RAM (Random Access Memory) is on silicon chips that are used by the computer while it is actively working. Short term memory is thousands of times faster than long term memory, but also much smaller. When you activate a program, the computer loads the program from long term memory into short term memory where information can be used quickly. When the program is done, the computer erases it (and its data) from short term memory, freeing up this faster memory for other programs.

1-0-1-0-1-0

Almost all computers use magnetic disk drives (hard drives) for long term memory. A hard drive is actually one or more circular plates made of glass or metal covered with a fine layer of magnetic film. The Read/Write Head uses a miniature coil to "write" information on the disk as a sequence of magnetic north and south poles. When electricity is passed through the coil, a magnetic field is produced. This magnetic field causes the magnetic film on the surface of the disk to "record" the polarity of the field. Since each spot on the disk can only be north or south, all information must be represented as on or off, like a switch. Schematically, a north pole means "on" while a south pole means "off".

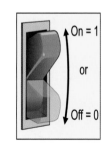

On = 1

or

Off = 0

The on-or-off language is called *binary*. Like a switch that can be turned "on" and "off," there are only two digits in the language: 0 and 1. In computer terms the word *bit* stands for "**bi**nary dig**it**." The binary language is used by all computers to store information.

Eight bits form a *byte*. A code represents each letter or number as a different one byte sequence of 0s and 1s. The diagram shows how the word 'face' is represented by 4 bytes or 32 bits. The binary code language used here is called the ASCII Code.

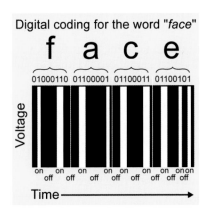

Digital coding for the word "*face*"

Reading memory

To read information, the changing magnetic poles on the disk induce tiny voltages on the coil in the read/write head as the disk spins. The voltages are amplified and turned into digital ones and zeros that are stored in short term memory (RAM).

Growing capacity

The smaller the individual north and south poles on a disk can be made, the more information you can fit on a single disk. The memory capacity of hard disks has increased more than 100 times in the past ten years as newer technologies use smaller areas to store each bit. As the space needed to store a bit decreases, the strength of each bit's field must also decrease so as not to influence the surrounding bits. This has been done by improving the magnetic recording film, by more precise manufacture of the disks themselves, and by developing smaller and more sensitive read/write heads.

The future of computer memory

Words and numbers are relatively compact in terms of storage. All the words in this entire textbook would take up less than 100 kilobits of disk memory. However, pictures and movies are another story. A *single* digitized picture can take up 5 megabits, or 50 times as much memory. Because of the increased graphical capabilities of today's computers, increasing the capacity of computer memory is critically important. Therefore, scientists continue to explore new ways to store digital information.

For example, some scientists are investigating the possibility of storing information on a protein found in a bacterium. Different twisting forms of the protein are used to record digital ones and zeros. Since proteins are so small it may be possible to get 100 or 1,000 times as much information into the same space used by a conventional hard drive today.

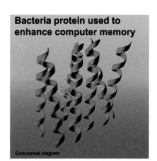

Bacteria protein used to enhance computer memory

Conceptual diagram

Questions:

1. The functions of a computer can be broken down into three basic steps. In which step does the CPU play a role?
2. What is the difference between short-term and long-term computer memory?
3. How many bits are used to write the word "congratulations" using the ASCII Code?
4. The trend in computer technology seems to be that computers are getting smaller while memory and speed increase. How would you illustrate this trend on a graph?

Chapter 17 Review

Understanding Vocabulary

Select the correct term to complete the sentences.

electric generator	electromagnetic induction	solenoid
electric motor	transformer	commutator
armature	Faraday's law of induction	coil
brushes	rotor	

Section 17.1

1. A wire looped into a circular _____ can be used to create a magnetic field that is stronger than that of a single wire.

2. A coil with many turns called a _____ is a device commonly used in speakers, motors, and many other devices.

Section 17.2

3. A(n) _____ is used to convert electrical energy into mechanical energy.

4. A _____ is used in a motor to switch the direction of the magnetic field created by the current.

5. The rotating part of a motor that holds the electromagnets is called the _____.

6. Electric current passes through the _____ and into the electromagnets in an electric motor.

Section 17.3

7. A(n) _____ is used to convert mechanical energy into electrical energy.

8. Using a magnet to create electric current in a wire is called _____.

9. _____ explains the relationship between the current created in a coil and the rate of change of the magnetic field through the coil.

10. A _____ uses two coils to change the voltage of the electricity coming into your home.

Reviewing Concepts

Section 17.1

1. How is magnetism created?

2. What exists in the region around a wire that is carrying current and that exerts a force on another current-carrying wire?

3. Explain how the right-hand rule can help you determine the direction of the magnetic field lines around a current-carrying wire.

4. What effect does increasing the current in a wire have on the magnetic field?

5. What effect does reversing the direction of the current in a wire have on the magnetic field?

6. What happens to the magnetic field as you move farther away from a current-carrying wire?

7. Why do we not use a single wire with a large current if we wish to create a strong magnetic field?

8. What is the advantage of using a coil to create a magnetic field?

9. Why don't we usually notice the force between the current-carrying wire in an extension cord?

Section 17.2

10. A motor turns _____ energy into _____ energy.

11. Why is it necessary to use at least one electromagnet in a motor instead of only permanent magnets?

12. What is the purpose of the commutator in a motor?

13. Why must the direction of the current in a motor's electromagnets be switched repeatedly?

14. List the three main parts of an electric motor.

Section 17.3

15. What happens as you move a magnet toward a coil of wire in terms of electricity?

16. If you hold a magnet still near a coil of wire, will current or voltage be induced? Explain your answer.

. State Faraday's law of induction in your own words.

. Why does a spinning coil near a magnet produce alternating current rather than direct current?

. What is the voltage provided by electrical outlets in buildings?

. The voltage of the electricity in outside power lines is much higher than the voltage of the electricity in buildings. How is the voltage reduced?

. The primary and secondary coils in a transformer have different voltages and currents but the same _____.

. A certain transformer has more turns in the secondary coil than in the primary coil. Does the transformer increase or decrease voltage?

olving Problems

ection 17.1

Copy the diagram of the wire shown to the right and draw the magnetic field lines in the region around the wire. Don't forget to include arrows to show the field's direction.

Current

What happens to the strength of the magnetic field near a wire if you double the current? Triple the current? Quadruple the current?

Copy the diagram of the coil shown to the right and draw the magnetic field in the region around it. Don't forget to include arrows to show the field's direction.

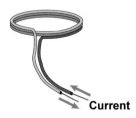

Current

4. Explain how each of the following would affect the current produced by a magnet moving toward a coil of wire:

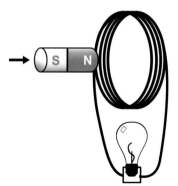

   a. using a stronger magnet
   b. moving the magnet toward the coil at a faster speed
   c. reversing the magnet's motion so it moves away from the coil
   d. adding more turns of wire to the coil
   e. moving the magnet's south pole toward the coil
   f. adding a second light bulb to the circuit

5. Decide whether each pair of wires or coils will attract or repel.

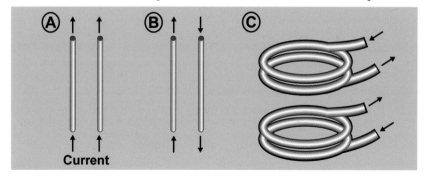

Section 17.2

6. At a certain instant, the electromagnet in the motor shown below has its north pole facing the rotor that holds the permanent magnets. In which direction is the rotor spinning?

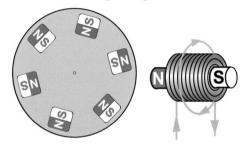

7. The rotor in the motor below is spinning clockwise. Is the direction of the current in the electromagnet from A to B or from B to A?

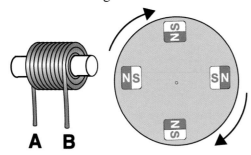

A B

Section 17.3

8. A transformer contains 1000 turns in the primary coil and 50 turns in the secondary coil.
   a. If the voltage of the secondary coil is 120 volts, what is the voltage of the primary coil?
   b. If the voltage of the primary coil is 120 volts, what is the voltage of the secondary coil?

9. A laptop computer uses a rechargeable 24 volt battery. A transformer is used to convert an electrical outlet's 120 volts to 24 volts.
   a. If the primary coil has 500 turns, how many turns must the secondary coil have?
   b. If the current in the primary coil is 1 ampere, what is the current in the secondary coil? (Hint: Calculate the power.)

Applying Your Knowledge

Section 17.1

1. Speakers use electromagnets and permanent magnets to create sound from electric currents. Research how electromagnets are used to produce the vibrations that create the music you listen to.

Section 17.2

2. The first motors were built to run on direct current. However, direct current could not be easily transmitted over long distances. In the late 1800's, Nikola Tesla invented a motor that ran on alternating current. Research Tesla's life and his invention of the AC motor.

Section 17.3

3. Suppose you have a transformer that provides a secondary voltage four times as great as the primary voltage. You have a cell phone that uses a 6 volt battery. Could you use a 1.5 volt battery and the transformer to power the phone?

4. A bicycle light generator is a device you place on the wheel of your bike. When you turn the wheel, the generator powers a light. When you stop, the light goes out. Explain how you think the generator makes electricity.

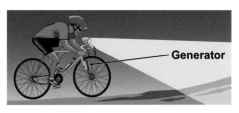

Generator

5. A clever inventor claims to be able to make an electric car that makes its own electricity and never needs gas. The inventor claims that as the car moves, the wind generated by the motion spins a propeller. The propeller turns a generator that makes electricity to power the car. Do you believe this car would work? Why or why not? (Hint: Think about conservation of energy.)

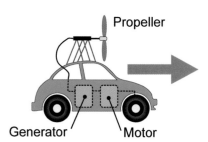

Propeller

Generator   Motor

6. Some electric toothbrushes contain rechargeable batteries that are charged by placing the toothbrush on a plastic charging base. Both the bottom of the toothbrush and the base are encased in plastic, so there is no connection between the circuits in the toothbrush and the base. How do you think the battery in the toothbrush gets charged?

Chapter 18

Fields and Forces

"Use the force, Luke" is a well-known quote from a very popular film series, which you have probably seen at least once. The force field in the movie is only imaginary but real force fields do exist and are very important in physics. Gravity, electricity, magnetism, and other important concepts in physics all depend on real force fields. All forces exist in what we call "fields." In fact, you are sitting in a virtual sea of fields right now. You are surrounded by light fields, electrical fields, magnetic fields, sound fields, and, of course, a gravitational field.

A group of scientists, physicians, and engineers formed a group in 1978 called the Bioeletromagnetics Society. Bioeletromagnetics is the study of how electromagnetic fields affect biological systems. With at least one-third of the U.S. population using cell phones, some researchers are exploring how the radiofrequency fields that exist around cell phone antennas might affect cell phone users. Although some studies in Sweden have shown some possible links between cell phone usage and increased headaches and fatigue, no studies have been able to conclusively show any harmful affects of cell phone usage.

Key Questions

✓ How does the force of gravity get from the sun to Earth?

✓ If all masses exert gravity on other masses, why don't you feel the gravitational pull between you and this textbook?

✓ How can electrical appliances, lightning, and even static electricity interfere with the operation of sensitive electronics?

18.1 Fields and Forces

In many chapters, you have read about forces. Some forces come from electricity or magnetism. Other forces come from pressure, motion, or gravity. What we have *not* discussed is how forces *actually act*. What carries the influence of a force from one place to another? How does the force of gravity get from the sun to Earth? How does the electrical force from a battery spread through a wire to cause current to flow everywhere in the wire? This chapter will answer these and other questions by discussing the concept of a *field*.

What is a field?

An example Think about listening to music from a portable stereo. You can hear the music for a long distance away from the stereo. However, the farther away you go, the softer the music gets. At some distance you can no longer hear the music at all because the volume has become too low. How do you describe the loudness of the music all around the stereo?

Definition of a field In physics, a **field** is a quantity that has a value everywhere in space. The loudness has a value everywhere around the stereo. That means you can describe the loudness with a *field*. Figure 18.1 shows what the *sound intensity field* might look like near a stereo. The circular lines represent places where the loudness is equal. The graph shows the loudness of the sound in decibels (dB). At a distance of 120 meters the sound has a loudness of 10 decibels, which is about the same loudness as hearing a whisper from one meter away.

You hear the field, not the stereo itself A person standing far away *does not hear the stereo directly*. If you were to switch the stereo off, the person would not know for several seconds. Instead, the person hears the sound field *created by the stereo*. This may seem like an unimportant detail, but it turns out to be fundamental to physics.

We experience fields, not their sources *All* interactions between matter and energy proceed through fields. Sound is a form of energy. The sound intensity field describes precisely how much sound energy a listener hears in every place. Like sound from the stereo, we only experience the *fields* created by things, *not the things themselves*.

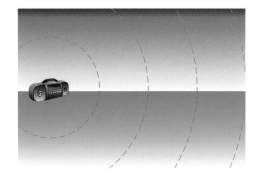

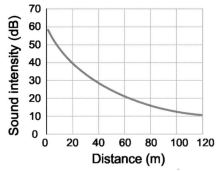

Figure 18.1: *The sound intensity field near a stereo.*

Fields and energy

Fields are everywhere

All of space is filled with fields. In fact, many different fields can occupy the same space. You are constantly immersed in fields, including radio and television broadcasts, microwaves, light, electricity, and gravity. There are fields everywhere (Figure 18.2)!

Fields contain energy

Any field is a form of energy that is distributed through space. You can easily show that a magnetic field has energy because it can exert force over distance (doing work) on another magnet. The stronger the field, the more energy is stored in the field. Where does the energy come from?

Energy must come from somewhere

The energy in the field of an electromagnet comes from the current in the wires. But what about a permanent magnet? Permanent magnets are not magnetic early in the manufacturing process because their atoms are randomly oriented. Powerful electromagnets are used to magnetize permanent magnets. The initial magnetization process is the source of the energy that creates the magnetic field of a permanent magnet.

Fields and forces

Fields create forces when they interact with matter. The force holding you to your chair comes from the gravitational field of Earth interacting with the matter in your body. You do not fall *through* the chair because electrons in the atoms of the chair repel electrons in atoms on *you* through electric fields.

You can add fields of the same type

Fields of the same kind can be added or subtracted. You can use two magnets to force a compass needle to point in any direction you wish. Figure 18.3 illustrates the effects of a permanent magnet and an electromagnet on a compass. The compass responds to the total magnetic field at its position. The total magnetic field is the sum of the magnetic fields from each magnet plus the magnetic field of Earth itself.

Add forces from fields of different types

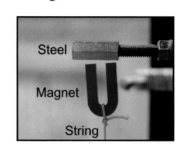

The total force acting on a body is the sum of all forces from all fields that are present. The photograph at left shows a small magnet that is being held up by a magnetic field. The magnet feels forces from several fields including gravity, magnetism, and the electric fields holding the atoms of the string together.

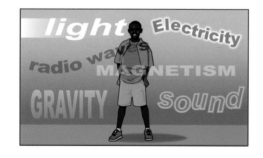

Figure 18.2: *Some of the fields that pass through you all the time.*

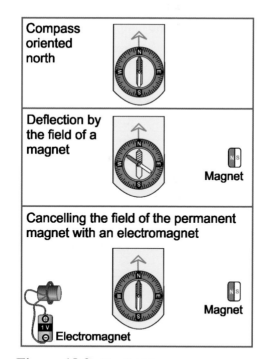

Figure 18.3: *The field from an electromagnet can either cancel the field from a permanent magnet or add to it.*

The inverse square law

Intensity Your hear only the sound energy that falls on the small area of the opening to your ear. This area is about one square centimeter (1 cm²). Because the conversion of electricity to sound is only 1% efficient, a 100-watt stereo puts out a sound power of one watt. As the sound spreads out, that single watt is spread over more and more area and loudness decreases. Close to the stereo, 0.01 watt is captured by the small opening of your ear. The **intensity**—the number of watts per unit area—reaching your ear is 0.01 watts per square centimeter. Because the power spreads out, far away from the stereo the intensity drops so the same square centimeter of your ear captures *less* than 0.01 watt of power (Figure 18.4).

The inverse square law The strength of a field decreases the farther you get from the source. For example, suppose a light bulb gives off 10 watts of light. The *light intensity* around the bulb is described by the number of watts per square meter of area. The area of a sphere is $4\pi r^2$, where r is the radius. If the radius is 1 meter, the area is 12.6 m². The light intensity is 0.8 W/m² (10 W ÷ 12.6 m²). If the radius is 2 meters (twice as far), the intensity is four times less because the same amount of light is spread out over 50.3 m² instead of 12.6 m². The intensity of light from a small source follows an **inverse square law** because its intensity diminishes as the square of the distance increases.

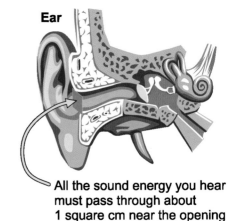

All the sound energy you hear must pass through about 1 square cm near the opening to the ear.

Figure 18.4: *The loudness of the sound you hear depends on the the number of watts per square centimeter that arrive at the opening of your ear.*

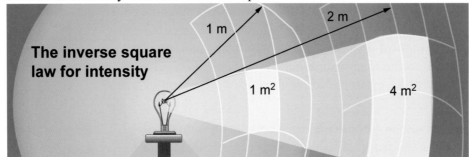

The inverse square law for intensity

1 m
2 m
1 m²
4 m²

Comparing force vs. distance
- - - - Electrical force and gravity *(inverse square law)*
—— Force between two magnets

Force

Distance ⟶

Figure 18.5: *The force from a magnet decreases faster than an inverse square law. This is because all magnets have two opposite poles, not just one.*

Fields and the inverse square law Many fields follow an inverse square law, including electricity and gravity as well as light. Magnetism is an exception because all magnets have two opposite poles, not just one. The magnetic field decreases much faster than an inverse square law (Figure 18.5) because the north and south poles cancel each other out as you move far away from the magnet.

The speed of a field

Some questions for thought

When you bring a magnet close to another magnet, how fast does the first magnet feel the other's force? Does one magnet instantly feel the other one? Does the force from one magnet reach the other instantly no matter what the distance is between them? The answers come from thinking about the interaction in two steps. First, the magnet creates a magnetic field. Second, the magnetic field creates forces on other magnets.

The speed of light

The magnetic field carries the force from one magnet to the other at the speed of light (Figure 18.6). The speed of light is 300,000,000 m/sec so it takes only a tiny fraction of a second for the force to get from one magnet to another when the distance is a few meters. However, when the distance is large the time delay is also large. If a giant magnet were to suddenly appear at the center of the Milky Way galaxy we would not feel its force for thousands of years.

Nothing is instantaneous

Nothing travels instantly from one place to another. Not force, not energy, and not even information! This applies to light, electricity, gravity, sound, and any other form of energy you can think of. All interactions are carried by fields and the fastest that *any* field can spread is the speed of light.

Time delays due to field speed

When you make a cell phone call, information like your number and the number you are calling is coded in pulses of energy. The information spreads out as an electromagnetic field expanding at the speed of light (Figure 18.7, see chapter 24). Since light can circle Earth 7 $\frac{1}{2}$ times in one second, there is not much time delay. However, talking to a space craft is another story! It takes 35 minutes for light to travel from Earth to Jupiter when the planets are at their closest. That is one reason why it is so difficult to control distant space craft. It takes 35 minutes for the space craft's signal to reach Earth and another 35 minutes for the response to get back. A lot can happen in 70 minutes!

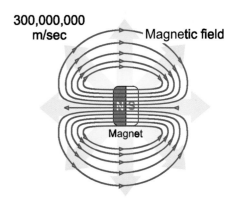

Figure 18.6: *The magnetic field moves outward at 300,000,000 m/sec carrying the magnetic force.*

Figure 18.7: *Information carried by a field cannot travel faster than the speed of light.*

18.1 Section Review

1. Name three quantities that are described by fields.

2. If you get 30 meters away from a light bulb, how does its intensity compare to when you are 10 meters away?

3. If the sun were to vanish instantly, would Earth immediately fly out of its orbit? Explain why or why not.

18.2 Gravity

When Newton first proposed the law of universal gravitation he was quoted as saying, "Though I have calculated its effect, exactly *how* gravity operates is still a mystery." He realized that it did not make sense that gravity should instantly transmit forces between planets regardless of their distance. The idea of a field had not yet been thought of during Newton's time. Therefore, his law of gravitation described the strength and direction of the force of gravity, but not how the force got from one body to the next.

The gravitational field

Mass creates the gravitational field
Like the force from a magnet, the force of gravity comes from a field. The gravitational field is created by mass. All mass creates a gravitational field, even a single atom. However, gravity is a relatively weak force and it takes a planet-sized mass to create a field strong enough to create a significant force.

The gravitational interaction between two masses proceeds in two steps. Mass creates a **gravitational field** first. Then, the gravitational field exerts forces on other masses (Figure 18.8).

The gravitational field around Earth

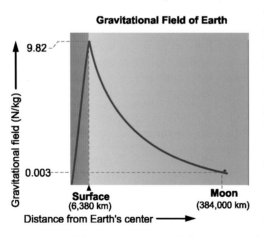

The gravitational field is a **force field** because it creates a force on a mass at all points in space. The force on an imaginary test mass, (m), is equal to the mass multiplied by the gravitational field (g). This is the familiar formula for an object's weight ($F = mg$). The graph shows the strength of Earth's gravitational field from Earth's center to the moon (*note: scale is not linear*).

Fields and relativity
The idea of the gravitational field is useful even within Einstein's theory of relativity. In chapter 12 you learned that the gravitational field is caused by distortions in space-time created by massive objects. That is why gravity can bend light even though light has no mass.

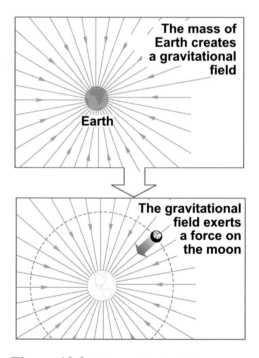

Figure 18.8: *The gravitational force between Earth and the moon acts in two steps: (1) Earth and the moon both create a gravitational field, and (2) the moon feels a force from the gravitational field that causes it to orbit Earth.*

The gravitational field of planets and stars

Gravity is a vector   The gravitational field is a vector field because the force has a direction at all points in space. Like the magnetic field, you can draw field lines to show the direction of the gravitational field. The field lines represent the force acting on an imaginary test mass. The field lines point toward the center of a large mass, such as Earth (Figure 18.9).

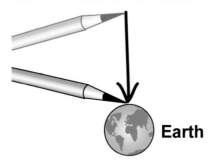

Choose a point to begin. Draw a vector showing the direction of the force of gravity at that point.

Earth

Calculating the field

LAW OF GRAVITATION

$(6.67 \times 10^{-11} \text{ N·m}^2/\text{kg}^2)$ *Mass (kg)*

Force (N)   Mass (kg)

$$F = m_1 \frac{Gm_2}{r^2}$$

Distance (m)

Gravitational field g, (N/kg)

Newton's law of gravitation, first presented in chapter 6, can be rearranged. The strength of the gravitational field (g) is given by the quantity, Gm_2/r^2. If we know the mass and radius of a planet, we can use this quantity to calculate the strength of gravity on that planet. The example problem illustrates how to find g for single objects like a planet or ball.

Repeat for other points around the Earth.

Calculate the gravitational field of Mars

The planet Mars has a mass of 6.4×10^{23} kg and a radius of 3,400,000 meters. Calculate the value of g (gravitational field) on the surface of Mars.

1. **Looking for:**   Value of g in N/kg
2. **Given:**   Mass in kilograms and radius in meters
3. **Relationships:** $g = Gm_2/r^2$ where $G = 6.67 \times 10^{-11}$ N·m^2/kg^2
4. **Solution:** $g = (6.67 \times 10^{-11} \text{ N·m}^2/\text{kg}^2)(6.4 \times 10^{23} \text{ kg})/(3.4 \times 10^6 \text{ m})^2$
                        $= 3.69$ N/kg compared to Earth's 9.8 N/kg

Your turn...

Calculate the gravitational field at the surface of a 1-kilogram ball with a radius of 0.10 meters. **Answer:** 6.67×10^{-9} N/kg

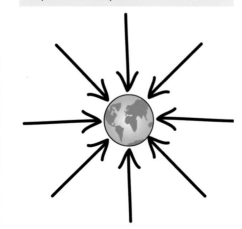

Figure 18.9: *Field lines show the direction of the force an object would feel if placed in any location around Earth.*

18.2 Section Review

1. If the earth were to vanish instantly, would the moon immediately fly out of its orbit or would there be a time delay? Explain.

2. Why don't you feel gravity between ordinary objects such as yourself and a bowling ball?

18.3 The Electric Field

In chapter 15 you learned that electric charges exert forces on each other. Unlike charges attract, and like charges repel. You also learned about Coulomb's law, which describes the strength of the force between two charges. Coulomb's law is one of the fundamental relationships in the universe because atoms are held together by the electrical attraction between protons (positive) and electrons (negative). Like gravity, the force between electric charges is carried by a field, called the electric field.

Drawing the electric field

Direction of an electric field   By convention, we draw the **electric field** to represent the force on an imaginary positive test charge. Because it is imaginary, the test charge itself does not change the electric field. The electric field therefore points *toward* negative charges and *away* from positive charges (Figure 18.10). Because of this convention, a positive charge placed in an electric field will feel a force in the direction of the field, and a negative charge will feel a force opposite the direction of the field.

Field lines   As we did with magnetic and gravitational fields, we use field lines to make a diagram of the electric field around one or more charges. Electric field lines follow the direction of the force on a positive test charge. The strength of the electric field is shown by the spacing of the field lines. The field is strong where the field lines are close together and is weak where the lines are far apart.

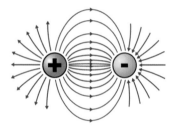

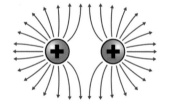

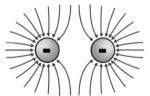

Figure 18.10: *The electric field around two or more charges can be found by imagining the force on an imaginary positive test charge at various points in the region.*

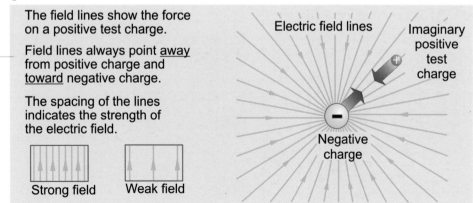

The field lines show the force on a positive test charge.

Field lines always point <u>away</u> from positive charge and <u>toward</u> negative charge.

The spacing of the lines indicates the strength of the electric field.

Strong field   Weak field

Electric field lines

Imaginary positive test charge

Negative charge

Calculating the electric field

Electric field strength The strength of the electric field determines the amount of force a charge feels near another charge. The object that creates the field is called the **source charge**. The charge you place to test the force is the *test* charge. The force (F) on the test charge is equal to the amount of charge (q) multiplied by the electric field (E), or $F = qE$. As we did with gravity, we can rewrite Coulomb's law so that the electric field is a separate quantity in the formula (Figure 18.11).

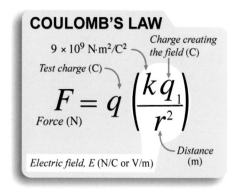

COULOMB'S LAW

$$F = q \left(\frac{kq_1}{r^2} \right)$$

9×10^9 N·m²/C² — Charge creating the field (C)
Test charge (C)
Force (N)
Electric field, E (N/C or V/m) — Distance (m)

Figure 18.11: *Coulomb's law can be written so that electric field and test charge (q) appear as separate quantities.*

Units of electric field With gravity, the strength of the field is in newtons per kilogram (N/kg) because the field describes the amount of force per kilogram of mass. With the electric field, the strength is in *newtons per coulomb* (N/C) for a similar reason. The electric field describes the amount of force per *coulomb of charge*. For example, a 10 C test charge feels 10 times as much force as a 1 C charge.

Volts per meter The electric field can also be written in more practical units. Remember, one volt is one joule per coulomb. A joule is equal to a newton·meter. By combining the relationships between units you can prove that one newton per coulomb is the same as one *volt per meter*. This is a prescription for how to make an electric field in the laboratory. A voltage difference of one volt over a space of one meter makes an electric field of 1 V/m. That same field exerts a force of one newton on a one-coulomb test charge (Figure 18.12). Note that in both Figure 18.12 and the graphic below, the 1-volt battery is hypothetical.

Current in a wire We can now explain how the voltage from a battery causes current to flow in a wire. Once the wire is connected, an electric field spreads very rapidly through the wire. The field spreads much faster than the movement of the electrons. Electrons throughout the wire begin moving and carrying current as soon as they feel the electric field. The electrons move slowly, at their drift velocity. The field however, moves at nearly the speed of light so it penetrates the entire wire almost instantaneously.

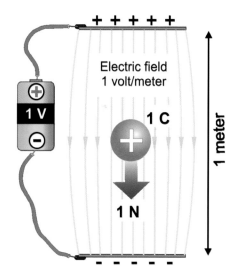

Figure 18.12: *A voltage difference of 1 volt across a distance of 1 meter makes an electric field of 1 volt per meter. This creates a force of 1 newton on a 1 coulomb test charge.*

The force on a charge in an electric field

The force on electrons in a wire

The force on a charge is equal to the charge in coulombs multiplied by the electric field in volts per meter (Figure 18.13). Like any force, the force from the electric field accelerates the charge on which it is acting. Inside a copper wire carrying current, the free electrons feel a force from the electric field. The force accelerates electrons in the direction of the field. Why don't the electrons get faster and faster and make the current go higher and higher? The answer is that the copper atoms get in the way. An electron only accelerates for a short distance before it collides with an atom. The electron bounces off and is accelerated for another short distance before it bounces off another atom. This is why the constant force from the electric field results in a constant drift velocity for electrons. In a similar way, we also see constant speed motion when the applied force equals the force of friction.

How to make an electron beam accelerator

An electric field is produced by any voltage difference across any insulating space, such as air or a vacuum. Many electrical devices use electric fields created in this way. For example, suppose voltage is created across a metal plate and screen (Figure 18.14). The plate repels electrons and the screen attracts electrons. Because the screen has holes, many of the electrons pass right through. Because the electrons feel a force between the plate and screen, this device is an *accelerator* for electrons. With such a device, electrons in the beam can easily move at speeds exceeding 1 million m/sec.

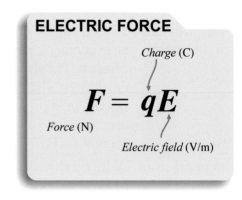

ELECTRIC FORCE

$$F = qE$$

Charge (C)

Force (N)

Electric field (V/m)

Figure 18.13: *The force on a charge in an electric field is equal to the charge in coulombs multiplied by the field strength in volts per meter.*

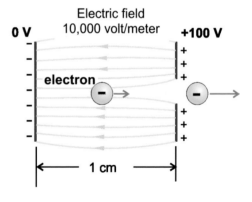

Figure 18.14: *An electric field between a plate and a screen makes an accelerator for charged particles like electrons.*

Calculating the electric force on a raindrop

A 1-gram drop of water has a static charge of 0.0001 coulombs. In a large thunderstorm, the drop might experience an electric field of 1,000 volts per meter. In this situation, what would be the force on the drop?

1. **Looking for:**   Force in newtons

2. **Given:**   Mass in grams and charge in coulombs

3. **Relationships:** $F = qE$

4. **Solution:** $F = (0.0001 \text{ C}) \times (1{,}000 \text{ V/m}) = 0.1 \text{ N}$

Your turn...

What is the force on a 0.005-coulomb charge in an electric field of 300 volts per meter? **Answer:** 1.5 N

Electric shielding

Conductors can block electric fields In a conductor, charges are free to move under the influence of any electric field. When a conductor is placed in an electric field, a very interesting thing happens. If the field is positive, negative charges move toward it until the field is neutralized. If the field is negative, electrons move away leaving enough positive charge behind to neutralize the field. *On the inside of the conductor, the field is zero*!

Computer network cable

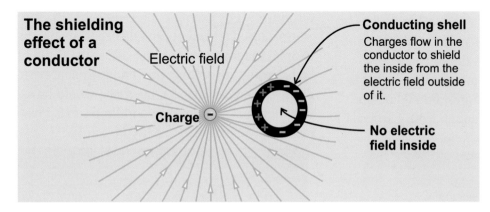

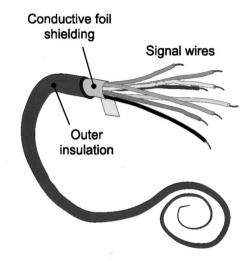

Figure 18.15: *Computer network cables have a conducting foil shield to keep out unwanted electric fields that could cause interference.*

Shielding out electrical interference Electric fields are created all around us by electric appliances, lightning, and even static electricity. These stray electric fields can interfere with the operation of computers and other sensitive electronics. Many electrical devices and wires that connect them are enclosed in conducting metal shells to take advantage of the **shielding** effect. For example, if you unwrap a computer network wire, you will find eight smaller wires wrapped by aluminum foil. The aluminum foil is a conductor and shields the wires inside from electrical interference (Figure 18.15).

18.3 Section Review

1. Draw the electric field around a negative charge. Do the field lines point toward or away from the charge?
2. What is the force on a 1-coulomb charge in an electric field of 1 volt per meter?
3. What is the electric field inside a good conductor which is not carrying current?

Space Weather is Magnetic

"Today's high will be 75°F with clear skies and sunshine. And it looks like the magnetic storm that on its way will affect our local electric power grid! More on this after a station break."

This fictional weather report includes information about space weather. The extent to which space weather affects Earth is actively investigated by scientists. Aiding this research is the Advanced Composition Explorer (ACE) satellite launched by NASA in 1997.

The ACE orbits one of a few unique points in space at which the gravitational pull on the satellite by Earth and the sun exactly cancel each other. For ACE, the center of its orbit is a point that is 148.5 million kilometers from the sun and 1.5 million kilometers from Earth. At this location, the ACE is far enough from Earth so that it is not affected by the planet's magnetic field.

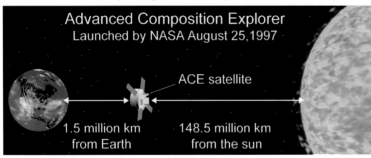

Advanced Composition Explorer
Launched by NASA August 25, 1997

ACE satellite

1.5 million km from Earth   148.5 million km from the sun

Storming Earth's atmosphere

The sun emits more than heat and light. The solar wind travels at 400 km/sec (about million miles per hour) and is composed of electrically charged particles. The solar wind comes from the sun's outer suface and is so hot that the sun's gravity cannot hold on to it. Evidence of solar wind comes from the tails of comets. A comet's tail acts like a "wind sock" and shows that there is a continuous flow of particles from the sun.

The Advanced Composition Explorer collects data on solar wind particles and provides one-hour advanced warnings of magnetic storms—events when solar wind is particularly intense due to massive solar eruptions. Magnetic storms can damage communications satellites orbiting Earth and cause electrical currents to flow through and overwhelm electric power grids on the ground. Potential consequences are disrupted radio, television, and telephone signals, and possible loss of electricity for homes and businesses. For example, on March 13, 1989, a major magnetic storm caused a blackout in Quebec, Canada, that affected 6 million people. Magnetic storms also affect the flight of spacecraft and can be hazardous to astronauts. If an astronaut performed a space walk during a magnetic storm, he or she would be exposed to space radiation that is more than a million times greater than the dose of radiation we experience daily on Earth!

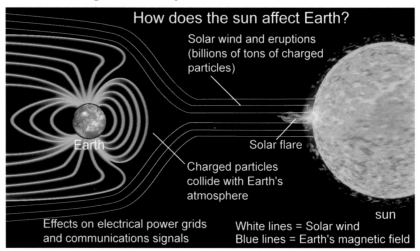

How does the sun affect Earth?

Solar wind and eruptions (billions of tons of charged particles)

Earth

Solar flare

Charged particles collide with Earth's atmosphere

sun

Effects on electrical power grids and communications signals

White lines = Solar wind
Blue lines = Earth's magnetic field

Gigantic magnetic spots

Solar wind and magnetic storms are associated with sunspots. Sunspots occur when magnetic fields—caused by the movement of gas within the sun—break the sun's surface. The spots which are cooler than surrounding areas appear dark because they give off less light than the than the gases around them. The magnetic field in a sunspot may be 5,000 times stronger than Earth's magnetic field!

Sunspots were observed by many early astronomers such as Galileo. In fact, Galileo harmed his eyesight by looking at the sun using a telescope. Remember, you should NEVER look directly at the sun. A safe method for viewing the sun is to project its image onto a white surface using a telescope or binoculars. When the sun is observed in this way, you can see the sunspots as dark areas. Although the areas look small, they can be as large as Earth.

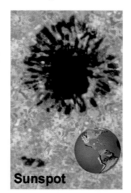
Sunspot

Occasionally, large "loops" of gas can be seen jumping up from groups of sunspots and extending far out into space. These are most easily observed during eclipses. Sometimes loops from different sunspot regions connect and become solar flares. The flares release such large amounts of heat and light that solar wind intensifies and causes magnetic storms.

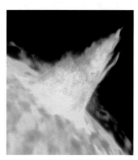

Sun activity in 11-year cycles

Not surprisingly, the occurrence of solar flares is related to the number of sunspots. The number of sunspots varies over an 11-year period known as the sunspot cycle. Many scientists speculate that there is a relationship between the sunspot cycle and variations in our global climate. Two decades of satellite research have shown that at times of high sunspot number, the amount of energy that reaches the edge of Earth's atmosphere increases slightly. However, only through further research will scientists be able to say how the sunspot cycle affects the global climate.

After a peak in the sunspot cycle, the sun emits billions of tons of gas referred to as coronal mass ejections (CMEs). As the gas leaves the sun's surface, its "magnetic skin" is shed as well. The result is that the sun's magnetic field lines are re-oriented and the build up of magnetism at the sun's surface begins again. Like solar flares, CMEs also cause magnetic storms on Earth.

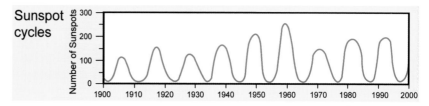

Magnetism shields Earth

Earth's magnetic field lines protect the planet from solar wind. The field lines, which exert force on moving charges, trap the electrical charges in solar wind and force them to move along the field lines particularly at the poles. When the charged particles encounter the upper atmosphere, they cause atmospheric atoms to emit light. The lights—called auroras—appear above the horizon in the night sky.

Auroras are a mild effect of solar wind. Magnetic storms are a dramatic form of space weather and scientists are very interested in predicting these storms since they can seriously disrupt our daily operations. For this reason, scientists pay close attention to space weather. You can too by getting a daily space weather report at the NASA-sponsored site www.spaceweather.com.

Questions:
1. Why is it important to have a satellite like the ACE in space? Research the ACE at http://www.srl.caltech.edu/ACE.
2. How can astronauts be protected from space radiation?
3. When are magnetic storms most likely to happen?
4. When will the next sunspot peak occur?

Chapter 18 Review

Understanding Vocabulary

Select the correct term to complete the sentences.

shielding	intensity	field
force field	gravitational field	test charge
inverse square law	source charge	electric field

Section 18.1

1. A quantity that has a value at every point in space is a _____.

2. _____ is a measure of power per area.

3. If two quantities are related by a(n) _____, as one increases the other rapidly decreases.

Section 18.2

4. Any object with mass creates a _____.

5. A _____ creates a force on any object placed in it that is sensitive to the force.

Section 18.3

6. The _____ points away from positive charges and toward negative charges.

7. Conductors have a _____ effect that causes the electric field inside a conductor to be zero.

8. A _____ creates an electric field.

9. It is helpful to imagine a positive _____ when drawing electric field lines.

Reviewing Concepts

Section 18.1

1. Interactions between _____ and _____ occur through fields.

2. List three types of fields that are affecting you right now.

3. What is stored in a field?

4. Why does a sound get quieter as you move away from its source?

5. In what units is intensity measured?

6. What does it mean to say a field follows an inverse square law?

7. Do all fields follow an inverse square law?

Section 18.2

8. Anything with _____ creates a gravitational field.

9. Why don't we notice the gravitational fields created by all of the objects around us?

10. What happens to the strength of Earth's gravitational field as you move away from Earth's surface?

11. Explain how you feel Earth's gravity even when you jump off the ground and are not directly touching the Earth.

12. In what units are gravitational fields measured?

13. In what direction do the gravitational field lines around the Earth point?

Section 18.3

14. A _____ charge in an electric field feels a force in the direction of the field. A _____ charge feels a force in a direction opposite the field.

15. What determines the strength of a charge's electric field at a certain point?

16. What two pieces of information can you get by looking at field lines?

17. What does the spacing of electric field lines tell you about the field strength?

18. In what units is electric field strength measured? List two possible answers.

19. What makes free electrons move through a wire in a circuit? Use the idea of electric fields in your answer.

20. Why are many electrical wires enclosed in a metal covering?

Solving Problems

Section 18.1

1. The light intensity 1 meter away from a bulb is 2 W/m^2. What is the intensity 2 meters away?

2. You stand 4 meters away from a light and measure the intensity to be 1 W/m^2. What will the intensity be if you move to a position 2 meters away?

Section 18.2

3. Gravitational fields follow an inverse square law. Suppose you weigh 600 newtons when you are on Earth's surface. How much would you weigh if you were to move away from the Earth so you doubled your distance from its center?

4. Jupiter has a mass of 1.9×10^{27} kilograms and a radius of 7.15×10^7 meters. Calculate the strength of Jupiter's gravitational field at its surface.

5. Jupiter's moon Io has a mass of 8.94×10^{22} kilograms and a radius of 1.82×10^6 meters. Calculate the strength of the gravitational field on Io's surface.

6. Use Newton's law of gravitation to show that Earth's gravitational field has a strength of 9.8 N/kg.

Section 18.3

7. Draw the electric field for each of the following.
   a. a single proton
   b. a single electron
   c. a proton a small distance away from an electron
   d. the region between two oppositely charged plates

8. The electric field in a region is shown below. At which marked point is the electric field the strongest? At which point is it the weakest?

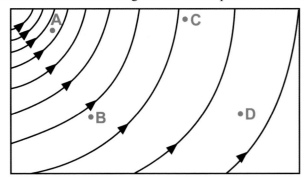

9. The electric field strength in a region is 2,000 N/C. What is the force on an object with a charge of 0.004 C?

10. What is the strength and direction of the force on each charge shown below?

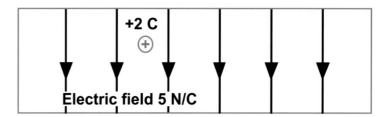

Applying Your Knowledge

Section 18.1

1. Are some types of fields vectors while others are scalars, or are all fields the same type of quantity? Explain using examples.

2. Fields cannot travel faster than the speed of light. List some examples of fields that travel slower than the speed of light and fields that travel at the speed of light.

3. Use the idea of intensity to explain why it is not a good idea to put your ear directly up to a loud stereo speaker.

4. If the Sun were to suddenly vanish, how long would it take for us to notice?

Section 18.2

5. A planet's gravitational field is represented with the letter g and is measured in N/kg. When you studied free fall, you measured g in m/sec^2. Show that the two units are equivalent.

6. Suppose you could double Earth's mass without changing its size. What would happen to the strength of the gravitational field? What if you instead doubled the radius but kept the mass at its current value?

Section 18.3

7. Research particle accelerators. How are they designed, and what are they used for?

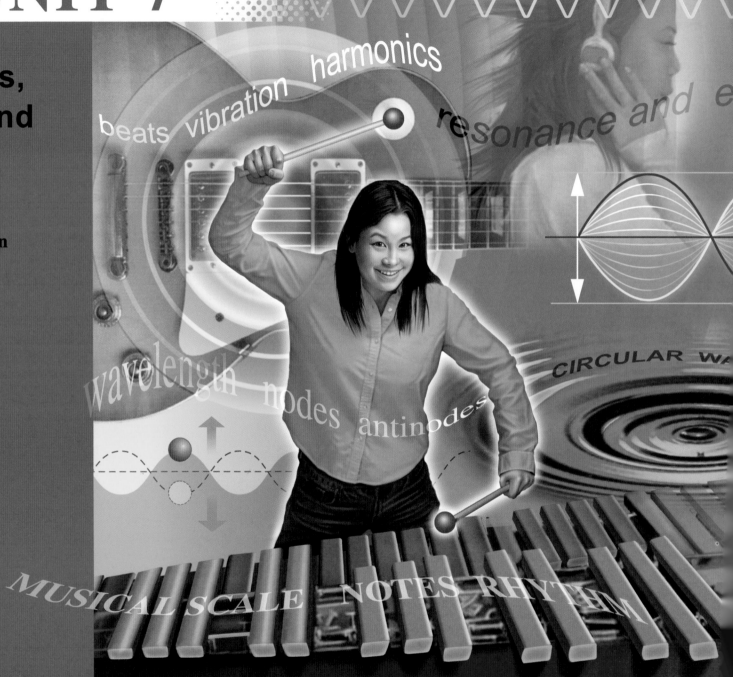

UNIT 7

Vibrations, Waves, and Sound

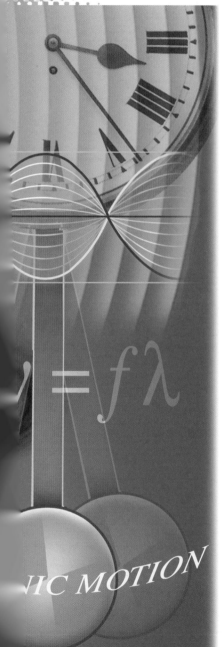

Chapter 19

Harmonic Motion

People often create habits that are repetitive because certain repetitive motions have regular comfortable rhythms. Babies like the feel of the back and forth motion of a rocking chair. It seems to make them feel happy and puts them to sleep. We see back and forth motion in many situations. Earth spins you around every 24 hours. Maybe this explains why we are often very comfortable with motions that have regular rhythms.

We see back-and-forth motion in many situations. A swing, the pendulum of a grandfather clock, and a rocking chair all have this kind of motion. Motion that repeats is called harmonic motion. Offered a choice to sit in a regular chair or a rocking chair, you might pick the rocking chair. For one thing, rocking back and forth is more fun than sitting still.

Harmonic motion includes motion that goes around and around. Earth orbiting the sun, the planet spinning on its axis, and a ferris wheel are all examples of this kind of harmonic motion.

Objects or systems that make harmonic motions are called oscillators. Think about where you see oscillators or oscillating systems in your school and home. Look around your classroom — where do you see oscillators? Where do you see back-and-forth motion or motion that goes around and around?

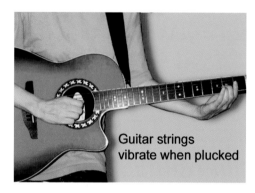

Guitar strings vibrate when plucked

Key Questions

✓ How many examples of harmonic motion exist in an amusement park?

✓ What do two "out of phase" oscillators look like?

✓ How is harmonic motion related to playing a guitar?

19.1 Harmonic Motion

The forward rush of a cyclist pedaling past you on the street is called *linear motion*. Linear motion gets us from one place to another whether we are walking, riding a bicycle, or driving a car (Figure 19.1). The pedaling action and turning of the cyclist's wheels are examples of harmonic motion. **Harmonic motion** is motion that repeats.

Motion in cycles

What is a cycle? In earlier chapters we used position, speed and acceleration to describe motion. For harmonic motion we need some new ideas that describe the "over-and-over" repetition. The first important idea is the **cycle**. A cycle is a unit of motion that repeats over and over. One spin of a bicycle wheel is a cycle and so is one turn of the pedals. One full back-and-forth swing of a child on a playground swing is also one cycle (Figure 19.1).

Looking at one cycle A pendulum's cycle is shown in the diagram below. Each box in the diagram is a snapshot of the motion at a different time in the cycle.

The cycle of a pendulum

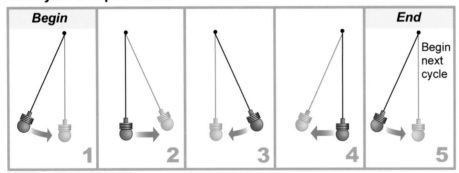

The cycle of a pendulum The cycle starts with (1) the swing from left to center. Next, the cycle continues with (2) center to right, and (3) back from right to center. The cycle ends when the pendulum moves (4) from center to left because this brings the pendulum back the the beginning of the next cycle. The box numbered "5" is the same as the one numbered "1" and starts the next cycle. Once a cycle is completed, the next cycle begins without any interruption in the motion.

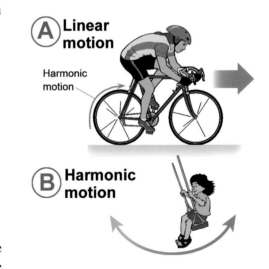

Figure 19.1: *(A) Real-life situations such as riding a bicycle can include both linear motion and harmonic motion. (B) A person on a swing is an example of harmonic motion in action.*

Where do you find harmonic motion?

Oscillators The word **oscillation** means a motion that repeats regularly. Therefore, a system with harmonic motion is called an **oscillator**. A pendulum is an oscillator; so is your heart and its surrounding muscles. Our solar system is a large oscillator with each planet in harmonic motion around the sun. An atom is a small oscillator because its electrons vibrate around the nucleus. The term **vibration** is another word used for back and forth. People tend to use "vibration" for motion that repeats fast and "oscillation" for motion that repeats more slowly.

Earth is part of harmonic motion systems Earth is a part of several oscillating systems. The Earth-sun system has a cycle of one year, which means Earth completes one orbit around the sun in a year. The Earth-moon system has a cycle of approximately 28 days. Earth itself has several different cycles (Figure 19.2). It rotates on its axis once a day, making the 24-hour cycle of day and night. There is also a wobble of Earth's axis that cycles every 22,000 years, moving the north and south poles around by hundreds of miles. There are cycles in weather, such as the El Niño Southern Oscillation, an event that involves warmer ocean water and increased thunderstorm activity in the western Pacific Ocean. Cycles are important; the lives of all plants and animals depend on seasonal cycles.

Music Sound is a traveling vibration of air molecules. Musical instruments and stereo speakers are oscillators that we design to create sounds with certain cycles that we enjoy hearing. When a stereo is playing, the speaker cone moves back and forth rapidly (Figure 19.3). The cyclic back-and-forth motion pushes and pulls on air, creating tiny oscillations in pressure. The pressure oscillations travel to your eardrum and cause it to vibrate. Vibrations of the eardrum move tiny bones in the ear setting up more vibrations that are transmitted by nerves to the brain. There is harmonic motion at every step of the way, from the musical instrument's performance to the perception of sound by your brain.

Color Light is the result of harmonic motion of the electric and magnetic fields (chapter 18). The colors that you see in a picture come from the vibration of electrons in the molecules of paint. Each color of paint contains different molecules that oscillate with different cycles to create the different colors of light you see (chapter 24).

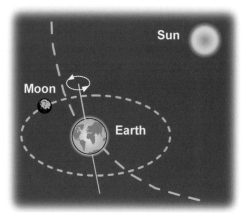

Figure 19.2: *The Earth-sun-moon system has many different cycles. The year, month, and day are the result of orbital cycles.*

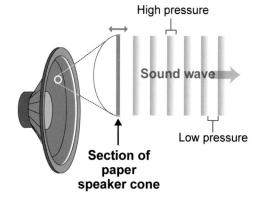

Figure 19.3: *As a speaker cone moves back and forth, it pushes and pulls on air, creating oscillating changes in pressure that we can detect with our ears. The dark blue bands in the graphic represent high pressure regions and the white bands represent low pressure regions.*

Describing harmonic motion

Oscillators in communications

Almost all modern communication technology relies on harmonic motion. The electronic technology in a cell phone uses an oscillator that makes more than 100 million cycles each second (Figure 19.4). When you tune into a station at 101 on the FM dial, you are actually setting the oscillator in your radio to 101,000,000 cycles per second.

Period is the time for one cycle

The time for one cycle to occur is called the **period**. The cycles of "perfect" oscillators always repeat with the same period. This makes harmonic motion a good way to keep time. For example, a clock pendulum with a period of one second will complete 60 swings (or cycles) in one minute. A clock keeps track of time by counting cycles of an oscillator.

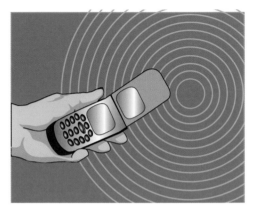

Figure 19.4: *The cell phone you use has an electronic oscillator at millions of cycles per second.*

A period is the time to complete one cycle of harmonic motion.

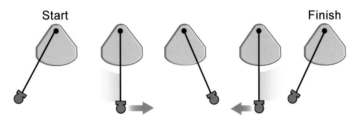

Start · Finish

Frequency is the number of cycles per second

The term **frequency** means the number of cycles per second. FM radio (the "FM" stands for frequency modulation) uses frequencies between 95 million and 107 million cycles per second. Your heartbeat has a frequency between one-half and two cycles per second. The musical note "A" has a frequency of 440 cycles per second. The human voice contains frequencies mainly between 100 and 2,000 cycles per second.

A hertz equals one cycle per second

The unit of one cycle per second is called a **hertz**. You hear music when the frequency of the oscillator in your radio exactly matches the frequency of the oscillator in the transmission tower connected to the radio station (Figure 19.5). A radio station dial set to 101 FM receives music broadcast at a frequency of 101,000,000 hertz or 101 megahertz. Your ear can hear frequencies of sound in the range from 20 Hz to between 15,000 and 20,000 Hz. The Hz is a unit that is the same in both the English and metric systems.

Figure 19.5: *You hear music from your car radio when the oscillator in your radio matches the frequency of the oscillator in the transmission tower connected to the radio station.*

Calculating harmonic motion

Frequency is the inverse of period
Frequency and period are inversely related. The period is the time per cycle. The frequency is the number of cycles per time. For example, if the period of a pendulum is 2 seconds, its frequency is 0.5 cycles per second (0.5 Hz).

PERIOD AND FREQUENCY

$$\text{Period (seconds)} \longrightarrow T = \frac{1}{f} \longleftarrow \text{Frequency (hertz)}$$

$$\text{Frequency (hertz)} \longrightarrow f = \frac{1}{T} \longleftarrow \text{Period (seconds)}$$

Calculating frequency

The period of an oscillator is 15 minutes. What is the frequency of this oscillator in hertz?

1. Looking for: You are asked for the frequency in hertz.

2. Given: You are given the period in minutes.

3. Relationships: Convert minutes to seconds using the conversion factor 1 minute/60 seconds; Use the formula: $f = {}^1/_T$;

4. Solution:

$$15\,\text{min} \times \frac{60\,\text{sec}}{1\,\text{min}} = 900\,\text{sec}; \quad f = \frac{1}{900\,\text{sec}} = 0.0011\,\text{Hz}$$

Your turn...

a. The period of an oscillator is 2 minutes. What is the frequency of this oscillator in hertz? **Answer:** 0.008 Hz

b. How often would you push someone on a swing to create a frequency of 0.20 hertz? **Answer:** every 5 seconds

c. The minute hand of a clock pendulum moves 1/60 of a turn after 30 cycles. What is the period and frequency of this pendulum? **Answer:** 60 seconds divided by 30 cycles = 2 seconds per cycle; the period is 2 seconds and the frequency is 0.5 Hz.

Keeping "perfect" time

The world's most accurate clock, the NIST-F1 Cesium Fountain Atomic Clock in Boulder, Colorado, keeps time by counting cycles of light waves emitted by a cluster of cesium atoms. This clock can run for more than 30 million years and not gain or lose a single second! The cesium atoms are cooled to near absolute zero by floating them in a vacuum on a cushion of laser light. The very low temperature is what makes the clock so stable and accurate. At normal temperatures the frequency of light waves would be affected by the thermal motion of the cesium atoms. Near absolute zero the thermal motion is all but eliminated. .

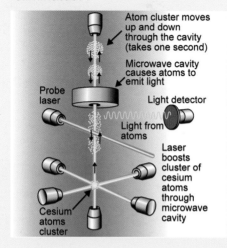

Amplitude

Amplitude describes the size of a cycle
You know the period is the time to complete a cycle. The **amplitude** describes the "size" of a cycle. Figure 19.6 shows a pendulum with small amplitude and large amplitude. With mechanical systems (such as a pendulum), the amplitude is often a distance or angle. With other kinds of oscillators, the amplitude might be voltage or pressure. The amplitude is measured in units appropriate to the kind of system you are describing.

How do you measure amplitude?
The amplitude is the maximum distance the oscillator moves away from its *equilibrium* position. For a pendulum, the equilibrium position is hanging straight down in the center. For the pendulum in Figure 19.7, the amplitude is 20 degrees, because the pendulum moves 20 degrees away from center in either direction.

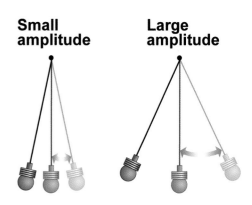

Figure 19.6: *Small amplitude versus large amplitude.*

Damping
Friction slows a pendulum down, as it does all oscillators. That means the amplitude slowly gets reduced until the pendulum is hanging straight down, motionless. We use the word **damping** to describe the gradual loss of amplitude of an oscillator. If you wanted to make a clock with a pendulum, you would have to find a way to keep adding energy to counteract the damping of friction.

19.1 Section Review

1. Which is the best example of a cycle: a turn of a bicycle wheel or a slide down a ski slope?
2. Describe one example of an oscillating system you would find at an amusement park.
3. What is the relationship between period and frequency?
4. Every 6 seconds a pendulum completes one cycle. What are the period and frequency of this pendulum?

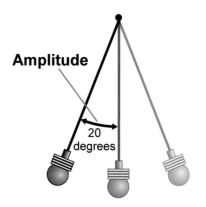

Figure 19.7: *A pendulum with an amplitude of 20 degrees swings 20 degrees away from the center.*

19.2 Graphs of Harmonic Motion

Harmonic motion graphs show cycles (Figure 19.8). Even without seeing the actual motion, you can look at a harmonic motion graph and figure out the period and amplitude. You can also quickly sketch an accurate harmonic motion graph if you know the period and amplitude.

Reading harmonic motion graphs

Repeating patterns
The most common type of graph puts position on the vertical (*y*) axis and time on the horizontal (*x*) axis. The graph below shows how the position of a pendulum changes over time. The repeating "wave" on the graph represents the repeating cycles of motion of the pendulum.

Finding the period
This pendulum has a period of 1.5 seconds so the pattern on the graph repeats every 1.5 seconds. If you were to cut out any piece of the graph and slide it over 1.5 seconds it would line up exactly. You can tell the period is 1.5 seconds because the graph repeats itself every 1.5 seconds.

Showing amplitude on a graph
The amplitude of harmonic motion can also be seen on a graph. The graph below shows that the pendulum swings from +20 centimeters to -20 centimeters and back. Therefore, the amplitude of the pendulum is 20 centimeters. Harmonic motion graphs often use positive and negative values to represent motion on either side of a center (equilibrium) position. Zero usually represents the equilibrium point. Notice that zero is placed halfway up the *y*-axis so there is room for both positive and negative values. This graph is in centimeters but the motion of the pendulum could also have been graphed using the angle measured relative to the center (straight down) position.

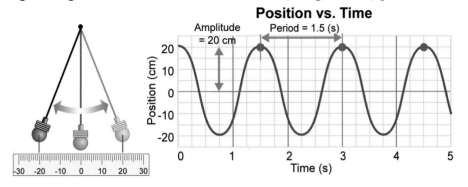

Vocabulary

phase

Objectives

✓ Recognize the difference between linear motion and harmonic motion graphs.
✓ Interpret graphs of harmonic motion.
✓ Determine amplitude and period from a harmonic motion graph.
✓ Recognize when two oscillators are in phase or out of phase.

Typical Linear Motion Graphs

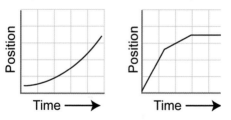

Typical Harmonic Motion Graphs

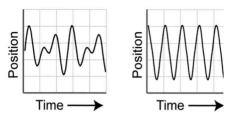

Figure 19.8: *Typical graphs for linear motion (top) and harmonic motion (bottom). Graphs of linear motion do not show cycles. Harmonic motion graphs show repeating cycles.*

Determining period and amplitude from a graph

Calculating period from a graph

To find the period from a graph, start by identifying one complete cycle. The cycle must begin and end in the same place in the pattern. Figure 19.9 shows how to choose the cycle for a simple harmonic motion graph and for a more complex one. Once you have identified a cycle, you use the time axis of the graph to determine the period. The period is the time difference between the beginning of the cycle and the end. Subtract the beginning time from the ending time, as shown in the example below.

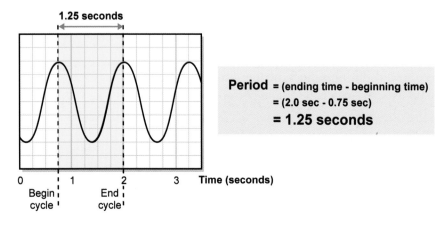

Period = (ending time - beginning time)
= (2.0 sec - 0.75 sec)
= **1.25 seconds**

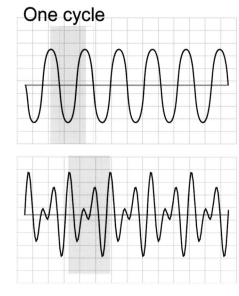

Figure 19.9: *The cycle is the part of the graph that repeats over and over. The yellow shading shows one cycle for each of the graphs above.*

Calculating amplitude from a graph

On a graph of harmonic motion, the amplitude is half the distance between the highest and lowest points on the graph. For example, in Figure 19.10, the amplitude is 20 centimeters. Here is the calculation:
[20 cm - (- 20 cm)] ÷ 2 = [20 cm + 20 cm] ÷ 2 = 40 cm ÷ 2 = 20 cm.

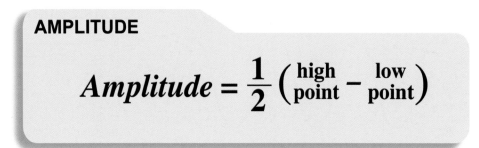

AMPLITUDE

$$Amplitude = \frac{1}{2}\left(\begin{matrix}\text{high}\\\text{point}\end{matrix} - \begin{matrix}\text{low}\\\text{point}\end{matrix}\right)$$

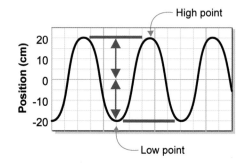

Figure 19.10: *The amplitude is one-half the distance between the highest and lowest points on the graph. In this graph of harmonic motion, the amplitude is 20 centimeters.*

Circular motion and phase

Phase How do you describe where a pendulum is in its cycle? Saying the pendulum is at a 10 degree angle is not enough. If the pendulum started at 10 degrees, then it would be at the start of its cycle. If the pendulum started at 20 degrees it would be part way through its cycle and could be near the start or the end. The **phase** tells you exactly where an oscillator is in its cycle. Phase is measured relative to the whole cycle, and is independent of amplitude or period.

Cycles of circular motion are 360° The most convenient way to describe phase is to think in terms of angles and circular motion. Circular motion is a kind of harmonic motion because rotation is a pattern of repeating cycles. The cycles of circular motion always measure 360 degrees. It does not matter how big the wheel is, each full turn is 360 degrees. Because circular motion always has cycles of 360 degrees, *we use degrees to measure phase*.

Phase is measured in degrees To see how degrees apply to harmonic motion that is not circular (such as a pendulum), imagine a peg on a rotating turntable (Figure 19.11). A bright light casts a shadow of the peg on the wall. As the turntable rotates, the shadow goes back and forth on the wall (A and B in Figure 19.11). If we make a graph of the position of the shadow, we get a harmonic motion graph (C). One cycle passes every 360 degree turn of the turntable. A quarter cycle has a phase of 90 degrees, half a cycle has a phase of 180 degrees and so on (Figure 19.11).

Two oscillators "in phase" The concept of phase is most important when comparing two or more oscillators. Imagine two identical pendulums. If you start them together, their graphs look like the picture below. We say these pendulums are *in phase* because their cycles are aligned. Each is at the same phase at the same time.

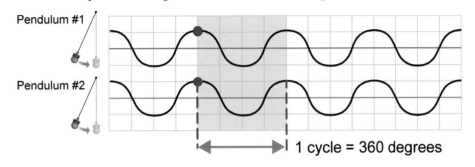

1 cycle = 360 degrees

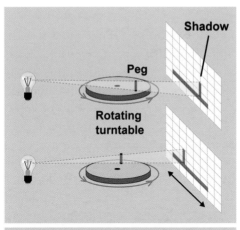

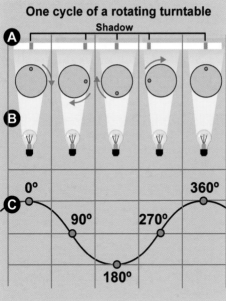

Figure 19.11: *The harmonic motion of a rotating turntable is illustrated by the back-and-forth motion of the shadow of the peg.*

Harmonic motion that is out of phase

Out of phase by 90 degrees
If we start the first pendulum swinging a little before the second one, the graphs look like Figure 19.12. Although, they have the same cycle, the first pendulum is always a little bit ahead of the second. Notice that the graph for pendulum number 1 reaches its maximum 90 degrees *before* the graph for pendulum number 2. We say the pendulums are *out of phase* by 90 degrees, or one-fourth of a cycle (90 degrees is one-fourth of 360 degrees).

Out of phase by 180 degrees
When they are out of phase, the relative motion of oscillators may differ by a little or by as much as half a cycle. Two oscillators that are 180 degrees out of phase are one-half cycle apart. Figure 19.13 shows that the two pendulums are always on opposite sides of the cycle from each other. When pendulum number 1 is all the way to the left, pendulum number 2 is all the way to the right. This motion is illustrated on the graph by showing that "peaks" of motion (positive amplitude) for one pendulum match the "valleys" of motion (negative amplitude) for the other.

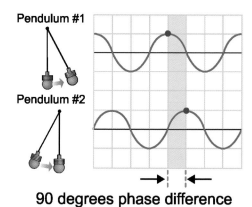

90 degrees phase difference

Figure 19.12: *The two pendulums are 90 degrees out of phase.*

19.2 Section Review

1. What is the difference between a graph of linear motion and a graph of harmonic motion?

2. A graph of the motion of a pendulum shows that it swings from +5 centimeters to -5 centimeters for each cycle. What is the amplitude of the pendulum?

3. A pendulum swings from -10 degrees to +10 degrees. What is the amplitude of this pendulum?

4. A graph of harmonic motion shows that one cycle lasted from 4.3 seconds to 6.8 seconds. What is the period of this harmonic motion?

5. A graph of harmonic motion shows that the motion lasted for 10 seconds and it included 5 cycles. What is the period of this harmonic motion?

6. Sketch the periodic motion for two oscillators that are 45 degrees out of phase.

7. If one oscillator were out of phase with another oscillator by 45 degrees, what fraction of a 360-degree cycle would it be out of phase? 1/8, 1/4, 1/2, or 3/4?

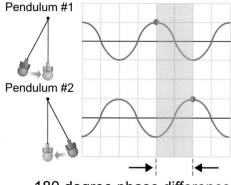

180 degree phase difference

Figure 19.13: *The two pendulums are 180 degrees out of phase.*

19.3 Properties of Oscillators

Why does a pendulum oscillate? A car on a ramp just rolls down and does not oscillate. What properties of a system determine whether its motion will be linear motion or harmonic motion? You will learn the answers to these questions in this section. You will also learn how to change the period of an oscillator by changing the ratio of a few important variables.

Restoring force and equilibrium

Different kinds of systems

If you set a wagon on a hill and let it go, the wagon rolls down and does not come back. If you push a child on a swing, the child goes away from you at first, but then comes back. The child on the swing shows harmonic motion while the wagon on the hill does not. What is the fundamental difference between the two situations?

A wagon rolling down a hill will **not** have harmonic motion.

Why?

A child on a swing <u>will</u> have harmonic motion.

Equilibrium

Systems that have harmonic motion always move back and forth around a central or **equilibrium** position. You can think of equilibrium as the system at rest, undisturbed, with zero net force. A wagon on a hill is *not* in equilibrium because the force of gravity is not balanced by another force. A child sitting motionless on a swing *is* in equilibrium because the force of gravity is balanced by the tension in the ropes.

Restoring forces

Equilibrium is maintained by restoring forces. A **restoring force** is any force that always acts to pull the system back toward equilibrium. If the child on the swing is moved forward, gravity creates a restoring force that pulls her back, toward equilibrium. If she moves backward, gravity pulls her forward, back to equilibrium again (Figure 19.14). Systems with restoring forces are the ones that move in harmonic motion.

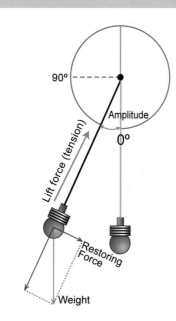

Figure 19.14: *Restoring force keeps a pendulum swinging. Restoring force is related to weight and the lift force (or tension) of the string of a pendulum.*

Inertia and mass

Inertia causes an oscillator to go past equilibrium

The restoring force of gravity always pulls a pendulum towards equilibrium. Why doesn't the pendulum just stop at equilibrium? Newton's first law of motion explains why. According to the first law, an object in motion tends to stay in motion. The pendulum has inertia that keeps it moving forward. Inertia causes the pendulum to overshoot its equilibrium position every time. The result is harmonic motion.

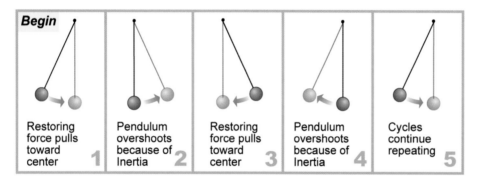

Begin

Restoring force pulls toward center **1**

Pendulum overshoots because of Inertia **2**

Restoring force pulls toward center **3**

Pendulum overshoots because of Inertia **4**

Cycles continue repeating **5**

Inertia is common to all oscillators

All systems that oscillate on their own (without a motor) have some property that acts like inertia and some type of restoring force. Harmonic motion results from the interaction of the two effects: inertia and restoring force.

Increasing mass may increase the period

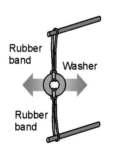

Rubber band

Washer

Rubber band

You can make a simple oscillator with a steel washer and two rubber bands (picture). What happens to the period if you increase the mass by adding more washers? The restoring force from the rubber band is the same. If the mass increases, then (by Newton's second law) the acceleration decreases proportionally. That means the oscillator moves slower and the period gets longer.

How mass affects the period

Changing the mass of a pendulum does *not* affect its period. That is because the restoring force on a pendulum is created by gravity. Like free fall, if you add mass to a pendulum the added inertia is exactly equal to the added force from gravity. The acceleration is the same and therefore the period stays the same.

Harmonic motion in machines

Natural harmonic motion results from restoring forces and inertia. However, harmonic motion can also be forced. When a machine is involved, cycles of motion can be created using an energy source to push or rotate parts. Mechanical systems usually do not depend on a restoring force or inertia to keep going.

For example, the piston of a car engine goes up and down as the crank turns. The piston is in harmonic motion, but the motion is caused by the rotation of the crankshaft and the attachment of the connecting rod. Gasoline provides the energy to keep this harmonic motion system going.

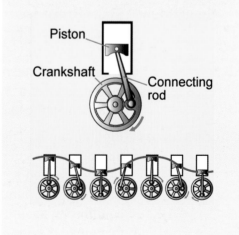

Piston

Crankshaft

Connecting rod

eriod and natural frequency

Natural frequency
A pendulum will have the same period each time you set it in motion. Unless you change the pendulum itself (such as changing its length) it will always swing with the same period. The **natural frequency** is the frequency (or period) at which a system naturally oscillates. Every system that oscillates has a natural frequency.

Why natural frequency is important
Microwave ovens, musical instruments, and cell phones are common devices that use the natural frequency of an oscillator. For example, the strings of a guitar are tuned by adjusting the natural frequency of vibrating strings to match musical notes (Figure 19.15). All objects can oscillate, and that means everything in the universe has a natural frequency. In fact, most things have several natural frequencies because they can oscillate in different ways.

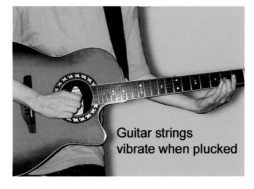

Guitar strings vibrate when plucked

Figure 19.15: *A guitar uses the natural frequency of strings to make musical notes. Here, the musician plays the musical note A. As a result, the string vibrates at 440 hertz.*

Natural frequency

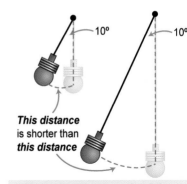

This distance is shorter than this distance

Changing the length of the string changes the period of a pendulum

The natural frequency depends on the balance between restoring force and inertia (mass). Any change that affects this balance will also change the natural frequency. The natural frequency of a pendulum depends on the length of the string. If you make the string longer, the restoring force is spread out over a proportionally greater distance. The period of the pendulum gets longer. Tuning a guitar changes the natural frequency of a string by changing its tightness (or *tension*). Changing the mass changes the natural frequency *only if restoring force is not due to gravity.*

Periodic force
You can keep a swing (pendulum) swinging for a long time by pushing it at the right time every cycle. A force that is repeated over and over is called a **periodic force**. A periodic force has a cycle with an amplitude, frequency and period, just like an oscillator. *To supply energy to an oscillator you need to use a periodic force.* A constant force will not have the same effect. If you push once per cycle (periodic force) the amplitude of a swing increases (Figure 19.16). If you applied a constant force of the same strength, the swing would move in the direction of your force and stay there, motionless.

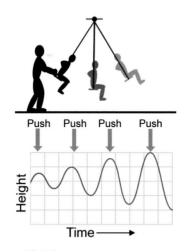

Figure 19.16: *Each push of a swing at the right time increases the amplitude (height) of the swing. Each push is a periodic force.*

Resonance

Force and natural frequency

Newton's second law ($a = F/m$) tells you how much acceleration you get for a given force and mass. While the second law is still true for harmonic motion, there is a new and important difference. Harmonic motion is motion that oscillates back and forth. What happens if the force is periodic and oscillates back and forth too? When you shake one end of a rope up and down in a steady rhythm you are applying a periodic force to the rope (Figure 19.17). The rope behaves very differently depending on the frequency at which you shake it up and down! If you shake it at *just the right frequency* the rope swings up and down in harmonic motion with a large amplitude. If you don't shake at the right frequency, the rope wiggles around but you don't get the large amplitude *no matter how strong a force you apply*.

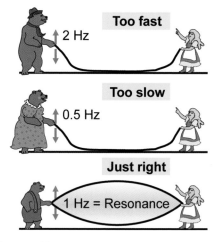

Figure 19.17: *A jump rope is a good example of resonance. If you shake it at the right frequency, it makes a big wave motion. If your frequency is too fast or too slow, the rope will not make the wave pattern at all.*

Resonance

Resonance occurs when a periodic force has the same frequency as the natural frequency of the system. If the force and the motion have the same frequency, each cycle of the force matches a cycle of the motion. As a result each push adds to the next one and the amplitude of the motion grows. You can think about resonance in three steps: the *periodic force*, the *system*, and the *response*. The response is what the system does when you apply the periodic force (Figure 19.18). In resonance, the response is very large compared to the strength of the force, much larger than you would expect. Resonance occurs when:

- there is a system in harmonic motion, like a swing;
- there is a periodic force, like a push;
- the frequency of the periodic force matches the natural frequency of the system.

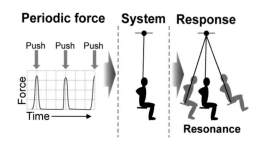

Figure 19.18: *When you push someone on a swing, you are using resonance. Small or big pushes at the right time in a swing's motion will make a person swing higher. If the periodic force (the push) is applied at the wrong time, the swing does not swing at all.*

A jump rope is a example of resonance

Like a swing, a jump rope depends on resonance. If you want to get a jump rope going, you shake the ends up and down. By shaking the ends, you are applying a periodic force to the rope. However, if you have tried to get a jump rope going, you have noticed that you have to get the right rhythm to get the rope moving with a large amplitude (Figure 19.17). The extra-strong response at 1 hertz is an example of resonance and happens only when the frequency (rhythm) of your periodic force matches the natural frequency of the jump rope.

Simple oscillators

A mass on a spring
You know from experience that springs resist being extended or compressed. Figure 19.19 shows how the restoring force from a spring always acts to return it to equilibrium. A system of a mass on a spring is a simple oscillator. When the spring is compressed, it pushes back on the mass. When the spring is extended, it pulls on the mass. The system is an oscillator because the push-pull of the spring is a restoring force and the mass supplies the inertia. An example of a mass on a spring is a car (mass) and its shock absorbers (springs). Wheels on springs can oscillate up and down over bumps without the whole car having to move up and down too. Along with springs, shock absorbers also have high friction *dampers* that quickly slow any oscillation down. A car that keeps bouncing after going over a bump has shock absorbers with dampers that are worn out and not providing enough friction.

A vibrating string
An example of a *vibrating string* oscillator is a rubber band stretched between two rods (Figure 19.20). If the middle of the rubber band is pulled to the side, it will move back toward being straight when it is released. Stretching the rubber band to the side creates a restoring force. When the rubber band is released, inertia carries it past being straight and it vibrates. Vibrating strings tend to move much faster than springs and pendulums. The period of a vibrating string can be one-hundredth of a second (0.01 second) or shorter.

Mass on a vibrating string
You can modify the rubber band oscillator by adding a bead to the middle of a stretched rubber band (Figure 19.20). The bead adds extra mass (inertia) to this simple oscillator. How would adding a bead to a rubber band change the natural frequency? Notice that gravity is not directly involved in the back and forth movement of this oscillator.

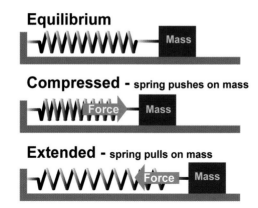

Figure 19.19: *A mass on a spring is an oscillating system. When the spring is compressed, it pushes back on the mass to return to equilibrium. When the spring is extended, it pulls the mass back toward equilibrium.*

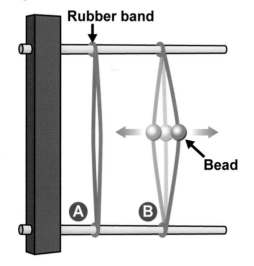

Figure 19.20: *A stretched rubber band is a good example of a vibrating string (A). You can modify this simple oscillator by adding a bead to the rubber band (B).*

19.3 Section Review

1. Identify the restoring force for a pendulum, a mass on a spring, and a vibrating string.
2. You change the amplitude of a pendulum from 10 centimeters to 30 centimeters. How does this change affect the period of the pendulum? Justify your answer.
3. Is a person jumping on a trampoline an oscillator? Justify your response.
4. If you wanted to increase the period of a pendulum, how would you change its length?

Skyscrapers and Harmonic Motion

The John Hancock Tower is one of the tallest skyscrapers in New England. This 60-story building is 240.7 meters (790 feet) tall and was completed in 1976. With 10,344 windowpanes, the most striking feature of this building is that it is completely covered in glass!

John Hancock Tower
Boston, Massachusetts

While this skyscraper was being built in 1972 and 1973, a disaster struck—windowpanes started falling out from all over the building and crashing to the ground. So many fell out that, with the boarded up window holes, the Hancock Tower was nicknamed the "plywood palace." Some people said the windows fell out because the building swayed too much in the wind—they thought the problem was due to the natural harmonic motion of the skyscraper.

Why does a skyscraper sway?

Just like trees which experience harmonic motion in strong winds, skyscrapers also sway side to side. Skyscrapers or any buildings, even though made of steel and concrete, begin to vibrate when the wind blows or an earthquake occurs. All buildings have a fundamental frequency of vibration. For example, the fundamental frequencies for buildings range as follows: 10 hertz for one-story buildings, 2 hertz for a three- to five-story buildings, 0.5 to 1 for tall buildings (10 to 20 stories high), and 0.17 hertz for skyscrapers.

On the top floor of some skyscrapers, with a strong wind, the amplitude of their side-to-side motion ("sway") can be several feet. Therefore, engineers have carefully designed skyscrapers to handle a large swaying motion. Engineers strive to keep the amplitude very small so that the people inside will not be disturbed. When the falling windowpanes of the Hancock Tower were blamed on the building's sway, engineers were quick to point out that the John Hancock Tower was designed to sway slightly. Engineers did not think the sway of this building was causing the falling windows.

Swaying is a form of simple harmonic motion. Swaying starts with a disturbing or force such as the wind pushing on the side of the building. A restoring force keeps the motion always accelerating back towards its equilibrium point. In a skyscraper, the equilibrium point is when the building is perfectly straight. For a skyscraper, the restoring force is provided by the mass of the structure of the skyscraper. The Hancock Tower has a stiff backbone made up of steel columns and beams in the skyscraper's core. That extra sturdiness allows the building to bend slightly and then ease back towards its center point. Some skyscrapers get their restoring force from hollow, rigid tubes at the perimeter of the structure. The advantage of the tubes is that they are a strong core design, with less weight.

The Citicorp Center in New York City was the first building to have a mechanical means for providing a restoring force to counteract swaying. A 410-ton concrete weight housed on the top floors of the building slides back and forth in opposition to the sway caused by wind. Thus, the restoring force in the Citicorp Center is accomplished by

Citicorp Center
New York, New York

shifting the center of mass of the building so that gravity pulls the building back towards its "straight" or equilibrium position. The device used in the Citicorp Center is called a wind-compensating damper or "tuned mass damper."

William LeMessurier, an innovative engineer, installed the tuned mass damper in the Citicorp Center. LeMessurier was also involved in installing a tuned mass damper in the Hancock Tower. This device wasn't necessary to stop windows from falling, but was used to keep the building from twisting as it swayed — a very disturbing affect felt by the people on the top floors of the building.

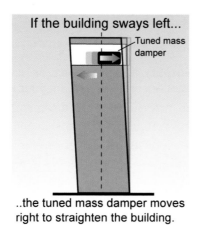

If the building sways left...

Tuned mass damper

..the tuned mass damper moves right to straighten the building.

What is the tallest building in the world?

The current world champion of skyscrapers (2004) is Taipei 101 located in Taiwan. It is 508 meters tall (1,667 feet) with 101 floors above ground. Since both earthquakes and wind are concerns in Taiwan, the building's engineers took extra precautions. The 800-ton wind-compensating damper at the top of the building is a large spherical shape hung as a simple pendulum. The damper is visible to the public on the 88th and 89th floors where there is a restaurant! When the building begins to sway either due to wind or an earthquake, the damper acts as a restoring force. The Taipei 101 is built to withstand an earthquake greater than 7 on the Richter scale!

Other countries are currently constructing skyscrapers that will be even taller than Taipei 101. So, this world record holder will not be the tallest building for very long. With modern materials, and future innovations yet to come, the main limitation to the height of future skyscrapers is the cost to build such tall buildings!

The reason for the falling windows

The windows of the Hancock Tower fell out because of how the double-paned glass was bonded to the window frame. The bonding prevented the glass from responding to temperature changes and wind forces. Because the windows were held too rigidly by the bonding, the glass fractured easily and fell out. The modern John Hancock Tower sways slightly in the wind just like before, but without twisting thanks to the tuned mass damper. Also, the bonding of the windows has been fixed, and now the windows stay in place.

Some of the world's tallest buildings

519 m (1703 ft)

508 m (1667 ft)

452 m (1486 ft)

449 m (1472 ft)

Sears Tower
Chicago, Illinois

Taipei 101
Taipei, Taiwan

Petronas Towers
Kuala Lumpur, Malaysia

Empire State Building
New York, New York

Questions:

1. From the reading, why were the windows falling out of the John Hancock Tower?

2. Describe the sway of a building. Use the terms force and harmonic motion in your answer.

3. Research and write a brief report about William LeMessier's work on the Citicorp Center.

4. Research the John Hancock Tower and find out what its tuned mass damper looks like and how it works.

5. Find out why Taipei 101 "beats" the Sears Tower as the world's tallest building.

Chapter 19 Review

Understanding Vocabulary

Select the correct term to complete the sentences.

oscillators	phase	harmonic motion
frequency	resonance	cycle
natural frequency	hertz	period
damping	restoring force	vibration
amplitude		

Section 19.1

1. Frequency is measured in ____.

2. A ____ is the building block of harmonic motion and has a beginning and an end.

3. The time it takes for one cycle is called the ____.

4. Motion that repeats itself over and over is called ____.

5. The number of cycles an oscillator makes per second is called the ____.

6. A pendulum, an atom, and the solar system are all examples of ____.

7. ____ describes the size of a cycle.

8. Swinging motion (back and forth motion that repeats) is an example of a ____.

9. Friction causes ____ in an oscillator.

Section 19.2

10. The ____ of an oscillator describes where it is in the cycle.

Section 19.3

11. When the frequency of a periodic force matches the natural frequency of the oscillating system, ____ occurs.

12. A guitar is tuned by adjusting the ____ of the vibrating string to match a musical note.

13. The ____ is a force that always acts to pull an oscillator back toward the center position.

Reviewing Concepts

Section 19.1

1. Identify the following as examples of harmonic motion, linear motion, or both. Explain your answer.
   a. A child moving down a playground slide one time
   b. An ocean wave rising and falling
   c. A car moving down the street
   d. A ball bouncing up and down

2. A system with harmonic motion is called an oscillator. Oscillators can be virtually any size. List at least one example of a very large oscillator and a very small oscillator.

3. Describe a single cycle of harmonic motion for the following situations:
   a. A spinning merry-go-round
   b. Earth's orbit around the sun
   c. A clock pendulum

4. Using a person on a swing as an example of harmonic motion, describe these terms:
   a. period
   b. frequency
   c. cycle
   d. amplitude

5. Your favorite radio station is 106.7. What are the units on this number and what do they mean in terms of harmonic motion?

6. What is the mathematical relationship between frequency and period for a harmonic motion system?

7. Name a unit used to measure the following:
   a. amplitude
   b. frequency
   c. period
   d. mass

Section 19.2

8. Describe how you would determine the period and amplitude of an oscillator from a graph of its harmonic motion. You may use a diagram to help you answer this question.

9. Two players dribble basketballs at the same time. How does the motion of the basketballs compare if they are in phase? out of phase?

10. Explain why circular motion, like the motion of a ferris wheel, is an example of harmonic motion.

Section 19.3

11. If the length of the rope on a swing gets longer:
    a. What happens to the period of the swing?
    b. What happens to the frequency of the swing?

12. Pushing a child on a playground swing repeatedly at the natural frequency causes resonance, which increases the amplitude of the swing, and the child goes higher. If the pushes provide the periodic force of the system, what provides the restoring force?

13. Identify the equilibrium position for the following situations.
    a. A person on a swing
    b. A person bungee jumping
    c. A guitar string being plucked

14. What is resonance and how is it created? Give an example of a resonant oscillating system in nature.

Solving Problems

Section 19.1

1. The wings of a honeybee move at a frequency of 220 Hz. What is the period for a complete wing-beat cycle?

2. If a pendulum's period is 4 seconds, what is its frequency?

3. What is the period of Earth spinning on its axis? What is its frequency? (Hint: How long does it take for one spin?)

4. Jason's heartbeat is measured to be 65 beats per minute.
    a. What is the frequency of heartbeats in hertz?
    b. What is the period for each heartbeat in seconds?

5. In the table below, fill in the period and frequency for the second hand, minute hand, and hour hand of a clock.

	Period (seconds)	Frequency (hertz)
Second hand		
Minute hand		
Hour hand		

Section 19.2

6. The graph shows the motion of an oscillator that is a weight hanging from a rubber band. The weight moves up and down. Answer the following questions using the graph.

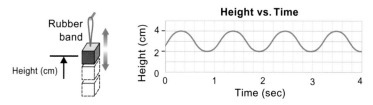

a. What is the period?
b. What is the frequency?
c. What is the amplitude?
d. If you count for 5 seconds, how many cycles would you count?

7. Make a graph of three cycles of motion for a pendulum that has a period of 2 seconds and an amplitude of 5 centimeters.

8. Which of the following graphs illustrates the harmonic motion of two children on swings 180 degrees out of phase. What fraction of a 360-degree cycle are these two graphs out of phase: $^1/_8$, $^1/_4$, $^1/_2$, or $^3/_4$?

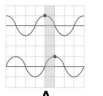 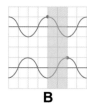 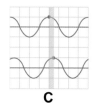

| A | B | C |

Section 19.3

9. The mass on a pendulum bob is increased by a factor of two. How is the period of the pendulum affected?

10. Describe how you might change the natural frequency of the following oscillating systems.

    a. a guitar string

    b. a playground swing

    c. a paddle ball game with a ball attached to a paddle with an elastic

    d. a diving board

11. How does decreasing the length of a pendulum affect its period?

Applying Your Knowledge

Section 19.1

1. The human heart is both strong and reliable. As a demonstration of how reliable the heart is, calculate how many times your heart beats in one day. Start by measuring the frequency of your pulse in beats per minute and use the result for your calculation.

2. Ocean tides rise and fall based on the position of the moon as it moves around Earth. The ocean's water is pulled in the direction of the moon by the moon's gravity. The sun's gravity also affects the tides, but because of its great distance from Earth, the effect is not as strong as the moon's. The graphic shows different positions of the moon relative to Earth and the sun.

    a. Which two positions of the moon result in greater tide amplitudes (these are called *spring tides*)? Which two positions result in smaller tide amplitude (these are called *neap tides*)? Refer to the graphic above.

    b. Challenge question: In many places on Earth there are two high tides and two low tides each day. Why do you think this happens?

3. The solar system is an oscillator with each of the planets in harmonic motion around the sun. Give five examples of cycles that relate to the solar system and also give the period and frequency of each example. Use your library or the Internet to find the answers to this question.

4. A sewing machine makes sewing stitches, a repeating task, easier. As a result, many parts of a sewing machine have harmonic motion. Find a sewing machine to examine. List two parts of this machine that use harmonic motion. If you don't know the names of certain parts, make a diagram of the machine to help you explain your answer.

Section 19.2

5. The graphic shows the harmonic motion of a pirate ship amusement park ride. Use what you know about kinetic and potential energy to answer the following questions.

    a. Where in its cycle does the pirate ship have its highest potential energy? its lowest potential energy?

    b. Where in its cycle does pirate ship have its highest kinetic energy? its lowest kinetic energy?

    c. Make a graph of the amount of kinetic energy the ride has during one cycle of motion. On the same graph, plot the amount of potential energy during one cycle of motion. Use the point at which the ride it at its highest as the starting point of the cycle. Is this graph like a harmonic motion graph? Why or why not?

Section 19.3

6. Buildings are not completely stiff — they sway side-to-side at their natural frequency. What do you think happens if the natural frequency of a building matches the frequency of an earthquake? How could a building's natural frequency be changed?

7. The cycle of motion of a pendulum is created by the restoring force of the weight of the bob. As with all motion, the harmonic motion of a pendulum must follow Newton's laws of motion.

    a. Newton's first law states that objects tend to keep doing what they are doing. How does the first law apply to a pendulum?

    b. Newton's second law states that $a = F \times m$. Which fact about the motion of a pendulum does the second law explain: (1) that changing the mass *does not* change the period, or (2) that changing the length *does* change the period.

    c. Name an action-reaction pair of the pendulum that illustrates Newton's third law.

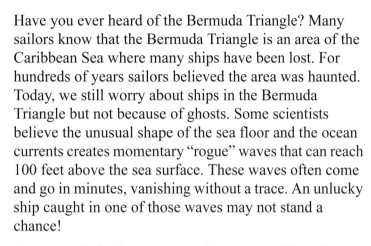

Chapter 20

20

Waves

Have you ever heard of the Bermuda Triangle? Many sailors know that the Bermuda Triangle is an area of the Caribbean Sea where many ships have been lost. For hundreds of years sailors believed the area was haunted. Today, we still worry about ships in the Bermuda Triangle but not because of ghosts. Some scientists believe the unusual shape of the sea floor and the ocean currents creates momentary "rogue" waves that can reach 100 feet above the sea surface. These waves often come and go in minutes, vanishing without a trace. An unlucky ship caught in one of those waves may not stand a chance!

Any coastal city has to worry about waves. Therefore, many harbors are designed to reduce the size of water waves. A quiet harbor allows for sailboats to sail, for goods to be brought in by big ships, and for coastal buildings to be safe. At beaches it is also important that waves not be too big so the water is safe for swimmers. Special computer programs allow designers of coastal areas to determine how to control waves. Usually, underwater structures are built to dampen waves. If you are a surfer, however, you want big waves. The same computer programs also predict the location of the biggest waves.

Water waves are useful for learning because they are easy to make and study. What you know about water waves applies to other waves too — including sound, light, and microwaves. The ideas even apply to gravity waves that occur when black holes crash into each other.

Key Questions

✓ How is your cell phone like a traffic light or a drum?
✓ Which wave interactions are involved in how sunglasses work?
✓ What is anti-noise?

20.1 Waves

A **wave** is an oscillation that travels from one place to another. A musician's instrument creates waves that carry sound to your ears. Dialing a cell phone to call a friend sends microwaves from the cell phone antenna; the microwaves carry the signal containing your voice to your friend. Similarly, when you throw a stone into a pond, the energy of the falling stone creates a waves in the water that carry the energy to the edge of the pond. In this section you will learn about waves.

Why learn about waves?

What is a wave? If you poke a ball floating on water it moves up and down in harmonic motion. But something else happens to the water as the ball oscillates. The surface of the water oscillates in response and the oscillation spreads outward from where it started. An oscillation that travels is a wave.

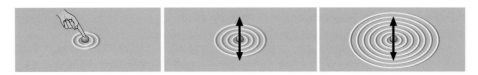

Energy and information Waves carry an oscillation from one place to another, causing oscillation in whatever they encounter. Because waves can change motion, we know that waves are a traveling form of energy. Waves also carry information, such as conversations, pictures, or music. Waves are used in many technologies because they can quickly carry information over great distances. The sound wave from a violin carries information about the vibration of the strings to your ear. Your ear hears the vibrations as music. In a similar way, a radio wave carries sounds from a transmitter to your car stereo. Another kind of radio wave carries television signals. All the information you receive in your eyes and ears comes from waves (Figure 20.1).

- The light from the traffic light is a wave.
- The ripples in the puddle of water are waves.
- The electricity flowing in the wires attached to the street lights is a wave.
- Waves carry radio, TV, and cell phone transmissions through the air all around you.

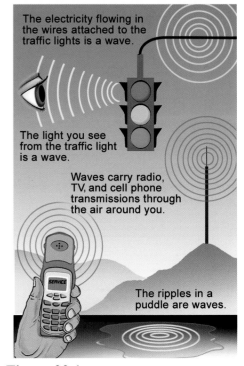

The electricity flowing in the wires attached to the traffic lights is a wave.

The light you see from the traffic light is a wave.

Waves carry radio, TV, and cell phone transmissions through the air around you.

The ripples in a puddle are waves.

Figure 20.1: *Many examples of waves.*

Recognizing waves

How do you recognize a wave? All waves are traveling oscillations that move energy from one place to another. The energy might be in actual motion, or it might be sound, light, or another form of energy. When you see the things in this list, you should suspect that there is some kind of wave involved.

Waves are present:

- when you see a vibration that moves.
  Example: A guitar string after it is plucked
- when something makes or responds to sound.
  Example: A drum or your ears
- when something makes or responds to light.
  Example: A light bulb or your eyes
- when technology allows us to "see through" objects.
  Examples: ultrasound, CAT scans, MRI scans, and X rays
- when information travels through the air (or space) without wires.
  Example: A satellite dish for receiving television signals

Waves transmit information Waves are present whenever information, energy, or motion is transmitted over a distance without anything obviously moving. The remote control on a TV is an example. To change the channel you can use the remote or you can get up and push the buttons with your finger. Both actions provide the information needed to change the channel on the TV. One action uses physical motion and the other uses a wave that goes from the remote control to the television. Your knowledge of physics and waves tells you there must be some kind of wave coming from the remote control because information traveled from one place to another, and nothing appeared to move. The wave from the remote control is infrared light that is invisible to the eye.

All waves have common properties. Like oscillations, waves have the properties of frequency, period, and amplitude. Information in waves is often transmitted in patterns of changing amplitude or frequency. For example, the number two might be represented by a wave whose amplitude was high for 2 seconds, then low again (Figure 20.3). Waves also have two new properties: *speed* and *wavelength*.

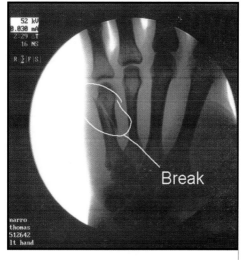

X ray

Figure 20.2: *An X ray is created by passing waves through the body. The calcium in bones absorbs X rays so bones show up as darker areas in an X ray photo. This photo clearly shows a broken finger.*

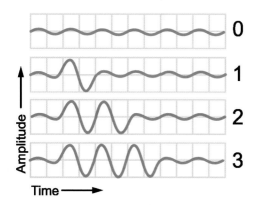

Figure 20.3: *One way to represent numbers using the amplitude of a wave.*

Transverse and longitudinal waves

How waves travel

How do waves travel through the air or down a string? For a wave to travel, molecules need to be connected or in contact with each other. Because air molecules collide, waves can travel in the air. A wave can travel along a string because molecules are connected. If you cut a string, a wave would not spread across the break.

Transverse waves

A **transverse** wave has its oscillations perpendicular to the direction the wave moves. For example, the wave pulse in the diagram below moves from left to right. The oscillation (caused by the girl's hand) is up and down. Water waves are transverse waves because oscillation of the water's surface is perpendicular to the direction of the wave's motion (Figure 20.4 top).

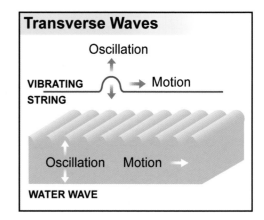

Making a transverse wave pulse

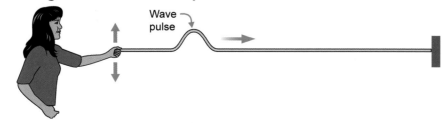

Longitudinal waves

A **longitudinal** wave has vibrations in the same direction as the wave moves (Figure 20.4 bottom). A large spring with one end fastened to a wall is a good way to demonstrate a longitudinal wave. A sharp push-pull on the end of the spring results in a traveling wave pulse as portions of the spring compress, then relax. The direction of the compressions are in the same direction that the wave moves. Sound waves are longitudinal waves. Like a wave pulse on a spring, air molecules oscillate back and forth as sound travels.

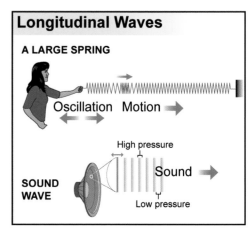

Figure 20.4: *(A) Transverse waves oscillate perpendicular to the direction the wave moves. A vibrating string and a water wave are transverse waves. (B) Longitudinal waves oscillate in the same direction the wave moves. A wave traveling along a large spring and a sound wave are longitudinal waves.*

Making a longitudinal wave pulse

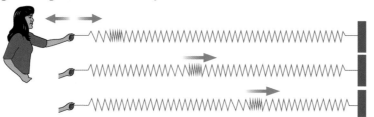

Frequency, amplitude, and wavelength

Waves are oscillators
Waves have cycles, frequency, and amplitude. However, unlike other kinds of oscillators, waves travel and have speed. On this page, you will learn how frequency and amplitude are defined and measured for waves.

Frequency
The frequency of a wave is a measure of how often it goes up and down (Figure 20.5). The frequency of the motion of one point on the wave is equal to the frequency of the whole wave. Distant points on the wave oscillate up and down *with the same frequency*. A wave carries its frequency to every place it reaches.

Frequency is measured in hertz
Wave frequency is measured in *hertz* (Hz). A wave with a frequency of one hertz (1 Hz) causes everything it touches to oscillate at one cycle per second. Water waves made in a large pan of water typically have low frequencies, between 0.1 and 10 hertz. Sound waves that we hear have higher frequencies, between 20 Hz and 20,000 Hz.

Amplitude
The amplitude of a wave is the maximum amount the wave causes anything to move away from equilibrium. Equilibrium is the average, or resting position (Figure 20.6) of the material the wave is moving through. You can measure amplitude as one-half the distance between the highest and lowest points.

Wavelength
You can think of a wave as a series of high points and low points. A **crest** is a high point of the wave, a **trough** is the low point. **Wavelength** is the distance from any point on a wave to the same point on the next cycle of the wave (Figure 20.7). One wavelength is the length of one complete cycle of the wave. We use the Greek letter "lambda" to represent wavelength. A lambda (λ) looks like an upside down "y."

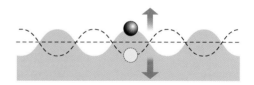

Figure 20.5: *The frequency of a wave is the rate at which every point on the wave moves up and down. The floating ball moves up and down at the frequency of the wave.*

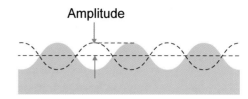

Figure 20.6: *The amplitude of a water wave is the maximum height the wave rises above the level surface. This is the same as half the distance between the lowest and highest places.*

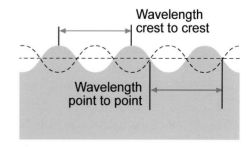

Figure 20.7: *The wavelength of a water wave can be measured from crest to crest. This is the same as the distance from one point on a wave to the same point on the next cycle of the wave.*

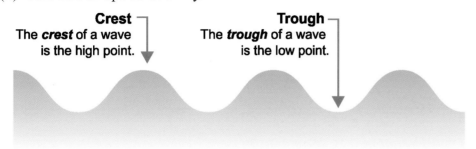

Crest ┐
The **crest** of a wave is the high point.

Trough ┐
The **trough** of a wave is the low point.

The speed of waves

What is moving? The speed of a wave is different from the speed of a moving object, like a ball. The speed of a ball is the speed at which the ball itself moves. The speed of a wave is the speed at which the wave's oscillations travel through a material. When a wave moves through water, *the water itself stays in the same average place*. The typical speed of a water wave is a few miles per hour. Light waves are extremely fast—186,000 miles per *second* (300,000 km/sec). Sound waves travel at about 660 miles per hour (about 1,000 km/h), faster than water waves and much slower than light waves.

What is the speed of a wave? The graphic below illustrates how to measure wave speed. You have to start a ripple in one place and measure how long it takes the ripple to affect a place some distance away. The speed of the wave is how fast the ripple gets from one place to the next, NOT how fast the wave surface moves up and down. As you learned on the previous page, the up-down speed of the water surface determines its frequency (Figure 20.8).

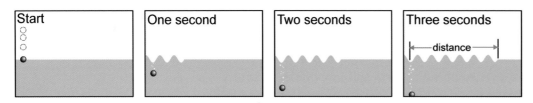

Speed is frequency times wavelength In one complete cycle, a wave moves forward one wavelength (Figure 20.8). The speed of a wave is the distance traveled (one wavelength) divided by the time it takes (one period). Since the frequency is the inverse of the period, it is easier to calculate the speed of the wave by multiplying wavelength and frequency. The result is true for all kinds of waves. Frequency times wavelength is the speed of the wave.

$$Speed = \frac{\text{Distance traveled}}{\text{Time taken}} = \frac{\text{Wavelength}}{\text{Period}} = \left(\frac{1}{\text{Period}}\right) \times \text{Wavelength}$$

$$Speed = Frequency \times Wavelength$$

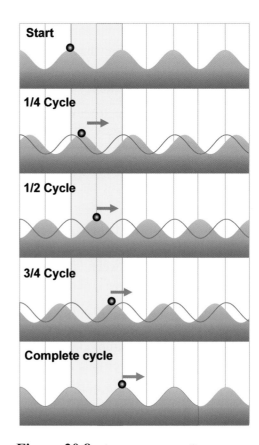

Figure 20.8: *A wave moves a distance equal to one wavelength in one cycle. Since a cycle takes one period, the speed of the wave is the wavelength divided by the period. The speed of a wave can also be calculated by multiplying frequency times wavelength.*

Calculating the speed of waves

Units You can calculate the speed of a wave if you know its frequency and wavelength. Recall that one hertz equals one cycle per second. The number of cycles is a pure number with no units. The *units* of Hz are 1 ÷ second. If wavelength is in meters, and frequency has units of 1 ÷ seconds, then the wave speed has units of meters per second (m/sec).

THE SPEED OF A WAVE

Speed (m/sec) ⟶ $v = f\lambda$ ⟵ *Wavelength* (meters)

Frequency (hertz)

Cooking with waves

A magnetron is a device in a microwave oven that creates a wave driven by electricity. Some of the energy of this wave enters the inside of the microwave and cooks food. The shape of the magnetron forces the wave to vibrate at exactly 2.4 billion cycles per second (2.4 gigahertz), This frequency is a natural frequency of water molecules. A microwave heats food by transferring wave energy to water molecules.

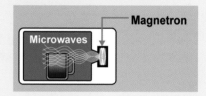

Magnetron

Microwaves

Finding wave speed

The wavelength for a wave is 0.5 meter, and its frequency is 40 hertz. What is the speed of this wave?

1. Looking for: The speed of the wave in meters per second.

2. Given: Wavelength is 0.5 meter and frequency is 40 hertz.

3. Relationships: speed = frequency × wavelength

4. Solution: speed = 40 Hz × 0.5 m = 40 ($^1/_{sec}$) × 0.5 m
speed = 20 m/sec
The speed of the wave is 20 m/sec.

Your turn...

a. The frequency of a wave is 50 hertz and the wavelength is 0.001 meter. What is the wave speed? **Answer:** 0.05 m/sec
b. The period of a wave is 10 seconds and the wavelength is 2 meters. What is the wave speed? **Answer:** 0.2 m/sec

Standing waves on a string

What is a standing wave?
A wave that is confined in a space is called a **standing wave**. It is possible to make standing waves of almost any kind, including sound, water, and even light. You can experiment with standing waves using a vibrating string. Vibrating strings are what make music on a guitar or piano.

Harmonics

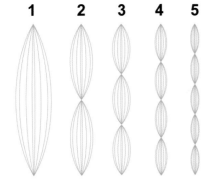

The first five harmonics of the vibrating string

A string with a standing wave is a kind of oscillator. Like all oscillators, a string has natural frequencies. The lowest natural frequency is called the **fundamental**. A vibrating string also has other natural frequencies called **harmonics**. The diagram shows the first five harmonics. You can tell the harmonic number by counting the number of "bumps" on the string. The first harmonic has one bump, the second has two, the third has three, and so on. Another name for the "bump" on a wave is *antinode* (Figure 20.9).

Wavelength
A vibrating string moves so fast that your eye sees a wave-shaped blur (Figure 20.10). At any one moment the string is in only one place within the blur. One complete "S" shape on the string is one wavelength. As frequency increases, wavelength decreases. Higher frequency waves have shorter wavelengths.

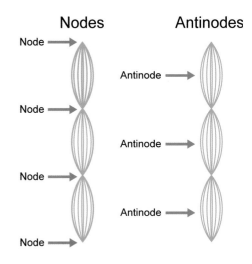

Figure 20.9: *Nodes and antinodes for the third harmonic of the vibrating string. Nodes are points where the string does not move. Antinodes are points of the greatest amplitude.*

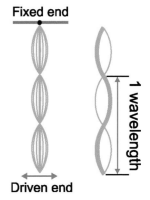

Figure 20.10: *A standing wave on a vibrating string. The wavelength is the length of one complete S shape of the wave.*

20.1 Section Review

1. Does a pair of walkie-talkies work using waves? Justify your answer.
2. Which is the fastest way to send information, using sound, light, or water?
3. Compare and contrast longitudinal and transverse waves in a short paragraph.
4. What is the speed of a wave that has a wavelength of 0.4 meter and a frequency of 10 Hz? Is this wave most likely to be a sound wave, light wave, or a water wave?
5. What is the period of a wave that has a wavelength of 1 meter and a speed of 20 Hz?

20.2 The Motion of Waves

Waves travel *through* substances, such as air or water. How do we know which direction a wave moves? What happens when a wave encounters an edge, or moves from one substance into another? We will find the answers by observing water waves because they are slow and easy to see. However, what we learn applies to all waves, including light and sound.

Wave patterns and directions

Why do waves travel?
Waves **propagate,** which means they spread out from where they begin. When you drop a ball into water, some of the water is pushed aside and raised by the ball (A). The higher water pushes the water next to it out of the way as it tries to return to equilibrium (B). The water that has been pushed then pushes on the water in front of *it*, and so on. The wave spreads through the interaction of each bit of water with the bit of water next to it (C).

Propagation of a water wave

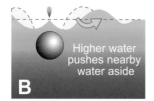

Plane waves and circular waves
The easiest waves to make and study are plane waves and circular waves (Figure 20.11). The crests of a **plane wave** form a pattern of parallel straight lines called **wave fronts**. The crests of a **circular wave** form a pattern of circular wave fronts. A plane wave is started by disturbing water in a line. Pushing the water with a ruler makes a plane wave. A circular wave is started by disturbing water at a single point. A fingertip touched to the water's surface makes a circular wave.

The direction a wave moves
The direction a wave moves depends on the shape of the wave front. Plane waves are straight and move in a line perpendicular to the crest of the wave. Circular waves move outward in a circle from the center. Anything that changes the shape of the wave front changes the direction the wave moves.

Vocabulary

propagate, plane wave, wave fronts, circular wave, boundaries, reflection, refraction, diffraction, absorption

Objectives

✓ Learn how waves propagate.
✓ Describe the four wave interactions.

Plane waves

Circular waves

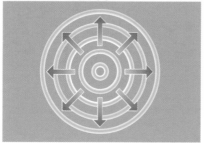

Figure 20.11: *Plane waves move perpendicular to the wave fronts. Circular waves radiate outward from the center.*

When a wave encounters objects

The four wave interactions

Have you ever heard a radio station fade out while driving into a tunnel or down into a valley? Radio signals are carried by radio waves. Like all waves, radio waves are affected by objects that get in their way. An FM radio wave can only propagate a short distance into a tunnel. Simple things like mirrors and complex things like X rays and ultrasound all depend on how waves behave when they encounter objects. When a wave hits an object or a surface, four things can happen. Sometimes all four happen at the same time, but to varying amounts. The four are listed below and illustrated in Figure 20.12.

Reflection *The wave bounces and goes in a new direction.*

Refraction *The wave bends as it passes into and through an object.*

Diffraction *The wave bends around an object or through holes in the object.*

Absorption *The wave is absorbed and disappears.*

Boundaries

Waves are affected by **boundaries** where conditions or materials change. A boundary is an edge or surface where things change suddenly. The surface of glass is a boundary. A wave traveling in the air sees a sudden change to a new material (glass) as it crosses the boundary. Reflection, refraction, and diffraction usually occur at boundaries. Absorption also occurs at a boundary, but usually happens more within the body of a material.

Reflection

When a wave bounces off an object we call it **reflection**. A reflected wave is like the original wave but moving in a new direction. The wavelength and frequency are usually unchanged. An echo is an example of a sound wave reflecting from a distant object or wall. People who design concert halls pay careful attention to the reflection of sound from the walls and ceiling.

Refraction

Refraction occurs when a wave bends as it crosses a boundary. We say the wave is *refracted* as it passes through the boundary. Eyeglasses are a good example where refraction is used to bend light waves. People with poor eyesight have trouble focusing images. Glasses bend incoming light waves so that an image is correctly focused within the eye.

Reflection
The wave bounces and goes in a new direction.

Refraction The wave bends as it passes into and through and object.

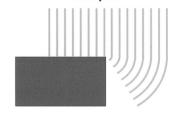

Diffraction The wave bends around an object or through holes in the object.

Absorption The wave is absorbed and disappears.

Figure 20.12: *The four basic interactions between waves and boundaries.*

Diffraction and absorption

Diffraction The process of bending around corners or passing through openings is called **diffraction**. We say a wave is *diffracted* when it is changed by passing through a hole or around an edge. Diffraction usually changes the direction and shape of the wave. When a plane wave passes through a narrow opening diffraction turns it into a circular wave. Diffraction explains why you can hear someone even though a door is open only a tiny crack. Diffraction causes the sound wave to spread out from the crack.

Diffraction through a small opening turns plane waves into circular waves.

Absorption **Absorption** is what happens when the amplitude of a wave gets smaller and smaller as it passes through a material. The wave energy is transferred to the absorbing material. A sponge can absorb a water wave while letting the water pass. Theaters often use heavy curtains to absorb sound waves so the audience cannot hear backstage noise. The tinted glass or plastic in the lenses of your sunglasses absorbs some of the energy in light waves. Cutting down the energy makes vision more comfortable on a bright, sunny day.

20.2 Section Review

1. If you threw a small rock into a pond, would plane waves or circular waves be created?
2. Does a mirror work by reflection or refraction?
3. Why is refraction important in how eyeglasses work?
4. One of the four wave interactions is very important in how plants use light to grow. Guess which one and write a couple of sentences justifying your answer.

Waves and earthquakes

Earth's crust is not one shell, but is broken up into huge slabs called "plates". The plates float on top of a deep layer of softer, partly melted rock. Where the plates hit each other they sometimes slip very suddenly, resulting in earthquakes. An earthquake releases powerful seismic waves that travel along the surface and also through the planet. One kind of seismic wave is a longitudinal wave. Another kind of seismic wave is transverse. The transverse wave shakes the ground sideways and causes damage to buildings and bridges. Because seismic waves travel through the planet, they are used to study what Earth is like deep below the surface. The refraction and reflection of seismic waves are like an X ray of the Earth's internal structure.

Site of earthquake
Seismic waves travel through Earth

20.3 Wave Interference and Energy

You almost never see (or hear) a single wave with only one frequency. That would be like seeing only one single color or hearing only one part of one note. Instead, you see (or hear) a complex mixture of waves of many different frequencies and amplitudes, all mixed together. **Interference** happens when two or more waves mix together. Interference mixes waves in ways that are very useful but can also be dangerous. For example, radio and television use the interference of two waves to carry music and video. In contrast, sometimes water waves add up to make a gigantic wave that may last only a few moments, but can sink even the largest ship.

The superposition principle

The superposition principle It is common for there to be many waves in the same system at the same time. For example, if you watch the ocean, you can see small waves on the surface of larger waves. When more than one wave is present, the **superposition principle** states that the total vibration at any point is the sum of the vibrations from each individual wave.

An example The diagram below illustrates the superposition principle. If there are two waves present (A and B), the total vibration at any point in time (C) is the sum of the vibrations from wave (A) and wave (B). In reality, single waves are quite rare. The sound waves and light waves you experience are the superposition of thousands of waves with different frequencies and amplitudes. Your eyes, ears, and brain separate the waves in order to recognize individual sounds and colors.

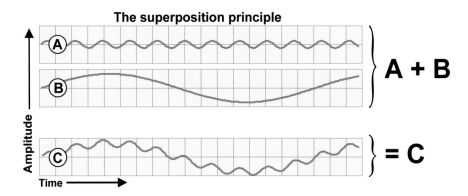
The superposition principle

Active noise reduction

In some environments, people wear headphones to muffle noise and protect their hearing. Headphones can also create "anti-noise." A microphone in the headphone samples the noise and generates anti-noise, or sound that is 180 degrees out of phase with the noise. The anti-noise cancels out or reduces noise by superposition.

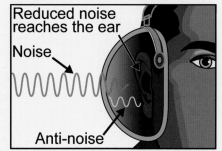

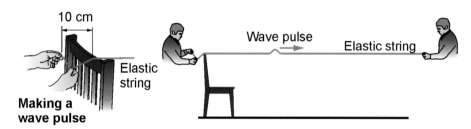

Constructive and destructive interference

Wave pulses A **wave pulse** is a short length of wave, maybe just a single oscillation. Imagine stretching an elastic string over the back of a chair (diagram below). To make a wave pulse, pull down a short length of the string behind the chair and let go. This creates a "bump" in the string that races away from the chair. The moving "bump" is a wave pulse. The wave pulse moves *on* the string, but each section of string returns to the same place after the wave moves past. The speed of the wave pulse is what we mean by the speed of a wave.

Constructive interference

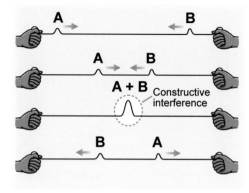

Figure 20.13: *Two wave pulses that are in phase can add up to make a single, bigger pulse when they meet. This is an example of constructive interference.*

10 cm

Elastic string

Wave pulse

Elastic string

Making a wave pulse

Constructive interference Suppose you make two wave pulses on a stretched string. One comes from the left and the other comes from the right. When the waves meet, they combine to make a single large pulse. **Constructive interference** occurs when waves add up to make a larger amplitude (Figure 20.13). Constructive interference is useful in working with light and sound. For example, when two sound waves constructively interfere, loudness increases.

Destructive interference There is another way to add two pulses. What happens when one pulse is on top of the string and the other is on the bottom? When the pulses meet in the middle, they cancel each other out (Figure 20.14). One pulse pulls the string up and the other pulls it down. The result is that the string flattens and both pulses vanish for a moment. In **destructive interference,** waves add up to make a wave with smaller or zero amplitude. After interfering both wave pulses separate again and travel on their own. This is surprising if you think about it. For a moment, the middle of the cord is flat, but a moment later, two wave pulses come out of the flat part and race away from each other. Waves still store energy, even when they interfere. Noise cancelling headphones are based on technology that uses destructive interference.

Destructive interference

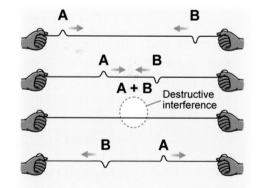

Figure 20.14: *Two equal wave pulses that are out of phase will subtract when they meet. The upward movement of one pulse exactly cancels with the downward movement of the other. For a moment there is no pulse at all. This is an example of destructive interference.*

Natural frequency and resonance

Natural frequency and resonance

As you learned in chapter 19, waves can have natural *frequency* and *resonance* just like oscillators. But first, a wave has to be caught in a system with boundaries. By itself, light keeps going in a straight line. There is no resonance. But catch the light between two perfect mirrors and you can get resonance of light waves, which is exactly how a *laser* works!

In free space a light wave travels in a straight line

Mirror   Mirror

Standing wave

Between mirrors light can form a standing wave

Resonance and reflections

Resonance in waves comes from the interference of a wave with its own reflections. To see how this works, think about making a pulse on an elastic string. One end of the string is tied to the wall, making a boundary. A pulse launched on the top reflects off the wall and comes back *on the bottom* of the string. When the pulse gets back to where it started, it reflects again, and is back on top of the string. After the second reflection, the pulse is traveling in the same direction, on the same side of the string as it started (Figure 20.15).

Resonance and constructive interference

To build up a large wave, you wait until a reflected pulse has returned to your hand before launching a new pulse. The new pulse adds to the reflected pulse to make a bigger pulse (constructive interference). The bigger pulse moves away and reflects again. You wait until the reflection gets back to your hand and then shake the string to add a third pulse. The total wave pulse is now three times as large as at the start. *Resonance is created by adding new pulses so that each adds to the reflected pulse in constructive interference.* After a dozen well-timed pulses, the string develops a single large wave motion, and you have resonance (Figure 20.16)! This is exactly how the standing waves on the vibrating string are formed.

Why resonance is important

The concepts of resonance and natural frequency apply to a huge range of natural and human-made systems. The tides of the oceans, musical instruments, the laser, the way our ears separate sound, and even a microwave oven are all examples of waves and resonance.

Reflection of a wave pulse

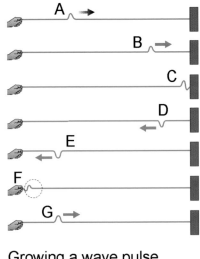

Growing a wave pulse

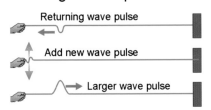

Figure 20.15: *Reflections of a wave pulse on an elastic string.*

Resonance

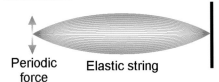

Figure 20.16: *A vibrating string in resonance has a single large wave pattern such as this.*

Waves and energy

A wave is a form of moving energy

What exactly moves in a wave? In a water wave, the water moves up and down, but stays, on average, in the same place. What moves is *energy*. A wave is an organized form of energy that travels. When you drop a stone into a pool, most of the stone's kinetic energy is converted into water waves. The waves spread out carrying the energy far from the place where the stone fell.

Frequency and energy

The energy of a wave is proportional to its frequency. Higher frequency means higher energy. This is obvious for a jump rope. You have to move the rope up and down twice, doing twice as much work, to make the rope swing at twice the frequency. Figure 20.17 shows three standing waves with the same amplitude and different frequencies. The wave with the higher frequency has more energy. The result is true for almost all waves. The energy of a wave is proportional to its frequency.

Amplitude and energy

The energy of a wave is also proportional to amplitude. Given two standing waves of the same frequency, the wave with the larger amplitude has more energy. With a vibrating string, the potential energy of the wave comes from the stretching of the string. Larger amplitude means the string has to stretch more and therefore stores more energy.

Why are standing waves useful?

Standing waves are used to store energy at specific frequencies. With the wave on the string you observed how a small input of energy at the natural frequency accumulated over time to build a wave with much more energy. Musical instruments use standing waves to create sound energy of exactly the right frequency. Radio transmitters and cell phones also use standing waves to create power at specific frequencies.

Frequency and energy

Lowest frequency = lowest energy

Double frequency = double energy

Triple frequency = triple energy

Amplitude and energy

Small amplitude = low energy

Large amplitude = high energy

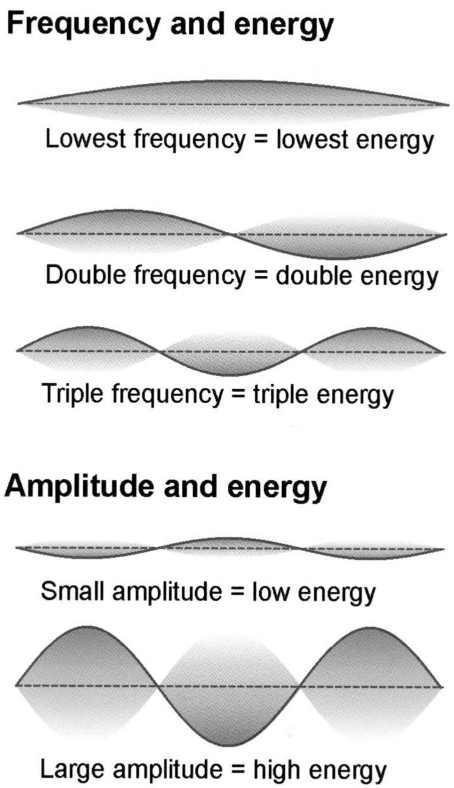

Figure 20.17: *The energy of a wave is proportional to its frequency and amplitude.*

20.3 Section Review

1. Explain the superposition principle in your own words.
2. Two waves combine to make a wave that is larger than either wave by itself. Is this constructive or destructive interference?
3. Can a wave have resonance when the wave is free to expand as far as it can go? Explain why or why not.
4. Which has more energy: a vibrating string at 30 Hz or the same vibrating string at 70 Hz?
5. If a wave is being absorbed, what would you expect to happen to the amplitude of the wave? Explain using the idea of energy.

Waves that Shake the Ground

In 1995, a severe earthquake struck Kobe, Japan. During the quake, about 86,000 buildings—like the one at right—were damaged and about 82,000 collapsed even though it lasted only 20 seconds! So, much damage in so short a time all caused by waves traveling through Earth.

Kobe earthquake 1995

You know how to cause water waves and cause a wave to travel along a string or a Slinky™. How do waves get started in the ground? Earthquakes begin in Earth's rocky crust. Pressure can build up in underground rocks causing them to expand and contract. Like a stretched rubber band or a compressed spring, the rocks store energy. When the rocks break or change shape, stored energy is suddenly converted to ground-shaking energy. The result is that seismic waves radiate from the place where the rocks inside Earth release stored energy and an earthquake occurs. During a quake, there is a strong burst of shaking that lasts from seconds to minutes. The longest ever recorded earthquake occurred in 1964 in Alaska and lasted for four minutes.

Earthquake waves

Seismic waves caused by an earthquake travel through the ground about 20 times faster than the speed of sound (about 5 kilometers per second). These waves can be slowed or bent depending on the properties of rock they encounter.

Two kinds of waves are released from the location that the earthquake starts. One kind of wave, called primary waves are faster and push and pull on rocks as they moves through Earth. The second kind of wave—secondary waves—move sideways and up and down, traveling a little slower than primary waves.

Because they are faster, primary waves reach Earth's surface first. When primary and secondary waves reach the surface they become surface waves. These waves move more slowly (about 10 percent slower than secondary waves), but can be very damaging. When these waves have a lot of energy, the ground rolls like the surface of the ocean. Surface waves can also move side to side and cause buildings to collapse.

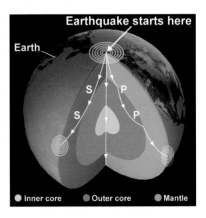

Seeing inside Earth

Seismic waves are recorded and measured by a seismograph. A worldwide network of seismographs at stations on land and in the oceans record earthquakes. The amplitudes of the recorded waves are related to the magnitude of the earthquake. People who record and interpret seismic waves are called seismologists. In addition to measuring earthquakes, seismologists use seismic waves to study Earth's internal structure. Primary and secondary waves travel through Earth and help identify the properties of the layers inside Earth. For example, primary waves but not secondary waves pass through the outer core of Earth. Secondary waves do not travel through liquids. Therefore, this observation indicates to seismologists that the outer core of Earth is liquid.

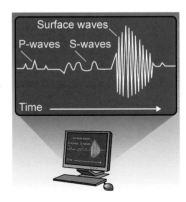

Where do earthquakes occur?

Earth is covered by a thin crust of rock. Rather than being continuous, the crust is broken into pieces called tectonic plates. These pieces constantly, although slowly, move. As edges of the plates move against each other, pressure builds up and an earthquake can occur. The graphic below shows the edges of Earth's "puzzle pieces" (white lines) and the red dots show common earthquake locations.

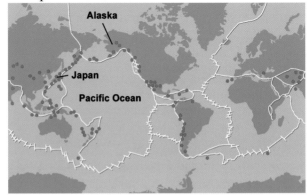

Dangerous underwater earthquakes

In the middle of the Pacific Ocean, earthquakes can occur on the ocean floor. When this happens, a huge and dangerous water wave called a tsunami can occur. The speed at which this wave travels can be about 700 kilometers per hour.

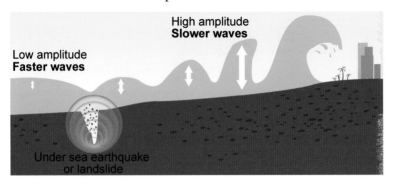

In the open ocean, you would not notice a tsunami because its amplitude is small. However, as the wave reaches a shallow area, the water piles up so that the wave amplitude greatly increases. The wave may get as high as 25 meters!

Tsunamis cause serious flooding and the power of their waves wrecks buildings and can cause loss of life. Tsunamis affect coastal areas and islands that experience earthquakes. To protect people from tsunamis, around the Pacific coastline of Alaska, Hawaii, and the west coast of the Lower 48 states, there are ocean-bound tsunami detectors and seismographs. Scientists use information from the detectors and seismographs to forecast tsunamis. Because scientists know how fast a tsunami can travel after it has been triggered by an earthquake, they can warn people in coastal places to evacuate to higher ground.

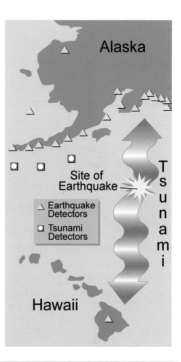

Questions:

1. List and describe the different types of seismic waves.
2. Research the Richter scale. What do the numbers on this scale represent?
3. Where are earthquakes most likely to occur on Earth?
4. If an earthquake occurs in the Pacific Ocean about 3,000 km from Hawaii and 1,900 km from Alaska, how much time do Hawaiians have to evacuate away from the coast? How much time do the Alaskans have? Use the speed for a tsunami from the reading.

Chapter 20 Review

Understanding Vocabulary

Select the correct term to complete the sentences.

harmonics	circular wave	absorption
reflection	waves	transverse waves
longitudinal waves	fundamental	trough
destructive interference	diffraction	constructive interference

Section 20.1

1. Waves on a string and water are examples of ____, and oscillate perpendicular to the direction the wave moves.

2. The low point of a wave is called its ____.

3. The lowest natural frequency of an object is known as the ____ frequency.

4. ____ carry energy and information from one place to another.

5. Sound waves are ____, and oscillate in the same direction as the wave motion.

6. Multiples of the natural frequency are called ____.

Section 20.2

7. By touching your finger at a single point of the surface of a smooth pond, you can create a(n) ____ pattern.

8. When waves bounce off an obstacle and change direction, it is known as ____.

9. A wave bending around obstacles and going through openings is called ____.

10. Using a heavy curtain in a theater to keep the audience from hearing backstage sound is an example of the ____ of sound waves.

Section 20.3

11. Two waves meeting and adding up to a larger wave is called ____.

12. Two waves meeting and cancelling each other out is called ____.

Reviewing Concepts

Section 20.1

1. Identify how each of the following situations involves waves. Explain each of your answers.
   a. A person is talking to someone on a cell phone.
   b. An earthquake causes the floor of a house to shake.
   c. A person listens to her favorite radio station on the car stereo.
   d. A doctor makes an X ray to check for broken bones.
   e. You turn on a lamp when you come home in the evening.

2. Compare transverse waves and longitudinal waves. Give two examples of each type of wave.

3. Arrange the equation relating wave speed, frequency, and wavelength for each of the following scenarios. Let v = wave speed, f = frequency, and λ = wavelength:
   a. You know frequency and wavelength. Solve for v.
   b. You know frequency and wave speed. Solve for λ.
   c. You know wave speed and wavelength. Solve for f.

4. Write a formula relating the speed of a wave to its period and wavelength.

5. Give one example of a wave with a very short wavelength and one one with a very long wavelength.

6. For the wave in the diagram, which measurement shows the amplitude? Which measurement shows the wavelength?

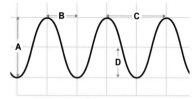

7. What causes a standing wave?

8. How many nodes and antinodes are in a single wavelength of the second harmonic of a vibrating string?

Section 20.2

Sketch the wave crests, indicating the direction of motion, for:

a. a circular wave
b. a plane wave

). Below are diagrams representing interactions between waves and boundaries. Identify each interaction by name.

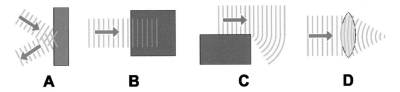

A   B   C   D

. What happens to the amplitude of a wave when the wave is absorbed?

2. Explain why you can hear a sound through a door that is only open a crack. Use the terms *wave* and *interaction* in your answer.

3. Read the descriptions below and indicate which of the four types of wave interactions (*absorption*, *reflection*, *refraction*, or *diffraction*) has occurred.

a. The distortion of your partially submerged arm makes it look "broken" when viewed from the air.
b. You hear the music even though you are seated behind an obstruction at a concert.
c. You see yourself in a mirror.
d. Water ripples passing through a sponge become smaller.
e. Heavy curtains are used to help keep a room quiet.

Section 20.3

4. What happens if two waves are in the same place at the same time? Use the term *superposition principle* in your answer.

5. Can two waves interfere with each other so that the new wave formed by their combination has *NO amplitude*? What type of interference is this?

6. What happens to the amplitude of two waves as the result of:

a. constructive interference?
b. destructive interference?

Solving Problems

Section 20.1

1. A wave has a frequency of 10 Hz and a wavelength of 2 meters. What is the speed of the wave?

2. A sound wave has a speed of 400 m/sec and a frequency of 200 Hz. What is its wavelength?

3. The wavelength of a wave on a string is 1 meter and its speed is 5 m/sec. Calculate the frequency and the period of the wave.

4. Draw at least one cycle of a transverse wave with an amplitude of 4 centimeters and a wavelength of 8 centimeters. If the frequency of this wave is 10 Hz, what is its speed?

5. The standing wave pattern in the graphic at right has a frequency of 30 Hz.

a. What is the period?
b. At what frequency will you find the fourth harmonic?
c. At what frequency will you find the fifth harmonic?
d. How many nodes are in this wave pattern?
e. How many antinodes are in this wave pattern?

30 Hz

6. You are doing a vibrating string experiment and observe the sixth harmonic at 48 Hz. At what frequency do you find the third harmonic?

7. How many nodes and antinodes does this standing wave have?

8. An A note played on a piano vibrates at a frequency of 440 Hz. Find the frequency for its second harmonic.

Section 20.2

9. The wave in the picture is about is about to pass through a small hole in a wall. Sketch what the wave front will look like after it passes through the hole.

10. Which graph shows the superposition of the two in-phase waves shown below?

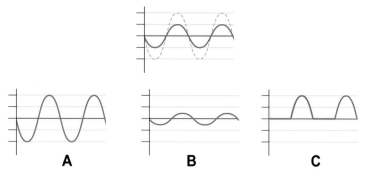

A   **B**   **C**

11. Which graph shows the superposition of the two out-of-phase waves shown below?

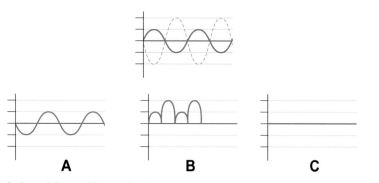

A   **B**   **C**

Applying Your Knowledge

Section 20.1

1. Tsunami waves are large ocean waves generated by disturbances like underwater earthquakes or landslides. Tsunamis can travel on the open ocean at speeds of 200 m/s, which is comparable to the speed of a jet airplane.

   a. What type of wave is a tsunami, transverse or longitudinal?

   b. If the period of a tsunami is one hour (= 3,600 seconds), what is its frequency?

   c. If a tsunami's wave speed is 200 m/s and its period is 3,600 seconds, what is its wavelength?

2. The "sweet spot" on a baseball bat is related to how the bat vibrates when it hits a baseball. If a ball hits the sweet spot, your hands do not feel the vibrations of the bat. Whereas, if the ball hits a place on the bat that is *not* the sweet spot, the vibrations cause your hand to hurt after you hit the ball. Find out why this happens. Use your library or on the Internet to research this phenomenon. Write a short paragraph with a diagram to summarize your findings.

Section 20.2

3. Eye doctors use a refraction test to measure your eyesight for glasses. The test is performed by having you look through a refractor device at an eye chart. The refractor device has different types of lenses for you to look through. When a lens is found that gives you clear vision, the doctor can prescribe the correct set of eyeglasses for you.

   a. Why do you think this is called a refraction test?

   b. What kind of wave is being refracted by the refraction device?

   c. How do eyeglasses help you to see more clearly?

4. The reflection of sound waves leads to echoes, where the listener hears a delayed repeat of the original sound. If a canyon wall is 34 meters away and the speed of sound in air is 340 m/sec, what would be the time delay of an echo in the canyon?

Section 20.3

5. In 1933 the US Navy steamship *Ramapo* reported seeing a 64 meter wave in the open ocean where the sea is 4,000 to 6,000 meters deep. How might this wave have been formed? Is this just a sea tale or is a wave this size possible?

6. Have you ever been in a situation that was too noisy? Choose one of the following research topics on the subject of noise. Research your topic and present your findings in a one-two page essay. Include in your essay information about how noise is reduced using understanding of sound waves.

   a. Noise from airports

   b. Noise from highways

   c. Use of hearing protection by teenagers

   d. Health problems related to noise

Chapter 21

Sound

Humans were making musical instruments to produce sounds 20,000 years before the wheel and axle were invented! Among instrument builders, perhaps Antonio Stradivari is the most famous. Between 1667 and 1730 Stradivari built violins in the small town of Cremona, Italy. A violin's sound is rich and complex because vibrations of its wooden parts create a unique blend of frequencies.

Stradivari worked tirelessly trying different woods and different varnishes, searching for the perfect sound. Over time he developed a secret formula for varnish, and special ways to carve and treat the all-important vibrating parts of the violin. In the 300 years since Stradivari, no one has figured out how he did it. Today, a Stradivarius violin is the most highly prized of all musical instruments. Its rich sound has never been duplicated.

Key Questions

✓ How do atoms make sound happen?
✓ Why is your voice unique?
✓ How do beats keep you in tune?

21.1 Properties of Sound

Like other waves, sound has the properties of frequency, wavelength, amplitude, and speed. Because sound is such a big part of human experience, you already know its properties — but by different names. You may never hear anyone complain about amplitude, but you have heard about sound being too *loud*. The loudness of sound comes from the amplitude of a sound wave.

The frequency of sound

Frequency and pitch
Sound is a wave, and like all waves it has a frequency. Your ear is very sensitive to the frequency of sound. The **pitch** of a sound is how you hear and interpret its frequency. A low-frequency sound has a low pitch, like the rumble of a big truck or a bass guitar. A high-frequency sound has a high pitch, like the scream of a whistle or siren. The range of frequencies humans can hear varies from about 20 hertz to 20,000 hertz.

Most sound has more than one frequency
Most sound that you hear contains many frequencies. In Chapter 20 we talked about the *superposition principle*. Complex sound is created by the superposition of many frequencies. In fact, the sound of the human voice contains thousands of different frequencies — all at once. (Figure 21.1).

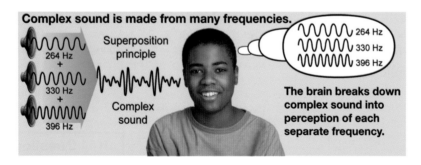

The frequency spectrum
Why is it easy to recognize one person's voice from another, even when people are saying the same word? The reason is that voices have different mixtures of frequencies. A *frequency spectrum* is a graph showing the different frequencies present in a sound. Loudness is on the vertical axis and frequency is on the horizontal axis. Figure 21.1 shows the frequencies of the voices for three individuals saying "hello."

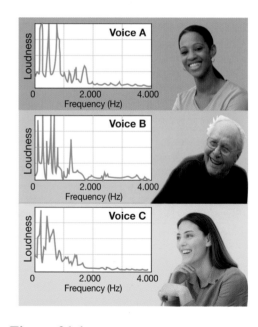

Figure 21.1: *The frequencies in three people's voices as they say the word "hello."*

The loudness of sound

The decibel scale
The loudness of sound is measured in **decibels** (dB). Loudness is determined mostly by the amplitude of a sound wave. Almost no one (except scientists) uses amplitude to measure loudness. Instead we use the decibel scale (Figure 21.2). Most sounds fall between zero and 100 on the decibel scale, making it a very convenient number to understand and use.

Table 21.1: *Common sounds and their loudness in decibels*

0 dB	The threshold of human hearing; the quietest sound we can hear
10-15 dB	A quiet whisper 3 feet away
30-40 dB	Background sound level at a house
45-55 dB	The noise level in an average restaurant
65 dB	Ordinary conversation 3 feet away
70 dB	City traffic
90 dB	A jackhammer cutting up the street 10 feet away; louder sounds than 90 dB cause hearing damage
100 dB	Walkman turned to its maximum volume
110 dB	The front row of a rock concert
120 dB	The threshold of physical pain from loudness

The sensitivity of the ear
How loud you hear a sound depends on both the amplitude of the sound wave and the response of your ear. The human ear is most sensitive to frequencies of sound between 500 and 5,000 Hz. It is no surprise that these are same the frequencies in voices! An *equal loudness curve* compares how loud you hear sounds of different frequencies (Figure 21.3). Sounds near 2,000 Hz seem louder than sounds of other frequencies, even at the same decibel level. According to this curve, a 40 dB sound at 2,000 Hz sounds just as loud as an 80 dB sound at 50 Hz. Almost no one can hear sound above 20,000 Hz no matter how large the amplitude is.

Acoustics
Acoustics is the science and technology of sound. Knowledge of acoustics is important in many situations. For example, reducing the loudness of sound is important in designing libraries so that sounds are absorbed to maintain quiet. Recording studios are designed to prevent sound from the outside from mixing with the sound inside.

Comparing Decibels and Amplitude

Decibels (dB)	Amplitude
0	1
20	10
40	100
60	1,000
80	10,000
100	100,000
120	1,000,000

Figure 21.2: *The decibel scale is a measure of the amplitude of sound waves. We use the decibel scale because our ears can hear a wide range of amplitudes. Every increase of 20 decibels (dB) means the sound wave has 10 times greater amplitude and it sounds about twice as loud.*

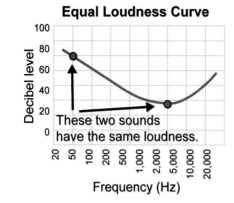

Figure 21.3: *All points on an equal loudness curve have the same loudness.*

The speed of sound

Sound moves about 340 meters per second
You have likely noticed that you hear thunder many seconds after you see lightning. Lighting is what creates thunder so they occur at the same time. You hear a delay because sound travels much slower than light. The speed of sound in air is 343 meters per second (660 miles per hour) at one atmosphere of pressure and room temperature. The speed varies some with temperature and pressure.

Subsonic and supersonic
Objects that move slower than sound are called **subsonic**. A passenger jet is subsonic because its speed ranges from 400 to 500 miles per hour. Objects that move faster than sound are called **supersonic**. Some military jets fly at supersonic speeds. If you were on the ground watching a supersonic plane fly toward you, there would be silence (Figure 21.4). The sound would be *behind* the plane, racing to catch up.

Sonic booms
A supersonic jet "squishes" the sound waves that are created as its nose cuts through the air. A cone-shaped **shock wave** forms where the wave fronts pile up. In front of the shock wave there is total silence. Behind the shock wave you can hear the noise from the plane. Right at the shock wave the amplitude changes abruptly, causing a very loud sound called a *sonic boom*.

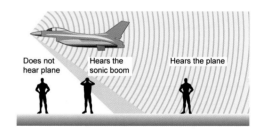

Figure 21.4: *If a supersonic jet flew overhead, you would not hear the sound until the plane was far beyond you. The boundary between sound and silence is called a "shock wave." It is almost as if all the sound were compressed into a thin layer of air. The person in the middle hears a sonic boom as the shock wave passes over him. Because the sonic boom can shatter windows, planes are not allowed to fly over cities at supersonic speeds.*

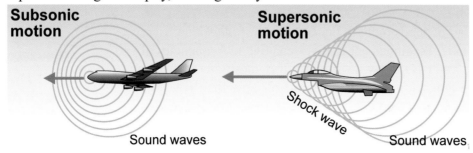

Sound in liquids and solids
The speed of sound in liquid and solid materials is usually faster than in air (Figure 21.5). Compared to air, sound travels about five times faster in water, and about 18 times faster in steel. This is because sound is really a travelling oscillation of the atoms in a material. Like other oscillations, sound depends on restoring forces and inertia, only on an atomic scale. The forces holding steel atoms together in a solid are much stronger than the forces between molecules in air. Stronger restoring forces raise the speed of sound.

Material	Sound speed (m/sec)
Air	330
Helium	965
Water	1530
Wood (average)	2000
Gold	3240
Steel	5940

Figure 21.5: *The speed of sound in various materials (helium and air at 0°C and 1 atmospheric pressure).*

The Doppler effect

Definition of the Doppler effect

If a sound-producing object is stationary, listeners on all sides will hear the same frequency. When the object is moving, the sound will *not* be the same to all listeners. People moving with the object or to the side of it hear the sound as if the object were stationary. People in front of the object hear sound of higher frequency; those behind it hear sound of lower frequency. The shift in frequency caused by motion is called the **Doppler effect** and it occurs when a sound source is moving at speeds below the speed of sound.

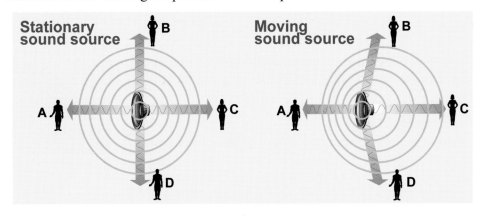

The cause of the Doppler effect

The Doppler effect occurs because an observer hears the frequency at which wave fronts arrive at his or her ears. Observer (A) in the graphic above hears a higher frequency. This is because the object's motion causes the crests in front to be closer together. The opposite is true behind a moving object, where the wave crests are farther apart. Observer (C) in back hears a lower frequency because the motion of the object makes more space between successive wave fronts. The greater the speed of the object, the larger the difference in frequency between the front and back positions.

Demonstrating the Doppler effect

You can hear the Doppler effect when you hear the siren of a fire engine coming toward you and then move past you. You can observe the Doppler effect if someone whirls a small battery-powered beeper around his head on a string. The frequency shifts up and down with each rotation according to whether the beeper is moving toward you or away from you.

Doppler radar

The Doppler effect also happens with reflected waves, including microwaves. With Doppler radar, a transmitter sends a pulse of microwaves. The microwaves reflect from a moving object, such as a car. The frequency of the reflected wave is increased if the car is moving toward the source and decreases if the car is moving away.

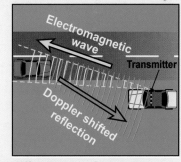

The difference in frequency between the reflected and transmitted wave is called the Doppler shift. Because Doppler shift is proportional to speed, Doppler radar is a way to measure speed accurately at a distance. Doppler radar is used to enforce speed limits, to measure the speed of wind in storms, and in many other applications where speed needs to be measured from a distance.

Recording sound

The importance of recorded sound
A hundred years ago the only way to hear music was to be within hearing range of the musicians as they played. The recording of sound was a breakthrough in technology that changed human experience.

The microphone
To record a sound you must store the pattern of vibrations in a way that can be replayed and be true to the original sound. A common way to record sound starts with a microphone. A microphone transforms a sound wave into an electrical signal with the same pattern of vibration (top of Figure 21.6).

Analog to digital conversion
In modern digital recording, a sensitive circuit called an "analog to digital converter" measures the electrical signal 44,100 times per second. Each measurement consists of a number between zero and 65,536 corresponding to the amplitude of the signal. One second of compact-disc-quality sound is a list of 44,100 numbers. The numbers are recorded as data on the disc.

Playback of recorded sound
To play the sound back, the string of numbers on the CD is read by a laser and converted into electrical signals again by a second circuit. This circuit is a digital to analog converter, and it reverses the process of the first circuit. The playback circuit converts the string of numbers back into an electrical signal. The electrical signal is amplified until it is powerful enough to move the coil in a speaker and reproduce the sound (bottom of Figure 21.6).

Stereo sound
Most of the music you listen to has been recorded in stereo. A stereo recording is actually two recordings, one to be played from the right speaker, the other from the left. Stereo sound feels almost "live" because it creates slight differences in phase between sound reaching your left and right ears.

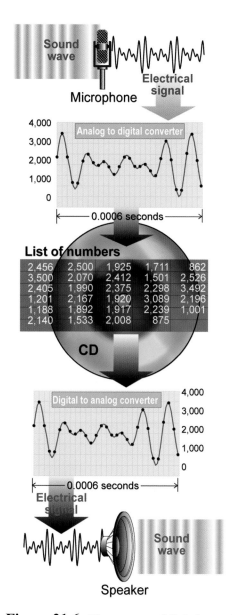

Figure 21.6: *The process of digital sound reproduction.*

21.1 Section Review

1. What is the relationship between pitch and frequency?

2. Do two sound waves that seem equally loud always have the same amplitude? Explain.

3. How do the amplitudes of a 120-decibel sound and a 100-decibel sound compare?

4. Would a car driving at 800 mph be supersonic or subsonic?

5. A paramedic in an ambulance does not experience the Doppler effect of the siren. Why?

6. How many numbers are involved in generating one minute of stereo sound on a CD?

21.2 Sound Waves

You can see the water move in a water wave, but sound waves are invisible. Sound is a wave because it has both frequency and wavelength. We also know sound is a wave because it does all the things other waves do. Sound can be reflected, refracted, and absorbed. Sound also shows interference and diffraction. Resonance occurs with sound waves and is especially important in how instruments work.

What is oscillating in a sound wave?

Sound in solids and liquids Sound is a traveling oscillation of atoms. If you push on one atom, it pushes on its neighbor. That atom pushes on the next atom, and so on. The push causes atoms to oscillate back and forth like tiny masses on springs. The oscillation spreads through the connections between atoms to make a sound wave.

Sound in air and gases In air the situation is different. Air molecules are spread far apart and interact by colliding with each other. The pressure is higher where atoms are close together and lower where they are farther apart. Imagine pushing the molecules on the left side of the picture below. Your push squeezes atoms together creating a layer of higher pressure. That layer pushes on the next layer, which pushes on the next layer, and so on. The result is a traveling oscillation in pressure, which is a sound wave. Sound is a *longitudinal* wave because molecules are compressed in the same direction the wave travels.

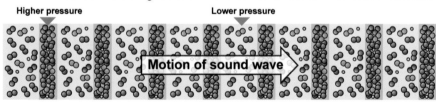

The frequency range of sound waves Anything that vibrates creates sound waves, as long as there is contact with other atoms. However, not all "sounds" can be heard. The oscillations we call sound waves cover a wide range of frequencies. Humans can hear only the narrow range between 20 Hz and 20,000 Hz. Bats can hear high frequency sounds between 40,000 and 100,000 Hz and whales hear very low frequency sounds that are lower than 10 Hz.

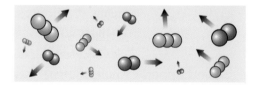

Figure 21.7: *Air is made of molecules in constant random motion, bumping off each other and the walls of their container.*

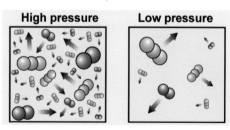

Figure 21.8: *At the same temperature, high pressure means more molecules per unit volume. Low pressure means fewer molecules per unit volume.*

Sound and air pressure

Speakers If you touch the surface of a speaker, you can easily feel the vibration that creates a sound wave. Figure 21.9 shows a magnified illustration of a speaker, a sound wave, and the oscillation of pressure. When music is playing, the surface of the speaker moves back and forth at the same frequencies as the sound waves. The back and forth motion of the speaker creates a traveling sound wave of alternating high and low pressure.

Air pressure You can feel the pressure in a soda bottle, so why can't you feel the pressure from a sound wave? You can! But you need your ears. Your skin is not nearly sensitive enough to detect sound waves. The change in air pressure created by a sound wave is incredibly small. An 80 dB sound, equivalent to a loud stereo, changes the air pressure by only 1 part in a million.

Frequency and pressure change The frequency of sound indicates how fast air pressure oscillates back and forth. The purr of a cat, for example, might have a frequency of 50 hertz. This means the air pressure alternates 50 times per second. The frequency of a fire truck siren may be 3,000 hertz. This corresponds to 3,000 vibrations per second (3,000 Hz) in the pressure of the air.

Sound speed depends on temperature In air, the energy of a sound wave is carried by moving molecules bumping into each other. Anything that affects the motion of molecules also affects the speed of sound. When the air gets cold, the molecules move more slowly and the speed of sound decreases. For example, at 0°C, the speed of sound is 330 meters per second, but at 21°C, the speed of sound is 344 meters per second.

Sound speed and pressure If the pressure of air goes up, molecules become more crowded. The speed of sound increases4 because the atoms collide with each other more often. If the pressure goes down, the speed of sound decreases. This affects airplanes. At high altitudes, both the pressure and temperature go down. A plane that is subsonic at low altitudes may become supersonic at higher altitudes.

Sound speed and molecular weight Remember, temperature measures the average kinetic energy of molecules. Lighter molecules go faster than heavier molecules at the same temperature. The speed of sound is higher in helium gas because helium atoms are lighter (and faster) than either oxygen (O_2) or nitrogen (N_2) molecules that make up air. That is why you sound funny when you talk after inhaling helium gas.

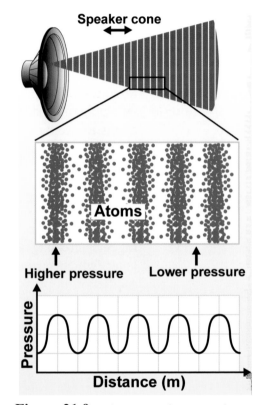

Figure 21.9: *What a sound wave might look like if you could see the atoms. The effect is greatly exaggerated to show the variation.*

The wavelength of sound

Range of wavelengths of sound

The wavelength of sound in air is comparable to the size of everyday objects. The chart below gives some typical frequencies and wavelengths for sound in air. As with other waves, the wavelength of a sound is inversely related to its frequency (Figure 21.10). A low-frequency 20-hertz sound has a wavelength the size of a large classroom. At the upper range of hearing, a 20,000-hertz sound has a wavelength about the width of your finger.

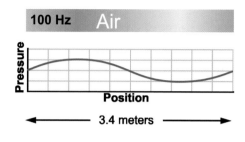

Table 21.2: *Frequency and wavelength for some typical sounds*

Frequency (Hz)	Wavelength	Typical source
20	17 meters	rumble of thunder
100	3.4 meters	bass guitar
500	70 cm (27")	average male voice
1,000	34 cm (13")	female soprano voice
2,000	17 cm (6.7")	fire truck siren
5,000	7 cm (2.7")	highest note on a piano
10,000	3.4 cm (1.3")	whine of a jet turbine
20,000	1.7 cm (0.67")	highest-pitched sound you can hear

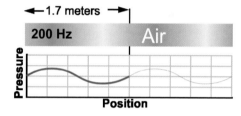

Wavelengths of sounds are important

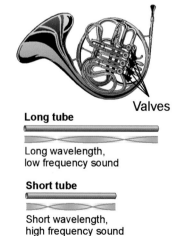

Although we usually think about different sounds in terms of frequency, the wavelength can also be important. If you want to make sound of a certain wavelength, you often need to have a vibrating object that is similar in size to the wavelength. That is why instruments like a French horn have valves. A French horn makes sound by vibrating the air trapped in a long coiled tube. Short tubes only fit short wavelengths and make high frequency sound. Long tubes fit longer wavelengths and make lower frequency sounds. Opening and closing the valves on a french horn allows the player to add and subtract different length tubes, changing the frequency of the sound.

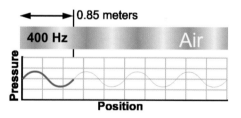

Figure 21.10: *The frequency and wavelength of sound are inversely related. When the frequency goes up, the wavelength goes down proportionally.*

Interaction between sound waves and boundaries

Interactions of sound and materials

Like other waves, sound waves can be reflected by hard surfaces and refracted as they pass from one material to another. Diffraction causes sound waves to spread out through small openings. Carpet and soft materials can absorb sound waves. Figure 21.11 shows examples of sound interactions.

Reverberation

In a good concert hall, the reflected sound and direct sound from the musicians together create a multiple echo called **reverberation**. The right amount of reverberation makes the sound seem livelier and richer. Too much reverberation and the sound gets muddy from too many reflections. Concert hall designers choose the shape and surface of the walls and ceiling to provide the best reverberation. Some concert halls have movable panels that can be raised or lowered from the ceiling to help shape the sound.

Constructing a good concert hall

Direct sound (**A**) reaches the listener along with reflected sound (**B, C**) from the walls. The shape of the room and the surfaces of its walls must be designed and constructed so that there is some reflected sound, but not too much.

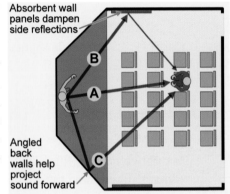

Absorbent wall panels dampen side reflections

Angled back walls help project sound forward

Interference can also affect sound quality

Reverberation also causes interference of sound waves. When two waves interfere, the total can be louder or softer than either wave alone. The diagram above shows a musician and an audience of one person. The sound reflected from the walls interferes as it reaches the listener. If the distances are just right, one reflected wave might be out of phase with the other. The result is that the sound is quieter at that spot. An acoustic engineer would call it a *dead spot* in the hall. Dead spots are areas where destructive interference causes some of the sound to cancel with its own reflections. It is also possible to make very loud spots where sound interferes constructively. The best concert halls are designed to minimize both dead spots and loud spots.

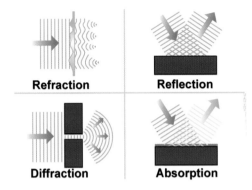

Refraction | Reflection

Diffraction | Absorption

Figure 21.11: *Sound displays all the properties of waves in its interactions with materials and boundaries.*

Ultrasound

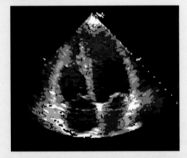

Ultrasound is sound that has high frequency, often 100,000 hertz or more. We cannot hear ultrasound, but it can pass through the human body easily. Medical ultrasound instruments use the refraction and reflection of sound waves inside the body to create images. Doctors often take ultrasound pictures of the human body. The ultrasound image pictured above is a heart.

Standing waves and resonance

Resonance of sound
Spaces enclosed by boundaries can create *resonance* with sound waves. Almost all musical instruments use resonance to make musical sounds. A panpipe is a good example of resonance in an instrument. A panpipe is a simple instrument made of many tubes of different lengths (Figure 21.12). One end of each tube is closed and the other end is open. Blowing across the open end of a tube creates a standing wave inside the tube. The frequency of the standing wave is the frequency of sound given off by the pipe. Longer pipes create longer wavelength standing waves and make lower frequencies of sound. Shorter pipes create shorter wavelength standing waves and therefore make higher frequencies of sound.

Standing wave patterns
The closed end of a pipe is a closed boundary. A closed boundary makes a node in the standing wave. The open end of a pipe is an open boundary to a standing wave in the pipe. An open boundary makes an antinode in the standing wave. Figure 21.12 shows a standing wave that has a node at the closed end and an antinode at the open end. The wavelength of the fundamental is four times the length of the pipe. The pipe resonates to a certain sound when its length is one-fourth the wavelength of the sound.

Designing a musical instrument
Suppose you wish to make a pipe that makes a sound with a frequency of 660 hertz (the note E). Using the relationship between frequency and wavelength, the required wavelength is (343 m/sec) ÷ (660 Hz) = 0.52 meters. The length of pipe needs to be one-fourth of the wavelength to make a resonance in the fundamental mode. One-quarter of 52 centimeters is 13 centimeters. If you make a thin pipe that is 13 centimeters long with one closed end, it will have a natural frequency of approximately 660 hertz. This is the principle on which musical instruments are designed. Sounds of different frequencies are made by standing waves. The length of a vibrating system can be chosen so that it resonates at the frequency you want to hear.

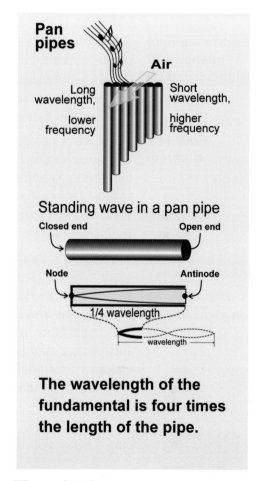

The wavelength of the fundamental is four times the length of the pipe.

Figure 21.12: *A panpipe is made from tubes of different length. The diagram shows the fundamental for a standing wave of sound in a panpipe.*

Wave speed = *Frequency* **×** *Wavelength*

Wave speed ÷ *Frequency* = **Wavelength**

Fourier's theorem

How are multiple frequencies of sound created? To make a single frequency of sound, a speaker vibrates back and forth in a simple pattern with a single wavelength and frequency. However, almost all the sound you hear is a combination of frequencies. What kind of motion should a speaker use to create multiple frequencies of sound at the same time, as there is in music or speech?

Fourier's theorem The answer involves **Fourier's theorem**. Fourier's theorem says a wave of any shape can be made by adding up single frequency waves. Remember that the superposition principle states that many single waves add up to one complex wave. Fourier's theorem works from the other direction. A complex wave can be made from a sum of single frequency waves, each with its own frequency, amplitude, and phase.

An example Figure 21.13 shows a "square wave" with a frequency of 100 Hz. A square wave does not have a single frequency, but instead contains many frequencies. In agreement with Fourier's theorem a pretty good reproduction of the square wave can be made by adding five waves of different frequencies and amplitudes. To produce multiple frequencies, a speaker vibrates back and forth with a complex motion. If a speaker were to vibrate back and forth with sudden jerks, like the square wave, it would create sound of all the frequencies it takes to make the square wave!

100 Hz square wave

Amplitude	Frequency
100	100 Hz

First five frequencies in a square wave

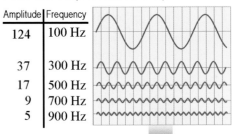

Amplitude	Frequency
124	100 Hz
37	300 Hz
17	500 Hz
9	700 Hz
5	900 Hz

Sum of the first five frequencies

Figure 21.13: *Making a square wave by adding up five single-frequency waves.*

21.2 Section Review

1. How could you increase the air pressure inside a bag containing a group of air molecules?

2. Is sound a longitudinal or transverse wave?

3. A 200-hertz sound has a wavelength about equal to the height of an adult. Would a sound with a wavelength equal to the height of a 2-year old child have a higher or lower frequency than 200 Hz?

4. In which situation does sound travel faster: (a) outside on a winter day, or (b) outside on a summer day?

5. Would a full concert hall have different reverberation from an empty hall? Explain.

6. The superposition principle states: wave A + wave B = wave C. Write an equation like this for Fourier's theorem.

21.3 Sound, Perception, and Music

Sound is everywhere in our environment. We use sound to communicate and we listen to sound for information about what is going on around us. Our ears and brain are constantly receiving and processing sound. In this section you will learn about how we *hear* a sound wave and how the ear and brain construct meaning from sound. This section will also introduce some of the science behind music. Musical sound is a rich language of rhythm and frequency, developed over thousands of years of human culture.

The perception and interpretation of sound

Constructing meaning from patterns

As you read this paragraph, you subconsciously recognize individual letters. However, the *meaning* of the paragraph is not in the letters themselves. The meaning is in the *patterns* of how the letters make words and the words make sentences. The brain does a similar thing with sound. A single frequency of sound is like one letter. It does not have much meaning. The meaning in sound comes from patterns of many frequencies changing together.

The ear hears many frequencies at once

When you hear a sound, the nerves in your ear respond to more than 15,000 different frequencies at the same time. This is like having an alphabet with 15,000 letters! The brain interprets all 15,000 different frequency signals from the ear and creates a "sonic image" of the sound. The meaning in different sounds is derived from the patterns in how the different frequencies get louder and softer.

Complex sound waves

Imagine listening to live music with a singer and a band. Your ears can easily distinguish the voice from the instruments. How does this occur? The microphone records a single "wave form" of how pressure varies with time. The recorded wave form is very complex, but it contains all the sound from the music and voice (Figure 21.14).

How the brain finds meaning

You ear is a living application of Fourier's theorem. The ear separates the sound into different frequencies. Your brain has learned to recognize certain patterns of how each frequency changes over time. One pattern might be a word. Another might be a musical note. Inside your brain is a "dictionary" that associates a meaning with a pattern of frequency the same way an ordinary dictionary associates a meaning from a pattern of letters (a word).

Vocabulary

frequency spectrum, sonogram, cochlea, rhythm, musical scale, note, octave, beat, consonance, dissonance

Objectives

✓ Describe how the meaning of sound is related to frequency and time.

✓ Learn how we hear sound.

✓ Describe the musical scale, consonance, dissonance, and beats in terms of sound waves.

✓ Learn about the role of harmonics in how instruments sound.

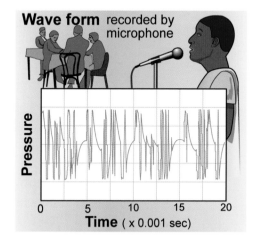

Figure 21.14: *The recorded wave form from 0.02 seconds of music.*

The frequency spectrum and sonogram

Frequency spectrum
A **frequency spectrum** is a graph showing the different frequencies present in a sound. The vertical axis tells you the loudness and the horizontal axis tells you the frequency. Sound containing many frequencies has a wave form that is jagged and complicated. The wave form in the Figure 21.15 is from an acoustic guitar playing the note E. The frequency spectrum shows that the complex sound of the guitar is made from many frequencies, ranging up to 10,000 Hz and beyond.

Wave form and spectrum change with time
Both the wave form and the spectrum change as the sound changes. The wave form and spectrum represent only a single moment of the sound. Since meaning comes from patterns of changing frequencies, we need another graph that can show three variables at once: frequency, amplitude, and time.

Sonograms
A **sonogram** shows how loud sound is at different frequencies over a period of time (Figure 21.16). The sonogram below is for a male voice saying "hello." The word lasts from 0.1 seconds to about 0.6 seconds. You can see lots of sound below 1,500 hertz and two bands of sound near 2,350 and 3,300 hertz. Every person's sonogram is different, even for the same word.

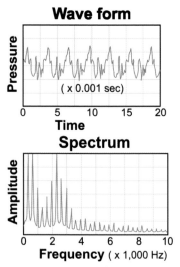

The **spectrum** shows the frequencies that make up a complex wave form.

Figure 21.15: *Each peak in the spectrum represents the frequency and amplitude of a wave that makes up the wave form.*

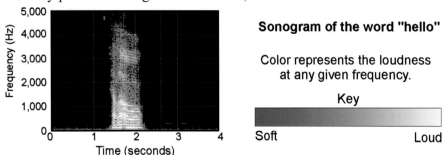

Sonogram of the word "hello"

Color represents the loudness at any given frequency.

Key

Soft — Loud

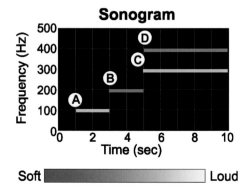

Sonogram

Soft — Loud

Figure 21.16: *A sonogram shows how the loudness of different frequencies of sound changes with time.*

Reading a sonogram
A sonogram shows frequency on the vertical axis and time on the horizontal axis. The loudness is shown by different colors. The sonogram above shows the word "hello" lasting from 1.4 to 2.2 seconds. You can see that there are many frequencies almost filling up the space between 0 and 5,000 Hz. Figure 21.16 shows a simpler sonogram to help you learn to read this complex graph. Which bar represents a loud sound of 100 Hz lasting from 1 to 3 seconds (A, B, C, or D)?

How we hear sound

Hearing sound   We get our sense of hearing from the **cochlea**, a tiny fluid-filled organ in the inner ear (Figure 21.17). The inner ear has two important functions: providing our sense of hearing and our sense of balance. The three semicircular canals near the cochlea are also filled with fluid. Fluid moving in each of the three canals tells the brain whether the body is moving left-right, up-down, or forward-backward.

How the cochlea works   The perception of sound starts with the eardrum. The eardrum vibrates in response to sound waves in the ear canal. The three delicate bones of the inner ear transmit the vibration of the eardrum to the side of the cochlea. Fluid in the spiral of the cochlea vibrates and creates waves that travel up the spiral. The spiral channel starts out large and gets narrower near the end. The nerves near the beginning see a relatively large channel and respond to longer-wavelength, lower-frequency sound. The nerves at the small end of the channel respond to shorter-wavelength, higher-frequency sound.

The range of human hearing   The range of human hearing is between 20 hertz and 20,000 hertz (or 20 kilohertz, abbreviated kHz). The combination of the eardrum, bones, and the cochlea all contribute to the limited range of hearing. You could not hear a sound at 50,000 hertz (50 kHz), even at a loudness of 100 decibels. Animals such as cats and dogs can hear much higher frequencies because of the design of their outer ears and the more sensitive structures in their inner ears.

Hearing ability changes with time   Hearing varies greatly with people and changes with age. Some people can hear higher-frequency sounds and other people cannot. People gradually lose high-frequency hearing with age. Most adults cannot hear frequencies above 15,000 hertz, while children can often hear to 20,000 hertz.

Hearing can be damaged by loud noise   Hearing is affected by exposure to loud or high-frequency noise. The nerve signals that carry sensation of sound to the brain are created by tiny hairs that shake when the fluid in the cochlea is vibrated. Listening to loud sounds for a long time can cause the hairs to weaken or break off. It is smart to protect your ears by keeping the volume reasonable and wearing ear protection if you have to stay in a loud place. In concerts, many musicians wear earplugs to protect their hearing.

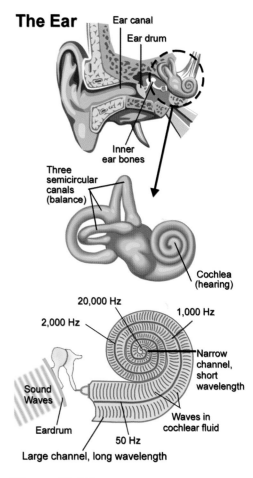

Figure 21.17: *The structure of the inner ear. When the eardrum vibrates, three small bones transmit the vibration to the cochlea. The vibrations make waves inside the cochlea, which vibrates nerves in the spiral. Each part of the spiral is sensitive to a different frequency.*

Music

Pitch The *pitch* of a sound is how high or low we hear its frequency. A higher frequency sound is heard as a higher pitch. However, because pitch depends on the human ear and brain. The way we hear a sound can be affected by the sounds we heard before and after.

Rhythm **Rhythm** is a regular time pattern in a sound. Here is a rhythm you can 'play' on your desk: TAP-TAP-tap-tap-TAP-TAP-tap-tap. Play 'TAP' louder than you play 'tap.' Rhythm can be made with sound and silence or with different pitches. People respond naturally to rhythm. Cultures are distinguished by their music and the special rhythms used in music.

The musical scale Music is a combination of sound and rhythm that we find pleasant. Styles of music are vastly different but all music is created from carefully chosen frequencies of sound. Most of the music you listen to is created from a pattern of frequencies called a **musical scale**. Each frequency in the scale is called a **note**. The range between any frequency and twice that frequency is called an **octave** (see sidebar). Notes that are an octave apart in frequency share the same name. Within the octave there are eight primary notes in the Western musical scale. Each of the eight is related to the first note in the scale by a ratio of frequencies (see sidebar). The scale that starts on the note C (264 Hz) is show in the diagram below.

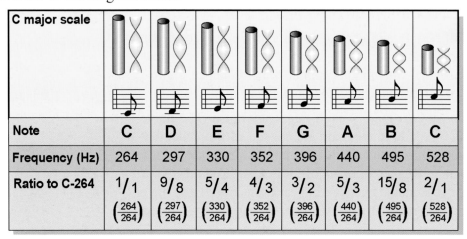

C major scale							
Note	C	D	E	F	G	A	B	C
Frequency (Hz)	264	297	330	352	396	440	495	528
Ratio to C-264	$\frac{1}{1}$ $\left(\frac{264}{264}\right)$	$\frac{9}{8}$ $\left(\frac{297}{264}\right)$	$\frac{5}{4}$ $\left(\frac{330}{264}\right)$	$\frac{4}{3}$ $\left(\frac{352}{264}\right)$	$\frac{3}{2}$ $\left(\frac{396}{264}\right)$	$\frac{5}{3}$ $\left(\frac{440}{264}\right)$	$\frac{15}{8}$ $\left(\frac{495}{264}\right)$	$\frac{2}{1}$ $\left(\frac{528}{264}\right)$

Notes on a musical scale

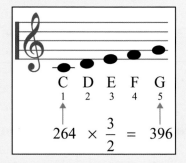

The notes on a musical scale are related to the first note by ratios of frequency. For example, the fifth note has a frequency 3/2 times the frequency of the first note. If the first note is C-264 Hz, then the fifth note has a frequency of 1.5 times 264, or G-396 Hz.

Octaves

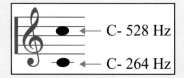

Two notes are an octave apart when the frequency of one note is double the frequency of the other. Notes that are an octave apart are given the same name because they sound similar to the ear. For example, the note C has a frequency of 264 Hz. Frequencies of 132 Hz and 528 Hz are also named "C" because they are an octave apart from C-264 Hz.

Consonance, dissonance, and beats

Harmony *Harmony* is the study of how sounds work together to create effects desired by the composer. From experience, you know that music can have a profound effect on people's moods. For example, the tense, dramatic soundtrack of a horror movie is a vital part of the audience's experience. Harmony is based on the frequency relationships of the musical scale.

Beats The frequencies in the musical scale are specifically chosen to reduce the occurrence of a sound effect called *beats*. When two frequencies of sound are close but not exactly equal, the loudness of the total sound seems to oscillate or **beat**. At one moment the two waves are in phase and the total sound is louder than either wave separately. A moment later the waves are out of phase and they cancel each other out, making the sound quieter. The rapid alternation in amplitude is what we hear as beats. The sidebar at right describe how bats use beats to locate insects. Beats are also useful for determining if an instrument is out of tune (see sidebar next page).

Adding two waves with different frequency

Why we hear beats

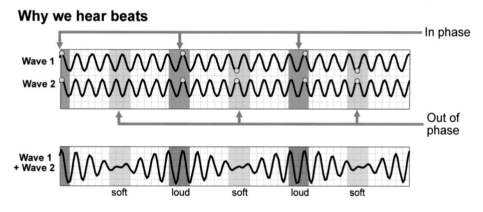

Consonance and dissonance When we hear more than one frequency of sound and the combination sounds good, we call it **consonance**. When the combination sounds bad or unsettling, we call it **dissonance**. Consonance and dissonance are related to beats. When frequencies are far enough apart that there are no beats, we get consonance. When frequencies are too close together, we hear beats that are the cause of dissonance. Dissonance is often used to create tension or drama. Consonance can be used to create feelings of balance and comfort.

Echolocation and beats

Bats navigate at night using ultrasound waves instead of light. A bat's voice is like a "sonic flashlight" shining a beam of sound. A bat emits short bursts of sound that rise in frequency and are called "chirps." When the sound reflects off an insect, the bat's ears receive the echo. Since the frequency of the chirp is always changing, the echo comes back with a slightly different frequency. The difference between the echo and the chirp makes beats that the bat can hear. The beat frequency is proportional to how far the insect is from the bat. A bat can even determine where the insect is by comparing the echo it hears in the left ear with what it hears in the right ear.

Voices and instruments

Voices
The human voice is a complex sound that starts in the larynx, a small structure at the top of your windpipe. The term *vocal cords* is a little misleading because the sound-producing structures are not really cords but are folds of expandable tissue that extend across a hollow chamber known as the larynx. The sound that starts in the larynx is changed by passing through openings in the throat and mouth (Figure 21.18). Different sounds are made by changing both the vibrations in the larynx and the shape of the openings.

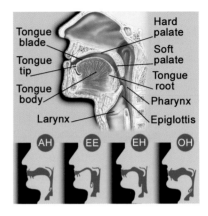

Figure 21.18: *The human voice is created by a combination of vibrating folds of skin in the larynx and the resonant shapes of the throat and mouth.*

The guitar

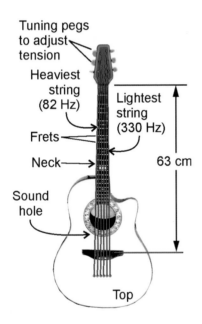

Tuning pegs to adjust tension

Heaviest string (82 Hz)

Lightest string (330 Hz)

Frets

Neck

63 cm

Sound hole

Top

The guitar has become a central instrument in popular music. Guitars come in many types but share the common feature of making sound from vibrating strings. A standard guitar has six strings that are stretched along the neck. The strings have different weights and therefore different natural frequencies.

The heaviest string has a natural frequency of 82 Hz and the lightest a frequency of 330 Hz. Each string is stretched by a tension force of about 125 newtons (28 pounds). The combined force from six strings on a folk guitar is more than the weight of a person (750 N or 170 lbs). The guitar is tuned by changing the tension in each string. Tightening a string raises its natural frequency and loosening lowers it.

Each string can make many notes
A typical guitar string is 63 centimeters long. To make different notes, the vibrating length of each string can be shortened by holding it down against one of many metal bars across the neck called frets (Figure 21.19). The frequency goes up as the vibrating length of the string gets shorter. A guitar with 20 frets and six strings can play 126 different notes, some of which are duplicates.

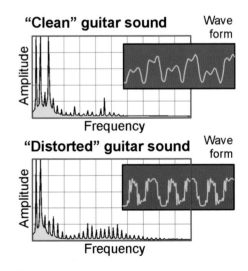

Figure 21.19: *Wave forms from "clean" and "distorted" guitar sounds. Notice that both sounds have the same fundamental frequency but the distorted sound has more high-frequency harmonic content.*

Harmonics and the sound of instruments

The same note can sound different

The same note sounds different when played on different instruments. As an example, suppose you listen to the note C-264 Hz played on a guitar and the same C-264 Hz played on a piano. A musician would recognize both notes as being C because they have the same frequency and pitch. But the guitar sounds like a guitar and the piano sounds like a piano. If the frequency of the note is the same, what gives each instrument its characteristic sound?

Instruments make mixtures of frequencies

The answer is that the sound from an instrument is not a single pure frequency. The most important frequency is still the fundamental note (C-264 Hz, for example). The variation comes from the *harmonics*. Remember, harmonics are frequencies that are multiples of the fundamental note. We have already learned that a string can vibrate at many harmonics. The same is true for all instruments. A single C note from a grand piano might include 20 or more different harmonics.

Recipes for sound

A good analogy is that every instrument has its own *recipe* for the frequency content of its sound. Another word for recipe in this context is *timbre*. In Figure 21.20 you can see how the mix of harmonics for a guitar compares to the mix for a piano when both instruments play the note C. This graphic illustrates that the timbre of a guitar is different from that of a piano.

Beat frequency

An "A" tuning fork produces vibrations for the note A at 440 hertz. Let's say the A string on a guitar is out of tune and its natural frequency is 445 hertz. This means that when you play the string and listen to the tuning fork, you will hear a beat frequency of 5 beats per second or 5 hertz! The beat frequency becomes zero, when the string is tuned to a natural frequency of 440 hertz.

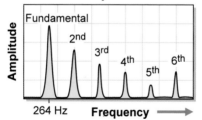

Piano spectrum

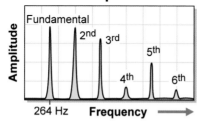

Guitar spectrum

21.3 Section Review

1. Explain how the cochlea allows us to hear both low-frequency and high-frequency sound.
2. What is the range of frequencies for human hearing?
3. If you were talking to an elderly person who was having trouble hearing you, would it be better to talk in a deeper voice (low-frequency sound) or a higher voice (high-frequency sound)?
4. What is the difference between the pitch of a sound and its frequency?
5. If two sound waves are in phase, do you hear beats? Why or why not?
6. A musician in a group plays a "wrong" note. Would this note disrupt the harmony or the rhythm of the song they are playing? Explain your answer.
7. Why does an A played on a violin sound different from the same note played on a guitar?

Figure 21.20: *The sound of the note C played on a piano and on a guitar. Notice that the fundamental frequencies are the same but the harmonics have different amplitudes.*

Sound Spaces

Loud and quiet places

In the study of acoustics, the science of sound, the focus is usually on enclosed spaces. Your living room or bedroom at home is an enclosed space, but so is your school cafeteria or auditorium. Physicists who specialize in acoustics study how sound acts in these spaces.

Think about the sound you hear in a school cafeteria or gymnasium versus the school library. From experience, you know that a cafeteria and gym are often loud places, and libraries are quiet. Now, think about the design of these spaces and the types of materials used in them. What comes to mind?

Most libraries and auditoriums have carpet on the floors. The walls and ceilings of these spaces may also have special materials that absorb sound. Of course, the sound in a library or auditorium is also controlled by rules and what types of events are happening.People study quietly in libraries and may listen to speeches or music in an auditorium.

In contrast, cafeteria's tend to be large spaces with tile floors and bare ceilings. Such flooring is easier to clean, but also provides a surface that reflects sound. The floor of a gymnasium is good for bouncing basketballs and for bouncing

sound. When sound is reflected rather than absorbed by a surface the space tends to be noisy rather than quiet.

Sound review

As you know, sound travels through a medium (solid, liquid, or gas) until the energy is absorbed by the medium. As sound travels the medium compresses and releases; in air, sound is characterized by waves of increasing and decreasing air pressure. The time that it takes for sound to be absorbed is called reverberation time. The sound waves move through a room and reflect off surfaces that they contact. The time varies depending upon many variables including the strength of the initial sound, the absorption rate of the walls of the room, and the size of the room. A *live room* is one whose materials have a low absorption rate and therefore a long reverberation time. Live rooms include gymnasiums and cafeterias where sounds easily reflect off walls, last a long time, even while many news sounds are made. A library or auditorium is an example of a *dead room*. In such rooms, the absorption rate of the materials is much higher. The reverberation time is decreased causing the space to be quieter.

Passive versus active noise reduction

In a library, passive noise reduction (PNR) is used to help make this enclosed space quiet. Carpet or heavy curtains or even ear plug are examples of passive noise reduction items. These materials absorb sound.

Another way to reduce sound is by active noise reduction (ANR). ANR technology tries to eliminate rather than absorb sound that is unwanted. Specially designed headphones are one part of the growing technology of ANR. There are three basic parts of ANR in a headphone: a microphone, processing electronics, and a speaker. These parts, which must all fit into the ear piece of the headphones, work together to cancel unwanted sound waves.

With carefully designed ANR, the microphone very near the ear canal continually detects noise. The frequency and amplitude profile of the noise is detected. The processing electronics create another noise that is just the opposite of the original. This new noise—or anti-noise—is sent into the ear canal by the speaker and cancels the offending sound.

To effectively address noise, scientists have learned that passive and active noise reduction are effective in different ways. ANR seems to work more efficiently with low frequency sounds while PNR is more efficient absorbing the higher frequencies. For example, studies have shown that the noise produced by propellers in airplanes is in the low frequency range. Therefore, specialized ANR headphones work well for airplane pilots. Extra soundproofing for passive noise reduction, although it would lessen high frequency noise, would add too much weight to a plane to be practical.

ANR technology is also available for headphones used with CD or MP3 players. These headphones are safe to wear because they only cancel the lower frequencies of sound, and not speech or warning sirens. Presently, ANR technology is being tested to lower the noise from the cooling fans inside electronic devices like your computer, tailpipes of cars, or inside the cabin of the car. As ANR technology grows, new uses for ANR will be discovered. Can you think of a new use for ANR technology?

How active noise reduction headsets work

PNR — Passive Noise Reduction

ANR — Anti-Noise Reduction

Noise

Loudness reduced by PNR. PNR can also remove high frequency sounds.

Anti-noise cancels noise, especially low frequency noise.

The ear covering provides passive noise reduction.

Noise is greatly reduced or eliminated.

Active noise reduction circuitry and power.

Headsets use a combination of passive and active noise reduction.

Questions:

1. What is the difference between a live room and a dead room in terms of sound?
2. If you wanted to create a recording studio for recording a new CD for your band, what would you do? You may want to do research on the Internet to find out the design features of recording studios.
3. Compare and contrast passive and active noise reduction.
4. Does active noise reduction work using constructive or destructive interference?

Chapter 21 Review

Understanding Vocabulary

Select the correct term to complete the sentences.

Doppler effect	acoustics	supersonic
consonance	musical scales	decibels
reverberation	sonogram	cochlea
Fourier's theorem	pitch	beat
	shock wave	dissonance

Section 21.1

1. The loudness of a sound wave is measured in ____.

2. The science and technology of sound is known as ____.

3. The ____ of a sound is how high or low we hear its frequency.

4. A ____ jet travels faster than sound.

5. The shift in sound frequency caused by a moving sound source is called the ____.

6. A sonic boom is caused by the pressure change across a(n) ____.

Section 21.2

7. Reflected sound waves added to direct sound create a multiple echo called ____.

8. ____ states that a wave form is the sum of single frequent waves.

Section 21.3

9. The ____ is the tiny fluid filled organ in the inner ear that provides our sense of hearing.

10. Most music is based on patterns of frequencies called ____.

11. When two frequencies of sound are close, but not exactly the same, the loudness of the sound seems to oscillate or ____.

12. A combination of sound frequencies that sound good is called ____.

13. A combination of unsettling-sounding frequencies is called ____.

14. A special kind of graph that shows how loud sound is at different frequencies is called a(n) ____.

Reviewing Concepts

Section 21.1

1. Imagine you are cruising in outer space in a spaceship when you notice an asteroid hurtling towards your ship. You fire a missile and score a direct hit. The asteroid explodes into a billion pieces. Would you hear the explosion? Explain your answer.

2. How do we recognize people's voices?

3. What does the decibel scale measure, and what scale does it use?

4. If a fire engine moves toward you, does the pitch of its siren increase or decrease?

5. How fast does an airplane need to be traveling to create a sonic boom? Is this speed supersonic or subsonic?

6. How is stereo sound recorded and why does it sound "live"?

Section 21.2

7. Explain how sound is caused at the molecular level. Sketch what a sound wave would look like at the molecular level.

8. What type of waves are sound waves?

9. How does pressure work as a restoring force to create a sound wave?

10. Which of the following sounds has the shortest wavelength?
    a. The rumble of thunder at 20 Hz
    b. A base guitar at 100 Hz
    c. A fire truck siren at 2,000 Hz
    d. The highest note on a piano at 5,000 Hz

11. If the temperature of a material increased, how would the speed of sound through this material be affected? Why?

12. In which space would it be easier to hear a musician and why—outdoors or in your classroom?

Section 21.3

13. What is the difference between a wave form graph and a sound spectrum graph for a complex sound? Which graph best illustrates the harmonic motion of sound. Which graph best illustrates which frequencies are the loudest in a complex sound?

4. Some musicians wear earplugs when playing in concerts. What happens when the inner ear is exposed to very loud noises?

5. Which part of the ear vibrates in response to sound in the ear canal?

6. How are the pitch and frequency of a sound related?

7. What gives different instruments their characteristic sound? For example, why does a note played on a piano sound different from the same note played on a guitar?

8. How are beats created?

9. Why can't you hear a dog whistle at 25,000 Hz, but your dog can?

Solving Problems

Section 21.1

1. The sound of ordinary conversation 3 feet away is 65 decibels and the sound in a restaurant is 45 decibels.
   a. To our ears, how much louder is the ordinary conversation than the restaurant?
   b. How much larger is the amplitude of the sound waves in ordinary conversation than in the restaurant?

2. The Doppler effect is used by astronomers to determine if stars are moving away from or toward Earth. Red light has a lower frequency than blue light. If light from a star is shifted to the red does that mean the star is moving toward or away from Earth?

Section 21.2

3. The speed of sound through air is approximately 340 m/sec. What is the wavelength of a sound wave with a frequency of 680 Hz?

4. The range of human hearing is between 20 Hz and 20,000 Hz. If the speed of sound is 340 m/sec, what is the longest wavelength you can hear? What is the shortest?

5. Suppose you stand in front of a wall that is 170 meters away. If you yell, how long does it take for the echo to get back to you if the speed of sound is 340 m/sec?

6. What is the fundamental frequency for an organ pipe that is one meter long? The pipe has one end that is open and another end that is closed. Use a wave speed of 340 m/sec.

Section 21.3

7. If middle C on a piano has a frequency of 264 Hz, what is the frequency of the C one octave higher? One octave lower?

8. Describe what you hear when a musical note at 440 Hz is played at the same time as another note at 443 Hz.

Applying Your Knowledge

Section 21.1

1. Some people have perfect pitch. Research in your library or on the Internet what it means to have perfect pitch. What are the pros and cons of having perfect pitch?

Section 21.2

2. Why is hanging heavy curtains a good way to decrease sound in a room? Use the terms *absorption* and *amplitude* in your answer.

3. Compare the superposition principle to Fourier's theorem.

Section 21.3

4. Compare the active noise reduction to traditional hearing protection, such as ear muffs or ear plugs.

5. At what level does sound become unsafe? What are some ways you can protect your hearing? Suggest three places where you might need to use hearing protection.

6. Harmonic synthesizers can mimic almost any sound and allow you to play it as music on a keyboard. A synthesizer can sound like a flute, a bell, or a piano. In a short paragraph, describe how the synthesizer is able to play the same keyboard notes with such different sounds.

7. The human voice is a complex sound that is created by a combination of vibrating folds of skin in the larynx and the resonant shapes of the throat and mouth. Humans can hear sounds at frequencies of 20 to 20,000 Hz. Research the range of human voice frequencies. How do the voice ranges compare to the hearing ranges?

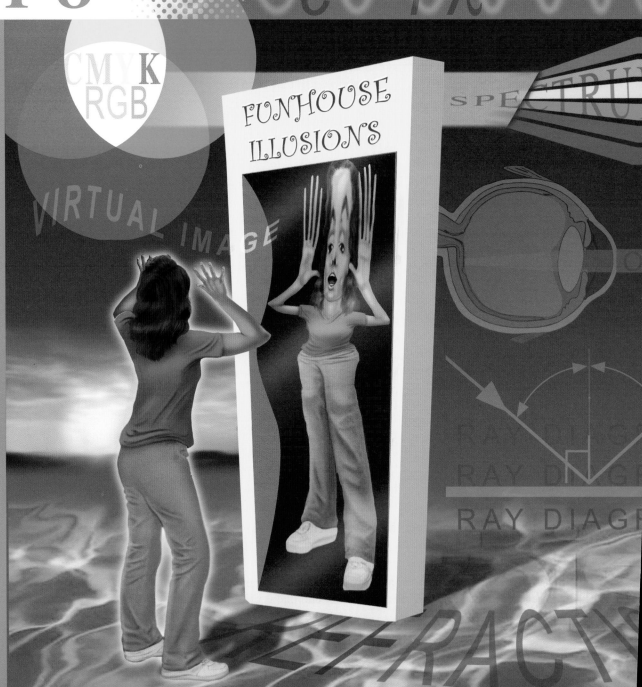

UNIT 8

Light and Optics

Chapter 22 Light and Color

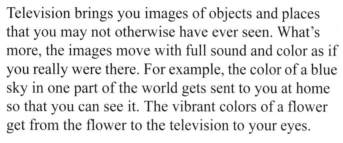

Television brings you images of objects and places that you may not otherwise have ever seen. What's more, the images move with full sound and color as if you really were there. For example, the color of a blue sky in one part of the world gets sent to you at home so that you can see it. The vibrant colors of a flower get from the flower to the television to your eyes.

What creates color? Does the flower give off red and orange light like a neon sign? How is color seen by our eyes?

To answer these questions, start with a short experiment. Take a colorful object like a shirt or a toy. Look at your object in the light. Then, look at the same object in a totally dark room. What do you see? How do the colors compare in the light versus in the dark? Your answer and your observations will prepare you for this chapter, where you will learn about light and color.

Key Questions

✓ How do computers and DVDs make color using just numbers?

✓ What is color and how do our eyes see color?

✓ Where does light come from?

22.1 Properties of Light

Every time you see something, light is involved. Whether you are looking at a light bulb or a car or this book, light brings visual information to our eyes. In fact, the very act of "seeing" means receiving light and forming images in your mind from the light received by your eyes. In complete darkness, we cannot see anything! This chapter is about light—where it comes from and its properties including color and its interactions.

What is light?

Light is a form of energy
Today we believe that light, like sound and heat, is a form of energy. We have learned how to make light and use light to do all sorts of useful things. Like most of science, our understanding of light starts with what light does and what its properties are (Figure 22.1). We know that:

- light travels extremely fast and over long distances,
- light carries energy and information,
- light travels in straight lines,
- light bounces and bends when it comes in contact with objects,
- light has color, and
- light has different intensities, and can be bright or dim.

Seeing and reflected light
What physically happens as you see this page? Light in the room reflects off the page and into your eyes. The reflected light carries information about the page that allows your brain to construct an image of the page. You see because light in the room *reflects* from the page into your eyes. If you were inside a perfectly dark room with no light, you would not be able to see this page at all because the page does not give off its own light. *We see most of the world by reflected light.*

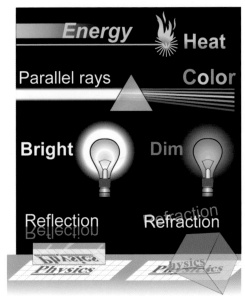

Vocabulary
incandescence, fluorescence, intensity

Objectives
✓ Describe the properties of light.
✓ Review the term light intensity.
✓ Learn about the speed of light.
✓ Be able to compare light and sound waves.

Figure 22.1: *Some words and properties that are associated with light. What words do you use to describe light?*

Light from atoms

The electric light

For most of human history people relied on the sun, moon, and fire to provide light. Thomas Edison's electric light bulb (1879) changed our dependence on fire and daylight forever. The electric light is one of the most important inventions in the progress of human development.

Light is produced by atoms

Whether in an electric bulb or in the sun, light is mostly produced by atoms. Remember from chapter 9, atoms absorb and emit energy by rearranging electrons. Eventually, any excess energy that an atom has is released. This energy release or transfer is analogous to a ball rolling down hill. Unlike a ball, an atom releases the extra energy usually — but not always — as light!

Incandescent light bulbs

In order to get light *out* of an atom you must put some energy *into* the atom first. One way to do this is with heat. When atoms get hot enough some of the thermal energy is released as light. The process of making light with heat is called **incandescence**. Incandescent bulbs pass electric current through a thin metal wire called a filament. The filament heats up and gives off light. The atoms of the filament, convert electrical energy to heat and then to light. Unfortunately, incandescent bulbs are not very efficient. Only a fraction of the energy of electricity is converted into light. Most of the energy becomes heat (Figure 22.2). Some incandescent bulbs are actually designed to make heat.

Fluorescent light bulbs

Another common kind of electric light is a fluorescent bulb (Figure 22.3). Fluorescent bulbs are used in schools, businesses and homes, because they are much more efficient than incandescent bulbs. Compared with a standard incandescent bulb, you get four times as much light from a fluorescent bulb for the same amount of electrical energy. This is possible because fluorescent bulbs convert electricity directly to light without generating as much heat.

How fluorescent bulbs make light

To make light, fluorescent bulbs use high-voltage electricity to energize atoms of gas in the bulb. These atoms release the electrical energy as light, in a process called **fluorescence**. The atoms in a fluorescent bulb give off high-energy ultraviolet light, the same kind that gives you a sunburn. The ultraviolet light is absorbed by other atoms in a white coating on the inside surface of the bulb. This coating re-emits the energy as white light that we *can* see. Even with the two-step process, fluorescent bulbs are still four times more efficient at producing light than incandescent bulbs.

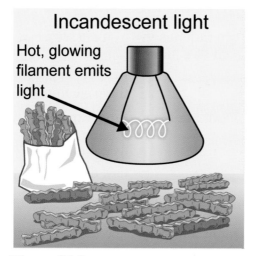

Figure 22.2: *An incandescent light bulb generates light by heating a metal filament. The atoms inside the filament convert electrical energy to heat and then to light.*

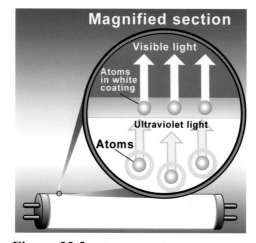

Figure 22.3: *Fluorescent lights generate light by exciting atoms with electricity in a two-step process. First invisible ultraviolet light is produced which causes atoms to emit visible white light.*

Light carries energy and power

Light radiates in all directions
You can see a bare light bulb from anywhere in a room because the bulb emits light in all directions. When the rays of light are represented by arrows, the light coming from a bulb looks like (Figure 22.4). You can see the paper of this page from different places because the page reflects light in all directions.

Light intensity
From experience, you know that as you move away from a source of light, the amount of light decreases. We use the word **intensity** to describe the amount of light energy per second falling on a surface. For example, on a summer day, the amount of sunlight falling on a single square meter of surface is 500 watts. The intensity of this light is 500 watts per square meter (500 W/m²). *Light intensity is the power of light per unit area* (Figure 22.5).

Light intensity follows an inverse square law
For a small source of light, the intensity decreases as the square of the distance from the source increases. In other words, light intensity follows an *inverse square law* — as the distance from a light source increases, the light intensity decreases by the square of the distance from the source.

The diagram below shows the inverse square law. At a radius of one meter, 8 watts of light fall on a one meter square area. The light intensity is 8 W/m². The intensity at 2 meters is one-fourth the intensity at one meter or 2 W/m². Increasing the distance by a factor of 2 *reduces* the intensity by a factor of 2^2 or 4. Tripling the distance (from 1 to 3 meters) would reduce the intensity by a factor of 3^2 or 9. The intensity at 3 meters would be 8/9 or 0.889 W/m².

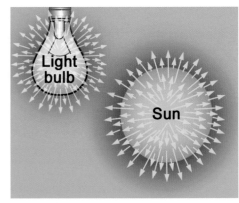

Figure 22.4: *Light emitted from the sun or from a light bulb travels in straight lines from the surface.*

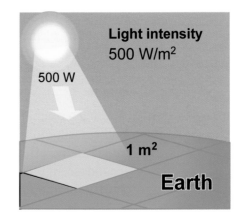

Figure 22.5: *Light intensity is the amount of energy per second falling on a surface. In the summer, the intensity of sunlight reaches 500 watts per square meter on Earth's surface.*

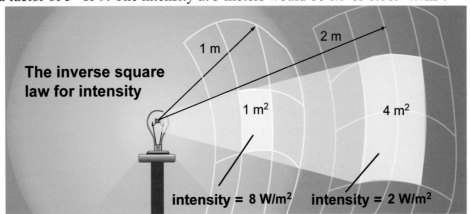

The inverse square law for intensity

1 m
2 m
1 m²
4 m²
intensity = 8 W/m²
intensity = 2 W/m²

The speed of light

Comparing the speeds of sound and light

Consider what happens when you shine a flashlight on a distant object. You do not see the light leave your flashlight, travel to the object, bounce off, and come back to your eyes. But that is exactly what happens. You do not see it because it happens so fast. For example, suppose you shine a flashlight on a mirror 170 meters away. The light travels to the mirror and back in about one millionth of a second (0.000001 sec). Sound travels much slower than light. If you shout, you will hear an echo one second later from the sound bouncing off a wall 170 meters away and back to your ears. Light travels almost a million times faster than sound.

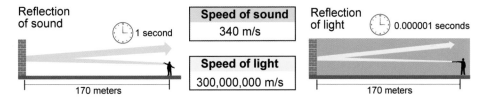

The speed of light, $c = 3 \times 10^8$ m/sec

The speed at which light travels through air is approximately 300 million meters per second. Light is so fast it can travel around the entire Earth 7 1/2 times in 1 second. The *speed of light* is so important in physics that it is given its own symbol, a lower case *c*. When you see this symbol in a formula, remember that $c = 3 \times 10^8$ m/sec.

Why you hear thunder after you see lightning

The speed of light is so fast that when lightning strikes a few miles away, we hear the thunder several seconds after we see the lightning. At the point of the lightning strike, the thunder and lightning are simultaneous. But just a mile away from the lightning strike, the sound of the thunder is already about 5 seconds behind the flash of the lightning. You can use this information to calculate how far you are away from a thunderstorm (see the sidebar at right).

Accurate measurement of *c*

Using very fast electronics, the speed of light can be measured accurately. One technique is to record the time a pulse of light leaves a laser and the time the pulse returns to its starting position after making a round trip. The best accepted experimental measurement for the speed of light in a vacuum is 299,792,458 m/sec. For most purposes, we do not need to be this accurate and may use a value for *c* of 3×10^8 m/sec.

Light is faster than sound

The speed of light is about 300 million meters per second or 186,000 miles per second. At 15°C, the speed of sound is about 340 m/sec or 0.21 miles per second. You can use the speed of sound to determine how far away a lightning strike has occurred. In one second, light travels 186,000 miles. Sound travels about one-fifth of a mile in a second. When you see lightning, begin counting seconds until you hear thunder. Multiply the number of seconds you count by 0.21. The result is the distance in miles between where you are and where the lightning struck.

Light can bounce (reflection) and bend (refraction)

Light rays can bounce and bend

When light moves through a material it travels in straight lines. Diagrams of light utilize one or more imaginary lines we call *light rays* to show how light travels. When light rays move from one material to another, the rays may bounce or bend. *Reflection* occurs when light bounces off of a surface. *Refraction* occurs when light bends crossing a surface or moving through a material. Reflection and refraction cause many interesting changes in the images we see.

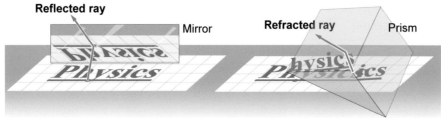

Light rays are reflected in a mirror, causing an inverted image.

Light rays are refracted (or bent) by a prism, causing the image to be distorted.

Reflection creates images in mirrors

When you look in a mirror, objects that are in front of the mirror appear as if they are behind the mirror. Light from the object strikes the mirror and reflects to your eyes. The image reaching your eyes appears to your brain as if the object really *was* behind the mirror. This illusion happens because your brain "sees" the image where it would be if the light reaching your eyes had traveled in a straight line.

Refraction changes how objects look

When light rays travel from air to water they refract. This is why a straw in a glass of water looks broken or bent at the water's surface. Look at some objects through a glass of water; move the glass closer and farther away from the objects. What strange illusions do you see?

Twinkling of stars

Another example of refraction of light is the twinkling of a star in the night sky. To reach your eyes, starlight must travel from space through Earth's atmosphere which varies in temperature and density. Cold pockets of air are more dense than warm pockets. Starlight is refracted as it travels through the various air pockets. Since the atmosphere is constantly changing, the amount of refraction also changes. The image of a star appears to "twinkle" or move because the light coming to your eye follows a zig-zag path to your eyes due to refraction.

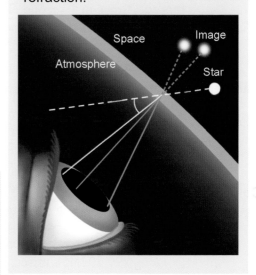

22.1 Section Review

1. Why can we see an object in a room from any position?

2. If a room were completely dark, could you see your hand? Explain using the idea of reflection.

3. List three observations that show light carries energy.

4. Can light be reflected and refracted at the same time? If so, give an example.

22.2 Vision and Color

Light reaches your eyes in one of two ways. Light can come directly from an object that produces its own light, such as a light bulb or glow stick. In this case the color of the light depends on the colors produced by the object. Light can also be reflected from objects that do not produce their own light, such as clothes or plants. With reflected light the color is produced by selectively subtracting out some colors. In this section, you will learn about color and how our eyes see color.

Color and energy

White light When all the colors of the rainbow are combined, we do not see any one color. We see light without *any* color. We call this combination of all the colors **white light** (below). White light is a good description of the ordinary light that is all around us most of the time. The light from the sun and the light from most electric lights is white light. The colors that make up white light are called *visible light*. There are other forms of light that we cannot see, such as infrared and ultraviolet light.

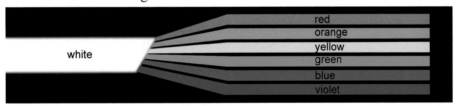

What is color? Why does some light appear red and other light appear blue? **Color** is how we perceive the energy of light. This definition of color was proposed by Albert Einstein. All of the colors in the rainbow are light of different energies. Red light has the lowest energy we can see, and violet light the highest energy. As we move through the rainbow from red to yellow to blue to violet, the energy of the light increases.

Color and energy What do we mean when we talk about the energy of light? Think about the very hot, blue flames from a gas stove or a gas grill. The atoms of gas in the flame have high energy so they give off blue light. The flame from a match or from a burning log in the fireplace is reddish-orange. These flames are not nearly as hot as gas flames, so the atoms have a less energy. The low energy light from a match flame appears red or yellow (Figure 22.6).

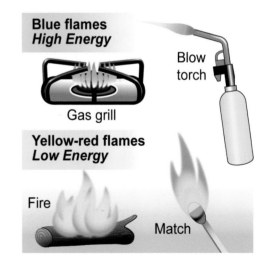

Figure 22.6: *High energy flames such as the ones from a gas grill produce blue light. Fire flames are lower energy and produce reddish-yellow light.*

How the human eye sees light

How we see color

The energy of light explains how we see colors. Light enters your eye through the lens (Figure 22.7) then lands on the retina. On the surface of the retina are light-sensitive cells called **photoreceptors**. When light hits a photoreceptor cell, the cell releases a chemical signal that travels along the optic nerve to the brain. In the brain, the signal is translated into a perception of color. Which signal gets sent depends on how much energy the light has. Some photoreceptors respond only to low energy, others to medium energy and a third type to higher energy.

Cone cells respond to color

Our eyes have two types of photoreceptors, called *cones* and *rods*. **Cones** (or *cone cells*) respond to color (Figure 22.8) and there are three types. One type responds best to red light. Another type responds best to green light and the last type responds best to blue light. We see a wide range of light colors depending on how each kind of cone cell is stimulated. For example, we see white light when all three types of cones (red, green, blue) are equally stimulated.

Rod cells respond to light intensity

The second kind of photoreceptor, **rods** (or *rod cells*), respond only to differences in intensity, and not to color (Figure 22.8). Rod cells detect black, white, and shades of gray. However, rod cells are more sensitive than cone cells especially at low light levels. At night, colors seem washed out because there is not enough light for cone cells to work. When the light level is very dim, you see "black and white" images transmitted from your rod cells.

Black and white vision is sharper than color vision

An average human eye contains about 130 million rod cells and 7 million cone cells. Each one contributes a "dot" to the total image assembled by your brain. The brain evaluates all 137 million "dots" about 15 times each second, creating the perception of motion. Because there are more rod cells, fine details are sharpest when there is high contrast between light and dark areas. That is why black and white print is easier to read than colored print. The cone cells are concentrated near the center of the retina, making color vision best at the center of the eye's field of view. Each cone cell "colors" the signals from the surrounding rod cells. Because there are fewer cone cells, and there are three kinds, our color vision is much less sharp than our black-and-white vision at recognizing fine details.

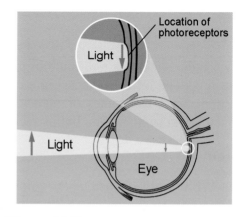

Figure 22.7: *The photoreceptors that send color signals to the brain are in the back of the eye.*

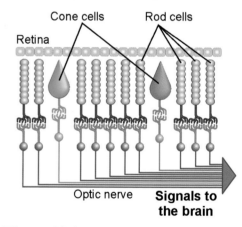

Figure 22.8: *The human eye has two types of photoreceptors—cones and rods. Cones respond to color and rods respond to the intensity of light.*

How we see colors

The additive color process

Our eyes work according to an **additive color process** — three photoreceptors (red, green, blue) in the eye operate together so that we see millions of different colors. The color you "see" depends on how much energy is received by each of the three different types of cone cells. The brain thinks "green" when there is a strong signal from the green cone cells but no signal from the blue or red cone cells (Figure 22.9).

How we perceive color

We perceive different colors as a combination of percentages of the three **additive primary colors**: *red*, *green*, and *blue*. For example, we see *yellow* when the brain gets an equally strong signal from both the red and the green cone cells at the same time. Whether the light is actually yellow, or a combination of red and green, the cones respond the same way and we perceive yellow. If the red signal is stronger than the green signal we see orange (Figure 22.10). If all three cones send an equal signal to the brain, we interpret the light we see as white.

The additive primary colors

Yellow
Red
Green
White
Magenta
Blue
Cyan

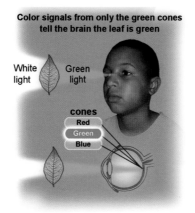

Figure 22.9: *If the brain gets a signal from only the green cone, we see green.*

Two ways to see a color

The human eye can see any color by adding different percentages of the three additive primary colors. Mixing red and green light is one way the eye sees the color yellow or orange, for example. Keep in mind that you perceive these colors even though the light itself is still red and green. You can also see pure yellow light or orange light that is not a mixture of red and green.

Do animals see colors?

To the best of our knowledge, primates (such as chimpanzees and gorillas) are the only animals with three-color vision similar to that of humans. Birds and fish—in particular, tropical varieties—have three or more kinds of photoreceptors. Some birds and insects can also see ultraviolet light which humans cannot detect. Dogs, cats, and some squirrels are thought to have at least two color photoreceptors. Although both octopi and squid can change color better than any other animal, they cannot detect color.

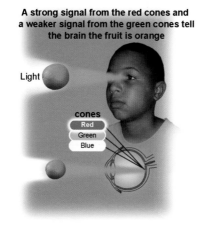

Figure 22.10: *If there is a strong red signal and a weak green signal, we see orange.*

The physics of color and light

Photons Just as matter is made of tiny particles called atoms, light energy comes in tiny bundles called *photons*. In some ways photons act like jellybeans of different colors. Each photon has its own color, no matter how you mix them up. The lowest energy photons we can see are the ones that appear a dull red in color (Figure 22.11). The highest-energy photons we can see are the color of blue tending to deep violet.

Waves Light is also a wave. Like other waves, the frequency of light is proportional to its energy. Red light has lower energy than blue light and also has a lower frequency (Figure 22.12). The frequency of light waves is *very* high compared to sound waves. Red light has frequencies in the range of 460 trillion hertz (460×10^{12}) and blue light in the range of 640 trillion hertz.

Colors You can think of a photon like a very short length of a light wave. Each photon carries the frequency of the light corresponding to its energy. An orange photon has a frequency of 490 trillion Hz, between red and yellow. This energy stimulates the red cone cells strongly and the green cone cells weakly, causing us to see orange. Mixing a little green light with more red light causes the same stimulation of the cone cells. This tricks the brain into "seeing" orange light even though the actual photons are red and green.

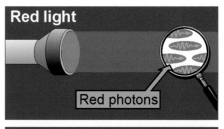
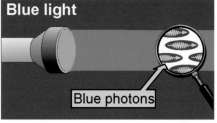

Figure 22.11: *Light is made of tiny bundles of energy called photons.*

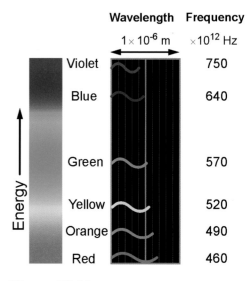

Figure 22.12: *The wavelength and frequency of colors of light.*

22.2 Section Review

1. How do we know that white light is composed of a rainbow of colors?
2. At a fireworks display on the fourth of July you see red, green, and blue fireworks. Which fireworks produce the highest light energy?
3. If humans have only three kinds of color photoreceptors, how can we see so many colors?
4. Why might it be a good idea to put a light in your clothes closet? (Hint: What kind of vision do we have in dim light?)

22.3 Using Color

You have read about how we see and interpret color. This section is about how a wide range of colors can be created by using a few colors. With the subtractive and additive color processes, color is created and used in publishing books, in television, and in video technology.

How things appear to be different colors

What gives objects their color?
Why does a blue shirt look blue? We see blue because chemicals (dyes) in the cloth absorbed the other colors in white light and *reflect only the blue to our eyes* (Figure 22.13). The color blue is not *in* the cloth! The blue light you see is the blue light mixed into white light that shines on the cloth. You see blue because the other colors in white light have been absorbed by the cloth.

The subtractive color process
Colored fabrics and paints get color from a **subtractive color process**. Chemicals known as *pigments* in the dyes and paints absorb some colors and reflect other colors. Pigments work by taking away colors from white light, which is a mixture of all the colors.

The subtractive primary colors

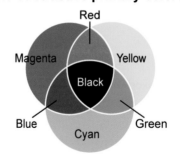

The subtractive primary colors
To make all colors by subtraction we need three primary pigments. We need one that absorbs blue, and reflects red and green. This pigment is called *yellow*. We need another pigment that absorbs green, and reflects red and blue. This is a pink-purple called *magenta*. The third pigment is *cyan*, which absorbs red and reflects green and blue. Cyan is a greenish shade of light blue. Magenta, yellow, and cyan are the three **subtractive primary colors** (Figure 22.13). By using different proportions of the three pigments, a paint can appear almost any color by varying the amount of reflected red, green, and blue light. For example, to make *black*, add all three and all light is absorbed, reflecting none.

Vocabulary

subtractive color process, subtractive primary colors, CMYK color process, RGB color process

Objectives

✓ Learn about the subtractive color process.
✓ Compare the CMYK and RGB processes.
✓ Learn about color blindness.
✓ Learn how plants use light and color to grow.

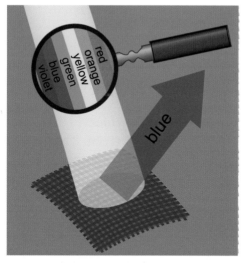

Figure 22.13: *The pigments in a blue cloth absorb all colors except blue. You see blue because blue light is reflected to your eyes.*

The CMYK color process

A subtractive color process Another name for the *subtractive color process* is the **CMYK color process** CMYK stands for cyan, magenta, yellow, and black. The letter K stands for black because the letter B is used to represent the color blue.

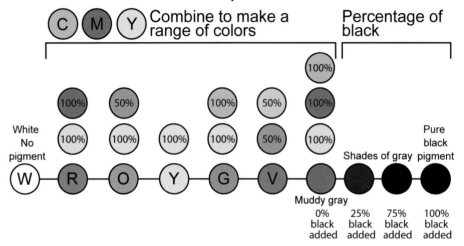

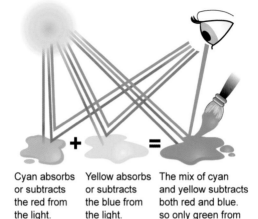

Figure 22.14: *Creating the color green using the cyan and yellow.*

CMYK are pigments The CMYK color process is used for making all colors that are seen in reflected light, including printing inks and fabric dyes. The three pigments, cyan, magenta, and yellow are combined in various proportions to make any color. Figure 22.14 shows how CMYK pigments can be combined to make green. Theoretically, mixing cyan, magenta, and yellow should make black, but in reality the result is only a muddy gray. This is why a fourth color, pure black is included in the CMYK process. Figure 22.15 shows how the CMYK process works with an ink-jet printer.

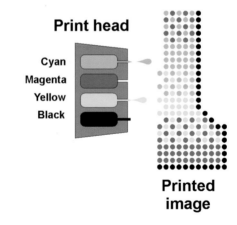

Figure 22.15: *An ink jet printer makes tiny dots of cyan, magenta, yellow, and black to print a full-color image. The dots are so small that your eye sees smooth colors. Look at an ink-jet print under a magnifying glass to see these dots.*

To make	Mix	Because	White light
Red	Magenta and yellow	Magenta absorbs green Yellow absorbs blue Red gets reflected	
Blue	Magenta and cyan	Magenta absorbs green Cyan absorbs red Blue gets reflected	
Green	Cyan and yellow	Cyan absorbs red Yellow absorbs blue Green gets reflected	

Making a color image

Making a color photograph

Modern printing presses use the CMYK color process to produce vivid colors from only four inks. To print a color photograph, the image is converted into four separate images in cyan, magenta, yellow, and black. Each separate image represents what will be printed with its matching CMYK ink. The cyan separation is printed with cyan ink, the magenta separation with magenta ink, and so on. Figure 22.16 shows the four color separations from a color image.

The RGB color process

Color images are also created using the **RGB color process**, an additive process that uses red, green, and blue light. The RGB process is used by television screens and computer monitors. A television makes different colors by lighting red, green, and blue pixels to different percentages. For example, a light brown tone is 88 percent red, 85 percent green, and 70 percent blue. A computer monitor works the same way. Each pixel (or dot) has three numbers that tell how much red, green, and blue to use. A digital video image is 720 dots wide times 480 dots high. If each dot has three numbers (R, G, B) a single image takes 1,036,800 numbers to store!

Video camera create color images

A video camera-recorder (also called a camcorder) uses the RGB process differently than a TV. Like the rods and cones in your retina, a video camcorder has 300,000 - 500,000 sensors on a small chip called a CCD (Charge-Coupled Device). The sensors on the CCD measure the light intensity and percentages of red, green, and blue in the light coming through the camera lens. This information is recorded 30 times per second. The CCDs in most video camera-recorders are typically 1 centimeter square or less.

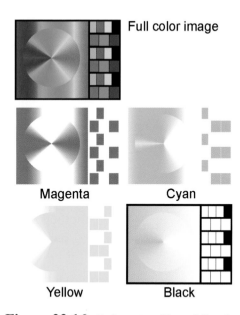

Full color image

Magenta   Cyan

Yellow   Black

Figure 22.16: *To be printed by a full-color press, an image is separated into separate cyan, magenta, yellow, and black images.*

Figure 22.17: *A television makes colors using tiny glowing dots of red, green, and blue.*

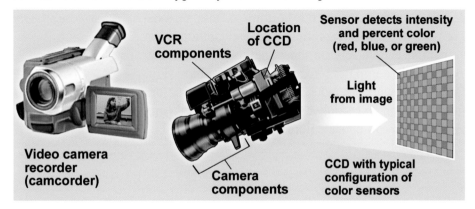

VCR components
Location of CCD
Sensor detects intensity and percent color (red, blue, or green)
Light from image
Video camera recorder (camcorder)
Camera components
CCD with typical configuration of color sensors

Color blindness

Not everyone sees color the same way

You may be surprised to learn that all people do not see color the same way. A condition called color blindness affects about 8 percent of males and 0.4 percent of females. This means that about one out of every 13 men has color blindness and about one out of every 250 women has color blindness.

Color blindness is inherited

Although color blindness can be caused by eye disease, it is most often an inherited condition. More males than females have color blindness because of how the genes that determine our sex are inherited. Males have a X and a Y chromosome; females have two X chromosomes. The genes that are related to color blindness are on the X chromosome which males receive only from their mothers; they receive the Y chromosome from their fathers. Because females receive two X chromosomes, they have two chances to inherit the genes for normal color vision.

What is color blindness?

People who are color blind have trouble seeing certain colors. The most common condition is red-green color blindness (Figure 22.18). People with this type of color blindness have trouble seeing reds and greens. Less common is blue-green color blindness. Complete color blindness means that the person can only see shades of gray. Fortunately, this condition is rare.

Living with color blindness

It is easy to lead a normal life with color blindness. Having color blindness just means that an individual must look for ways to adapt to situations where color is involved. For example, color is extremely important when driving because traffic lights and street signs are color-coded. Fortunately, in most states, the traffic lights are vertical and the colors are in the same position— red on top, yellow in the center, and green on the bottom. A less serious situations where color is important is in interpreting maps and purchasing clothes. In these cases, color blind people rely on other methods to interpret colors. Interestingly, working with computers requires lots of color. For example, if you are going to make a web site, you will want to include color. For a color blind person this can be tricky. Fortunately, colors are standardized and a color blind person can chose colors using numbers.

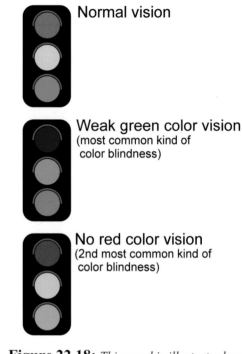

Normal vision

Weak green color vision
(most common kind of color blindness)

No red color vision
(2nd most common kind of color blindness)

Figure 22.18: *This graphic illustrates how red-green color blindness affects seeing a traffic light. The top of the graphic shows what the traffic light looks like with normal color vision. The middle and bottom graphic show what a traffic light looks like with two of the common forms of color blindness.*

Plants use color

Light is necessary for photosynthesis

Plants absorb energy from light and convert it to chemical energy in the form of sugar. The process is called *photosynthesis*. The vertical (*y*) axis of the graph in Figure 22.19 shows the percentage of light absorbed by a plant. The *x*-axis on the graph shows the colors of light. The heavy line shows how much and which colors of visible light are absorbed by plants. Based on this graph, can you explain why plants look green?

Why most plants are green

The important molecule that absorbs light in a plant is called *chlorophyll*. There are several forms of chlorophyll in a plant and they absorb mostly blue and red light, and reflect green light. This is why most plants look green. This graph also shows that plants need red and blue light to grow. A plant will die if placed under only green light!

Plants reflect some light to keep cool

Why don't plants absorb all colors of light? The reason is the same reason you wear light colored clothes when it is hot outside. Like you, plants must reflect some light to avoid absorbing too much energy and overheating. Plants use visible light because the energy is just enough to change certain chemical bonds, but not enough to completely break them. Ultraviolet light has more energy but would break chemical bonds. Infrared light has too little energy to change chemical bonds.

Why leaves change color

The leaves of some plants, such as sugar maple trees, turn brilliant red or gold in the fall. Chlorophyll masks other plant pigments during the spring and summer. In the fall when photosynthesis slows down, chlorophyll breaks down and red, orange, and yellow pigments in the leaves are revealed!

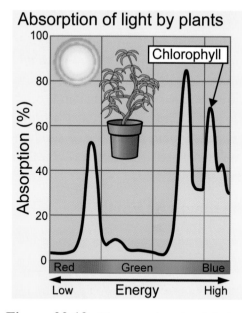

Figure 22.19: *Plants need to absorb light to grow. The plant pigment chlorophyll absorbs red and blue light, and reflects green light. This is why plants look green! Challenge: All plants that use sunlight to grow have chlorophyll, but some do not look green. Come up with a hypothesis to explain this observation.*

22.3 Section Review

1. Do you think this text book was printed using the CMYK color process or the RGB color process? Explain your answer.

2. If you were going to design the lighting for a play, would you need to understand the CMYK color process or the RGB color process? Explain your answer.

3. Why does static on a television set appear white?

4. How is the color black produced in the CMYK color process versus the RGB color process?

5. Some plants that grow in shady areas have dark green or even purple leaves. Come up with a hypothesis to explain this observation.

The Northern Lights

The northern lights, or *Aurora Borealis* is the northern version of an amazing show of light and color in the sky of Earth's polar regions. Aurora Borealis is Latin for "dawn of the north." The southern hemisphere has a matching show, often the mirror image of what is seen in the north; *Aurora Australis* means "the dawn of the south." The aurora (both northern and southern) owes its existence to the magnetosphere, which protects Earth from dangerous particles given off by the sun.

The magnetic Earth

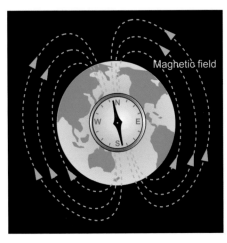

Magnetic field

The *magnetosphere* is a giant magnetic field created by Earth that extends thousands of miles into space. You can see evidence of it when you use a compass. The needle points north, aligning with the magnetic field lines. The aurora is caused by interactions between the magnetosphere and the atmosphere—the layer of gases that surrounds our planet.

The stretched out part of the magnetosphere is called the magnetotail. Instead of being empty space, the magnetosphere is populated by ions. These ions are mainly electrons and protons, but also consist of oxygen and nitrogen atoms stripped of an electron, giving them a positive net charge.

Solar wind

The solar wind is a stream of particles that moves away from the sun in all directions. The magnetosphere acts like a giant shield against almost all of the particles of the solar wind, diverting them around Earth. At about a million miles an hour, the solar wind pushes against the magnetosphere causing Earth's magnetosphere to be compressed on the sun side and stretched out on the other side.

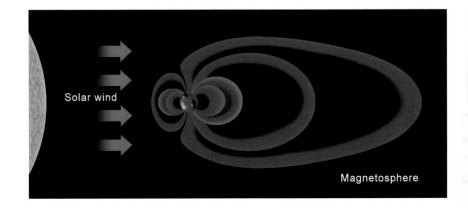

Solar wind

Magnetosphere

Let the light show begin

Since ions are charged, they are influenced by the electrical force of the magnetosphere and move along its magnetic field. As ions in the magnetosphere travel along the magnetic field lines toward Earth, a gigantic electric current is produced. The particles get closer to Earth as the magnetic field lines converge at the poles and begin to encounter the outer reaches of the atmosphere called the ionosphere. Instead of continuing on through the ionosphere and hitting Earth, the particles begin to collide with the atoms and molecules of the ionosphere.

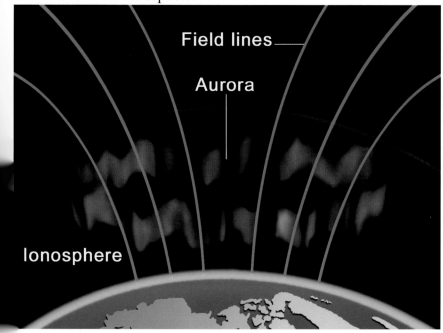

The energy released during those collisions creates the light of the aurora. Each collision bumps an electron in the struck atom to a higher energy level. When the electron drops back down to a lower energy level it emits a distinctive color of light. Different colors of light are created depending on the element and the energy of the collision.

The effect is like a neon sign. As electrons move through the neon gas in the sign the neon atoms produce a reddish glow. During an aurora, oxygen in the ionosphere emits a green or greenish-yellow light at lower altitudes, but at higher altitudes a brilliant red color. Nitrogen emits a red color at lower altitudes, but higher up in the ionosphere it can produce purple and even blue light. The whole effect can look like ribbons or curtains of colored light.

The sun's influence

Solar flares, coronal mass ejections, and coronal holes all produce huge amounts of particle emissions from the sun. They add to the steady flow of the solar wind and disturb Earth's magnetosphere, resulting in dramatic auroral displays. Hovering hundreds of miles above the north and south magnetic poles is a ring of auroral activity called the auroral oval. Even when we can't see the shimmering curtains of light in the sky, they are still there, extremely dim and detected only with special electronic equipment in satellites. Solar activity also causes the auroral oval to change size and shape during very active periods.

Questions:

1. Based on what you learned in Unit 6, what causes Earth to have a magnetic field?
2. Why is the aurora observed only in regions that are closer to the north and south poles and not near the equator?
3. Why is a gigantic electric current produced along the field lines? (Hint: think about the definition of electric current)
4. What causes the different colors of light associated with the aurora?
5. Do some research to find out what causes solar flares, coronal mass ejections, and coronal holes.

Chapter 22 Review

Understanding Vocabulary

Select the correct term to complete the sentences.

photoreceptors	subtractive process	incandescent
CMYK color process	intensity	color
fluorescent	cones	rods
additive primary colors	white light	RGB color process
subtractive primary colors	additive process	

Section 22.1

1. _____ light bulbs produce light by heating a metal filament.

2. The power of light per unit area is light _____.

3. _____ light bulbs produce light by passing electricity through a gas.

Section 22.2

4. _____ in the back of the eye absorb light and create a sense of vision.

5. Creating color by changing the strengths of the signals of three primary colors is a(n) _____ used by TVs.

6. _____ are photoreceptors that respond to color.

7. _____ is made up of all the possible colors of light.

8. A prism separates light into different wavelengths of _____.

9. The three _____ are red, green, and blue.

10. _____ are photoreceptors that respond to black, white, and shades of gray.

Section 22.3

11. Another name for the subtractive color process is the _____.

12. Creating color by relying on the reflected and absorbed light of three primary colors is a(n) _____ used to dye fabric.

13. Another name for the additive color process is the _____.

14. The three _____ are cyan, yellow, and magenta.

Reviewing Concepts

Section 22.1

1. How is an incandescent bulb different from a fluorescent bulb?

2. Why do we see lightning before we hear thunder?

3. Which of the following is *NOT* a quality of light?
   a. high speed
   b. acceleration
   c. color
   d. intensity

4. Describe the role of atoms in producing light in a fluorescent light bulb.

5. In terms of the absorption and reflection of light, describe the difference between a black piece of cloth and a white piece of cloth.

6. What is the difference between reflection and refraction of light?

Section 22.2

7. What is white light in terms of other colors?

8. What determines the color of an object?

9. What are the three additive primary colors?

10. What color of visible light has the least energy? The most energy?

11. Which photoreceptors in your eye respond the most in dim evening light? Which respond the least? How does this explain your vision in this type of light?

Section 22.3

12. Answer *True* or *False* for each of the following sentences. If the answer if *False*, correct the highlighted word to make the sentence *True*.
   a. _____ A green object *reflects* green light. _____
   b. _____ A blue object *absorbs* red and yellow light. _____
   c. _____ A yellow object *reflects* red light. _____
   d. _____ A white object *absorbs* red light. _____

13. What are the three subtractive primary colors?

14. If a store clerk adds more colorants (pigment) to a can of white paint, what happens to the light we use to view the paint?

15. Why is mixing pigments called color subtraction?

16. What colors of light are reflected by the color magenta?

17. In the CMYK color process, why is black pigment used instead of mixing cyan, magenta, and yellow pigments?

18. How does a color printing press produce all the colors of a printed picture?

19. How does a color television screen produce all the colors you see on the screen?

20. An image of a sunset is displayed on a computer screen. This image is then printed onto a piece of paper by a printer. When the paper is held up next to the screen, the images are almost identical. What is the difference between the processes used to create these two images?

Solving Problems

Section 22.1

1. Rewrite the following false statements so that they are true.
    a. Light intensity is measured in units of power per volume of space.
    b. If the intensity of light at 1 meter from a source is 1 W/m^2, it will be 2 W/m^2 at 2 meters from the source.
    c. At 1 meter from a light source, a 1 m^2 area has a light intensity of 0.8 W/m^2. At 3 meters from a light source, a 1 m^2 area will have a light intensity that is 0.4 W/m^2.

2. You are reading a book by the light of a lamp. Compare the intensity of the light on your book at one meter away from the lamp to the intensity of the light on your book at two meters away from the lamp.

3. If four seconds passes between seeing a lightning strike and hearing thunder, about how far away was the lightning?

4. Arrange the following in order of speed from fastest to slowest: sound waves, light waves, water waves

Section 22.2

5. Which star would be hotter, a star that produces blue light or a star that produces red light?

6. Your brain perceives color by an additive process. How would you see the following combinations of light colors?
    a. red + blue
    b. blue + green
    c. red + green
    d. red + blue + green

7. For stage lighting for a play in a theater, a magenta spot of light is created and a green spot of light. What happens when these two spots of light combine?

Section 22.3

8. Using what you know about the subtractive color process, fill in the rest of the table.

The Three Subtractive Primary Colors		
Color	Absorbs	Reflects
Cyan	Red	
Magenta		
Yellow		Red	Green

9. If you wanted to make green paint, what combination of pigments would you use?

10. How would you create the following colors using inks on paper?
    a. red   b. green   c. blue   d. white

11. If a cloth that appears blue in white light is viewed in a room filled with only blue light, what color will it appear?

12. Identify the color process (RGB or CMYK) used in each step:
    a. Taking a photograph with a digital camera.
    b. Transferring the image to a computer. The image appears on a computer monitor.
    c. Printing the image using a laser printer.
    d. Seeing the image on the paper with your eyes.

13. Answer the following questions using the absorption graph in Figure 22.19 in the text.

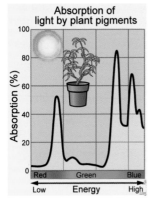

Absorption of light by plant pigments

a. Which colors of light are most absorbed the by plants?

b. Which colors of light are reflected the most by plants?

c. Based on the information from the absorption graph, explain why a plant will grow more quickly if it is grown in white light rather than green light.

d. When green pigments in the plants break down in the fall, you can see that leaves have other pigments like red and orange pigments. This effect is very noticeable in the northeastern United States. Come up with a hypothesis to explain why plants might have other pigments in addition to green?

Applying Your Knowledge

Section 22.1

1. A common misconception in physics is related to how we see objects. You have learned in this chapter that it is only possible to see an object under two conditions: (1) when light is present, and (2) if an object gives off its own light. To help address this misconception, do the following:

   a. Conduct a survey of 20 people you know. Ask them the following question: If there is no light in a completely dark room, could you see your hand in front of your face?

   b. What is the correct answer to this question? How many people answered the question correctly? How many people answered it incorrectly?

   c. Make an engaging and creative flyer that would help people understand how we see objects.

2. Even with a two-step process for producing light, fluorescent bulbs are still four times more efficient at producing light than incandescent bulbs. Among the types of incandescent bulbs, the halogen bulbs are most efficient. Find out why and write a short paragraph about halogen bulbs explaining how they work.

3. Calculate the time it takes light and sound to travel the distance of one mile, which is 1,609 meters. Use 340 m/sec for the speed of sound.

4. The distances between stars in space are huge. Because of this, scientists have developed units other than kilometers or meters to measure them. A *light year* is a common measurement unit in astronomy. Even though the name may sound like it, this unit does not measure time. One light year is the distance that light can travel through space in one year. How long is a light year in meters?

Section 22.2

5. Research which colors of light the human eye is most sensitive to. It has been suggested that fire engines be painted with yellow-green paint instead of red paint. Explain why this might be a good idea.

6. Research the color vision of nocturnal animals. What is different about the photoreceptor in the eyes of nocturnal animals?

Section 22.3

7. A blue filter contains blue pigments. What happens to white light the is shone through a blue filter? Explain why.

8. Why do clothes that you try on in a store under fluorescent lighting look different when you get home and try them on under incandescent lighting?

9. Design an improvement to a common product to make it easier for color blind people to use.

10. A color TV makes colors using just red, green, blue light. The following table illustrates how the colors are made. Part of the table is filled in to get you started. Using your understanding of the RGB process, fill in the rest of the table.

Dot color on TV monitor	The color you see on the TV monitor					
	Black	White	Red	Yellow	Green	Blue
Red	off		on	on		
Green		on	off			
Blue						

Chapter 23 Optics

Why do people catch colds? For thousands of years people believed that colds and other illnesses came from evil spirits. The world changed in 1673 when Anton Leeuwenhoek peered through a primitive microscope he had made. To his astonishment he saw tiny creatures swimming around! Leeuwenhoek's discoveries revealed a miniature universe no human had ever seen before. He was the first to see that a drop of pond water contains a tiny world of plants and animals.

Once the microscopic world was discovered, the causes of sickness could be investigated. Today, we know that small forms of life, bacteria and viruses, are usually what make you sick. Microscopes and telescopes are based on optics, the science and technology of light. By manipulating light, optical devices greatly enhance our eyesight so that we can see things that are miniscule or astronomically far away.

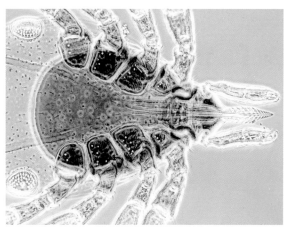

Key Questions

✓ Why can I see myself in a mirror but not when I look at the floor or a bare wall?

✓ Is it possible to make an object disappear?

✓ How do lenses work?

23.1 Optics and Reflection

Look at your thumb through a magnifying glass. It looks huge. Of course, your hand is the same size it always was, even though what you see is a giant thumb (Figure 23.1). Explaining how magnification occurs is part of the science of optics. **Optics** is the study of how light behaves. Optics also includes the study of the eye itself because the human eye forms an image with a lens. Devices that rely on optics include mirrors, telescopes, eyeglasses, contact lenses, and magnifying glasses. This section introduces you to optics and how images are formed.

Optics is the study of light

Light travels in straight lines

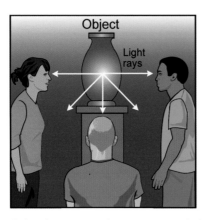

As light moves through a material such as air, the light normally travels in straight lines. If three people in a room see the same vase, it is because light travels straight from the vase to their eyes. To trace the movement of light we draw lines and arrows called light rays. A **light ray** is an imaginary line that represents a thin beam of light. The arrow head on a light ray shows you the direction light is moving.

Lines and angles describe the path of light

Light does not *always* go straight from an object to your eyes. For example, light may bend when it crosses the boundary between glass and air. A magnifying glass uses the bending of light rays to make things appear larger (or smaller) than they really are. The curved surface of a magnifying glass bends light rays so they appear to come from a much larger thumb. That is the magnified thumb that you see!

A magnifying glass bends light rays so they *appear* to come from a larger thumb

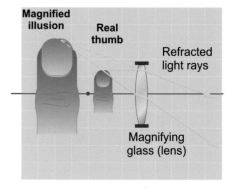

Figure 23.1: *How a magnifying glass creates the illusion of a giant thumb by bending light rays.*

Simple optical devices

Optical devices are common

Almost everyone has experience with optical devices. For example, trying on new glasses, checking your appearance in a mirror, or admiring the sparkle from a diamond ring all involve optics. Through experiences like these, most of us have seen optical effects created by three basic devices: the lens, the mirror, and the prism.

Lenses

A lens bends light in a specific way. A **converging lens** (or convex lens) bends light so that the light rays come together to a point. This is why a magnifying glass makes a hot spot of concentrated light (Figure 23.2). The human eye has a single converging lens. A **diverging lens** (or concave lens) bends light so it spreads light apart instead of coming together. An object viewed through a diverging lens appears smaller than it would look without the lens.

Mirrors

A mirror reflects light and allows you to see yourself. Flat mirrors show a true-size image (Figure 23.3). Curved mirrors distort images by causing the light rays to come together or spread apart. The curved surface of a fun house mirror can make you look appear thinner, wider, or even upside down!

Prisms

A **prism** is another optical device. It is made of a solid piece of glass with flat polished surfaces. A common triangular prism is shown in the diagram below. Prisms can both bend and/or reflect light. Telescopes, cameras, and supermarket laser scanners use prisms of different shapes to bend and reflect light in precise ways. A diamond is a prism with many flat, polished surfaces. The "sparkle" that makes diamonds so attractive comes from light being reflected many times as it bounces around the inside of a cut and polished diamond.

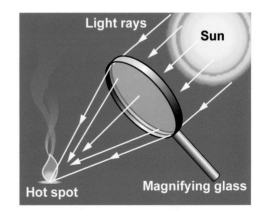

Figure 23.2: *A magnifying glass is a converging lens. This is why a magnifying glass can be used to makes a hot spot of concentrated light.*

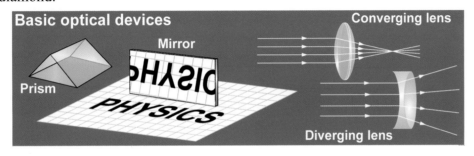

Figure 23.3: *The image you see in a flat mirror is life-size.*

Four ways light is affected by matter

The four interactions
When light interacts with matter, like glass, wood, or anything else, four things can happen.

- The light can go through almost unchanged (transparency).
- The light can go through but be scattered (translucency).
- The light can bounce off (reflection).
- The light can transfer its energy to the material (absorption).

Transparent
Materials that allow light to pass through are called **transparent**. Glass is transparent as are some kinds of plastic. Air is also transparent. You can see an image though a transparent material if the surfaces are smooth, like a glass window.

Translucent
An object is **translucent** if some light can pass through but the light is scattered in many directions (Figure 23.4). Tissue paper is translucent, and so is frosted glass. If you hold a sheet of tissue paper up to a window, some light comes through the paper, but you cannot see an image clearly through tissue paper.

Reflection
Almost all surfaces reflect some light. In chapter 22 you learned that color comes from reflecting some light but absorbing other light. A mirror is a very good reflector but a sheet of white paper is also a good reflector. The difference is in how they reflect (see the next page).

Absorption
When light is *absorbed*, its energy is transferred to the material. That is why a black road surface gets hot on a sunny day. A perfect absorber looks black because it reflects no light at all. Black paper and black velvet cloth are good absorbers of light.

All interactions at once
All four interactions of light with matter almost always happen at the same time. An ordinary glass window is mostly transparent but also absorbs about 10% of light. The glass scatters some light (translucency) and reflects some light. The same material also behaves differently depending on how well the surface is polished. Frosted glass has a rough surface and is translucent. Clear glass has a polished surface and is transparent. Colored paper absorbs some light, reflects some light, and is partly translucent (Figure 23.5).

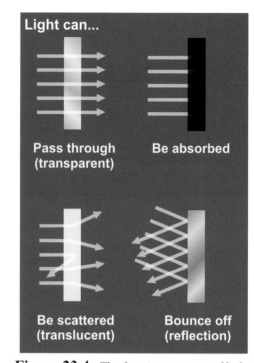

Figure 23.4: *The four interactions of light with matter.*

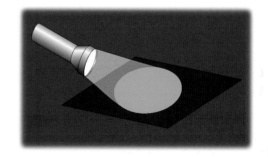

Figure 23.5: *Colored objects reflect some colors of light and absorb other colors. Can you tell which colors are absorbed and which are reflected?*

Reflection

The image in a mirror

When you look at yourself in a mirror, you see your own image as if your exact twin were standing in front of you. The image appears to be the same distance from the other side of the mirror as you are on your side of the mirror (Figure 23.6). If you step back, so does your image. Images appear in mirrors because of how light is reflected by mirrors.

Specular reflection

Light is reflected from all surfaces, not just mirrors. But not all surfaces form images. The reason is that there are two types of reflections. A ray of light that strikes a shiny surface (like a mirror) creates a single reflected ray. This type of reflection is called **specular reflection**. In specular reflection each ray of light bounces off in a single direction (Figure 23.7). Images are produced in polished surfaces that create specular reflection, such as on the surface of a mirror. If you look closely at a mirror illuminated by a light bulb, somewhere the reflected light forms an image of the light bulb itself. In fact, a surface which has perfect specular reflection is invisible. If you look at that surface, you see reflections of other things, *but you don't see the surface itself.*

Diffuse reflection

A surface that is not shiny creates **diffuse reflection**. In diffuse reflection, a single ray of light scatters into many directions (Figure 23.7). Diffuse reflection is caused by the roughness of a surface. Even if a surface feels smooth to the touch, on a microscopic level it may be rough. For example, the surface of a wooden board creates a diffuse reflection. In a lighted room, you see the board by reflected light, but you cannot see an image of a light bulb in the board. When you look at a diffuse reflecting surface *you see the surface itself.*

One surface can be both types of reflection

Many surfaces are in between rough and smooth. These kinds of surfaces create both kinds of reflection. For example, a polished wood tabletop can reflect some light in specular reflection, and the rest of the light in diffuse reflection. The specular reflection creates a faint reflected image on the table surface. You also see the table surface itself by light from diffuse reflection.

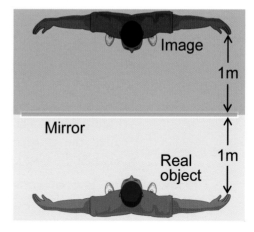

Figure 23.6: *The image you see in a flat mirror is the same distance behind the mirror as you are in front of it.*

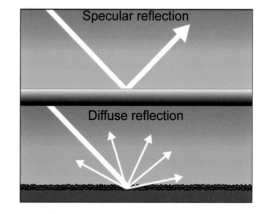

Figure 23.7: *Specular and diffuse reflections.*

The law of reflection

Incident and reflected rays Consider a ray of light coming from a light bulb and striking a mirror. The **incident ray** is the light ray that strikes the mirror. The **reflected ray** is the light ray that bounces off the mirror (Figure 23.8).

The normal line Between the incident and reflected rays, there is an imaginary line called the **normal line** which is perpendicular to the surface of the mirror (Figure 23.8). The angle between the incident ray and the normal line is called the **angle of incidence**. The **angle of reflection** is the angle between the normal line and the reflected ray.

The law of reflection The **law of reflection** says *the angle of incidence equals the angle of reflection.* Light rays reflect from a mirror at the same angle at which they arrive. Angles are always measured relative to the normal line. The law of reflection applies to any surface with specular reflection.

An example Imagine that a light ray strikes a flat mirror with a 30-degree angle of incidence (Figure 23.9). What would be the angle of reflection? According to the law of reflection, the angle of reflection is 30 degrees.

Drawing a ray diagram A **ray diagram** is an accurately drawn sketch showing how light rays interact with mirrors, lenses, and other optical devices. Incident and reflected rays are drawn as arrows on a ray diagram. A mirror is drawn as a solid line. The normal line is drawn as a dotted line perpendicular to the mirror surface; this line starts where the incident ray strikes the mirror. The angle of incidence and angle of reflection are measured between the light rays and the normal line as shown in Figure 23.8.

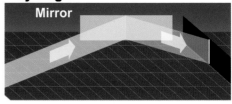
Ray diagram

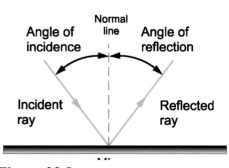
Figure 23.8: *The angle of incidence is equal to the angle of reflection.*

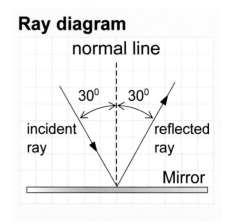
Ray diagram

Figure 23.9: *This ray diagram illustrates that the angle of incidence equals the angle of reflection.*

23.1 Section Review

1. Make a list of all the optical devices you use on an average day.

2. Name an object that is mostly transparent, one that is translucent, one that is mostly absorbent, and one that is mostly reflective.

3. Why can you see your own reflected image in a mirror but not on dry, painted wall?

4. A light ray leaving a mirror has a 15-degree angle of reflection. What is the angle of incidence?

23.2 Refraction

Light rays may bend as they cross a boundary from one material to another. For example, light waves bend from air to water. *Refraction* is the bending of light rays. Whenever you use eyeglasses, a telescope, binoculars, or fiber optics technology, you are using the refraction of light.

The index of refraction

An example of refraction A glass rod in a glass of water makes a good example of refraction (Figure 23.10). The glass rod appears to break where it crosses the surface of the water. It is obvious that the rod has not *actually* broken. The illusion is caused by refracted light rays. The light rays from the glass rod are refracted (or bent) when they cross from water back into air before reaching your eyes.

The index of refraction The ability of a material to bend rays of light is described by a value called the index of refraction. The **index of refraction (n)** for a material measures the ability of the material to bend light. The index of refraction is represented by a lowercase letter n. The index of refraction for air is approximately 1.00. Water has an index of refraction of 1.33. A diamond has an index of refraction of 2.42. Diamonds sparkle because of their high index of refraction. Table 23.1 lists the index of refraction for some common materials.

Table 23.1: *The index of refraction for some common materials*

Material	Index of refraction
Vacuum	1.0
Air	1.0001
Water	1.33
Ice	1.31
Glass	1.5
Diamond	2.42

Why refraction occurs Refraction occurs when light rays cross a surface between two materials that have a different index of refraction. The "broken rod" illusion happens because the index of refraction of water and air and different.

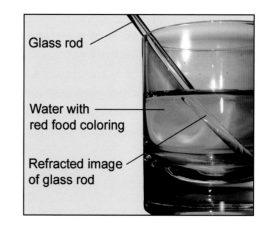

Glass rod

Water with red food coloring

Refracted image of glass rod

Figure 23.10: *A glass rod appears broken at the point it enters the water. This illusion is created because light is refracted as it travels from air to water.*

How much does refraction bend light rays?

The angles of incidence and refraction

As we did with reflection, we will look at angles that light rays make as they are refracted by a surface. The angle of incidence is the angle between the incident ray and the normal line, the same as for a mirror. The **angle of refraction** is the angle between the refracted ray and the normal line.

The direction a light ray bends

The direction in which a light ray bends depends on whether it is moving from a high index of refraction to a lower index or vice versa. A light ray going from a low index of refraction into a higher index bends *toward the normal line*. A light ray going from a high index of refraction to a low index bends *away from the normal line*.

Light path	How light is refracted
High n to low n	Bends away from normal line
Low n to high n	Bends toward normal line

The index of refraction in both materials

The angle that light is refracted depends on the index of refraction on both sides of a surface. The diagram below shows light crossing a piece of glass. When light goes from air into glass (A) it bends toward the normal line because glass has a higher index of refraction than air. When the light goes from glass into air again (B) it bends away from the normal line. Coming out of the glass the light ray is going into air with a lower index of refraction than glass.

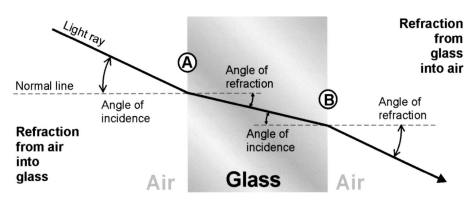

Refraction can make objects seem invisible

When light travels from one material to another, the light rays bend. This is because most any two materials will have different indices of refraction.

However, if two materials have the same index of refraction, the light doesn't bend at all. This makes for a neat trick you can do with a glass rod. Glass is transparent, so you only see the edges of the rod because of refraction. The edge appears dark because light is refracted away from your eyes.

Vegetable oil and glass have almost the same index of refraction. If you put a glass rod into a cup of vegetable oil, the rod seems to disappear! Light travels through the oil and glass as if the two materials were the same!

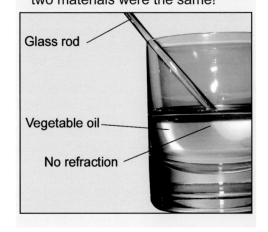

Total internal reflection

When light goes from one material to another

When light goes from one material into another that has a lower refractive index, it bends away from the normal line. The angle of refraction that occurs when the light bends from the normal line is always greater than the angle of incidence. For example, in water when the angle of incidence is 45 degrees, the angle of refraction in air is 70 degrees. The refractive index of water is 1.33, for air it is 1.00.

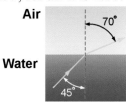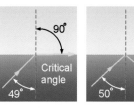

Air

70°   81°   90°

Water   Critical angle   Total internal reflection

45°   48°   49°   50°

Total internal reflection

As the angle of incidence increases, there is a point at which the light will not enter the air but reflect back into the water! This effect is called **total internal reflection.** Total internal reflection happens when the angle of refraction becomes greater than 90 degrees. As you can see in the diagram above, when the angle of refraction reaches 90 degrees, the refracted ray is traveling straight along the surface of the water. In water, this happens when the angle of incidence is 49 degrees. At angles greater than 49 degrees, *there is no refracted ray.* All of the light is reflected back into the water!

The critical angle

The angle of incidence at which the angle of refraction is 90 degrees is called the **critical angle**. The critical angle depends on the index of refraction of the material. The critical angle for water is about 49 degrees. The critical angle for glass is about 42 degrees. At angles of incidence greater than the critical angle for a material, total internal reflection occurs.

Fiber optics are pipes for light

The sidebar at right explains how a glass rod can be used as a *light pipe*. If glass rods are made very thin, they are flexible, but still trap light by total internal reflection. **Fiber optics** are thin glass fibers that use total internal reflection to carry light, even around bends and corners. Because light can be used to transmit information as images or data, fiber optics technology is very important in the communications industry. A bundle of optical fibers can even make an *image pipe,* where each fiber transmits one dot of an image from one end of the bundle to the other end.

A light pipe

A solid glass rod can become a light pipe that carries light. This can happen if light enters the rod at an angle of incidence greater than the critical angle. Inside the rod, light continues to reflect off the inside walls and bounce back into the rod because of total internal reflection. Fiber optic technology uses glass fibers to carry information on laser beams (light) including internet data and telephone calls .

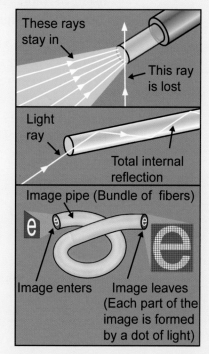

These rays stay in

This ray is lost

Light ray

Total internal reflection

Image pipe (Bundle of fibers)

Image enters   Image leaves (Each part of the image is formed by a dot of light)

Refraction and colors of light

Index of refraction varies for different colors of light

The index of refraction for most materials varies by a small amount depending on the color of light. For example, glass has an index of refraction slightly greater for blue light than for red light. A glass prism splits white light into its spectrum of colors because each color is bent slightly differently. For example, blue light is bent more than red (Figure 23.11). Colors between blue and red are bent proportional to their position in the spectrum. Remember, the order of colors in the visible light spectrum is red, orange, yellow, green, blue, violet (or ROY-G-BV). Yellow rays, in the middle of the spectrum, are bent about halfway between red and blue rays.

Dispersion

The "rainbow" you see when light passes through a prism and a real rainbow in the sky are examples of dispersion. **Dispersion** describes how refractive index varies depending on the color of light. The refractive index values listed in Table 23.1 are based on the bending of a specific color of yellow light. Yellow light was chosen because it is the center of the visible light spectrum.

Rainbows

Rainbows occur when white light from the sun passes through water droplets in the atmosphere. Like a prism, each drop splits white light into the spectrum of colors. However, we see bands of colors in the sky because each color of light that reaches your eyes come from droplets at different heights in the sky (Figure 23.12). This is because of how the light is bent by the curved surface of each droplets. The colors you see follow ROY-G-BV from top to bottom.

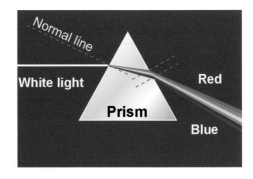

Figure 23.11: *A prism separates the colors of white light by dispersion. Blue light bends more than red light.*

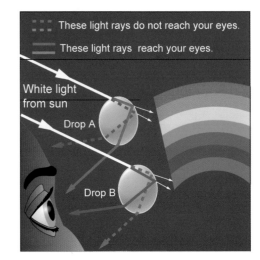

Figure 23.12: *Water droplets in the sky act as prisms. However, we see bands of color because red light reaches your eyes from higher in the atmosphere and blue light reaches your eyes from lower in the atmosphere.*

23.2 Section Review

1. A glass rod seems to disappear when it is place in vegetable oil. Based on this observation and Table 23.1, predict the index of refraction for vegetable oil.

2. Fill in the blank: When light travels from water into the air, the refracted light ray bends _____ (away or toward) the normal line.

3. Describe the refracted ray when the angle of incidence is at the critical angle. What happens to an incident light ray when the angle of incidence is greater than the critical angle?

4. In which situation might dispersion be a problem in focusing a camera lens: (a) taking a color photograph, or (b) taking a black and white photograph? Explain your answer.

23.3 Mirrors, Lenses, and Images

An *image* is a picture that represents the way light is organized somewhere else. For example, the image of an ice cream cone created by your eye or a camera matches the pattern of light from real ice cream cone. In this section, you will learn how images are created. You will learn how to use lenses and mirrors to make images larger or smaller, upright or upside down, near or far away.

Images

Objects and images

It is helpful to think about optics in terms of objects and images. **Objects** are real physical things that give off or reflect light rays. **Images** are "pictures" of objects that are formed in space where light rays meet. Images are formed by our eyes, and by mirrors, lenses, prisms, and other optical devices (Figure 23.13). Images are not objects you can touch; they are just illusions created by organizing light *collected* from objects.

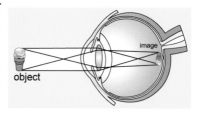

Rays come together in an image

Each point on an object gives off light rays in all directions. That is why you can see an object from different directions. Images are created by collecting many rays from each point on an object and bringing them back together again in a single point. For example, a camera works by collecting the rays from an object so they form an image on the film. In the diagram below many rays from a part of the bridge railing are *focused* to a single point by the camera lens, forming the image of that part of the railing. A camera captures some but not all the rays. This is why a photograph only shows one side of an object — you can't turn a photograph over and see the back of any object!

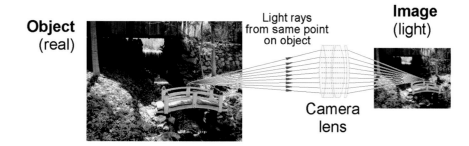

Object (real)

Light rays from same point on object

Image (light)

Camera lens

Vocabulary

object, image, virtual image, optical axis, focal point, focal length, real image, focus, magnification, refracting telescope

Objectives

✓ Learn how images are formed.
✓ Learn the difference between a real and a virtual image.
✓ Learn the parts of a ray diagram and how to draw one.

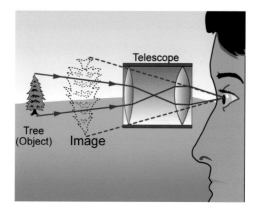

Telescope

Tree (Object)   Image

Figure 23.13: *You see the tree because light from the tree reaches your eye. The image of the tree in a telescope is not the real tree, but instead is a different way of organizing light from the tree. A telescope organizes the light so that the tree appears bigger but also upside down!*

The image in a mirror

Seeing your reflection

If you stand in front of a flat mirror, your image appears the same distance behind the mirror as you are in front of the mirror. If you move back the image seems to move back too. If you raise your left hand, the hand on the left side of the image is raised. How does this happen?

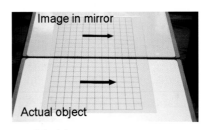

Figure 23.14: *The image in a flat mirror*

The image of an arrow in a mirror

The photograph in Figure 23.14 shows a mirror in front of a piece of graph paper that has an arrow drawn on it. The arrow on the graph paper is an *object* because it is a physical source of (reflected) light. The image of the arrow appears in the mirror. Look carefully and you see that the image of the arrow appears the same number of squares *behind* the mirror as the paper arrow is in front of the mirror.

A ray diagram of an image in a mirror

Figure 23.15 shows a ray diagram of the arrow and mirror. The head of the arrow is a source of light rays. The ray diagram traces three light rays that leave the tip of the arrow and reflect from the mirror. These rays obey the law of reflection. We see an image of the arrow in the mirror because the reflected rays *appear* to come from behind the mirror. To see where the rays appear to come from, you extend the actual rays using dotted lines. The image of the tip of the arrow is formed at the point where the dotted lines meet. Remember, an image forms when many rays on an object come together again, *or appear to come together again*. The diagram shows the image appears the same distance behind the mirror as the arrow is in front of the mirror.

Ray diagram

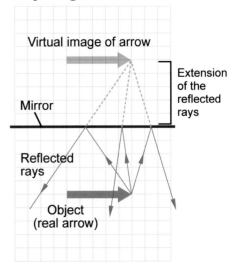

Figure 23.15: *A ray diagram of the arrow in the mirror, showing the location of the virtual image.*

Virtual images

The image in a mirror is called a **virtual image** because the light rays do not *actually* come together to form the image. They only *appear* to come together. The virtual image in a flat mirror is created by your eyes and brain. Your brain "sees" the arrow where it would be if the light rays reaching the eye had come in a single straight line.

Real and virtual images

Because the light rays do not actually meet, a virtual image cannot be projected onto a screen or on film. Virtual images are illusions created by your eye and brain. To show a picture on a screen or record an image on film you need a *real image*. Real images form where light rays actually come together again. The images formed by a camera lens or projector lens are real images. If the difference seems confusing, turn the page for an explanation!

Lenses

A lens and its optical axis
A lens is made of transparent material with an index of refraction different from air. The surfaces of a lens are curved to refract light in a specific way. The exact shape of a lens's surface depends on how strongly and in what way the lens needs to bend light. Nearly all lenses are designed with an **optical axis**, an imaginary line that goes through the center of the lens. Light traveling along the optical axis is not bent at all by the lens.

Focal point and focal length
Light rays that enter a converging lens parallel to its axis bend to meet at a point called the **focal point** (Figure 23.16). Light can go through a lens in either direction so there are always two focal points, one on either side of the lens. The distance from the center of the lens to the focal point is the **focal length**. The focal length is usually (but not always) the same for both focal points of a lens.

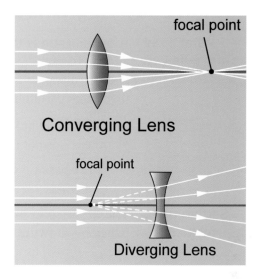

Figure 23.16: *Converging and diverging lenses.*

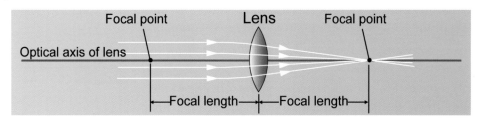

Converging and diverging lenses
Figure 23.16 shows how light rays enter and exit two types of lenses. The entering rays are parallel to the optical axis. A *converging lens* the rays bends exiting rays toward the focal point. A *diverging lens* bends the rays outward, away from the focal point.

How light travels through a converging lens
Most lenses have surfaces that are shaped like part of a sphere. Any radius of a sphere is also a normal line to the surface. When light rays fall on a spherical surface from air, they bend *toward* the normal line (Figure 23.17). For a converging lens, the first surface (air to glass) bends light rays toward the normal. At the second surface (glass to air), the rays bend *away* from the normal line. Because the second surface "tilts" the other way, it also bends light rays toward the focal point. Both surfaces of a diverging lens bend light away from the optical axis (Figure 23.16).

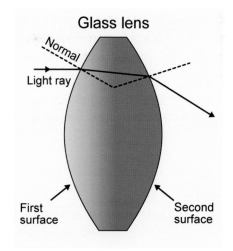

Figure 23.17: *Most lenses have spherically shaped surfaces.*

Drawing a ray diagram for a converging lens

What a ray diagram tells you   A ray diagram is the best way to understand what type of image is formed by a lens. To draw a ray diagram for a lens, you need to know the focal length and the distance of the object from the lens. If the lenses are not too thick, then three particular rays of light follow rules that make them easy to draw.

1. A ray passing though the center of the lens is not bent at all.
2. A ray parallel to the axis bends to pass through the far focal point.
3. A ray passing through the near focal point comes out of the lens parallel to the axis.

Setting up to make a ray diagram   The first step in making an accurate ray diagram is to set up a sheet of graph paper by drawing a straight horizontal line to be the optical axis. The lens itself is drawn as a vertical line crossing the axis. The last step in setting up is to draw the two focal points, *f*, on the axis. The focal points should be the same distance on either side of the lens. It is important that the ray diagram be drawn to *scale*. For example, a scale often used with graph paper is one box equals 1 centimeter.

Drawing the object   An upward arrow is used to represent the object, usually on the left side of the lens. The distance from the arrow to the lens must be correctly scaled. For example, an object 20 centimeters away from a lens is drawn 20 boxes to the left of the lens in a ray diagram.

The three principal rays   To find the location of the image, draw the three rays listed above, starting each from the tip of the arrow. Figure 23.18 shows how to draw each ray.

Step 1: Draw a light ray passing through the center of the lens.

Step 2: Draw a light ray that starts parallel to the axis and bends at the lens to pass through the far focal point.

Step 3: Draw a light ray passing through the near focal point. This light ray bends so it is parallel to the axis on the far side of the lens.

The point where these three rays intersect on the far side of the lens is where the image of the tip of the arrow will be. Remember, an image forms where many rays from an object come together again.

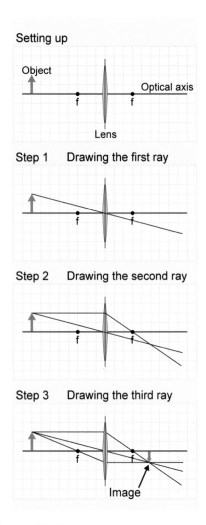

Figure 23.18: *The process of drawing a ray diagram.*

The image formed by a lens

Real images

A converging lens can form a **real image** (diagram below). In a real image, light from each single point on an object comes back together again at a single point in another place to make an image. The place where the light comes back together again is called the **focus**. The focus is where you see the image clearly.

Ray diagrams

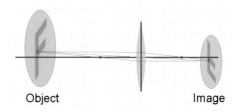

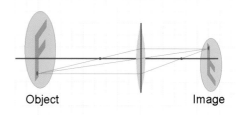

Figure 23.19: *Each point of the F in the image is formed by collecting light from a single point on the real F (object).*

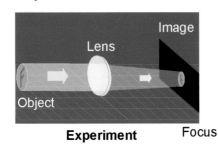

Experiment

Ray diagram

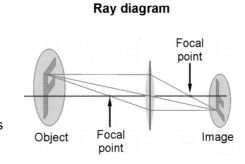

Projecting an image on a screen

The ray diagram shows how the real image is formed. Following the rules on the preceding page, three light rays are drawn starting from the same point, the upper corner of the "F". Notice that these three rays all meet together again at a single point on the other side of the lens. That point is the *image* of the upper corner of the "F". You can put a screen at that distance from the lens to see the image.

Single lenses invert images

Notice that the image of the "F" is upside down. A real image made by a single lens is always upside down. The lens in a movie projector also makes an upside down image. To make the image right side up, the film is put in the projector upside down!

How a lens makes an image

To make an image, a lens collects rays from every point on an object. Rays from *each point* on the object are brought back together again to make *each point* of the image. Even when you cover half the lens, you still see the whole image. The uncovered half still works the same way, but the image is dimmer since less light from the object is used to form each point of the image. Your eye does a similar thing in very bright light. The pupil of the eye gets smaller, covering part of the lens (Figure 23.20).

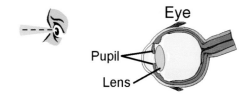

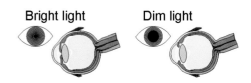

Figure 23.20: *The pupil of your eye gets smaller, blocking more of the lens in bright light. However, your field of vision does not get smaller!*

Magnification and telescopes

Lenses can form virtual images
Both converging and diverging lenses can form virtual images. For example, a converging lens used as a magnifying glass creates an image that is virtual and larger than life (magnified). Light is bent by the lens so that it appears to come from a much larger object (Figure 23.21).

Magnification
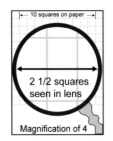

Images may be smaller than life size, or equal to or larger than life size. The **magnification** of an image is the ratio of the size of the image divided by the size of the object. For example, a lens with a magnification of 4 creates an image that appears 4 times larger than the real-life object.

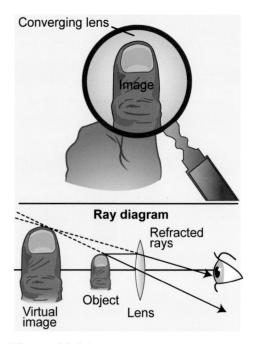

Figure 23.21: *A magnifying glass is a lens that forms a virtual image that is larger-than-life and appears behind the lens.*

A magnifying glass is a single converging lens. A magnified virtual image forms when you look at an object that is *closer* than one focal length from the lens. If the object is farther than one focal length you see a real image that is smaller than actual size (and upside down). The focal-length limit is why magnifying glasses should be held fairly close to the objects you are looking at.

The refracting telescope
To get higher magnification, microscopes and telescopes use more than one lens. A **refracting telescope** has two converging lenses with different focal lengths. The lens with the shorter focal length is nearer to the eye.

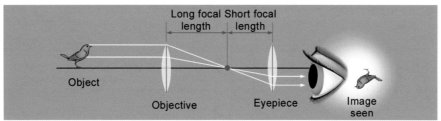

Reflecting telescope
Because large lenses are nearly impossible to make, most modern telescopes use a concave mirror instead of one lens. The diagram shows a reflecting telescope, much like the one used by the Hubble Space Telescope and almost all astronomical observatories (Figure 23.22).

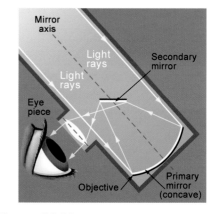

Figure 23.22: *A lens showing an image magnified by 4.*

Characteristics of images

Real or virtual images
Images can be real or virtual. If the image is real, it can be projected on a screen, like the image from a movie projector. If the image is virtual, it is created by the eye and brain and cannot be projected on a screen. The image in a mirror is virtual.

Inverted and magnified images
Images can be inside down (inverted) or right-side-up. Images can also be life sized, smaller or larger than life sized. The real image from a single lens is upside down and can be smaller or larger than real life. The image from a simple telescope is upside down, but can be much larger than real life. The image from a magnifying glass is right-side-up and larger than life (Figure 23.23). The image in a diverging lens is right-side-up and always smaller than real life (Figure 23.24).

Images from a single lens
The characteristics of the image depend on the design of your optical system. Eyeglasses, projector lenses, binoculars, and microscopes are all optical systems that produce different kinds of images. Figure 23.25 gives a summary of the characteristics of images made by single lenses.

The compound microscope

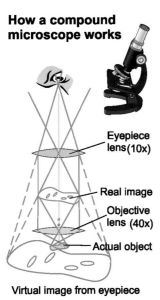

How a compound microscope works

Eyepiece lens(10x)

Real image

Objective lens (40x)

Actual object

Virtual image from eyepiece

The microscope that you use in biology class is probably a compound microscope. Like a telescope, a compound microscope uses two converging lenses. The lens closest to the object has a very short focal length and makes a real, larger, inverted image of the object inside the microscope.

The lens you look through (the *eyepiece*) has a longer focal length. The real image from the first lens is closer than one focal length to the eyepiece. That means the eyepiece acts like a magnifying glass, magnifying the (already larger) real image from the first lens. The overall magnification is the magnification of the objective multiplied by the magnification of the eyepiece. For example, a 10× eyepiece lens with a 40× objective lens produces an overall magnification of 400 (10 × 40).

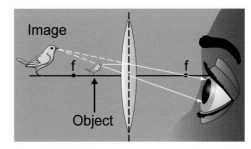

Figure 23.23: *A converging lens becomes a magnifying glass when an object is located inside the lens's focal length.*

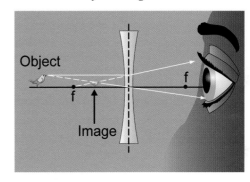

Figure 23.24: *A diverging lens always has the same ray diagram, which shows a smaller image. It doesn't matter where the object is, the image will always be smaller.*

Lens	Position of object	Image
Converging	Beyond the focal length	Real
Converging	Inside the focal length	Virtual and larger
Diverging	Anywhere	Virtual and smaller than object

Figure 23.25: *Image summary table*

Optical systems

Optical systems *Optical systems* are built from lenses, mirrors, and prisms. Optical systems do two things. First, an optical system must collect light rays. Second, the system changes the light rays to form an image, or process light in other ways. A camera is an optical system that collects light to record an image. Your eye is also an optical system. A photocopy machine is another optical system. The more light an optical system collects, the brighter the image it can form.

The image from a pinhole camera A simple optical system can be made with a pinhole in a box (Figure 23.26). No image forms on the front of the box because rays from many points of the object reach the same point on the box. An image *does* form inside the box, however. The image inside the box forms because light rays that reach a point on the box surface are restricted by the pinhole to come from only a pinhole-sized point on the object.

A lens makes a brighter image than a pinhole The image formed by a pinhole is very dim because the pinhole is small and does not allow much light to come through. The image formed by a lens is brighter because a lens is larger and collects more light (Figure 23.26). Each point on the image is formed by a cone of light collected by the lens. With a pinhole, the cone is much smaller and therefore the image has a much lower light intensity.

The larger the lens, the brighter the image. This is because a larger lens collects more light rays. Compared to smaller lenses, larger lenses can make good images with less light. That is why inexpensive cameras with small lenses need a flash to take pictures indoors. The small lens does not capture enough light by itself.

Why multiple lenses are useful Multiple lenses are useful because they allow an optical system to change the size of an image. The size of the image from a single lens depends on the distance between the object and the lens. If you are looking at a bird through a lens, you cannot easily change the distance between you and the bird! It is much easier to change the optical system. The telephoto lens in a camera is really two or more lenses that can move relative to one another. When you zoom in and out, the camera changes the separation between the lenses. As the separation changes, the magnification also changes.

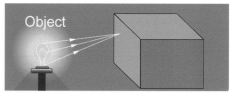

No image forms on the face of the box because light from many points on the object falls on the same point on the box.

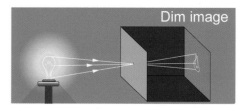

A pinhole forms a dim image by restricting light from each point on the object to a single point on the back of the box.

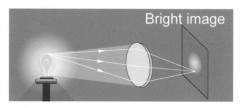

A lens forms a bright image by focusing more light from each point on the object to the equivalent point on the image.

Figure 23.26: *The images formed by a pinhole camera and a lens are different in brightness because different amounts of light are collected to form each point of the image.*

Recording images

Recording images on film

One technique for recording images uses film. Film uses special inks that respond to light. For a black and white photograph, the ink darkens in response to the intensity of light. Where light on the image is intense, the ink becomes dark. Where the image is dark, the ink remains light. Because dark and light are inverted, this image is known as a *negative* (Figure 23.27). A positive image is created by shining light through the negative onto photographic paper, also coated with light-sensitive ink. Light areas on the negative allow light through and darken corresponding areas on the photograph. A color film uses three colors of light-sensitive ink.

Recording images electronically

The second technique for recording an image is electronic. A digital camera, like a video camera-recorder, uses a sensor called a CCD, which is located at the focal plane of the camera lens. On the surface of the CCD are thousands of tiny light sensors. There are separate light sensors for red, blue, and green (Figure 23.28). For each sensor, the amount of light is recorded as a number from 0 to 255. For example, if the red sensor records 255, it is seeing the most red light it can handle. A recording of 0 means the sensor sees no light. A color image is recorded as a table of numbers. Each point on the image has three numbers corresponding to the amount of red light, blue light, and green light. The *resolution* of a digital camera is the number of points, called *pixels*, that can be recorded by the CCD. A *2 megapixel* camera stores 2 million pixels per image. Since each pixel is three numbers, a 2 megapixel image actually requires 6 million numbers to be stored.

Figure 23.27: *Recording an image on film is a two-step process.*

23.3 Section Review

1. If an object is 1 foot away from a mirror, how far behind the mirror surface does the image appear to be? Is this image a real or virtual image?

2. What is the difference between a real and virtual image?

3. Is a pair of binoculars a simple optical device or an optical system? Explain your answer. You may want to research how binoculars work to answer this question.

4. Compare how images are recorded on film to how they are made using a digital camera.

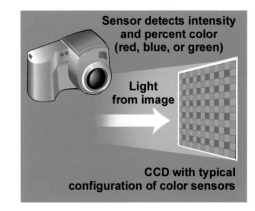

Figure 23.28: *A digital camera records an image as intensity of red, green, and blue light.*

Retinal Implants: Hope for the Blind

Mike, a 28 year old blind man, lies awake on an operating table, while surgeons place a three-millimeter square electrode panel on the retina of his anesthetized eye. Soon, a medical research team will stimulate the electrodes, in hopes that these electrical impulses will do what the rods and cone cells in his eye once did: send a message from the ganglion cells through the optic nerve to the visual cortex of his brain, forming an image.

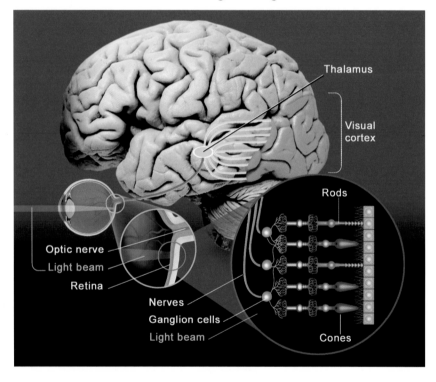

Legally blind since age 17, Mike volunteered for this study knowing that he may not see anything, and even if he does, the electrode panel will have to be removed at the end of the four-hour operation, since engineers are still working to develop materials that will protect the delicate electronics from the salty, wet environment of the eye for a long time.

Ready? asks the head surgeon. Mike gives a "thumbs-up" and the room falls quiet. The electrical stimulation machine emits a tone and then activates one of the electrodes on the panel.

"I can see something...a pea-sized circle of light, at about arm's length!" Mike's voice crackles with excitement.

After the next tone, two electrodes are activated. "This time it's about the size of a dime, and twice as bright."

The experiments continue, varying the amount of current and the placement of the activated electrodes. Mike sees a banana-shaped curve when four electrodes in a row are activated. He cannot yet distinguish the patterns that form an "L" and a "T" however. He sees blobs of light, but not distinct shapes.

Mike was one of six participants in this first human trial of the Boston Retinal Implant Project. The project's team of doctors, biologists, engineers, and rehabilitation specialists has been working since 1988, with the goal of producing a safe, long-lasting method to stimulate the retina. They want to generate images detailed enough to enable a blind person to, for example, walk by herself in an unfamiliar place.

How artificial vision works

The vision system consists of a special pair of glasses with a tiny video camera attached. The camera sends information about an image via wireless transmission to a chip surgically implanted on the outside of the eye. The chip in turn decodes the image and activates electrodes in order to stimulate the ganglion cells that normally send messages to the visual cortex of the brain.

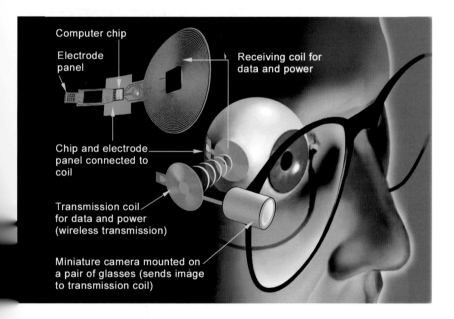

Computer chip

Electrode panel

Receiving coil for data and power

Chip and electrode panel connected to coil

Transmission coil for data and power (wireless transmission)

Miniature camera mounted on a pair of glasses (sends image to transmission coil)

This technology will most likely help people who have damaged photoreceptors (rod and cone cells) but whose ganglion cells and optic nerves are still functioning. Researchers expect that people with adult-onset blindness will adjust most easily to the vision system, because the visual cortex of their brain is used to organizing information about light, dark, and colors into recognizable pictures.

While the vision system won't be a cure for every type of blindness, it does hold promise for people affected by two of the most common causes of adult-onset blindness, retinitis pigmentosa and macular degeneration. Both of these diseases damage the eye's photoreceptors but usually leave the other parts unharmed.

A look ahead

The Boston Retinal Implant Project team knows that there is much work to be done in order to create a vision system that can improve the quality of life for blind patients. Biologists are researching how to lower the amount of electrical current needed to get ganglion cells to send messages, while engineers are exploring different ways to transmit information to the eye's interior. However, they have proven that electrical stimulus of the ganglion cells does activate the body's remaining intact visual system and allows the patient to perceive light. This is a crucial first step toward the formation of images, which is the ultimate goal of the project.

And as the technology develops there is hope that one day this artificial vision system may be so fine-tuned that the video camera could serve as a pair of binoculars or even a microscope. Someday, perhaps, this system will not only restore Mike's ability to see, but even extend his range of vision beyond the normal capabilities of the human eye.

Questions:

1. Why do you think the team's biologists are seeking the lowest effective amount of current?
2. Explain a significant breakthrough the Boston Retinal Implant project team has accomplished.
3. Describe at least two challenges that the team faces.

Chapter 23 Review

Understanding Vocabulary

Select the correct term to complete the sentences.

dispersion	fiber optics	incident ray
reflected ray	diffuse reflection	focal length
law of reflection	virtual image	specular reflection
converging lens	index of refraction	normal line

Section 23.1

1. A light ray that strikes a mirror is called a(n) _____.

2. A light ray that bounces off a mirror is called a(n) _____.

3. The light reflected off carpet or another rough surface is an example of _____.

4. The _____ predicts that light rays bounce off a mirror at the same angle from which they arrive.

5. A lens that bends light rays together, toward the focal point is called a _____ lens.

6. The _____ is an imaginary line drawn perpendicular to the surface of a mirror or any surface.

7. Your reflection in a mirror is an example of _____.

Section 23.2

8. _____ describes the effect of white light splitting into different colors because of the different refractive indices for the different colors.

9. The number that describes a material's ability to bend light is the _____.

10. _____ are glass fibers that use total internal reflection to transmit information.

Section 23.3

11. An image in a mirror that appears to come from behind the mirror is called a(n) _____.

12. The distance between the focal point and the center of the lens is called the _____.

Reviewing Concepts

Section 23.1

1. What is a light ray? What are light rays used for?

2. Can you predict how far away the image of an object will appear in a mirror?

3. How does the size of your image in a flat mirror compare to your size?

4. Describe the four interactions light can have with matter. Give an example of a situation where more than one interaction happens at the same time.

5. Distinguish between a transparent object and a translucent object.

6. Glare from headlights can make it harder to see when driving at night. Glare is worse when roads are wet from rain versus when roads are dry. Explain why, in terms of the two types of reflection.

7. What happens to light when it travels through a prism or a lens?

8. When drawing a ray diagram, what is the *normal* line?

9. State the law of reflection in your own words.

10. Describe how you measure the incident angle?

Section 23.2

11. What happens to light as it moves from one material to another that has a different index of refraction?

12. Refer to Table 23.1 in the text. For light moving from air, which material has a greater ability to bend light toward the normal line: ice or glass? How do you know?

13. A glass rod appears to disappear when placed in vegetable oil. Why?

14. Describe what happens in total internal reflection.

15. Fiber optics are glass fibers that carry light. You know from experience that light shines through glass. Why doesn't light escape from these glass fibers?

Section 23.3

16. Mirrors and lenses both produce images that your eye can see. How are mirrors and lenses similar? How are mirrors and lenses different?

17. Describe how objects, real images, and virtual images are different.

18. What happens to light traveling along the optical axis of a lens?

19. What happens to light rays entering a converging lens parallel to the optical axis?

20. If you've used a camera, you may have noticed that you can't have both a close object and a far away object in focus at the same time. Why not?

21. An optical system has a magnification of 100. What does 100 mean in this context? Use the terms *object* and *image* in your answer.

22. Explain the differences between a converging lens and a diverging lens. For each lens: discuss the shape, how each bends parallel light rays, and how the images are formed.

Solving Problems

Section 23.1

1. A ray of light strikes a mirror. Which of the following rays (a, b, c, or d) best describes the path of the light ray leaving the mirror?

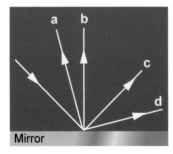

   A light ray strikes a mirror and is reflected. The angle between the incident ray and the reflected ray is 60°. What is the angle of reflection for this ray?

   If you stand two meters in front of a mirror, what is the apparent distance between you and your image?

4. A light ray strikes a mirror and is reflected as shown.

   a. Copy the sketch and draw the normal line to the mirror.
   b. On your sketch, label the angle of incidence and the angle of reflection.
   c. If the angle of incidence is 20 degrees, what is the angle of reflection?

Section 23.2

5. The graphic shows a ray of light travels from air into water.

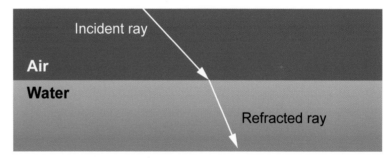

   a. Copy the sketch and draw the normal line at the boundary between the air and water.
   b. On your sketch, label the angle of incidence and the angle of refraction.
   c. Find and label the index of refraction for each material on your sketch.

6. A light ray crosses from a piece of glass into a liquid. You observe that the light ray bends closer to the normal passing from the glass to the liquid. Based on this observation, how does the index of refraction for the liquid compare to the index of refraction for the glass?

Section 23.3

7. A 2-centimeter tall object is positioned 10 centimeters from a converging lens with a focal length of 5 centimeters.

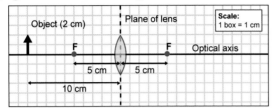

a. Copy the graphic to scale on your own graph paper. Trace the rays and predict where the image will form.
b. Is the image real or virtual?
c. What is the image size compared to the object size?
d. Is the image upright or inverted?

8. A 2-centimeter tall object positioned 4 centimeters from a converging lens. The focal length of this lens is 5 centimeters.

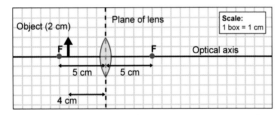

a. Copy the graphic to scale on your own graph paper. Trace the rays and predict where the image will form
b. Is the image real or virtual?
c. What is the image size compared to the object size?
d. Is the image upright or inverted?

9. If a 1-centimeter diameter coin is viewed under a lens with a magnification of 2.4, what will the diameter of the image be?

Applying Your Knowledge

Section 23.1

1. The phrase "MY MOM" is held in front of a flat mirror. When you read it in the mirror, what do you read? Try it and find out. Make sure you use capital letters.

2. Why do ambulances often have the reversed lettering for "AMBULANCE" on the front of their vehicles?

Section 23.2

3. In section 23.2, you learned that it is possible for objects to appear invisible. Write a short science fiction story that includes this phenomenon in the plot. Be sure to explain accurately the science behind why and how this can happen.

4. Chromatic aberration is a common optical error found in simple lenses. It causes colored images to appear blurry instead of in sharp focus. Use what you know about prisms and rainbows to explain why chromatic aberration occurs. Research how chromatic aberration can be corrected using lenses.

5. A microscope is a tool scientists use to magnify cells and very small objects. Find and study a labeled diagram of a microscope. Magnification for this tool depends on the eyepiece and objective lenses. Describe these parts and explain where they are located on a microscope. How do you calculate the magnification of a microscope?

Section 23.3

6. Your eye is an entire optical system that works together with the optic nerve and your brain to help you see images. Research the human eye and write a report that answers the following questions:

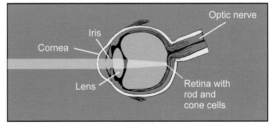

a. What is the purpose of the iris in the eye?
b. What is the purpose of the optic nerve?
c. What is the purpose of rod and cone cells?
d. What is the purpose of the lens?
e. How does the flexibility of the lens affect your ability to see?

7. A telescope can be used for looking at objects on Earth as well as in the sky. What do the following words mean when used to describe the working of a telescope: aperture, magnification, reflector, and refractor?

Chapter 24

The Physical Nature of Light

How is a radio like a flashlight? How can microwaves act like rays of light? While these may seem like strange questions, they are not. Radio, microwaves, and light are all three forms of the same kind of wave. They just have different frequencies — like chocolate, vanilla, and strawberry are different flavors of ice cream. The same processes of reflection and refraction work with microwaves as with ordinary light. That is why cell phone towers have funny-shaped dishes on them. The dishes act like mirrors and lenses for microwaves that carry cell phone transmissions. Human technology has found uses for almost every frequency of "light" including frequencies we cannot see.

Light is a form of energy, and in this chapter, you will learn about the electromagnetic spectrum and how electromagnetic radiation, including visible light, behaves. Microwave ovens, laptop computer screens, sunglasses, and lasers are all different types of technology that take advantage of the unique properties of the electromagnetic spectrum.

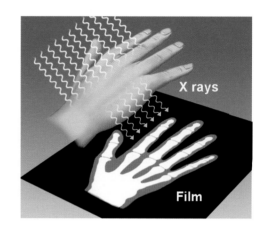

X rays

Film

Key Questions

✓ What does the acronym "ROY-G-BV" refer to?
✓ Why do radio broadcast towers have to be so tall?
✓ How does glow-in-the-dark plastic work?

24.1 The Electromagnetic Spectrum

Common objects can range in size. For example, a rock can be bigger than your fingernail but smaller than a truck. While harder to imagine, the whole range of rock sizes actually includes objects as big as the moon and smaller than a grain of sand. Wavelengths of light also come in a range of sizes. We see the range of wavelengths from red to violet (ROY-G-BV), but this visible light is just a small part of a much larger range of light waves called the electromagnetic spectrum. This section explores the whole spectrum, most of which is used by humans in one way or another.

Light is an electromagnetic wave

What is an electromagnetic wave?
Light is a wave, like sound and the ripples on a pond. What is oscillating in a light wave? Imagine you have two magnets. One hangs from a string and the other is in your hand. If you wave the magnet in your hand back and forth, you can make the magnet on the string sway back and forth. How does the oscillation of one magnet get to the other one? In Chapter 18 you learned that magnets create an invisible magnetic field around them. When you move a magnet up and down, you make a wave in the magnetic field. The wave in the magnetic field makes the other magnet move.

The frequency of the wave
However, the wave in the magnetic field also keeps travelling outward at the speed of light as an **electromagnetic wave**. If you could shake your magnet up and down 100 million times per second (100 MHz) you would make an FM radio wave. If you could shake the magnet up and down 450 trillion times per second, you would make waves of red light (Figure 24.1). Light and radio waves are waves of electromagnetism.

Oscillations of electricity or magnetism create electromagnetic waves
Anything that creates an oscillation of electricity or magnetism also creates electromagnetic waves. If you switch electricity on and off repeatedly in a wire, the oscillating electricity makes an electromagnetic wave. This is exactly how radio towers make radio waves. Electric currents oscillate up and down the metal towers and create electromagnetic waves of the right frequency to carry radio signals. Tapping a stick up and down in a puddle makes ripples that spread out from where you tap. Oscillating electric current in a radio tower makes ripples of electricity and magnetism that spread out from the tower at the speed of light as electromagnetic waves.

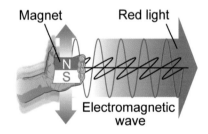

Figure 24.1: *If you could shake a magnet up and down 450 trillion times per second, you could make an electromagnetic wave that you would see as red light.*

The electromagnetic spectrum

Properties of electromagnetic waves
Like all waves, electromagnetic waves (like light) have frequency, wavelength, amplitude, and speed. Also like other waves, electromagnetic waves carry energy in proportion to their frequency. Shaking a magnet one million times per second (1 MHz) takes more energy than shaking it once per second (1 Hz). That is why a 1 MHz electromagnetic wave has a million times more energy than a 1 Hz electromagnetic wave of the same amplitude.

Why visible light is different
Almost all electromagnetic waves are invisible for the same reason you cannot see the magnetic field between two magnets. The exception is visible light. Visible light includes only the electromagnetic waves with the range of energy that can be detected by the human eye.

The electromagnetic spectrum
The entire range of electromagnetic waves, including all possible frequencies, is called the **electromagnetic spectrum**. The electromagnetic spectrum includes radio waves, microwaves, infrared light, ultraviolet light, X rays, and gamma rays. Visible light is a small part of the spectrum in between infrared and ultraviolet light.

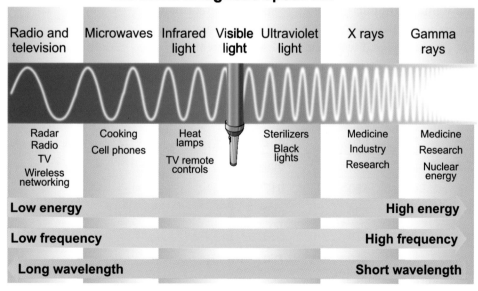

The electromagnetic spectrum

How does an electromagnetic wave spread?

Electromagnetic waves have both magnetic and electrical qualities. The two qualities exchange energy back and forth like a pendulum exchanges potential and kinetic energy back and forth. In chapter 17 you learned about induction; a changing magnetic field induces an electric field and vice versa. Induction is how electromagnetic waves propagate and spread. Each cycle of the electric part of the wave creates a magnetic wave as it changes. Each cycle of the magnetic wave in turn creates a new cycle of the electric wave. The electric and magnetic parts of the wave keep regenerating each other as the wave propagates.

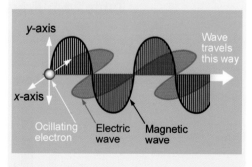

The wavelength and frequency of visible light

Wavelength of light
The wavelength of visible light is very small. For example, waves of orange light have a length of only 0.0000006 meter (6×10^{-7} m). Because wavelengths of light are so small, wavelengths are given in nanometers. One nanometer (nm) is one billionth of a meter (10^{-9} m). Figure 24.2 shows the size of a light wave relative to other small things. Thousands of wavelengths of red light would fit in the width of a single hair on your head!

Frequency of light
The frequency of light waves is very high. For example, red light has a frequency of 460 trillion, or 460,000,000,000,000 cycles per second. To manage these large numbers, units of terahertz (THz) are used to measure light waves. One THz is a trillion hertz (10^{12} Hz), or a million megahertz.

Wavelength and frequency are inversely related
Wavelength and frequency are inversely related to each other. As frequency increases, wavelength decreases. Red light has a lower frequency and longer wavelength than blue light. Blue light has a higher frequency and shorter wavelength than red light.

Energy and color of light
The energy of waves is proportional to frequency. Higher-frequency waves have more energy than lower-frequency waves. The same is true of light. The higher the frequency of the light, the higher the energy. Since color is related to energy, there is a direct relation between color, frequency, and wavelength. Table 24.1 shows the color, frequency, and wavelength of visible light.

Table 24.1: *Frequencies and wavelengths of light*

Energy	Color	Wavelength (nanometers)	Frequency (THz)
Low	Red	650	462
	Orange	600	500
	Yellow	580	517
	Green	530	566
	Blue	470	638
High	Violet	400	750

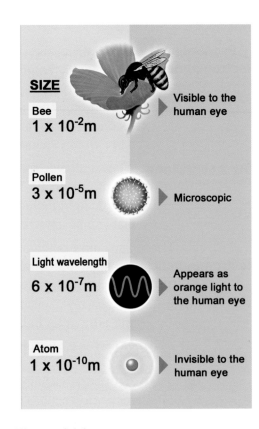

Figure 24.2: *The length of a bee is about 1×10^{-2} m; a grain of pollen is about 3×10^{-5} m wide; the wavelength of orange light is 6×10^{-7} m; and an atom is about 1×10^{-10} m in diameter.*

The speed of light waves

The speed of light

All electromagnetic waves travel at the same speed in a vacuum, the speed of light — 3×10^8 m/sec. As with other waves, the speed of light is the frequency multiplied by the wavelength.

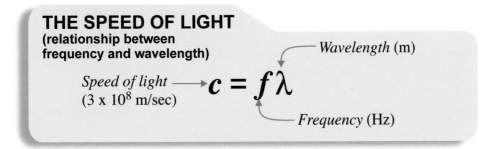

THE SPEED OF LIGHT
(relationship between frequency and wavelength)

Speed of light
(3 x 10⁸ m/sec)

Wavelength (m)

$$c = f\lambda$$

Frequency (Hz)

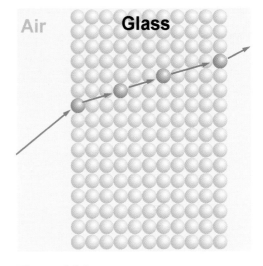

Air   **Glass**

Figure 24.3: *It takes light more time to pass through a material because the light must continuously be absorbed and re-emitted by each atom in turn.*

Light travels slower through materials where *n* >1

When passing through a material, light is continuously absorbed and re-emitted by the atoms that make up the material (Figure 24.3). Light moves at 3×10^8 m/sec *between* the atoms. However, the process of absorption and emission by the atoms causes a delay that makes the light take longer to move through the material. The speed of light in a material is equal to the speed of light in a vacuum divided by the refractive index (*n*) of the material. For example, the speed of light in water (*n* = 1.33) is 2.3×10^8 m/sec (3×10^8 m/sec ÷ 1.33). The refractive index of a material is the speed of light in a vacuum divided by the speed of light in the material (see sidebar at right).

Wavelengths are shorter in refractive materials

When moving through a material, the frequency of light stays the same. Because the frequency stays the same, the wavelength of light is reduced in proportion to how the speed changes. That means the wavelength of red light is shorter in water than in air.

Finding the wavelength of light

You can find the wavelength of light from the frequency and speed. For example, the frequency of red light is 4.6×10^{14} hertz (Hz). If you used the speed of light in a vacuum, 3×10^8 m/sec, then wavelength is 6.5×10^{-7} m (3×10^8 m/sec ÷ 4.6×10^{14} Hz). Use this calculation to find the wavelength of blue-green light in a vacuum. The frequency of blue-green light is 6.0×10^{14} hertz. The answer is that blue-green light has a wavelength of 5×10^{-7} meter.

Index of refraction

The index of refraction (n) for a material is the ratio of the speed of light in a vacuum to the speed of light in that material.

$$n = \frac{speed\ of\ light\ in\ a\ vacuum}{speed\ of\ light\ in\ the\ material}$$

Low-energy electromagnetic waves

What does "low-energy" mean?

We classify the energy of electromagnetic waves by comparing it to the energy it takes to remove an electron from an atom. Energy great enough to remove an electron can break the chemical bonds that hold molecules together. Low energy waves (like visible light) do not have enough energy to break most chemical bonds.

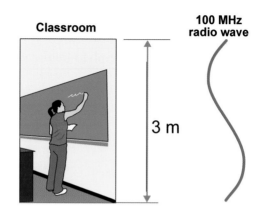

Figure 24.4: *A 100-megahertz radio wave, 100 FM on your radio dial, has a wavelength of 3 meters, about the height of a classroom.*

Radio waves

Radio waves are the lowest-frequency waves. They have wavelengths that range from kilometers down to tens of centimeters (Figure 24.4). Radio broadcast towers are tall because they need to be one-quarter of a wavelength high to efficiently create the large wavelengths of radio waves.

Microwaves

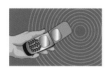

Microwaves range in length from approximately 30 cm (about 12 inches) to about 1 mm (the thickness of a pencil lead). Cell phones and microwave ovens use microwaves (Figure 24.5). The waves in a microwave oven are tuned to the natural frequency of liquid water molecules. The high intensity of microwaves inside an oven rapidly transfers energy to water molecules in food. Microwaves heat up and cook food by heating water molecules.

Infrared waves

Infrared light includes wavelengths from 1 millimeter to about 700 nanometers. Infrared waves are often referred to as radiant heat. Although we cannot see infrared waves, we can feel them with our skin. Heat from the sun comes from infrared waves in sunlight.

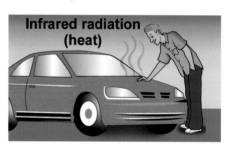

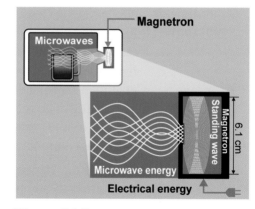

Figure 24.5: *A microwave oven uses microwaves to cook food. A device called a magnetron generates microwaves in the oven from a standing wave powered by electricity.*

Visible light

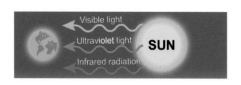

Visible light has wavelengths between 700 and 400 nanometers and includes all the colors of light (ROY-G-BV) we see when white light is split by a prism. The term "light" commonly refers to this part of the spectrum. However, any part of the electromagnetic spectrum from radio waves to gamma rays can be considered as "light." Earth receives almost the whole spectrum of electromagnetic waves from the sun, including infrared, ultraviolet, and visible light.

High-energy electromagnetic waves

Ultraviolet light   **Ultraviolet light** has a range of wavelengths from 10 to 400 nanometers. Like other forms of high energy electromagnetic waves, ultraviolet light has enough energy to remove electrons and break chemical bonds. Sunlight contains ultraviolet waves (Figure 24.6). A small amount of ultraviolet radiation is beneficial to humans, but larger amounts cause sunburn, skin cancer, and cataracts. Most ultraviolet light is blocked by ozone in Earth's upper atmosphere (Figure 24.6). A hole in the Earth's ozone layer is of concern because it allows more ultraviolet light to reach the surface of the planet, creating problems for humans, plants, and animals.

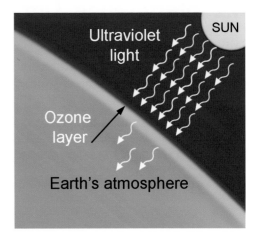

Figure 24.6: *Most of the ultraviolet light from the sun is absorbed by the Earth's ozone layer.*

X rays   **X rays** are high-frequency waves that are used extensively in medical and manufacturing applications (Figure 24.7). Their wavelength range is from about 10 nanometers to about 0.001 nm (or 10-trillionths of a meter). When you get a medical X ray, the film darkens where bones are because calcium and other elements in your bones absorb the X rays before they reach the film. X rays show the extent of an injury such as a broken bone.

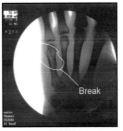

x ray

Gamma rays   **Gamma rays** have wavelengths of less than about ten-trillionths of a meter. Gamma rays are generated in nuclear reactions, and are used in many medical applications. Gamma rays can push even the inner electrons right out of an atom and completely disrupt chemical bonds. You do not want to be around strong gamma rays without a heavy shield.

24.1 Section Review

1. Describe an electromagnetic wave. How is one made?
2. What is the relationship between the frequency of light and its wavelength?
3. What is the speed of light in air ($n = 1.0001$)? What could you do to make light slow down?
4. Compare and contrast a radio wave and ultraviolet light.
5. Why might an infrared camera be able to "see" a person in the dark?

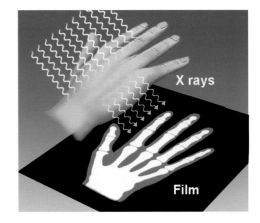

Figure 24.7: *X rays have a high enough energy to go through your soft tissue but not through your bones.*

24.2 Interference, Diffraction, and Polarization

The wave-like properties of light cannot be seen directly. In this section you will learn about experimental evidence that demonstrates how we know light is a wave. Like sound and water waves, light shows interference and diffraction. Light also has the property of polarization. Many inventions use the properties of light. Lasers use interference of light waves. We separate colors with a diffraction grating. Sunglasses and LCD screens use polarization.

Diffraction and shadows

Shadows Imagine shining a flashlight on a wall though a slot in a piece of cardboard. On the wall, you see bright light where the light rays pass through the slot. You see shadow where the cardboard blocks the light rays. If the light bulb is very small, there is a sharp edge to the shadow, showing you that light rays travel in straight lines (Figure 24.8).

Thin slits can cause diffraction If the slot is very narrow the light on the screen looks very different. The light spreads out after passing through the opening. The spreading is caused by diffraction. Diffraction is a wave behavior. We saw the same spreading of water waves when they passed through a small opening. Diffraction occurs when a wave passes through an opening not too much wider than the wavelength of the wave. A small opening acts like the center of a new circular wave. Seeing diffraction with light is evidence that light is a wave.

The fuzzy edge of a shadow
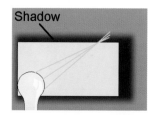
An ordinary shadow often has a fuzzy edge for a different reason. When light comes from a light bulb, light rays from many points on the bulb cast shadows in slightly different places. The width of the fuzzy edge depends on how far away the light bulb is, how large it is, and how far the screen is.

Diffraction in a shadow
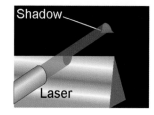
You can see diffraction in a shadow cast by a sharp edge with light from a laser. The edge of the shadow has ripples in it! The ripples are caused by diffraction. You do not see this in white light because of the mixture of wavelengths. A laser makes a pure color with a single wavelength.

Ordinary shadow
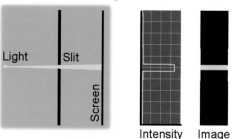

Diffraction shadow
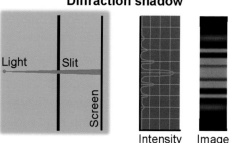

Figure 24.8: *Light and an ordinary shadow compared to diffraction.*

The interference of light waves

Young's double-slit experiment

Interference is a property of waves. In 1807, Thomas Young proved light was a wave when he showed that two beams of light could interfere with each other. In a famous experiment, Young let a beam of light pass through two very thin slits. After passing through the slits, the light fell on a screen.

Interpreting the experiment

If light were NOT a wave, then the pattern should look like the diagram on the left (below). The light at any point on the screen is simply the light from one slit plus the light from the other. However, when the experiment is done, the pattern looks like the diagram on the right. There are bright and dark bands across the screen caused by the interference of the two light beams

Constructive interference

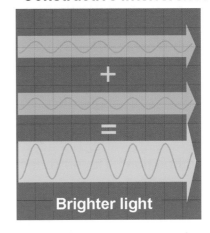

Brighter light

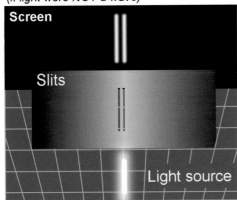

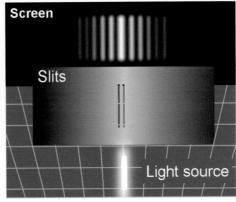

Destructive interference

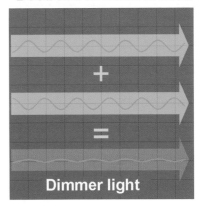

Dimmer light

Interference of light waves

The double slit experiment is strong evidence that light is a wave because an interference pattern can only be created by the addition of waves. Think of each slit as the source of a circular wave. The waves from both slits are exactly in phase when they leave the slit, because light from both slits is from the same wave front. Straight ahead (in line with the slits), the waves reach the screen in phase and there is a bright area on the screen. Next to this bright area, the light from each slit hits the screen out of phase because one of the two waves has to go a longer distance than the other. The bright bands in an interference pattern are where the light waves from both slits are in phase at the screen (constructive interference). The dark bands appear where the light waves reach the screen out of phase (destructive interference, Figure 24.9).

Figure 24.9: *The interference pattern (bands) comes from the interference of light as waves from each slit add up at each point on the screen. Constructive interference creates brighter light. Destructive interference creates dimmer light.*

Diffraction gratings and spectrometers

Diffraction grating A **diffraction grating** creates an interference pattern similar to the pattern for the double slit. A grating is actually a series of thin parallel grooves on a piece of glass or plastic. When light goes through a diffraction grating, each groove scatters the light so the grating acts like many parallel slits.

The central spot When you shine a laser beam through a diffraction grating most of the light goes straight through. A bright spot called the *central spot* appears directly in front of the grating where the light passes straight through (Figure 24.10). Some light is also scattered off many grooves. The interference of the light scattered from the grooves is what causes the additional bright bands on either side of the central bright spot.

The diffraction pattern The **diffraction pattern** is the series of bright spots on either side of the central bright spot. The closest bright spots to the center are called the *first order*. The light waves that produce the first order are one whole wavelength different in phase from each other. The second closest set of bright spots are called second order because these are made by the constructive interference of light waves that are two wavelengths different. You can often see third order, and even fourth order spots as well.

The location of bright spots is related to wavelength Like the double slit, a bright spot forms when the light waves from two adjacent grooves arrive in phase at the screen. The two waves travel a slightly different distance. They arrive in phase when the difference in distance between the two waves is exactly one wavelength. Because the location of the bright spots depends on wavelength, different wavelengths of light make bright spots at different distances from the central spot (Figure 24.11).

The spectrometer When light with a mixture of wavelengths passes through a diffraction grating, each wavelength makes a bright spot at a different place on the screen. As a result the grating spreads the light out into its separate wavelengths. That is why you see a rainbow when looking at a bright white light through a diffraction grating. A spectrometer is a device that uses a diffraction grating to create a spectrum (Figure 24.12). The spectrometer has a printed scale that allows you to read different wavelengths of light directly from the pattern of light made by the grating.

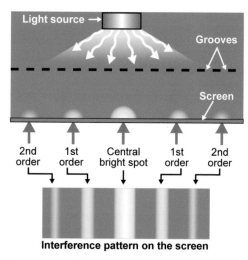

Figure 24.10: *The interference pattern from a diffraction grating.*

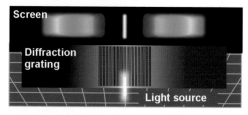

Figure 24.11: *Different wavelengths of light make bright spots at different distances from the central spot.*

The visible spectrum of hydrogen

397 nm (ultraviolet)
410 nm (violet)
434 nm (blue-violet)   656 nm (red)
486 nm (blue-green)

400   450   500   550   600   650   700
Wavelength (λ, nm)

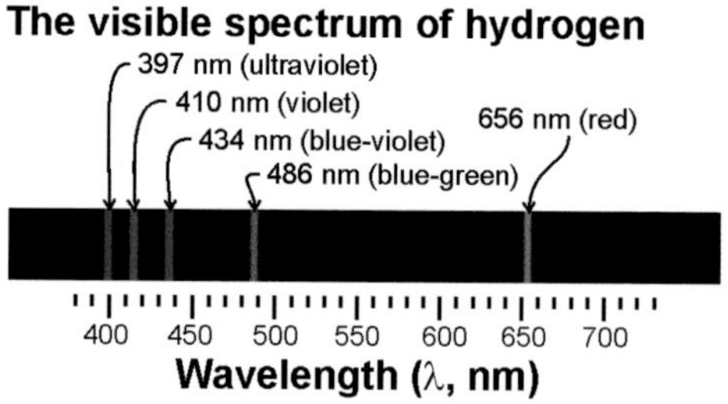

Figure 24.12: *The spectrum of light from by hydrogen gas seen in a spectrometer.*

Polarization

Polarization of a wave on a spring

An easy way to think about polarization is to think about shaking a spring back and forth. Waves move *along* the spring in its long direction. The oscillation of the *transverse* wave is perpendicular to the direction the wave travels. If the spring is shaken up and down it makes *vertical polarization*. If the spring is shaken back and forth it makes *horizontal polarization*. The polarization is the direction of the oscillation of the wave perpendicular to the direction the wave moves. Only transverse waves can have polarization. Longitudinal waves (like sound) cannot have polarization since they oscillate in only one direction, along the direction the wave moves.

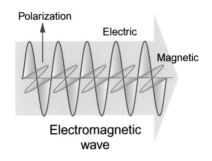

Figure 24.13: *The orientation of light is called its polarization. The polarization of light always refers to its electrical component.*

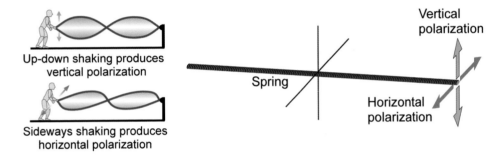

Polarization of light waves

The polarization of a light wave is the direction of the electric part of the wave oscillation (Figure 24.13). Polarization is another wave property of light. The fact that light shows polarization tells us that light is a *transverse wave*. Like a spring, the polarization of a light wave may be resolved into two perpendicular directions we usually call *horizontal* and *vertical*.

Unpolarized light

Most of the light that you see is *unpolarized*. That does not mean the light has no polarization. Unpolarized light is really just an equal mixture of all polarizations. We call ordinary light unpolarized because no single polarization dominates the mixture.

Polarizers

A **polarizer** is a material that allows light of only one polarization to pass through. Light that comes through a polarizer has only one polarization — along the *transmission axis* of the polarizer. Light with a single polarization is called *polarized light*. (Figure 24.14).

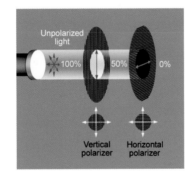

Figure 24.14: *Ordinary light is unpolarized. If this light passes through a vertical or horizontal polarizer, 50 percent of the light will pass through the polarizer. The light that passes will be horizontally or vertically polarized depending on the polarizer.*

Applications of polarization

Polarized sunglasses   Light that reflects at low angles from horizontal surfaces is polarized mostly horizontally. Polarized sunglasses reduce glare because they selectively absorb light with horizontal polarization (Figure 24.15) while letting other light through. Using polarized sunglasses, you can still see the light reflected from other objects, but the glare off a surface such as water is blocked.

LCD computer screens   Images on a laptop computer's LCD (liquid crystal diode) screen are made using polarized light (see diagram below). Unpolarized light first comes from a lamp. This light passes through a polarizer. The resulting polarized light then passes through numerous pixels of liquid crystal that act like windows.

Dark dots are made by crossing polarizers   Each liquid crystal window can be electronically controlled to act like a polarizer, or not. When a pixel is *not* a polarizer, the light comes through and you see a bright dot. When a pixel becomes a polarizer, light is blocked and you see a dark dot. The picture is made of light and dark dots. To make a color picture there are separate polarizing windows for each red, blue, and green pixel.

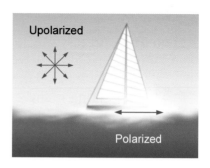

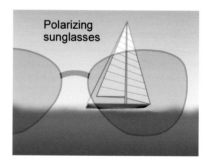

Figure 24.15: *Unpolarized light from the sun is polarized horizontally when it reflects off the water. Polarized sunglasses block out this light; regular sunglasses do not.*

How an LCD display works

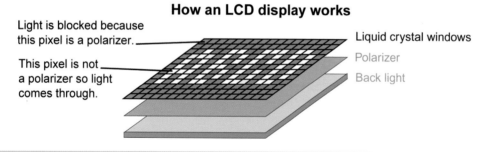

Light is blocked because this pixel is a polarizer.

This pixel is not a polarizer so light comes through.

Liquid crystal windows
Polarizer
Back light

24.2 Section Review

1. Why do sound waves spread out after passing through a partly open door while light waves make a beam of light that does not spread nearly as much?

2. Suppose you shine white light through a filter that absorbs a certain color of green. What will the spectrum of this light look like after passing through a diffraction grating?

3. Look at an LCD screen through polarizing sunglasses. Explain what you see when you rotate the sunglasses to change the angle of the transmission axis of the polarizing lenses.

24.3 Photons

Light has both wave-like and particle-like properties. By "particle-like" we mean that the energy of a light wave is divided up into little bundles called *photons*. Each atom that makes light gives off one photon at a time. Each atom that absorbs light absorbs one photon at a time. A beam of light consists of trillions of photons travelling at the speed of light.

The photon theory of light

Photons   The energy of a light wave is divided up in tiny bundles called *photons*. Each photon has its own color, no matter how you mix them up. Orange light is made of orange photons, red light of red photons, and so on. You can almost think of photons as colored jelly beans, except they have no mass.

Color and photons   The lowest-energy photons we can see are the ones that appear red to our eyes (Figure 24.16). The highest-energy photons we can see are the color of deep violet. Low-energy atoms make low-energy photons and high-energy atoms make high-energy photons. As atoms gain energy, the color of the light they produce changes from red to yellow to blue and violet.

White light   White light is a mixture of photons with a range of energy. This is because white light is created by atoms that also have a range of energy. For example, when a dimmer switch is set very low, the filament of an incandescent bulb is relatively cool (low energy) and the light is red. As you turn up the switch, the filament gets hotter and makes more green and blue light. At full power the filament is bright white—which means it is producing photons of all colors.

Temperature and energy   The atoms in a material have a range of energy depending on temperature. At room temperature (20°C) a rock gives off no visible light. At 600°C, some atoms have enough energy to make red light. At 2,600°C, atoms can make all colors of light, which is why the hot filament of a light bulb appears white.

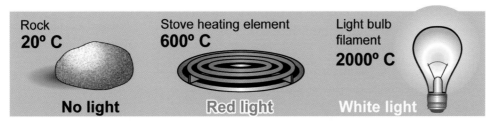

Vocabulary

photoluminescence

Objectives

✓ Define a photon.
✓ Explain how energy is related to the color of light.
✓ Learn that a one photon affects one electron at a time.
✓ Understand that seeing objects and color depends on how light is reflected and absorbed.

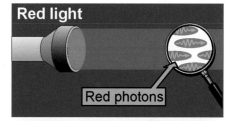

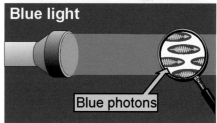

Figure 24.16: *Blue photons have a higher energy than red photons.*

The energy and intensity of light

Energy, color, and intensity
The intensity of light is a combination of both the number of photons and the energy per photon. There are two ways to make light of high intensity. One way is to have high-energy photons. A second way is to have a lot of photons even if they are low-energy (Figure 24.17). In practical terms, to make a red light with an intensity of 100 watts per meter squared (W/m^2) takes a lot more photons then it does to make the same intensity with blue light.

Glow-in-the-dark plastic
If glow-in-the-dark plastic is exposed to light, it stores some energy and later is able to release the energy by giving off light. The plastic can only make light if it is "charged up" by absorbing energy from other sources of light. You can test this theory by holding your hand on some "uncharged" glow-in-the-dark plastic and then exposing it to bright light. If you then bring the plastic into a dark area and remove your hand, you can see that the areas that were covered by your hand are dark while the rest of the plastic glows (Figure 24.18).

Photo luminescence
The glow-in-the-dark effect comes from phosphorus atoms that are in the plastic. When photons of light collide with phosphorus atoms, the energy from the photons is stored in the atoms. Slowly, the stored energy is released as pale green light. The process of releasing stored light energy is called **photoluminescence**.

An experiment with photon energy
Glow-in-the-dark plastic demonstrates that *a single atom only absorbs a single photon at a time*. Let's say we want a phosphorus atom to give off a green photon. To give off green light, the atom must absorb equal or greater energy. If one red photon is absorbed the atom does not get enough energy to make a green photon, and cannot glow. However, if a single atom could absorb two or more red photons it might get enough energy to emit a green photon. If you try the experiment you find that even very bright red light does not make the atoms of phosphorus glow. However, even dim blue light causes the atoms to glow. This is because one blue photon has more than enough energy to allow a phosphorus atom to release a green photon. If you try different colors, you find that only photons with more energy than those of green light will cause the glow-in-the-dark plastic to glow.

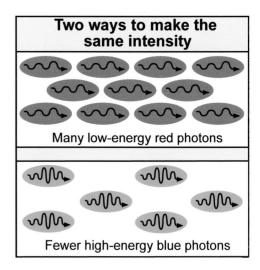

Figure 24.17: *The number and energy of photons determine the intensity of the light.*

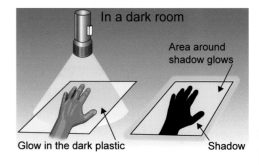

Figure 24.18: *The light from the flashlight cannot energize the phosphorus atoms that your hand blocks. These atoms will not glow because they did not receive any energy from photons from the flashlight.*

Absorbing, reflecting, and creating light

Light reflects off surfaces
Light reflected off a wall in a room started at a light source like a light bulb. Atoms in the wall first absorb and then re-emit the light energy. This process of absorbing and re-emitting light happens so fast that we may accurately describe the light as reflecting off the surfaces.

The process of how light is reflected
The atoms on the surface of this paper in the white areas absorb the light from the room and immediately emit almost all of the light back in all directions. You see a white page because the atoms on the surface of the paper absorb and re-emit light of all colors equally (Figure 24.19). The black letters are visible because light falling on black ink is almost completely absorbed and no light is re-emitted.

Most atoms absorb and emit light
Almost all atoms absorb and emit light. For most atoms, the absorption and emission of light happens in less than one millionth of a second. This is so fast that only the most sensitive instruments can detect the time delay. However, a phosphorus atom in glow-in-the-dark plastic is different. Phosphorus atoms have a special ability to delay the emission of a photon for a relatively long time after they have absorbed light.

Light from chemical reactions
Many chemical changes release energy. Some of the energy is absorbed within atoms and re-emitted as light. For example, the warm flickering glow from a candle comes from trillions of atoms in the wick giving up photons as they combine with oxygen atoms in the air (Figure 24.20). The light that comes from a glow stick is also made through chemical changes.

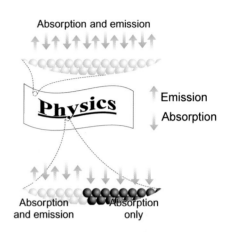

Figure 24.19: *White paper absorbs and immediately re-emits photons of all colors in all directions. Black ink absorbs photons of all colors and emits none, which is why it looks black.*

24.3 Section Review

1. Give one example where light acts like a wave and one example where light acts like a particle.
2. Is it possible for two beams of light to have the same number of photons per second yet have different amounts of power? Explain.
3. Give at least 3 differences between a photon and an atom.
4. A piece of wood does not produce light. However, a log on a fire some times glows with reddish light. Explain this observation.

Figure 24.20: *The light from a candle flame comes from energy released by chemical changes.*

The Electromagnetic Spectrum in the Sky

For thousands of years, people have looked up at the sky and wondered what the sun, moon, and planets were made of, how they were created, and what kept them going. Did you know they emit much more radiation than just visible light?

Electromagnetic radiation has helped scientists learn more about our solar system, galaxies and the universe around us. For example, astronomers confirmed the existence of black holes — very dense objects in space that have huge gravitational fields — using X-ray telescopes.

Visible light

The earliest observations were made using visible light because very little special equipment was required. The human eye makes a good observation device, and with a telescope, it's even better!

Astronomers use telescopes to do more than just magnify images. For very dim or distant objects, very little light reaches Earth. Telescopes act as "light buckets" and collect as much light from a dim source as possible. Bigger telescopes can collect more light than smaller ones and allow scientists to see objects that are farther away and dimmer.

A different approach to getting better pictures of the sky in the past 50 years is to launch telescopes mounted on satellites into orbit beyond the atmosphere. These new telescopes, like the Hubble Space Telescope, can show us crystal clear views we could never obtain on Earth.

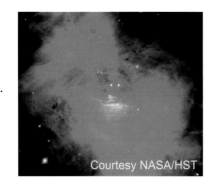

Courtesy NASA/HST

Emissions spectra

Another way in which scientists learn about celestial objects is by observing emitted light. Astronomers use spectrometers to determine which frequencies of electromagnetic radiation are present in light from stars. Patterns of spectral lines can be associated with chemical elements, so when a particular pattern appears in the spectrum of light from a star, it's a good sign that element is present in the star.

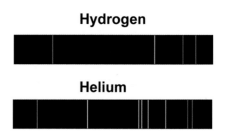

Hydrogen

Helium

Radio telescopes

While performing a study on radio communications in the early 1900's, an engineer discovered an unknown source of interference. It turned out that the source of the radiation was located in the sky at the center of the Milky Way galaxy.

To further investigate the sources of radio waves in space, scientists built radio telescopes. Because radio waves have a much longer wavelength than visible light, equipment used to accurately detect radio waves must be much bigger. The biggest radio telescope in the world is the Arecibo Radio Telescope in Puerto Rico; it's over 300 meters across and built into a huge sinkhole in the ground! In the 1960's, new theories predicted the existence of a certain kind of pulsing star, and astronomers found them by observing radio waves.

Courtesy NASA

Gamma rays and X rays

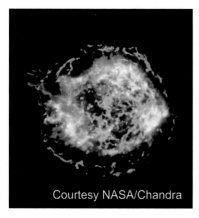

Courtesy NASA/Chandra

Other objects in the sky emit high energy electromagnetic radiation, like X rays and gamma rays. Unlike most visible light and lower energy radiation, high energy electromagnetic waves do not usually pass through the atmosphere, so observations of this radiation are made from satellites. This image of the supernova remnant Cassiopeia A was taken by the NASA satellite Chandra.

Infrared telescopes

Because water vapor in the atmosphere absorbs much of the infrared radiation from space, infrared telescopes are often built high in the mountains, like the Mauna Kea Observatory in Hawaii, which is about 4,000 meters above sea level.

Scientists also mount infrared sensors on an airplane and fly above 99% of the atmospheric water vapor to take more sensitive readings than on the ground. While observing a star passing behind Uranus, they saw it blinking in and out of view, and it was discovered that Uranus has rings, similar like Saturn.

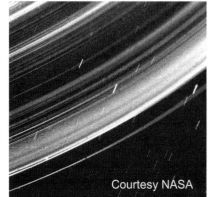

Courtesy NASA

Astronomers learned that the surface of the moon was covered with a fine powder years before anyone set foot there by making observations of reflected infrared light.

Electromagnetic variety show

Below are four images of the Crab Nebula: clockwise, starting in the top left, the images were taken in the X-ray region of the spectrum, the optical range, with a radio telescope, and in the infrared spectrum.

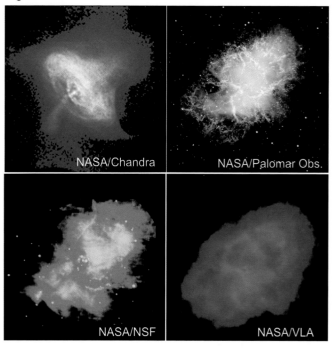

NASA/Chandra   NASA/Palomar Obs.
NASA/NSF   NASA/VLA

Questions:

1. What device could you use to help you observe objects in the night sky?
2. How much light can a "light bucket" hold?
3. What elements are likely present in our sun?
4. What conclusions could you make about the Crab Nebula, given the four different images above?

Chapter 24 Review

Understanding Vocabulary

Select the correct term to complete the sentences.

spectrometer	photoluminescence	electromagnetic spectrum
photons	ultraviolet radiation	infrared waves
diffraction grating	gamma rays	X rays
visible light	polarization	electromagnetic waves
polarizer		

Section 24.1

1. Radio waves, X rays, gamma rays, and visible light are all part of the _____.

2. _____ is the type of electromagnetic wave that can cause sunburn.

3. _____ are produced by oscillations of electricity or magnetism.

4. _____ is the type of electromagnetic wave we feel as heat.

5. The part of the electromagnetic spectrum we can see with our eyes is called _____.

6. _____ are high frequency waves with a wavelength of 10 nanometers to 0.001 nanometers.

7. _____ are the highest frequency waves in the electromagnetic spectrum and are generated in nuclear reactions.

Section 24.2

8. Light passes through a _____ and comes through with only one orientation.

9. A(n) _____ measures the wavelength of light.

10. The orientation of light vibrations, either horizontal or vertical, is called a _____.

11. A(n) _____ creates interference patterns when light is passed through it.

Section 24.3

12. The process of releasing stored energy as light is known as _____.

13. Particles of light energy are known as _____.

Reviewing Concepts

Section 24.1

1. Compare red light and blue light in terms of the energy, wavelength, and frequency of both types of light.

2. The speed of light changes as it passes through different materials due to the absorption and emission of the light by atoms. As the speed changes, does its frequency, wavelength, or both change?

3. How is the index of refraction for a material dependent upon the speed of light? Is it possible for a material to have an index of refraction less than 1? Why or why not?

4. Write the equation for the speed of light that you would use in each of the following scenarios. Let c = the speed of light, f = frequency, and λ = wavelength:
   a. You know frequency and wavelength.
   b. You know the speed of light and frequency.
   c. You know the speed of light and wavelength.

5. List two different ways that microwaves are used.

6. When a beam of X rays is passed through a person's body and onto a special film, a radiograph (or X-ray photograph) is created. How do radiographs enable a doctor to "see" a broken arm?

Section 24.2

7. List *four* pieces of evidence that light is a wave.

8. How is an interference pattern of light created? In your answer, use the terms *constructive interference* and *destructive interference*.

9. Thomas Young demonstrated that light is a wave. What experiment did he use and what evidence did his experiment create?

10. What is a spectrometer used for?

11. What causes the central spot when light goes through a diffraction grating? What causes the first order bright spots?

12. Is an electromagnetic wave a transverse or longitudinal wave?

13. What does it mean to say a light wave is *polarized*?

14. Explain what a polarizer does to unpolarized light.

Section 24.3

15. How is the intensity of light related to photons?

16. How is a photon's color related to its energy?

17. What "charges up" glow-in-the-dark plastic? Does it matter what color light you use to charge up the plastic?

18. In the subtractive color process, pigments absorb some colors and reflect some colors of light. Explain the absorption and reflection of colors of an object in terms of atoms and electrons.

Solving Problems

Section 24.1

1. The following are different types of electromagnetic waves: Gamma rays, visible light, X rays, microwaves, radio waves, infrared light, ultraviolet light. Arrange these waves in order from:
   a. LOWEST energy to HIGHEST energy.
   b. SHORTEST to LONGEST wavelength.

2. For the electromagnetic waves in question (1), does it make sense to order them by their speed? Why or why not?

3. Calculate the wavelength of violet light that has a frequency of 7.5×10^{14} Hz.

4. What is the frequency of a microwave with a 30-centimeter wavelength?

5. The speed of light in a vacuum is 3×10^8 m/sec. What is the speed of light in flint glass whose index of refraction is 1.65?

6. Light travels at 1.56×10^8 m/sec through zircon. What is the index of refraction of zircon?

Section 24.2

7. A polarizer transmits 50% of a light's intensity, and the transmitted light is oriented horizontally. How much of the light intensity was absorbed, and what is the orientation of this light?

. A red laser with a wavelength of 650 nanometers is passed through a diffraction grating. What would you expect to see?

Section 24.3

9. Photographers use a special scale called Color Temperature for comparing the colors of light sources when they take pictures. Color temperature is the temperature in Kelvins at which that color light would be emitted. Which would have the higher color temperature, a sunset or a blue flashbulb?

10. At 600°C, a heating element produces red light. Is red light also present when a light bulb filament makes white light at 2000°C?

11. A blacksmith can tell the temperature of a metal piece by looking by its color. You know that the order of colors in a rainbow is ROYGBIV. Which color would a blacksmith see first, red or white, as he heats up the metal to the highest temperature of 2600°C?

Applying Your Knowledge

Section 24.1

1. What would the world look like if your eyes could see all the different wavelengths of the electromagnetic spectrum—from radio waves to gamma waves—and not just visible light? What would your experience be like if you were able to see all kinds of electromagnetic waves? Write a short essay that answers these questions.

Section 24.2

2. Unlike humans, who sense only brightness and color, some animals in the animal kingdom use polarized vision for a variety of uses. Research an animal that uses polarized vision and, in a poster, describe how this animal uses polarized vision to its advantage. What is special about the eyes of animals with polarized vision?

3. Edwin Land (1909-1991), a physicist, invented the first filters to polarize light and held many patents in the fields of optics and photography. Research his life and inventions. Write a short paper or give a presentation that summarizes your findings about this inventor.

Section 24.3

4. The trick in building fireworks is to find materials that release light at the specific color you want to see. Research which materials are used to produce the different colors of fireworks. Make a table of the materials and the frequency and color they produce.

Glossary

A

absolute zero – the lowest possible temperature where molecules have the lowest energy they can have; 0 K on the Kelvin temperature scale.

absorption – the decrease in amplitude of a wave as it passes through a material and loses energy.

acceleration – the change of speed over time.

acceleration due to gravity (g) – an acceleration of an object due to Earth's gravitational field strength; equal to 9.8 m/sec^2.

acoustics – the science and technology of how sound behaves.

activation energy – the energy needed for a chemical reaction to break the chemical bonds in the reactants.

additive color process – a process that creates color by adding proportions of red, green, and blue together.

additive primary colors – red, green, and blue.

air resistance – the opposing force on a moving object due to friction of air.

alpha decay – radioactive decay that results in an alpha particle (a helium nucleus) being emitted from the nucleus of an atom.

alternating current (AC) – an electric current (or voltage) that oscillates in direction. Household AC reverses its voltage 60 times per second.

ammeter – an instrument for measuring electric current flow.

amorphous – a type of solid matter in which the atoms have no repeating order, the opposite of crystalline.

ampere (amp or A) – the unit for measuring electrical current.

amplitude – the maximum distance from the average in harmonic motion; amplitude is often a distance or an angle.

analysis – the detailed interpretation of experimental results to determine what they mean.

angle of incidence – the angle between the incident ray and the normal line.

angle of reflection – the angle between the normal line and the reflected ray.

angle of refraction – the angle between a refracted ray and the normal.

angular speed – the rate at which an object rotates or revolves.

antimatter – matter which has the opposite charge (and other properties) from normal matter; an anti-electron (positron) has a positive charge while a normal electron has a negative charge.

B

Archimedes' principle – a principle that states that the force exerted on an object in a liquid is equal to the weight of the fluid displaced by the object.

armature – the rotating part of an electric motor

atom – the smallest particle of an element that can exist alone or in combination with other atoms.

atomic number – the number of protons that an atom contains.

atomic theory – a theory that states that all matter is composed of tiny particles called atoms.

axis of rotation – the line around which an object rotates.

B

battery – a device that transforms chemical energy to electrical energy.

beat – the oscillation of amplitude that results from the interference of two sound waves with frequencies that are close but not exactly equal

Bernoulli's principle – the law of conservation of energy as applied to fluid flow; height, pressure and speed of a fluid are related by energy conservation along a streamline.

beta decay – radioactive decay that results in a beta particle (an electron) being emitted from the nucleus of an atom.

big bang – a theory of the origin of the universe in which the universe was once smaller than an atom and began to expand with a huge explosion.

black hole – a compact, astronomical object with such strong gravity that its escape velocity is equals or exceeds the speed of light.

boundaries – an edge or surface where conditions or materials change.

Boyle's law – states that the pressure of a gas is inversely proportional to its volume at constant temperature.

brittleness – a measure of a material's tendency to break rather than stretch.

brushes – allow current to flow into the coil of an electric motor.

buoyancy – a measure of the upward force a fluid exerts on an object.

C

calorie – a unit of energy equal to 4.184 joules; the quantity of heat energy required to raise the temperature of one gram of water by 1°C.

capacitance – a measure of a capacitor's ability to store charge.

capacitor – a device that stores electric charge by keeping positive and negative charges separated.

Celsius scale – a temperature scale on which zero equals the temperature that water freezes (0°C) and 100 is the temperature that water boils (100°C).

center of gravity – the average position of an object's weight.

center of mass – the point at which an object naturally spins.

centrifugal force – the effect of inertia on an object moving in a curve; centrifugal force is not a true force.

centripetal force – a force that causes an object to move in a circle.

chain reaction – occurs when the fission reaction of a single atom triggers more nuclear reactions and results in the continuous release of nuclear energy.

charge – a fundamental electrical property of matter that can be positive, zero, or negative; causes electrons (-) and protons (+) to attract each other.

charged – an object whose net charge is not zero.

charging by contact – the transfer of electric charge between two different objects by touching them together.

charging by friction – the transfer of electric charge between two different objects by rubbing them together.

charging by induction – the transfer of electric charge between two objects without direct contact.

Charles' law – states that the volume of a gas increases with increasing temperature if pressure is held constant.

chemical bond – the strong attractive force that holds together atoms in molecules and crystalline salts.

chemical energy – the energy that is stored in the chemical bonds that join atoms.

chemical equation – chemical formulas and symbols that represent a chemical reaction.

chemical properties – properties that can only be observed through a chemical change.

chemical reaction – the breaking and/or forming of chemical bonds that arrange or re-arrange atoms into different molecules or compounds; relationship between reactants and products.

circuit diagram – a schematic drawing of an electric circuit.

circular wave – waves whose crests form a pattern of circular wave fronts.

circumference – the measure of the distance around a circle.

closed circuit – a circuit in which there is a complete path for current to flow.

CMYK color process – another name for the subtractive color process that uses cyan, magenta, yellow, and black pigments.

cochlea – a tiny, fluid-filled structure in the inner ear that contains the nerves that create your sense of hearing.

coil – a current-carrying wire made into loops.

collision – occurs when two or more objects hit each other.

color – the perception of the energy of light; red light has the lowest energy that we can see, and violet light the highest.

commutator – the device that switches the direction of electrical current in the electromagnets of an electric motor.

compass – a device containing a magnet that interacts with Earth's magnetic field to indicate direction.

components – the set of perpendicular vectors that add up to a given vector.

compound – a substance made of two or more elements that cannot be separated by physical means.

conductor – a material that easily carries electrical current.

cones – photoreceptor cells in the eye that respond to color.

consonance – a combination of sound frequencies that is agreeable or harmonious.

constant speed – a speed that does not change.

constructive interference – occurs when waves add up to make a larger amplitude.

control variable – a variable in an experiment that is kept the same throughout the experiment.

convection – the transfer of thermal energy by the motion of a fluid.

converging lens – a lens that bends light rays so they come together; usually a convex lens.

coulomb (C) – the unit of electric charge.

Coulomb's law – the formula that says the force between two electric charges is proportional to the product of the two charges divided by the square of the distance between them.

covalent bond – a type of chemical bond that is formed when two atoms share electrons.

crest – the top or highest points on a wave.

critical angle – the angle at which light is totally reflected back into a material.

crystalline – a solid having an orderly, repeating pattern arrangement of atoms or molecules.

cycle – a unit of oscillation that repeats over and over.

D

damping – the gradual loss of amplitude of an oscillator.

deceleration – a decrease in speed.

decibel (db) – the unit for measuring the loudness of sound.

density – a property that describes the ratio of mass to volume.

dependent variable – the variable in an experiment that changes in response to choices made by the experimenter; the dependent variable is plotted on the *y*-axis of a graph.

destructive interference – occurs when waves add up to make a smaller amplitude.

diamagnetic – a type of matter in which the magnetic fields of individual electrons cancel out, leaving each atom with zero magnetic field.

diffraction – the change in shape of a wave as it passes through openings or bends around an edge.

diffraction grating – an optical device with a series of thin, parallel grooves that creates an interference pattern of light.

diffraction pattern – the interference pattern of bright and dark bands of light created by a diffraction grating.

diffuse reflection – the scattering of light into many directions off a non-shiny surface.

direct current (DC) – electrical current flowing in one direction only.

dispersion – describes the variation in the refractive indices of different colors of light.

displacement – the distance and direction between the starting and ending points of an object's motion; displacement is a vector quantity.

dissonance – a combination of sound frequencies that is discordant or unsettling.

distance – the length of space between two points.

diverging lens– a lens that bends light rays so they spread apart; usually a concave lens.

Doppler effect – the shift in frequency caused by the relative motion of the sound source and observer.

E

efficiency – the ratio of a machine's output work to input work.

elastic collision – occurs when objects collide so that the total kinetic energy remains the same before and after the collision.

elasticity – a measure of a solid's ability to stretch and then return to its original shape and size.

electric circuit – any complete path through which electricity travels.

electric current – the flow of electric charge.

electric field – the electric force in newtons per coulomb created in the space around an electric charge.

electric motor – a machine that converts electrical energy into mechanical energy.

electrical energy – the type of energy resulting from electric current.

electrical symbol – a simple symbol used for parts of a circuit in circuit diagrams.

electrically neutral – an object that has equal amounts of positive and negative charges and whose net charge is zero.

electromagnet – a magnet created by electric current flowing in wires; a simple electromagnet can be made by inserting an iron core into a wire coil that is conducting an electrical current.

electromagnetic force – a force created by electricity (charge) or magnetism.

electromagnetic induction – the process of using a moving magnet to create a current or voltage.

electromagnetic spectrum – the entire range of electromagnetic waves, including all possible frequencies.

electromagnetic wave – a wave of oscillating electric and magnetic fields that moves at the speed of light; light is an example.

electron – a low-mass particle with a negative charge that occupies the energy levels in an atom outside the nucleus; electrons are involved in chemical bonds and reactions.

electroscope – an instrument used to detect charged objects.

element – a pure substance that contains only atoms with the same atomic number (number of protons in the nucleus).

ellipse – a particular mathematical kind of "oval" shape; an ellipse is the shape of the orbit of a comet.

endothermic reaction – a chemical reaction in which requires a net input of energy.

energy – a fundamental quantity of the universe; measure of ability to change or create change; energy is required to make a force do work, change motion, raise temperature, create new matter, break chemical bonds, or push electric current through a wire.

energy conversion – also energy transformation; the changing from one kind of energy to another kind of energy; for example, an energy conversion occurs when potential energy is converted to kinetic energy.

energy flow diagram – a diagram showing the transformations and conversions of energy in a system.

energy level – one of the discrete values of energy that electrons in an atom are allowed to have.

energy of pressure – the energy stored in the pressure of a fluid.

English system – a system of measuring that uses distance units of inches, yards, and miles.

equilibrium – (1) occurs when the forces on an object are balanced and the net force equals zero; (2) in harmonic motion, the resting position of the system where the system is undisturbed with no net force.

evaporation – the process by which atoms or molecules leave a liquid and become a gas at a temperature below the boiling point.

exothermic reaction – a chemical reaction in which there is a net release of energy.

experiment – any situation that is specifically set up to observe what happens.

experimental variable – a variable in an experiment that is changed by the experimenter; the variable which is plotted as an independent variable on the x-axis of a graph.

F

Fahrenheit scale – a temperature scale on which water freezes at 32 degrees Fahrenheit (or 32°F) and water boils at 212°F.

farad (F) – the unit of capacitance.

Faraday's law of induction – states that the voltage induced in a coil is directly proportional to the rate of change of the magnetic field through the coil.

ferromagnetic – a material (like iron) with very strong magnetic properties.

fiber optics – thin glass fibers that use total internal reflection to carry light.

field – a quantity that has a value everywhere in space; how forces are transmitted from one object to another.

first law of thermodynamics – that energy cannot be created or destroyed, only converted from one form into another; a form of the law of conservation of energy.

fluid – a form of matter that flows when any force is applied, no matter how small the force is; liquids and gases are fluids.

fluorescence – a process by which atoms release light energy.

focal length – the distance from the center of a lens to the focal point.

focal point (f) – a point in an optical system at which many light rays actually meet or appear to meet.

focus – the place where light rays from each point on an object come together again at a corresponding point to form an image.

food chain – a series of steps through which energy and nutrients are transferred from organism to organism in an ecosystem.

force – a push, a pull, or any action that has the ability to change motion.

force field – a distribution of energy in space that causes a force on objects within it; includes magnetic fields, gravitational fields, and electrical fields.

Fourier's theorem – says that any complex wave can be made by adding up single frequency waves.

free fall – the acceleration of a falling object under the sole influence of Earth's gravitational force.

free-body diagram – a diagram showing all the force vectors that are acting on an object.

frequency (f) – the number of cycles per second; measured in hertz (Hz).

frequency spectrum – a graph showing the distribution of different frequencies in a complex signal, like a sound wave.

friction – the force that always resists motion and is caused by relative motion between objects (like the wheel and axle of a car).

fulcrum – a fixed point on a lever about which the lever rotates.

fundamental – the lowest natural frequency of a standing wave.

G

gamma decay – a process by which the nucleus of an atom emits a gamma ray.

gamma rays – electromagnetic waves with wavelengths of less than 0.001 nm; high energy photons emitted spontaneously in nuclear reactions.

gas – a phase of matter that flows and can expand or contract to fill any container.

gauss (G) – a unit used to measure the strength of a magnetic field; Earth's average magnetic field strength is approximately 0.3-0.5 G.

general relativity – Einstein's theory in which gravity is an effect created by the curvature of space and time.

generator – a device that converts kinetic energy into electrical energy using the law of induction.

gravitational constant – the constant in Newton's law of universal gravitation; equal to 6.67×10^{-11} Nm^2/kg^2; it is the same everywhere in the universe.

gravitational field – a force field created by mass and acting on mass.

group – elements that exhibit similar chemical properties; arranged in vertical columns on the periodic table.

H

half-life – the length of time it takes for half of any sample of a radioactive isotope to change into other isotopes (or elements).

hard magnet – a material whose magnetic domains remain aligned for a long time, making them more difficult to demagnetize.

harmonic motion – motion that repeats itself over and over.

harmonics – frequencies that are multiples of fundamental frequency.

heat – a flow of thermal energy from one object to another object due to a temperature difference.

heat conduction – the transfer of thermal energy by the direct contact of particles of matter.

hertz (Hz) – the unit of one cycle per second; frequency is measured in hertz.

Hooke's law – says the force exerted by a spring is proportional to its change in length.

horsepower (hp) – a unit of power; one horsepower is equal to 746 watts.

hypothesis – a prediction that can be tested by experimentation; a hypothesis is the starting point for future investigation.

I

image – an illusion or "picture" of a real object; images are created by bending light rays in an optical system.

impulse – the product of force × time that causes a change in momentum.

incandescence – the process of creating light with heat.

incident ray – a light ray that strikes a surface.

independent variable – the variable in an experiment that is manipulated by the experimenter and that causes changes in the dependent variable in the experiment; the independent variable is plotted on the x-axis of a graph.

index of refraction (n) – a ratio that gives a measure of a material's ability to bend light.

inelastic collision – a type of collision where the total kinetic energy after the collision is less than it was before the collision; usually involves objects sticking together or changing shape.

inertia – the resistance of a body to change its state of motion.

infrared light – a type of electromagnetic wave with a wavelength between 1 mm and 700 nm; infrared light is invisible to the human eye; the form of radiant heat.

input – the force, work, energy, or power applied to a machine.

input arm – the side of a lever between the fulcrum and the input force.

insulator – a material that poorly conducts electrical current or heat.

intensity – (1) the field strength at a certain point in space; (2) a measure of the amount of light energy per second falling on a surface.

interference – the pattern of pressure, brightness, amplitude, or other wave characteristic that comes from adding more than one wave of the same kind.

intermolecular forces – the medium-strength forces between atoms and/or molecules that determine phase (solid, liquid, gas) at any given temperature.

inverse square law – describes a quantity that varies inversely with the square of the distance.

ion – an atom that has gained or lost one or more electrons and therefore has a net electrical charge.

ionic bond – a type of chemical bond between atoms that transfers electrons; a bond between ions.

irreversible – a process that can only run forward and cannot run backward; a process for which the efficiency is less than 100%.

isotopes – forms of the same element that have different numbers of neutrons and different mass numbers.

J

joule (J) – a unit of energy (and work); a joule is equal to one newton of force times one meter of distance.

K

Kelvin – temperature scale starting at absolute zero and measuring the actual energy of atoms; on this scale water freezes at 273 K and boils at 373 K.

kilowatt (kW) – a unit of power equal to 1,000 watts or 1,000 joules per second.

kilowatt-hour (kWh) – a unit of energy equal to one kilowatt of power used for one hour; equal to 3.6 million joules.

kinetic energy – energy that comes from motion.

Kirchhoff's current law – the total current flowing into any branch point in a circuit equals the total of current flowing out of the branch point.

Kirchhoff's voltage law – the voltage changes (including the battery) around any loop of a circuit must total to zero.

L

law of conservation of energy – energy cannot be created or destroyed although it can be changed from one form to another; also called the first law of thermodynamics.

law of conservation of momentum – in the absence of external forces, the total momentum of a system remains constant.

law of reflection – when a light ray reflects off a surface, the angle of incidence is equal to the angle of reflection.

of universal gravitation – the force of gravity between two objects is proportional to the product of their masses divided by the square of the distance between them.

ngth – a measured distance; a fundamental property of space (along with time).

ver arm – the perpendicular distance between the line of action of a force and the axis of rotation.

ht ray – an imaginary line that represents a thin beam of light.

e of action – an imaginary line in the direction of the force and passing through the point where the force is applied.

ear speed – the distance traveled per unit of time.

uid – a phase of matter that holds its volume but can change its shape and flow.

ngitudinal – a wave whose oscillations are in the same direction as the wave travels.

oricant – a substance used to reduce friction between parts or objects moving against each other.

M

achine – a mechanical system capable of performing work.

acroscopic – large enough to be observed and measured directly.

agnetic – the ability to exert forces on magnets or other magnetic materials.

agnetic declination – the difference between the direction a compass points and the direction of true (geographic) north.

agnetic domain – a region of a material in which atoms magnetically align in the same direction, increasing the magnetic field strength.

agnetic field – the magnetic force that surrounds a magnetic object at all points in space.

agnetic field lines – the arrows used to show the direction of magnetic force in a magnetic field; magnetic field lines always point away from a magnet's north pole and toward a magnet's south pole.

agnetic poles – north and south; the two opposite places on a magnet where the magnetic field is the strongest; all magnets have at least one north pole and one south pole.

agnification – the ratio of the size of the image to the size of the object.

agnitude – a quantity's size or amount without regard to its direction; the "length" of a vector.

ass – the amount of matter an object has; a measure of an object's inertia; measured in grams or kilograms.

ass number – the total number of protons and neutrons in the nucleus of an atom.

mechanical advantage – the ratio of output force to input force.

mechanical energy – energy an object or system has due to motion or position.

metal – a category of elements that are usually shiny, opaque, and a good conductors of heat and electricity.

metalloids – a category of elements that have properties of both metals and nonmetals.

metric system – a system of measuring based on the meter and the kilogram and using multiples of 10.

microwave – a type of electromagnetic wave with a wavelength between 30 cm and 1 mm; cell phones and microwave ovens use microwaves.

mixture – a substance that contains more than one kind of matter.

model – a method of representing a relationship between variables.

molecule – the smallest particle of a compound that retains the identity of the compound.

momentum – the mass of an object multiplied by its speed or velocity.

multimeter – an instrument used for measuring voltage, current, and resistance.

musical scale – a series of frequencies arranged in a special pattern.

N

natural frequency – the frequency at which a system naturally oscillates.

natural law – a rule that every process in the universe obeys.

net force – the sum of all forces acting on an object.

neutron – an uncharged particle found in the nucleus of an atom; one of three particles in normal atoms, along with protons and electrons.

newton (N) – the metric unit of force; one newton causes a mass of one kilogram to accelerate at one meter per second per second.

Newton's first law – an object at rest will remain at rest unless acted on by an unbalanced force; an object in motion continues with constant speed and direction in a straight line unless acted on by an unbalanced force.

Newton's second law – the acceleration of an object is directly proportional to the net force acting on it and inversely proportional to its mass.

Newton's third law – whenever one object exerts a force on another, the second object exerts an equal and opposite force on the first.

noble gases – elements in group 18 of the periodic table; they usually do not form chemical bonds with other elements and are chemically inert.

nonmetals – a category of elements that are typically poor conductors of heat and electricity.

normal force – the force perpendicular to an object's surface.

normal line – an imaginary line drawn perpendicular to a surface.

note – a musical sound; from a musical scale.

nuclear energy – a form of energy that is stored in the forces within the nucleus of an atom; may be absorbed or released by nuclear reactions.

nuclear reaction – a reaction that changes the nucleus of at least one atom; may change one element into another element; involve much more energy than chemical reactions.

nucleus – the center core of an atom that contains protons and neutrons.

O

object – real things that give off or reflect light rays.

octave – the interval between a frequency and twice that frequency; two notes an octave apart sound similar to the ear and have the same letter name.

ohm (Ω) – the unit of electrical resistance; one volt causes a current of one amp to flow in a circuit with a resistance of one ohm.

Ohm's law – a formula that says the current flowing in a circuit is the voltage divided by the resistance.

open circuit – a circuit in which there is a break so that current cannot flow.

optical axis – an imaginary line that goes through the center of a lens; light traveling along the optical axis is not bent by the lens.

optics – the science and technology of the behavior of light.

orbit – a regular, repeating path that an object in space follows around another object caused by the influence of gravity.

oscillation – a motion that repeats regularly.

oscillator – a system that shows harmonic motion.

output – the force, work, energy, or power produced by a machine.

output arm – the side of a lever between the fulcrum and the output force.

P

parabola – the distinctive, arched shape of a projectile's trajectory; a particular mathematical curve.

parallel circuit – a circuit in which the current can take more than one path.

paramagnetic – a material where the magnetism of electrons in individual atoms does not cancel completely; paramagnetic materials are nonmagnetic, but can show signs of weak magnetism in the presence of a magnet.

period – (1) a horizontal row of the periodic table; (2) the amount of time it takes to repeat one cycle.

periodic force – an oscillating (repetitive) force.

periodic table – a table that organizes the known elements by increasing atomic number into rows (periods) and groups (columns).

permanent magnet – a material that retains its magnetic properties even when no external energy is supplied.

phase – where an oscillator is in its cycle.

photoluminescence – the releasing of stored light energy.

photon – the smallest possible quantity of light energy.

photoreceptors – highly specialized, light-sensitive cells in the retina of the eye.

photosynthesis – a chemical reaction performed by plants in which energy from the sun is converted to chemical energy; carbon dioxide and water are converted to sugar and oxygen in this reaction.

physical properties – properties that can be observed directly without changing the identity of the substance.

pitch – the perceived frequency of a sound.

Planck's constant (**h**) – a fundamental constant equal to 6.6×10^{-34} joule/sec.

plane wave – waves whose crests form of pattern of straight line wave fronts.

plasma – an ionized gas phase of matter; examples of plasma include stars, lightning, and neon-type lights.

polarization – (1) the separation of the positive and negative charge in an object's atoms due to the effect of an electric field; (2) a property of transverse waves (like light) that describes the direction of oscillations.

polarized – (1) when positive and negative charge in an object's atoms have been slightly separated; (2) light in which the oscillations of the electric field of the wave are all of the same orientation.

polarizer – a device or material that polarizes light by allowing light of only one polarization through.

potential energy – stored energy that comes from position.

potentiometer – a variable resistor.

power – the rate at which work is done; rate at which energy flows; equal to work ÷ time or energy ÷ time; measured in watts; one watt is a joule per second.

pressure – force per unit area; measured in newtons per square meter (Pa) or pounds per square inch (psi).

prism – an optical device used to refract and reflect light in precise ways; prisms can be used to separate white light into its component colors by dispersion.

probability – the mathematical rules describing the chance for an event occurring.

product – (1) substance(s) formed as the result of a chemical reaction; (2) the result of multiplying two quantities together.

projectile – any object moving through space and affected only by gravity.

propagate – to spread out or travel.

proton – positively charged particle found with neutrons in the nucleus of an atom; one of three particles in normal atoms, along with neutrons and electrons.

Q

quantum state – the discrete values of energy and momentum which are allowed for a particle as described by quantum theory.

quantum theory – the theory that describes the behavior of matter and energy on the atomic scale.

R

radiant energy – another term for electromagnetic energy.

radiation – energy that travels through space in the form of particles or pure energy.

radio wave – the lowest frequency of electromagnetic waves with a wavelength greater than tens of centimeters; radio waves are used for carrying radio and television signals.

radioactive – describes atoms which are unstable and spontaneously change into other atoms by the emission of particles and/or energy from the nucleus.

radioactive decay – the spontaneous changing of the nucleus of atoms through the release of radiation.

range – the distance a projectile travels horizontally.

ray diagram – a diagram that uses lines and arrows to show how light rays travel through an optical system.

reactant – one of the starting materials in a chemical reaction.

real image – an image formed by rays of light coming together.

reference frame – a perspective from which the position and motion of a system can be described.

reflected ray – a light ray that bounces off a surface.

reflection – the bouncing of a wave off a surface.

refracting telescope – a telescope that uses two converging lenses with different focal lengths to make objects look bigger.

refraction – the bending of a wave as it travels across a boundary.

relative humidity – the percent of water vapor in the air compared to the amount of water vapor the air could potentially hold at a given temperature.

resistance – the measure of an object's ability to conduct electrical current; measured in ohms.

resistor – an electrical device with a fixed resistance.

resonance – occurs when a periodic force has the same frequency as the natural frequency; the amplitude of a system in resonance is much larger than the strength of the force would normally produce.

respiration – the process of obtaining energy from glucose and oxygen while producing carbon dioxide and water.

restoring force – a force that always acts to pull an oscillating system back toward equilibrium.

resultant – a single vector that is the sum of a group of vectors.

reverberation – multiple echoes of sound caused by reflections of sound building up and blending together.

reversible – an ideal process that can run forward or backward.

revolve – to move around, or orbit, an external axis.

RGB color process – an additive color process that uses red, green, and blue light.

rhythm – the organization of sound into regular time patterns.

right-hand rule – the rule used to figure out a magnetic field's direction; when the thumb of your right hand points in the direction of electrical current, your fingers wrap in the magnetic field's direction.

rods – photoreceptor cells in the eye that respond to differences in intensity.

rotate – to spin around an axis of rotation that passes through an object.

rotational equilibrium – occurs when the torques on an object are balanced.

rotor – the rotating disk of an electric motor or generator.

S

satellite – an object in orbit around another object with gravity providing the centripetal force.

scalar – a quantity having magnitude only, and no direction; examples are mass, temperature, and time.

scientific method – a process that is used to gather evidence that leads to understanding.

second (sec) – a commonly used unit of time; $\frac{1}{60}$ of a minute.

second law of thermodynamics – states that when work is done by heat flowing, the output work must be less than the amount of heat flow.

semiconductor – a material between conductor and insulator in its ability to carry current.

series circuit – a circuit in which the current only has one path.

shielding – reducing or blocking electric fields.

shock wave – the "piled up" wave fronts that form in front of a supersonic object; the boundary between sound and silence.

short circuit – a branch in a circuit with zero or very low resistance.

simple machine – an unpowered mechanical device, such as a lever, that works by a single movement.

sliding friction – a resisting force created when two surfaces slide against one another.

slope – a line's vertical change divided by its horizontal change.

soft magnet – a magnetic material that is relatively easily magnetized or demagnetized; an example is iron.

solenoid – a coil of wire that acts as an electromagnet when current passes through it.

solid – a phase of matter that holds its volume and shape and does not flow.

sonogram – a graph showing how the loudness of different frequencies of sound changes with time.

source charge – the charge that creates an electric field.

specific heat – a property of a substance that tells us how much heat is needed to raise the temperature of one kg by 1°C.

spectral line – each individual line of color appearing in a spectrometer.

spectrometer – a device that spreads light into its different colors.

spectrum – the characteristic pattern of colors emitted by a pure element.

specular reflection – "shiny surface" reflection in which each incident ray creates only one reflected ray; opposite of diffuse reflection.

speed – the rate at which position changes; the distance traveled divided by the time taken.

speed of light (c) – the speed of light is a constant equal to about 300,000,000 m/sec in a vacuum.

spring constant – a constant that represents the relationship between the force exerted by a spring and its change in length.

standing wave – a resonance created by trapping a wave between boundaries that cause the wave to interfere with its own reflections.

static electricity – a buildup of either positive or negative charge; consists of isolated motionless charges, like those produced by friction.

static friction – the force that keeps two surfaces from sliding across each other when neither surface is moving relative to the other.

steady state – occurs in a system when the variables describing the system remain constant over time.

stress – the ratio of force acting through a material divided by the cross-section area through which the force acts.

strong nuclear force – the force that holds protons and neutrons together when they are very close together in the nucleus of atoms.

subsonic – motion that is slower than the speed of sound.

subtractive color process – a process that creates color by subtracting colors from white light using absorption.

subtractive primary colors – yellow, magenta, and cyan.

superconductor – a conductor with zero electrical resistance; certain materials can become superconductors at very low temperatures.

superposition principle – when two or more waves overlap, the resulting wave is the sum of the individual waves.

supersonic – motion that is faster than the speed of sound in air.

switch – a device for turning electricity on and off in a circuit.

system – a collection of matter and processes that occur in a certain space and can be studied.

T

tensile strength – a measure of how much pulling, or tension, a material can withstand before breaking.

tension – a force that stretches or pulls.

terminal speed – the maximum speed reached by an object in free fall; the speed at which the forces of gravity and air resistance are equal.

theory of special relativity – a theory by Albert Einstein describing what happens to matter, energy, time, and space at speeds close to the speed of light.

thermal conductor – a material that easily conducts heat.

thermal energy – the sum of all the kinetic energy of a material's atoms and molecules.

thermal expansion – the expansion of materials with an increase in temperature and the contraction with a decrease in temperature.

thermal insulator – a material that conducts heat poorly.

thermal radiation – heat transfer in the form of electromagnetic waves including light.

thermodynamics – the branch of physics that deals with heat, energy, and work.

thermometer – an instrument that measures temperature.

time dilation – according to Einstein's theory of special relativity, time runs slower for objects in motion than for objects at rest.

time interval – the time separating two events.

torque (τ) – a measure of how much a force acting on an object causes the object to rotate.

total internal reflection – occurs when light within a material approaches a surface at greater than the critical angle and reflects back.

trajectory – the curved path a projectile follows.

transformer – a device that uses induction to convert one AC electrical current and voltage to another AC current and voltage while keeping power about the same.

translucent – describes a material that allows some light to pass through and scatter.

transparent – describes a material that allows light to pass through with little or no scattering.

transverse – a type of wave with oscillations that are perpendicular to the direction the wave travels.

trough – the bottom or lowest points on a wave.

U

ultraviolet light – electromagnetic waves with a wavelength shorter than visible light but longer than X rays; cannot be seen by the human eye; have high enough energy to remove electrons and break chemical bonds.

uncertainty principle – it is not possible to precisely know a particle's position, momentum, energy, and time in a quantum system.

V

valence electrons – the electrons in an atom that are involved in the formation of chemical bonds.

variable – (1) a factor that affects the results of an experiment; (2) a named quantity that can have many values.

vector – a quantity that has both magnitude and direction; examples are weight, velocity, and magnetic field strength.

velocity – the vector form of speed; a quantity that specifies both speed and direction.

vibration – rapid oscillation.

virtual image – is formed when light rays are bent so they appear to come from a point in space different from where they actually come from; a virtual image cannot be projected on a screen.

viscosity – a measure of a fluid material's resistance to flow.

visible light – a type of electromagnetic wave with a wavelength between 700 and 400 nm; includes all the colors of light the human eye can see.

volt (V) – the measurement unit for voltage; one volt provides one watt of power for each amp of current that flows.

voltage – a measure of electric potential energy.

voltage drop – the difference in voltage across an electrical device that has current flowing through it.

voltmeter – an instrument used for measuring voltage.

W

watt (W) – the metric unit of power; one watt is a joule per second.

wave – an oscillation that travels, moving energy from one place to another.

wave fronts – another term for the crests of a wave.

wave pulse – a short length of wave or a single oscillation.

wavelength – the length of one complete cycle of a wave.

weight – a force created by gravity acting on mass.

white light – the equal combination of all the colors of light.

work – a form of energy; calculated as force × distance when both force and distance are in the same direction.

Index

A

Index

553

Index

Index

Index

559